Creating and Contesting
Social Inequalities

Creating and Contesting Social Inequalities

Contemporary Readings

Edited by

Carissa M. Froyum
University of Northern Iowa

Katrina Bloch
Kent State University at Stark

Tiffany Taylor
Kent State University at Kent

New York   Oxford
OXFORD UNIVERSITY PRESS

Oxford University Press is a department of the University of Oxford.
It furthers the University's objective of excellence in research,
scholarship, and education by publishing worldwide.

Oxford   New York
Auckland   Cape Town   Dar es Salaam   Hong Kong   Karachi
Kuala Lumpur   Madrid   Melbourne   Mexico City   Nairobi
New Delhi   Shanghai   Taipei   Toronto

With offices in
Argentina   Austria   Brazil   Chile   Czech Republic   France   Greece
Guatemala   Hungary   Italy   Japan   Poland   Portugal   Singapore
South Korea   Switzerland   Thailand   Turkey   Ukraine   Vietnam

For titles covered by Section 112 of the US Higher Education
Opportunity Act, please visit www.oup.com/us/he for the
latest information about pricing and alternate formats.

Published by Oxford University Press
198 Madison Avenue, New York, New York 10016
http://www.oup.com

Library of Congress Cataloging-in-Publication Data

Names: Froyum, Carissa M., editor. | Bloch, Katrina, editor. | Taylor,
    Tiffany, 1972- editor.
Title: Creating and contesting social inequalities : contemporary readings /
    co-edited by Carissa M. Froyum, Katrina Bloch, Tiffany Taylor.
Description: Oxford ; New York : Oxford University Press, [2017] | Includes
    bibliographical references.
Identifiers: LCCN 2015034923 | ISBN 9780190238469
Subjects: LCSH: Social stratification. | Equality. | Social policy.
Classification: LCC HM821 .C74 2017 | DDC 305--dc 3 LC record available at http://lccn.loc.gov/2015034923

Printing number: 9 8 7 6 5 4 3 2 1

Printed in the United States of America
on acid-free paper

Dedication

For Isak, Hans, and Linnea (CF)

CONTENTS

Part V. Why Do People Go Along with Inequalities?

Why are we enemies of the Jews?

We are enemies of the Jews because we are warriors for the freedom of the German people. THE JEW IS THE CAUSE AND BENEFICIARY OF OUR SLAVERY. . . .

[THE JEW] HAS RUINED OUR RACE, ROTTED OUR MORALS, CORRUPTED OUR TRADITIONS AND BROKEN OUR POWER. . . .

The Jew is the plastic demon of the decline of mankind. . . .

The Jew is uncreative. He does not produce anything, HE DEALS ONLY WITH PRODUCTS. With junk, clothes, pictures, precious stones, grain, stocks and bonds, shares, people and states. And he has STOLE somewhere everything he uses in his trading. . . .

The Jew is indeed ALSO A HUMAN BEING. Certainly, and none of us has ever doubted it. We only doubt that he is a DECENT person. He doesn't belong to us. He lives according to other inner and outer laws. . . . He is indeed a human being—BUT WHAT KIND? —1920s pamphlet by Paul Joseph Goebbels (1991)

Introduction

Joseph Goebbels was a fanatical Jew hater and henchman of Adolf Hitler. As an early member of the National Socialist Movement, Goebbels vilified Jews, as he did in the 1920s pamphlet that opens this preface and in other writings and speeches. He berated Jews as immoral and indecent—views which allowed him to sidle up to Hitler and earn the contempt of envious others in the National Socialist German Workers Party who derided him as "The Little Mouse Doctor" (Snyder 1991,

53). Goebbels eventually became the Reich Minister for Public Enlightenment and Propaganda, which allowed him to profligate official Nazi ideologies through the book burnings and propaganda journalism and film he masterminded.

Nazis blamed Jews for the decline and economic ills of Germany following the humiliation and reparations of World War I. National Socialism's vision of a pure Aryan "master race" was built on ridding Germany of the "demon" Jewish contaminant. As historian Klaus P. Fischer (1999) explains:

Many German racial thinkers had sounded shrill notes of alarm, warning that the population of Germany was being degraded by biological inferiors—the poor, the weak, the insane, the asocial—who were multiplying in far greater numbers than the gifted few upon whom progress depended. . . . In the words of Rudolf Hess, National Socialism was basically "applied racial science"
—Angewandte Rassenkunde (383, 384)

National Socialists were particularly adept and ruthless in their mixing of racism and eugenics, even in their early days before they fully implemented "the final solution" to the "Jewish question." For instance, they created a series of race laws, including the Nuremberg Laws, designed to grow and protect German Nordics (Fischer 1999). The Entitled Law for the Prevention of Progeny with Hereditary Diseases (1933) mandated sterilization of people with broadly defined diseases. The Law for the Protection of German Blood and German Honor (1935) prohibited sexual relations and marriage between Germans and Jews. The Reich Citizenship Law (1935) provisioned citizens of German or related blood with full political rights but subjects with only protections but not political rights. The Law for the Protection of the Genetic Health of the German People (1935) required marrying couples to undergo medical exams and prohibited marriage to someone with disease.

As scholars of social inequalities, we have much to study and learn from Nazi Germany. From its using propaganda to dehumanize groups of people to transforming workers into obedient cogs to institutionalizing racist, ableist, heterosexist, and misogynistic ideologies, Nazi Germany epitomizes how individual people recreate categorical inequalities—and the exploitation, abuse, and genocide they accompany. Seventy years after the Soviet liberation of Auschwitz on January 27, 1945, the post-9/11 world remains engulfed in social conflicts, wars, and genocide connected to divisions of race, creed, nativity, nationality, and other categories of differences. The lessons of the Holocaust are as important as ever. Inequality scholars and prominent Jewish voices are sounding alarms about a renewed rise of anti-Semitism and violence against Jews in Europe, especially France, leading Jeffrey Goldberg to question "Is It Time for the Jews To Leave Europe?" on the cover of the April 2015 edition of *The Atlantic*.

We have designed this reader to answer students' pressing questions about why people categorize themselves and each other into social groups, how they transform these categories into real-world differences in life chances, and what people have done and can do to make a difference to change things. We discuss the results of the latter collectively as "social inequalities" or "categorical inequalities."

Social inequalities are when one social category of people has unearned advantages over and at the expense of another group (Schwalbe 2008). These advantages are most easily seen as differences in access to resources (e.g., money, land, jobs, status, well-being, mobility, psychological health, etc.), quality of resources, rewards, or returns on investment, and consequences for similar actions or beliefs. They are unearned in the sense that they are not accounted for through hard work, better skill, or other meritocratic differences between groups of people. Rather, the groups themselves are social elaborations of otherwise arbitrary or non-meritocratic differences among people, differences dwarfed by their influence on people's life chances. Inequalities have an ideological component in that extensive belief systems develop to explain and justify exploitation and domination of others. Dominant groups of people manipulate and coerce subordinated people into participating in their own oppression so that they may not recognize their own oppression or, worse yet, may agree with it.

Inequalities are a sociological matter. They are necessarily systematic: They occur through regular and repeated actions and beliefs by many people across areas of social life (e.g., in workplaces, families, on the street, etc.). Acting in ways that recreate them is often habitual. Inequalities are also institutionalized into rules, laws, and practices governing social institutions. Because inequalities are engrained in habit and institutions, people often struggle to see how an individual person's actions relate to the broader problem. Or they may think inequalities are inevitable or natural. But inequalities are neither natural nor inevitable. This book is designed to demonstrate how they work, piece by piece.

This reader takes an integrated approach to studying inequality so that as the book progresses, students will connect the pieces to each other. Using contemporary theoretical and empirical readings arranged intuitively around big-picture questions, this book facilitates seeing how our actions in one dimension of social life relate to other areas of social life. We aren't workers one minute and then family members another minute. But we are actors whose decisions and beliefs at work relate to, shape, and are influenced by home life. Similarly, rather than thinking of different forms of inequality as separate and unrelated, we approach racialization, gender inequality, heterosexism, ableism, and class inequality *intersectionally* (Collins 2000; Crenshaw 1991), that is, as interconnected and sometimes mutually dependent. Even so, various forms of inequality manifest from similar social processes, and so we focus on demonstrating those mechanics to you. Finally, this reader is integrative in that it connects the local and the global. It also places the United States within global context.

Organization of the Book

Creating and Contesting Social Inequalities has five sections, which we call Parts. Each part is a collection of readings which address the basic questions students have about why and how inequalities exist and change.

Part I. Where do inequalities come from? Does it have to be this way?

When students first begin the study of social inequalities, they often think that inequalities somehow exist in their own right, outside of our actions. Many believe inequalities have and always will exist. Part I challenges students' perceptions of the inevitability of inequalities by illustrating their socio-historic construction. This part emphasizes that people's actions create inequalities. It provides an historical and cross-cultural picture of how inequalities develop and change, thereby orienting students toward thinking of them as dynamic and changeable. Students learn to contextualize inequalities within time and space, and in relation to each other. Part I introduces students to intersectionality.

Part II: Why do we categorize people into groups? How does differentiation transform into inequality?

Part II illustrates how we come to think about people as part of distinctive groups, some of which are afforded more status, power, and opportunity than others. Part II illustrates three social processes. First, "Thinking and Believing" introduces students to the notion of implicit, cognitive biases and shows how our beliefs play out, even without our knowledge, within particular social contexts. This section raises the question of the necessity of intention in creating inequalities. In "Creating Boundaries," students examine how our media, interactions, and laws create borders between groups so that one group is seen as deserving of social benefits while the other is undeserving. Social actors put boundaries into practice in "Policing Boundaries": assessing each other based on classification, collectively organizing around boundaries, and discriminating. "Contesting and Changing" illustrates how people challenge the social categorizing of people into superior and inferior groups through the lens of contestation or acceptance of the new medical label for intersexuality and challenging unconscious biases and racial discrimination among police.

Part III: How do dominant groups get and hoard resources?

Inequalities result in vast differences in life chances by ensuring the dominant groups' access to material, social, and psychological resources while limiting subordinates' access. Part III examines the practices through which dominant group members secure resources and protect their interests through three social processes. First, when exploiting people, dominant group members use subordinate members for their economic, political, social, or emotional gain. Second, they exclude subordinates. Dominant group members, for example, restrict subordinates' access to resources through discrimination, and people hold the subordinate group to cultural standards of the dominant group. Third, dominant group members threaten and enact violence to control subordinate members and reduce or eliminate their influence. The social change readings present laws, law enforcement, food justice activism, and unionization as potential agents of resistance and change. Taken as a whole, Part III shows how dominant groups come to monopolize valued or scarce resources.

Part IV: How do inequalities become institutionalized?

Inequalities are often hard to recognize because they are diffused across social environments and are deeply embedded within social structures. This embeddedness normalizes inequalities and renders them invisible—they appear to exist outside of the action of any particular individuals. Yet it is the routines and practices of people acting out roles that often perpetuate inequalities. Part IV examines how inequalities become embedded in institutional practices and culture, that is, how they become part of the various ways we organize the social world, producing institutional inertia that is hard to challenge. The section "Bureaucratizing" reveals how inequalities become part of the means of administration (Schwalbe 2008). It demonstrates how supervision and work requirements to be efficient and routinized constrain subordinates while bolstering superordinates and deflecting their attention away from inequalities. In "Controlling Spaces," social ties become the point of analysis. Readers see how elites cultivate exclusive social networks, ensuring their ties to each other and shoring up their resources. This section also demonstrates how controlling spaces isolates subordinates and restricts their access to resources. "Instituting Social Policy" examines how social policies can be instruments that equalize or exacerbate inequalities. The "Contesting and Changing" section of Part IV highlights the empirical effects of various diversity policies and how marginalized groups mitigate the negative consequences of inequalities through their personal networks and by creating safe spaces.

Part V: Why do people go along with inequalities?

Inequalities are powerful because they organize social life, and they shape how we think about ourselves and each other. We may even come to see the very categories that differentiate us as central to who we are as people, or we may believe that some people truly deserve particular experiences and opportunities while others do not. That is, part of the power of inequalities is that people become invested in them. They value the social and material benefits that accompany them. Part V explores these dynamics of inequality by looking at how people maintain identities through inequality, how controlling discourses gives them meaning and influence, and how the suppression and control of emotions serves to reproduce inequalities. The section on changing and contesting shows how people refashion their senses of self, ideologies, and emotions in ways that orient them toward acceptance and social change.

On top of the readings about how inequalities work and change, each part has two additional features: data analysis exercises and a collection of projects and resources for creating change. We have designed the data analysis exercises so that students answer a provocative question about the state of social inequalities today by analyzing data presented in an easy-to-understand format, such as tables and figures. Students apply what they have learned about how inequalities work and change to new areas of social life. Projects and resources to make a difference provide students a way to put into action outside of the classroom what they have learned.

Some of the questions and answers in *Creating and Contesting Social Inequalities* may seem like minutiae in comparison to the grandiosity of the problems. That is by design. Inequalities result from many people's small and mundane actions coming together over and over again. Each of us plays a part, and looking at our own and others' actions allows us to stave off the impulse to "do nothing because nothing can be done." We can and must take action to make a difference.

One final note about this reader. We have chosen to capitalize "Black" and lowercase "white." As Crenshaw (1991) writes "Blacks, like Asians, Latinos, and other 'minorities,' constitute a specific cultural group and, as such, require denotation as a proper noun" (1244). While potentially imperfect, we capitalize "Black" to indicate the shared marginalization and history amongst a group that may or may not identify as African and because of slavery, cannot identify an ethnic heritage. However, white people often identify as additional ethnicities, such as Irish, Italian, German, etc.

Acknowledgments

This book began as a conversation with Sherith Pankratz about how to do an inequality book differently. Thank you to her and to Katy Albis for seeing us through this project. We would also like to thank the following reviewers commissioned by Oxford University Press: Debjani Chakravarty, Grand Valley State University; Margaret S. Crowdes, California State University, San Marcos; Cherise Harris, Connecticut College; Daphne Henderson, University of Tennessee at Martin; Karyn Loscocco, State University at Albany; Geraldine Manning, Suffolk University; Stephanie McClure, Georgia College & State University; Debarashmi Mitra, Central New Mexico Community College; Jana Sladkova, University of Massachusetts, Lowell; and Ahoo Tabatabai, Columbia College.

References

Collins, Patricia Hill. 2000. *Black Feminist Thought: Knowledge, Consciousness, and the Politics of Empowerment.* 2nd ed. New York: Routledge.

Crenshaw, Kimberle. 1991. "Mapping the Margins: Intersectionality, Identity Politics, and Violence against Women of Color." *Stanford Law Review* 43:1241–1299.

Fischer, Klaus P. 1999. *Nazi Germany: A New History.* New York: Continuum.

Goebbels, Paul Joseph. 1991. "Dr. Paul Joseph Goebbels, Later to Become Propaganda Minister of the Third Reich, Writes a Pamphlet Excoriating the Jews." In *Hitler's Third Reich: A Documentary History* (ed. and trans. Louis L. Snyder), 53–55. Chicago: Nelson-Hall.

Goldberg, Jeffrey. 2015. "Is It Time for the Jews to Leave Europe?" *The Atlantic.* April.

Schwalbe, Michael. 2008. *Rigging the Game: How Inequality Is Reproduced in Everyday Life.* New York: Oxford University Press.

Snyder, Louis L., ed. and trans. 1991. *Hitler's Third Reich: A Documentary History.* Chicago: Nelson-Hall.

Creating and Contesting
Social Inequalities

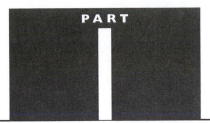

Where Do Inequalities Come From? Does It Have to Be This Way?

People often mistake inequalities for naturally occurring social facts, as if racism, patriarchy, class inequality, ableism, heterosexism, and nativism are natural states which exist in their own right, outside of our actions. When we make this mistake, inequalities are like a thick smog, surrounding us, hanging in the air, no cause apparent and no direct way to rid ourselves of it. Our attention to the smog heightens during crises: when we have somewhere we desperately want to go but are choked by the polluted air. But the smog blocks out the full context of the hills, trees, and water in the broader environment, illuminating most clearly our immediate surroundings, the few steps behind us, and the few before us. We overlook the mundane habits of life—driving our SUVs to run errands, dumping pollutants, relying on electricity from coal plants, consumption of

beef—which seem removed from dirty particles in the air. We may even conclude, "Well, smog has always been here. Nothing is ever going to change." Or, "I'm only one person. There's nothing I can do about it."

Inequalities too are entrenched, hidden, and often taken for granted. Like smog, they are not natural; nor are they inevitable.

As scholars of the social world, we use our sociological imaginations to analyze inequality as the by-product of our collective thoughts and actions, as something, as Michael Schwalbe (2008) explains, we accomplish together. Sociologists refer to this approach to understanding the social world as social constructionism (Berger and Luckman 1966). Social constructionism is the analysis of how people create shared meanings and ways of organizing the world. It treats social categories and systems as sociohistoric byproducts of human thought and action with clear—and potentially discernable—histories. Rather than throwing our hands up in the air and declaring, "The smog is simply here to stay," a social constructionist approach pushes researchers to study when and how people formed, changed, maintained, and challenged systematic inequalities.

Part I of this book introduces us to a social construction approach to studying social inequalities. We learn that:

- *Inequalities are created by people. So is equality.* Both only occur because we continue to maintain them through our thoughts and actions. To understand what inequalities are and how they work, thus, we must study people's behavior and thinking.

- *Understanding inequalities is an empirical task.* We look to data to identify the origins of inequalities; trace their development across time; recognize variations across cultures; determine who benefits from particular social arrangements, social groupings, or belief systems; analyze who is most influential in creating social categories and the tools they use; and see how people contest and adapt to oppression and domination. Part I tells the origin stories of inequalities.

- *The social world shapes biological realities.* While there are some true biological differences between people's genetics, physical capabilities, and even appearances, they are small and utterly dwarfed in size compared to the differences in people's life chances often attributed to them. In fact, there is vastly more biological diversity within social categories (e.g., among females) than across them (e.g., between females and males). What we do with minute differences— the attention we afford them, the classification systems we do or do not draw around them, the extent to which we arrange our social worlds accordingly—are matters of social construction. Moreover, sociologists challenge the notion that biology is destiny, demonstrating instead that how we think about, categorize, and treat people

actually shapes our bodies. Scientists, politicians, and the elite have long used biological explanations as justifications for oppressing people *ex post facto*. Biology is an ideology.

- *Different forms of inequality are interconnected.* Black feminist scholars challenged the understanding of each type of inequality as a stand-alone system of oppression, arguing instead that they "intersect" (Collins 2000; Crenshaw 1989) for individual people's identities and as social structures. "Intersectionality" challenges us to understand people's experiences complexly, as existing within racism, class inequality, patriarchy, heterosexism, and ableism simultaneously and unevenly. People may be advantaged in one arena of social life (e.g., be heterosexual and therefore receive the benefits afforded to heterosexuals) but disadvantaged by another (e.g., be poor). Moreover, different systems of inequality *interact* with each other. Capitalism, for example, draws on racist ideologies for women and men differently. So while social constructionism helps us understand how people create shared meanings and ways of organizing the world, intersectionality shows how race, gender, and class inequalities influence the shared meanings and organization of the world. Systems of domination work with, through, and against each other. How important one dimension of inequality is in a given setting (e.g., within families) or for a particular life outcome (e.g., getting a fulfilling, well-paying job) is an empirical matter.

- *How people dominate each other and resist domination is common across systems of inequality.* Despite the complexity of inequalities, certain ways of acting and thinking maintain all of them. This book identifies those common practices.

The historical foundations of inequalities, their cross-cultural variation, and the elaboration of ideologies to justify dominating others demonstrates how repeated, coordinated, mundane actions of individual people establish systems of inequality. The smog lifts. Because we together recreate inequalities, we can also together accomplish equality.

References

Berger, Peter. L., and Thomas Luckmann. 1966. *The Social Construction of Reality: A Treatise in the Sociology of Knowledge.* New York: Doubleday.

Collins, Patricia Hill. 2000. *Black Feminist Thought: Knowledge, Consciousness, and the Politics of Empowerment,* 2nd ed. New York: Routledge.

Crenshaw, Kimberle. 1989. "Demarginalizing the Intersection of Race and Sex: A Black Feminist Critique of Antidiscrimination Doctrine, Feminist Theory and Antiracist Politics." *University of Chicago Legal Forum* 139–167.

Schwalbe, Michael. 2008. *Rigging the Game: How Inequality Is Reproduced in Everyday Life.* New York: Oxford University Press.

I

The Roots of Inequality

MICHAEL SCHWALBE

The achievement ideology, the aspirational belief that each individual can make the sort of life s/he wants through skill and hard work, is deeply entrenched in American culture. Songs, movies (e.g., *An American Tail, The Blind Side, Citizen Kane, Coming to America, Maid in America, Pretty Woman, The Pursuit of Happyness*), and cultural heroes (e.g., Barack Obama, John Wayne, Rocky) valorize upward mobility, overcoming obstacles, and individualized effort. The achievement ideology, sometimes referred to as meritocracy or the American dream ideology, is also embedded in social policy debates, such as the attack on affirmative action under the guise of "reverse discrimination." The underlining assumption is that individuals are no longer prejudiced and public policies have eradicated discrimination so that each individual now faces a level playing field. Inequalities, insofar as they exist, the thinking goes, result not from the exploitative, coordinated actions of the dominant group but from the individualized failures of subordinated people themselves. They didn't work hard enough or do well enough. In essence, we get what we deserve. The people at the top are there because they've earned it.

People who benefit from inequalities have developed elaborate belief systems like the achievement ideology to make exploitation and deprivation seem natural and normal—and the fault of oppressed people. The achievement ideology, and other belief systems such as biological essentialism (the belief that biological differences create different, justifiably unequal social realities for people) and even multiculturalism, obfuscate the reality that inequalities are socially constructed and can only exist because of inertia: We continue to think and act in ways that keep them in place and reinvent them. These systems exist to exploit people. Ideologies leave people who dominate feeling they deserve to and people who are oppressed hoping to one day escape through their own individual effort.

In the reading that follows, Michael Schwalbe introduces readers to the idea that inequalities are human accomplishments in which people steal from, exploit, and extort from others so that they can hoard social and material resources. He encourages readers to think of inequalities as *verbs*, as things we do together (e.g., racializing or gendering), rather than as nouns, static states of being (e.g., classes). Rather than asking, "What do inequalities look like?" this social constructionist approach challenges us to ask, "What do we do to create them?"

The accomplishment of inequalities is often difficult to see for other reasons. We take inequalities for granted because we, at least to some degree, have inherited them. We did not make up the racial categories we see or to which we try to be colorblind. Nor did we originally invent the ideas that men should be powerful and women, caring. Rather, we are socialized into beliefs and social systems that already categorize people into different social classes, abilities, racial groups, and genders. Anyone who

Excerpted from Schwalbe, Michael. 2008. "The Roots of Inequality." In *Rigging the Game: How Inequality Is Reproduced in Everyday Life* Second Edition. New York: Oxford University Press. Pp. 25–47. Reprinted by permission Oxford University Press USA.

takes a trip to a mainstream toy store immediately sees this socialization at work. Even into the second decade of the twenty-first century, toy aisles are gender segregated for small children. Not only are the aisles color coded—dark primary colors and black for boys and pink and other pastels for girls—but the toys themselves give boys practice building and destroying things and dominating other boys, while girls learn to relate to others, take care of them, and be appealing. We didn't invent these toys or the two categories they reflect and reinforce, even if we play with them.

We also fail to see how everyday actions maintain inequalities because human beings are creatures of habit. What we experience every day feels far removed from complicated social histories of exploitation of Chinese workers and extermination of native peoples. Our everyday concerns—maintaining our grades, having fun, securing a good job—deflect our attention from the complex realities in the background. We may also feel we have no choice but to play with the toys that we're given, or as adults to be deferent to our bosses. We go along to get along.

Moreover, we each want to maintain a meaningful sense of self. We want to be valued for who we are and to feel important. Implicating ourselves in racializing or gendering severely challenges our notions of self and leads us to wonder, "If I am a part of recreating these awful systems, which rely on exploiting others and create pain and suffering, then what kind of person am I?"

But seeing inequalities as social constructions, or as accomplishments people do together, as Michael Schwalbe explains in this selection, is the first step to understanding—and dismantling—them, in the face of the moral, personal, and social risks involved. Thinking of inequalities as social constructions isn't easy. One way to see what is otherwise hidden is to list the types of evidence that point to social constructionism and then apply those criteria to racialization, gendering, and other forms of inequality. How would we know if something is socially constructed? People in different places and times doing things differently (cross-cultural and cross-time variation). Having an origin story of inequality and tracing its historical development. Seeing people make the categories and attach resources to them in real time. Uncovering who benefits from particular social arrangements and at whose expense. Identifying the tools that people use to exploit others and create ideologies that justify inequalities. You may be able to think of more. With the right sorts of data, we can then apply these criteria to understand how we make inequalities together. We're in luck! Sociologists and other social scientists have done some of this empirical work for us already. In the reading that follows, Schwalbe introduces us to this research.

The other obstacles to understanding inequalities as something we create through coordinated action on an ongoing basis are social and psychological. And as students of inequality, we have to deal with these too. Our loyalty to our families or our own senses of self make it easier to claim, "My ancestors were immigrants who came here legally and made it on their own. *They* didn't have slaves or kill native peoples. What does racism have to do with me?" than to deal with the implications of knowing one's family homesteaded on stolen land. Or the challenge of acknowledging the role that government programs played in helping white families accumulate wealth and pass it along to their children and grandchildren. If we know these things, then we feel compelled to act—to look in the mirror, to do things differently, to organize for change. On the flip side, it hurts to think of others exploiting us, of using us or people we love so that people like them can have more and feel better about themselves.

With the revelations of studying the accomplishment of inequalities come no easy answers and often a sense of discomfort. These feelings are normal and, we would argue, necessary in order to create a better, more just society.

Most sociologists who study inequality, whether they look at how much inequality there is or how it's reproduced, discuss it in terms of race, class, and gender. Class is typically defined as a matter of *economic* inequality, whereas race and gender are seen as matters of *status* inequality.[1] One snag that sociologists and others who write about inequality then run into is figuring out how race, class, and gender are related. These forms of inequality are often said to be "intersecting" or "interlocking" or "mutually reinforcing." Noting this connectedness is important, because doing so reminds us that an analysis of one form of inequality cannot ignore the others.

Yet it has proved difficult to say precisely how these forms of inequality are linked. Part of the problem is a tendency to immediately think about inequality in terms of abstract categories like race, class, and gender instead of looking first at how people actually do things together to create and distribute resources. In this chapter I'm going to start in a different place and show how inequality is rooted in relationships, practices, and processes.

Think of it this way. A log and a candle can both burn, but if we want to understand what is going on in both cases, we need to know some basic chemistry (specifically, about oxidation). The same principle applies to inequality. To understand what race, class, and gender are all about, we need to look beneath the surface of things and try to see the processes that create them. Then we can better understand how they are similar, how they are different, and how they are linked.

At first I'm not going to talk about race, class, and gender at all. Instead I'm going to start with resources. My claim, in a nutshell, is this: *Inequality is created and reproduced by institutionalizing imbalanced flows of socially valued resources. . . .*

Resources

Inequality means, by definition, that some people have more of something than others. But what exactly is this "something" that they have more of? Merely to say that they have more resources isn't very informative; that's like saying they have more "stuff." So the first thing it's necessary to do is to be more specific about what counts as a resource and why these resources matter. I'll start with the easiest and best example: money.

Money is a resource because it can help us satisfy our needs and desires. That's what a resource is: something that either directly satisfies, or helps us to satisfy, a need or a desire. We can't eat money, or wear it, or live in it, but we can use it to buy food, clothing, and shelter and thereby satisfy our physical needs. We can also use it to buy just about any other kind of object or experience that might help to make us happy and healthy. That's why it's often said that money is a "universal resource."

Because money can be converted into so many other things, it's the resource that people who study inequality, especially in capitalist societies, pay the most attention to. But we can also broaden our notion of resources. For instance, land can be a valuable resource if you can grow food on it or charge people to live on it. In some places, animals, if you can eat them or use them to do work, are important resources. Tools—from stone axes to wooden plows to computers to satellites to cruise missiles—are also resources.

The value of a resource depends on what can be done with it. It depends on whether there exist human needs and desires it can satisfy or help to satisfy. If so, then you may be able to use the resource yourself or trade it (presumably for something of equal value) to someone who can use it. You might have more belly button lint than anyone else in the world. But unless you can gain some benefit from it, it's not much of a resource.

Material resources are not the only ones that matter. Knowledge and skill are also important. So are degrees and credentials. In some contexts, a male body and light skin can be valuable because of the responses they elicit from others. There are also what we might call "inner resources." Feelings of confidence and self-worth, for example, are resources that can help us act effectively and thereby satisfy our needs and desires.

The language of resources will also be helpful later for seeing why it's easier for some people to get ahead than others. In brief, getting ahead is easier for folks who are given the right kind of resources for making money, achieving status, or acquiring power. Implied here is another key idea: resources are often convertible, meaning that having one kind can lead to getting other kinds. This is why many people go to college. They seek to convert knowledge into a degree, a degree into a job, a job into income, and income into happiness.

Finally, the value of a resource depends on the situation. On a medieval battlefield, a long arm, a sharp sword, and fighting skill were no doubt of great value. In a college classroom, you will be better served by a sharp mind and skill with a pen. In a working-class bar, a Ph.D. might be more of a liability than an asset. The value of a resource depends, in other words, not only on the needs and desires it can satisfy or help to satisfy, but on the obstacles one faces in trying to satisfy those needs and desires.

In the end, resources matter because they make the difference between living well and barely living, which is why it's important to look at how various kinds of resources are distributed in our society (and around the world).[2] An unequal distribution of resources produces an unequal distribution of experiences—of health and illness, of pain and pleasure, of security and insecurity, of opportunity and despair. The distribution of resources matters, in other words, because it roughly corresponds to the distribution of suffering and chances to live a satisfying human life.

Creating an Imbalance of Resources

For the sake of illustration, imagine a society in which all the important material resources are *equally* distributed. By material resources I mean food, clothing, shelter, land, tools, and whatever counts as money. In this imaginary society, even though people have different personalities, tastes, values, and ideas, everybody has about the same level of resources needed for living a safe, comfortable, healthy life. How, then, out of this hypothetical state of equality, could a state of inequality be created?

Theft is one possibility. An individual, or, more likely, a group of people, could try to take resources away from other people in the community. This might be done through trickery or through the use or threat of violence. It might involve taking some or most of the resources possessed by others. A successful resource grab by an aggressive person or group is thus one way the condition of equality could be spoiled.

Stealing from outsiders is another possibility. This might require building weapons and developing skill in using them, and perhaps also devising a transportation technology (e.g., seafaring ships). Piracy and plunder offer the advantage of generating less internal, day-to-day conflict than robbing one's neighbors. Resources taken from outsiders can also be shared with one's neighbors, perhaps thereby gaining their support, or at least tolerance, for the enterprise and the inequality it creates.

Equality could be spoiled by extortion. This might take the form of running a protection racket, that is, extorting one's neighbors to pay a fee for protection against outside raiders. Such a method presumes that there's an outside threat, that an individual or group has the skill and resources to provide protection, and that those being extorted are vulnerable. If these conditions prevail, then extortion might work very well to create an imbalanced

flow of resources. It might even lead those doing the extorting to form what we call a "government."

Yet another possibility is forced labor. Again, the victims could be insiders or outsiders. In either case, one group must be strong enough to coerce the labor of another group and to take away whatever is produced. This strategy allows the exploiting person or group to accumulate more resources than the exploited group. Those who merely worked for themselves would probably also fall behind those who were able to exploit the labor of others.

A person or group might also accumulate extra resources by controlling a resource that other people desire and can't get elsewhere. The resource in question could be material (e.g., food, land, water, oil, medicine) or symbolic (e.g., craft knowledge, spiritual wisdom). If enough people want it badly enough to pay a high price, the person or group with a monopoly on the resource could become rich.

It is also possible that a person or group might decide to work harder or longer than anyone else. This presumes that extra effort—at whatever kind of work the person or group is able to do—would be rewarded. There wouldn't be much advantage to making more of something that wasn't usable, tradable, or preservable (unless the work process itself was enjoyable). Still, there is the possibility, in principle, of inequality arising from above-average effort.

Proposing a society that begins in a state of equality might seem unrealistic. Because inequality is all that most of us alive today have ever known, it's hard to imagine a state of equality. And if we've been taught to see inequality as the natural result of individual differences in ability and effort, it might be even harder to accept that inequality results from theft, extortion, and exploitation. But if we take a longer view of human history, the illustration I've offered, starting from a state of equality is not unrealistic at all.

Our species, *Homo sapiens*, emerged about 150,000 years ago. But it's only in about the last 12,000 years that humans have lived in societies based on settled agriculture and mechanical industry. Prior to this humans lived in hunting-and-gathering societies. In these societies there was little, if any, inequality; every adult did a share of the work necessary to survive, and there were no surplus material resources for anyone to accumulate. This means that for about 90 percent of the time our species has existed, we lived in a state of rough equality.[3]

Neolithic Revolution

Developed

Surplus

Things changed with the advent of settled agriculture. Once humans learned to domesticate plants (and animals) and harvest an annual crop in one place, it became possible to accumulate more food than was needed to survive. Now it was possible for some people to survive without being direct producers (hunters/gatherers/farmers) themselves. A strong minority could also grab an unequal share of the resources for themselves, because there was a surplus to be grabbed. With settled agriculture there arose the possibility of a complex, stratified society in which some people could be kings and queens, soldiers and priests—while most others did the direct labor.

Settled agriculture also changed the value of other resources. Land, water (for irrigation), draft animals, and forced labor became more valuable. Weapons and military skill became more valuable for both offense—taking other people's land, water, etc.—and defense—protecting the resources one already controlled. Technical knowledge related to farming, warfare, and transport became more valuable. Even philosophical and religious knowledge became more valuable, because this kind of knowledge was often used to justify inequality.

The emergence of settled agriculture was thus a turning point in human history. By making it possible to generate a substantial surplus, settled agriculture made possible the complex systems of inequality we see today. It accelerated the growth of science and technology. It also gave rise to problems that still exist in modern capitalist societies: how to control workers; how to control and distribute the resources produced by workers; and how to explain and legitimate inequality.

Inequality Closer to Home

When we look back over a long sweep of time, it's not hard to see that theft, extortion, and exploitation have played a large part in creating inequality.[4] In fact, much of human history can be read as a series of stories about powerful groups taking control of land and other natural resources, enslaving militarily weaker peoples, creating laws and governments to serve their interests, and inventing ideas to justify their actions. None of this should be news to anyone who has studied ancient or modern history.

But as we get closer to the present-day United States, it becomes harder for many people to see what theft, extortion, and exploitation have to do with

inequality. In part this is because we're taught that inequality arises only because some people are smarter or work harder than others. . . . I'll point to two bits of history that, if not forgotten, remind us how our present state of inequality is hardly a result of fair play on a level field. Think first about the days before Europeans arrived in what we now call North America.

There is dispute among anthropologists about how many people lived here before 1492. Credible estimates range from 7 million to 18 million.[5] But regardless of the precise figure (and it is hard to be precise), one thing is sure: All the land here—all 3,537,438 square miles—belonged to the native people. And then, in only a few hundred years, nearly all of the vast wealth constituted by this land ended up in the hands of Europeans. Today Native Americans possess only a tiny fraction of the land that is now the United States.

How did this happen? Most Americans know the story. The land was simply taken, through deception and force, over a period of about 400 years. European diseases that decimated the indigenous people and made them too weak to resist further aided the process.[6] It would be fair to say that this is a story not merely of theft but of what we now call "genocide," the extermination (or nearly so) of an entire people.

Many Americans of European descent readily admit that native people were the victims of theft and fraud and slaughter. What may be harder to admit is that everyone who owns land today has benefited from that ugly history. If the Eno, Occaneechi, Cherokee, and Tuscarora peoples had not been forced out, once upon a time, I would not have a deed that says I own the land on which my house sits.

The whole story of how inequality was created through the theft of land from Native Americans is more complicated. For instance, the British government and later the U.S. government did not parcel out land equally; some settlers got bigger and better "land grants" than others, and thus found it easier to build fortunes. Changes in markets (see, for example, the history of tobacco) and in technology also affected the value of land, no matter how it was acquired. All of this history is pertinent to understanding how the theft of land at one time led to great inequalities later. If we want to see how exploitation operated to create inequality during the same historical period, the obvious example to consider is slavery.

Although exploitation often involves some form of coercion, it is not merely a matter of forcing people to do what they would rather not do. To exploit a person or a group of people is to use them unfairly.[7] This means using people's bodies and minds to create valuable resources of some kind without compensating them fully for what they've created. If someone works for you and creates, say, $100 worth of goods, but you can get away with paying them only $50—perhaps because they have no other way to earn money, or because they don't realize how much wealth they've created—that's exploitation.

People who are *enslaved* are used unfairly in ways that are not hard to see. Their bodies and minds, their energy and skill are used to create valuable resources, which are then taken for use or sale by some group with a greater capacity for violence. It doesn't matter if the people who are enslaved appear to accept their circumstances. The arrangement is still exploitative, because one group uses another to create valuable resources and then takes an inequitable share of those resources for itself.[8]

In the pre–Civil War American South, people of African descent who were enslaved created enormous value for their owners. Slaves built buildings and roads, raised crops, tended animals, and did much of the other work—including child care, housecleaning, and cooking—that made southern agrarian society possible. Slave labor created wealth for slave owners precisely because this labor was not fully paid for. The food, clothing, and shelter slaves received was worth only a small fraction of the value their labor created. Slave owners thus accumulated wealth by keeping most of the value created by other people's labor.

The wealth created by slave labor in the South also helped to enrich northerners.[9] Textile manufacturers in the North made extra profits in part because of the low cost of slave labor. Shipbuilders sold the ships that transported slaves and the products of their labor. The wealth of slave owners was also spread around when they bought materials from northern manufacturers. And before slavery was outlawed in northern states, some northerners owned slaves and benefited from their labor. The important point is that the wealth created by slaves ended up in many hands *other than their own*.

People of African descent who were enslaved could not simply say, "We're getting a raw deal here, so we'll just move on and try a more pleasant way to make a living." Laws written by and for slave owners, and the use of organized violence to enforce those laws, made it impossible for slaves to opt out of the system, other than by escape or suicide. But force per se isn't what made slavery exploitative. It was exploitative because one group of people took an unfair share of the value created by other people's labor. Because the system was unfair and inhumane, force was needed to hold it in place.

As with the theft of Native American land, most Americans today, including those who identify as "white," recognize the injustice of slavery. It's hardly controversial to say that enslaved African peoples created great wealth for their owners and for others with whom slave owners did business. But we see this sort of thing more easily in retrospect. It's easier to say, "Yes, a lot of inequality was created long ago through theft and exploitation," than it is to admit that similar processes operate today. It is even harder to admit that we might be implicated in such processes.

Inequality as an Accomplishment

One way to sum up what I've been saying is this: Inequality is an *accomplishment*. It doesn't just happen, like the wind or the rain; it happens because of how people think and act. This means, for one thing, that we need not accept inequality as a mysterious fact about the social world. We can understand it by studying what people think and do. But if we say that inequality is an accomplishment, and that it often arises out of theft, extortion, and exploitation, does this mean that it's caused solely by the conscious acts of mean and selfish people?

The simple answer is no. It is fair to say, however, that inequality is *sometimes* the intended result of actions consciously undertaken by people who would qualify, by modern standards, as "mean and selfish." There are plenty of historical examples. In fact, some people would think of land theft from Native Americans and the enslavement of Africans as examples. But here's why things are more complicated: Even people who strive to create inequality for their own benefit rarely think of themselves as mean or selfish, and usually they deny that what they are doing is wrong—even if this seems clear to people on the outside.

Another complication is that people who are robbed and exploited may come to accept their plight. They might see it, for example, as ordained by God or nature. (Of course, we must look at where such beliefs come from.) Still another complication is that creating inequality on a large scale involves many people doing things that seem to have no connection to theft, extortion, or exploitation. They might see themselves as merely doing their jobs, or doing what's necessary to make a living, with no intention of harming anyone.

So while inequality is an accomplishment, it's not always obvious to the people involved, as they go about their everyday lives, *how* it's being accomplished. This suggests that to understand how inequality is reproduced, we will have to look at processes that people may not even realize they are caught up in. We will also have to look at processes that result in inequality, even when that's not what most people intend to make happen. . . .

Relationships, Practices, and Processes

Earlier I said that sociologists usually think of class as a matter of economic inequality. The idea is that people can be ranked on the basis of wealth and income. This way of thinking accords with common sense in U.S. society. We have no trouble thinking of rich people as being in a different—and usually we think "higher"—class than people who are middle class or poor. Yet there is something missing from this view.

Certainly it's important to look at the economic resources that people have acquired and how much they regularly take in, because income and wealth are hugely consequential in many ways. But, as I've argued, "How much?" isn't the only important question. We should also ask, "How?" This question calls for looking at what it is that people do within the economic system, especially how they *relate to others* within the system.

In the previous section I discussed some possibilities: steal from others, extort others, exploit others, work for others and hope to get some value in return, produce things of value for use or trade. If we think in these terms, it makes less sense to think of "class" simply as a matter of ranking based on income or wealth. If we think in terms of what people do and how they relate to others, different labels come to mind. It might even be helpful to avoid referring to classes at all, at least for the moment.

One reason to forgo using the term "class" is that it brings to mind a group that operates at the societal level. Referring, for instance, to a "ruling class" implies a group that dominates a whole society. But the processes through which resources accumulate can operate on smaller scales, and it's those processes we need to understand. It might be more useful, then, to refer to a group—of any size, operating on any scale, in any context—in terms of what it does. We might thus think of an exploiting group, a working group, and a collaborating group that helps the exploiting group keep the working group under control.

While such terms are too simple to describe any modern society, they can help us think about class as a matter of process; that is, as a matter of how people relate to each other in ways that create and sustain resource inequalities.[10] The idea is to shift from looking at how much stuff people possess to looking at what they are able to do—with, for, and to others—by virtue of the kind of resources they control. Popular terms such as "upper class," "middle class," and "lower class" aren't helpful in this regard. Such terms tell us nothing about how these groups relate to each other, nor about where their resources come from.

Looking at economic inequality in terms of relationships and practices also suggests questions that might not arise if we think solely in terms of grouping and ranking people on the basis of accumulated resources. For instance: How do people get into a position from which they can exploit others? How do they actually use the resources they control? What kind of cooperation is required from whom? How are others rendered vulnerable to exploitation?

This isn't to say it's never useful to talk about class or classes. On the contrary, these terms remind us that *many people are in similar positions when it comes to how they generate and accumulate resources*. To talk about classes also reminds us that we're looking at a system of relationships and collective practices, not the idiosyncratic, uncoordinated actions of individuals. It's important to keep this "system view" in mind, lest it seem that inequality is simply the result of conniving by a few mean and nasty people. We should remain cautious, however, in using language that can obscure the practices and processes through which exploitative economic relationships are created and sustained.

Race

There is still a lot of discussion among sociologists (and others) about the best way to think of race and gender. One source of confusion is the tendency to talk about race and gender as if they were natural objects. This way of talking implies that we can gaze into the social world and see race and gender just like astronomers see stars in the sky. But while natural objects exist apart from human action, race and gender do not. Unlike stars, race and gender are social constructions, which means that they exist only because of what people think and do.[11]

When people claim that they can see "race," all they are seeing are external bodily differences (e.g., skin color) on the basis of which they have learned to categorize others. Because bodily differences are biological, people mistakenly believe that racial categories are biological, even though this notion has been discredited for at least 50 years. While some racial categorization schemes loosely correspond to gene pools, "race" is a political notion.[12] It is best thought of as a myth invented for the sake of creating or reinforcing inequality.

The term "race" itself is part of the problem, because the term masks the action that goes into constructing the myth and keeping it alive. A better term to use is racializing, which implies action.[13] This term reminds us that race does not exist as part of nature but is a result of how people define and treat each other. What we think of as the obvious fact of "race" is thus really a product of human imagining. This does not mean, however, that the consequences of racial categorization schemes are imaginary.

So why would a person or group try to racialize anyone else? Why invent race schemes and use them to impose identities on others and to claim an identity for one's self? The answer lies in seeing that these schemes do not merely describe difference; rather, they inscribe inequality.

The racial categorization schemes invented in the late nineteenth and early twentieth centuries were based on the idea that human groups had evolved at different rates. Intelligence, creativity, industry, and morality were seen as the hallmarks of human evolution. These criteria were then used to rank human groups from least evolved to most evolved. Since it was Europeans dreaming up these schemes and doing the judging, it's not surprising that they put themselves at the top of the list. The "races" of Africa, Asia, North and South America, the South Pacific, and so on were seen as less fully evolved, and hence inferior.[14]

This way of dividing people helped to justify colonialism and slavery. If Europeans were the superior race, it made sense that they should be in charge. The inferior races would do better, it was argued, if they submitted to control by Europeans, whose greater intelligence and morality would hasten the advance of global civilization. In this view, it made sense for Europeans to take other people's resources and to put those people to work in fields and mines. It also made sense to use whips and guns to maintain control, since that was often the only way to deal with people who could not grasp that they were better off being enslaved.

Colonialism and slavery existed long before Darwin's ideas about evolution were invoked to justify these practices. In earlier times, mythology and religion were used to define some people as inferior and thus as legitimate targets of conquest and exploitation. Those who attempt to racialize others tend to use the ideas that are most respected in a given place and time.

Whether mythology, religion, or science provides the background ideas, the principle is the same. One group defines itself as superior as a way to justify exploiting others and to make the process easier. If people can be convinced that they are inferior, or that God wants them to suffer on earth, they are more likely to accept being exploited. Racializing can also be used to cause division and conflict within an exploited group, thus making it harder for members of the group to fight back in an organized way. The exploiting group then laughs, as the saying goes, all the way to the bank.

In sum, we must be careful if we talk about "race" as part of trying to understand how inequality is reproduced. If inequality is an accomplishment, we need language that calls our attention to what it is that people do. And one thing that groups striving for dominance have often done is to invent schemes to divide and rank people. If embraced, these schemes serve to justify exploitation and make people easier to control. What we think of as "gender" works much the same way.

Gender

Many people balk at seeing gender as socially constructed. "Look," they will say, "women and men are fundamentally and undeniably *different*. Women get pregnant and have babies, and men don't. Get it? So the idea that gender is social rather than natural is silly." While it's true that women can give birth and men can't, gender is no more a simple matter of reproductive anatomy than race is a matter of skin color. To sort this matter out, it helps to reexamine some things we usually take for granted.

Certainly we can group human beings based on differences in reproductive anatomy. We can call humans with penises "males" and those with vaginas "females." Some people would say that there is nothing suspect about this practice; it is self-evidently true, they would insist, that some humans are males and others are females.

It's true that bodily differences exist in nature, but the *categories* "male" and "female" are human inventions, created with language.[15] Even more clearly an invention is the idea that males and females are different kinds of people. It is one thing to say that humans come in two types with regard to reproductive anatomy, and another thing to say that therefore there are two types of people, each type possessing distinct aptitudes, inclinations, and abilities. To arrive at the latter belief takes a lot of imagination.[16]

When infants are born, they are inspected and assigned to a sex category: male or female. Then begins a long process through which they are taught to do what they are supposed to do as members of the gender category that corresponds to their assigned sex category. Just to state what we all know: Males are supposed to become boys, then men; females are supposed to become girls, then women. In U.S. culture, no other options are approved.

What we usually overlook about this process is how much defining, teaching, rewarding, and punishing it takes, over many years, to create gendered beings. Males do not automatically turn into boys and men. They must be taught, first of all, that sex and gender categories exist and are important; that people can and should be sorted into these categories; and that they belong to one set of categories (males/boys/men) and not the other (females/girls/women).

But learning the categories is just a beginning. Males must then be taught, through punishment and reward and by example, to think, feel, and behave in ways that are culturally prescribed for boys and men. Along the way, they also learn to punish and reward others for their proper or improper displays of gender. Females learn analogous lessons as they are molded into girls and women. (Again, just to acknowledge the obvious: Not everyone passively accepts the standard cultural prescriptions regarding gender; there is resistance, negotiation, and improvisation.)

So, just as there are schemes that impose racial identities on people, there are schemes that impose sex and gender identities on people. These identities in turn shape people's experiences in profound ways. And while bodily differences are indeed natural, the meanings attached to these differences are cultural. If no one thought to divide humans into the categories male/female or women/men, or if these categories had no bearing on what people were taught to think, feel, and do, then gender—at least as we know it—would not exist.

Does this mean that gender schemes, like racial categorization schemes, were invented to divide and rank people as a way to aid exploitation? For some people, the answer is yes. According to this view, the first exploitative relationship in the history of our species was between males and females. Males, the argument goes, used their greater size and strength to force females to do a disproportionate share of the work necessary to survive. The argument goes on to suggest that it was a small step from males exploiting females within their own clans and tribes to groups of males using organized violence to enslave and exploit other clans and tribes.

In this view, large-scale exploitative systems, such as slavery and feudalism, and later capitalism, are seen as outgrowths of patriarchy.[17] It's hard to nail down this kind of causal link. But two things are clear from the historical record: Patriarchy predates feudalism and capitalism; and males have often used their greater size and strength—and thus their greater capacity for physical violence—to dominate society. There have of course been powerful women, but their power has always depended on the ability to mobilize men who could use violence effectively.[18]

In principle, a "sexual division of labor"—that is, dividing the necessary societal labor along male/female lines—need not be exploitative. Males and females could do an equal amount of different kinds of work, for which they were rewarded equitably, with neither group benefiting at the other's expense. In modern industrial societies, however, gender remains a scheme for dividing humans into types based on anatomy, ranking them based on their capacity for dominance, and then using this ranking to determine who will be stuck doing the least desirable, lowest-paid work.[19] To the extent that this scheme allows males to accrue an unequal share of resources at the expense of females, it can be called exploitative. . . .

It should be apparent that it's hard to talk about inequality in U.S. society, or anywhere else, without using the familiar terms "race," "class," and "gender."

As handy and indispensable as these terms are, they can keep us from seeing inequality as a result of what people think and do. What I've thus been arguing for is a shift from thinking about inequality in terms of categories to thinking about it in terms of relationships, practices, and processes. The danger is that if we treat race, class, and gender as things that are somehow just there, like features of the natural world, we might mistakenly conclude that it is beyond human ability to change them. . . .

Notes

1. Status refers to prestige, *esteem in the eyes of others*, or, as Max Weber called it, "social honor." Generally speaking, a person with higher status receives more deference and respect than a person with lower status. How much status a person has depends on what is valued in a culture. In the contemporary United States status is determined by occupation, education (and other forms of achievement), fame and visibility, and wealth and power. It is also determined by the values attached to racial and gender categories, sexual identities, and physical capability.

2. For information about inequality on a global scale, see the University of California–Santa Cruz Atlas of Global Inequality (http://ucatlas.ucsc.edu/).

3. For a variety of perspectives on the economics of hunter-gatherer societies, see John Gowdy (ed.), *Limited Wants, Unlimited Means* (Island Press, 1997).

4. See Charles Tilly, *Durable Inequality* (University of California Press, 1998).

5. These estimates are for the land mass that lies north of present-day Mexico. See William Denevan (ed.), *The Native Population of the Americas in 1492* (University of Wisconsin Press, 1992, 2nd ed.). For a wider discussion of life on the North American continent before the European invasion, see Charles Mann, *1491: New Revelations of the Americas before Columbus* (Knopf, 2005).

6. See Jared Diamond, *Guns, Germs, and Steel* (Norton, 1997).

7. My analysis of exploitation draws from Erik Wright, "Class Analysis," pp. 1–42 in *Class Counts* (Cambridge University Press, 1997). See also Tilly, *Durable Inequality*, pp. 117–146.

8. Those who do the bossing often claim that their work is essential and that it too creates value. This argument is superficially plausible, though it's often the case that those who benefit primarily from *owning* the means of production do very little coordinating or creating themselves (see David Schweickart, *After Capitalism* [Rowman and Littlefield, 2002], pp. 31–39). There is also the issue of proportionality. One can acknowledge the utility of coordinative work and still question the rate at which such work is rewarded. Finally, there is the matter of who determines the rates at which various kinds of work are rewarded. A lack of democracy in making such determinations is the hallmark of an exploitative economic system.

9. See Anne Farrow, Joel Lang, and Jenifer Frank, *Complicity: How the North Promoted, Prolonged, and Profited from Slavery* (Ballantine, 2005).

10. There is, of course, more than one way to conceptualize class and class relations. For discussions of various ways to do so, see Erik Wright (ed.), *Approaches to Class Analysis* (Cambridge University Press, 2005).

11. The classic expression of the social constructionist perspective in sociology is found in Peter Berger and Thomas Luckmann's *The Social Construction of Reality* (Doubleday Anchor, 1966).

12. See the statement of race by the American Anthropological Association (http://www.aaanet.org/stmts/racepp.htm); and Howard Winant, "Race and Race Theory," *Annual Review of Sociology* (2000) 26: 169–185. Recent research has found patterns of gene pool variation that roughly correspond to continental groupings of humans. It is a mistake, however, to use the archaic, baggage-laden term "races" to refer to these groups, since they do not constitute racial groups in the pernicious way that such groups are popularly understood. For an example of this mistake, see Nicholas Wade, *Before the Dawn* (Penguin, 2006), pp. 181–201.

13. Michael Omi and Howard Winant use the term "racializing projects" to discuss the historical construction of racial categories and identities. See Omi and Winant, *Racial Formation in the United States: From the 1960s to the 1990s* (Routledge, 1994, 2nd ed.).

14. For a critical analysis of scientific racism, see Stephen Jay Gould's *The Mismeasure of Man* (Norton, 1981).

15. See Suzanne Kessler and Wendy McKenna, *Gender: An Ethnomethodological Approach* (University of Chicago Press, 1978).

16. Stereotypes about gender differences lead us to imagine far greater differences between women and men than actually exist. For an overview of the research showing how slight these differences are, see R. W. Connell, *Gender* (Polity Press, 2002), pp. 40–46. See also Cynthia Epstein, *Deceptive Distinctions* (Yale University Press, 1988).

17. On the relationship between capitalism and patriarchy, see Michele Barrett, *Women's Oppression Today* (Verso, 1980); Zillah Eistenstein (ed.), *Capitalist Patriarchy* (Monthly Review Press, 1979); Gerda Lerner, *The Creation of Patriarchy* (Oxford University Press, 1986); and Maria Mies, *Patriarchy and Accumulation on a World Scale* (Zed Books, 1986).

18. Allan Johnson examines women's place and power under patriarchy in *The Gender Knot* (Temple University Press, 2005, 2nd ed.), pp. 8–9, 15–19, 59–66.

19. See Judith Lorber, *Paradoxes of Gender* (Yale University Press, 1994), pp. 13–36; and "Shifting Paradigms and Challenging Categories," *Social Problems* (2006) 53: 448–453.

Questions

1. What does Schwalbe mean by inequality? What resources are at stake in inequalities? What nonmaterial resources are important for leading meaningful lives? Are all forms of resource imbalance—where one group has more resources than others—problematic? What makes "inequality" problematic?

2. Schwalbe explains that there is nothing natural about inequalities—that human beings create inequalities by thinking and acting together. If people create equality or inequality, how do inequalities arise in the first place? What is settled agriculture, and why did inequality arise with this economic system? Why do inequalities seem natural and inevitable when, in fact, they are relatively recent historical phenomena?

3. What is exploitation, and what role does it play in inequalities? How do people go about exploiting each other? What tools do they use? What resources do they exploit?

4. What are "class," "race," and "gender?" How is thinking of them as verbs different from thinking of them as nouns? Is class a different type of inequality? Why doesn't Schwalbe want us to think about class as upper-, middle-, and lower-class groups of people? What does Schwalbe mean when he says that race and gender are social constructions? If race and gender are not the natural result of biological differences, what are they? What is their relationship to economic resources? What if we extend this thinking to disabilities? How does thinking of disabilities as social phenomena shape the questions we ask?

5. If something is socially constructed, does that mean it isn't real? That it is simply in people's heads?

6. In 1998, the American Anthropological Association (AAA) released a statement on race, explaining the cultural—rather than biological—origins of race. Read the statement on the AAA's web page or here: http://www.understandingrace.org/about/statement.html. Then examine the link (or lack thereof, more accurately) between race and biology at http://www.understandingrace.org/humvar/index.html. What is the relationship between race and the body, especially skin color and genes? How well does genetic variation match with racial categories? How much genetic variation exists across racial groups? What about within them? What roles do genes and environment play in creating diseases such as sickle cell anemia and hypertension? If sociologists mean something other than biological variation when they talk about race, what *are* races? By extension, what are disabilities?

2

Origins of Inequality and Uneven Development

JAMES W. RUSSELL

In the previous reading, Michael Schwalbe argued for thinking of inequality as an accomplishment—something individuals create and recreate together, through repeated, coordinated actions. Considering inequality something *we do* shifts our thinking. Rather than viewing inequality as a natural state of being, one that has always existed and will always exist—regardless of our best efforts otherwise—an accomplishment approach pushes us to understand inequality empirically as anything but inevitable. We look to explain how and why inequality exists. If inequality is an accomplishment, it is an historical phenomenon, whose creation and development we can trace across time. Rather than taking inequality for granted, then, we seek answers: When did inequality develop? How did people maintain equality at other times in history? When did things change? What changed them? What tools did people use to dominate others, and how have they changed over time? How did people resist subordination, and what was most successful?

These are some of the questions that James Russell's historical examination of the European conquest of North America addresses. Russell demonstrates the economic and racial foundations of inequality. The history begins with indigenous peoples who maintained systems of equality until relatively recently. Their communal approach to economics and reproduction, shared property ownership, nomadism, and lack of surplus allowed for interdependence and mutuality that we today recognize as social equality. The advent of horticulture, settled agriculture and plowing, private property, surplus, and a management class, however, brought about economic stakes to be monopolized and people to be exploited to do so.

Russell then traces the conquest of native peoples across North America by the Spanish, Dutch, British, and French. His account draws a complex picture of what undergirds inequality. Among other social processes, Russell shows how Europeans played on native belief systems, appropriated local social systems for their own use, exploited existing tensions, exposed people without immunity to new diseases, and decimated kinship systems to conquer new lands and people. His work forces readers to consider the variation in domination based on the economic systems of the conquerors.

Finally, Russell's piece illustrates for the reader the close interconnection of racialization and what we know of as class. He argues that Europeans fostered racial groupings and racist beliefs to justify the extermination, domination, and enslavement of other people. Essentially, race served an economic end.

Russell's account is the historical embodiment of Schwalbe's accomplishment approach. It applies empiricism to understand the social origins of inequalities as a historically contingent story of domination. Europeans created vast systems of inequality, structural and ideological in form, in order to accrue material and cultural resources. There was nothing natural or inevitable about it.

Excerpted from Russell, James W. 2009. *Class and Race Formation in North America*. Toronto. University of Toronto Press. Pp. 13–33. Reprinted with permission of the publisher.

The modern history of class and race in North America begins with the violent imposition of European colonial rule over pre-existing indigenous societies. Never before or after has world history witnessed human devastation on this scale. Across all of the Americas as many as 150 million Indians succumbed within a century to the guns, forced labor, or diseases of their conquerors. During the same period, millions of Africans were kidnapped and brought to the Americas to work as slaves. It is impossible to understand the contemporary class inequality of Indians and African Americans without first examining these historical antecedents.

It is further no accident that racism—the ideological belief that there are superior and inferior races—developed during this period of conquest and colonization. Europe had had only small-scale trading relationships with non-Europeans from Africa and Asia until colonization brought them into extensive contacts and exploitative class relationships with indigenous peoples. The colonization of the Americas represents the first time in world history that different races were combined in class structures on a large scale. It is in this context that Europeans developed the modern ideology of racism as a pseudoscientific attempt to rationalize and justify the social fact that they were forcing non-whites into the lowest economic and class positions.

Racist ideologists first questioned the degree to which indigenous peoples were human beings at all. In the decades following the conquest of the Aztec empire, there were actual debates in Europe over the question of whether Indians were fully human beings or beings lower on the scale of development. If they were lower beings, then Christian moral principles would not apply to them. Pope Paul III resolved the dispute in 1537, at least for the Church, when he issued a bull proclaiming Indians to be fully human beings. That decree, of course, did not end white racist attitudes toward Indians.

The next targets of racist ideology were Black slaves. Racists justified their enslavement on the grounds that they were inferior creatures to be treated not much differently from farm animals. New world slave masters agreed with the Roman distinction that an animal was an *instrumentum mutum* while the slave was an *instrumentum semi-vocale*.

The modern history of North American class and racial inequality thus begins with European conquest and colonization. The full history of North America,

though, begins with the peoples who migrated from Asia across the Bering Strait and inhabited the continent for at least 22,000 years and perhaps as much as 50,000 years prior to European arrival.[1]

Indigenous Societies on the Eve of the Conquest

The earliest indigenous societies of North America were made up of nomadic hunters and gatherers. These types of societies continued for millennia. Among the most important were the Chichimecas in northern Mesoamerica—the area from about 100 miles north of present-day Mexico City to Panama—and the Apaches, Navajo, Plains Indians, Sioux, Iroquois, and Cree further to the north. They lived and moved together in small bands that rarely exceeded 50 persons.

There was an essential economic and social equality among these hunters and gatherers, making them, in social and economic terms, communal societies. There was no sense of ownership of land or any other type of means of production. There could be possession of tents and other articles, but because all possessions had to be moved from place to place as hunting territories shifted, these possessed articles were, of necessity, simple, and the opportunity to accumulate personal wealth was limited. The social differentiation that did exist was restricted to non-class status or prestige bases. The leader of a band enjoyed more prestige than the others but did not possess significantly more material wealth.

These were also stateless societies in the sense that there was no regular group of officials who lived off taxing the rest. Political decision-making certainly existed as adults within the bands met to deliberate over common problems such as when to move or how to confront enemies. However, because of the small band populations, it was possible and desirable for all members to participate. In this sense, communal societies were essentially democratic, not out of ideological conviction but because their small population bases made any other form of common decision-making unworkable.

Throughout Mesoamerica and in some regions to the north, beginning as long as 8,000 years ago—the dawn of the Neolithic revolution of the Americas[2]—groups of indigenous peoples achieved technological mastery of elementary farming. They lived within sedentary villages and cultivated the soil as their means of producing food, with supplements coming from hunting, fishing, and gathering. These village communities were the first locations of class differentiation in North America. Typically, as land became valuable as a means of production, households and families sought to obtain control over greater quantities of it and reserve for themselves the most fertile parcels. Land-rich families had the means to produce more for themselves and thus enjoyed greater levels of consumption and social class standards of living than land-poor families.

Land-rich families at first relied on their own labor. Only later were they able to monopolize possession of enough land so that other community members became landless and forced into the subordinate economic class positions of being either renters or laborers. In this sense, social class differentiation preceded economic class differentiation in both world and North American history. Most of these village communities were within the Mesoamerican part of North America.

North of Mesoamerica, there were two important groups. Spanish colonizers originally applied the term "Pueblo" to describe all the Indians in their northern territories (centered mostly in present-day New Mexico) who lived within village communities. The Pueblos thus were not a culturally unified single tribe or nation but rather a heterogeneous grouping of village communities. At the time of first Spanish contact, there were between 130,000 and 248,000 Indians living within approximately 100 Pueblo village communities.[3] They practiced horticulture—use of hoes to cultivate small garden-sized plots of land—and there is evidence of elementary social class differentiation, with an elite having privileged access to consumption items.

The Iroquois, who lived across parts of what today is eastern Canada and the northeastern United States, were more developed than the Pueblos. They practiced horticulture, from which as much as 80 percent of their food supplies came, the balance coming from hunting, fishing, and gathering.[4] Several families lived together within longhouses, and a number of longhouses were grouped together within village communities. At the end of the fifteenth century, well before permanent European settlement, five of the Iroquois tribes or nations, including the Mohawk, joined together in the Iroquois Confederation, the most complex indigenous political formation north of Mexico. The basic purposes of the confederation were to suppress internal warfare and join forces for an effective military alliance against other tribes.

State empires, which grouped together large numbers of village communities, were the largest in scale and the most complex societies of pre-Columbian North America. A number of these, of which the Aztec and Mayan are only the most well-known, existed for some 2,000 years prior to the Conquest in the three main zones of Mesoamerica: the *altiplano* or central highlands spreading outward from the Valley of Mexico, where Mexico City is located today; the Gulf Coast, where the Mexican states of Veracruz and Tabasco are today; and the area that now contains the Mexican Yucatan peninsula, Belize, and Guatemala. The first state society of which there is evidence was the Olmec, centered in Veracruz beginning approximately in 1500 BC. The classic period of the Maya was from 300 to 900 AD. In the central highlands the Aztec empire (1350–1522) was preceded by the Tula (856–1168) and Teotihuacan (200–650).

The state empires were class-based societies in which the dominant class exercised its domination by virtue of controlling the state, which in turn financed itself by collecting exploitative tribute payments from the village communities that it dominated. Roger Bartra, who systematically studied Aztec documents and generalized his findings to other similar types of pre-Columbian empires, concluded that "the exploitation took the form of a tribute imposed on the communities (paid in kind, work, or primitive forms of money) that was in reality a rent paid to the sovereign for the use of the land of which, because of divine grace, he was the absolute owner."[5] Jared Diamond concluded that "the tribute received by the Aztecs each year from subject peoples included 7,000 tons of corn, 4,000 toris of beans, 4,000 tons of grain amaranth, 2,000,000 cotton cloaks, and huge quantities of cacao beans, war costumes, shields, feather headdresses, and amber."[6]

The Aztec empire was by far the largest and most developed of the state societies. It encompassed a territory the size of Italy and contained as many as 25 million people.[7] Its capital city, Tenochtitlan, where Mexico City lies today, had a population of between 250,000 and 500,000, making it one of the world's largest cities of its day—as Mexico City is today.

A fused ruling class of military, political, and religious leaders sat at the top. The economic role of this ruling class was to accumulate and direct the investment of tribute payments in products and labor.

The leaders had their own tribute-collecting bureaucracy. Once collected, tributes were invested in—aside from consumption needs of the ruling class—military and infrastructure (roads, aqueducts, etc.) maintenance and expansion. At the base of Aztec society were peasants living in largely self-sufficient households and village communities. Most household food supplies came from horticulture, with supplements coming from hunting and gathering, fishing and herding. Surpluses—what was produced beyond household consumption needs—were destined to be tribute payments and trade.

Village communities generally had at least sporadic market days when peasants would gather to exchange their surpluses. This gave rise to an economic class of merchants and craft workers who serviced the markets. The merchants specialized in buying and selling for a profit, and the craft workers sold their products and services. In addition to the economic classes of the ruling class, merchants, and peasants, there was also a small slave class drawn mainly from war captives, debtors, and criminals. Unlike the slavery of Ancient Greece and Rome or the slavery that would later come after the European conquest, this slavery was limited. The condition of slavery did not pass on to the children of slaves, and slave labor and products were not essential bases of the Aztec economy.

In terms of consumption levels—that is, social classes—Aztec society spread from the lower classes of poor peasants and slaves to the rich upper class, which was made up of the members of the ruling households. In between was a small middle class made up mainly of prosperous merchants in Tenochtitlan.

To this economic and social portrait of Aztec society must be added an account of the Aztec worldview and profound religiosity, both of which played important institutional roles in daily life and which became key factors that would influence the course of the Conquest. The Aztecs deeply believed that they lived within a divine order that governed every aspect of their lives—from the positioning of the stars to their personal destinies. That was what made sense to them and what gave purpose to their lives. Within this order, the god Huitzilopochtli, the incarnation of the sun, continually had to fight against the forces of darkness and death. The sun had to emerge victorious or life would be completely extinguished. Each darkening, from sunsets to eclipses, marked the beginning of the sun's battle with the forces of darkness, and each dawn indicated that the sun had emerged victorious and life would go on.

According to Aztec belief, the purpose of all activities—making war, harvesting, and sacrificing victims—was to maintain this divine order. Any failure could disrupt its functioning. If a drought came, that was a sign as well as punishment, indicating that the Aztecs had not complied enough with their divine obligations. Sacrifices of their own blood were necessary to put themselves back in place in the divine order. This fatalistic worldview explains why the Aztecs went to the extremes of carrying out human sacrifices. They deeply believed both that it was true and that they were powerless to do anything but comply, otherwise the whole cosmological order would collapse. That was their obligation if both they, not as individuals but as a people, and the whole divine order were to survive. The Aztecs also believed that their cosmological world—that of the Fifth Sun—had been preceded by four previous worlds, each one of which had ended in calamity. Their world also was destined to end apocalyptically—as it did.

Europe on the Eve of the Conquest

Europe at the time of the conquest was at distinctly different levels of technological and social development than the societies of North America. In contrast to North America, where horticulture that relied on humans wielding hoes was the highest level of technology achieved, Europe had known for more than a millennium more sophisticated and productive agricultural technologies that employed animal-drawn plows to cultivate fields. The Europeans would bring the animal-drawn plow with them and introduce it to the Americas. In terms of social development, unlike North America where the Aztec state society was the highest level of complexity, Europe in the sixteenth century was passing from feudalism to capitalism.

European feudalism, as described most completely by Marc Bloch, was composed of essentially precommodity natural and self-sufficient manorial economies in which landlords controlled use of the land, which they rented out to peasants.[8] Peasants for the most part produced products for their own household consumption. Their surplus products were divided between those that were used for rent payments and those that were marketed.

Capitalism required a radical transformation of feudalism, necessitating the development of free markets in labor, the means of production (capital), and products. That meant that peasant labor had to be divorced from the land in order to be available for hire. Land—the principal feudal means of production—had to become available for sale. Products of labor were sold in markets rather than consumed directly by their producers. All three types of markets were already at various stages of development in Europe at the time of the Conquest to such an extent that it was possible to speak of the emergence of market-organized capitalist societies.

The Conquest

In North America the Spanish, British, French, and Dutch took control of different areas and the indigenous peoples within them. The largest scale and most spectacular of the conquests took place, logically, in what today is Mexico, where the indigenous population was the most numerous and developed. One of the great mysteries that has puzzled generations of historians was how it was possible for Hernán Cortés with just 500 soldiers to overthrow a warrior empire that controlled experienced armies with hundreds of thousands of men. The puzzle has generally been answered in three ways.

First, the Aztec empire did not offer unified resistance to the invaders. The Aztecs had enemies on their borders and discontented peoples within. As they continually sought to expand their boundaries and tributary areas, they met resistance from smaller state societies, such as Tlaxcala. Within the areas that they had conquered, there was resentment and discontent among many of the village communities and subject peoples. Cortés was able to take advantage of these fissures and enlist the Aztecs' enemies in his own armies. In other cases, he defeated smaller indigenous armies on the periphery of the Aztec empire and then added their ranks to his own. In part they combined with the conquistador cause as armies that have been thoroughly routed on the battlefield by overwhelming forces often do. In part Cortés obliged them to join his armies as a term of surrender. By the time he made his final assault on Tenochtitlan, his 500 men were backed up by over 100,000 indigenous soldiers.

There is a certain racial mythology surrounding these events. Because Cortés had substantial numbers of Indian allies, it is misleading to see the initial conquest as entirely a battle between Spanish and Indians. Cortés marched into a situation in which the indigenous peoples were not united. They belonged to different, and often warring, state empires (such as the Aztecs and Tlaxcalans); they were simple oppressed subjects of one or another empire; or they lived outside of the control of empires and only had localized identities. To believe that they could have developed a unity that overrode all of these divisions is to believe that common racial identity is (or should be) the moving force of history.

In this respect, Mexican nationalism and national identity have been largely formed out of a particular interpretation of the Conquest: They begin with the indigenous peoples long before the arrival of the Spanish who tragically ended their civilizations. The dominant interpretation views Cortés as an invader. . . . Even more disdained in Mexican history is Cortés's Indian interpreter and lover, Malintzin or *Doña* Marina, as the Spanish called her, whose advice significantly aided his victories. Referred to as *La Malinche*, a variation of her Indian name, she is seen as the great betrayer of pre-Hispanic Mexico. Today, many Mexicans denounce as *malinchistas* those compatriots whom they accuse of identifying more with foreigners than with their own country. The interpretation of the role of Malinche is also related to the cultural complex of *machista* ideas in which men see and fear all women as potential betrayers. The problem, as Roger Bartra has pointed out, is that there was no pre-Hispanic Mexican homeland to be betrayed. Mexico as a nation developed after, not before, the Conquest.[9]

The second factor instrumental in the defeat of the Aztecs was disease. When the Spanish arrived in the Americas, they unwittingly brought with them the germs of diseases that had spread earlier through Europe. The Spanish themselves over generations had built up relative resistances to these diseases, but the Americas had had no biological experience with them. Hence, when contact was made, diseases spread rapidly through the indigenous populations. Alfred M. Crosby, among others, has concluded that one of the reasons why the Aztecs could not put up stronger resistance to the conquistadores was that many of them were very sick or dying from European diseases during decisive battles.[10]

The third influencing factor was the Aztec world-view or belief system. As mentioned, the Aztecs deeply believed that sooner or later their world would end apocalyptically. It was within this context that the Aztec ruler Montezuma and most of his advisors initially believed that the Spanish conquistadores were gods and harbingers of a divinely ordered destruction of their world, against which there was nothing that could be done except to accept it fatalistically. This subjective factor weakened the Aztec defenses and allowed the conquistadores a relatively easy conquest. Even if the Aztecs were not completely sure that their doom had already been divinely ordained, there was enough of a generalized doubt throughout the ranks of their armies to vitiate resistance. The Aztecs had never seen guns or horses before. The deafening sounds and deadly fire spit out by the guns as well as the size and speed of the beasts that carried their bearers were terrifying. In addition, disfiguring diseases descended upon them. All these unsettling events confirmed their belief that the apocalyptic end was indeed near. Once conquered, the Aztecs were fatalistically pre-disposed, because of their deeply rooted belief system, to accept that the world of the Fifth Sun was no more and that a new world with a new god had taken its place.

Soon after conquering Tenochtitlan, the Spanish began their military push northward, provoking a series of wars with the fiercely independent Chichimeca peoples. Further north, in the areas that would become the Southwest of the United States, the Spanish encountered further resistance, especially from the Apaches. As for the Pueblo village communities, the Spanish made peace with them at first. Then, in 1680, the Pueblos revolted and expelled the Spanish from New Mexico. Later the Spanish were able to return and coexist with the Pueblos, but they never were able to completely subdue the Apaches and other nomadic Indians, especially in western New Mexico, which is today Arizona.[11] The final submission of all of the indigenous bands came only with the U.S. military presence after the 1846–1848 Mexican-American War.

The other conquests that took place on the North American continent were less epic than what took place in Mexico but were as consequential for the indigenous peoples. The first permanent British settlements on the east coast of what would become the United States, the Jamestown and Plymouth colonies, were not established until nearly a century after the Spanish conquest of Tenochtitlan. The British settlement differed from the Spanish in three ways. First, unlike the Spanish, who confronted relatively densely populated areas, the British encountered sparse populations. Second, again unlike the Spanish, who sought to take advantage of abundant Indian labor to construct their colonial cities and later farm their lands, the British from the beginning arrived with an enclave mentality. They built their cities like fortresses, always seeking to keep the Indians beyond the limits of where they lived. Finally, unlike the Spanish, who lived with, and who with increasing frequency [had sexual relationships] with, indigenous people, the British strictly segregated themselves. There was one similarity: as in Mexico, European diseases took a heavy toll among the indigenous people. For example, diseases reduced the population of Northwest Coast Indians from 180,000 to 40,000 within a century of contact.[12]

As more settlers arrived seeking choice land for planting, the colonies expanded at the expense of the Indians. In time, expansion provoked resistance and wars broke out. Around Plymouth in 1675, King Phillip's War, named after the English name for the Indian chief, broke out. After defeating and capturing the Indians, the settlers executed the chief and placed his head on a stake, where it remained for 25 years. His wife and children were shipped to the West Indies and sold into slavery.[13]

The first permanent European settlers of the area of New York were the Dutch who founded New Netherlands. They too expanded their holdings violently at the expense of the Indians. In 1641, Dutch soldiers massacred all of the occupants of two Indian villages on Staten Island, a part of present-day New York City, while they slept. They then burned the villages to the ground.[14]

French settlers founded Canada's first permanent European colony at Quebec in 1608, approximately the same time as the founding of the Jamestown colony. The French settlers pursued a different policy with the Indians than the British did. For the most part, instead of segregating themselves, they formed alliances with different Indian groups in various internecine Indian wars. The largest of these was between the Algonquians and the Iroquois; beginning in 1609, the French sided with the Algonquians for a half century of fighting over control of the fur trade in the lower Great Lakes and St. Lawrence.

What sugar was to the Caribbean, fur was to New France. The French generally obtained furs, for which there was a growing world market subject to the dictates of fashion, from Indians, who often obtained them from other Indians further inland or collected them themselves. The French were thus the traders and the Indians the producers of furs. Unlike sugar, however, furs could not be produced under plantation conditions where a subjugated slave labor force could be concentrated. It had to be trapped over wide wooded areas. In 1649 the French decided to trap the furs themselves and dispense with the Indian middlemen, who were essentially "fur-collecting mercenary warriors."[15]

In most cases, the French attempted to work with Indian allies to defeat other Indians for the interests of France. The general policy of entering into alliances with one or another side of warring Indian tribes was not without exceptions, though. The first contact between the Beothuk people on Newfoundland and French fishers ended in confrontation, with the French attempting to hunt down and annihilate the entire Beothuk population.[16] As in all areas of North America, European diseases also took a heavy toll among the indigenous peoples in the north: In 1639, for example, a smallpox epidemic killed two-thirds of the 30,000 members of the Huron Confederacy.[17]

The indigenous societies of North America on the eve of the European conquests thus ranged, in developmental terms, from hunting and gathering bands of nomads to horticultural village communities to the state empires of Mesoamerica. Europe, by contrast, at that time was composed of agricultural societies in varying degrees of transformation from feudalism to capitalism. The conquest of North America started first in its most highly developed area, the Aztec Empire, and then over the next three centuries spread to remoter regions of the continent.

For the first time in North America class and race became correlates, with Indians being forced into the lower rungs of the colonial class systems as slaves, peasants, peons, and, certainly, the poor.

Colonial Reconstruction

After the Conquest, capitalism as an economic system, based on expanding markets and profit-oriented businesses, grew and developed unevenly across the North American continent. That much is obvious from its contemporary features in the United States, Mexico, and Canada. This uneven development came in large part because the Spanish and British, as well as the Dutch and French, imported different varieties of it and did so under different conditions.

Capitalism as such had developed unevenly across Europe as it displaced feudalism. Markets and workshops located in cities were its original centers, while the country remained mired in traditional feudal relationships. The economies of such countries as Britain and Holland became proportionately more capitalistic and less feudalistic at faster rates than countries like Spain and Portugal. Hence, the main colonizers of the areas of North America that would become the United States, Mexico, and Canada came from countries that represented significantly different hybrids of feudal and capitalist economic features.

In Spain, feudal features were proportionately more present than in Britain; thus, what the Spanish institutionally implanted in North America was proportionately more feudalistic than what the British implanted. In addition, the Spanish had to graft their economic practices onto those of the indigenous peoples who always greatly outnumbered them by ratios as great as 20 to 1. The British were not so encumbered by pre-existing indigenous practices since they quickly outnumbered the native population, which their colonists could push aside and economically marginalize. It followed that capitalism could and did develop much more rapidly in the British than Spanish areas.

The Spanish confronted large and complexly organized indigenous societies. They found it useful and relatively easy to absorb many of these indigenous state institutions into their own semifeudal forms of organization. The Aztec tribute payment, for example, was easily continued as a payment to the new Spanish authorities. This blending of two types of social organizations was possible because in many respects the prior indigenous state empires and the conquering feudal societies were similarly structured. In both, the ruling classes received payments of surplus products from subject classes, as tribute payments in the case of the indigenous state empires and as rent payments in the case of feudal societies. The main difference between the two was that the rule was centralized in the former and decentralized in the latter. But the form of domination, if not the source, was very similar.[18] Neither form of society, though, was compatible with capitalistic development. The noncapitalist aspects of Aztec and Spanish social and economic organization reinforced each other and acted as brakes on capitalism.

In contrast, in the British areas of North America, the indigenous peoples were from the beginning pushed away from the areas of colonization. Their forms of social and economic organization played no part in the social and economic organization of the colonies. In a double sense the conditions for capitalist development were much more favorable in the British than Spanish areas of North America. The British were more inclined to be capitalistic in the first place because their home country was experiencing rapid capitalist development. Second, North America represented a kind of institutional *tabula rasa* for them: they had a free hand to form the kinds of social and economic institutions that they wanted. They were not forced to absorb whole indigenous populations and take into account their pre-existing institutions, as were the Spanish colonizers.

To all of this must be added the different roles and consequences of religious institutions. The Spanish brought and deeply institutionalized a medieval Catholic creed that, as Max Weber powerfully argued, fettered capitalist development.[19] It held that the community had to devote a considerable amount of its labor and time to religious pursuits such as prayer and the construction of churches and viewed with suspicion labor directed at producing worldly wealth.

The Protestant theologies that reigned in British North America had a different view of economic activity. They found success in worldly pursuits to be positive signs of righteousness, and they were not so demanding of labor, time, and resources. The Protestant work ethic, the most important economic consequence of this worldview, resulted in generations of overproducers and underconsumers. Business owners reinvested their profits rather than spending them on luxury consumption items. Protestant workers were the answer to the capitalist dream: They worked hard without demanding high wages. Both classes of Protestants significantly accelerated the accumulation of capital. If the ornately constructed Catholic Church was the symbol of colonial culture in the Spanish-dominated areas, the no-nonsense simple New England church was the symbol of Puritan culture.

It followed that the Spanish and British areas developed unevenly at different speeds and with different features. Mexico inherited the institutional features of large haciendas, communal land holdings, significant natural economies, and a church that drained economic resources. The United States and Canada inherited an economic ethic more in tune with capitalist needs and an almost wide-open territory within which capitalism could develop, once it was cleared of the obstacles posed by the presence of its relatively few original inhabitants.

The indigenous populations were integrated into the social bases of the colonial class system in New Spain, composed of present-day Mexico and Central America, as slaves, laborers, peons, and peasants. The Spanish sought their labor. In the British areas, though, the dynamic was different. Indians were always outside of the evolving economic system. All that the new settlers wanted from them was their land.

If feudal and semifeudal institutions slowed the development of capitalism in part of North America, slavery, which existed in both the Spanish and southern British colonies, played a more supporting role. North American slavery, unlike peasant agriculture, was always related to capitalist development. The basic purpose of having a slave labor force was to produce products for which there was a market demand. Owners used slaves to mine silver and plant sugar, tobacco, and other crops for the world market. Slaves produced profits for their owners and significantly contributed to the overall accumulation of capital that launched international capitalism. . . .

In sum, the sixteenth-century varieties of capitalism that the Europeans brought with them were hybrids of feudal, slave, and capitalist formations. The three major varieties that developed were: a capitalism with significant feudal features in New Spain and New France; a slavery-based capitalism in the British southern colonies; and an elementary agrarian capitalism in the British northern colonies.

Spanish Colonial Society

New Spain represented both a radical uprooting and restructuring of Aztec society and an adaptation to it. The Spanish took over as the new ruling class and razed Aztec cities and places of worship in order to construct a new society in their own image. One of the most graphic monuments to this policy is at Cholula in

Puebla where the Spanish constructed a church precisely at the apex of the ruins of an indigenous pyramid. The visual symbolism of this act of cultural domination was paralleled later in the United States, when within a couple of decades of the final military conquest of the Sioux, the conquering power carved the faces of four of its presidents on the top of Mount Rushmore, a mountain sacred to the conquered. In both cases, conquerors through physical defacement of an indigenous shrine attempted to symbolize their power while simultaneously erasing the cultural pasts of the conquered.

The sheer size and cultural depth of the conquered indigenous population, though, forced the Spanish to include them within their institutions. They could not simply push Indians to frontier areas, as was done in the northern British colonies. Spanish feudal institutions were fairly easily transplanted and adapted to the new colonial conditions because, as mentioned earlier, the pre-existing Aztec state and the Spanish feudal economies shared a number of similar features. Peasant labor was the base of both types of economies, and, in both, peasants were accustomed to making tribute or rent payments to overlords. The Spanish, once they had lopped off the Aztec occupants of the ruling positions within the economic and social pyramids, simply took their places. . . .

The Spanish initially implanted the *encomienda* system. The Crown granted an individual, the *encomendero*, the right to collect tributes from the individuals, the *encomendados*, within an area. This was the first landlord-peasant economic class structure established by the Spanish in New Spain. The *encomienda* system represented not so much a break from as a continuation of the old pre-Hispanic state society forms of collecting tributes.[20] . . .

Angel Palerm Vich argues that not only were there institutional continuities between the pre-Hispanic and Spanish colonial economic class structures, but there were also continuities of individuals. According to him, during this period substantial numbers of the old Indian upper class remained largely intact. The Spanish allowed them to keep some of their properties and political authority and to continue collecting tributes from the Indian masses. The Spanish did not totally displace them at first but rather moved in alongside them in the class structure. "The Spanish and the superior indigenous class," writes Palerm Vich, "lived over the mass of aboriginal agriculturalists from whom they wrested part of their product by means of tribute payments."[21] In time, though, the Indian component of the early colonial upper class was almost completely edged out, with the Spanish taking over virtually all opportunities for acquiring upper-class incomes.

The *encomienda* system did not last long. Instead of being content with collecting tributes from Indians who continued their economic activities as they always had, the Spanish sought to develop and exploit the land and other natural resources. Toward that end they built their own haciendas to control both agriculture and ranching; took over mining operations; and seized control of state administration, commerce, and some production in the cities. The major economic actors were the hacienda owners, whose labor force consisted mainly of indigenous peasants; the church, which was a large landowner in its own right and holder of credit capital; and the colonial state, which controlled lucrative political and military positions.

Men could make their fortunes and insure their upper-class membership from the exploitation of peasant labor on the land they owned or from the exploitation of income opportunities afforded by controlling state posts. Although the church was a powerful economic actor, it did not so much generate upper-class members as receive them; that is, because of celibacy vows as well as the corporate organization of the institution, rich priests could not pass on fortunes to heirs. However, it was customary for at least one son of a rich family to become a priest who would quickly move into the upper echelons of the church. The church was thus a part of a colonial class society in which its priests along with landlords and state authorities ran the economic structure.

The colonial labor force was dualistic, as emphasized by Palerm Vich and others.[22] The core of the economy consisted of the hacienda, mining, and urban labor forces, but outside of that core existed subsistence-level villages and farms in which mainly Indians lived. These were in a double sense peripheral labor forces. First, they generated mostly subsistence products for household consumption. Such surplus products as they generated did not circulate beyond local markets. Second, they were outside of the control of the landlords and mine owners and thus outside of the main systems of exploitation.

A middle class—in both the economic and social senses—of professionals and merchants sputtered into existence in the cities by the late colonial period. Economically they were small business owners, and socially their businesses were prosperous enough to afford incomes above those received by the Indian and mestizo lower classes.

The New Spain colonial economy was feudal to the extent not only that a significant amount of peasant production was for self and household consumption rather than market sale but that the church's power as a large land controller and accumulator of capital acted as a brake on capitalist development. It was capitalist to the extent that increasing amounts of production were oriented to both domestic and international markets and that labor and capital markets were developing.

Slave labor was employed in households, plantation fields, sugar mills, and mines. It was legal and existed for the entire colonial period, but it was never practiced as extensively as in the southern areas of British North America. The first slaves were Indians. Some had been slaves before the Conquest and simply changed owners after it. Others were newly enslaved by the Spanish. Indian slavery legally ended in 1551 by order of the Spanish court. In practice, though, it continued in frontier areas of New Spain.

The burden of slave labor passed from Indians to Africans, as in the rest of Latin America, by the middle of the sixteenth century. During the colonial period, as many as 250,000 African slaves were imported through the ports of Veracruz and Acapulco into Mexico.[23] Some had already been slaves in the Spanish possessions within the Caribbean, while others were brought from Africa. There was also a much smaller trade in Asian slaves transported from the Philippines, also a colony of Spain, to the Pacific port of Acapulco. These were all referred to as "Chinos," though the majority were Filipinos.[24]

David M. Davidson calculated the distribution of Mexican slaves during the height of their use in the mid-seventeenth century. There were four main areas. The first was centered in the city of Veracruz, where about 5,000 slaves worked mostly as transporters and dock workers. Outside of Veracruz another 3,000 slaves worked on sugar plantations and ranches. The second area was north and west of Mexico City, where some 15,000 slaves worked in mines and as herders of cattle, sheep, and mules. The third area was in a belt from Puebla to the Pacific Coast, where some 3,000 to 5,000 slaves worked on sugar plantations, on ranches, and in mines. The fourth and largest area was in Mexico City itself, where between 20,000 and 50,000 slaves worked in urban occupations.[25]

Significant numbers of slaves rebelled and escaped during the colonial period. The fear of slave rebellion was always an undercurrent in colonial society. In 1537, as the African slave population of Mexico City was growing rapidly, rumors spread among the Spanish inhabitants that a rebellion was about to break out. They responded by publicly executing several dozen slaves through quartering.[26] That same year a number of escaped slaves—referred to collectively as *cimarrones* in New Spain—attacked a Spanish village.[27] Because New Spain contained many remote mountainous areas, *cimarrones* were able to establish themselves relatively easily and fend off attempts at recapture. Some of the mountain villages originally established by *cimarrones* in Veracruz, Oaxaca, and Guerrero continue today to be inhabited by their descendants.[28] The Spanish authorities attempted to deter escapes by establishing severely repressive punishments, including castration.[29]

There was a close correlation between race and social class position in New Spain. As Alexander von Humboldt, who traveled extensively through New Spain, famously noted, "The skin, more or less white, decides the rank that a man occupies in society."[30] The upper classes were completely white, but they were not without divisions. The top social class positions belonged to leading landlord, political, and military families, as well as the top echelons of the clergy, who were Spanish-born *peninsulares*. Below them in status, but still upper class, were wealthy landlords and merchants who were *criollos* (Spaniards born in New Spain). The small middle class was made up of moderately prosperous *criollo* merchants and landowners. The two lower classes were made up of the free poor (mixed race and Indians) and Black slaves.

Throughout the colonial period the Spanish authorities attempted to categorize people racially, with people of mixed backgrounds being placed in what they called castes.[31] Europeans, Indians, and Africans constituted the three racial trunk lines and originating caste positions. Cross-racial unions produced three general mixed-race caste positions: *mestizos* (European-Indian), *mulattoes* (European-African), and *zumbaigos* or *mulattoes pardos* (Indian-African). The attempt to categorize the colonial population, though, did not stop with these six positions. Cross-caste unions among the different mixed-race castes produced still new combinations, which received their own labels. The offspring of whites and mulattoes were called *moriscos*. The offspring of a particular type of mixed union could also be labeled differently according to which parent had one of the particular racial backgrounds, such as whether it was the father or the mother who was the white in a white-Indian union. In time, as new types of combinations increased, the number of labels generated to describe their offspring multiplied to as many as 56 in the highly race-conscious discourse of colonial society.

Catholic missionary work moved in tandem with the consolidation of Spanish economic and political power. The Indians' fatalistic receptivity to the rule of new gods facilitated the work of the church. Nevertheless, the conversion of millions of Indians to Catholicism was an extraordinary evangelical feat seldom if ever matched in world history, before or since. The depth of Catholic religiosity among the Mexican Indian population today, as evidenced by the huge crowds that turn out to see visiting popes, bears testimony to the success of the missionary effort.

A fortuitous and, in the eyes of some colonial critics, suspicious miracle greatly aided the conversion effort. In 1532, just 11 years after the final conquest of Tenochtitlan, the Virgin Mary appeared in transfigured form as an Indian on a hill that today is within the limits of Mexico City. An Indian peasant, Juan Diego, witnessed her appearance. As evidence, she left her image on a piece of cloth. From that incident spread belief in the miracle of the Virgin of Guadalupe, which facilitated conversion of the indigenous population and which continues to be deeply embraced in Mexico, especially among the indigenous peoples.

In addition to allowing that divinity could take the form of an Indian, Spanish Catholicism had to adapt itself to some pre-existing Indigenous beliefs and practices while attempting to uproot those that were judged to be heathen. For instance, celebration of the indigenous Day of the Dead was incorporated into and became a part of the church's customary festivities, but adoration of idols had to end.

From the 1530s onward, the Spanish pushed northward, attempting to colonize frontier areas. The north was inhabited by a large variety of nomadic bands who spoke different languages. The Aztecs had pejoratively called them collectively *Chichimecas*—descended from dogs—and the Spanish adopted the term. Their hunting and gathering technology required large areas in which to search for sustenance, especially given the arid and semi-arid characteristics of the Mexican north. The Spanish sought to use that land in a different way for agriculture, ranching, and mining.

Two different uses of land thus competed. There is no question that the Spanish sought to use it more efficiently. A square hectare of land devoted to agriculture can support more people than can the same unit of land used for hunting and gathering. At the same time, because the nomadic bands required so much territory to survive, any intrusion by foreigners undercut their economic means of survival. The very presence of the Spanish created problems for the Indians.

Spanish colonization of the north followed a pattern. As haciendas, mines, and towns formed, the authorities established a presidio or fort near them for protection. The church in turn established a mission in its attempt to convert and pacify the nomads. As the frontier advanced and old towns disappeared, presidios moved, marking the progress of Spanish colonization.[32]

Spanish policy attempted to make the Indians sedentary and transform them from hunters and gatherers into a hacienda and mining labor force. None of these efforts proceeded peacefully. Almost continual warfare accompanied the Spanish colonization of its northern territories up through the nineteenth century. The sword and the cross were the primary Spanish instruments for overcoming nomadic Indian resistance and opening up the northern territories to agricultural, ranching, and mining exploitation.

Capitalism, Feudalism, and New France

Almost a century after New Spain was founded, Spain's neighbor, France, established its own colony in the northern reaches of the continent. Colonial New France was centered in Quebec and the St. Lawrence Valley. French explorers, traders, and military outposts extended its influence further west and south down through what is now the U.S. Midwest to Louisiana.

Since France, like Spain and unlike Britain, still had significant feudal economic vestiges slowing capitalist development in the sixteenth and seventeenth centuries, its North American colony was partially constructed according to feudal principles. An important part of agriculture in seventeenth-century New France, like that of New Spain, remained firmly embedded in feudal customs. The colonial authorities granted land as estates (*seigneuries*) to landlords (*seigneurs*) in the St. Lawrence Valley. The landlords inhabited the estates with French-origin peasants (*censitaires* or *habitants*). The estate economies followed almost completely French feudal precedent. The peasants owed rent (about 10 percent of their yearly income, which was less severe than in France), military service, and, in some cases corvée labor, that is, compulsory work for the landlord. They were also required to work for the Crown a few days a year to maintain roads and bridges. Approximately half of the peasants produced only enough for subsistence and rent payments.[33]

At the same time, the fur trade was organized according to capitalist principles. French merchants bought pelts from Indian trappers that were then shipped for sale in France. The early fishing industry also was carried out on a profit-making basis, with the crews being paid wages.

New France, like New Spain, had a history of slavery on the margins of its economy, but it was even more marginal. No more than 4,000 persons were slaves in the entire history of the colony. The majority of these were Indians rather than Blacks. There was even less of a basis for plantation slave systems in New France than there was in New Spain.[34]

Relations between whites and Indians developed in New France in a number of ways that paralleled those of New Spain. While there was no conquest comparable to that of Tenochtitlan, the early military history of New France saw French settlers aligning themselves with one or another Indian tribe against another. There was significant intermarriage among French and indigenous persons with the resulting offspring sharing the same racial characteristics as Mexican mestizos. This was one of the roots of what would later become known as the Canadian *Métis* population.

Agrarian and Slave Capitalism in the British Colonies

The British colonists[35] who came to North America brought with them the attitudes of early capitalist development so that their colonies originated and developed much more in capitalistic conditions than did either the Spanish or French colonies. The Britain they left was in the late stages of its economic transition from medieval feudalism to capitalism. When they arrived, they encountered sparse populations of Indigenous peoples with communal modes of production that were distinctly different from either feudalism or capitalism. These peoples were mostly hunters and gatherers with no concept of private property. Two different economic and social ways of life thus confronted each other.

The colonists immediately sought land to develop into farms; to get it they had to, in one way or another, push the indigenous peoples back from the shore lands. This push immediately triggered resistance, touching off a series of coastal wars. By the eve of the War of Independence, Indian resistance in the 13 colonies had been practically eliminated. But with more land-hungry settlers continually arriving and with the most fertile lands already claimed, pressure mounted for further expansion westward. The British colonial authorities, though, had negotiated a series of treaties with Indian tribes that limited such expansion. This was one of the grievances of the colonists that set off the War of Independence.

Indigenous peoples were always marginalized in the colonies. Unlike in colonial New Spain where the Spanish colonists encountered densely populated areas, the labor of whose people they sought to exploit, in the British colonies there was virtually no attempt to exploit indigenous labor. The only thing that the colonists wanted from the Indians was their land. The violent expropriation and appropriation of that land was the original condition for the economic development of what would become the United States.

From the beginning—also unlike in the Spanish or French areas—market production dominated colonial farming practices in the British colonies. Farmers produced for household consumption as well—mainly in remote areas, such as Appalachia, where peasant subsistence economic and cultural ways of life took hold—but that was never their primary goal. Market-oriented farming was the rule, a subsistence-oriented peasantry, as in New Spain, the exception.

Because of the increasing production of market-oriented agricultural surplus products, there was enough food to support immigration and population growth in colonial cities such as Boston, New York, Philadelphia, and Halifax. Within those and other cities, in turn, important industries such as shipbuilding and rum-distilling developed. These industries were both the seeds of the later development of industrial capitalism and sites of the original development of the urban economic classes of capitalists and workers.

The northern colonies thus developed predominantly—but not exclusively—with independent businesses and free labor. But not all labor was free. There were some Black slaves. More significant economically, there were large numbers of indentured servants who were required to work for masters for seven years before becoming free laborers. As much as half of the white population in the northern colonies came originally as indentured servants.

The use of indentured servants eventually died out for economic reasons. Investment in them was costly, considering that the owner would have to free them in seven years. Many escaped, causing immediate loss of investment. Finally, Britain ceased to encourage the indentured servant trade when it realized that it was having a harmful effect on its own domestic profits. Originally, British mercantile policy assumed that exporting the unemployed into the indentured servant trade would help insure social stability. However, this changed in the eighteenth century when it was realized that the maintenance of an unemployed population at home had a salutary effect on wages from the point of view of employers—that is, the greater the relative size of the unemployed population, the greater the downward pressure on the wages of the employed population due to the law of supply and demand.

The northern economic and class structure, although it rested for a long period on unfree indentured labor, always developed in the context of the primary capitalist goal of profitability and insuring growth through reinvestment of profits. If in New Spain spectacular amounts of wealth were made and squandered episodically, in British North America capital was accumulated methodically. However, it was no less accompanied by violence. The Massachusetts and Pennsylvania colonies established scalp bounties for Indians who stood in the way; and, as we will see, once the many small streams and rivulets of methodical accumulation joined together into an institutionalized national economy and self-evident national purpose, means of violence on a far larger scale would be accumulated to remove other obstacles.

The southern British colonies from 1660 to 1782 functioned within a world capitalist context. They employed slave labor to produce particular crops, such as sugar, tobacco, cotton, and indigo, for which there was a strong demand on the world market. In this sense, new world slavery was a necessary complement to the early development of capitalism. The trade in slaves themselves was exceptionally lucrative, with the profits generating capital formation; slave products were profitably sold on the world market; and, in many cases, slaves produced the raw materials that free labor in factories transformed into finished products.

In the New World as a whole, sugar was the most important slave-produced crop for the world market during the colonial period, but it was of minimal importance in the southern colonies because their climatic and soil conditions were not appropriate. For the entire colonial period, tobacco was the leading slave-produced crop. It was only after independence that the invention of the cotton gin facilitated the orientation of southern agriculture toward meeting the skyrocketing world demand for cotton. Because the demand for tobacco was considerably less than that for sugar, the southern colonies only counted a very small percentage of New World slaves. By 1700, they had imported no more than 30,000 African slaves, a small number compared to, for example, Brazil which had imported 500,000 to 600,000.[36] Nevertheless, the bases of the southern slave economy were established during the colonial period. These would allow the expansion of the system as world economic demands changed in the late eighteenth century.

The British followed the practice of systematically separating slaves from the same African linguistic groups so that they would not be sold together for work in the same area. This practice forced the slaves to learn the English language quickly. With no one to speak to in their native tongue, the languages eventually were lost. So too were African regional and tribal customs. British policy thus led to a rapid cutting of the slaves' African cultural heritage.

Notes

1. Charles C. Mann, *1491: New Revelations of the Americas before Columbus* (New York: Vintage, 2006), 18.
2. The Neolithic revolution of the Americas occurred about 3,000 years after that of the Middle East; Mann 19.

3. Thomas D. Hall, *Social Change in the Southwest, 1350–1880* (Lawrence: University Press of Kansas, 1989), 40.

4. R. Douglas Francis, Richard Jones, and Donald B. Smith, *Origins: Canadian History to Confederation* (Toronto: Holt, Rinehart and Winston, 1988), 15.

5. Roger Bartra, "Tributo y Tenencia en la Tierra en la Sociedad Azteca," in Roger Bartra, ed., *El Modo de Producción Asiática* (Mexico City: Ediciones Era, 1969), 215.

6. Jared Diamond, *Guns, Germs, and Steel: The Fates of Human Societies* (New York: W.W. Norton, 1999), 292.

7. Michael Meyer and William L. Sherman, *The Course of Mexican History* (New York: Oxford University Press, 1979), 89.

8. Marc Bloch, "Feudalism, European," in *Encyclopedia of the Social Sciences* (New York: Macmillan, 1933) and *Feudal Society*, volumes 1 and 2, trans. L. A. Manyon (1940; Chicago, IL: University of Chicago Press, 1961).

9. Roger Bartra, *La Jaula de la Melancolia: Identidad y Metamórfosis del Mexicano* [The Cage of Melancholy: Identity and Metamorphosis of the Mexican] (Mexico City: Grijalbo, 1987).

10. Alfred M. Crosby, *The Columbian Exchange: Biological and Cultural Consequences of 1492* (Westport, CT: Greenwood Press, 1972).

11. See Carey McWilliams, *North from Mexico* (1949; Westport, CT: Greenwood Press, 1968).

12. Robert Boyd, *The Coming of the Spirit of Pestilence: Introduced Infectious Diseases and Population Decline among Northwest Coast Indians, 1774–1874* (Seattle: University of Washington Press, 1999), 3.

13. George W. Ellis and John E. Morris, *King Philip's War* (New York: Grafton Press, 1906), 274; James Truslow Adams, *The Founding of New England* (Boston: Atlantic Monthly Press, 1921), 362.

14. Dee Brown, *Bury My Heart at Wounded Knee* (New York: Henry Holt and Company, 1970), 4.

15. George Brown and Ron Maguire, "Indian Treaties in Historical Perspective," in James S. Frideres, ed., *Native People in Canada* (Scarborough, ON: Prentice-Hall Canada, 1983), 49.

16. Brown and Maguire, 40.

17. Francis, Jones, and Smith (see note 5), 47.

18. I have discussed the similarities and differences of the feudal and state modes of production in *Modes of Production in World History* (London: Routledge, 1989), 50–51.

19. Max Weber, *The Protestant Ethic and the Spirit of Capitalism* (1905; New York: Scribner's, 1948).

20. Cf. "During these first years after the conquest the Spanish simply substituted themselves for the old indigenous sovereigns and took advantage of the native systems of exploitation" (Roger Bartra, "Tributo y Tenencia en la Tierra en la Sociedad Azteca," ["Tributes and Land Ownership in Aztec Society"] in Roger Bartra, ed., *El Modo de Producción Asiática [The Mode of Asiatic Production]* [Mexico City: Ediciones Era, 1969], 216).

21. Angel Palerm Vich, "Factores Históricos de la Clase Media en México," ["Historical Factors of the Mexican Middle Class] in Miguel Othon de Mendizábal et al., eds., *Ensayos Sobre las Clases Sociales en México [Essays on Mexican Social Class]* Mexico City: Editorial Nuestro Tiempo, 1968), 93–94.

22. Palerm Vich 93–94.

23. Gonzalo Aguirre Beltrán, *Cuijla: Esbozo Etnográfico de un Pueblo Negro, [Cuijla: Ethnographic Outline of a Negro Town]* (Mexico City: Fondo de Cultura Económica, 1958), 8.

24. Rolando Mellafe, *Negro Slavery in Latin America* (Berkeley: University of California Press, 1975), 69.

25. David M. Davidson, "El Control de los Esclavos Negros y su Resistencia en el México Colonial, 1519–1650," ["Control and Resistance of Negro Slaves in Colonial Mexico, 1519–1650"] in Richard Price, ed., *Sociedades Cimarronas* (Mexico City: Siglo Veintiuno Editores, 1981), 87.

26. José L. Franco, "Rebeliones Cimarronas y Esclavas en los Territorios Españioles" ["Runaway and Slave Rebellions in the Spanish Territories"], in Price (ed.), *Sociedades Cimarronas* 43.

27. Mellafe, 105.

28. See Aguirre Beltrán, *Cuijla*.

29. Aguirre Beltrán, *Cuijla*, 59.

30. Alexander von Humboldt, *Ensayo Politico Sobre el Reino de la Nueva España [Political Essays on the New Spanish Empire]*, vol. 1 (Paris, 1822), 262.

31. Aguirre, Beltrán, *La Población Negra de México, 1518–1810 [The Negro Population of Mexico, 1519–1810]*, Ediciones Fuente Cultural, México, D. F., 1946; Miguel Othon de Mendizábal et al., eds., *Ensayos Sobre las Clases Sociales en México [Essays on Mexican Social Class]*, Mexico City: Editorial Nuestro Tiempo, 1968). . . .

32. Cf. "[Colonization of the north involved] exploration and possession of new lands, founding of population centers, exploration for natural resources, forced submission of the Indian, and once the enterprise was

consolidated, defense of the acquired possessions" (María Teresa Huerta Preciado, *Rebeliones Indígenas en el Noreste de México en la Epoca Colonial* [Indigenous Runaways in the Northeast of Mexico During Colonialism] [Mexico City: Instituto Nacional de Antropología e Historia, 1966], 103).

33. Francis, Jones, and Smith (see note 5), 78–79; Allan Greer, *Peasant, Lord, and Merchant: Rural Society in Three Quebec Parishes 1740–1840* (Toronto: University of Toronto Press, 1985).

34. Francis, Jones, and Smith; also Robin W. Winks, *The Blacks in Canada* (New Haven, CT: Yale University Press, 1971).

35. Until 1783 the British colonies of North America were referred to as British America. The term "British North America" came into use to refer to Britain's remaining North American colonies after the independence of those that became the United States. To avoid confusion of terms, I am referring to them simply as the British colonies.

36. Herbert S. Klein, *African Slavery in Latin America and the Caribbean* (New York: Oxford University Press, 1986), 53.

Questions

1. What were nomadic and hunter-gatherer societies in North America like prior to colonization? Why was there relative equality among these groups? What happened? What economic relationships facilitated the development of inequality? Later on, how did feudalistic conquerors compare to capitalist ones? What property systems undergirded widespread categorical inequality? Political systems? Status systems? Why? What tools did the dominant class use to rule over others? How do these processes relate to those put forth by Schwalbe in "Roots of Inequality?"

2. What was happening in Europe prior to conquest? What social factors facilitated European conquests of native peoples in North America? What role did belief systems play in creating and sustaining inequality? Which belief systems were important and how? Were they causes? Justifications? Facilitators? Or something else?

3. One social process for establishing and maintaining dominance is appropriation. Russell describes, for example, how Spaniards appropriated the Aztec tribute system in ways that facilitated their domination yet slowed down capitalist development. How else did Europeans use native peoples, their land, their culture, and their social systems to help defeat other native peoples? Why is appropriation so powerful as a tool of domination? What effect did it have on resistance? How else did Europeans thwart resistance?

4. Russell demonstrates a foundational relationship between class oppression and racialization in North America. What was the nature of the relationship? Was one more elemental than the other? Was one status-based and the other material? Do race and class as systems relate to each other in the same ways today? If not, what is their relationship today?

5. Russell points out the unique positionality of people of "mixed race" historically. How does Russell interpret the experience of people of mixed race? What are miscegenation laws? What role did they play in racialization? When were they outlawed in the United States? When did the U.S. Census allow for people to classify themselves as multiracial? How many people classified themselves as part of at least two racial or ethnic groups then? What about now? What are some potential political ramifications of more people classifying themselves as multiracial? How were miscegenation laws similar to and/or different from same-sex marriage bans?

6. Examine the American Anthropological Association's timeline on race in the United States online (you can find it here: http://www.understandingrace.org/history/index.html). The timeline dates back to 1600 and provides brief articles on racialization through government, science, and society. Pick a time in U.S. history that you know little about. Scroll to that time and read the relevant articles. How was race accomplished during that time period? Who were the major players? What tools did they use? How did people resist racialization?

3

Stratified Societies

NANCY BONVILLAIN

One way to better understand how people create inequalities is to study cross-cultural variation in how people categorize each other, allot resources, and accomplish the economic activities necessary for sustaining life. In "Stratified Societies," Nancy Bonvillain provides a rich, detailed, and nuanced portrait of four different societies with varying degrees of organizing around gender. The Haidi and Tlingit of Canada had foraging economies in which women and men did different tasks but were interdependent and valued equally for their contributions. An elaborate potlatch feasting system celebrated women and men. Matrilineality and inheritance rights for women assured their relatively high status.

The Kpelle of Liberia, alternatively, mixed male dominance with female autonomy. Both women and men contributed to farming, albeit sometimes to different tasks. Men held rights over land, while women retained control over production, the goods produced, and income. Women initiated divorce, but men manipulated women and children in marriage.

Male dominance characterized the South African Mpondo. Men alone owned cattle, the marker of wealth; women had no role in economic exchange but instead specialized in subsistence work for household consumption. Wives deferred to their husbands, and Mpondo enforced a strict sexual double standard—where boys had premarital sex freely but girls could not.

Relative equality marked the Tonga of the South Pacific—before extensive European contact. Here again, women controlled economic relations to their benefit. Women's wealth, called *koloa*, was more valued than men's wealth, named *ngaue*. Koloa was the medium for public exchange. Men did the cooking, a lowly valued task. Sisters enjoyed *fahu* rights, which included controlling brothers' work and family. Premarital sex was common for boys and girls, and husbands and wives afforded each other respect. When the Tonga encountered European traders, however, the value of *koloa* dissipated. As their products lost value in the global marketplace and Wesleyan Methodist missionaries granted property rights to male heads of households and reassigned cooking to women, women were relegated to second-class status.

Looking across the four societies draws into focus the importance of economic relations to gender-based stratification. Women's control over land, production decisions, the products to exchange with others, and the production process afforded them access to material and social resources. Readers will wonder how women's status across the globe varies today in relation to economic resources. Bonvillain's piece also draws our attention to the role that ideology plays in solidifying inequalities. When women controlled material resources, ideologies of difference were not enough to oppress women, yet ideologies of male dominance were crucial to legitimizing women's subordination among societies where women had less control over production and reproduction.

Bonvillain, Nancy. *Women and Men: Cultural Constructs of Gender,* 4th Edition, © 2007. Printed and Electronically reproduced by permission of Pearson Education, Inc., New York, New York.

In societies characterized by systems of social stratification, relations among individuals and kinship groups are founded not on egalitarian principles but rather on hierarchical ranking of people. The degree of segmentation and the strength of hierarchy vary cross-culturally. In some cultures, rank is of less consequence for social, economic, and political functioning than in others. In some chiefdoms, egalitarian ethics continue to organize relationships among people; in others, inequality and differentiation dominate societal interactions. Effects of stratification on gender constructs also vary. In some, gender relations are relatively egalitarian. Principles of men's and women's autonomy and worth may be socially recognized and ideologically supported. However, stratification in many chiefdoms may be based on the exercise of economic and political control by individual men competing with each other and/or by men as a group acting to restrict women's rights.

The Haida and Tlingit of the Canadian Pacific Coast

. . . Unlike the scarcity of resources endured by many foragers, the Pacific Northwest provides an abundant variety of foods in different seasons. . . . People living in this region are able to collect enough food not only for their daily survival but also for accumulation of large surpluses used in trade and in ceremonial displays and feasts.

The Tlingit (TLING-git) of Alaska and the Haida (HAI-da) of the Queen Charlotte Islands off the coast of British Columbia exemplify many cultural elements common to Pacific coast peoples. . . . Economic activities were allocated according to gender. . . . Men were primarily engaged in fishing and hunting these varied resources. Women were responsible for gathering the abundant wild plants, seaweed, fruits, and nuts. Their work also included the vital task of preserving and storing fish and meat caught during the summer. Fruits and some plants were also dried and stored. Large surpluses amassed in a short period of time were kept for use throughout the year. People were then freed of most subsistence activities and spent a good deal of time in social, ceremonial, and political activities.

Tlingit and Haida society was organized through matrilineal clans that determined descent, restricted marriage possibilities through rules of clan exogamy, and influenced patterns of residence. Clans were corporate groups, owning large plank houses in which their members lived and controlled access to resource areas. . . . Households were based on matrilineal affiliation, with a preference for avunculocal residence. Houses were ideally inhabited by a man, his own nuclear family, and his sisters' sons and their families. . . . Lineages and clans were led by chiefs—that is, men who bore hereditary titles owned by their kin group.

When a man assumed a new title or chieftainship, he sponsored a public communal feast, called a *potlatch*. . . . Prestige accrued to a potlatch giver who was able to amass and distribute more wealth than had been given at previous feasts.

. . . Although chieftainships were held primarily by men, women sometimes became chiefs, principally if their lineages had no capable man to assume the position. But even in the absence of women's roles as chiefs, women's labor was crucial to the potlatching system. [W]omen were responsible for preserving fish and other foods that could later be consumed or distributed to guests at potlatches. Women, then, not only were involved in household production but also had publicly recognized roles as distributors of resources in their communities. In addition, women were said to be responsible for protecting the household supplies that were given at potlatches. . . .

Gender equality in the potlatching system was demonstrated by the fact that sons and daughters were equally recognized through feasts given by their parents. A son's or daughter's birth, naming, puberty, marriage, and other accomplishments were publicly celebrated. The Haida expressed preferences for the birth of daughters, recognizing women's responsibility for procreation and continuity of matrilineages, but boys were also desired because they aided their maternal uncles in amassing wealth and eventually succeeded to uncles' titles and positions.

Even though Tlingit and Haida cultural constructs validated the equality of women and men, women were socialized to be somewhat deferential toward their husbands. Wives were expected to "show respect" to their husbands and to acquiesce to them in daily activities. . . . Men did not abuse their wives or deprive them of their essential autonomy.

Women owned property and had recognized rights to dispose of it as they chose. A woman's property remained her own after marriage and did not merge with that of her husband. The principle of individual control of goods and houses worked against women, though, in the event of divorce or the death of husbands. Divorce was fairly common and could be initiated by either spouse. Because men owned the houses in which they and their families lived, a divorced wife returned to her father's or brother's residence.

The Kpelle of Liberia

. . . West African cultures offer examples of the combination of men's dominance and women's autonomy. For instance, the Kpelle (KPE-lay) of Liberia exemplify some characteristic West African cultural practices. Among the Kpelle, gender constructs support the "belief in the formal superiority of men over women" (Gibbs, 1965, p. 230). But examination of the roles and rights of women and men reveals that women make significant recognized contributions to their families and have both economic and social independence despite public control exercised by men.

. . . Men cut down trees in fields in preparation for planting, and then women and men clear the fields of undergrowth. Men and women engage in farming, although the crops produced are distinct: men are responsible for producing rice; supplies of other foods are in women's domain and are obtained by their labor.

A couple farms on land allotted to men as heads of households within patrilineages. . . . Women work on land allocated to their husbands. Although men are the holders of land use rights, women have a great deal of control over the produce of the land. They make decisions about which crops to grow and in what amount. . . . In addition, women determine the planting of other crops on acreage allotted to them by their husbands. They "have complete control over the income from these individual plots" (Gibbs 1965, p. 201).

Women obtain income from the sale of surplus produce. . . . [M]any women sell a portion of their crops to people in their villages or to travelers who stop by to purchase food from displays in front of a woman's house. . . . Income derived from market sales is controlled by the woman who earns it.

Kpelle households consist of nuclear families residing in proximity to kin based on principles of patrilineal descent and affiliation. That is, nuclear dwellings headed by men are located near those of their fathers and/or brothers. Members of a polygynous family all live in the same house, although each wife has her own room that she shares with her children. A man's economic responsibilities include his obligation to supply his wife (or wives) and children with rice and to fulfill other material needs such as provision of clothing and household goods.

Kpelle marriages, then, are basically differentiated in terms of the legal status of women and the ensuing rights that men and their lineages may claim over a woman's children. If a woman is a full legal wife—that is, in a standard marriage with payment of bridewealth—her children belong to her husband's patrilineage. If a woman's legal status is in transition—that is, during the period of bride service—her children belong to her patrilineage and cannot be claimed by her husband. If a woman is the legal wife of a patron even though she lives with another man, her children belong to the patron.

Rates of divorce among the Kpelle are "moderately high" according to Gibbs (1965). . . . Women usually initiate divorce, in part because fixing of blame is most often placed on the initiator, and men are reluctant to be publicly criticized. Even though women are characteristically blamed for failure of their marriages, their request to be divorced is usually granted. A man who wishes a divorce may mistreat his wife so she will seek a formal divorce in court. In this manipulative manner, he obtains his objective but is not publicly faulted.

Despite ideological constructs supporting male dominance, Kpelle women exercise their autonomy stemming from critical roles in household economies. Moreover, their productive roles are not confined to the domestic sphere. Women sell crops they plant and crafts they create. And they control the dispersal of income derived from their labor. Women's contributions are acknowledged by their husbands' lack of interference in their pursuits. If a woman experiences abuse or extreme personal domination from her husband, she has the option of seeking a divorce.

The Mpondo of the Transkei

. . . The Mpondo (PON-do) chiefdom, located in the Transkei region of South Africa, illustrates patterns of marked social stratification and male dominance. Economic and political factors intersect and combine to endow chiefs with power over commoners and to give men rights to dominate women.

Mpondo land is said to be owned by paramount and district chiefs. Chiefs in turn allocate use rights to portions of land to other men who are heads of lineages and households. . . .

Wealth in Mpondo society is measured by individual ownership of cattle. Cattle, owned exclusively by men, literally and figuratively embody a man's wealth. . . . [C]attle are given in bridewealth transactions by men in a husband's lineage to those in a wife's kin group. Cattle are thus economic symbols of bonds created through social relationships. Cattle are also received by men as payment for services rendered. In addition, cattle function in Mpondo ritual life when they are distributed at public feasts and on ceremonial occasions marking rites of passage such as marriages and funerals.

. . . Whereas Mpondo men are distributors and recipients of cattle, women have no direct roles in this vital system of exchange. They do not own cattle, cannot obtain them through raiding, and do not direct their distribution. In fact, women are themselves exchanged for cattle in transfers of bridewealth.

Women's roles are restricted to direct subsistence production. They produce crops grown on land under their husbands' control. Women's labor therefore benefits the patrilineage into which they marry. But their labor is for household consumption only. A significant contrast between women's and men's productivity, therefore, is that while women work to produce goods for use, men work to produce and distribute goods (namely, cattle) that have value both for use and for exchange. . . .

Wives are expected to be deferential toward their husbands. Many ritualized restrictions affect their actions. For example, a woman must not walk too close to an elder man in her husband's lineage. When outdoors, she must walk behind, rather than in front, of the huts in the village. And she cannot drink milk from her husband's cows during the first year of marriage. . . .Ideological constructs supporting male prerogatives are expressed in Mpondo culture by a double standard in regard to sexual activity. Premarital sexual behavior on the part of girls is severely criticized and punished, whereas boys' premarital sexual behavior is considered normal and acceptable. Similarly, adultery is more sternly condemned when committed by wives than by husbands.

Attitudes toward divorce are ambiguous. Either a husband or a wife may initiate divorce. Marital conflicts are often motivated by adultery, although such acts are not considered legitimate grounds for divorce. That is, a husband who divorces his wife because of her affair cannot claim a return of bridewealth from her kin. If a divorce is considered legitimate—that is, for dereliction of a wife's duty—the woman's kin must return bridewealth to her husband. Even if a wife initiates a divorce, bridewealth is returned by her family if she is deemed to be at fault.

A husband's dominance over his wife is extended to encompass her interactions with his kin. A woman defers to her husband's relatives. . . .

The Tonga of the South Pacific

. . . Data from Tonga [from a group of Polynesian islands in the South Pacific] demonstrate how differentiated gender roles and relations in a chiefdom society can become increasingly hierarchical as a chiefdom is transformed into a kingdom. In this process, women's rights are undermined, and the social value traditionally bestowed on them is demeaned.

Traditional Tongan society was based on a system of ranking in which no two individuals were of equal rank. Three abstract principles were used to determine an individual's status relative to others: seniority, an older person outranking a younger; gender, a man outranking a woman; and sisterhood, a sister outranking her brother (Gailey, 1987).

Tongan economy entailed a strict division of labor based on gender. Two kinds of goods were therefore produced: women's products, called *koloa*, or "valuables, wealth"; and men's products, called *ngaue*, or "work" (Gailey, 1987, pp. 97, 101). . . . Because they were made by women, *koloa* items were considered more valuable than *ngaue*. . . .

Tongan subsistence was based on horticulture and fishing. Nonchiefly men carried out farming tasks, producing crops such as yams, coconuts, and a variety of vegetables. They supplied their families with fish and turtles obtained in the open seas. Nonchiefly women collected shellfish in shallow waters and reefs and also fished in lagoons. They extracted oil from coconuts and blended it with flowers to be used as a salve to protect the skin.

In addition to subsistence activities, men were responsible for cooking, an occupation that carried low prestige in Tongan society. Other household tasks were not linked to gender but were performed by both women and men. These included child care and building of houses. . . .

Koloa, or women's wealth, was employed as the medium of exchange in social, economic, political, and ritual contexts. In other words, women's work provided the means for publicly demonstrating underlying societal relationships and obligations. *Koloa* thus gave visible evidence of women's roles in integrating the multifaceted networks of Tongan society.

. . . Premarital sexual activity was common for both girls and boys. Only among the chiefly strata were restrictions placed on girls' behavior. High-ranking daughters were watched closely to assure their chastity, but among the majority of Tongans, most people engaged in sexual relations prior to marriage. . . .

Tongan marriages were monogamous for nonchiefly people, but chiefly men often had several wives. The highest-ranking men additionally had concubines.

In Tongan marriages, husbands and wives were expected to show respect toward each other. A wife's behavior was customarily deferential toward her husband, but if a wife outranked her husband, he often deferred to her.

Violence against women in the form of beatings and rape was extremely rare. . . .

Tongan society, however, did not remain static. . . . [C]ontact with Europeans beginning in the seventeenth century accelerated processes of change and channeled subsequent cultural shifts in particular directions. Among the consequences was a reworking of gender constructs so as to increase men's authority while women's social, economic, and political claims were undermined. . . .

Expansion of trade throughout the nineteenth century had a crucial impact on the traditional division of labor and especially on the value of *koloa*, or women's wealth. At first, coconut oil, processed by women, was an important trade item. . . . Concomitantly, women's importance in commerce enhanced their status. . . . However, after the middle of the nineteenth century, the world market for coconut oil declined. Instead, Europeans sought dried coconut, called *copra*. But because collection and processing of coconuts was *ngaue*, or men's work, the shift to trade in copra began a realignment of traditional Tongan beliefs about the inherent value of women's and men's products.

As *copra* production intensified throughout the rest of the nineteenth century, men spent more time in this endeavor and less time in fulfilling other subsistence and domestic tasks. As a result, women were compelled to engage in work such as farming and cooking that carried low status.

. . . Two interrelated factors led to undermining women's roles. First, cotton and wool replaced traditional bark cloth, one of the most highly valued *koloa* items. Second, because cotton cloth was purchased with cash, men's access to money from copra production changed Tongan concepts of value. . . . [M]en's labor was used to procure a valuable trade item. Women's wealth was thus undermined in a dual process of material replacement and ideological reconstruction.

Codification of laws and enactment of a Tongan constitution in the mid-nineteenth century solidified the state's power and men's authority over women. Many Tongan laws and government policies were instigated under the influence of Wesleyan Methodist missionaries from Great Britain who began their mission activities in Tonga in the 1820s.

. . . First, use rights to land were granted individually to men as heads of their households.

Second, domestic economic tasks were shifted by assigning the responsibility of cooking to women. Men were drawn out of household work into producing copra and bananas for export and/or into wage-earning occupations. Women's work roles were restricted, thus rendering them increasingly dependent on their husbands for support.

Women's authority was further harmed by legal bans against the exercise of *fahu* rights. A woman can no longer lay claims to her brothers and their families. This shift resulted in dependence of a woman on her husband because other means of support were eliminated.

Finally, Wesleyans attempted to alter Tongan attitudes and behaviors concerning sexuality and marriage. By legal statutes, women who engaged in premarital or extramarital sexual activities were punished by fines, imprisonment, or forced labor on royal plantations (Gailey, 1987).

References

Gailey, Christine. 1987. *Kinship to Kingship: Gender Hierarchy and State Formation in the Tongan Islands*. Austin: University of Texas Press.

Gibbs, James. 1965. "The Kpelle of Liberia." In *Peoples of Africa* (ed. James L. Gibbs), 197–240. New York: Holt, Rinehart & Winston.

Questions

1. Summarize the characteristics of each group studied by Bonvillain. Then plot each group on the spectrum shown here:

complete equality   extreme exploitation and hierarchy

1. Where does each go? Why? Did they change? What caused change? Where would you plot the United States? Why? Pick one other country. Where would you put it, and why?

2. Looking across the groups, what social factors are associated with more (or less) stratification? What is the relationship between gender inequality and economic relations? What can we learn about how people accomplish equality and inequality through these cross-cultural examples?

3. Naming babies is an awesome responsibility. Parents revel in the ability to shape an identity for someone—and also fear messing it up. Go to the Social Security Administration's (SSA) website on the most popular baby names (http://www.ssa.gov/oact/babynames/). How many gender categories does the SSA list? What patterns do you notice in the lists? That is, what do the names have in common? How are they different? What social meanings are associated with the traits of the names? Now, do a bit of historical research on names. Examine the trends across the twentieth century. Find your own name. What do the names reveal about gender in the United States? Power and domination? Race and immigration?

4. Anthropological research has revealed several societies with more than two genders. Go to the website for PBS's film *Two Spirits* (http://www.pbs.org/independentlens/two-spirits/map.html). Examine the map and find three different ways that people have constructed gender outside of the male/female–man/woman binary. How did people organize gender in each? What social roles did people of other genders take on? For a contemporaneous example, read the work of Jenny Nordberg about females raised as boys in Afghanistan (in the *New York Times* here: http://www.nytimes.com/2010/09/21/world/asia/21gender.html?pagewanted=all) or in her book *The Underground Girls of Kabul* [Crown Publishing 2014]). How do people go about raising a bacha posh? What resources does a bacha posh offer access to for his family that girls do not? What role does gender segregation play in the practice? What unique problems does a bacha posh face? Does this third gender upend the gender order, recreate it, or something else? Why?

4

Frameworks of Desire

ANNE FAUSTO-STERLING

In January 2000, President Bill Clinton touted the complete mapping of the human genome. During a White House press conference (Clinton 2000), he said, "Without a doubt, this is the most important, most wondrous map ever produced by humankind." This "epic-making triumph of science and reason," as he described it, would also "revolutionize the diagnosis, prevention and treatment of most, if not all, human diseases." Classifying genes, their mutations, and the proteins they produced offered a brave new frontier in medicine: cancer treatment could be individualized and rare disease etiology finally identified. Other scientists devoted themselves to uncovering assumed biological underpinnings of human behavior: identifying genes which inclined some people toward addiction or obesity, or discovering the genetic roots of sexual desire.

Genes are the latest in the long line of biological factors researchers, physicians, and politicians have used to justify social hierarchies. Cranial variation, IQ, sex differences in brain size, hormonal variations—scientists have used them all to account for some people having more political power than others. They have done so assuming that the social systems of domination which people create to secure and hoard resources are explainable through their individual biological variation. The body of work by renowned geneticist Anne Fausto-Sterling, however, challenges biological determinism and categorizing people into binaries of imbued haves and have-nots. For example, her research (Fausto-Sterling 2000) demonstrates the rich variation of biological realities. We are many more than two sexes, so why two gender categories? She also argues (Fausto-Sterling 2008) that social circumstances actually produce rather than reflect biological variation. For example, an assortment of social factors—geography, breastfeeding versus formula-feeding babies, malnutrition due to poverty, smoking and drinking during pregnancy, and others—mediate vitamin D production, which turns off or on genes related to bone development. Studies of racial difference in bone density ignore these complex interactions, falsely reducing them to "racial differences." Fausto-Sterling's research flips the common understandings of the relationship between biology and social categories on its head. According to Fausto-Sterling, the scientific status quo is asking the wrong questions and using the wrong analytic framework.

In the following piece, Fausto-Sterling applies her critique to the study of human sexuality, particularly the search for a gay gene. The science uses bad samples, with one-dimensional definitions of sexuality, which exclude most people. They use a "normal versus mutant" oppositional approach which by definition leaves "heterosexuals" unexamined and their superiority unreflectively reinforced. They treat cellular processes as simplistic and static, despite having the analytic tools to offer more complex and dynamic models. They ignore the dynamic nature of sexuality, and they use badly conceived science to do so. Given these flaws in the research, why do genetic explanations for sexuality hold so much sway—for opponents and proponents of gay rights alike?

References

Clinton, Bill. 2000. "President Clinton, British Prime Minister Blair Mark Completion of the First Survey of the Entire Human Genome." *White House briefing*, June 26, 2000. http://www.genome.gov/10001356 (accessed October 10, 2014). (http://www.genome.gov/10001356)

Fausto-Sterling, Anne. 2000. "The Five Sexes, Revisited." *The Sciences*. 40(4):18–23.

Fausto-Sterling, Anne. 2008. "The Bare Bones of Race." *Social Studies of Science*. 38(5):647–694.

Genes versus choice. A quick and dirty search of newspaper stories covering scientific research on homosexuality shows that the popular press has settled on this analytic framework to explain homosexuality: Either genes cause homosexuality, or homosexuals choose their lifestyle.[1]

The mischief that follows such a formulation is broad-based and more than a little pernicious. Religious fundamentalists and gay activists alike use the genes–choice opposition to argue their case either for or against full citizenship for homosexuals. Biological research now arbitrates civil legal proceedings, and the idea that moral status depends on the state of our genes overrides the historical and well-argued view that we are "endowed by [our] Creator with certain unalienable Rights. . . ." Moreover, rather than framing research projects in terms of the whole of human desire, we neglect to examine one form, heterosexuality, in favor of uncovering the causes of the "deviant" other, homosexuality.

Intellectually, this is just the tip of the iceberg. When we invoke formulae such as oppositional rather than developmental, innate versus learned, genetic versus chosen, early-onset versus adolescent experience, a gay gene versus a straight gene, hardwired versus flexible, nature versus nurture, normal versus deviant, the subtleties of human behavior disappear.

Linear though it is, even Kinsey's scale has six gradations of sexual expression; and Kinsey understood the importance of the life cycle as a proper framework for analyzing human desire. Academics—be they biologists, social scientists[2], or cultural theorists—have become locked into an oppositional framework. As a result, they are asking the wrong questions and offering intellectually impoverished accounts of the emergence and development of human desire.

A steady patter of research papers linking genes to homosexuality rains down on us, hitting first the scientific journals; then soaking through to the newspapers, blogs, and television news; and finally growing like mold, often wildly reshaped from the initial tiny spore into the mycelia of popular discourse. As intellectual efforts, each of these articles has technical strengths and weaknesses—one can always criticize the sample size, or the method of recruiting study subjects, or the statistical test employed. But most of them share a similar—and problematic—analytical framework.

We can expose this general framework by considering one recent and widely reported article, "A Genomewide Scan of Male Sexual Orientation," authored by six scientists from five prestigious research institutions dotting the United States from California to Washington, D.C.[3] The article introduces the problem by citing scholarly research linking biological events or genetic structures to male-male sexual orientation. While the authors, Brian Mustanski and his colleagues, concede that the evidence is incomplete (they note the limited number of studies that attempt to locate specific genes related to homosexuality) and that nonbiological factors must also be involved (they mention, for example, two recent studies of twins that "report moderate heritability estimates[4] with the remaining variability being explained by nonshared environmental influences"[5]), they ultimately argue that the linkages suggested by such studies are important. Since they believe that many genes are likely to be involved, they decided to scan the entire genome (X, Y, and all of the autosomes) in an attempt to fish out a set of genes related in some way to male sexual orientation.

The authors hoped to avoid false positives caused by "gay men who identify as heterosexual"[6] by only studying self-identified gay men. But the idea that there are gay men who identify as heterosexual suggests that there is some biological essence of gayness that can exist genetically and therefore be measured independently of identity and behavior. This begs the definitional question. The state of being gay (in adulthood) might, in fact, reasonably include identity, behavior, and/or desire.

Indeed, in their groundbreaking work, *The Social Organization of Sexuality*, E. O. Laumann and his colleagues studied the interrelation of these components of homosexuality in 143 men who reported any inkling of same-sex desire. Of the men surveyed, 44 percent expressed homosexual desire but not identity or behavior, while 24 percent reported having all three of these components. Another 6 percent expressed desire and behavior but not identity, 22 percent expressed behavior but not desire or identity, 2 percent had only the identity, and 1 percent had the identity and desire but not the behavior.

So Mustanski and colleagues selected a subset of men who, judging from the Laumann survey, would comprise only 27 percent of men expressing some component of homosexuality. Thus, even if the authors were to find genetic linkages, genetic studies of this sort give insufficient theoretical attention to the possible meanings of such findings.

The study also compares the DNA of gay men with those of their heterosexual brothers. Since all siblings share 50 percent of their DNA, the DNA regions (genes) that are present in higher frequency in the genomes of the gay brothers then become regions of interest, as potentially related to male homosexuality. But to find the brothers for the study, the authors advertised in homophile publications, and the mean Kinsey score for their sample was 5.46.[7] Again, this sample would represent, according to the Laumann study, only about one quarter of men expressing or feeling some aspect of homosexuality.

As Mustanski and his colleagues freely acknowledge, their findings are merely suggestive, providing trails to be followed rather than explanations to be had. In their own words, they identify "candidate genes for further exploration" and hope that any future molecular analysis of "genes involved in sexual orientation could greatly advance our understanding of human variation, evolution and brain development."[8] But here, they reflect the point of view of most classical genetic studies. From Thomas Hunt Morgan's first analysis of the white-eyed fruit-fly mutant to present-day dissection of genes involved in embryo formation or disease, the geneticist's method is to study the mutant in order to understand normal processes. Although Mustanski and his colleagues prefer to consider homosexuality as part of the natural variation of the human species, this fig leaf cannot hide the basic framework of "normal versus mutant," which emphasizes fixed typologies rather than biological processes and life cycle analyses.

If some sociologists can frame homosexuality in ways that better appreciate its complexities, why can't biologists? After all, the tools exist within their field: biologists know how to look at behavior or cellular states as processes or emergences rather than as static categories. In studying the role of gene networks in the process of embryonic development, for example, Eric Davidson and his colleagues have pinpointed "feed-forward" genetic networks that define cell transitions as the fertilized egg divides and the resulting cells differentiate into specialized tissues. The process is self-generating, involves hundreds of genetic elements and their feedback loops, and progresses historically—each new cellular state provides the necessary conditions for the next one until a stable feedback loop is established.[9] Using a more complex version of a cybernetic thermostat regulation loop, the system maintains a stable differentiated state under a broad range of (though not all) conditions. Conceptually similar approaches have been employed to devise models of the emergence of perceptual competence in developing human infants.[10] Such dynamic models have room for specific information about gene action during neural development—the sort of information Mustanski and his colleagues seek—but they provide a more productive framework for understanding human desire as a developmental process rather than a typological state.[11]

The Mustanski article illustrates one other—and quite central—component used in biological approaches to the study of homosexuality: the imposition of a sex/gender schematic. The formal analogies are (1) "male:female" is as "heterosexual male: homosexual male;" (2) "male:female" is as "lesbian:heterosexual female;" and (3) "masculinity:femininity" is as "straight male or lesbian:gay male or straight woman." This is the logic that led Simon LeVay to study the hypothalamus in gay men, hoping to find the same differences in the brains of gay versus straight men that others had reported when comparing the brains of (presumably straight) men and women.[12] The Mustanski paper cites a number of studies based on this concept—a concept that is also often embraced by and acted out within the gay community. The stereotypes seen on *Will and Grace*, or in discussions about butch and femme lesbians, may derive from particular, but certainly far from universal, practices within the gay community. But are they a reasonable basis for biological investigations of homosexuality?

Theo Sandfort recently reviewed academic accounts of the relationship between gender and sexual orientation.[13] He argues that we now understand homosexuality to have multiple and not always synchronous components (attraction, orientation, behavior, self-identification) and varied expression according to gender, ethnicity, social class, and culture. In other words, the concepts of masculinity and femininity are no longer seen as bipolar. Rather, "it has become good practice to discuss them as multidimensional phenomena . . . [as] femininities and masculinities."[14] He then places the origin, in American psychology, of the idea that homosexual men are feminine and lesbians masculine, in the work of Lewis M. Terman and Catherine C. Miles, published in 1936. Sandfort reminds us that Terman and Miles identified homosexual men who did not fit this pattern of opposites, but failed to theorize about masculine gay men. Subsequent citations of their work followed suit, and the unquestioned link of male homosexuality to femininity was born. More recent and more multifaceted attempts to correlate gender expression with sexual orientation have yielded correspondingly more complex results. . . .

Sandfort recommends three research areas that, if carefully investigated, might help us add gender intelligently to a framework for understanding the development of human desire. First, he suggests we learn more about how different groups (men, women, homosexual, heterosexual) understand the concepts of masculinity and femininity. Do self-perceptions correlate with external perceptions? Second, he asks how the social and cultural environment (including gay subcultures that value male femininity and female masculinity) influence individual perceptions of masculinity and femininity. Third, he wonders what the consequences of gender perception and identification are. How do they contribute to sexual practices and desires? And, I would add, do the behaviors train brain circuits or otherwise influence brain development rather than (or in addition to) vice versa?

The "genes versus choice" opposition is also wanting on the "choice" side. Most people can understand why the word "choice" is bad in this context. First, it is easily used—especially in the popular and political arena—to deny rights. This usage implies that just as a person can "choose" not to commit a crime and thus avoid prosecution, so, too, a person can choose not to be gay and thus avoid homophobic violence or losing out on social benefits afforded to straight people. "Choice" also carries with it the connotation of conscious control and easy changeability; yet few homosexuals believe that they chose their state of desire. Indeed, the history of homosexuality is filled with stories of people who tried for years to become straight before accepting that, for whatever reasons, they felt how they felt.[15] Nor can heterosexuals choose to change their states of desire.

Rather than defend this oversimplification of choice, academics prefer to frame the opposition to biology in terms of social construction. They point out that regardless of where our sexual desires and our gender senses originate, they are not easily changed. . . . But, as with the biologist, the social constructionist has yet to offer a coherent account of the development of individual desire. The conventional constructionists do not explain how the body comes to feel desire, to respond to touch, or to quiver when a person to whom it is attracted walks through the door. Indeed, to date, attempts to offer such accounts have found little empirical support. . . .

What evidence exists for the varieties of experiential theories of desire? In the now classical study *Sexual Preference: Its Development in Men and Women*, Alan Bell, Martin Weinberg, and Sue Hammersmith interviewed hundreds of gay, lesbian, and straight men and women living in San Francisco. The bulk of interviewees said that childhood and adolescent sexual expression reflected their felt desires but did not determine them. The results also did not find evidence for the Freudian family dynamic or the parental manipulation theories of sexual formation. Subsequent studies have confirmed these findings.

The San Francisco project found what they claimed was a "powerful link between [childhood] gender nonconformity and the development of homosexuality."[16] Men and women who reported childhood gender atypical behaviors were more likely to become homosexual than those who did not. . . . Its conclusions, however, cannot be taken at face value. . . .

Two anecdotes, one personal and one from a recent longitudinal study of coming-out stories, illustrate the "memory as evidence" problem. When I was a little girl I went off to camp in the country. I was interested in natural history and also navigated socially by developing a niche and staying in it. One summer, I combined niche development with a crush on the (male) camp counselor in charge of the nature "museum" (a little cabin with found natural objects), and I devoted myself to catching snakes and insects and collecting mushrooms and the like. At the end of the summer, some of the group of girls I had met made little wooden gravestones for each of us. Mine read: "In memory of Anne who liked bugs better than boys." I was twelve at the time. I understood the comment to be about my interest in nature (nobody knew about my crush on the counselor) and remembered it in that way as I made my way through graduate school in biology, met and married my biologist husband, and became a professor of genetics. But fast forward thirty-odd years from the day my little girl friends wrote my epitaph, and I could be found separated from my husband, living on my own, and courting women (one of whom I eventually married). During that transitional courting period, I came upon my miniature grave marker lying in a box of childhood treasures and read it with new insight. Of course it meant that I had been pegged as gay all along. My little friends knew it, but it took me all that time to understand their message. (Or could they have just been writing about bugs after all?) Memories get rewritten; new narratives are scripted.

Lisa M. Diamond offers a more theoretical and formal version of my story as she reflects on her own research on sexual identity formation.[17] Consider three interviews over five years with the same lesbian woman. In the first interview the woman remembers being different as a child, a tomboy, uninterested in dating men. But she only began to think of difference in terms of sexuality in college, after meeting a lot of gay people. Two years later, in the second interview, she remembers being scared by her childhood crushes on female camp counselors. This time around she remembers linking her difference to sexual feelings even as a child. In the five-year follow-up interview her memories are quite explicitly sexual. Diamond asks if one of the versions is the "true" one, and concludes that "the very process of telling self-stories . . . engages multiple psychological

mechanisms that promote later consistency by organizing and consolidating preferred versions of events."[18]

Retrospective accounts, be they in formal academic studies or stories swapped with friends or collections of coming-out tales, present a dilemma. On the one hand, how better to find out about experiences and emotions than from the very people who are doing and feeling. . . . And yet, memory is unreliable. It is not an objective arbiter of past truths but rather a reconciler of past and present. Reconciliation is a lifelong process, and it matters both when in the life cycle a memory is elicited as well as in what culture and historical period.

So what do we want to know, and how do we find it out? First, I suggest that we take a page from contemporary dynamic-systems theories. Dynamic systems are complex and interactive. They are also self-organizing and self-maintaining. In some periods of their development they are unstable in that each current state produces the conditions for the next developmental moment[19]—the so-called feed-forward networks. But dynamic systems can also be self-stabilizing. And stability is one feature of human desire that requires explanation. Sexual preference, while not necessarily a permanent feature of a person's psyche, is very stable, as the failure of many decades of efforts to "cure" people of same-sex desire shows.

On the other hand, dynamic systems can destabilize. If enough of the inter-supporting subunits are disrupted, the entire system can become chaotic; eventually it restabilizes. The new stable state can produce the same types of desire, or a new set of desires may emerge. This, I would argue, is what happens when someone "changes" sexual preference. The current way of explaining a change in desire appeals to a hidden essence that finally works its way to the surface. Hence people "discover" that they were always gay but did not know it, and announce that their true nature has finally been revealed. The revelation model is at the heart of endless hours of friendly gossip within the gay community about so-and-so who is surely gay but doesn't know it. It's fun, but offers little substance with which to understand human development—both its stability and its mutability.

If we are to understand desire as a dynamic system, we must learn more about the underlying components that produce a stable state (or become destabilized). There are many levels of organization to consider, from the subcellular to the sociocultural. Here I want to displace genes. They don't belong at the bottom of the pyramid or as the first arrow in a linear array of causes. Rather, they belong in the middle. Genes don't cause; they respond. It is important to understand gene activity as a reaction to a particular environment or experience. I use environment very broadly here to include both a cellular environment, say, in the developing embryo, and behaviors and experiences that stimulate gene activity.

The enormous and growing literature on neural plasticity is exemplary. From birth through adolescence, the density of synapses in the human brain—a measure of increasing complexity, connectivity, and specificity—more than doubles. Recent work in the neurosciences shows that central nervous system development is dynamic and activity-dependent. In other words, throughout childhood, the brain grows, and nerve cells make and lose and remake and stabilize multiple connections in response to experiences and behaviors. Gene activity mediates these events but does not cause them in a directional sense.

A dynamic approach, potentially, can give us purchase on the question of how we come to embody desire. While the early and mid-twentieth-century work of philosophers, physiologists, psychiatrists, and psychologists such as Paul Schilder, Douwe Tiersma, and M. Merleau-Ponty should be revisited in this context, I want in this shorter piece to consider the idea of incorporating practices. N. Katherine Hayles[20] distinguishes between inscription, which she likens to Foucauldian discourse, and incorporation. Incorporating practices are repeated actions that become part of bodily memory. Learning to ride a bike is an archetypal example. We start out unable to balance on two wheels, but by trying and trying again, we eventually learn to balance without conscious thought. Our body has memorized the feeling; our muscles and nerves know what to do. Let me articulate the concept in the language of contemporary neuroscience: We form new neural networks, and we expand and train neuromuscular connections. Sometimes the memory is maintained primarily in the peripheral nervous system; other times the neural network involves the brain.

Several features of incorporated knowledge are conceptually interesting for an understanding of the development of human desire. First, there are improvisational elements: Incorporation is contextual rather than abstract. Second, incorporated knowledge is, literally, sedimented in the body and thus resists change. Third, because it is habitual, it is not part of conscious memory. But—and this is the fourth point—because it is contextual, sedimented, and nonconscious, it is possible, through the human capacity to narrate our own lives, for it to become a part of our conscious thought as well. In proper cybernetic thinking our narrations of desire can in turn modify incorporated knowledge.

I urge scholars from the sciences, social sciences, and humanities to devote their energies to developing newly framed analytical projects in discussion with one another. I believe we can recoup the energy lost by continued devotion to the old nature-versus-nurture, genes-versus-choice debate and charge our batteries with ideas that promise an understanding of human sexuality as something complex, ever changing, and more delectable for its very dynamism.

Notes

1. I used the keywords "genes" and "homosexuality" in the Lexis-Nexis academic database and searched general newspaper articles for the past two years. In well over one hundred articles, this is the framework for analysis.

2. I except some anthropologists from the broad-brush claim.

3. Brian S. Mustanski et al., "A Genomewide Scan of Male Sexual Orientation," *Human Genetics* 116, no. 4 (2005): 272.

4. See Kaplan's discussion of the use and misuse of the concept of heritability in Jonathan Kaplan, *The Limits and Lies of Human Genetic Research: Dangers for Social Policy* (New York: Routledge, 2000). See also Steven E. Lerman, Michael J. McAleer, and George W. Kaplan, "Sex Assignment in Cases of Ambiguous Genitalia and Its Outcome," *Urology* 55 (2000): 8–12.

5. Mustanski et al., "A Genomewide Scan," 273.

6. Ibid.

7. Zero = exclusively heterosexual, and 6 = exclusively homosexual.

8. Mustanski et al., "A Genomewide Scan," 277.

9. Eric H. Davidson et al., "A Genomic Regulatory Network for Development," *Science* 295, no. 5560 (2002): 1669–1678; Eric H. Davidson, *The Regulatory Genome: Gene Regulatory Networks in Development and Evolution* (New York: Academic Press, 2006).

10. Denis Mareschal and Scott P. Johnson, "Learning to Perceive Object Unity: A Connectionist Account," *Developmental Science* 5, no. 2 (2002): 151–172.

11. Marc D. Lewis, "Self-Organizing Individual Differences in Brain Development," *Developmental Review* 25 (2005): 252–277.

12. Simon LeVay, "A Difference in Hypothalamic Structure between Heterosexual and Homosexual Men," *Science* 253 (1991): 1034–1037; William Byne et al., "The Interstitial Nuclei of the Human Anterior Hypothalamus: An Investigation of Sexual Variation in Volume and Cell Size, Number and Density," *Brain Research* 856, nos. 1–2 (2000): 254–258.

13. Theo G. M. Sandfort, "Sexual Orientation and Gender: Stereotypes and Beyond," *Archives of Sexual Behavior* 34, no. 6 (2005): 595–611.

14. Ibid., 599. For a longer discussion of some of the subtleties involved, see also John H. Gagnon, *An Interpretation of Desire: Essays in the Study Sexuality* (Chicago: University of Chicago Press, 2004).

15. Martin B. Duberman, *Cures: A Gay Man's Odyssey* (New York: Dutton, 1991).

16. Alan P. Bell, Martin S. Weinberg, and Sue Kiefer Hammersmith, *Sexual Preference: Its Development in Men and Women* (Bloomington: Indiana University Press, 1981), 188.

17. Lisa M. Diamond, "Careful What You Ask For: Reconsidering Feminist Epistemology and Autobiographical Narrative in Research on Sexual Identity Formation," *Signs* 31, no. 2 (2006): 471–489.

18. Ibid., 478.

19. For general reading on dynamic systems, consult Esther Thelen and Linda B. Smith, *A Dynamic Systems Approach to the Development of Cognition and Action* (Cambridge, MA: MIT Press, 1994) and Scott Camazine et al., *Self-Organization in Biological Systems* (Princeton, NJ: Princeton University Press, 2001).

20. N. Katherine Hayles, "The Materiality of Informatics," *Configurations: A Journal of Literature Science and Technology* 1 (Winter 1993): 147–170.

Questions

1. What are the wrong questions that scientists keep asking? What is wrong with them? What is the assumed relationship between sexuality and gender? Where did this understanding come from—who specifically started it? What does it mean to examine sexuality as multidimensional?

2. What is a better analytic framework, according to Fausto-Sterling? What does a dynamic systems approach look like? What does Fausto-Sterling mean when she says that genes *respond* to human activity and experience? What is incorporated knowledge? What are the implications for our understanding of sexual desire? For social inequality in general?

3. This piece points out the role that scientists play in answering questions with deep political and social ramifications. Around what other debates about inequality have scientists engaged? Watch Part II of *Race: The Power of an Illusion* by California Newsreel (you may access companion materials at: http://www.pbs.org/race/000_General/000_00-Home.htm). How do scientists shore up their legitimacy? What debates with political ramifications are scientists participating in now? What role do they play? What other authorities have legitimized inequality, and how?

4. In *The Invention of Heterosexuality* (Dutton Books, 1995), historian Jonathan Ned Katz delineates how "heterosexuality" as a concept originated and developed. Read an excerpt on PBS's *Frontline* page (http://www.pbs.org/wgbh/pages/frontline/shows/assault/context/katzhistory.html). When did "heterosexuality" first appear in the dictionary? How did the concept of heterosexuality change across the twentieth century? What caused those changes? Why does Katz trace "heterosexuality" as a category rather than "homosexuality?" How do other social categories get framed as normative?

5

Intersectionality: Multiple Inequalities in Social Theory

SYLVIA WALBY, JO ARMSTRONG, AND SOFIA STRID

Black women scholars like Patricia Hill Collins (2000) and Kimberlé Crenshaw (1989) draw our attention to their unique positionality not just as women or Blacks but as *Black women*. Crenshaw's early work (e.g., 1989) pointed out the invisibility of Black women as targets of domestic violence. Collins' work (1986) argued convincingly that Black women, who had so often worked in white elite spaces (as nannies and cooks, for example), were "outsiders within." They developed unique knowledge about power structures—which Black men and white women were blinded to. These early works also demonstrated that while people could be oppressed in one dimension of social inequality (e.g., gender as a woman), they could be advantaged by others (e.g., class as a manager). Inequalities, Crenshaw explained, *intersect*. Unidimensional analyses were always incomplete from Black feminists' perspective, because they necessarily prioritized one form of inequality over another, ignored how inequalities interact with each other, and glossed over important power differentials within groups (e.g., class variation among women). To understand inequalities, thus, we had to examine them as matrices of domination.

Intersectionality scholars have examined not just individual identities or experiences of oppression at the nexus of race, class, and gender but also the institutional and interactional dimensions as well. That requires studying empirically the relationship among various systems of oppression: how they fit together, draw on each other, change each other, usurp each other, adapt to each other, and so on.

Accordingly, intersectionality theory has dramatically changed and complicated how researchers think about inequalities and collect and analyze data about them. Rather than assuming that experiences of the dominant group ring true for everyone, sociologists empirically test how social processes are inflected by various forms of inequality working together. For example, early studies on intergenerational social mobility drew conclusions from data comparing sons' class positions to those of their fathers (e.g., Blau and Duncan 1967). Early studies not only neglected women as social actors who might themselves have mobility, but they also neglected women's contributions to household economics and variation across race or class groups. More recently, the Pew Charitable Trusts' Economic Mobility Project (you can access information on their website, www.pewtrusts.org), examined mobility in the aftermath of the Great Recession—not just for men but for women and various racial/ethnic groups, and based on one's starting class position (i.e., how mobile are people who start at the bottom compared to people who start at the top or in the middle), and even in relation to place of residence. Similarly, studies on the education achievement gap examine racialization and class simultaneously to understand how they work together to affect educational attainment—and if they play out differently for boys and girls (see Condron

Excerpted from Walby, Sylvia, Jo Armstrong, and Sofia Strid. 2012. "Intersectionality: Multiple Inequalities in Social Theory." *Sociology* 46:224–240. Copyright © 2012, © SAGE Publications.

2009 for an excellent example of complex modeling). For scientists documenting the extent and processes of social equality, their models are much more complex and nuanced than they used to be.

In the piece that follows, Walby, Armstrong, and Strid lay out the dominant threads of intersectionality theory today, the debates which have arisen, and proposed resolutions of those issues. They tackle the "Oppression Olympics," in which researchers seem to be besting each other by claiming that one form of inequality is more fundamental or worse than others (usually, social class). They also discuss whether to think of intersectionality as systems of inequality that mutually constitute each other or as something else. Their piece challenges the reader to seriously consider how we conceptualize the relationships among racial, class, gender relations, and other forms of inequality.

Perhaps most interestingly for our purposes here, the authors raise the question of how our understanding of inequalities should relate to the political agenda of eradicating them. Here, the contributions of intersectionality have been monumental for making a difference in people's lives. Intersectionality calls us to think outside of simplistic binaries into gradations of gray. Rather than clumping women's experience into a single box and men's experience into another, intersectionality calls into question if there is "women's experience" in the first place. But intersectionality also challenges us to relate the experiences of people to each other. One's social justice work in one area may have consequences, albeit unintentionally, for inequality in another. We now must consider if and when that is the case, to make our work for change more effective.

Finally, intersectionality also provides a way for people to relate to each other emotionally by building empathy based on hidden commonalities and by showing how interconnected we really are. Where white middle-class girls in rural communities otherwise seem to have little in common with inner-city boys of color, we can relate their lives to each other and show how inequalities function to create oppressive conditions for both of them, albeit in different ways: They face some of the same educational struggles related to resource deprivation, lack of quality teachers, transportation issues, and isolation. And here intersectionality theory offers a promising avenue for working toward social justice on the ground: through empathy, networking, and coalition building.

References

Blau, Peter M., and Otis Dudley Duncan. 1967. *The American Occupational Structure.* New York: Wiley and Sons.

Collins, Patricia Hill. 1986. "Learning from the Outsider Within: The Sociological Significance of Black Feminist Thought." *Social Problems* 33(6): S14–S32.

Collins, Patricia Hill. 2000. *Black Feminist Thought: Knowledge, Consciousness, and the Politics of Empowerment,* 2nd ed. New York: Routledge.

Condron, Dennis J. 2009. "Social Class, School and Non-School Environments, and Black/White Inequalities in Children's Learning." *American Sociological Review* 74:683–704.

Crenshaw, Kimberlé. 1989. "Demarginalizing the Intersection of Race and Sex: A Black Feminist Critique of Antidiscrimination Doctrine, Feminist Theory and Antiracist Politics." *University of Chicago Legal Forum* 139–167.

The theorization of the intersection of multiple inequalities has become a central issue in gender theory. These developments potentially have much broader applications for wider social theory. Feminist analysis has moved beyond the longstanding critique of the focus on class in classical sociology, beyond the construction of a special set of studies of gender parallel to sub-fields of ethnicity, disability, age, sexual orientation, and religion and towards the theoretical recognition of the importance of the intersection of multiple inequalities, although there remain significant differences as to how this should proceed (Acker, 2000; Anthias and Yuval-Davis, 1992; Bhopal, 1997; Brah and Phoenix, 2004; Collins, 1998; Crenshaw, 1991; Felski, 1997; Hancock, 2007; Hartmann, 1976; Jakobsen, 1998; Lundström, 2006; Lykke, 2004; McCall, 2001, 2005; Medaglia,

2000; Mirza, 1997; Mohanty, 1991; Phizacklea, 1990; Phoenix and Pattynama, 2006; Verloo, 2006; Walby, 2009; Yuval-Davis, 2006).

The subject matter that is core to intersectionality is analyzed in other social science literature using concepts such as cosmopolitanism (Beck, 2006), multiculturalism (Phillips, 2009), anti-racism, hybridity (Gilroy, 2004), identity, and nationalism (Brubaker, 1996; Calhoun, 1995). There is a common interest in how to conceptualize and theorize the relationship between different social groups and between projects that shape each other. Recent gender theory has addressed these issues under the heading of "intersectionality," though there has been a long tradition of similar analysis before this term was coined (e.g., Hartmann, 1976).

The theoretical questions concerning intersectionality are linked to debates in the "real" world, of which the following are some examples. Has the merger of the equality commissions with the formation of the Equality and Human Rights Commission in the UK in 2007 led to more effective ways of addressing inequalities, because of greater organizational capacity to address their intersection, or has it reduced its functioning to the lowest common denominator? Are the particular forms of gender-based violence against women at the intersection of gender inequality, nation, ethnicity, and religion (e.g., forced marriage, female genital mutilation, trafficking, and "honor" crimes) best addressed by focusing on the particularity at the intersection, for example with special legislation for each form of violence, or by their inclusion in more general policies and politics to address violence against women? Is the gender pay gap best addressed by paying attention to its gender-specific aspects, for example through gender pay audits, or by focusing on class-led mechanisms such as the minimum wage?

This chapter addresses the theoretical debates that underlie different approaches to the analysis of intersectionality. It does not address the empirical detail of the substantive issues but rather is focused on the conceptual and theoretical issues that are interwoven through these discussions. The chapter starts by reviewing the major conceptual and theoretical literature on intersectionality, especially writings by Crenshaw (1989, 1991), McCall (2005), and Hancock (2007), in order to identify the main theoretical dilemmas in the field. Six dilemmas are identified, which are subjected to extended

conceptual and theoretical discussion in order to resolve them.

Key Questions in the Intersectionality Debates

Three texts—Crenshaw (1991), McCall (2005) and Hancock (2007)—have become central to the debates about gender and intersectionality and hence are the focus of this section which identifies the remaining dilemmas in the debates. These texts share a common starting point in the rejection of a focus on gender only and of generalizations from some women to all women (Mohanty, 1991), but they diverge in how they conceptualize the relationship between multiple inequalities.

Crenshaw

Crenshaw's (1989, 1991) work in developing the field of intersectionality is sufficiently significant that her work is very frequently cited in later literature. She produced not only a critique of the invisibility of Black women at the intersection of gender and race/ethnicity, but also a critique of identity politics for its over-stabilization of discrete groups and categories. Crenshaw (1991) regarded the invisibility of Black women in the domestic violence projects she analyzed as a weakness for both the gender equality project and the anti-racist project. Crenshaw (1989) also uses the concept of intersectionality to grasp the ways in which the interactions of gender and race limit Black women's access to the American labor market and how a lack of understanding of this intersection led to the marginalization of Black women and Black women's experiences. Crenshaw (1991: 1244) argues that the experiences faced by women of color were "not subsumed within the traditional boundaries of race or gender discrimination as these boundaries are currently understood." She suggests that previous academic, political, and civil societal engagements with the intersections of gender and race/ethnicity have not been sufficiently careful. One identity category is instead treated as dominant; social power "works to exclude or marginalize those who are different" (Crenshaw, 1991: 1242). "Contemporary feminist and anti-racist discourses have failed to consider intersectional identities such as women of color" (Crenshaw, 1991: 1243). Groups at the intersection of two or more identity categories are left out of focus in both analysis and politics: Black women, ethnic minority women, or "women of color," groups positioned at the intersection of gender and race/ethnicity, become marginalized as a group. . . . In the example of domestic violence, the experiences of African-American women are made invisible, with activists not supporting the public release of data on this group at the intersection of gender and ethnicity for fear that "the statistics might permit opponents to dismiss domestic violence as a minority problem" (Crenshaw, 1991: 1253). "Women of color can be erased by the strategic silences of anti-racism and feminism" (Crenshaw, 1991: 1253).

Crenshaw makes a distinction between structural intersectionality and political intersectionality. Structural intersectionality concerns the intersection of unequal social groups. Political intersectionality concerns the intersection of political agendas and projects.

Crenshaw considered groups at the point of intersection to be mutually constituted, for example, by gender and ethnicity. Crenshaw's critique of the invisibility of domestic violence against Black women focuses on two main actors—white women and Black men—for their hesitation at publicly identifying this violence. However, in this focus on the agency of these two disadvantaged groups her analysis curiously loses sight of the actions of the powerful and the racist structures. Maintaining the focus on the larger structures is an issue raised by McCall (2005) (see next section).

Substantively, Crenshaw's analysis led the way to a host of studies of the particularities of groups at the point of intersection, which had been previously underexamined.

McCall

There are now many different approaches to intersectionality. McCall (2005) reviews the plethora of studies using the concept of intersectionality and identifies three distinct approaches: intra-categorical, anti-categorical, and inter-categorical (1773–1774). The intra-categorical is concerned to "focus on particular social groups at neglected points of intersection . . . in order to reveal the complexity of lived experience within such groups" (McCall 2005: 1774). This approach

draws inspiration from Crenshaw's work in order to examine groups, often small ones, which had not been previously analyzed. This has the disadvantage of displacing the focus from the larger social processes and structures that might be causing the inequalities. The anti-categorical approach is "based on a methodology that deconstructs analytical categories." This approach considers the stabilization of categories to be problematic in essentializing and reifying the social relations that the analyst may be seeking to change. It thus prioritizes fluidity over stability of categories. This is problematic in that it makes practical analysis difficult. The inter-categorical approach "provisionally adopt[s] existing analytical categories to document relationships of inequality among social groups and changing configurations of inequality among multiple and conflicting dimensions" (McCall 2005: 1773). McCall recommends the inter-categorical, for its power in engaging with the larger structures that generate inequalities. McCall's (2001) analysis is interesting for its attention to inequalities within the categories, not only between them.

Hancock

Hancock (2007: 64, 67) also reviews the many studies of intersectionality in order to build a typology of approaches, but one that is different from McCall's. She identifies three approaches to the study of race, gender, class, and other categories of difference: unitary, multiple, and intersectional. In the "unitary" approach, only one category is examined, and it is presumed to be primary and stable. In the "multiple" approach more than one category is addressed, and these matter equally; the categories are presumed to be stable and to have stable relationships with each other. In the "intersectional" approach more than one category is addressed; the categories matter equally; the relationship between the categories is open; the categories are fluid, not stable; and they mutually constitute each other. Within this typology, Hancock places considerable emphasis on the issue of fluidity, suggesting that only in the last category is there any analytic presumption of fluidity of the categories. She presumes that a category is either dominant (unitary) or equal to other categories (multiple, intersectional); this omits any notion of asymmetry.

Unresolved Theoretical Dilemmas

The many studies of intersectionality inspired or reported by Crenshaw, McCall, and Hancock show important differences in approach. Six major theoretical dilemmas remain unresolved in these debates:

1. How to address the relationship between structural and political intersectionality without reducing political projects to social structures. Crenshaw introduces this distinction, but it is rarely addressed in the subsequent literature on intersectionality.

2. How to conceptualize the intersections so that bringing the agency of the disadvantaged into focus does not leave the actions of the powerful out of sight. Crenshaw's analysis loses sight of the actions of the powerful and the racist structures, while McCall's (2001) early work deliberately looks at the inequality within "categories"; much of the work that uses concepts of "category" and "strand" tends to obscure the powerful within them.

3. How to balance the stability and fluidity of inequalities so they are sufficiently stable as to be available for empirical analysis, while recognizing that they change. The emphasis on fluidity in Hancock poses challenges for practical analysis.

4. How to neither leave class out of focus nor treat it as of overwhelming importance. Much current literature has addressed the previous neglect of ethnicity, but this is often at the expense of class.

5. How to bring into focus the projects of small minorities, while not making the normative assumption (as Hancock does) that all projects are equally important.

6. How to simultaneously identify the intersecting inequalities while recognizing that their intersection changes what they are. The notion of mutual constitution invoked by Hancock is in tension with the demand from Crenshaw that the component inequalities are made visible.

Structural and Political Intersectionality

There is a tension between a focus on structural inequalities and a focus on the political projects. One way of attempting to resolve this tension is by reducing one to the other, for example, assuming that political projects can be "read off" from structural inequalities. This is one of the problems identified by Crenshaw in "identity" politics. As Crenshaw (1991) notes, structural intersectionality is not the same as political intersectionality. They are not reducible to each other. Further, there are many actually existing intersections in social structures, but only some of these become the focus of political and policy attention. The relationship between "structural intersection" and "political intersection" (Crenshaw, 1991) and reasons for the selection of some intersectional strands and not others as politically relevant are significant for the analysis of intersectionality in equality policies. However, most writers on intersectionality focus on sets of unequal social relations, and insofar as they address political intersectionality assume that this can be derived from the associated social relations. Yet, not all intersectionality issues directly concern sets of social relations in the way discussed so far. There are also projects and policy fields, which are informed by but not reducible to strands.

A focus on the different constructions of policy projects and arenas provides additional insights to the analysis. Here there is interest in the implications of intersectionality for the constitution of the project and indeed of the policy field itself (rather than only the clients within that policy field). An example is the extension of the policy field of gender-based violence to include forced marriage, in which the constitution of the policy arena itself is structured by the approach to intersectionality within the policy terrain. There are projects where differently constituted civil society groups come together, for example, in the project to end child poverty in the UK, or to promote human rights. Projects are the sites of alliances and shifting coalitions of different social forces that come together on one issue and may stand in opposition on others. In many public services, such as health and education, there are policy fields that are informed by the interests of multiple equality strands but which are not reducible to any one of these.

The tension between structural and political intersectionality is best addressed by noting that these issues are separate, as well as having a relationship with each other. They should not be conflated, or reduced to each other.

Categories or Social Relations?

What are the structural "things" that are intersecting? Hancock (2007) uses the term "category" in her summary table. McCall (2005) organizes her typology around whether writers are anti-, intra-, or inter-category. Crenshaw uses the concept of intersectional groups to challenge the concept of "identity" that underlies identity politics, and she most often speaks of "women of color." The use of these terms does not focus on the nature of the social relations within the category but rather on the relations between the categories, especially relations at the point of intersection.

A problem with these approaches is the curious tendency to neglect analysis of the power of the actions of the dominant group within the "category." The analysis of intersectionality has often focused on the actions of the disadvantaged groups. For example, there has been a focus on the actions of white women rather than white men in the context of an intersectional issue facing Black women. Indeed Crenshaw (1991: 1258), in her analysis of violence by Black men against Black women, states, "Not only do race-based priorities function to obscure the problem of violence suffered by women of color; feminist concerns often suppress minority experiences as well." However, such an approach inappropriately ignores the role of the more powerful groups in these divisions. In relation to issues of ethnicity, it is important not to neglect the role of racists in the politics of silencing ethnic minority women in issues of domestic violence. Noting the importance of the powerful in each of the intersections might shift some of the focus from the inactions of white feminists to the actions of white racists. Indeed it is hard to understand the silence on domestic violence against Black women outside of an account of the racist structuring of the policy terrain.

It is important not to focus only on the disadvantaged people since this obscures the role of the powerful within sets of unequal social relations. Rather than using concepts such as "category" or "strand" that offer connotations of unified blocks, it is important, when the focus of the analysis is inequality, for unequal social relations to remain central to the specification of the units or ontology of the analysis. Hence here the term "inequality" or "set of unequal social relations" is preferred, rather than category or strand. In order to understand the relationship between inequalities it is necessary to understand the nature, or ontology (Bhaskar, 1997), of the social relations through which it is constituted. The ontology of the inequality needs to be specified as a prior step to addressing the nature of the relationship between sets of unequal social relations. However, it is common in analyses of intersectionality for the ontology of inequalities to be left out of focus, with most of the attention being placed instead on the relations between them. The consequence of this focus of attention is that the ontology of the inequality is often too shallow and unitary. This means that the inequalities are treated in practice as if they were relatively holistic and leave out of focus the inequality that is central to this set of social relations.

Fluidity or Stability?

There is a tension between the use of stable concepts or whether the priority should be given to the use of fluid and changing ones. Hancock (2007) advocates fluidity, while McCall (2005) argues for stabilization. Hancock (2007) is critical of approaches to the relations between multiple inequalities that stabilize the categories. Indeed only analyses that treat categories as fluid are considered by her to truly merit the term "intersectional." This is linked to her insistence that at the point of intersection . . . of the initial categories are changed beyond recognition. . . . McCall (2005), by contrast, argues for the use of stabilized macro categories in order to analyze "inter-categorical" intersectionality. This is because the destabilization of concepts makes actual analysis of substantive matters very difficult (Felski, 1997; Sayer, 1997).

How is this tension between fluidity and stability to be resolved? The way forward is to recognize the historically constructed nature of social inequalities and their sedimentation in social institutions (Choo and Ferree, 2010; Ferree, 2009; Walby, 2009). At any one moment in time, these relations of inequality have some stability as a consequence of their institutionalization, but over a period of time they do change. The institutionalization of social relations often provides a degree of relative stability to the experience of social inequality. As social institutions change so does the environment within which specific sets of social inequalities are negotiated and struggled over. Changes in social institutions may be gradual, for example, as gendered rates of employment change, or they may be sudden, even revolutionary. It is important to note their historical dynamics, as well as temporarily stabilizing the categories for analysis at any one point in time.

Class and Non-Class Inequalities

There is ambivalence as to the location of class in the analysis of the intersection of gender with other inequalities. In earlier debates on gender inequality there was interest in the intersection of gender and class relations (Acker, 2000; Hartmann, 1976), and indeed with the intersection of gender, ethnicity, and class (Anthias and Yuval-Davis, 1992; Collins, 1998; Davis, 1981; Phizacklea, 1990; Westwood, 1984), but this interest in class has faded, though not entirely disappeared (McCall, 2005). In consequence, the intersection of gender and class is relatively neglected in current debates. Much of the debate on intersectionality has been concerned with the intersection of gender and ethnicity (Collins, 1998; Crenshaw, 1991; Medaglia, 2000; Mirza, 1997).

Class is not a justiciable inequality under EU legislation, while US writings have often (though not always) focused on ethnicity and race. In an EU context, the six inequalities (gender, ethnicity, disability, age, religion/belief, and sexual orientation) that are the subject of legislation have been subject to the most analysis. . . . However, class is an important aspect of the structuring of inequalities, intersecting in complex ways with all inequalities (Hills et al., 2010). It is important in the structuring of the employment laws and institutional machinery of tribunals and courts that implement these laws. The implementation of the laws on non-class justiciable inequalities takes place in institutions that were originally established to secure justice and good relations for class-based relations between employers and employees. . . . [I]ssues of discrimination in pay and working conditions are still central to legal interventions in inequalities, despite their extension to the supply of goods and services. Class-based oppositional institutions, such as trade unions, have developed complex internal committees and practices to address the intersection of class with other inequalities. Class has continuing effects on the equality architecture.

The conclusion drawn here is that class should be systematically included in the discussions on the intersection of gender and other inequalities. However, it is also important that its significance should not be overstated and to retain the distinction between different forms of inequality.

Competing or Cooperating Projects?

There is a tension between the normative position of treating all equality projects as if they are of equal importance and the analytic stance of treating their relative importance as a matter for empirical investigation.

Hancock (2007) is vehement in her claim that all equality issues should be treated as if they were of equal importance. She is scathing about the development of an "Oppression Olympics," in which some inequalities claim to be more important than others. She treats the construction of a hierarchy of projects in equality politics as a normative issue, and regards this as a pernicious practice to the detriment of equality overall. In Hancock's typology, either one project is dominant (as in the unitary approach) or they are equally important (as in the multiple and intersectional approaches).

An alternative approach is to analyze the actual relations between projects, so as to understand their implications. This opens up to view the possibility that the relations between different projects are highly varied, and do not fit neatly into a dichotomy of "dominant" or "equal." This is the potential outcome of varied processes of competition and alliance of social groups and projects. Different equality projects may have different priorities for the use of resources and the shaping of the definition of an ostensibly common equality project. These may result in competition, alliance, hierarchy, or hegemony.

There are different forms of competition among equality projects, ranging from competitive political organizing to active and acrimonious hostility. There has been concern that the integration of policy machinery on different equality grounds may lead to greater competition for a superior place in a hierarchy of inequality projects, and that competition would become more important than cooperation (Bell, 2004; Verloo, 2006). This may occur when projects associated with some inequalities have stronger legal powers for remedying discrimination than others (Bell, 2004; Hepple, Coussey, and Choudhury, 2000).

An example of discursively organized competition between projects is that of the agenda surrounding "choice," which is currently associated with the neoliberal project but has at some times been adopted by feminists, as in "a woman's right to choose." The choice agenda can be used in opposition to the agenda of equality in circumstances where women are deemed to have freely chosen options even though these options have implications for greater inequality (Hakim, 1991). For example, if women freely choose specific jobs because they are "caring" and have part-time hours, then they can be described within the choice agenda as if they have simultaneously accepted the associated lower pay. The agenda of choice can also in some circumstances invoke the discourse of "diversity," which tends to prioritize difference over equality (Hankivsky, 2005). This means that "choices" made on the basis of "diversity" may be claimed to take priority over claims on the basis of equality. Other forms of competition can involve a sharper clash of values; for example, in the UK in 2007, churches fought the application of anti-discrimination laws to adoption by gay couples.

Rather than competition, the relations between social groups and projects may involve those of alliance (Jakobsen, 1998), coalition (Ferree and Hess, 1995), or network (Keck and Sikkink, 1998; Moghadam, 2005). In addition, they may take the form of a shared project, as in the case of some forms of social democracy (Huber and Stephens, 2001). Some alliances cross the boundary between state and civil society, as in the important alliances identified between elected women politicians, feminist bureaucrats, and feminists in civil society such as academics and activists (Halsaa, 1998; Vargas and Wieringa, 1998; Veitch, 2005), sometimes in "velvet triangles" (Woodward, 2004). The development of practices and institutions at the inter-face of state and civil society is important in increasing the impact of feminist developments in civil society on the state (Walby, 2011).

Alliances and coalitions often involve partners that are asymmetrical in their resources. This may mean that one set of social relations or project (such as class) may achieve hierarchy or hegemony over the others. The movement of an equality project into the mainstream in order to secure the resources of the mainstream for the equality project is a common if contested practice (Walby, 2005). If successful, there are rewards for the equality project. However, there is a risk that the equality project merely becomes absorbed or integrated into the mainstream, eroding its own project (Jahan, 1995). A parallel issue emerges if several equality projects merge; they may each gain from the support of the others, but it is also the case that one can become hegemonic at the expense of the rest.

The implications of the varying forms of competition, cooperation, hierarchy, and hegemony between inequalities, between projects, and between policy fields are challenging for theories of intersectionality. It challenges the search for a single best way of characterizing these relationships. It is not a choice between intra-categorical or inter-categorical (McCall, 2005). Nor is it a choice between unitary or multiple or intersectional (Hancock, 2007). Rather, the extent of the separation or integration of the inequalities (and projects) is empirically variable by context. These are best thought of as variations in the extent to which sets of social relations (and projects) mutually shape each other, rather than mutually constitute each other. These forms of competition and cooperation produce different types of relations between multiple inequalities.

In conclusion, while there are normative aspects to the relations between projects, it is important that these are addressed analytically. There are many ways in which projects may intersect, which are more complex than those of competition and cooperation including complex forms of asymmetrical alliances. Some social relations of inequality are more important than others in structuring the environment which shapes these social relations.

Mutual Shaping Rather than Mutual Constitution

There is a tension over whether naming specific inequalities is the best approach in the analysis of intersectionality or not. Crenshaw is critical of the invisibility of domestic violence against Black women and shows that this is bound up with the disadvantaged position of the intersectional group of Black women. She treats "Black" and "women" as relevant categories, as well as that of "Black women."

Hancock prefers to focus only on what she sees as a new category that is produced at the point of intersection, not on the prior components. She makes a distinction between an approach that is "multiple parallel," and one that is "mutual constitution." Approaches that adopt "mutual constitution" treat the original entities that intersect as transformed into something new, which is not the same as either of the originating forms. For example, "Black women" cannot be understood as the mere addition of "women" and "Black" but is instead a distinctive category. In the typology proposed by Hancock, only "mutual constitution" counts as "intersectional." This is contrasted with the notion that inequalities are simply added together at the point of intersection, "multiple," and with the notion that there is one over-arching inequality, "unitary."

The issue of "visibility" sits awkwardly with the concept of "mutual constitution." Writers that appear to prioritize the "mutual constitution" approach to intersectionality nevertheless often also argue for separate naming, which might appear somewhat inconsistent (Crenshaw, 1991; Hancock, 2007). McCall avoids this problem by considering both "intra-categorical" and "inter-categorical" approaches to be types of intersectionality; mutual constitution is not necessary for the relation between multiple inequalities to be counted as "intersectional" in her account.

Further, the concept of mutual constitution is too simple and insufficiently ambitious to grasp the varying and uneven contribution of sets of unequal social relations to the outcome. For purposes of analysis it is useful to be able to specify the particularity that each inequality brings to each instance, without resorting to the notion of infinite variety suggested by the anti-categorical approach that precludes systematic and explanatory analysis. While it might appear that naming or not-naming is a simple dichotomy, in practice many concepts are in between, with inequalities implicitly named rather than erased or named explicitly. For example, in relation to gender, the concepts of "carer" and "domestic violence" are implicitly gendered, in that most speakers would understand the asymmetric gender relations implied by these terms. In relation to the gender/ethnicity/religion intersection, the concept of "forced marriage" is implicitly gendered, ethnicized, and religious, but not explicitly so. In the context of gender mainstreaming, where the goal is the inclusion of the gender equality project into the mainstream and the aspiration is to change the mainstream, it is as likely that the gender equality project will itself be modified (Jahan, 1995; Moser, 2005; Rees, 2006; Walby, 2011). Success may involve the submerging of the named project (gender equality) within a larger project (human rights, social democracy) in alliance with other projects, which, while including feminist goals, is not named as gendered. It is possible that in some circumstances making a group less visible can be an important strategy in optimizing chances of success. Whether degendering is part of a successful integration of a gender equality project into a larger project or part of its defeat depends upon the resources available to the gender constituency, the resources of allies and opponents, and the context.

Dichotomizing analysis into either additive or mutual constitution approaches is a mistake. In order to move forward in this debate it is necessary to develop the greater depth in the ontology of the intersecting inequalities as well as developing greater sophistication in the analysis of the way in which these sets of social relations, or systems of social relations, affect each other. This requires not only the depth of ontology that is developed in critical realism (Archer, 1995; Sayer, 2000) but also the analysis of complex adaptive systems that is developed in complexity theory (Urry, 2005; Walby, 2007). Complexity notions of the intersection of systems assume that each system is changed as a result of its interaction with other systems, but that it is not destroyed or turned into something totally new. There is mutual adaptation, or mutual shaping of these systems of social relations.

The way forward through the dilemma of both making visible the separate components at the point of intersection while also recognizing that social relations and projects are changed at the point of intersection is to adopt the concept of "mutual shaping" and to reject that of "mutual constitution." "Mutual shaping" is a better concept than that of "mutual constitution" since it enables the retention of naming of each relevant inequality or project while simultaneously recognizing that it is affected by engagement with the others. It acknowledges the way that systems of social relations change each other at the point of intersection, but do not become something totally different.

Conclusions

The analysis of intersectionality has been considerably advanced by Crenshaw, McCall, and Hancock and many others, but six remaining dilemmas were identified. Resolutions to these six dilemmas have been proposed that draw on the insights of critical realism and complexity theory.

The first dilemma is how to address the relationship between structural and political intersectionality so that one is not simply reduced to the other even while recognizing that there is a connection. This is best addressed by separately identifying and addressing the intersection of sets of unequal social relations and the intersection of projects in addition to examining the relationship between structures and projects. It is important not to conflate a set of social relations and a related project, but to recognize the distinction between them.

The second dilemma is how to address the relations between the inequalities without leaving the actions of the powerful within each set of unequal social relations out of focus. The way forward is to draw on the insights of critical realism to deepen the ontological depth of the objects that are intersecting, so that the inequalities in these sets of social relations can be made more available for analysis. It is also useful to change the terminology, so as to avoid terms that carry the connotations of unity, such as "strands" and "categories" and to replace them with terms such as inequalities, sets of unequal social relations, regimes and social systems. When the focus is on the set of social relations of inequality rather than on a unitary concept of a "strand" or "category," then it is easier to identify the significance of the actions of the powerful as well as of the disadvantaged.

The third dilemma is how to balance the stability and fluidity of the concepts capturing the sets of social relations. The way forward is to recognize that concepts need to have their meaning temporarily stabilized at the point of analysis, even while recognizing that their social construction is the outcome of changes and interactions over time and to note the historically varied construction of these categories. Identifying the historically changing relations between social institutions is important in providing the appropriate context of current inequalities. This approach draws on notions of ontological depth from critical realism.

The fourth dilemma is how to address class, which appears to be differently situated in intersectionality debates from other inequalities. It is important to systematically consider the reinsertion of class in analyses of the intersection of gender with other inequalities, even though there are differences in their ontological construction. Class needs to be included, without becoming dominant in the analysis of multiple intersecting inequalities.

The fifth dilemma is how to address the issue of the so-called "Oppression Olympics" and the tension between a normative tendency to declare all inequality projects equal and an analytic stance that treats this as an empirical question. The way forward is substantive investigation and the recognition that the relations between the projects may be competitive or cooperative, hierarchical or equal, asymmetrical or hegemonic. Some projects may be more important than others in shaping the social environment in some contexts.

The sixth dilemma is how to address the preference for the visibility of each inequality in the context of an emerging hegemonic conceptualization of intersectionality as "mutual constitution." The way forward is to reject the concept of mutual constitution and to replace it with the concept of mutual shaping of equalities and projects. This approach draws not only on critical realism but also on complexity theory approaches to the intersection of complex adaptive systems. At the point of intersection complex systems mutually adapt, each changing the other, but they do not usually destroy each other. Each remains visible, although each is changed. It is thus more appropriate to conclude that inequalities mutually shape each other rather than mutually constitute each other at their point of intersection. Underpinning this approach to the resolution of debates in intersectionality theory lies the utilization of a version of critical realism (in the approach to ontological depth, to social relations, and to the distinction between structural inequalities and political projects) and the selective deployment of complexity theory (especially in relation to social systems). This enables a move beyond some of the limitations of the previous debates on intersectionality, enabling their potential deployment to a wider range of social phenomena.

References

Acker, J. 2000. Revisiting Class. *Social Politics* 7(2): 192–214.

Anthias, F., and N. Yuval-Davis. 1992. *Racialized Boundaries*. London: Routledge.

Archer, M. S. 1995. *Realist Social Theory*. Cambridge: Cambridge University Press.

Beck, U. 2006. *The Cosmopolitan Vision*. Cambridge: Polity.

Bell, M. 2004. *Critical Review of Academic Literature Relating to the EU Directives to Combat Discrimination*. Brussels: European Commission.

Bhaskar, R. 1997. *A Realist Theory of Science*. London: Verso.

Bhopal, K. 1997. *Gender, "Race" and Patriarchy*. Aldershot: Ashgate.

Brah, A., and A. Phoenix. 2004. Ain't I a Woman? Revisiting Intersectionality. *Journal of International Women's Studies* 5(3): 75–86.

Brubaker, R. 1996. *Nationalism Reframed*. Cambridge: Cambridge University Press.

Calhoun, C. 1995. *Critical Social Theory*. Oxford: Blackwell.

Choo, H. Y., and M. M. Ferree. 2010. Practicing Intersectionality in Sociological Research. *Sociological Theory* 28(2): 129–149.

Collins, P. H. 1998. It's All in the Family: Intersections of Gender, Race, and Nation. *Hypatia* 13(3): 62–82.

Crenshaw, K. W. 1989. Demarginalizing the Intersection of Race and Sex: A Black Feminist Critique of Antidiscrimination Doctrine, Feminist Theory, and Antiracist Politics. *University of Chicago Legal Forum* 14: 538–554.

Crenshaw, K. W. 1991. Mapping the Margins: Intersectionality, Identity Politics, and Violence against Women of Color. *Stanford Law Review* 43(6): 1241–1299.

Davis, A. Y. 1981. Women, Race, and Class. New York: Random House.

Felski, R. 1997. The Doxa of Difference. *Signs* 23(1): 1–22.

Ferree, M. M. 2009. Inequality, Intersectionality and the Politics of Discourse: Framing Feminist Alliances. In *The Discursive Politics of Gender Equality: Stretching, Bending and Policymaking* (ed. E. Lombardo, P. Meier, and M. Verloo), 86–104. London: Routledge.

Ferree, M. M., and B. B. Hess. 1995. *Controversy and Coalition: The New Feminist Movement across Three Decades of Change,* 2nd ed. New York: Simon and Schuster, Macmillan.

Gilroy, P. 2004. *Between Camps.* London: Routledge.

Hakim, C. 1991. Grateful Slaves and Self-Made Women: Fact and Fantasy in Women's Work Orientations. *European Sociological Review* 7(2): 101–121.

Halsaa, B. 1998. A Strategic Partnership for Women's Policies in Norway. In *Women's Movements and Public Policy in Europe, Latin America, and the Caribbean* (ed. G. Lycklama, A. Nijeholt, V. Vargas, and S. Wieringa, 167–189. New York: Garland.

Hancock, A.-M. 2007. When Multiplication Doesn't Equal Quick Addition. *Perspectives on Politics* 5(1): 63–79.

Hankivsky, O. 2005. Gender vs. Diversity Mainstreaming: A Preliminary Examination of the Role and Transformative Potential of Feminist Theory. *Canadian Journal of Political Science* 38(4): 977–1001.

Hartmann, H. 1976. Capitalism, Patriarchy and Job Segregation by Sex. *Signs* 1:137–170.

Hepple, B., M. Coussey, and T. Choudhury. 2000. *Equality: A New Framework.* London: Hart Publishing.

Hills, J., et al. 2010. *An Anatomy of Economic Inequality in the UK: Report of the National Equality Panel.* London: Government Equalities Office. http://eprints.lse.ac.uk/28344/1/CASEreport60.pdfAccessed September 16, 2015.

Huber, E., and J. D. Stephens. 2001. *Development and Crisis of the Welfare State.* Chicago: Chicago University Press.

Jahan, R. 1995. *The Elusive Agenda: Mainstreaming Women in Development.* London: Zed Books.

Jakobsen, J. R. 1998. *Working Alliances and the Politics of Difference.* Bloomington: Indiana University Press.

Keck, M. E., and K. Sikkink. 1998. *Activists beyond Borders.* Ithaca, NY: Cornell University Press.

Lundström, C. 2006. "Okay, but We Are Not Whores You Know": Latina Girls Navigating the Boundaries of Gender and Ethnicity in Sweden. *Young: Nordic Journal of Youth Research* 14(3): 203–218.

Lykke, N. 2004. Between Particularism, Universalism and Transversalism: Reflections on the Politics of Location of European Feminist Research and Education. *NORA: Nordic Journal of Women's Studies* 12(2): 72–82.

McCall, L. 2001. *Complex Inequality.* New York: Routledge.

McCall, L. 2005. The Complexity of Intersectionality. *Signs* 30(3): 1771–1800.

Medaglia, A. 2000. *Patriarchal Structures and Ethnicity.* Avebury: Ashgate.

Mirza, H. S. (ed.). 1997. *Black British Feminism.* London: Routledge.

Moghadam, V. M. 2005. Globalizing Women. Baltimore, MD: Johns Hopkins University Press.

Mohanty, C. T. 1991. Under Western Eyes. In *Third World Women and the Politics of Feminism* (ed. C. T. Mohanty, A. Russo, and L. Torres). Bloomington, IN: Indiana University Press. Pp. 51–80.

Moser, C. 2005. Has Gender Mainstreaming Failed? *International Feminist Journal of Politics* 7(4): 576–590.

Phillips, A. 2009. *Multiculturalism without Culture.* Princeton, NJ: Princeton University Press.

Phizacklea, A. 1990. *Unpacking the Fashion Industry.* London: Routledge.

Phoenix, A., and P. Pattynama. 2006. Editorial: Intersectionality. *European Journal of Women's Studies* 13(3): 187–192.

Rees, T. 2006. *Mainstreaming Equality in the European Union.* London: Routledge.

Sayer, A. 1997. Essentialism, Social Constructionism and Beyond. *Sociological Review* 45(3): 453–487.

Sayer, A. 2000. *Realism and Social Science.* London: Sage.

Urry, J. 2005. The Complexity Turn. *Theory, Culture and Society* 22:1–14.

Vargas, V., and S. Wieringa. 1998. The Triangles of Empowerment. In *Women's Movements and Public Policy in Europe, Latin America and the Caribbean* (ed. G. Lycklama, A. Nijeholt, V. Vargas, and S. Wieringa), 3–23. New York: Garland.

Veitch, J. 2005. Looking at Gender Mainstreaming in the UK Government. *International Feminist Journal of Politics* 7(4): 600–606.

Verloo, M. 2006. Multiple Inequalities, Intersectionality and the European Union. *European Journal of Women's Studies* 13(3): 211–228.

Walby, S. 2005. Gender Mainstreaming: Productive Tensions in Theory and Practice. *Social Politics* 12(3): 1–25.

Walby, S. 2007. Complexity Theory, Systems Theory, and Multiple Intersecting Social Inequalities. *Philosophy of the Social Sciences* 37(4): 449–470.

Walby, S. 2009. *Globalization and Inequalities: Complexity and Contested Modernities.* London: Sage.

Walby, S. 2011. *The Future of Feminism.* Cambridge: Polity.

Westwood, S. 1984. *All Day, Every Day.* London: Pluto Press.

Woodward, A. 2004. Building velvet triangles. In *Informal Governance in the European Union.* (ed. T. Christiansen and S. Piattoni), 76–93. Cheltenham: Edward Elgar.

Yuval-Davis, N. 2006. Intersectionality and Feminist Politics. *European Journal of Women's Studies* 13(3): 193–209.

Questions

1. What is "intersectionality?" How did it develop, and who founded it? What does intersectionality add to the study of inequality?

2. Reexamine the pieces by Russell and Bonvillain, using the author's framework. What sort of intersectional analysis is being done? What do we learn about how inequalities in general work? About how inequalities interact with each other?

3. The authors argue that intersectionality research has at times devolved into an "Oppression Olympics." Why? What is problematic about that, and how do the authors suggest dealing with the issue instead? What do the authors mean by "mutual constitution" of inequalities? How is this different from an "additive" approach to intersectionality? Why do the authors reject "mutual constitution" in favor of "mutual shaping?"

6

Slaves, Immigrants, and Suffragists: The Uses of Disability in Citizenship Debates

DOUGLAS BAYNTON

Inequalities are elaborate systems of domination in which one group of people imposes their will on others and hoards resources. The resources secured by dominant groups include the obvious—money, land, decision-making power. But less visible social resources are also important, especially stability, respect from others, psychological well-being, and the ability to define reality as one sees it. Inequality scholars point out that categorical inequalities are necessarily relational: One group gains at another's expense. Dominant groups develop elaborate systems to secure resources and justify their doing so.

Max Weber ([1922] 1978) described one system of social hoarding as "social closure." Social closure is when a group uses exclusivity to raise its status. It works the same way a monopoly does—by restricting competition—but the payoff is social rather than financial. Consider the elaborate credentialing process that American physicians undergo, for example. They have to graduate from high school, obtain a four-year college degree, take the MCAT exam and score well, get into medical school, pass coursework and clinicals, pass Step 1 of the board exam, pass Step 2 of the board exam, graduate from medical school (Congratulations, you are now a doctor!), apply to and get matched with a residency program, complete at least three years of residency, pass Step 3 of the board exam, and take a board licensure exam to practice medicine independently and with licensure in their field of specialization. Through this elaborate process, physicians demonstrate their value by making sure not just anyone can be one of them. By positioning themselves as different from and better—more skilled—than EMTs, nurses, physicians assistants, midwives, nurse practitioners, and other medical personnel, physicians protect their group's ability to garner respect from others, prescribe medications, impose their decision making, justify high salaries, and so on. It is through their superior relationship to these other groups that physicians hoard resources.

When we understand inequalities as systems people create in relationship to other people in order to hoard resources, inequality scholars direct their inquiry to several questions. Who benefits from organizing social life or belief systems a particular way? Who writes the social history that becomes common knowledge? How do they gain by it from others? How do people adapt to changing political, economic, or social environments? What tools do people use to challenge their own or others' oppression? How does using those tools affect other forms of inequality?

The piece that follows pushes the reader to ask several of these questions and apply an intersectional analysis. Douglas Baynton is an historian who considers disability a central form of stratification, one implicated—and too often overlooked—in the development and contestation of other forms of inequality during the key debates of the nineteenth and twentieth centuries in the United States: over African American freedom, women's suffrage, and immigration. Baynton shows how people without disabilities framed disability as a tool for social exclusion. Moreover, social justice advocates used their typicality to challenge their marginalization due to race, gender, and nativity. In other words, opponents and proponents alike used disability, often in the form of intellectual capability or lack thereof, to justify or challenge the subordinate groups' exclusion or exploitation. Disabilities became a foil against which groups proved their deservedness to human rights. Baynton's inclusion of disability as an intersection of analysis challenges the marginalization of people with intellectual and developmental disabilities and forces the reader to center them in the understanding of history.

Reference

Weber, Max. [1922] 1978. *Economy and Society: An Outline of Interpretive Sociology* (ed. Guenther Roth and Claus Wittich). Berkeley and Los Angeles: University of California Press.

In an article published nearly three decades ago, Joan Scott (1986) discusses the difficulty of persuading historians to take gender seriously. A common response to women's history was that "women had a history separate from men's, therefore let feminists do women's history, which need not concern us," or "my understanding of the French Revolution is not changed by knowing that women participated in it." Despite the substantial number of works on women's history, the topic remained marginal in the discipline. Simply adding women to history, Scott argues, while necessary and important, would not be sufficient to change the paradigms of the profession. To accomplish that, feminists had to demonstrate that gender was "a constitutive element of social relationships" and "a primary way of signifying relationships of power" (1055, 1067).

I argue that disability is likewise a constitutive element of social relationships. That is to say, not only are disabled people significant actors in history, but the concept of disability has functioned rhetorically to structure thought about social hierarchies in general. I want to make that argument by talking briefly about each of the three great citizenship debates of the nineteenth and early twentieth centuries: African American freedom and civil rights, women's suffrage, and immigration restriction.

Disability arguments were prominent in justifications for slavery in the nineteenth century and, after the demise of slavery, were used to justify other forms of unequal relations between white and Black Americans. One of the most common arguments for slavery was simply that the intelligence of African Americans was impaired to such an extent that they were unable to live in freedom on an equal basis with white Americans. Doctors warned that education of African Americans came "at the expense of the body, shortening the existence" and resulting in bodies "dwarfed or destroyed" by the unnatural exertion (Van Evrie 1868, 121, 181, 221).[1] An article on the "diseases and physical peculiarities of the negro race" in the New Orleans Medical and Surgical Journal explained that it is the "defective hematosis, or atmospherization of the blood, conjoined with a deficiency of cerebral matter in the cranium, and an excess of nervous matter distributed to the organs of sensation and assimilation, that is the true cause of that debasement of mind, which has rendered the people of Africa unable to take care of themselves" (Cartwright 1851, 693).

A second line of disability argument was that African Americans, because of their inherent physical and mental weaknesses, were prone to become disabled under conditions of freedom and equality. Samuel Cartwright, in 1851, described two types of mental illness to which African Americans were especially susceptible. The first was "drapetomania," a condition that caused slaves to run away, "as much a disease of the mind as any other species of mental alienation." It apparently was common among slaves whose masters had "made themselves too familiar with them, treating them as equals." The second was dysaesthesia aethiopis, a "mental disease . . .

accompanied with physical signs or lesions of the body," a symptom of which was a strong desire to avoid work and cause mischief. Its cause was similarly a lack of firm governance and was therefore nearly universal among free Blacks as well as a "common occurrence on badly-governed plantations." Cartwright explained that the need of African Americans to submit to a master was evident in "the physical structure of his knees, being more flexed or bent, than any other kind of man" (707–710).[2] John C. Calhoun, senator from South Carolina and one of the most influential spokesmen for the slave states, argued in defense of slavery that the "number of deaf and dumb, blind, idiots, and insane, of the negroes in the States that have changed the ancient relation between the races" was seven times higher than in the slave states ([1844] 1888, 337).

Physicians were still claiming at the turn of the century that African Americans were disabled by freedom and therefore in need of greater oversight. An article in the North Carolina Medical Journal inquired whether "the effect of freedom upon the mental and physical health of the negroes of the South" had been "damaging." It concluded that there were "more congenital defects" and a dramatic increase in mental illness and tuberculosis, which supposedly had been rare among enslaved African Americans. Freedom, for which the African American's weak mind and frail constitution were ill suited, had brought to the former slave a "harvest of mental and physical degeneration and he is now becoming a martyr to an heredity thus established" (Miller 1896, 286, 289, 290). To justify slavery, it was sufficient to claim that free Blacks were more likely to be disabled. The contention had to be countered, and no argument on other grounds could trump it. Writing in opposition to slavery in the *New York Journal of Medicine* in 1844, for example, one doctor responded to this argument by maintaining that if free Blacks in the North did experience more disability than slaves, the cause might instead be the climate. "The whole constitution of the Black is adapted to a tropical region," he wrote, and their health was therefore bound to suffer in the northern climate (Forry 313). He understood that to effectively oppose slavery, he had to produce an alternative explanation for the supposedly higher rates of disability among free Blacks. The notion that a people might be enslaved to protect them from disability he did not question.

During the long-running debate over women's suffrage in the nineteenth and early twentieth centuries, one of the rhetorical tactics of suffrage opponents was to point to the physical, intellectual, and psychological flaws of women—their frailty, irrationality, and emotional instability. Paralleling the arguments made in defense of slavery, two types of disability arguments were used: that women have disabilities that make them incapable of using the franchise responsibly and that, because of their frailty, women would become disabled if exposed to the rigors of political participation. The American antisuffragist Grace Goodwin, for example, spoke of the "great temperamental disabilities" with which women had to contend: "woman lacks endurance in things mental. . . . She lacks nervous stability" (1913, 91–92). The second line of argument is identified most closely with Edward Clarke, author of *Sex in Education; or, A Fair Chance for Girls.* Clarke's line of reasoning chiefly concerned education but was often applied to suffrage as well. He maintained that overuse of the brain among young women was responsible for the "numberless pale, weak, neuralgic, dyspeptic, hysterical, menorrhagic, dysmenorrhoeic girls and women" of America with "bloodless female faces, that suggest consumption, scrofula, anemia, and neuralgia" ([1873] 1972, 18, 22). An appropriate education designed for women's frail constitutions would ensure "a future secure from neuralgia, uterine disease, hysteria, and other derangements of the nervous system" (62).

Similarly, William Warren Potter, addressing the Medical Society of New York in 1891, suggested that many a woman was incapacitated for motherhood by inappropriate education: "her reproductive organs are dwarfed, deformed, weakened, and diseased, by artificial causes imposed upon her during their development" (1891, 48). A. Lapthorn Smith asserted in *Popular Science Monthly* that educated women were increasingly "sick and suffering before marriage and are physically disabled from performing physiological functions in a normal manner" ([1905] 1985, 149). A prominent late-nineteenth-century neurophysiologist, Charles L. Dana, estimated that enfranchising women would result in a 25-percent increase in insanity among them and "throw into the electorate a mass of voters of delicate nervous stability . . . which might do injury to itself without promoting the community's good" (qtd. in Camhi 1994, 18).[3]

Disability figured not just in arguments against the equality of women and minorities but also in feminist arguments for equality. Instead of challenging the notion that disability justified political inequality, like antislavery writers feminists maintained that women did not have the disabilities attributed to them and therefore deserved the rights of citizenship. Suffrage rhetoric was replete with references to the intelligence and abilities of women, countering the imputations of female inferiority. Although more common later in the century, this form of argument was already in evidence in 1848 at the Seneca Falls Woman's Rights Convention. Delegates there resolved that "the equality of human rights results necessarily from the fact of the identity of the race in capabilities and responsibilities" and further that "being invested by the Creator with the same capabilities . . . it is demonstrably the right and duty of woman" to participate in public political life (*Woman's Rights Convention* [1870] 1969, 4).

Suffragists turned the rhetorical power of the disability argument to their own uses, charging that women were being erroneously and slanderously classed with disabled people who were legitimately denied suffrage. Suffrage posters depicted thoughtful-looking women surrounded by slope-browed, wild eyed men identified implicitly or explicitly as "idiots" and "lunatics," with captions that read, "Women and her Political Peers" (Tickner 1988, illus. 4), or "It's time I got out of this place. Where shall I find the key?" (Sheppard 1994, 30). The suffrage supporter George William Curtis, speaking before a New York convention in 1867, demanded to know why women should be classed with "idiots, lunatics, persons under guardianship and felons" (qtd. in Stanton, Anthony, and Gage [1881] 1969, 288), and Elizabeth Cady Stanton in 1869 turned to the same rhetorical device when she objected that women were "thrust outside the pale of political consideration with minors, paupers, lunatics, traitors, [and] idiots" ([1869] 1978, 256).

The exclusion of disabled people has long been one of the fundamental imperatives of American immigration policy. The first major federal immigration law, the 1882 Act to Regulate Immigration, prohibited entry to any "lunatic, idiot, or any person unable to take care of himself or herself without becoming a public charge." Those placed in the categories "lunatic" or "idiot" were automatically excluded. The "public charge" provision was intended to encompass people with disabilities more generally and was left to the examining officer's discretion. The criteria for excluding disabled people were steadily tightened over the next four decades, as the eugenics movement and popular fears about the decline of the national stock gathered strength. The Immigration Act of 1891 replaced the phrase "*unable* to take care of himself or herself without becoming a public charge" with "*likely* to become a public charge" (emphasis added). The Immigration Act of 1907 denied entry to anyone judged "mentally or physically defective, such mental or physical defect being of a nature which *may affect* the ability of such alien to earn a living" (emphasis added).

In 1917, regulations for medical inspectors directed them to exclude persons with "any mental abnormality whatever" and listed diseases and physical disabilities that could be cause for exclusion. Among them were arthritis, asthma, bunions, deafness, deformities, flat feet, heart disease, hernia, hysteria, poor eyesight, poor physical development, spinal curvature, vascular disease of the heart, and varicose veins (United States Public Health Service 1917, 28–29). In short, the exclusion of disabled people was central to the laws and the work of the immigration service. In 1907, the commissioner general of immigration proclaimed that "the exclusion from this country of the morally, mentally, and physically deficient is the principal object to be accomplished by the immigration laws" (United States Bureau of Immigration 1907, 8).

Once the laws and procedures restricting the entry of disabled people were firmly established, attention turned to restricting the entry of undesirable ethnic groups, and for this task the concept of disability was a powerful tool. In 1924, a quota system was instituted that severely limited the numbers of immigrants from southern and eastern Europe. Behind this law lay decades of warnings from superintendents of institutions, philanthropists, immigration reformers, and politicians that immigrants from these nations were disproportionately prone to congenital defects (Trent 1994, 166–169). A rhetoric of "defective races" was an essential element in configuring the image of the inferior immigrant. References to "the slow-witted Slav," the "neurotic condition of our Jewish immigrants," and the "degenerate and psychopathic types, which are so

conspicuous and numerous among the immigrants" were pervasive in the debate over restriction (Grayson 1913, 103, 107–109). The earlier laws forbidding entry to defectives were motivated in part by the desire to limit immigration from inferior nations and were used to target particular ethnic groups. According to Jewish organizations, for example, the diagnosis of "poor physique" was used particularly against Jewish immigrants (Sanders 1909). Conversely, it was assumed that the 1924 quota law would reduce the number of defective immigrants. As one sociologist noted, "the physiognomy of certain groups unmistakably proclaims inferiority of type." Among new immigrants whom he observed landing at Ellis Island, "in every face there was something wrong." Italians were "dwarfish," Portuguese, Greeks, and Syrians were "undersized," and Jews were "very poor in physique . . . the polar opposite of our pioneer breed" (Ross 1914, 285–290). The issues of ethnicity and disability were so intertwined in the immigration debate as to be inseparable.

The attribution of disease or disability to oppressed groups has a long history. Yet while many have pointed out the injustice of this, few have asked why these attributions are such powerful tools for inequality, why they are so furiously denied and condemned by their targets, and what this tells us about our attitudes toward disability. When historians note the uses of disability in citizenship debates, they focus entirely on issues of gender, race, and ethnicity and not on the ways disability is used to constitute and maintain social hierarchies. For example, Daryl Michael Scott has described how both conservatives and liberals long used an extensive repertoire of "damage imagery" to describe African Americans. Conservatives worked "within a biological framework and argued for the innate inferiority of people of African descent" to justify inequality. Liberals maintained that social conditions were responsible for Black inferiority and used damage imagery to argue for rehabilitation, thereby reinforcing "the belief system that made whites feel superior in the first place" (D. M. Scott 1997, xi–xvii). The "contempt and pity"—a phrase that also describes historically prevalent attitudes toward disabled people—of conservatives and liberals defined Americans of African descent as defective. Scott cites Charles S. Johnson, president of Fisk University, who in a 1928 speech complained that "the sociologists classify Negroes with cripples, persons with recognized physical handicaps" (208nl2). Like Johnson, Scott laments the fact that "African Americans were often lumped with the 'defective,' 'delinquent,' and dependent classes" (12). This is obviously a bad place to be "lumped." He does not ask why that might be the case; to be associated with disability is self-evidently discrediting.

In the case of women's suffrage, Lois Magner (1992) has described how women were said to bear the "onerous functions of the female," which brought on a "mental disability that rendered women unfit" for political engagement or an "active life" (119–120). Nancy Woloch (1994) has noted that a "major antisuffragist point was that women were physically, mentally, and emotionally incapable of duties associated with the vote. Lacking rationality and sound judgment, they suffered from 'logical infirmity of mind.' . . . Unable to withstand the pressure of political life, they would be prone to paroxysms of hysteria" (339). Aileen Kraditor (1981) has observed that antisuffragists "described woman's physical constitution as too delicate to withstand the turbulence of political life. Her alleged weakness, nervousness, and proneness to fainting would certainly be out of place in polling booths and party conventions"(20). While such stereotypes are justifiably derided, historians generally leave unchallenged the notion that weakness or a tendency to faint might legitimately disqualify one from suffrage.[4]

Historians have also scrutinized the common attribution of mental and physical inferiority to new groups of immigrants, but only to condemn it as slander. With their attention confined to racial and ethnic stereotypes, what this might also tell us about attitudes toward disabled people has gone largely ignored, and prejudice against people with disabilities passes unremarked. While it is certain that immigration restriction rested in good part on a fear of "strangers in the land," as John Higham (1955) described it, this and other forms of inequality in American history have been fueled also by a pervasive and deep-seated fear of defectives in the land.

Notes

1. Van Evrie (1868) notes in his preface that the book was completed "about the time of Mr. Lincoln's election"

and was therefore originally an argument in favor of the continuation of slavery but now constituted an argument for its restoration.

2. See also Szasz (1971).

3. Goodwin (1913) echoed this rhetoric, warning that the "suffragists who dismay England are nerve-sick women" (92).

4. See also Digby (1989), 192–220.

References

Act to Regulate Immigration. 1882, August 3. Stat. 22.214.

Calhoun, John C. [1844] 1888. "Mr. Calhoun to Mr. Pakenham," April 18, 1844. In *The Works of John C. Calhoun* (ed. Richard K. Cralle), Vol. 5, 333–339. New York: Appleton.

Camhi, Jane Jerome. 1994. *Women against Women: American Anti-Suffragism, 1880–1920.* New York: Carlson.

Cartwright, Samuel A. 1851. "Report on the Disease and Physical Peculiarities of the Negro Race." *New Orleans Medical and Surgical Journal* 7:691–715.

Clarke, Edward. [1873] 1972. *Sex in Education; or, A Fair Chance for Girls.* New York: Arno.

Digby, Anne. 1989. "Woman's Biological Straitjacket." In *Sexuality and Subordination: Interdisciplinary Studies of Gender in the Nineteenth Century* (ed. Susan Mendas and Jane Randall). New York: Routledge. Pp. 192–220.

Forry, Samuel. 1844. "On the Relative Proportion of Centenarians, of Deaf and Dumb, of Blind, and of Insane in the Races of European and African Origin." *New York Journal of Medicine and the Collateral Sciences* 2:310–320.

Goodwin, Grace Duffield. 1913. *Anti-Suffrage: Ten Good Reasons.* New York: Duffield.

Grayson, Thomas Wray. 1913. "The Effect of the Modern Immigrant on Our Industrial Centers." In *Medical Problems of Immigration* (ed. American Academy of Medicine), 103–110. Easton, PA: American Academy of Medicine Press.

Higham, John. 1955. *Strangers in the Land: Patterns of American Nativism, 1860–1925.* Piscataway, NJ: Rutgers University Press.

Immigration Act. 1891, March 3. Stat. 26.1084.

Immigration Act. 1907, February 20. Stat. 34.899.

Kraditor, Aileen S. 1981. *The Ideas of the Woman Suffrage Movement.* New York: Norton.

Magner, Lois. 1992. "Darwinism and the Woman Question: The Evolving Views of Charlotte Perkins Gilman."

In *Critical Essays on Charlotte Perkins Gilman* (ed. Joanne Karpinski), 115–128. New York: Hall.

Miller, J. F. 1896. "The Effects of Emancipation upon the Mental and Physical Health of the Negro of the South." *North Carolina Medical Journal* 38:285–294.

Potter, William Warren. 1891 "How Should Girls Be Educated? A Public Health Problem for Mothers, Educators, and Physicians." In *Transactions of the Medical Society of the State of New York* (ed. Medical Society of the State of New York), 42–56. Albany: Medical Society of the State of New York.

Ross, Edward Alsworth. 1914. *The Old World and the New: The Significance of Past and Present Immigration to the American People.* New York: Century.

Sanders, Leon. 1909. "Letter to Surgeon General of the Public Health and Marine Hospital," November 14, 1909. National Archives, Washington. RG 90, entry 10, file 219.

Scott, Daryl Michael. 1997. *Contempt and Pity: Social Policy and the Image of the Damaged Black Soul, 1880–1996.* Chapel Hill: University of North Carolina Press.

Scott, Joan. "Gender: A Useful Category of Historical Analysis." *American Historical Review* 91:1053–1075.

Sheppard, Alice. 1994. *Cartooning for Suffrage.* Albuquerque: University of New Mexico Press.

Smith, A. Lapthorn. 1905, March. "Higher Education of Women and Race Suicide." *Popular Science Monthly.* Rpt. in *Men's Ideas / Women's Realities: Popular Science, 1870–1915* (ed. Louise Michele Newman), 147–151. New York: Pergamon.

Stanton, Elizabeth Cady. [1869] 1978. "Address to the National Woman Convention, Washington, D.C., January 19, 1869." *The Concise History of Woman Suffrage* (ed. Mari Jo Buhle and Paul Buhle), 249–256. Chicago: University of Illinois Press.

Stanton, Elizabeth Cady, Susan B. Anthony, and Matilda Joslyn Gage, eds. [1881] 1969. *History of Woman Suffrage*, Vol. 2. New York: Arno.

Szasz, Thomas S. 1971. "The Sane Slave: A Historical Note on the Use of Medical Diagnosis as Justificatory Rhetoric." *American Journal of Psychotherapy* 25:228–239.

Tickner, Lisa. 1988. *The Spectacle of Women: Imagery of the Suffrage Campaign, 1907–1914.* Chicago: University of Chicago Press.

Trent, James W. 1994. *Inventing the Feeble Mind: A History of Mental Retardation in the United States.* Berkeley: University of California Press.

United States Bureau of Immigration. 1907. *Annual Report of the Commissioner of Immigration.* Washington, DC: U.S. Government Printing Office.

United States Public Health Service. 1917. *Regulations Governing the Medical Inspection of Aliens.* Washington, DC: U.S. Government Printing Office.

Van Evrie, John H. 1868. *White Supremacy and Negro Subordination: Or, Negroes a Subordinate Race.* New York: Van Evrie.

Woloch, Nancy. *Women and the American Experience.* Vol. 1: To 1920. New York: McGraw.

Woman's Rights Convention. [1870] 1969. *Woman's Rights Conventions: Seneca Falls and Rochester, 1848.* New York: Arno.

Questions

1. How did opponents of civil rights, women's suffrage, and immigration rights use disability to enhance the status of the dominant group and deplete the status of subordinate groups? Did proponents use the same rhetorical devices or different ones? What resources were implicated in each debate?

2. One of the key arguments of intersectionality is that mainstream social movements have excluded people on the margins who had other subordinated statuses. Is that what has happened with people with disabilities? What has made them invisible? Why was their subordination legitimized by people who were challenging the legitimacy of oppression of others? In what ways are the interests of people oppressed by race, gender, or immigration status the same as people with disabilities? Why have subordinated groups so readily used other subordinated groups as foils against which to prove their own deservedness?

3. Do only the victors write history? How do they get to do so? What role does writing the history play in sustaining inequalities? Who and what has effectively challenged a singular writing of history?

4. Baynton demonstrates the power of words to demarcate groups of people as inferior and unworthy of respect and status. What words have been used to demean people with disabilities? How have those words changed over time? As Baynton demonstrates, stigmatizing words can be applied to groups outside of the target group. What words do people use to describe people without disabilities or their actions that implicate disabilities? What terms do people with disabilities prefer to describe themselves or their conditions? Why?

5. In 1990, 171,897 people with developmental disabilities lived in institutional settings (with 16 or more residents) in the United States, according to David Braddock's "State of the States 2011" report (available on the Web at stateofthestates.org). Within many states, disabilities advocates have successfully argued or sued for deinstitutionalization, pushing to incorporate people with disabilities into communities so that they gain more self-sufficiency and self-governance. By 2009, the number had dropped 46 percent to 92,314. Carissa, as a college student, spent summers doing direct care of adults with developmental disabilities in such a community setting: with four clients in their own rented house in a typical residential neighborhood in a small town. Her job consisted of helping clients with daily tasks such as cooking and cleaning, getting ready for work, and fulfilling their care plans, which they devised along with their support team. One of the best parts of her job was helping clients prepare for annual summer vacations, a trip the clients saved money for and enthusiastically anticipated every year. During one summer, Carissa got to accompany several clients on their trip to a vacation home in woods country. During a stop at a fast food restaurant, she stood beside David as he ordered his food and paid for it. When the order came up, the worker behind the counter turned to Carissa, and in a caring voice, said to her, "Tell him to be careful. The fries are hot." She reached out to hand the bag to Carissa. What assumptions was the fast food worker making about David? About Carissa? Where did those assumptions come from? How do people use their body language, postures, and gestures to signify other people's competence and value or lack thereof? How should Carissa have responded? What about David? If we take an intersectional approach to analyzing this interaction, how is social class complicating disability-based inequality? What benefits do people with developmental disabilities derive from being fully integrated into their communities? What benefits do communities get? What does full integration look like?

A. Data Analysis Exercise: How Does the United States Compare to Other Economically Advanced Countries?

Part I introduced you to the idea that inequality is a social construction. In other words, inequality is something that people do. In this data analysis exercise, you will apply that framework to recognize and understand inequality around the world. Chart 1 provides data on income inequality, unemployment, democracy, well-being, food insecurity, life expectancy, incarceration rates, and student math and science scores across several countries (Blow 2011). Use the information provided to answer the following questions.

Best   Worst
                                    Worst of the worst

	Income inequality (Gini Index) Higher numbers represent more income inequality	Unemployment rate Most recent estimates	Level of Democracy Scale of 1 to 10	Gallup Global Wellbeing Index Percentage thriving, 2010	Food Insecurity "Have there been times in the past 12 months when you did not have enough money to buy food that you or your family needed?" Percentage answering yes.	Life Expectancy at Birth	Prison Population Per 100,000 citizens	Student Performance Math Scale Score	Science Scale Score
Australia	30.5	5.1	9.22	62		81.72	133	514	527
Canada	32.1	8.0	9.08	62	8	81.29	117	527	529
Norway	25.0	3.7	9.8	69		80.08	71	498	500
Netherlands	30.9	5.5	8.99	68		79.55	94	526	522
Germany	27.0	7.1	8.38	43	6	79.41	85	513	520
Austria	26.0	4.5	8.49	57		79.65	103	496	497
Switzerland	33.7	3.9	9.09	62	4	80.97	79	534	517
Denmark	29.0	4.2	9.52	82	3	78.47	71	503	499
Finland	29.5	7.9	9.19	75		79.13	60	541	554
Belgium	28.0	8.1	8.05	56		79.37	97	515	507
Malta	26.0	7.0	8.28	40		79.59	140		
Japan	38.1	5.2	8.08	19	7	82.17	59	529	539
Sweden	23.0	8.3	9.5	68	5	80.97	78	494	495
Hong Kong	53.3	4.6	5.92	65	6	81.96	141	555	549
Iceland	28.0	8.6	9.65	47		80.79	60	507	496
New Zealand	36.2	6.5	9.26			80.48	203	519	532
Luxembourg	26.0	5.5	8.88	45		79.48	139	489	484
United Kingdom	34.0	7.9	8.16		9	79.92	206	492	514
Ireland	30.7	8.6	8.79	49	7	80.07	99	487	508
Singapore	48.1	2.3	5.89	19	2	82.06	273	562	542
Cyprus	29.0	6.0	7.29	45	10	77.66	105		
South Korea	31.4	3.7	8.11	28	16	78.81	98	546	538
Italy	32.0	8.4	7.83	39	15	80.33	113	483	489
France	32.7	9.5	7.77	35	9	81.09	365	497	498
Czech Republic	26.0	9.3	8.19	39		77.01	211	493	500
Slovenia	28.4	10.6	7.69	27	11	77.12	67	501	512
Taiwan		5.2	7.52	22		78.15	282		
Slovakia	26.0	12.5	7.35	21		75.62	185	497	490
Israel	39.2	6.4	7.48	62	15	80.86	325	447	455
Spain	32.0	20.0	8.16	36	14	81.07	159	483	488
Greece	33.0	12.0	7.92	31	9	79.8	102	466	470
Portugal	38.5	10.7	8.02	22	10	78.38	110	487	493
United States	45.0	9.0	8.18	57	16	78.24	743	487	502

Sources: The C.I.A.'s "The World Factbook," U.S. unemployment rate from the Bureau of Labor Statistics, the Economist Intelligence Unit's "Democracy Index 2010." Gallup, Unicef, King's College London's World Prison Brief, Organization for Economic Cooperation and Development's Program for International Student Assessment.

Chart 1 Health, Education, Criminal Justice, and Economic Measures by Countries Considered "Advanced Economies" by the International Monetary Fund.

Questions:

1. One way that researchers measure inequality is by creating a Gini index. The Gini index uses family income to determine the level of inequality among households in a given country. Higher Gini scores indicate greater inequality across households within a country (i.e., some households are really rich while others are very poor), with a score of 100 indicating complete inequality. Lower Gini scores indicate greater equality; a score of 0 indicates that all households have the same income in a given country. Which three countries on this list have the highest Gini index scores? What do these countries have in common? Which three countries have the lowest? What do these countries have in common? Identify three countries that have an economy most similar to the United States. What is the United States' Gini score, and how does it compare to those countries?

2. How does the unemployment rate in the United States compare to other countries? How does the life expectancy in the United States compare to other countries? Which countries had the highest reports of food insecurity? Finally, how do incarceration rates vary by country?

3. The Wellbeing index in column four is a subjective measure of well-being. Gallup asked individuals to rank their well-being from 0–10, with higher numbers indicating higher well-being. The table presents the percentage of people in a country who rated their well-being at 7 or higher. How does the United States compare to other countries? Is there a relationship between perceived well-being and the level of inequality in the country? If so, what relationship exists? If not, what could explain this pattern? Be sure to use information from the table to support your answer.

4. On which indicators is the United States doing the best? The worst? How does the United States compare to other like economies? What historical realities, political structures, and other social structures account for the United States's position in relation to other countries?

5. What is meant by the term "social construction"? How does the information you reported from Chart 1 illustrate the social construction of inequality?

Reference

Blow, Charles M. 2011. "Empire at the End of Decadence." *New York Times,* February 19, A23. http://www.nytimes.com/2011/02/19/opinion/19blow.html?r=0; chart at: http://graphics8.nytimes.com/images/2011/02/19/opinion/19blowcht/19blowcht-popup-v5.gif (accessed September 11, 2015).

B. Data Analysis Exercise: Is the United States the Land of Opportunity?

A hallmark of American society is the promise of opportunity to create a better life for oneself. Social mobility refers to people's movement from one social class to another across their lifetime. People can be upwardly mobile—moving from the poorer class they are born into to a richer class later in life—or they can, as many people did during the Great Recession, move downward. This data analysis exercise provides data on the likelihood of upward mobility in the United States.

1. What do people mean when they describe the United States as the land of opportunity? What is the American dream? If you believe in the American dream, what specifically do you believe?

2. From where did you learn about the American dream? How do people learn to believe in the American dream? What role do the media play? Politicians? Parents? Religion? The education system? Provide specific examples.

3. Many sociologists think of the American dream as an ideology, or a belief system. What social contexts are most likely to conjure up beliefs about the American dream? How does the American dream ideology

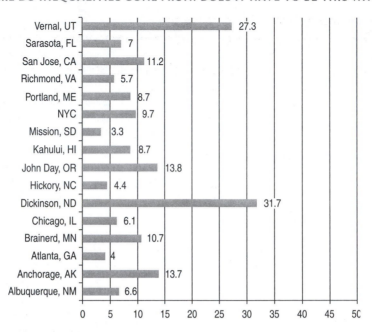

Figure 1 The Chance That a Child Raised in the Poorest 20% of American Households Will Rise to the Richest 20%.*

* Data compiled from David Leonhardt, "In Climbing Income Ladder, Location Matters," *New York Times,* July 22, 2013, http://www.nytimes.com/2013/07/22/business/in-climbing-income-ladder-location-matters.html?emc=eta1&_r=2& (accessed December 10, 2014). Original source: Chetty, R., N. Hendren, P. Kline, and E. Saez. "Where is the Land of Opportunity? The Geography of Intergenerational Mobility in the United States." *Quarterly Journal of Economics* 129(4): 1553-1623, 2014.

influence how people judge each other and them-selves? How does it shape people's interpretations of success and failure?

4. Before looking at Figure 1, what do you think is the likelihood of becoming part of the richest 20 percent of households in the United States if someone is raised in the poorest 20 percent? If the American dream is true, what do you think it should be?

5. Figure 1 shows the chance a child raised in the poorest 20 percent of households is going to rise to the highest 20 percent in various cities in the United States. How do the rates compare to your expectations from question 4? Do they support the interpretation of the American dream as reality or ideology?

6. Go to the *New York Times* and locate the story "In Climbing Income Ladder, Location Matters," by David Leonhart (http://www.nytimes.com/2013/07/22/busi-ness/in-climbing-income-ladder-location-matters.html?emc=eta1&_r=2&) to see a map of the entire United States. Blue spots on the map indicate a higher chance of being upwardly mobile, while red spots represent a small chance. In what areas of the United States are the chances for upwardly mobility the highest? Lowest? Why is there so much varia-tion? What do they have to do with race/ethnicity and the local economies? Is the American dream more accessible to some Americans than others? If so, what does that mean for our understanding of the American dream?

Projects and Resources to Make a Difference

Here are some projects you can do to make a difference.

Project 1: Critiquing and rewriting history. Choose an important historical social justice event or movement in your area. (You can ask a history professor, social justice activist, or women's and gender studies professor for an idea of an event.) Collect news articles covering the event or movement. To what extent are women or people of color visible in the coverage? Disabilities? Are disabilities used to add legitimacy to human rights claims? How so? If not, what frames or rhetoric are used to claim legitimacy? Using news coverage, locate an activist involved or a local expert on the issues. Set up an interview with this person. Get a detailed history of the event from the person's perspective. Be sure to inquire about the extent to which disabilities were visible, considered, discussed, and used. Rewrite a brief history of the event using an intersectional perspective. Disseminate your history.

Project 2: Analysis of history books. Locate a copy of the history book you last used in high school or a copy of the books used in local high schools. Conduct a content analysis of the books' inclusion and use of inequality and disability as a point of analysis. How visible is inequality or people with disabilities, people of color, or women? Which kinds of inequality are prominent, and how are they used? What is missing? How can disability and other forms of inequality be included into curriculum in ways that challenge inequality rather than foster it? What is the process for adopting specific textbooks in your area? Partner with relevant stakeholders—teachers, local historical society, library, local advocacy groups, school board—to make history in your city more inclusive.

Additional Resources:

- For an accessible exploration of race and biology watch *Race: The Power of an Illusion Part I* (San Francisco: California Newsreel, 2003). Visit the companion website on pbs.org for interesting Q & A with experts, discussion, and additional resources.
- *Guns, Germs and Steel: The Fates of Human Societies* (New York: W. W. Norton, 1997) by Jared Diamond and the documentary of the same title (visit its PBS website at http://www.pbs.org/gunsgermssteel/index.html) further explain conquest.

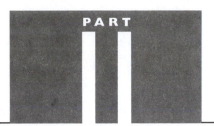

Why Do We Categorize
People into Groups?
How Does Differentiation
Transform into Inequality?

After Martin Luther King Jr. was assassinated, Jane Elliott walked into the third-grade class she was teaching in Riceville, Iowa, and conducted a class exercise later dubbed "the blue-eyes/brown-eyes exercise." She broke the all-white class into two groups based on their eye color, branded one group inferior and the other superior, and then treated the groups accordingly. A *Frontline* documentary (Peters 1985) illustrates how Elliott's exercise (repeated in other classes) transformed an otherwise overlooked physical difference into a consequential categorical inequality in the classroom.

In the video, Elliott put collars on the inferior group to visibly mark them and then attached resources to being in the superior group: extra recess time, special lunch, and drinking privileges. She also drew attention to eye color and interpreted students' (and their family members') behavior in relation to it. For example, when kids performed well, Elliott attributed their success to their eye color. When students misbehaved, she drew attention to their eye color. Over time, the kids described each other as "blue eyes" and "brown eyes," quarreled over what it meant to be of a particular group, and performed more/less well on a card sorting exercise depending on their designation as superior/inferior that day. As Elliott describes in the video, perfectly caring kids who got along well one day turned into bigoted discriminatory kids the next.

Social categories get inside our heads in the real world, too, shaping how we perceive ourselves and others. We together actively create those categories using many of the interactional tools that Elliott did.

Part II shows how the social categories of inequality become internalized by individuals and enacted, even unconsciously, when interacting with others. It also shows how people police and codify categorical inequalities through law and corporate policy.

In Part II, we learn:

- *While some people are overtly bigoted, bias can be subtle and unconscious.* Our brains naturally create cognitive shortcuts to help us navigate the social world without being overwhelmed by too much data. Some of this stereotyping is rather harmless. However, entrenched cultural beliefs have trained our brains to categorize people according to race, gender, age, and perhaps class instantaneously when we interact with each other. This categorization can activate stereotypes about people, thus influencing our assessment of people's competence, social status, and warmth. One need not have animus toward a particular group in order for him/her to be biased against someone of the group.

- *Biases are intersectional.* Recall from Part I that people create shared meanings and ways of organizing the world and that intersectionality shows how race, gender, class, disability, and other inequalities influence both the shared meanings and organization of the world. Extending this idea, in Part II, we learn that the content of stereotypes exists at the intersection of multiple forms of inequality. Stereotypes—and in turn expectations for behavior and assessments of people's competence—are different for Native American/American Indian women and Black women, for example. They are different for men with visible disabilities and women with visible disabilities.

- *Some social settings activate people's biases.* All of our interactions happen in a particular place with particular people. Three social contexts make stereotyping more salient: those in mixed status group, those involving stereotypical tasks, and those with people who appear prototypical.

- *We recreate the boundaries between groups using an assortment of social tools.* Othering is the social process of marking groups as different from each other and one group as morally superior. Social policy, law, and media codify who belongs in what group and the consequences of group membership for people's status and access to resources, such as pay, promotion, and well-being.

- *Boundaries, however, are fluid.* People shift boundaries as the dominant group's needs change and subordinated peoples resist being othered and the targets of discrimination.

- *We police the boundaries between groups.* Discrimination is one way we enforce category designations and ensure that some people get more opportunities and resources than others. Harassment and objectification of subordinated group members are other ways. Dominant groups also appropriate the culture of subordinated groups in exploitive ways. They consume cultural products in ways that reinforce their own superiority and the subordinated groups' inferiority.

- *Othering and discrimination can be subtle and hidden.* Stigmatizing bigotry and outlawing discrimination have not made inequalities disappear. Rather, othering and discrimination have changed forms.

- *Undoing social categories takes conscientious, persistent effort.* Because social categories are deeply enmeshed in our cultural images, social policies, and even our brains, we must vigilantly guard against social biases in our assessments of people and our decision making. Counteracting cognitive biases depends on creating situations and encounters that destabilize stereotyping. Having repeated, consistent contact with people from stereotyped groups is important. So is contact with counter-stereotypical images and people. Additionally, we need to create and enforce social policies that position us to make decisions based on individualized knowledge of people. What works to effect social change is an empirical question, one we must constantly study given how adept dominant groups are at changing tactics. It is important to remember that social categories, as we have learned, are social constructions. Since they are created and reinforced by the actions of people, they can also be undone by people's actions.

Together, the readings, data analysis exercises, and resources in Part II show us how we create categories so that we may work to destroy them.

Reference

Peters, William, producer and director. 1985. *A Class Divided*. Yale University Films for *Frontline*. http://www.pbs.org/wgbh/pages/frontline/shows/divided/ (accessed December 10, 2014).

7

Intersecting Cultural Beliefs in Social Relations: Gender, Race, and Class Binds and Freedoms

CECILIA L. RIDGEWAY AND TAMAR KRICHELI-KATZ

Chris, a Black man, walks into the room and greets the patient before him. Chris is dressed in a white uniform and introduces himself by name. He tells the patient he is her nurse. The patient, a white woman, asks, "Are you from housekeeping?"

This anecdote, paraphrased from Adia Harvey Wingfield's (2009:18–19) study on Black men in women's professions, illustrates how racial, gender, and class expectations collide in interactions. The patient's assumption that Chris must clean the room rather than care for patients stems from deep-seated stereotypes about Black people's competence and class position. They also reflect widespread cultural beliefs stating that women are naturally nurturing and expressive while men are instrumental. Yet despite her obvious, inaccurate biases, the patient would likely deny that she is racist or sexist or that she holds racist or sexist beliefs. She may even consider herself to be antiracist or feminist. She is not alone: As we'll see in Data Analysis Exercise D, overt racism has sharply diminished across time. How can people hold socially progressive attitudes and yet act in biased ways? How can overt racism be politically incorrect and yet racial and gender discrimination, endemic?

Ridgeway and Kricheli-Katz answer the preceding questions using the social psychological theory "expectation states." Expectation states explains how entrenched stereotypes become activated in interaction—so that we act in biased ways without even knowing it. Stereotyping is essentially a cognitive shortcut; it allows our brains to size up a situation and determine how to act. Shortcutting of some sort is necessary because our brains otherwise would become paralyzed by data overload.

But widespread entrenched cultural beliefs have trained our brains to categorize people in ways most of us would otherwise, more consciously, reject—according to their race, gender, age, and perhaps class. Whenever we interact with people, our brains automatically and instantaneously categorize others according to these status characteristics. Our assessment of who is what and our perception of their appropriate social roles (e.g., nurse, patient, housekeeper, doctor) are also shaped by these perceived identities. In certain social settings, what the authors term "situational relational contexts," racial and gender categorization activates stereotypes, especially about people's competence and degree of status. These stereotypes in turn bias our assessment of the person and our expectations for interacting with them. Students may assume, for example, that a 20-something-year-old Latina entering a classroom is another student rather than the mathematics professor she is. They may call her by her first name or "Mrs." rather than as "Doctor" or "Professor." They may assume that she isn't an expert at math until she *proves* to them that she is. Or they may

Excerpted from Ridgeway, Cecilia L. and Tamar Kricheli-Katz. 2013. "Intersecting Cultural Beliefs in Social Relations: Gender, Race, and Class Binds and Freedoms." *Gender & Society* 27:294–318. Copyright © 2013, Sociologists for Women in Society.

comment on her looks or mastery of language in their student assessments of her teaching. All of these biased behaviors can happen implicitly and cognitively, without having to espouse overt racist or sexist beliefs.

Three contexts bring stereotypes to the forefront. Settings which have mixed status groups, for example, students and professors, activate stereotyping. So do circumstances that involve stereotypical tasks, such as math or caretaking. Third, stereotypes become more salient when a person appears prototypical. Ridgeway and Kricheli-Katz demonstrate how stereotypes activated in these social contexts create social binds for some actors and social freedoms for others.

Readers of this piece will be nudged to consider new directions for counteracting biases. Rather than changing people's overt attitudes, readers may consider disrupting the categorization process, countering stereotypes, bringing other statuses to the forefront, and explicitly analyzing the social context as points for social change.

Reference

Wingfield, Adia Harvey. 2009. "Racializing the Glass Escalator Reconsidering Men's Experiences with Women's Work." *Gender & Society* 23(1): 5–26.

Gender and Race as Primary Frames

Social relations, whether in person or even in imagination, require us to find a way to coordinate with the other. To do that, we need some way to anticipate the other's behavior so we can decide how to act ourselves. A diverse range of research suggests that people solve this problem by categorizing the other, and, by comparison, themselves, according to widely shared, "common knowledge" cultural codes of social difference (Chwe 2001; Ridgeway 2011; Stryker and Vryan 2003; West and Fenstermaker 1995). These cultural beliefs about social difference are shared stereotypes, but their significance conveys more than many associate with that term. Because they provide an initial basis for deciding "who" the other is, who we are in comparison, and therefore how each of us is likely to behave, they play a powerful role in organizing social relations.

To organize interaction in real time, some of these cultural codes for categorizing others must be so simplified that they can be applied to virtually any other in order to initiate the process of defining "self" and "other" in that situation. Social cognition research suggests that only a small number—about three or so—of category systems act as such primary frames for social relations in a given culture (Brewer 1988). These frames are "primary" not because they are necessarily most important for personal identity or most determinative of social outcomes but because they act as simplified, culturally provided starting points for sociocognitive person construal. Evidence suggests that sex, race, and age are primary

categories of person perception in the United States (Brewer and Lui 1989; Schneider 2004, 96).

Further evidence shows that people in the United States automatically and nearly instantly categorize any person they deal with in terms of sex and race (Ito and Urland 2003; Macrae and Quadflieg 2010). People will categorize others on sex and race on the basis of quite minimal cues even though they may then recategorize a person if more cues become available. A person's automatic sex and race categorization of another is important because it implicitly frames the person's subsequent understanding of that other. Further categorizations of the other in terms of institutional roles (a clerk, a coworker) or contextual identities (pedestrian) are nested in the prior understanding of the person as a man or woman and as a given race, and take on a slightly different meaning as a result (Brewer 1988; Freeman and Ambady 2011). Speed of racial categorization has been studied almost entirely in terms of Black–white distinctions (Ito and Urland 2003), but other racial categorizations, such as Asian or Latino, are likely to be similarly fast and automatic. Although we fully recognize the problems of doing so, we limit our analysis of race in this chapter to Black–white and Asian–white distinctions, due to space limitations and the restricted body of sociocognitive studies of other racial distinctions.

In social relational contexts ["situations in which actors must take the expected reactions of others into account in deciding how to act themselves" (Ridgeway and Kricheli-Katz 2013: 295)], sex and race categorization unconsciously prime gender and race stereotypes in the perceiver's mind, making those cultural beliefs cognitively available to implicitly shape the perceiver's judgments and behaviors in response to the other (Macrae and Quadflieg 2010). Importantly, however, the extent to which these mentally primed stereotypes actually do bias the perceiver's responses varies from negligible to substantial depending on features of the *context* and, thus, context is fundamental to their effects (Kunda and Spencer 2003). What matters is the extent to which the sex or race categorization of the other seems to the perceiver to offer usefully diagnostic information about the other in that situation. At the least, evidence indicates that gender and race stereotypes are *effectively salient* (i.e., sufficiently salient to measurably bias judgments and behavior) in contexts in which the participants differ on the characteristic (mixed-sex or mixed-race settings) or that are culturally linked to the characteristics (gender- or race-associated contexts, which can include same-sex or same-race contexts) (see Berger and Webster 2006). In addition, perceivers apply stereotypes more strongly in their responses to others who appear more *prototypical* of the category (Macrae and Quadflieg 2010).

Thus, the more gender or race stands out in a situation because it differentiates the people there and/or seems relevant to the goals of the setting or to the characteristics of a participant, the more a perceiver's responses will be biased by widely shared gender and race stereotypes. This means that although both gender and race are virtually always cognitively available to shape judgments and behavior in social relational contexts, they need not do so equally in a given situation. Depending on the context, one or the other may have a stronger impact.

The contents of widely known gender and race stereotypes differ in many ways, but research suggests that they have in common the inclusion of beliefs that people in one category of the difference (men, whites) are of higher status and diffusely more competent, especially at the things that count most in society, than are those in the other category (women, people of color) (Fiske 2010). Thus, to the extent that gender or race stereotypes are salient in a setting, they bias expectations for one person's competence and suitability for leadership compared to another (Berger and Webster 2006). These biased expectations tend to have self-fulfilling effects on behavior in the setting and to create inequalities in evaluations of performance, influence, and attributions of ability (Berger and Webster 2006). In this way, among others,

implicitly salient gender and race stereotypes shape interpersonal hierarchies of influence, status, and perceived leadership potential in ways that reproduce and maintain gender and race as systems of inequality. Since these interpersonal hierarchies constitute a shared resource domain for the gender and race (and class) systems, when the hierarchies that emerge in a given relational context are shaped by both gender and race stereotypes, the gender and race systems intersect in that context.

Class in Social Relations

Although we have known since Bourdieu (1984) that class can be highly consequential for interpersonal relations, social cognition studies have not examined class categorization in detail. Sociocognitive studies of the superordinate, "master," versus secondary categories into which people place others (e.g., Brewer and Lui 1989; Stangor et al. 1992) clearly demonstrate that gender and race are primary (i.e., superordinate) cultural frames for person perception but are less definitive about class. Studies show that one class indicator, occupation, is a subordinate category of person perception in comparison to gender (Brewer 1988; van Kippenenburg and Dijkhuis 2000), but there is less evidence about other aspects of class categorization in relation to either gender or race. More research is necessary to determine if class is a primary, "master" category of person perception in the United States or whether class indicators are cognitively nested within prior categorizations of a person in terms of gender and race (and age).

Whether or not people automatically and instantly categorize one another on class as they do sex and race, a variety of research suggests that people are quite sensitive to cues of class difference (e.g., accent, dress, and speech) in everyday interaction (Fiske 2010). Therefore, if class differences are present among interactants, they are likely to become implicitly salient in the situation before very long (Ridgeway and Fisk 2012). There are also widely shared cultural stereotypes about class that closely link class standing with status and competence (Cuddy, Fiske, and Glick 2007; Fiske et al. 2002). We would expect, then, that once class difference becomes salient for people in a situation, class stereotypes implicitly bias their behaviors and judgments of each other's competence in a similar process to what we have described for gender and race stereotypes (Fiske 2010; Ridgeway and Fisk 2012). Research clearly shows that class indicators, such as occupational status and education, systematically bias competence expectations, social influence, and leadership in interactional contexts (Webster and Foschi 1988). More subtle indicators of differences in cultural class background likely create similar biasing effects (Stuber 2006).

Yet, despite these similarities, we argue that an important difference remains between the ways that cultural beliefs about class shape interpersonal relations compared to cultural beliefs about gender and race. Dominant American beliefs view class as an achieved and potentially transient attribute in contrast to the highly essentialized popular views of sex and race (Kluegel and Smith 1986; Morning 2011; Prentice and Miller 2006), despite the fact that, in social relations, gender, race, and class are all interactional accomplishments (West and Fenstermaker 1995). The essentialized cultural conception of gender and race, compared to class, is real in its consequences. The cues on which we categorize people on sex and race are commonly seen as stable, inherent, visually apparent, and trans-situationally present aspects of a person, attributes that would always be there if we imagined the person, in contrast to the cues by which we class categorize, such as education, occupation, or accent, which are viewed as more acquired and potentially changeable.

This difference in essentialization, we argue, has important implications for intersectionality. Culturally essentialized attributes are traits that a culture deems "always there" in a person. If both gender and race are essentialized in the United States, then they must *both* be always there in any cultural prototype of a "person." The more essentialized the cultural image of "men" or "women" is, the more that gender image in the U.S. context must also be implicitly raced. Similarly, an essentialized image of "Black" or "white" or "Asian" must also be implicitly gendered. If cultural beliefs about class are less essentialized, as we have argued, then class is a little different from gender and race in this sociocognitive regard, even though class, too, when salient in a situation, powerfully shapes behavioral inequalities among the participants. We argue that this sociocognitive difference is significant because it causes aspects of class meanings to sometimes additively combine while also intersecting in other ways as race and gender do.

OVERLAPPING HEGEMONIC STEREOTYPES

Widely shared gender, race, and class stereotypes are hegemonic beliefs because they are not simply held by individuals but institutionalized in the media, in the images of people implied in organizational structures, in laws, and in the arrangement of public spaces (Acker 2006; Ridgeway 2011). Indeed, the power of these gender, race, and class beliefs to coordinate behavior in social relations derives not so much from individuals' personal endorsement of them (and many do not) as from individuals' sense that these beliefs are what "most people" believe and thus are the public rules by which they will be judged and expected to act. The hegemonic nature of these beliefs is what allows them to act as cultural schemas for enacting systems of inequality (Sewell 1992). An obvious implication, however, is that the versions of gender, race, and class beliefs that become institutionalized and, therefore, shared as cultural knowledge by dominants and subdominants alike, are likely to be the versions that most closely represent the experiences of these distinctions by dominant social groups. These are the groups who have the most power to shape these social institutions.

Gender and Race

If difference is defined from the perspective of dominant (white male) groups, it seems clear that the prototypical images that become embedded in widely shared and institutionalized images of "men" and "women" should implicitly correspond to white men and white women. And, since gender is "marked" by the implicit contrast of the "feminine" against the male standard, femininity as a marker of the gender hierarchy should be implicitly linked most prescriptively to white women.

If race is embedded in hegemonic gender beliefs, gender is also embedded in the prototypical images associated with widely shared, hegemonic white–Black and white–Asian racial stereotypes. Our arguments about how difference is defined from the perspective of dominant groups imply that race is another sort of contrast against the white male standard. As a different dimension of contrast, it is almost by definition not focused on men's difference from women. But as a result, it implicitly becomes a difference between types of men hierarchically defined as superior (white) and lesser (Black or Asian). This suggests that white–Black and white–Asian racial hierarchies are likely to be implicitly represented as subordinated types of masculinities (either too masculine or not masculine enough) that are contrasted against the hegemonic, "just right" masculinity of the white male standard (Chen 1999; Connell 1995; Messner 1992).

The contrasting masculinities embedded in white–Black American stereotypes distinctively reflect their historical origins in the violence of slavery. Research suggests that the implicit Black image is of physically powerful masculinity that is relatively extreme and potentially threatening compared to the white standard of "civilized," constrained, and socially based masculine power (Goff, Eberhardt, et al. 2008). In contrast, while cultural beliefs about Asians have changed over historical periods, contemporary racial stereotypes implicitly prototype Asians as more feminine than the white male standard and irreducibly "foreign" (Chen 1999; Espiritu 1997; Wu 2002).

These arguments about the implicit prototypical images evoked by hegemonic stereotypes of gender and white–Black and white–Asian race are troubling for the shameful racism they reveal behind these "common knowledge" stereotypes. Yet, they are supported by recent evidence. Documenting the implicitly gendered images of racial stereotypes, Galinsky, Hall, and Cuddy (2013) found that Black men and women were rated as more masculine (vigorous, strong, masculine) and less feminine (gentle, feminine), while Asian men and women were rated as less masculine and more feminine compared to white men and women. Wilkins et al. (2011) report similar results and also found that the more stereotypically Asian a man's appearance, the less masculine he was rated as appearing (although there were no such associations for Asian women). Galinsky et al. (2013) also found an association between gender and race stereotypes at the implicit level. When subliminally primed with "Black," subjects responded more quickly to masculine trait words; when primed with "Asian," they responded more quickly to feminine trait words, compared to when primed with "white."

In a provocative study, Goff, Thomas, and Jackson (2008) found that Black faces (male and female) were rated as more masculine than white faces. Strikingly, they also found that pictures of Black women's faces were much more likely to be mistaken as male (about 13 percent errors) than were those of white women (2 percent errors) even though sex categorization errors were low overall. There were no such race differences in the likelihood that Black men's and white men's faces (errors about 1.75 percent vs. 0.75 percent) were incorrectly sex categorized.

In a sophisticated set of studies, Johnson, Freeman, and Pauker (2012) investigated how the overlap between race (Black, white, Asian) and gender stereotypes shape sex categorization. Like Goff et al. (2008), they found that male faces were more easily sex categorized overall (reflecting the male standard), and outright errors in sex categorization were low. But in comparison to whites, Black faces were easier to classify as male and harder to classify as female, while Asian faces were more easily classified as female and slower to be classified as male. They found these associations at both the implicit and explicit levels.

Adding Class

Stereotypes of class represent the perspective of dominant groups as well, but we have argued that class stereotypes do not evoke as highly essentialized prototypical images as gender and race do. Perhaps for that reason, it is our impression that stereotypes of "middle class" and "working class" do not carry within them strong implications about the gendered characteristics of the prototypical member of the category.

On the other hand, it seems clear that class is deeply embedded in our essentialized prototypes of Black–white (cf. Feagin 1991) and Asian–white (Espiritu 1997; Wu 2002) race, reflecting the strong association between race and socioeconomic standing in the United States. Fiske et al. (2002), in their study of how a variety of social groups clustered together on stereotypical competence and warmth, found that "whites" and "middle-class people" were closely clustered, as were "Blacks" and "blue-collar people." Class is part of what it means to be "white" or "Black."

While, in the Fiske et al. (2002) study, whites as a group clustered with "middle class," "Asians" clustered together with "professionals" and the "educated," a slightly higher-class image. Thus, there is less of a class contrast in cultural beliefs about whites and Asians in that both are seen as middle-class. Yet, as many have observed, the stereotype of Asians as class advantaged, yet "foreign," is a sometimes dangerous source of envy and resentment by the dominant group (Fiske 2010; Wu 2002).

These studies of the deep linkage between class and white–Black and white–Asian race suggest that the automatic racial categorization of another also implicitly evokes a default assumption about that person's class location. The default assumptions about class embedded in racial prototypes create intersectional effects. A white person dressed in jeans and a T-shirt can shop comfortably at an expensive store, but a similarly dressed Black person, even if affluent, arouses suspicion (Feagin 1991). Dominant American beliefs that class is a less essentialized and potentially more variable attribute than race matter here, however. Contextual cues of class, if sufficiently salient, can weaken default class assumptions based on racial categorization. The same Black person treated with suspicion in the store may be accepted as middle-class when encountered at work in a hospital dressed as a surgeon.

Perhaps because Americans view class (and its dominant indicators of occupation, education, and income) as fundamentally achieved rather than ascribed, it seems to be especially strongly associated with beliefs about differences in competence. In major stereotype studies, correlations approach .90 (Fiske 2010). Both the close association of class with competence and the less essentialized nature of class stereotypes may sometimes allow class to act as a more "fungible" social difference than race or gender. That is, an individual's particular class "accomplishments" (education, a prestigious job), when salient in an interactional context, may partially compensate for race or gender status disadvantages in a more additive way than is typical for the complex intersections of race or gender, even though class also intersects with race through the default class assumptions that are embedded in racial prototypes. This suggests that in the workplace and other task- and competence-oriented contexts, the competence implications of class accomplishments (although not necessarily other implications of class) may combine with the competence implications of race or gender to affect the perceived competence and influence of individuals.

INTERSECTIONAL BINDS AND FREEDOMS

Gender and Race Binds

In social relational contexts, such as the workplace or a social gathering, not only will people have automatically sex- and race-categorized one another, but gender and race stereotypes will have become effectively, if implicitly, salient for them as they begin to relate to one another in the setting. The essentialized, prototypical images evoked by these stereotypes will correspond to the individuals in the situation in significantly different degrees. Other things being equal, white men mostly fit the prototype of both "men" and "whites," white women correspond to the prototype of "women," and Black men match the prototype of "Blacks." Because of overlapping stereotype content, Asian women fit reasonably well with the prototype of both "Asians" and "women." But Asian men, while they match the prototype of "Asian," are distinctly "off diagonal" and nonprototypical as men. As many have commented, however, it is Black women who fit poorly into the implicit prototypes of both gender and white–Black race (e.g., Collins 1990; Crenshaw 1989; hooks 1989). They are the doubly "off diagonal" people in contexts in which race and gender are both salient.

Recall that prototypicality is one of the factors that affects how strongly stereotypes evoked by sex and race categorization shape the perceiver's judgments and behaviors toward the categorized person. Interestingly, this suggests that white men and women and Black men will be judged and treated in more gender- and race-stereotypic terms than Asian men or Black women. (For white men, of course, this stereotypic treatment will often be advantaging.) Other things being equal, Asian men, in contrast, will be responded to as less like a typical man. Black women will be responded to as less like either a typical woman or a typical Black person (Purdie-Vaughns and Eibach 2008). Whether this is good or bad depends on the context, but it creates a characteristic set of "binds" and freedoms. Note that the Asian man is unprototypical of an advantaging status, male sex, while the Black woman is unprototypical of two disadvantaging statuses, female sex and race. While all forms of unprototypicality create binds, it may be that freedoms result from being unprototypical of disadvantaging statuses.

One set of "binds" develops from the "intersectional invisibility" that results from being unprototypical of one (Asian men) or two (Black women) of American culture's three or four primary frames for making sense of others and organizing social relations. It is literally harder to be "seen," for your perspective to be heard, or your contributions credited when you don't fit easily with people's automatic lenses for noticing, making sense of, and understanding others, lenses that are institutionalized as well as held by individuals (Cheng 1996; Collins 1999; hooks 1989; Purdie-Vaughns and Eibach 2008; Sesko and Biernat 2010).

Another set of binds develops in a particular type of relational context: one in which gender stereotypes are intensely salient (even though race may also be highly salient) because the setting is focused on heterosexual attraction. Hegemonic stereotypes cast prototypically masculine and prototypically feminine people as the public standard of attractiveness in such contexts, and even though many do not personally endorse these standards, they nevertheless have social effects. Wilkins et al. (2011), for instance, found that for men, being rated as more "stereotypically Asian" in appearance was associated with being seen as less physically attractive and masculine, while Asian appearance did not affect the perceived attractiveness of women. While most marriages are within race, both Wilkins et al. (2011) and Galinsky et al. (2013) suggest that the gender–race binds faced by Asian men in contexts of heterosexual attraction may contribute to the fact that, in 2000, 75 percent of Asian–white intermarriages were between white men and Asian women rather than white women and Asian men.

Because Black women are seen as less stereotypically feminine than white or Asian women (Galinsky et al. 2013; Wilkins et al. 2011), they also face cultural binds created by intersecting gender and race stereotypes that put them at a disadvantage in heterosexual relationship markets in comparison to white women, Asian women, and even Black men (who are seen as highly masculine). Galinsky et al. (2013) argue that this set of intersectional binds plays a role in the fact that 73 percent of Black–white interracial marriages in the 2000 U.S. Census were between Black men and white women and 86% of Black–Asian marriages were between Black men and Asian women.

Other sorts of cultural binds and, sometimes, freedoms develop for "off diagonal" people in workplace contexts and institutional roles. Cultural binds that create distinctive biases against Black women compared to white or Asian women may develop in roles or jobs that expect a (feminine) deferential, polite manner. These would include institutional roles that are consequential for inequality, such as "patient" dealing with medical authorities or "applicant" dealing with authorities that run government programs. They would also include feminized service jobs like secretary or nurse. Kilbourne, England, and Beron (1994), for instance, found that the wage penalty for working in a predominantly female occupation is twice as large for Black women as for white women.

In other, typically powerful, institutional contexts, however, the advantages are not with being seen as

politely feminine but instead as forceful and dominant. Many achievement-oriented contexts focus on agentic behavior and leadership that, in turn, is culturally linked to hegemonic masculinity. This creates a characteristic set of binds for Asian men in the work world. Cheng (1996) reports that when asked to select group leaders, participants prefer those with masculine traits, and when given a choice of several gender and race groups, were least likely to select Asian men. Chen (1999) describes how Asian men develop strategies to "bargain" with these gender–race binds in such settings.

For Black women, in contrast, being outside both gender and race prototypes can create certain freedoms and opportunities in work or other contexts that value agentic behavior and leadership (Livingston, Shelby, and Washington 2012; Richardson et al. 2011). White women face a well-documented "double bind" when they seek to act highly assertively in order to prove agentic competence and suitability for authority. Such behavior is perceived to violate their prescriptive gender requirement of being femininely "nice" and deferential. As a result, assertive efforts to act authoritatively are perceived as "domineering" coming from white women (but not from white men) and provoke a "backlash" of dislike and resistance from others (Rudman et al. 2012). Although we know of no "backlash" studies of Asian women, our argument suggests that they too would face resistance and dislike when they violate stereotypic gender and race expectations of deference. Indeed, observations that Asian women, though typically stereotyped as docile, are sometimes also viewed as "dragon ladies" may reflect just such a backlash reaction to assertive Asian women (Espiritu 1997).

Dominant behavior from Black men similarly challenges the racial hierarchy. Black men who succeed in the corporate world seem to have had to present a mild appearance to counter stereotypic race expectations that they will be threateningly aggressive (Livingston and Pearce 2009). In contrast, assertively dominant behaviors from Black women, at least in institutional contexts that value agentic behavior, may not provoke such resistance and backlash precisely because they are not seen as either prototypical (white) "women" or prototypical (male) "Blacks." For this reason, their dominance in agentic contexts does not centrally challenge the gender or the racial hierarchy.

In a study that supports these arguments, Livingston et al. (2012) experimentally varied whether a Black or white, male or female Fortune 500 executive was described as handling a meeting with subordinates in an assertive, tough way or in a communal, encouraging way. Participants rated the dominant Black male and white female bosses as less effective, less respected, and likely to have a lower salary compared to the dominant white male boss. But this was not the case for the dominant Black female boss. Like the white man, she was seen as quite effective, respected, and well paid. In a similar study, Richardson et al. (2011) found that a dominant Black female consultant, just like the dominant white male consultant, was perceived as more hireable than a dominant white woman or Black man and was also less disliked.

Other studies of agency-oriented contexts suggest similar effects. Ong (2005) reports that Black women who were physics graduate students strategically adopted a "loud Black girl" persona as a means of breaking through their intersectional invisibility in order to demonstrate their competence as scientists. Wingfield (2008) found that while Black professionals experienced workplace feeling rules against anger to be more constraining of them than of whites, Black women could get away with expressions of anger when Black men could not.

The ability to act highly assertively and authoritatively in agentic contexts without triggering a gender or race backlash is a social relational opportunity created for Black women by intersecting hegemonic gender and race stereotypes. It is not easy to take advantage of this opportunity, however, due to further problems created by the effects of these intersecting stereotypes in relational contexts. Black women must first gain access to relational contexts that value and reward agency and leadership, contexts typically associated with higher-level business and professional jobs. Black women's access to these jobs is made more difficult by the default class assumptions embedded in racial prototypes.

Once within such contexts, Black women must break through their relative invisibility to get others to notice them and take them seriously. They must also counter another aspect of the stereotype of Blacks that creates challenges that are different from those faced by white women. While both "women" and "Blacks" are stereotyped as diffusely less competent at desirable skills than white men, the basis of the presumed competence difference for the two groups is a little different. In contemporary gender stereotypes, (white) "women" are now seen as similar to "men" in the softer

aspects of agency associated with intellectual skills (e.g., intelligent, analytic), but still behind men in the forceful agency presumed to be necessary to master events and exercise authority (Prentice and Carranza 2002; Rudman et al. 2012). In current stereotypes, "Blacks," however, are seen as having forceful agency but as either explicitly or implicitly lagging behind "whites" in intellectual skills (Fiske 2010; Goff et al. 2008). Although likely to be less strongly stereotyped in this way (because they are less prototypical) than Black men, Black women are still likely to have to work harder to prove their underlying ability in the workplace and elsewhere than are similar white women. Proving high ability, in turn, is likely a necessity for Black women to take full advantage of their opportunity to act highly assertively in an effort to achieve a position of leadership in a work or other context. Finally, because they do face a type of "double jeopardy" in proving competence, once in a leadership position, they are likely to have little margin for errors in performance. Rosette and Livingston (2012) found that leaders who were Black women were judged more harshly for mistakes made on the job compared to those who were white women and Black men.

It is clear, then, that being off diagonal of the two primary frames of gender and race creates considerably more social relational binds for Black women than freedoms. If Black women manage to achieve access to a context and role that rewards agency, their distinctive intersectional position affords them some unexpected freedoms to act authoritatively. Yet, because of their same intersectional position, the barriers Black women face in gaining access to such contexts are more formidable than those faced by other groups (McGuire and Reskin 1993).

Class and Race Binds

What about the characteristic intersectional "binds" created by class in social relational contexts? We have argued that because class is a culturally less essentialized difference, some class indicators that become salient in a given context (dress, education) combine more simply with other social differences than do race and gender. On the other hand, class also has intersectional effects through the default assumptions about class that are embedded in the essentialized prototypes of white–Black race in particular. As a result, poor whites or whites in low-status jobs are also "off diagonal" people.

In social relational contexts in which white–Black race is salient, poor whites should also find themselves subject to distinctive cultural "binds" created by intersecting hegemonic beliefs about class and race. Cultural assumptions about whiteness, shared by whites and Blacks alike, have embedded within them the presumption of individual responsibility for class outcomes. That is, to be white is to be a free player, one who enjoys full agency, in the American dream of the self-made person. As free players, however, poor whites may be held fully accountable for a personal "failure" to achieve and may be treated with contempt. McDermott (2006) makes this argument about the interactions she observed with white clerks working in dead-end jobs in convenience stores on the boundary between Black and white neighborhoods in Boston and Atlanta. The clerks were often subjected to dismissive remarks from Black customers. In most cases, the white clerks reacted submissively, feeling they had little cultural ground on which to defend themselves. In an even clearer illustration of the "bind" of poor whites, McDermott (2010), in another study, describes a community of poor Appalachian whites who have embraced an identity as "Black" on the grounds that they may have distant ancestors of African-Indian origin. As her interview evidence shows, they have reidentified as Black as a way of stepping aside from the social disparagement they felt at being poor whites.

McDermott (2006, 2010) also shows, however, that context matters in how poor whites react to the cultural binds they feel in settings in which race and class are both salient. The racially homogeneous environment of the Appalachian whites meant that they were freer to re-identify as "Black" since they paid little social cost for doing so compared to what they would experience in a racially mixed context. Also, in the convenience stores in Atlanta, which has few institutions of white working-class solidarity, white clerks were more likely to react submissively to dismissive remarks from Blacks than in Boston, which has a tradition of such institutions. . . .

References

Acker, Joan. 2006. *Class Questions*. Lanham, MD: Rowman & Littlefield.

Berger, Joseph, and Murray Webster. 2006. "Expectations, Status, and Behavior." In *Contemporary Social Psychological Theories* (ed. Peter J. Burke). Stanford: Stanford University Press. pp. 268–300.

Bourdieu, Pierre. 1984. *Distinction* (trans. Richard Nice). Cambridge, MA: Harvard University Press.

Brewer, Marilynn B. 1988. "A Dual Process Model of Impression Formation." In *Advances in Social Cognition*, Vol. 1 (ed. Thomas K. Srull and Robert S. Wyer, Jr.). Hillsdale, NJ: Lawrence Erlbaum. pp. 1–36.

Brewer, Marilynn B., and Layton N. Lui. 1989. "The Primacy of Age and Sex in the Structure of Person Categories." *Social Cognition* 7:262–274.

Chen, Anthony. 1999. "Lives at the Center of the Periphery, Lives at the Periphery of the Center: Chinese American Masculinities and Bargaining with Hegemony." *Gender & Society* 13:584–607.

Cheng, Cliff. 1996. "'We Choose Not to Compete': The 'Merit' Discourse in the Selection Process and Asian and Asian American Men and Their Masculinity." In *Masculinities in Organizations* (ed. C. Cheng). Thousand Oaks, CA: Sage. pp. 177–200.

Chwe, Michael S. 2001. *Rational Ritual*. Princeton, NJ: Princeton University Press.

Collins, Patricia Hill. 1990. *Black Feminist Thought*. Boston, MA: Unwin Hyman.

Collins, Patricia Hill. 1999. "Moving Beyond Gender: Intersectionality and Scientific Knowledge." In *Revisioning Gender* (ed. Judith Lorber, Myra Marx Ferree, and Beth Hess). Thousand Oaks, CA: Sage. pp. 261–284.

Connell, R. W. 1995. *Masculinities*. Berkeley: University of California Press.

Crenshaw, Kimberle W. 1989. "Demarginalizing the Intersection of Race and Sex: A Black Feminist Critique of Antidiscrimination Doctrine, Feminist Theory and Antiracist Politics." *University of Chicago Legal Forum*: 139–167.

Cuddy, Amy J., Susan T. Fiske, and Peter Glick. 2007. "The BIAS Map: Behaviors from Intergroup Affect and Stereotypes." *Journal of Personality and Social Psychology* 92:631–648.

Espiritu, Yen Le. 1997. *Asian American Women and Men*. Thousand Oaks, CA: Sage.

Feagin, Joe R. 1991. "The Continuing Significance of Race: Antiblack Discrimination in Public Places." *American Sociological Review* 56:101–116.

Fiske, Susan T. 2010. "Interpersonal Stratification: Status, Power, and Subordination" In *Handbook of Social Psychology* (eds. Susan T. Fiske, Daniel T. Gilbert, and Gardner Lindzey). New York: John Wiley. pp. 941–982.

Fiske, Susan T., Amy J. Cuddy, Peter Glick, and Jun Xu. 2002. "A Model of (Often Mixed) Stereotype Content: Competence and Warmth Respectively Follow from

Perceived Status and Competition." *Journal of Personality and Social Psychology* 82:878–902.

Freeman, Jonathan B., and Nalini Ambady. 2011. "A Dynamic Interactive Theory of Person Construal." *Psychological Review* 118:247–79.

Galinsky, Adam D., Erika V. Hall, and Amy J. C. Cuddy. 2013. "Gendered Races Implications for Interracial Marriage, Leadership Selection, and Athletic Participation." *Psychological Science* 24(4): 498–50.

Goff, Phillip A., Jennifer L. Eberhardt, Melissa Williams, and Matthew C. Jackson. 2008. "Not Yet Human: Implicit Knowledge, Historical Dehumanization, and Contemporary Consequences." *Journal of Personality and Social Psychology* 94:292–306.

Goff, Phillip A., Margaret Thomas, and Matthew C. Jackson. 2008. "Ain't I a Woman?" *Sex Roles* 59:392–403.

hooks, bell. 1989. *Talking Back.* Boston, MA: South End Press.

Ito, Tiffany A., and Geoffrey R. Urland. 2003. "Race and Gender on the Brain." *Journal of Personality and Social Psychology* 85:616–626.

Johnson, Kerri L., Jonathan B. Freeman, and Kristin Pauker. 2012. "Race Is Gendered: How Co-Varying Phenotypes and Stereotypes Bias Sex Categorization." *Journal of Personality and Social Psychology* 102:116–131.

Kilbourne, Barbara, Paula England, and Kurt Beron. 1994. "Effects of Individual, Occupational, and Industrial Characteristics on Earnings: Intersections of Race and Gender." *Social Forces* 72:1149–1176.

Kluegel, James R., and Elliott R. Smith. 1986. *Beliefs about Inequality.* Edison, NJ: Aldine Transaction.

Kunda, Ziva, and Steven J. Spencer. 2003. "When Do Stereotypes Come to Mind and When Do They Color Judgment?" *Psychological Bulletin* 129:522–554.

Livingston, Robert W., and Nicholas A. Pearce. 2009. "The Teddy-Bear Effect: Does Having a Baby Face Benefit Black Chief Executive Officers?" *Psychological Science* 20:1229–1236.

Livingston, Robert W., Rosette Ashleigh Shelby, and Ella F. Washington. 2012. "Can an Agentic Black Woman Get Ahead? The Impact of Race and Interpersonal Dominance on Perceptions of Female Leaders." *Psychological Science* 23:346–353.

Macrae, C. Neil, and Susanne Quadflieg. 2010. "Perceiving People." In *Handbook of Social Psychology*, 5th ed., Vol. 1 (ed. Susan T. Fiske, Daniel T. Gilbert, and Gardner Lindzey). New York: John Wiley. pp. 428–463.

McDermott, Monica. 2006. *Working Class White.* Berkeley: University of California Press.

McDermott, Monica. 2010. "Ways of Being White." In *Doing Race* (ed. Hazel Markus and Paula Moya). New York: Norton. pp. 415–438.

McGuire, Gail M., and Barbara F. Reskin. 1993. "Authority Hierarchies at Work." *Gender & Society* 7:487–506.

Messner, Michael A. 1992. *Power at Play.* Boston, MA: Beacon.

Morning, Ann. 2011. *The Nature of Race.* Berkeley: University of California Press.

Ong, Maria. 2005. "Body Projects of Young Women of Color in Physics." *Social Problems* 52:593–617.

Prentice, Deborah A., and Erica Carranza. 2002. "What Women and Men Should Be, Shouldn't Be, Are Allowed to Be, and Don't Have to Be." *Psychology of Women Quarterly* 26:269–281.

Prentice, Deborah A., and Dale T. Miller. 2006. "Essentializing Differences between Women and Men." *Psychological Science* 17:129–135.

Purdie-Vaughns, Valerie J., and Richard P. Eibach. 2008. "Intersectional Invisibility." *Sex Roles* 59:377–391.

Richardson, Erika V., Katherine W. Phillips, Laurie A. Rudman, and Peter Glick. 2011. Double Jeopardy or Greater Latitude: Do Black Women Escape Backlash for Dominance Displays? Working paper, Northwestern University.

Ridgeway, Cecilia L. 2011. *Framed by Gender.* New York: Oxford University Press.

Ridgeway, Cecilia L., and Shelley J. Correll. 2004. "Unpacking the Gender System: A Theoretical Perspective on Cultural Beliefs and Social Relations." *Gender & Society* 18:510–531.

Ridgeway, Cecilia L., and Susan R. Fisk. 2012. "Class Rules, Status Dynamics, and 'Gateway Interactions.'" In *Facing Social Class* (ed. Susan T. Fiske and Hazel Markus). New York: Russell Sage. pp. 131–151.

Ridgeway, Cecilia L., and Tamar Kricheli-Katz. 2013. "Intersecting Cultural Beliefs in Social Relations Gender, Race, and Class Binds and Freedoms." *Gender & Society* 27(3): 294–318.

Rosette, Ashleigh S., and Robert W. Livingston. 2012. "Failure Is Not an Option for Black Women: Effects of Organizational Performance on Leaders with Single- Versus Dual-Subordinate Identities." *Journal of Experimental Social Psychology* 48:1162–1167.

Rudman, Laurie A., Corinne A. Moss-Racusin, Julie E. Phelan, and Sanne Nauts. 2012. "Status Incongruity and Backlash Effects: Defending the Gender Hierarchy Motivates Prejudice against Female Leaders." *Journal of Experimental Social Psychology* 48:165–179.

Schneider, Donald J. 2004. *The Psychology of Stereotyping.* New York: Guilford.

Sesko, Amanda K., and Monica Biernat. 2010. "Prototypes of Race and Gender: The Invisibility of Black Women." *Journal of Experimental Social Psychology* 46:356–360.

Sewell, William H. 1992. "A Theory of Structure." *American Journal of Sociology* 98:1–29.

Stangor, Charles, Laure Lynch, Changming Duan, and Beth Glass. 1992. "Categorization of Individuals on the Basis of Multiple Social Features." *Journal of Personality and Social Psychology* 62:207–218.

Stryker, Sheldon, and Kevin D. Vryan. 2003. "The Symbolic Interactionist Frame." In *The Handbook of Social Psychology* (ed. J. Delamater). New York: Kluwer Academic/Plenum. pp. 3–28.

Stuber, Jenny M. 2006. "Talk of Class: The Discursive Repertoires of White Working- and Upper-Middle-Class College Students." *Journal of Contemporary Ethnography* 35:285–318.

van Knippenberg, Ad, and Ap Dijkersterhuis. 2000. Social Categorization and Stereotyping. *European Review of Social Psychology* 11:105–44.

Webster, Murray, Jr., and Martha Foschi. 1988. "Overview of Status Generalization." In *Status Generalization* (ed. M. Webster and M. Foschi). Stanford, CA: Stanford University Press. pp. 1–20.

West, Candace, and Sarah Fenstermaker. 1995. "Doing Difference." *Gender & Society* 9:8–37.

Wilkins, Clara L., Joy F. Chan, and Cheryl R. Kaiser. 2011. "Racial Stereotypes and Interracial Attraction: Phenotypic Prototypicality and Perceived Attractiveness of Asians." *Cultural Diversity and Ethnic Minority Psychology* 17:427–431.

Wingfield, Aida. 2008. Are Some Emotions Marked "Whites Only?" *Gender & Society* 57:251–268.

Wu, Frank. 2002. *Yellow.* New York: Basic Books.

Questions

1. What are the three primary frames for categorizing people? How do primary frames work in interaction? (That is, what is their relationship to stereotypes? How do they influence people's assessments of others in interaction?) Ridgeway and Kricheli-Katz argue that the degree to which race and gender activate stereotypes depends on the social context in which interactions take place. What are the three interactional contexts which activate stereotyping? Provide examples of these contexts from your own life. Why do these situations in particular prime people to stereotype?

2. What do race and gender stereotypes include? From where do people learn these stereotypes? Provide specific examples. Provide specific examples of counter-stereotypical lessons from your own life. From where did you learn them? Why do stereotypes matter? What effect do they have? What binds and freedoms do various stereotypes afford people? Do people have to believe in stereotypes (agree with them) in order for stereotypes to have an effect? Why or why not?

3. In what ways does class function similarly to and differently from race and gender to implicitly bias people? What social cues do people use to determine someone's class? When someone has competing statuses (a female lawyer interacting with male clients, a male nurse interacting with male doctors), what determines which status is most important in setting expectations for behavior? How are racial stereotypes affected by gender and class?

4. Ridgeway and Kricheli-Katz neglect to talk about categorization of people based on their physical health or ability statuses. How should researchers add this dimension of inequality to their analyses? What research questions should they ask? How would a consideration of ability change their argument?

5. Create a list of words that you associate with authority. Have several friends generate their own lists. On the master list, circle the words that are culturally identified as feminine. Put a square around the words that are identified as masculine. Leave plain any that are associated with neither. What is the relationship between cultural beliefs about competence and authority and gender? From where did you learn these beliefs? How do those beliefs influence people's expectations for women? For men? How might people bolster their authority in ways that counteract gender expectations? What about racial expectations? What about stereotypes based in (dis)ability?

6. What are the implications of implicit bias research for social change?

8

Engendering Racial Perceptions: An Intersectional Analysis of How Social Status Shapes Race

ANDREW M. PENNER AND ALIYA SAPERSTEIN

Sociologists have long contended that we develop a sense of self by interacting with other people. We learn to think of ourselves by reading other people's cues about what they think about us, and we develop generalized ideas of who we are based on our reading of their assessments. These senses of self, in turn, guide how we label ourselves, what we value about ourselves, how we feel, and how we approach our interactions with others. When teachers repeatedly call on someone to answer questions aloud in class, for example, a student sees that others consider her smart, and over time she will likely come to see herself that way. She may even adopt the label of "smart." When she interacts with other students, she often does so in ways that confirm her sense of self as smart, perhaps by tutoring them or teaching them tough concepts in small groups. A smart identity guides the student's interactions with others and provides her life order and meaning.

Identities attached to inequalities do the same thing: They facilitate how to think, feel, act, and interact. As we learned in the previous reading, we automatically assess who people are in part by categorizing them, especially in terms of sex, race, age, and physical ability. Stereotypes add a layer of complication to our senses of self. The labels we give are laden with meanings about people's competence, warmth, and morality. They position groups of people in relation to each other, with the subordinate category of people being fundamentally different from and inferior to the dominant category of people. Then women and men aren't just different from each other, for example, but men are thought to be superior beings because of their supposed rationality and competence to lead. In sociology, we refer to ways people position one group as different and inferior as "othering."

Because people come to think of themselves in racial, class, gender, sexuality, nationhood, and ability terms, even when their identity is subordinated, social justice movements always contest the negative meanings associated with subordinated groups. "Black is beautiful," the reclamation of "queer," and "murderball" challenge the othering that positions subordinated identities as *lesser than*. They also protect people's senses of self embedded in the labels themselves. Subordinated people take pride in the identities they and others cast upon them.

In the following study, Penner and Saperstein unpack the identity categorization process, raising the questions of how stereotypes impact labeling itself and the consequences of identity fluidity for disrupting institutionalized inequalities. In the preceding example, a girl developed a sense of self as "smart" because others thought of and treated her as smart. Penner and Saperstein reverse the process, wondering how stereotypes about girls being bad at math, for example, might impact how likely someone is to view the smart student as a girl at all. What's more, would getting a job as an engineer at age 22 change how people later labeled her? And would such shifts in label disrupt the broader gender system?

The authors draw an even more interesting and complex picture than the smart-girl example. Rather than looking at how identities changing relates to gender stereotypes alone (or gender identities, which are largely binary and particularly sticky), they examine how racializing, classing, and gendering come together to influence racial and gender identities both. Using data from the National Longitudinal Survey of Youth (NLSY), which follows the same research participants across decades, allows researchers to track changes in racial categorization across time (and gender, but there were too few to study). Penner and Saperstein test whether having stereotypic experiences (e.g., going on welfare, incarceration, long-term unemployment) influences the interviewers' racial classification of the participant. Does going on welfare, being incarcerated, or being unemployed for a long time lead to more identification as Black and less as white? Does living in the suburbs lead to more identification as white and less of Black? Do they work the same way for women and men?

The authors find a surprising degree of variability in racial classification across time. Stereotypic experiences do influence racial classification, with higher-status experiences leading to more identification as white and lower-status experiences leading to more identification as Black. Perhaps more challenging, however, the authors question the effectiveness of counteracting stereotypes to disrupt systemic inequality altogether. Rather, they argue that inequalities incorporate atypical people into the existing power structure. Succeeding at math alone, then, may not dismantle the categories of boys and girls, even if it may mean success for that individual. So what does?

Race, Gender, and the Content of Our Stereotypes

In the United States, Black people are stereotyped as musical and athletic, but also lazy, unintelligent, and unethical (Blair, Judd, and Fallman 2004; Devine and Elliot 1995). Simply mentioning the phrase "inner city" cues racial stereotypes and affects whites' attitudes toward crime policy (Hurwitz and Peffley 2005). Even biracial Blacks (Harris and Khanna 2010) and new immigrants of African descent (Waters 1999) accept these negative stereotypes and use them to explain why native (and monoracial) Blacks are overrepresented at the bottom of the social hierarchy.

However, American racial stereotypes, from Ronald Reagan's "Welfare Queen" to Willie Horton on a prison furlough, have never been only about race. These ostensibly racial cues have both social class and gender dimensions. Like racial stereotypes, gender stereotypes and perceptions of innate difference reinforce hierarchies between women and men. Women are expected to be warm, sensitive, and interested in children, but not stubborn, controlling, or promiscuous, while men are supposed to be self-reliant and assertive, but not weak or gullible (Prentice and Carranza 2002). These widespread, "hegemonic" ideals facilitate gendered status distinctions, such that those who are unable to meet stereotypic expectations are relegated to subordinate or "pariah" positions in the social order (Schippers 2007).

A growing body of research highlights the importance of understanding how race and gender stereotypes and their associated value judgments intersect. For example, while men are typically perceived to be more competent than women (Correll and Ridgeway 2003), these evaluations do not necessarily hold for Black men (Wingfield 2009). Pervasive stereotypes of Black men in the United States portray them as shiftless (Kirschenman and Neckerman 1991), irresponsible fathers (Glauber 2008), and prone to violence and criminal behavior (Eberhardt et al. 2004). Black women, on the other hand, are widely perceived as single mothers (Kennelly 1999), loud and confrontational (Weitz and Gordon 1993), and undeserving of government benefits (Gilens 1999).

Even where men and women of the same race face similar stereotypes, there are often differences in the degree to which the stereotypes are thought to apply. For example, although Blacks are stereotyped as less intelligent than whites, Black women are seen as more intelligent than Black men (Steinbugler, Press, and Dias 2006). These persistent associations led Browne and Misra (2003) to conclude that women and men of color face different stereotypes that lead to discrimination.

Experimental research in social psychology provides support for this perspective as well. Studies show that when race and gender are cued simultaneously, people combine the characteristics to generate categorizations (Freeman and Ambady 2011) and behavioral expectations (Correll and Ridgeway 2003), rather than rely on one piece of information or the other. This research also demonstrates that evaluations related to a person's organizational roles "become nested within the prior, automatic categorization of that person as male or female and take on slightly different meanings as a result" (Ridgeway 1997).

At the same time, although category attributions of race and gender are largely automatic and occur within the first few seconds of perceiving someone, research shows that introducing other, seemingly contradictory characteristics or status cues can alter these perceptions (Freeman et al. 2011; Purdie-Vaughns and Eibach 2008). For example, racially categorizing admired Blacks and disliked whites takes longer and prompts more "mistakes" than categorizing admired whites and disliked Blacks (Richeson and Trawalter 2005). In this study, we examine whether similar processes occur during nonexperimental interactions, as Americans sort through a host of information to help them determine how to racially categorize someone. In particular, we are interested in whether the effects of social status on racial perceptions vary significantly by the target's gender.

Data and Methods

Our data come from the 1979 cohort of the National Longitudinal Survey of Youth 1997 (NLSY79), a representative sample of 12,686 U.S. men and women who were 14 to 22 years of age when first surveyed in 1979. Respondents were eligible to be interviewed every year thereafter, until 1994, when interviews began occurring biennially. We utilize data from 1979 to 1998, the most recent year in which the interviewers recorded their racial classification of the respondents. To define our study populations, we use the respondent's self-reported sex from 1979.

Racial Classification

Our dependent variable is the interviewer's classification of the respondent's race, which was collected in all but one survey year from 1979 to 1998. Interviewers were instructed to classify the respondent's race at the end of the interview. Thus, we do not have their first impression of the respondent's race; we have a classification colored by the respondent's answers during the survey interview. This is ideal for assessing the effects of social status on racial classification, because the interviewer heard a range of information about the respondent, from their income and education to their employment and marital history, prior to recording the respondent's race.

Interviewers were not given any special instructions as to how to classify the respondents by race (NLS 2006); the categories available to them were "Black," "White," and "Other." Descriptive statistics on how respondents were racially classified by the interviewer are reported in Table 1, along with our other key variables. Of the observations where respondents have racial classifications in consecutive survey years, 6 percent are described by a different race than in the previous person-year, and 20 percent of the individuals in the sample experienced at least one change in how they were racially classified between 1979 and 1998.[1]

It is possible that these changes in respondents' racial classification from one survey year to the next were the result of mistakes made by the interviewers if, for example, they were in a hurry to complete their remarks and meant to check "White" but mistakenly checked "Black.". . . For additional discussion of why changes in the racial perceptions of the same individual should not be interpreted primarily as errors, see Saperstein and Penner (2012).

However, we do not assume that the interviewer's classification is "true" or correct in any objective sense. We also do not assume that the interviewer's racial classification necessarily aligns with how the respondent would self-identify; rather, we view self-identification and classification by others as capturing different information about an individual's race and racial experiences (Saperstein 2008). We regard the interviewer's racial classification as a measure of how the respondent is likely to be perceived, and presumably treated, by others. Indeed, some scholars have argued that racial classification is actually a more appropriate measure than self-identification for understanding phenomena such as discrimination (Telles and Lim 1998). For this reason, understanding who gets racially classified as what, and under what circumstances, is an important question for sociological analysis.

Table 1 Descriptive Statistics.

	Women	Men
Racial classification		
Percentage classified as white by interviewer	67.8	67.2
Percentage classified as Black by interviewer	26.6	27.1
Percentage classified as other by interviewer	5.6	5.7
Respondent characteristics		
Percentage unemployed over 4 months	8.9	10.1
Percentage below poverty line	22.9	17.1
Percentage incarcerated	0.2	2.6
Percentage receiving welfare	17.5	6.8
Percentage married with children	31.5	24.9
Percentage married without children	11.2	10.0
Percentage unmarried with children	19.9	3.8
Percentage unmarried without children	37.4	61.3
Percentage with 4 or more children in household	3.2	1.5
Percentage living in an inner city	18.2	19.0
Percentage living in a suburb	30.4	30.0
Mean years of education	12.4	12.2
Percentage self-identified as Hispanic in 1979	17.3	16.5
Percentage self-identified as multiple races in 1979	11.8	9.1
Percentage born outside the United States	6.8	7.0
Percentage living in the South	39.5	37.4
Mean age	25.9	25.7
Interviewer characteristics		
Percentage female	95.8	88.7
Percentage self-identified as white	84.2	84.6
Percentage self-identified as Black	11.4	10.9
Percentage self-identified as other	4.4	4.5
Mean age	49.4	49.6
Percentage less than a high school degree	1.3	1.5
Percentage high school graduate	22.1	20.3
Percentage some college/vocational degree	37.9	38.7
Percentage bachelor's degree or more	38.7	39.4

Source: 1979 National Longitudinal Survey of Youth.

Note: Statistics for person-years (N = 182,224; representing as many as 12,686 unique persons in a given year).

Social Status

Our primary independent variables are repeated measures of the respondent's social position, such as long-term unemployment, poverty, incarceration, and welfare receipt. Because of widespread racialized stereotypes regarding who goes to prison or collects welfare benefits (Timberlake and Estes 2007), we expect that people who experience a loss of status on any of these dimensions will be more likely to be classified as Black, and less likely to be classified as white. Further, given the gendered nature of these stereotypes, we expect some changes in social position to have different effects on the racial classifications of women compared to men.

Our measure of unemployment indicates whether the respondents ever reported being unemployed for more than 16 weeks in the previous calendar year, and welfare receipt indicates whether the respondents, or their partners, ever reported receiving Aid to Families with Dependent Children (AFDC and later TANF), food stamps, Supplemental Security Income (SSI), or any other public assistance during the previous calendar year. To capture the experience of poverty, we examine whether the NLSY ever indicated that the respondent's total family income was below the poverty level in the previous calendar year. To measure incarceration, we use data on whether respondents were ever interviewed in jail or prison. These factors are not particularly common in any given year (e.g., in all person-years, just 1 percent of the sample is incarcerated on average, and 12 percent receive welfare benefits), so we focus on differences between respondents who have and have not ever experienced these changes in their social position. Given evidence of the lasting effect of incarceration on racial classification (Saperstein and Penner 2010), we suspect that these status cues not only operate directly—as when the interview takes place in prison, or information is given explicitly in response to a question—but also shape perceptions of respondents indirectly and might accumulate over time.

We also examine other class-relevant factors linked to racial stereotypes, such as marital and parity status (indicators for "married with children," "married without children," and "unmarried with children," with "unmarried without children" as the omitted category), family size (an indicator for having four or more children living in the household), neighborhood type (indicators for living in the inner city and living in the suburbs, with all else as the omitted category), and years of completed education. Changes in these characteristics are more common, so we allow these measures of status to vary from one year to the next. These factors are also likely to be immediate status cues during the survey interview, as the vast majority of interviews take place in the respondent's home.[2]

Other Respondent Controls

Both the likelihood of being racially classified in a particular way and experiencing the changes in social status detailed previously are related to other characteristics of the respondent. Thus, we include controls for the respondent's age (in years), country of birth (an indicator for born outside the United States), whether the respondent gave multiple racial/ethnic origin responses or reported a Hispanic origin in 1979, and whether the respondent currently lives in the South.[3]

Interviewer Characteristics

We control for demographic characteristics of the interviewer, in part because of research noting differences in interviewers' perception of respondents' skin tone (Hill 2002). These controls include age, race (self-identification as white, Black, or other), sex (an indicator for identifying as female), and education (indicators for some college and college graduates compared to everyone else). We also include year-fixed effects (i.e., indicators for the year of interview) in each model. These account for trends in classification caused by changes in the social meaning of race (e.g., due to increased immigration or the multiracial movement), changes in the salience of racial stereotypes due to media coverage of current events (e.g., the OJ Simpson trial), as well as year-to-year changes in survey design, question wording, or interviewer training....

Models

To examine the effects of social position on racial classification, we estimate logistic regression models predicting whether respondents are classified as white (vs. nonwhite) or Black (vs. non-Black) in a given year. We use dichotomous outcome variables to explore which characteristics move individuals either toward or away from the traditional poles of racial privilege and stigma in the United States: whiteness and Blackness.[4] The models examining whiteness control for whether the respondent was racially classified as white (vs. non-white) in the previous year, while the models examining Blackness control for whether the respondent was racially classified as Black (vs. non-Black) in the previous year. This allows us to isolate, for example, which factors are related to the likelihood of being classified as white in the current year, net of how the respondent was racially classified previously.

We estimate models separately for men and women to examine whether there are differences in which characteristics are related to the interviewer's racial classification. We also use fully interacted models to test whether the effects of social position on racial classification are statistically significantly different between women and men. These results are based on models that include all of our status variables together, which indicate, for example, whether there is an effect of unemployment on racial classification net of the other factors. With the exception of education (discussed later), the results are similar when we examine models that include only one status variable at a time.[5]

Results

We begin by presenting descriptive evidence that racial classification changes over time with similar frequency for women and men. We then estimate regression models to determine whether changes in perceived race are related to differences in social status, net of characteristics of both the survey interviewer and respondent—and whether or not the patterns differ between women and men.

Changes in Race over Time

Previous research has documented the existence of fluidity in racial classification in the United States for the same individuals at different points in their life course (Brown, Hitlin, and Elder 2007; Saperstein and Penner 2012). However, whether the level or patterns of change differ by gender has yet to be empirically explored. Table 2 presents year-to-year changes in racial classification in percentage terms. Each row is restricted to respondents who were classified as white, Black, or other, respectively, in the previous year and reports how they were classified by the interviewer in the current year. These categories are mutually exclusive as measured in the NLSY; thus, if racial classifications did not change over time, all of the observations would be in the diagonal cells. Observations in the off-diagonal cells indicate, for example, that on average 1.3 percent of women who were classified as Black in the previous year are classified as white in the current year. Similarly, on average 3.7 percent of women classified as white in the previous year are currently classified as other. Comparing the results for women (Panel A) and men (Panel B) reveals that the overall level of change in racial classification is

Table 2 Changes in Interviewers' Racial Classification of Respondents between Two Interviews.

	Current Year's Race			
Previous Year's Race	White	Black	Other	Total
Panel A: Women				
White (%)	95.8	0.5	3.7	100
(N)	52,656	294	2,040	54,990
Black	1.3	98.2	0.5	100
	290	21,365	109	21,764
Other	44.9	2.6	52.5	100
	2,016	117	2,353	4,486
Total	67.7	26.8	5.5	100
	54,962	21,776	4,502	81,240
Panel B: Men				
White (%)	95.8	0.5	3.7	100
(N)	51,065	260	1,996	53,321
Black	1.2	98.4	0.4	100
	263	21,185	90	21,538
Other	45.3	2.0	52.7	100
	2,025	88	2,355	4,468
Total	67.3	27.1	5.6	100
	53,353	21,533	4,441	79,327

Source: 1979 National Longitudinal Survey of Youth.

Note: Observations represent person-years. Percentages sum across rows.

almost identical. It is not the case that only women, or only men, experience changes in racial classification. Rather, racial fluidity characterizes the lived experience of race equally for women and men.[6]

When interpreting the results in Table 2, it is important to remember that we are pooling data for individuals over time, so our unit of analysis is a person-year [each person, each year]. Thus, the percentages describe, on average, how an individual classified as a particular race in the previous year will be seen in the current year, and not what proportion of people who have ever been classified as a particular race will ever make the transition in question (e.g., change their racial classification from Black to white between two years). These percentages are higher: Among respondents who have ever been classified as Black, 14 percent of individuals experience a change in classification from Black to white in consecutive interviews, and 4 percent experience a change from Black to other. Among respondents ever classified as white, 5 percent experience a change from white to Black in consecutive interviews, while 19 percent experience a change from white to other. Finally, among respondents ever classified as other, 88 percent experience at least one classification shift from other to white, and 8 percent experience a shift from other to Black in consecutive interviews. Like the fluidity observed in the year-to-year changes, the likelihood of ever experiencing a particular racial transition does not vary by gender.

The Effects of Social Status on Race

Having established that both women and men experience racial fluidity, we now turn to modeling which social factors influence racial classification. Though changes in race are equally likely for women and men overall, it does not necessarily follow that the changes for men and women are driven by the same factors, as we demonstrate next.

For both women and men, racial classification is influenced by a wide variety of status characteristics. . . . The odds ratio for having ever experienced long-term unemployment (.705) indicates that, net of all other measured factors, including whether she was classified as white in the previous year, having been unemployed reduces the odds of a woman being classified as white in the current year by roughly 30 percent. In fact, for women, all but one of our status variables is a significant

predictor of being classified by the interviewer as white. . . . [Eight] of the 11 status variables are statistically significant predictors of being classified as white among men. . . . Overall, 30 of the 44 possible associations between social position and racial classification are statistically significant and in the expected direction, demonstrating the inextricable link between race and class in the United States.

Poverty, for example, decreases both women's and men's odds of being classified as white, but the p value indicates that having ever been in poverty has a stronger effect (indicated by the odds ratio furthest from 1) on the racial classification of men compared to women. Finding that poverty has a stronger effect for men is consistent with traditional gender roles that emphasize men's responsibility as breadwinners (Reskin and Padavic 1994). Likewise, consistent with gendered stereotypes around welfare (Timberlake and Estes 2007), we see that women who ever received welfare benefits have lower odds of being seen as white and higher odds of being seen as Black, whereas men's racial classifications are not affected by reporting a history of welfare receipt (e.g., food stamps, SSI, and other public assistance).

However, there are also characteristics that significantly predict racial classification for both women and men where the estimated effects do not differ significantly by gender. . . . For example, both women and men are significantly more likely to be seen as white if they are married (with or without children) or live in the suburbs, and significantly less likely to be seen as white if they live in the inner city.

It is also worth noting that the factors that affect whether people are seen as white are not necessarily the same factors that affect whether they are seen as Black. For example, living in a suburb increases both women's and men's odds of being classified as white, but it does not affect their odds of being classified as Black. We also find that the odds ratio for having been classified as Black in the previous year is significantly larger for men. This suggests that "Blackness" in general is stickier for men: net of the status variables examined here, a man classified as Black this year has higher odds of being classified as Black again next year than a woman who is classified as Black this year.

Perhaps the most puzzling findings are for education. The results suggest education has a significant effect on the odds of both women's and men's racial classifications, but it affects these perceptions in different ways. For men, more educational attainment significantly increases the odds of being classified as white, as one might expect given the controversial but oft-repeated association between academic success and "acting white" (see Tyson, Darity, and Castellino 2005). However, for women, being more educated significantly decreases their odds of being classified as white, and increases their odds of being classified as Black. In interpreting these results, it is important to remember that the odds ratios represent the effects of education net of all other factors in the model. Models including only education—along with year-fixed effects, the previous year's racial classification, and self-identification as Hispanic or multiracial—indicate that more education is positively associated with whiteness and negatively associated with Blackness for both women and men (results available on request).

The difference between the education-only and full models suggests that the effect of education on women's racial classification operates through other demographic characteristics or aspects of social status; once factors such as welfare, poverty, unmarried parenthood,

and living in the South are taken into consideration, the positive association between education and whiteness becomes negative. In contrast, for men, education remains positively associated with whiteness even when other considerations are held constant. Our data are unable to speak to the specific mechanisms behind these differing results. However, finding that greater educational attainment is less incongruent with Blackness for women is in keeping with previous research that highlights gender differences in perceived intelligence (Steinbugler, Press, and Dias 2006).

Discussion

The results from our analysis of gender differences in the relationship between social position and racial classification can be summarized by three broad patterns, illustrated in Figure 1. First, as depicted in the pair of bars on the left, there are some status distinctions, such as living in the inner city, that are gender neutral; they affect racial classification similarly for women and men, in terms of both their magnitude and their statistical significance. Second, some factors have statistically significant effects for both women and men, but the magnitude of the effect differs. For example, as depicted in the

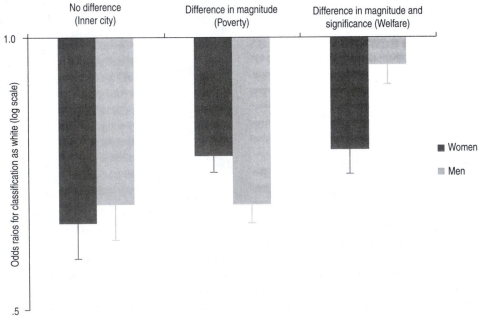

Figure 1 Gendered Patterns in How Social Status Shapes Race.
Note: Odds ratios are from models predicting classification as white separately for women and men.

middle pair of bars, having ever lived in poverty reduces the odds of being classified as white for both women and men, but the effect is significantly stronger for men. Third, some factors differ in both magnitude and statistical significance, as seen in the pair of bars on the right, where a history of welfare receipt affects the odds of women being classified as white, but has no significant net effect for men.

Overall, the results are consistent with a priori expectations of how common racial stereotypes are gendered. For status distinctions that tend to affect men and women equally, such as being married, we find no gender differences in their effects on racial classification. However, where status distinctions and their associated stereotypes are strongly gendered, as with welfare or incarceration, we find significant status effects on racial classification only for the expected group. Between these extremes are factors like poverty and parenthood, with stereotypes that can be applied to both men and women but are often deployed unequally (or asymmetrically), as when out-of-wedlock births are seen as a problem only for women of color (Furstenberg 2003).

We can also read the content of our racial stereotypes and their gendered dimensions backward, inferring them from the significant effects. . . . From this perspective, our results suggest that Blackness is associated with unemployment, poverty, unmarried parenthood, and inner-city residence, for both men and women. Whiteness, on the other hand, is associated with living in the suburbs and being married (regardless of parental status). . . . [O]ne can also infer the degree to which racial stereotypes are gendered. The primary example here is welfare, which has significant gender differences in its effects on being classified as white or Black, with significant effects for women but not men.

Our results imply that the stereotypes shaping racial classifications vary by gender, and thus suggest that factors triggering racial discrimination are also likely to vary. This echoes social psychological research on racial prototypicality showing that the more characteristics someone has that are associated with Blackness the more likely they are to be discriminated against (Eberhardt et al. 2006). However, our work also supports previous research finding that the prototypical Black woman and Black man (or white woman and

white man) are not identical (cf. Timberlake and Estes 2007). Taken together, our study calls attention to the fact that before racial discrimination can occur, potential discriminators must first racially classify their targets, and the factors that inform these classifications vary by gender. Revealing a history of welfare receipt may put a woman at greater risk for racial discrimination, because it increases the likelihood that she will be perceived as Black, but the same is not true for men. From a policy perspective, it is important to understand how the antecedents of discrimination might vary, especially if other axes of difference (e.g., gender, sexuality, class, disability) are subject to similar classification processes.[7]

Destabilizing Categories or Reinforcing Hierarchy?

The micro-level processes discussed in this chapter do not simply reflect macro-level structures of inequality, they actively "(re)constitute broader relations of inequality" (Pyke 1996, 546). As such, finding that changes in race are tied to social mobility in gendered ways has important implications for how we think about macrostructural aspects of intersectionality. In particular, our results highlight that changes in race, gender, or class status do not necessarily imply a significant weakening of boundaries or an undermining of categories, as has often been predicted in previous research (e.g., see Alba 2005; Wilkins 2004). Instead, our findings reveal a deeply intertwined system of inequality in which individual fluidity can perversely reinforce existing structural inequalities.

To illustrate, we take Collins's (1990) metaphor of the "matrix of domination" literally, invoking a multidimensional array of cells that encode a hierarchy of social status (though using "geometrical" images also has its limitations; see West and Fenstermaker 1995). Typically, the boundaries separating categories, or cells, along the dimension of race (or gender) are seen as static and rigid, restricting mobility and causing individuals' experiences to be shaped or constrained by their social location. So, when people experience class mobility, moving into the cells above or below their current structural position, it is assumed their trajectory is restricted to the same racialized column of cells. Our results reveal the potential for diagonal movement between cells, as social mobility can involve multiple dimensions of stratification simultaneously. For example, when a man's income falls below the poverty line, our results show that this not only affects his class position but also lowers his odds of being classified as white and raises his odds of being classified as Black.

However, highlighting the permeability of racial boundaries is not necessarily the same as saying they become blurred or unstable. We argue instead that these unexpected patterns of mobility are serving, intentionally or not, to maintain perceived differences between groups. When confronted with counter-stereotypical status shifts, the larger system of inequality can be stabilized by redefining individuals—moving them between cells of the existing matrix—instead of redefining the categories or their associated stereotypes and lived experiences. Rather than revise tropes about Black women and welfare, the matrix is reinforced as the racial categorizations of women who are (and are not) on welfare get reinterpreted.

Indeed, we suggest that the strength of these social boundaries is in their selectivity, not their impermeability per se. If the movement of individuals across cell (or category) boundaries is selective and based on status characteristics, the social meaning of the categories will remain in equilibrium, and their associated stereotypes will continue to be reinforced over time. To the extent that individual boundary crossing increases homogeneity within a given category or cell, this process can also increase social distance, as selective fluidity slowly redefines shared experiences. Thus, our findings suggest that the micro-level mobility we observe not only maintains the content of a particular social category but also positions cells vis-à-vis other cells in the larger structure of inequality.[8]

By highlighting the relationship between selective racial fluidity and the maintenance of hierarchy, our study provides an important counterpoint to the claim, common in literary criticism and cultural studies, as well as among members of the multiracial movement, that the existence of multiplicity and flexibility has the potential to undermine categorical racial distinctions. In a similar vein, Wilkins asserts that revealing the racial performances of individuals "destabilizes racial categories, adding elasticity to their boundaries and molding their content" (Wilkins 2004, 119). As performances imply an audience, studies of racial classification and identity performance effectively examine

opposite sides of the same coin. While we agree that acts of performing race, class, and gender offer the potential to destabilize categories through individual agency at any given point in time, our results suggest that over a longer period, identity performances (or at least the racial classifications that follow from them) are not transformative of the larger system. We echo Butler (1993) in noting that, theoretically, the fact that norms are reproduced through individual actions introduces the possibility of revolutionary change, but most of the time people give normatively "correct" performances, which help to maintain stability and affirm the existing hierarchy.

For example, the "wannabes" in Wilkins's study perform Puerto Rican-ness (rather than whiteness) to gain entrée into hip-hop culture and access to relationships with Black and Puerto Rican men. Although their behavior both calls into question the putative biological and cultural foundations of "race" and exposes the norms and stereotypes that circumscribe authentic membership, it leaves the overall hierarchy that frowns upon interracial relationships intact. In the long run, to the extent that their performances are successful (i.e., they are accepted and categorized as Puerto Rican by others), any normative transgression in their presentations of self will fade away into the appearance of compliant racial homogamy. This micro-level fluidity helps to reinforce inequality by concealing challenges to the hegemonic order; or, put another way, our expectations literally shape what we see and do not see, rendering potential points of incongruity effectively invisible.

Our examination of how micro-level fluidity reinforces the macro-level structures of inequality also stands in contrast to standard research on inequality, which focuses on how being located in a particular gender and/or race category constrains upward mobility and other forms of status attainment. Placing racial (and gender) fluidity alongside class mobility both recasts previous research and raises new research questions. From this perspective, it becomes important not only to examine how interlocking axes of oppression shape the experiences and opportunities of individuals in a particular social location, but also to ask who moves between which categories, how mobility is experienced, and what are the barriers to (or the avenues that facilitate) this movement (cf. Bettie 2002). Learning that some social boundaries are easier to cross while others are less permeable, or that movement along one dimension of status is likely to result in movement on another, helps us to better understand how various cells (or different axes of stratification) are organized in relation to each other and illuminates otherwise invisible aspects of the structure of the matrix.

Notes

1. We are referring to the previous *survey* year; after 1994, the comparison is to the interviewer's classification from two calendar years prior. Also, in 1987 the survey was conducted primarily by telephone and did not include interviewer-classified race. Thus, the 1988 data are compared to the data from two calendar years prior. See Saperstein and Penner (2012) for additional methodological details.

2. Of course, there are other observable status cues, such as how people dress and their voice or accent (Freeman et al. 2011; Giles and Bourhis 1976), that also influence racial classification. Although we cannot tease apart the effects of these kinds of status cues directly in this study, they likely mediate the relationships we identify and are an important focus for future research.

3. We use the respondents' "origin or descent" in 1979 to control for whether they reported multiple races or a Hispanic origin. In 2002, respondents were also asked whether they are of Hispanic origin and the "race or races" they consider themselves to be. Supplemental analyses showed no substantive difference when we controlled for identification in 1979 and 2002, and because the interviewer classification spans 1979–1998, we present results with controls based on the 1979 responses.

4. Multinomial logistic regression models examining the relative odds of being seen as white vs. other and white vs. Black provide similar results (available on request), suggesting that the effects of social position on racial classification discussed here are not being driven by movement into or out of the "other" category.

5. We did not present analogous models for racial self-identification because the information was recorded just twice by the NLSY (in 1979 and not again until 2002)—compared to up to 17 observations for interviewer classification. However, it is worth noting that the estimates for self-identification are substantively similar to the classification results. This suggests that our findings for racial classification are not an artifact of solely perceptual factors, such

as physical appearance, but capture broader class and gender stereotypes that Americans use to understand and apply racial categories to themselves and others.

6. These patterns of fluidity also suggest that there is considerable ambiguity around the distinction between "other" and "white." Some of the fluidity we observe is likely due to variation in how different interviewers define these categories. (Sixty-six percent of the sample was surveyed by a different interviewer in the previous and current years.) However, even when we examine classifications made by the same interviewer, 23 percent of respondents classified as "other" in the previous year are classified as "white" in the current year.

7. These classification processes are likely to be important, given work by Freeman et al. (2011) suggesting that stereotypes subtly shape how people are perceived even when they do not change how people are classified. That is, revealing a history of welfare receipt will matter to some extent for all women, not just the ones who are classified differently as a result.

8. Increasing selective fluidity could also reinforce the system of inequality by removing atypical exemplars. Ridgeway and Kricheli-Katz (2013) argue that counter-stereotypical exemplars represent a challenge to the intersectional structure of inequality because their existence forces observers to confront its ideological underpinnings. To the extent that this is true, recasting women who receive welfare as Black will act as a safety valve, resolving the stress or pressure created by stereotype-inconsistent individuals (e.g., white women on welfare).

References

Alba, Richard. 2005. "Bright vs. Blurred Boundaries: Second-Generation Assimilation and Exclusion in France, Germany, and the United States." *Ethnic and Racial Studies* 28:20–49.

Bettie, Julie. 2002. "Exceptions to the Rule: Upwardly Mobile White and Mexican American High School Girls." *Gender & Society* 16:403–422.

Blair, Irene V., Charles M. Judd, and Jennifer L. Fallman. 2004. "The Automaticity of Race and Afrocentric Facial Features in Social Judgments." *Journal of Personality and Social Psychology* 87:763–778.

Brown, J. Scott, Steven Hitlin, and Glen H. Elder, Jr. 2007. "The Importance of Being Other: A Natural Experiment about Lived Race over Time." *Social Science Research* 36:159–174.

Browne, Irene, and Joya Misra. 2003. "The Intersection of Gender and Race in Labor Markets." *Annual Review of Sociology* 29:487–513.

Butler, Judith. 1993. *Bodies that Matter*. New York: Routledge.

Collins, Patricia Hill. 1990. *Black Feminist Thought*. London: HarperCollins.

Correll, Shelley J., and Cecilia L. Ridgeway. 2003. "Expectation States Theory." In *Handbook of Social Psychology* (ed. John Delamater). New York: Kluwer Academic/Plenum. pp. 29–51.

Devine, Patricia G., and Andrew J. Elliot. 1995. "Are Racial Stereotypes Really Fading? The Princeton Trilogy Revisited." *Personality and Social Psychology Bulletin* 11:1139–1150.

Eberhardt, Jennifer L., Paul G. Davies, Valerie J. Purdie-Vaughns, and Sheri Lynn Johnson. 2006. "Looking Deathworthy: Perceived Stereotypicality of Black Defendants Predicts Capital-Sentencing Outcomes." *Psychological Science* 17:383–386.

Eberhardt, Jennifer L., Phillip Atiba Goff, Valerie J. Purdie, and Paul G. Davies. 2004. "Seeing Black: Race, Crime and Visual Processing." *Journal of Personality and Social Psychology* 87:876–893.

Freeman, Jon B., and Nalini Ambady. 2011. "A Dynamic Interactive Theory of Person Construal." *Psychological Review* 118:247–279.

Freeman, Jon, Andrew M. Penner, Aliya Saperstein, Matthias Scheutz, and Nalini Ambady. 2011. "Looking the Part: Social Status Cues Shape Racial Perception." *PLoS One* 6:e25107.

Furstenberg Jr., Frank E. 2003. "Teenage Childbearing as a Public Issue and Private Concern." *Annual Review of Sociology* 29:23–39.

Gilens, Martin. 1999. *Why Americans Hate Welfare*. Chicago, IL: University of Chicago Press.

Giles, Howard, and Richard Y. Bourhis. 1976. "Voice and Racial Categorization in Britain." *Communication Monographs* 43:108–114.

Glauber, Rebecca. 2008. "Race and Gender in Families and at Work: The Fatherhood Wage Premium." *Gender & Society* 22:8–30.

Harris, Cherise A., and Nikki Khanna. 2010. "Black Is, Black Ain't: Biracials, Middle-Class Blacks, and the Social Construction of Blackness." *Sociological Spectrum* 30:639–670.

Hill, Mark. 2002. "Race of the Interviewer and Perception of Skin Color." *American Sociological Review* 67:99–108.

Hurwitz, Jon, and Mark Peffley. 2005. "Playing the Race Card in the Post-Willie Horton Era: The Impact of Racialized Code Words on Support for Punitive Crime Policy." *Public Opinion Quarterly* 69:99–112.

Kennelly, Ivy. 1999. "That Single-Mother Element: How White Employers Typify Black Women." *Gender & Society* 13:168–192.

Kirschenman, Joleen, and Kathryn Neckerman. 1991. "'We'd Love to Hire Them but . . .': The Meaning of Race for Employers." In *The Urban Underclass* (ed. Christopher Jencks and Paul E. Peterson). Washington, DC: Brookings Institution. pp. 203–232.

Prentice, Deborah A., and Erica Carranza. 2002. "What Women and Men Should Be, Shouldn't Be, Are Allowed to Be, and Don't Have to Be: The Contents of Prescriptive Gender Stereotypes." *Psychology of Women Quarterly* 26:269–281.

Purdie-Vaughns, Valerie, and Richard P. Eibach. 2008. "Intersectional Invisibility: The Ideological Sources and Social Consequences of Non-Prototypicality." *Sex Roles* 59:377–391.

Pyke, Karen D. 1996. "Class-Based Masculinities: The Interdependence of Gender, Class, and Interpersonal Power." *Gender & Society* 10:527–549.

Reskin, Barbara F., and Irene Padavic. 1994. *Women and Men at Work*. Thousand Oaks, CA: Pine Forge Press.

Richeson, Jennifer A., and Sophie Trawalter. 2005. "On the Categorization of Admired and Disliked Exemplars of Admired and Disliked Racial Groups." *Journal of Personality and Social Psychology* 89:517–530.

Ridgeway, Cecilia L. 1997. "Interaction and the Conservation of Gender Inequality: Considering Employment." *American Sociological Review* 62:218–235.

Ridgeway, Cecilia L., and Tamar Kricheli-Katz. 2013. "Intersecting Cultural Beliefs in Social Relations: Gender, Race, and Class Binds and Freedoms." *Gender & Society*.

Saperstein, Aliya. 2008. (Re)Modeling Race: "Moving from Intrinsic Characteristic to Multidimensional Marker of Status." In *Racism in Post-Race America: New Theories, New Directions* (ed. Charles Gallagher). Chapel Hill, NC: Social Forces. pp. 335–349.

Saperstein, Aliya, and Andrew M. Penner. 2010. "The Race of a Criminal Record: How Incarceration Colors Racial Perception." *Social Problems* 57:92–113.

Saperstein, Aliya, and Andrew M. Penner. 2012. "Racial Fluidity and Inequality in the United States." *American Journal of Sociology* 118:676–727.

Schippers, Mimi. 2007. "Recovering the Feminine Other: Masculinity, Femininity, and Gender Hegemony." *Theory and Society* 36:85–102.

Steinbugler, Amy C., Julie E. Press, and Janice Johnson Dias. 2006. "Gender, Race, and Affirmative Action: Operationalizing Intersectionality in Survey Research." *Gender & Society* 20:805–825.

Telles, Edward, and Nelson Lim. 1998. "Does It Matter Who Answers the Race Question? Racial Classification and Income Inequality in Brazil." *Demography* 35:465–474.

Timberlake, Jeffrey M., and Sarah Estes. 2007. "Do Racial and Ethnic Stereotypes Depend on the Sex of Target Group Members?" *Sociological Quarterly* 48:399–433.

Tyson, Karolyn, William Darity, Jr., and Domini R. Castellino. 2005. "It's Not 'a Black Thing': Understanding the Burden of Acting White and Other Dilemmas of High Achievement." *American Sociological Review* 70:582–605.

Waters, Mary. 1999. *Black Identities*. Cambridge, MA: Harvard University Press; New York: Russell Sage Foundation.

Weitz, R., and L. Gordon. 1993. "Images of Black Women among Anglo College Students." *Sex Roles* 28:19–34.

West, Candace, and Sarah Fenstermaker. 1995. "Doing Difference." *Gender & Society* 9:8–37.

Wilkins, Amy C. 2004. "Puerto Rican Wannabes: Sexual Spectacle and the Marking of Race, Class, and Gender Boundaries." *Gender & Society* 18:103–121.

Wingfield, Adia Harvey. 2009. "Racializing the Glass Escalator: Reconsidering Men's Experiences with Women's Work." *Gender & Society* 23:5–26.

Questions

1. What is the authors' research question? How do they go about testing it? What data do they use, and why is this data set so interesting? What is the dependent variable being measured? What are the experiences used to measure "social status" (the independent variables)? Explain who is targeted by each stereotype.

2. How likely was a person to ever change race categories during the study? Were women or men more likely to have a change in racial categorization from one year to the next? How did having a racially stereotypic class experience affect people's racial classification? Which experiences were associated with whiteness? Blackness? Which experiences did that for women? Which for men? What was the relationship between education and racial classification for men? For women? What do the authors conclude?

3. What are the implications of this research for our understanding of discrimination?

4. Go to the Harvard University's "Project Implicit" website (https://implicit.harvard.edu/implicit/takeatest.html). Take one of the Implicit Association Tests. Were your results what you expected? Why or why not? Are they what you wanted? How do people end up with implicit associations that they may not want? Go to the "Education" tab and then FAQs. What was the test measuring, and how did it do it? This test is done in an artificial setting. How would interacting in the real world affect whether someone's biases are activated and acted upon?

5. Watch PBS's *Scientific American Frontiers* program "Hidden Motives Part II: Hidden Prejudice." What is the model for social change suggested in the video? Is this enough to counteract stereotyping or discrimination, by extension from Penner and Saperstein's research? Why or why not? From the authors' perspective, does playing with identity (e.g., changing identities or having seemingly fuzzy boundaries) destabilize systems of inequality? The authors suggest that when we encounter people who challenge stereotypes we may simply reclassify their identities rather than disassociate the stereotype from them. How so? Why don't they think that multiracialness or racial fluidity will necessarily lead to real social change? Do you agree? What model of social change that addresses hidden prejudice might work better?

9

Hetero-Romantic Love and Heterosexiness in Children's G-Rated Films

KARIN A. MARTIN AND EMILY KAZYAK

In his book *The Gender Knot*, Allan Johnson (2005) identifies three characteristics of patriarchal societies: male-dominance, male-centeredness, and male-identification. Male-dominance is when men control decision making and wield power over non-men. Male-centeredness is when men command attention, for example in interactions (e.g., by interrupting others) and the media (e.g., movies being about men, from men's point of view, for men's enjoyment). Male-identification is the alignment of the most desired characteristics with males, manhood, and masculinity. For example, leadership is associated with instrumentality and rationality in decision making. Male-identification disseminates the characteristics of manhood into ones valued across social settings. It aligns the social standard with the dominant group. It also defines the characteristics that serve as the boundary marker between what is desirable and what is not. Leadership is "making the tough decisions," regardless of the consequences—not failing to act because it will hurt people's feelings. Valuing leadership solidifies the boundaries between real men and not-men, even when women do it, without ever having to talk about men directly at all.

People create and normalize social boundaries whenever there are categorical inequalities. In order for an inequality to stick, social actors have to know who is in and who is out, as well as the characteristics that define the boundary. Once a category is created, people transmit and impose those categories—and their boundaries—into new social settings (Tilly 1999). The media play a key, albeit varied and contested, role in defining social standards, generating shared meanings, and transmitting social boundaries.

As Karin Martin and Emily Kazyak show in the following selection, many U.S. children have widespread access to television and movies, even from early ages. Despite the fractured media environment, children's movies are more popular than ever. The seeming ubiquity of particular characters and storylines raises questions about what meanings about social standards, categories of people, and social boundaries children's movies disseminate.

In this reading, Martin and Kazyak examine how high-grossing children's movies portray sexuality, despite being rated G. G-rated movies are supposed to be devoid of sexuality, yet Martin and Kazyak find sexuality themes in nearly every successful movie. Moreover, sexuality in movies is decidedly heterosexual. Two themes in particular were present across movies: a transformative, powerful hetero-romance and heterosexiness. Hetero-romance was a major plot line in 8 of 20 films and a minor plot line in 7 of 20 films. Through these plot lines, music, staging, and expressions, children's movies portrayed heterosexual love as uniquely powerful in nature: It was a tool of expression, rebellion, and freedom in ways that parent-child, sibling, and friend relationships were not. Finding and securing love, then, was a magical and trans-formative experience that could change people's lives, sometimes even their social circumstances.

The second theme, heterosexiness, had two dimensions. First, movies sexualized and exoticized women at the pleasure of men in the movie. This was especially true for women of color. Second, movies portrayed men ogling women, sometimes making a joke of it.

Rather than normalizing heterosexuality as mundane, hetero-romance and heterosexiness demar-cate heterosexuality as exhilarating, visceral, and emotionally and socially compelling. Look how enjoy-able heterosexuality is! Look how it can make your life better! Look how, well, sexy it is!

Finally, the reading points to the importance of how dominant groups in particular establish social boundaries and elevate the characteristics associated with them. Scholars of manhood and whiteness have especially challenged researchers to study dominant groups and how they maintain their social advantages. This study similarly draws our attention to heterosexuality, rather than leaving it unlabeled and therefore taken for granted.

Reference

Johnson, Allan G. 2005. *The Gender Knot: Unraveling Our Patriarchal Legacy*. Philadelphia, PA: Temple University Press.
Tilly, Charles. 1999. *Durable Inequality*. Berkeley: University of California Press.

The role that Disney plays in shaping individ-ual identities and controlling fields of social meaning through which children negotiate the world is far too complex to be simply set aside as a form of reactionary politics. If edu-cators and other cultural workers are to in-clude the culture of children as an important site of contestation and struggle, then it be-comes imperative to analyze how Disney's animated films powerfully influence the way America's cultural landscape is imagined.

—GIROUX (1996, 96)

Multiple ethnographic studies suggest that by elemen-tary school, children understand the normativity of het-erosexuality. That is, by elementary school, children have a heteronormative understanding of the world (Best 1983; Renold 2002, 2005; Thorne 1993). Yet we know little about what children bring with them to the peer cultures these ethnographers describe and how these understandings develop before elementary school. Martin (2009) finds that mothers' conversations with young children normalize heterosexuality, but children's social worlds are larger than the mother-child dyad. Re-search on adolescence suggests that alongside parents and peers, the media are important in shaping cultural understandings of sexuality (Kim et al. 2007; Ward 1995,

2003). This chapter provides a beginning step toward un-derstanding the role of the media in the development of children's heteronormativity. We ask, How are hetero-normativity and heterosexuality constructed in chil-dren's top-selling G-rated movies between 1990 and 2005? Before answering this question, we sketch our un-derstanding of heteronormativity and explain why we chose this genre of media, why we analyze the content of these films, and the limits of such analysis. We then review the existing literature on children's movies and finally turn to our study, which finds heterosexuality in children's movies is not entirely as theorists of hetero-normativity describe. That is, heterosexuality within the context of romantic relationships in G-rated movies is not ordinary or mundane but, rather, is powerful, excep-tional, and magical. Outside of romantic relationships, heterosexual desire is much less serious.

Heteronormativity

Heteronormativity includes the multiple, often mundane ways through which heterosexuality overwhelmingly structures and "pervasively and insidiously" orders "ev-eryday existence" (Jackson 2006, 108; Kitzinger 2005). Heteronormativity structures social life so that hetero-sexuality is always assumed, expected, ordinary, and privileged. Its pervasiveness makes it difficult for people to imagine other ways of life. In part, the assumption and expectation of heterosexuality is linked to its status as natural and biologically necessary for procreation (Lancaster 2003). Anything else is relegated to the non-normative, unusual, and unexpected and is, thus, in need of explanation. Specifically, within heteronormativity, homosexuality becomes the "other" against which heterosexuality defines itself (Johnson 2005; Rubin 1984). But not just any kind of heterosexuality is privileged. Heteronormativity regulates those within its boundaries as it marginalizes those outside of it.

According to Jackson (2006), heteronormativity works to define more than normative sexuality, insofar as it also defines normative ways of life in general. Heteronormativity holds people accountable to reproductive, procreative sexuality and traditional gendered domestic arrangements of sexual relationships, and it is linked to particular patterns of consumerism and consumption (Ingraham 1999). In other words, while heteronormativity regulates people's sexualities, bodies, and sexual relationships (for both those nonheterosexuals on the "outside" and heterosexuals on the "inside"), it regulates nonsexual aspects of life as well.

Heteronormativity also privileges a particular type of heterosexual. Among those aspects desired in heterosexuals, Rubin (1984) includes being married, monogamous, and procreative. We might also include that heterosexuality is most sanctioned when it is intraracial and that other inequalities, like race and class, intersect and help construct what Rubin calls "the inner charmed circle" in a multitude of complicated ways (e.g., Whose married sex is most sanctioned? Whose reproductive sex is most normal?). Heteronormativity also rests on gender asymmetry, as heterosexuality depends on a particular type of normatively gendered women and men (Jackson 2006). In this chapter, we examine how children's movies construct heterosexuality to better understand what information is available in media that might contribute to children's heteronormative social worlds.

Children, Media, and Movies

The media are an important avenue of children's sexual socialization because young children are immersed in media-rich worlds. Thirty percent of children under three years old and 43 percent of four- to six-year-olds

have a television in their bedrooms, and one-quarter of children under six years old have a VCR/DVD player in their bedrooms (Rideout, Vandewater, and Wartella 2003). Since the deregulation of television in the 1980s, there has been more and more content produced on television for children. Children's programming produced for television, however, must still meet educational regulations. Films produced with young children as a significant intended portion of the audience are under no such obligations. However, to attract young children (and their parents) to films, filmmakers must get their movies a G-rating. Film producers are interested in doing this because the marketing advantages that accompany a successful children's film are enormous (S. Thomas 2007). The Motion Picture Association of America rates a film G for "General Audience" if the film "contains nothing in theme, language, nudity, sex, violence or other matters that, in the view of the Rating Board, would offend parents whose younger children view the motion picture. . . . No nudity, sex scenes or drug use are present in the motion picture" (Motion Picture Association of America 2010: 7). Thus, a G-rating signals that these films expect young children in their audience.

We examine the top-selling G-rated movies to challenge the idea that these movies are without (much) sexual content and the notion that young children are therefore not exposed to matters relating to sexuality. As theorists of heteronormativity suggest, heterosexuality is pervasive, and we want to examine how it makes its way into films that are by definition devoid of sexuality. If heteronormativity structures social life well beyond the sexual arena, then it is likely at work even in films that announce themselves as free of sexuality.

We look at movies themselves rather than children's reception of them because of the difficulty of research with young children generally, especially around issues of sexuality (Martin, Luke, and Verduzco-Baker 2007) and around media (Thomas 2007). Parents, human subjects review boards, and schools all serve as barriers to research with children on these topics. Given that we know little about how heteronormativity is constructed for children, examining the content of these films seems a logical first step before asking what children take from them. Although we will not be able to say whether or which accounts of heteronormativity children take away with them after watching these movies, current research about children's relationships to such movies indicates that children are engaged with these media and the stories they tell. Enormous numbers of children watch Disney and other G-rated children's movies. In a 2006 survey of more than 600 American mothers of three- to six-year-olds, only 1 percent reported that their child had not seen any of the films we analyze here; half had seen 13 or more (Martin et al. 2007).

Many children also watch these movies repeatedly (Mares 1998). The advent of videos made it possible for children to watch and rewatch movies at home. In fact, preschool children enjoy watching videos/DVDs repeatedly, and this has implications for the way they comprehend their messages. Crawley et al. (1999) discovered that children comprehended more from repeated viewing. Repeated viewing may also mean that jokes or innuendo intended for adults in these films become more visible and curious, if not more intelligible, to young children. Further work by Schmitt et al. (1999) also suggests that young children's attention is most focused and content best understood when watching media that includes animation, child characters, nonhuman characters, animals, frequent movement, and purposeful action (as opposed to live action; adults, especially adult men; and characters who only converse without much action). These are prominent features of most of the G-rated films we analyze here, suggesting that they are certainly vehicles for children's attention and comprehension.

We also know young children are engaged by many such films, as the plots and toys marketed from them are used in many creative ways in children's fantasy and play. Not only do movies make social worlds visible on screen, but the mass marketing surrounding these movies invites young people to inhabit those worlds (Giroux 1996). These media not only offer what is normal but also actively ensure that children understand it and compel them to consume it (Schor 2004). Researchers have demonstrated the depth of children's engagement with such media and how they adapt it for their own uses. For example, Hadley and Nenga (2004) find that Taiwanese kindergartners used everything from Snow White to Digimon to demonstrate and challenge their Confucian values at school. Gotz et al. (2005) similarly find that eight-year-old children across the United States, Israel, Germany, and South Korea make use of the media in

constructing the "fantasylands" they imagine and play in. Thus, while we must look at particular groups of children's reception of particular media to see what they do with it (Tobin 2000), there is evidence that children certainly incorporate such media into their learning and play.

Finally, with respect to heterosexuality specifically, there is some evidence that suggests even young children learn from media accounts. Kelley, Buckingham, and Davies (1999) find that six- to eleven-year-old children incorporate what they learn about sexuality on television into their talk and identity work in their peer groups. Martin (2009) finds mothers of children ages three to six years old suggest that children, especially girls, know about heterosexual falling in love, weddings, and marriage from "movies," "princesses," and "Disney." Again, our research cannot address what children take away from their repeated viewings of such movies, but given that the extant research suggests they take something, we analyze what is there for the taking.

Some scholarship has begun to look at what kinds of narratives, accounts, and images are available in children's movies, and especially in Disney movies. Most useful for our purposes is the research on gender (Thompson and Zerbinos 1995; Witt 2000) and on gender and race stereotypes in young children's media (Giroux 1996; Hurley 2005; Mo and Shen 2000; Pewewardy 1996; Witt 2000). Most of this research indicates that there are fewer portrayals of women and of nonwhites than of men and whites and that those portrayals often rely on stereotypes. Analyses of the stereotypes and discourses of race and gender sometimes embed some discussion of sexuality within them. A smattering of research on race examines how some racial/ethnic groups are portrayed as exoticized and more sexualized than white women (Lacroix 2004). Research that examines gender construction in the media sometimes links heterosexuality and romantic love to femininity and discusses the importance of finding a man/prince for the heroines (Junn 1997; Thompson and Zerbinos 1995). But heterosexuality is a given in such analyses. The existing research does not fully analyze how heterosexuality is constructed in these films.

In a different vein, media scholars have offered queer readings of some children's and especially Disney films (Byrne and McQuillan 1999; Griffin 2000). Employing a poststructuralist lens that privileges the radically indeterminate meaning of texts, Byrne and McQuillan (1999) highlight how certain characters and storylines in Disney movies can be read as queer. They discuss the many queer or ambiguous characters populating these films, such as Quasimodo and the gargoyles in *The Hunchback of Notre Dame*. They describe the character Mulan as a "transvestite bonanza," representing "Disney's most sustained creation of lesbian chic" (1999, 143). Moreover, they highlight the queerness of certain storylines in Disney movies. For instance, they argue that homosocial desire and bonds between men structure many of the films, and they explicate the queerness of the portrayal of monstrous desire, a desire that threatens the family unit, in *Beauty and the Beast*. These readings do not argue that particular characters or plots are gay or lesbian per se; rather, they emphasize their queer potential. Similarly, Griffin (2000) aims to queer Disney by analyzing how gay and lesbian viewers might understand these films with gay sensibilities. He highlights how Disney characters who do not fit into their societies echo the feeling of many gays and lesbians. He also argues that many characters (especially villains) lend themselves to queer readings because of how they overperform their gender roles. Villainesses often look like drag queens, such as Ursula in *The Little Mermaid*, a character modeled after the transvestite star Divine. These analyses rest on the desire to destabilize the meanings of characters and storylines in movies to open them up and discover their queer potential. This scholarship, however, presumes a sophisticated and knowledgeable reader of culture. It does not consider children as the audience or address whether such readings are possible for young children. It overlooks, for example, that while there are transvestite characters like Mulan, the Mulan toys marketed to children were feminine, long-haired, non-sword-wielding ones (Nguyen 1998), perhaps making such readings less sustainable for children even if they are possible. Again, we will need research on what children take away from such media to address these issues.

Our Research

In this chapter, we do not aim to do a queer reading of these films, as such readings have already been done. Instead, we analyze how heterosexuality is constructed in children's G-rated films. We ask not how characters might be read as queer but what accounts these films offer of heterosexuality and how such accounts serve heteronormativity. Unpacking the construction of heterosexuality in these films is a first step toward understanding what social-sexual information is available to the children who watch them.

Sample and Method

The data for this study come from all the G-rated movies released (or rereleased) between 1990 and 2005 that grossed more than $100 million in the United States (see Table 1).[1] Using this sample of widely viewed films overcomes the limitations of previous analyses of children's, and especially Disney, movies, which often focus on a few particular examples. Here we have tried to examine all the most-viewed films within this genre and time period. The films in our sample were extremely successful and widely viewed, as evidenced by their sales numbers in theaters. Home videos/DVDs sales and rentals of these films are also very high (Arnold 2005), including direct-to-video/DVD sequels of many of these films, for example, *Lion King 1.5, Ariel's Beginning*, and *Beauty and the Beast's Enchanted Christmas*. While the audience for these films is broader than children, children are certainly centrally intended as part of the audience. G is the rating given to films that contain nothing that "would offend parents whose younger children view the motion picture" according to the Motion Picture Association of America (2010: 7). Sixteen (80 percent) of these films are animated, and 17 are produced by Disney, a major producer of children's consumption and socialization (Giroux 1997).

After collecting this sample, the first author screened all the films and then trained three research assistants to extract any storylines, images, scenes, songs, or dialogue that depicted anything about sexuality, including depictions of bodies, kissing, jokes, romance, weddings, dating, love, where babies come from, and pregnancy. The research assistants then wrote descriptions of the scenes in which they found material related to sexuality. They described the visuals of the scenes in as vivid detail as possible and transcribed the dialogue verbatim. Two research assistants watched each film and extracted the relevant material. The first author reconciled the minimal differences between what each research assistant included by rescreening the films herself and adding or correcting material.

Table I Sample: $100 Million G-Rated Movies, 1990–2005.

Movie	Year	Produced By	Any Reference	Major Plot	Minor Plot	Sexiness	Ogling of Women's Bodies
				Hetero-Romantic Story Line		Heterosexuality	
Chicken Little	2005	Disney	X		X	X	
The Polar Express	2004	Castle Rock					
Finding Nemo	2003	Disney/Pixar	X				
The Santa Clause 2	2002	Disney	X	X			
Monsters, Inc.	2001	Disney/Pixar	X		X		X
The Princess Diaries	2001	Disney	X	X		X	X
Chicken Run	2000	Dreamworks	X		X		X
Tarzan	1999	Disney	X		X		
Toy Story 2	1999	Disney/Pixar	X			X	X
A Bug's Life	1998	Disney/Pixar	X		X		X
Mulan	1998	Disney	X		X		X
The Rugrats Movie	1998	Nickelodeon					
101 Dalmatians	1996	Disney	X		X		
The Hunchback of Notre Dame	1996	Disney	X	X		X	X
Toy Story	1995	Disney/Pixar	X			X	
Pocahontas	1995/2005	Disney	X	X			
The Lion King	1994/2002	Disney	X	X			
Aladdin	1994	Disney	X	X		X	X
Beauty and the Beast	1991/2002	Disney	X	X		X	X
The Little Mermaid	1989/1997	Disney	X	X		X	X

This text describing the material in each film was then inductively coded using the qualitative software program QSR-Nvivo. The themes that emerged from this open-coding were then developed in a series of initial and then integrative memos. The movies were re-viewed again by both authors as needed to further explicate the categories of understanding that emerged from first-round coding. The memos were then developed into the results discussed next (Emerson, Fretz, and Shaw 1995).

Results and Discussion

We describe two ways that heterosexuality is constructed in these films. The primary account of heterosexuality in these films is one of hetero-romantic love

and its exceptional, magical, transformative power. Secondarily, there are some depictions of heterosexuality outside of this model. Outside of hetero-romantic love, heterosexuality is constructed as men gazing desirously at women's bodies. This construction rests on gendered and racialized bodies and is portrayed as less serious and less powerful than hetero-romantic love.

Magical, Exceptional, Transformative Hetero-Romantic Love

Hetero-romantic love is the account of heterosexuality that is most developed in these films. Only two films have barely detectable or no hetero-romantic references (see Table 1). In eight of these films hetero-romance is a major plot line, and in another seven films it is a secondary storyline. Those films not made by Disney have much less hetero-romantic content than those made by Disney.

Films where we coded hetero-romantic love as a major plot line are those in which the hetero-romantic storyline is central to the overall narrative of the film. In *The Little Mermaid*, for instance, the entire narrative revolves around the romance between Ariel, a mermaid, and Eric, a human. The same is true of movies like *Beauty and the Beast, Aladdin,* and *Santa Claus 2*. There would be no movie without the hetero-romantic storyline for these films. In others, the hetero-romantic storyline is secondary. For example, in *Chicken Run* the romance develops between Ginger and Rocky as they help organize the chicken revolt—the heart of the movie—although the movie ends with them coupled, enjoying their freedom in a pasture. While removing the hetero-romantic storyline would still leave other stories in place in such films, the romance nonetheless exists. In other movies, like *Toy Story*, references are made to hetero-romance but are not developed into a storyline. For instance, this film suggests romantic interest between Woody and Little Bo Peep, but their romance is not woven throughout the film.

While our focus is on the construction of heterosexuality, we recognize that other stories exist in these films. For instance, there are stories about parent-child relationships (e.g., Chicken Little wants his father to be proud of him; Nemo struggles against his overprotective father). Stories about workers, working conditions, and collective revolt also appear, for instance, in *Monsters, Inc.* (whose characters, working for the city's power company that relies on scaring children to generate electricity, successfully stop an evil corporate plan to kidnap children and eventually change their policy to making children laugh) and *Chicken Run* (whose main character, Ginger, successfully organizes all of her fellow chickens to escape their farm after learning of the farmers' plan to begin turning them into chicken pies). Though certainly there is much analysis that could be done around such stories, we do not do so here. Rather, we turn our attention to the hetero-romantic storylines and the work they do in constructing heterosexuality.

Theorists of heteronormativity suggest that the power of heteronormativity is that heterosexuality is assumed, mundane, ordinary, and expected. In contrast, we find that in these films, while it is certainly assumed, heterosexuality is very often not ordinary or mundane. Rather, romantic heterosexual relationships are portrayed as a special, distinct, exceptional form of relationship, different from all others. Characters frequently defy parents, their culture, or their very selves to embrace a hetero-romantic love that is transformative, powerful, and (literally) magical. At the same time, these accounts are sometimes held in tension with or constructed by understandings of the naturalness of heterosexuality. In the following text, we describe how the films construct these relationships as distinct, set apart, and different from others. We also describe how they are constructed as powerful, transformative, and magical.

These films repeatedly mark relationships between cross-gender lead characters as special and magical by utilizing imagery of love and romance. Characters in love are surrounded by music, flowers, candles, magic, fire, ballrooms, fancy dresses, dim lights, dancing, and elaborate dinners. Fireflies, butterflies, sunsets, wind, and the beauty and power of nature often provide the setting for—and a link to the naturalness of—hetero-romantic love. For example, in *Beauty and the Beast*, the main characters fall in love frolicking in the snow; Aladdin and Jasmine fall in love as they fly through a starlit sky in *Aladdin*; Ariel falls in love as she discovers the beauty of earth in *The Little Mermaid*; Santa and his eventual bride ride in a sleigh on a sparkling snowy night with snow lightly falling over only their heads in *Santa Claus 2*; and Pocahontas is full of allusion to water, wind, and trees as a backdrop to the characters falling in love. The characters often say little in these scenes. Instead, the scenes are overlaid with music and song that tells the viewer more abstractly what the characters are feeling. These scenes depicting hetero-romantic love are also paced more slowly with longer shots and with slower and soaring music.

These films also construct the specialness of hetero-romantic love by holding in tension the assertion that hetero-romantic relationships are simultaneously magical and natural. In fact, their naturalness and their connection to "chemistry" and the body further produce their exceptionalness. According to Johnson (2005), love and heterosexuality become interwoven as people articulate the idea that being in love is overpowering and that chemistry or a spark forms the basis for romantic love.

These formulations include ideas about reproductive instincts and biology, and they work to naturalize heterosexuality. We see similar constructions at work in these G-rated movies where the natural becomes the magical. These films show that, in the words of Mrs. Pots from *Beauty and the Beast*, if "there's a spark there," then all that needs to be done is to "let nature take its course." However, this adage is usually not spoken. Rather, the portrayal of romantic love as occurring through chemistry or a spark is depicted by two characters gazing into each other's eyes and sometimes stroking each other's faces. The viewer usually sees the two characters up close and in profile as serious and soaring music plays as this romantic chemistry is not explained with words but must be felt and understood via the gazing eye contact between the characters. Disney further marks the falling in love and the triumphs of hetero-romantic love by wrapping the characters in magical swirls of sparks, leaves, or fireworks as they stare into each other's eyes. The music accompanying such scenes is momentous and triumphant.

We asked whether all sorts of relationships might be magical, special, and exceptional in similar ways, as it is possible that many types of relationships have these qualities in these imaginative fantasies where anything is possible. However, we found that romantic heterosexual relationships in G-rated movies are set apart from other types of relationships. This serves to further define them as special and exceptional. All other love relationships are portrayed without the imagery just described. The pacing of friendship scenes is also faster and choppier, and the music is quicker and bouncy. Nor do friendships and familial relationships start with a "spark."

Parent-child relationships are portrayed as restrictive, tedious, and protective. The child is usually escaping these relationships for the exciting adolescent or adult world. Friendships are also set aside as different from romantic love. There are many close friendships and buddies in these stories, and none are portrayed with the imagery of romantic love. Cross-gender friends are often literally smaller and a different species or object in the animated films, thus making them off limits for romance. For example, Mulan's friend is Mushoo, a small, red dragon; Pocahontas is friends with many small animals (a raccoon; a hummingbird); Ariel is looked after by Sebastian (a crab) and Flounder (a fish); and Belle is befriended by a range of small household items (teapot, candlestick, broom). Same-sex friendships or buddies are unusual for girls and women unless the friends are maternal (e.g., Willow in *Pocahontas*, Mrs. Pots in *Beauty and the Beast*). The lead male characters, however, often have comical buddies (e.g., Timon in *The Lion King*, Abu in *Aladdin*, the gargoyles in *The Hunchback of Notre Dame*, Mike in *Monsters, Inc.*). These friendships are often portrayed as funny, silly, gross, and fun but certainly not as serious, special, powerful, important, or natural. For example, in *The Lion King*, Timon (a meerkat), Pumba (a boar), and Simba (a lion) all live a carefree life together in the jungle as the best of friends, but Simba quickly deserts them for Nala, a female lion, once he is an adolescent. Throughout the film, Timon and Pumba provide comic relief from the serious business of the lions falling in (heterosexual) love and saving the kingdom. Thus, the construction of friendships and family relationships reveals that hetero-romantic relationships in contrast are serious, important, and natural.

Furthermore, while friendships provide comic relief and friends and family are portrayed as providing comfort or advice to lead characters, these relationships are not portrayed as transformative, powerful, or magical. Hetero-romantic love is exceptional in these films because it is constructed as incredibly powerful and transformative. Throughout many of these films with a primary plot about hetero-romantic love, such love is depicted as rebellious, magical, defiant, and with a power to transform the world. This is quite different from our understanding of heterosexuality as normative, ordinary, and expected. The hetero-romantic relationships in these films are extraordinary. Falling in heterosexual love can break a spell (*Beauty and the Beast*) or cause one to give up her identity (*The Little Mermaid*). It can save Santa Claus and Christmas (*Santa Claus 2*). It can lead children (e.g., Ariel, Jasmine, Pocahontas, Belle) to disobey their parents and defy the social rules of their culture (e.g., Jasmine, Pocahontas). It can stop a war that is imminent (*Pocahontas*) or change an age-old law (*Aladdin*).

Hetero-romantic love is constructed as being in a realm of freedom and choice, a realm where chemistry can flourish and love can be sparked and discovered. Thus, romantic love is so exceptional it is positioned "outside of the control of any social or political force" (Johnson 2005, 37). This construction appears in G-rated movies and intertwines race and heteronormativity as characters who are nonwhite critique arranged marriages as backward and old-fashioned and celebrate a woman's ability to choose her own husband. For example, in *Aladdin*, Jasmine protests the law that dictates that she must marry a prince and says, "The law is wrong. . . . I hate being forced into this. . . . if I do marry, I want it to be for love." Later, Aladdin agrees with her that being forced to be married by her father is "awful." Pocahontas faces a similar dilemma, as her father insists that she marry Kocoum. When she disagrees and asks him, "Why can't I choose?" he says, "You are the daughter of the chief . . . it is your time to take your place among our people." While arranged marriages are portrayed as something outdated, these characters "choose" whom they will love, thus simultaneously securing hetero-romantic love's naturalness and extraordinariness and its position beyond the prescriptions of any social-political context. In fact, their love changes these prescriptions in both of these examples. Jasmine and Aladdin's love overturns the age-old law that the princess must marry a prince when she is of age, and Pocahontas's love for John Smith ends the war between her tribe and colonizers. This transformative power of hetero-romantic love is echoed throughout these films.

Finally, we observe that hetero-romantic love is not sexually embodied in these films except through kissing. The power of hetero-romantic love is often delivered through a heterosexual kiss. A lot of heterosexual kissing happens in G-rated films. *Princess Diaries*, with its live-action teenage characters, contains the most explicit kissing, as the main character daydreams that a boy kisses her passionately, open-mouthed as she falls back against the lockers smiling and giggling. Most animated kisses are with closed mouths (or the viewer cannot fully see the mouths) and of shorter duration, but they are often even more powerful. Throughout these films, but especially in the animated ones, a heterosexual kiss signifies heterosexual love and in doing so is powerful. Ariel of *The Little Mermaid* must secure a kiss from the prince to retain her voice and her legs. In *The Lion King*, when Nala and Simba kiss (lick and nuzzle) as they are reunited, they not only realize their love, but Simba realizes he must return to his rightful place as king and save his family and the entire kingdom. We often see these powerful kisses first very close-up and in profile and then

moving outward to show the wider world that the powerful kisses are transforming. For example, once the Beast is transformed back into a man by Belle's declaration of love, they kiss, and the entire kingdom appears to turn from winter to springtime, flowers bloom, and others who had been damaged by the same spell as the Beast are restored to their personhood.

In one case, the kiss of love initially leads to making the world worse. When Pocahontas kisses John Smith, others see them, and this leads to the death of the man Pocahontas's father wanted her to marry. Eventually, however, their love is what brings peace between the Native Americans and European colonizers. Even this negative transformation brought on by a kiss is different from kisses outside of hetero-romantic love. Take, for example, the only same-gender kiss in these films. In *The Lion King*, Pumba and Timon are eating dinner and sucking on opposite ends of a worm (reminiscent of the classic Lady and the Tramp spaghetti vignette). When they reach the middle, their lips touch with a smooch, and they both look toward the camera aghast, seemingly both at the deed (the "kiss") and having been "caught" by the camera. This kiss is treated as humorous and not as serious or powerful as the kisses of hetero-romantic love. Even heterosexual kisses outside of love relationships are not serious, powerful, or transformative. For example, Jasmine kisses the evil Jafar in *Aladdin*, but she does so to trick him. It works as a trick and distraction, but it is not powerful or transformative. Only hetero-romantic kissing is powerful in that it signifies love and in doing so can change the world.

Heterosexiness and the Heterosexual Gaze: Heterosexuality Outside of Love

Thus far, we have described how heterosexuality is constructed through depictions of hetero-romantic love relationships in these films. There is also heterosexuality depicted outside of romantic relationships, though this heterosexuality is quite different and more ordinary. As such, it is depicted not as earnest or transformative but as frivolous, entertaining, and crude. This nonromantic heterosexuality is constructed through the different portrayals of women's and men's bodies, the heterosexiness of the feminine characters, and the heterosexual gaze of the masculine ones.

Heteronormativity requires particular kinds of bodies and interactions between those bodies. Thus, as heterosexuality is constructed in these films, gendered bodies are portrayed quite differently, and we see much more of some bodies than others. Women throughout the animated features in our sample are drawn with cleavage, bare stomachs, and bare legs. Women of color are more likely to be drawn as young women with breasts and hips and white women as delicate girls (Lacroix 2004). Men are occasionally depicted without their shirts, such as in *Tarzan*; or without much of a shirt, as in *Aladdin*; and in one scene in *Mulan*, it is implied that men have been swimming naked. However, having part of the body exposed is more common among the lead women characters and among the women who make up the background of the scenes.

Women's nudity is also often marked as significant through comment or reaction. Women are often "almost caught" naked by men. For example, Mia of the *Princess Diaries* has her dressing area torn down by jealous girls, almost revealing her naked to a group of male photographers. Mulan bathes in a lake when she thinks she is alone, but when male soldiers come to swim, Mushoo refers to her breasts, saying, "There are a couple of things they're bound to notice," and she sneaks away. Similarly, Quasimodo accidentally stumbles into Esmeralda's dressing area, and she quickly covers up with a robe and hunches over so as not to expose herself. She ties up her robe as Quasimodo apologizes again and again and hides his eyes. However, as he exits, he glances back toward her with a smile signifying for the viewer his love for her. A glimpse of her body has made her even more lovable and desirable.

Men's bodies are treated quite differently in these films. Male bodies, to the extent they are commented on at all, are the site of jokes. Men's crotches, genitals, and backsides are funny. For example, in *Hunchback of Notre Dame*, a cork from a bottle of champagne flies between a man's legs and knocks him over and the man yells in pain; later in that movie, during a fight, someone says, "That's hitting a little below the belt," and the woman says, "No this is!" and aims to strike him in the groin but is deflected by a sword. A boy in *Princess Diaries* is doubled over in pain as a baseball hits him in the groin. This scene is played as funny and the result of another character extracting her vengeance. *The Rugrats Movie* is full of

jokes and images of boys' bare bottoms and penises. There are also references in other films to "a limp noodle" (*Mulan*) and "a shrinky winky" (*101 Dalmatians*). Mushoo in Mulan also jokes about male nudity, saying, "I hate biting naked butts." Women's genitals are never mentioned or invoked in any way. Their bodies are not the sites of jokes. Rather, women's bodies become important in the construction of heteronormative sexuality through their "sexiness" at which men gaze.

Much of the sexuality that these gendered bodies engage in has little to do with heterosexual sex narrowly defined as intercourse or even behaviors that might lead to it, but rather with cultural signs of a gendered sexuality for women. These signs are found in subplots, musical numbers, humorous scenes, and scenes depicting women's bodies, rather than in the main storylines of hetero-romantic true love. Such scenes contain sexual innuendo based in gesture, movement, tone of voice, and expression. Importantly, in all cases, sexiness is depicted as something women possess and use for getting men's attention. Sexiness is more often an attribute of female characters of color (e.g., Esmeralda, Jasmine, Ursula) (Hurley 2005) and is implicitly heterosexual given that the films construct the intended spectator of this sexiness as male (Mulvey 1975).

The best example of the representation of sexiness appears in *The Hunchback of Notre Dame*. Esmeralda, the Gypsy female lead, is drawn with dark hair, big green eyes, a curvy body, cleavage, and a small waist. She is also drawn with darker skin than other lead Disney characters like Belle (*Beauty and the Beast*) and Ariel (*Little Mermaid*). Darker skin and hair and "exotic" features are part of the representation of heterosexual sexiness for women. Moreover, Esmeralda spends much time in this film swaying her hips and dancing "sexily" while men admire her. An early scene in the film resembles a striptease, although all the character's clothes do not come off. The scene begins with the song, "Come one, come all! Hurry, hurry, here's your chance. See the mystery and romance . . . See the finest girl in France . . . Make an entrance to entrance . . . Dance la Esmeralda . . . Dance!" Esmeralda begins to dance. She is dressed seductively, and her dancing is provocative. We then see the men who are watching her. Frollo says, "Look at that disgusting display" to which Captain replies, "YES SIR!" and opens his eyes wider. She perches in front of Frollo and then tosses her scarf around his neck, pulls him in as if she is going to kiss him, puts her lips on his nose, and then pushes his hat over his face. She dances back to the stage where she does a split in front of Quasimodo and gives him a wink. She then steals a large spear from a security guard, stabs it into the stage and begins to swing and twist around the pole. The men in the crowd are all wide-eyed, screaming and cheering, and then they all toss money on stage for her performance.

Not all scenes with the signification of sexiness are so elaborated. When the candlestick and duster are turned back into people in *Beauty and the Beast*, the now-voluptuous maid prances bare-shouldered in front of the chef who stares. Throughout *Aladdin*, especially in fast-paced musical scenes, sexy women prance, preen, bat their eyelashes, shake their hips, and reveal their cleavage. When Genie sings to Aladdin, he produces three women with bare stomachs and bikini-like outfits who dance around him, touch him, bat their eyes at him, and kiss him. He stares at them sometimes unsure, but wide-eyed and smiling. When Prince Ali comes to ask Princess Jasmine for her hand in marriage, his parade to the castle is adorned with writhing, dancing women with bare stomachs and cleavage. Later, Jasmine sees Prince Ali as a fraud and tricks him with similarly sexy moves. Heterosexiness in *Aladdin* is delivered through the bodies of women of color who are exoticized.

There are a few examples of white women depicted as "sexy," although these are more delimited and do not involve the main white women/girl characters. In *Princess Diaries*, a group of teenage friends are shown doing many of the same things as the animated women in *Aladdin*. They dance, shake their hips, make faces with curled and puckered lips and squinting eyes, play with their hair, and slap their hips. In *Beauty and the Beast*, a man is hit on the head for talking to a large-breasted woman with cleavage and much lipstick who moves and speaks in a sexy, flirtatious manner. *Toy Story 2* has a group of singing, dancing, nearly all-white Barbies who are ogled by the masculine toys. These scenes make it clear that women move and adorn their bodies and contort their faces for men.

While the women are being sexy, the (usually white) men are performing a different role as these films construct heterosexuality. As is evident from some of the preceding examples, there is much explicit heterosexual gazing at or ogling of women's bodies in these films. Sometimes such gazing establishes that a woman is worth the pursuit of men and the fight for her that will develop the plot of the film, as in *Beauty and the Beast*. In an early scene in this film, when Belle walks out of a bookshop, three men who had been peering through the window turn around as if to pretend that they had not been staring. The man in the middle is then held up by the other two so that he can stare at Belle's backside as she walks away. All three men stare and then start to sing of her beauty. In other films, sexualized gazing is not so tightly attached to beauty but to the performance of heterosexual masculinity. In one instance in *Chicken Run,* the chickens are "exercising," and Rocky (a chicken) stares at Ginger's (a chicken) backside. She catches him, and he smiles, slyly. When the main characters refrain from overt ogling and sexual commentary, the "sidekicks" provide humor through this practice. For example, in *Toy Story 2,* Rex, Potato Head, Slinky Dog, and Piggy Bank drive through aisles of a toy store and stop at a "beach party" where there are many Barbies in bathing suits, laughing and dancing. As the male characters approach, a jackpot sound ("ching") is heard, and all four male characters' jaws drop open. Then "Tour Guide Barbie" acrobatically lands in their car and says she will help them. They all stare at her with open eyes and mouths. Mr. Potato Head recites again and again, "I'm a married spud, I'm a married spud, I'm a married spud," and Piggy Bank says, "Make room for single fellas" as he jumps over Potato Head to sit next to Barbie. They remain mesmerized by Barbie as she gives them a tour of the store.

The objectifying gaze at women's bodies is often translated into objectifying, sexist language. Girl/women characters are called doll face, chicks, cuties, baby doll, angel face, sweet cheeks, bodacious, succulent little garden snail, tender oozing blossom, temptress snake, and tramp; and the boys/men say things like "I'll give you a tune up any time" and "give her some slack and reel her in." The desiring gazes, the commentary, and the depictions of them (large eyes, staring, open mouths, sound effects, and anxiousness) are constructed as competitive and conquering or frivolous, in stark contrast to the exceptional, magical, powerful hetero-romantic love described earlier. These depictions of heterosexual interactions have the effect of normalizing men's objectification of women's bodies and the heterosexual desire it signifies.

Conclusion

Despite the assumption that children's media are free of sexual content, our analyses suggest that these media depict a rich and pervasive heterosexual landscape. We have illustrated two main ways that G-rated films construct heterosexuality. First, heterosexuality is constructed through depictions of hetero-romantic love as exceptional, powerful, transformative, and magical. Second, heterosexuality is also constructed through depictions of interactions between gendered bodies in which the sexiness of feminine characters is subjected to the gaze of masculine characters. These accounts of heterosexuality extend our understandings of heteronormativity.

First, the finding that heterosexuality is constructed through heterosexiness points to the ways that heteronormativity intersects with gender, race, and class in its constructions. While heterosexuality is normalized and expected, it takes different forms for different sorts of bodies, and this is especially true for heterosexuality outside of romantic relationships. Second, the finding that hetero-romantic love is depicted as exceptional, powerful, and transformative runs counter to current theoretical understandings of heteronormativity's scaffolding being the ordinary, expected, everydayness of heterosexuality. These films show heterosexuality to be just the opposite. Heterosexuality achieves a taken-for-granted status in these films not because it is ordinary but because hetero-romance is depicted as powerful. This finding in no way negates previous understandings of heteronormativity but rather extends another theoretical tenet—that is, that heterosexuality and its normativity are pervasive. Heterosexual exceptionalism extends the pervasiveness of heterosexuality and may serve as a means of inviting investment in it. Furthermore, heterosexuality is glorified here in mass culture but is also ordinary and assumed in everyday life. Thus, its encompassing pervasiveness lends it its power. Both ordinary and exceptional constructions of heterosexuality work to normalize its status because it becomes difficult to imagine anything other than this form of social relationship or anyone outside of these bonds.

Finally, we want to again emphasize that we cannot know what understandings and interpretations children might take away from these films or how they make sense of them alongside all the other social and cultural information they acquire. Others have shown that queer readings of such films are possible for adults (Griffin 2000). Children may have their own queer readings of such films. Without future work with children directly, we cannot know. However, these films are widely viewed by many very young children who are engaged with media-rich worlds. It is likely that these accounts of heterosexuality make it into their understanding of the world in some way, albeit likely with layers of misunderstanding, reinterpretation, and integration with other information. Regardless, these films provide powerful portraits of a multifaceted and pervasive heterosexuality that likely facilitates the reproduction of heteronormativity.

NOTE

1. http://www.washingtonpost.com/wp-srv/style/daily/movies/100million/article.htm.

REFERENCES

Arnold, Thomas K. 2005. "Kids' DVDs Are in a Growth Spurt." *USA Today.* http://www.usatoday.com/life/movies/news/2005-04-04-kids-dvds_x.htm.

Best, Raphaela. 1983. *We've All Got Scars: What Boys and Girls Learn in Elementary School.* Bloomington: Indiana University Press.

Byrne, Eleanor, and Martin McQuillan. 1999. *Deconstructing Disney.* London: Pluto Press.

Crawley, Alisha M., D. R. Anderson, A. Wilder, M. Williams, and A. Santomero. 1999. "Effects of Repeated Exposures to a Single Episode of the Television Program *Blue's Clues* on the Viewing Behaviors and Comprehension of Preschool Children." *Journal of Educational Psychology* 91:630–637.

Emerson, Robert, Rachel Fretz, and Linda Shaw. 1995. *Writing Ethnographic Fieldnotes.* Chicago: University of Chicago Press.

Giroux, Henry A. 1996. "Animating Youth: The Disneyfication of Children's Culture." In *Fugitive Cultures: Race, Violence, and Youth.* New York: Routledge.

———. 1997. "Are Disney Movies Good for Your Kids?" In *Kinderculture: The Corporate Construction of Childhood* (ed. Shirley R. Steinberg and Joe L. Kincheloe). Boulder, CO: Westview. pp. 53–67.

Gotz, Maya, Dafna Lemish, Amy Aidman, and Hyesung Moon. 2005. *Media and the Make Believe Worlds of*

Children: When Harry Potter Meets Pokemon in Disneyland. Mahwah, NJ: Lawrence Erlbaum.

Griffin, Sean. 2000. *Tinker Belles and Evil Queens: The Walt Disney Company from the Inside Out.* New York: New York University Press.

Hadley, Kathryn Gold, and Sandi Kawecka Nenga. 2004. "From Snow White to Digimon: Using Popular Media to Confront Confucian Values in Taiwanese Peer Cultures." *Childhood* 11(4): 515–536.

Hurley, Dorothy L. 2005. "Seeing White: Children of Color and the Disney Fairy Tale Princess." *Journal of Negro Education* 74:221–232.

Ingraham, Chrys. 1999. *White Weddings: Romancing Heterosexuality in Popular Culture.* New York: Routledge.

Jackson, Stevi. 2006. "Gender, Sexuality and Heterosexuality: The Complexity (and Limits) of Heteronormativity." *Feminist Theory* 7:105–21.

Johnson, Paul. 2005. *Love, Heterosexuality, and Society.* London: Routledge.

Junn, Ellen N. 1997. Media Portrayals of Love, Marriage & Sexuality for Child Audiences. Paper presented at the biennial meeting of the Society for Research in Child Development, Washington, DC.

Kelley, P., D. Buckingham, and H. Davies. 1999. "Talking Dirty: Sexual Knowledge and Television." *Childhood* 6:221–242.

Kim, J. L., C. L. Sorsoll, K. Collins, and B. A. Zylbergold. 2007. "From Sex to Sexuality: Exposing the Heterosexual Script on Primetime Network Television." *Journal of Sex Research* 44:145.

Kitzinger, Celia. 2005. "Heteronormativity in Action: Reproducing the Heterosexual Nuclear Family in After-Hours Medical Calls." *Social Problems* 52:477–498.

Lacroix, Celeste. 2004. "Images of Animated Others: The Orientalization of Disney's Cartoon Heroines from *The Little Mermaid* to *The Hunchback of Notre Dame.*" *Popular Communication* 2:213–229.

Lancaster, Roger. 2003. *The Trouble with Nature.* Berkeley: University of California Press.

Mares, M. L. 1998. "Children's Use of VCRs." *Annals of the American Academy of Political and Social Science* 557:120–131.

Martin, Karin A. 2009. "Normalizing Heterosexuality: Mothers' Assumptions, Talk, and Strategies with Young Children." *American Sociological Review* 74:190–207.

Martin, Karin A., Katherine Luke, and Lynn Verduzco-Baker. 2007. "The Sexual Socialization of Young Children: Setting the Agenda for Research." In *Advances in Group Processes,* vol. 6, *Social Psychology of Gender* (ed. Shelly Correll). Oxford, UK: Elsevier Science. pp. 231–260.

Mo, W., and W. Shen. 2000. "A Mean Wink at Authenticity: Chinese Images in Disney's *Mulan.*" *New Advocate* 13:129–142.

Motion Picture Association of America. 2010. "Classification and Rating Rules." Motion Picture Association of America, Inc. Sherman Oaks, CA: National Asosciation of Theatre Owners, Inc. http://filmratings.com/downloads/rating_rules.pdf. Accessed September 18, 2015.

Mulvey, Laura. 1975. "Visual Pleasure and Narrative Cinema." *Screen* 16:6–18.

Nguyen, Mimi. 1998. "A Feminist Fantasia, Almost." *San Jose Mercury News,* July 5.

Pewewardy, Cornel. 1996. "The Pocahontas Paradox: A Cautionary Tale for Educators." *Journal of Navajo Education* 14:20–25.

Renold, Emma. 2002. "Presumed Innocence: (Hetero) Sexual, Heterosexist and Homophobic Harassment among Primary School Girls and Boys." *Childhood* 9:415–434.

———. 2005. *Girls, Boys, and Junior Sexualities: Exploring Children's Gender and Sexual Relations in the Primary School.* London: Routledge Falmer.

Rideout, V., E. A. Vandewater, and E. A. Wartella. 2003. *Zero to Six: Electronic Media in the Lives of Infants, Toddlers, and Preschoolers.* Washington, DC: Henry J. Kaiser Family Foundation.

Rubin, Gayle. 1984. "Thinking Sex: Notes for a Radical Theory of the Politics of Sexuality." In *Pleasure and Danger* (ed. Carol Vance). Boston: Routledge. pp. 100–133.

Schmitt, K. L., D. R. Anderson, and P. A. Collins. 1999. "Form and Content: Looking at Visual Features of Television." *Developmental Psychology* 35:1156–1167.

Schor, Juliet B. 2004. *Born to Buy: The Commercialized Child and the New Consumer Culture.* New York: Scribner.

Thomas, Susan Gregory. 2007. *Buy, Buy, Baby: How Consumer Culture Manipulates Parents.* New York: Houghton Mifflin.

Thompson, T. L., and E. Zerbinos. 1995. "Gender Roles in Animated Cartoons: Has the Picture Changed in 20 Years?" *Sex Roles: A Journal of Research* 32:651–673.

Thorne, Barrie. 1993. *Gender Play: Girls and Boys in School.* New Brunswick, NJ: Rutgers University Press.

Tobin, Joseph. 2000. *"Good Guys Don't Wear Hats": Children's Talk about the Media.* Williston, VT: Teachers College Press.

Ward, L. Monique. 1995. "Talking about Sex: Common Themes about Sexuality in the Prime-Time Television Programs Children and Adolescents View Most." *Journal of Youth and Adolescence* 24:595–615.

———. 2003. "Understanding the Role of Entertainment Media in the Sexual Socialization of American Youth: A Review of Empirical Research." *Developmental Review* 23:347–388.

Witt, Susan D. 2000. "The Influence of Television on Children's Gender Role Socialization." *Childhood Education* 76:322–24.

Questions

1. Aren't movies just for fun? Why study media? What aspects of social life do media inform? How do media influence people? Does studying media imply that we are passive consumers who simply emulate what we see? In what ways are children's media different from adult media? How are they similar?

2. What are the two themes regarding heterosexuality identified by the researchers? How do G-rated movies portray heterosexuality as both exceptional and natural? How do films portray friendships and family relationships differently? What transformative powers does hetero-romantic love bring to its bearers? How do these films portray women and men's bodies differently? What roles do race, ethnicity, and skin tone play in portrayals of sexiness?

3. How do the two themes identified here create and reinforce categorical boundaries between people? How are they related to power and resource control?

4. Think back to your own childhood. If you watched movies, which was your favorite? In your memory, how did the movie portray heterosexuality? Race? Class? Disability? Go back and re-watch it. Were your recollections accurate? How do you remember interacting with the movie as a child? Did you purchase merchandise from it? Did you pretend to be characters? Did you act out heterosexual romance when doing so? How did you adapt your play? How does your form of interacting with media compare to the research on how people interact with it? If you are a parent, how do your children interact with movies and children's characters? Have you tried to shape their consumption of these movies and their related products? Why or why not? How easy or hard has it been? Have you been successful? Why or why not?

5. The authors restricted their analysis to films between 1990 and 2005. In the decade or so since, attitudes about sexuality and civil rights have shifted dramatically, as has the political and legal landscape for people who identify as GLBT or are in same-sex relationships. Do you think that the authors' data are thusly out of date? How do you think that children's movies have changed since then? Now, do some analysis as a class. Since 2005, several G-rated movies (*Toy Story 3, Monsters University, Cars, WALL-E, Ratatouille, Cars 2, Dr. Seuss' Horton Hears a Who!, Rio, Rio 2, Alvin and the Chipmunks: Chipwrecked*) have grossed over $100 million. But PG-rated movies have become even bigger business: *Frozen, Despicable Me, Despicable Me 2, Alice in Wonderland, Shrek the Third, Harry Potter and the Half-Blood Prince, Up, The LEGO Movie, Night at the Museum, Maleficent, Shrek Forever After, Brave, Oz the Great and Powerful, National Treasure: Book of Secrets, Alvin and the Chipmunks, Alvin and the Chipmunks: The Squeakquel, How to Train Your Dragon, Madagascar 3: Europe's Most Wanted, Kung Fu Panda, Dr. Seuss' The Lorax,* and *Tangled* have each grossed over $200 million. What are the restrictions on PG movies? Do production companies now prefer a PG rating? Do some research to find out. Then, break your class into pairs (or 3s/4s), and have each group analyze a different G/PG movie from the preceding list. Examine the themes around hetero-romance described in this article but also as related to social class and disability. How are the themes the same as and different from those described by Martin and Kazyak? Now construct a grid of themes with the entire class. What is the broader significance of your findings?

10

Diversity in the Lean Automobile Factory: Doing Class through Gender, Disability, and Age

PATRIZIA ZANONI

In April 2013, the Associated Press announced it was dropping "illegal immigrant" from its stylebook, and it would no longer characterize people themselves as "illegal." Senior Vice President and Executive Editor Kathleen Carroll explained that this decision followed earlier ones to drop "undocumented immigrants" because of its vagueness and inaccuracy and "schizophrenics" in favor of people-first language that reserved labels for actions (e.g., "someone diagnosed with schizophrenia"). (You can read about this decision on the AP's April 2, 2013 blog or here: http://blog.ap.org/2013/04/02/illegal-immigrant-no-more/.) Instead of describing people as illegal, then, the AP decided to use "illegal" to label people's actions only. And rather than assuming that people were in the United States illegally or accepting the carte blanch label of groups as illegally in the United States, they would be specific about people's actual situations and provide attribution to back up claims about legal status. The AP dropped the term "alien" entirely (outside of when directly quoting someone).

Why the fuss? Because "words matter," as Kleinman, Ezzell, and Frost (2009) eloquently explained in their extended criticism of "bitch." Kleinman et al. show that words not only reflect social life but shape it. Words are symbols, which illuminate shared meanings; and we use them to stake out claims about what is the truth, who matters, and how people should react to each other. Language is one tool used by the powerful to maintain their control. They use it to define reality as they see it (e.g., the victors write the history), to discredit others (e.g., those people are unqualified to have a say), and to justify their own hoarding of resources (e.g., only people like me should vote).

Language is also a tool used by the oppressed to challenge their subordination. By reclaiming words, shifting their cultural meanings, and presenting new and positive meanings, people together boldly claim, "I am not who you say I am! I have humanity! Treat me like the equal that I am!"

Language choice is central to the process of othering, or the creation of outsiders as fundamentally different from and inferior to insiders. When people describe newcomers as "aliens," a term derived from the Latin *alius,* meaning "other," they are claiming that newcomers are the other. They are not just unwelcome but undesirable and unworthy of what they, the insiders, are worthy of.

As Zanoni shows in the following selection, othering is a complex process of boundary making accomplished through language, interpretation, interaction, resource allocation, and policy. Her ethnography of a Belgian plant of a U.S.-based multinational car company analyzes how CarCo management and policy used "diversity" to position anyone who was not a fit and able middle-aged white man into an unproductive and therefore less valuable worker. While the ubiquity of "diversity" at the plant and the company's commitment to it seem progressive on the surface, Zanoni's analysis shows how "diversity" became a tool for exploiting workers. Pressure to be increasingly efficient and productive led management to characterize "diverse" workers as different from and less capable than the workers around whom the work was built. Because "diverse" workers were seen as problematic and less valuable, their work was outsourced and they were laid off during restructuring. Language was a tool for accomplishing material oppression.

Zanoni's study leads the reader to question what is otherwise taken-for-granted at the plant: How did striving for diversity get flipped on its head from an empowering act to an oppressive one? Why did only one employee question defining dominant workers as the norm that CarCo built the work around? Should efficiency be valued above all else? If diversity itself isn't the cure-all, what, if anything, is?

Finally, Zanoni's research raises the important issue of how being othered gets internalized in ways that divide people who have common material interests. The workers themselves came to adopt the perspectives about diversity of management, even though it led to increasingly more work. This demonstrates how othering in part produces a sense of superiority in the dominant group.

References

Kleinman, Sherryl, Matthew Ezzell, and Corey Frost. 2009. "Reclaiming Critical Analysis: The Social Harms of 'Bitch.'" *Sociological Analysis* 3(1): 46–68.

[Organizational] studies show that inequality results from discursive and material practices systematically associating high-rank, high-status jobs with white, male identities, and, conversely, constructing white males as being suitable for high-rank, high-status jobs—that is, organizations and social identities are seen as mutually constitutive. On the one hand social identities are re-defined through the social relations in the organization, so that categories such as "woman," "Black," "Muslim," and "old" acquire new, context-specific meanings and connotations reflecting such relations (Janssens and Zanoni 2005; Zanoni and Janssens 2004). On the other, social identities are themselves seen as structuring principles of organizations (Nkomo 1992).

This study intends to make an empirical and theoretical contribution to the critical literature by analyzing how "diversity" at once reflects underlying class relations and is implicated in their reproduction. I first show how the meanings acquired by socio-demographic identities in an organization are shaped by the specific positions of "different" workers, that is, labor, within the capitalist mode of production. I then demonstrate how such meanings in turn inform managerial practices that reproduce unequal class relations. The theoretical argument is made by drawing on empirical data from CarCo, an automobile factory located in Belgium which is, paradoxically, renowned for being a "best case" for diversity. A class-centered analysis allows unveiling structural

exclusion practices behind a highly developed diversity management program.

Conceptual Approaches to Class and Socio-Demographic Identities

Overall, understandings of class can be grouped under two main types.

A first type conceives of class as the exploitative relation between capital and labor resulting from their distinct position in the capitalist mode of production. According to Marx, in capitalism one group of individuals—labor—is forced to sell its labor power for a wage for its subsistence as it does not own the means of production. Another group of individuals—capitalists—owns the means of production and hires labor to produce goods and services. Capital is in the position of exploiting labor by paying wages lower than the value of the product of labor. Exploitation thus refers to the illegitimate appropriation by capital of the surplus-value produced by labor in the labor process (Braverman 1974; Marx 1976).

Class relations are further inherently tense because of the so-called "indeterminacy of labor," that is, the fact that "the precise amount of effort to be extracted cannot be 'fixed' before the engagement of workers, machinery and products for purposeful (profitable within capitalism) action in the labor process" (Smith 2006: 390). As a result, labor struggles for more compensation for less effort, and management, for less compensation for more effort. So conceptualized, class refers to a historically specific type of instrumental, exploitative relation between capital and labor resulting from the capitalist mode of production. In Marxist theory, individuals located in similar positions within the capitalist mode of production are expected to develop a common class consciousness reflecting such positioning, although this assumption has been the object of much critique (Wills 2008).

A second type of understanding conceives of class in a broader sense, at the macro-level of society. Here too individuals are classified into two groups: the working class and the bourgeoisie, although sometimes the middle class or petite bourgeoisie is added as a third social group. Yet in this case such classification is not directly tied to the relations of production. Rather, it is based on the grounds of property and power (E. O. Wright 1997), consciousness (Thompson 1983), style, accent, and attire (Anthias 2001; Bourdieu 1984; Scully and Blake-Beard 2006), or various combinations of these (Resnick and Wolff 2003). Independent of the criterion used to put individuals in either the working class or the bourgeoisie, class stands in this case as a specific type of social stratification (Anthias 2001).

There is a long tradition of scholarly work attempting to theorize the relation between socio-demographic identities—above all gender and "race"—and class, regardless of how the latter might be conceptualized. Positions vary on whether these are separate systems of oppression and how they interlock (i.e., Acker 2006; Collins 1986; Hartmann 1981; Young 1980). Often the debate has revolved around which system should be given theoretical primacy. For instance, unsatisfied with classical Marxist interpretations of patriarchal relations as ancillary to class relations (Engels [1884] 1972), "radical feminists" see patriarchal sexual relations as the main source of women's oppression (Eisenstein 1977). Others, inspired by Marxian materialism, conceive patriarchy as a specific mode of class relations (Gimenez 1978). Underlying different positions are more fundamental debates on the relation between the "economic" and the "cultural" or the "material" and the "ideological" (Bernans 2002; Butler 1998; Fraser 1998).

More recently, under the impulse of the scholarly work of Black feminists, standpoint theory (Hill Collins 2000; Harding 2004) and intersectionality theory (Crenshaw et al. 1995; McCall 2005; McDowell 2008;

Minow 1997; Yuval-Davis 2006) have been advanced as new ways to conceptualize power relations as emerging from individuals' simultaneous position at the "crossroad" of different social identities—that is, gender, "race"/ethnicity, and class—in a variety of contexts, including the workplace (i.e., Adib and Guerrier 2003; Boogaard and Roggeband 2010; Holvino 2010). Regardless of their distinct accents, in all of these arguments single identities do not have ontological primacy over one another, but rather are seen as interlocking in specific ways depending on the historical context and the specific situation in which relations take place.

Following these views, in this study, I investigate the interlocking of a number of socio-demographic identities—"diversity"—with class within an organization. Acknowledging the key role of context, and drawing on the insights from my previous work (Janssens and Zanoni 2005; Zanoni and Janssens 2004, 2007), I argue that in work settings class relations operate as a master matrix of power onto which other social identities become anchored. Class is here conceptualized as the social identity (capital versus labor) that defines individuals in organizations by virtue of their distinct positions within the capitalist relations of production (Braverman 1974; Marx 1976; Resnick and Wolff 2003). Class relations operate as a master matrix of power because organizations are fundamentally structured by labor processes constituting individuals as either labor—resources to be deployed for the generation of economic value and profit-making—or as capital—those entitled to that profit because of their ownership of the means of production.

The study applies this theoretical perspective to show how, on the one hand, the meanings of socio-demographic identities such as gender, age and (dis)ability—that is, diversity—at CarCo are informed by underlying class relations and, on the other, how in turn such meanings inform class relations between labor and capital. In the following paragraphs I introduce the company and elaborate on the methodology of the study; next I describe and analyze the case. Finally, I reflect on the theoretical insights and contributions that may be derived from it.

CarCo: A "Best Case" of Diversity Management

CarCo, the local branch of a U.S. multinational corporation, is renowned in Belgium for its diversity management. At the time of the study it had a broad array of diversity management initiatives including a local diversity council, an anti-discrimination clause in the company bylaws, regular reports to a worldwide diversity manager about the composition of personnel by gender, nationality, and age, an initiative to recruit more young female engineers, yearly monitoring of line managers' initiatives and perceptions on diversity, a printed diversity newsletter in various languages, and e-mail diversity news. The company had a diversity plan to promote the employment of ethnic minorities, had screened the selection procedures for biases, had an "action plan" to develop best diversity management practices, had diversity training for line managers, HR personnel, and trade union delegates, had a community project connecting supervisors and young migrants, and had integration projects for young migrants and migrants with higher education.

At the time of the study, CarCo had 9,000 employees and produced about 400,000 vehicles a year on two production lines. One of the largest employers in the region, it did not have a tradition of social conflict, despite a negative trend in employment since the early 1990s, when it counted almost 14,000 employees. The company was located in a historical immigration area, and at the time of the study 17 percent of its personnel were foreign nationals and—according to an estimation of the HR manager—about 40 percent had foreign origins. Different from other automobile factories in Belgium, CarCo had no history of inter-ethnic conflict despite the high share of personnel with a foreign background. The average age was 40 years for blue-collar employees and 45 years for white-collar ones, reflecting CarCo's origins in the mid-1960s and low personnel turnover. Similar to other automobile factories, only 10 percent of the employees were women, mostly in administrative functions. Altogether women represented only 8 percent of blue-collar workers and 5 percent of factory supervisors. Finally, 2 percent of the employees had a certified disability, yet the HR department estimated about 7 percent suffered from work-specific and temporary physical impairments.

The Ethnographic Study

The case study is based on data collected through participant observation, semi-structured interviews, internal and external documentation, and photographs. I first came in contact with the company in the early 2000s when I interviewed the HR director and the HR manager on their diversity policies. I later joined a study on diversity and diversity management in five "best case" companies, one of which was CarCo. Twenty semi-structured interviews from that study are part of the data included here. These interviews included employees with diverse demographic profiles in terms of gender, culture, or religion. Already familiar with the company, in 2003 I extended the original study through fieldwork, collecting additional data through interviews and participant observation in the factory.

The fieldwork lasted three months, during which I spent three to four days a week at the CarCo factory, following the work schedule of the assembly personnel working one of the two day shifts Monday through Friday, from 6 am to 2 pm or from 2 pm to 10 pm on alternate weeks. I had free access to the factory premises, made lots of informal contacts, and became relatively familiar with the workers and team leaders of various teams and all supervisors. Observation and informal communication started in the factory parking lot and continued through the factory gate, into the locker rooms, the shop floor, the cafeteria, the factory offices, and the grounds around the factory. I regularly attended supervisors' meetings and spent all breaks with employees. I did about 200 hours of participant observation, writing down my observations and impressions in a log book. During my fieldwork I carried out 40 interviews with supervisors, team leaders, operators, the HR manager, HR clerks, the company doctor, and one of the company nurses. The interviews covered respondents' personal background, professional experience, current job, relations with team members, team leader, and superiors, general questions about working at CarCo, as well as specific questions on diversity and diversity management. I also collected internal documents on the company and its history, the HR and diversity management, training programs, and the production system, and I took 150 photographs of the shop floor.

The line I studied assembled many different models of one type of vehicle, a mature product. It was a rather outdated line with many physically demanding jobs. Within some months, production was to be transferred to a low-cost country with a growing market for this vehicle. Employees were aware these were their last months in their jobs and with their colleagues and that they would be soon moved, either to the other assembly line or the promised new line. During my fieldwork, production was cut back and state-subsidized unemployment days were introduced. Yet, on the positive side, the mother company had promised major investments on a new production line, for which substantial public financial support had been made available. The atmosphere changed dramatically, however, in the fall, when CarCo announced it would cut 3,000 jobs, mostly in production. Though this restructuring was not completely unexpected—automobile sales were stagnant and competitors had also heavily cut production and personnel—employees had not imagined a downsizing of this scale. Since the restructuring, I have been collecting articles in the national press and kept informal communication with some of my informants.

In a first phase of the data analysis, I identified all excerpts on diversity in the transcripts of the interviews and the CarCo internal documentation. These excerpts referred either to diversity as a general category or to specific socio-demographic identities such as gender, disability, age, physical characteristics (i.e., height, strength, dexterity), language, religion, and culture. Next to a large number of excerpts that related diversity and identities to generally unproblematic interpersonal relations in the factory, a smaller, yet substantive number of excerpts (160) constructed diversity and identities in relation to production. This case study focuses on the latter. Within this data, most (130) constructed diversity by relating socio-demographic groups' specific (physical) characteristics or skills to the requirements of lean production. In 87% of the cases, they pointed to the problems they created for production, while the remaining 13% simply mentioned the differences as such. In this category of excerpts, mentioned differences were, in decreasing order of frequency, gender (female workers), disability, bodily characteristics, language, age (older workers), religion, culture, and a general diversity category. In many excerpts, various differences were mentioned at once. A smaller, yet significant, group of excerpts (30) constructed diversity as workers' strategy to resist work. These abstracts mostly mentioned, in decreasing order of frequency, the following "differences": disability, age (young workers), gender (female workers), culture, religion, and bodily characteristics. Finally, I identified all the excerpts in which diversity and "differences" were connected to organizational action to increase the

company's profitability and competitiveness. These data included two categories: outsourcing and restructuring.

The Dark Side of the Best Case: Instrumental Constructions of Diversity at CarCo

At CarCo, diversity was frequently constructed in instrumental terms by connecting differences to lean production. To contextualize these discursive constructions, I first describe the production system the company had introduced in the early 2000s, based on just-in-time and total quality management (JIT/TQM). Widely utilized in the automobile industry, lean production is a way of substantially cutting costs by "producing only the necessary products in the necessary quantities at the necessary times" (Miltenburg 1989, 192; Tsai 1995) and is notorious for its effectiveness in intensifying work (Barker 1993; Delbridge 1995; Graham 1994; Sewell 1998).

At CarCo, work was intensified by evening out production through line balancing and product sequencing. That is, the line was balanced by designing jobs as to keep cycle time—the time interval separating consecutive products on the line—on different models as constant as possible, so that operators could carry out different tasks on each vehicle always within the time at their disposal. Product sequencing—"the mix"—meant that models were fed into the assembly line in an optimal order, such that lack of time for tasks on one vehicle was tentatively compensated by exceeding time for tasks on the next. A more stable production sequence allowed standardizing jobs through formal job descriptions prescribing how each task was to be carried out and in which order, stimulating workers to develop routines and work faster, increasing their productivity. Twice a year productivity gains were harvested by the company by eliminating jobs and redistributing tasks over the remaining ones, a process called, ironically, "commitment." At the same time, labor was made more flexible. Operators were split up into small teams and expected to know at least three jobs on their station so that they could be optimally deployed on the line according to changing production needs and absences. Operators on the same team were encouraged to rotate to keep their handiness on different jobs.

With the introduction of TQM, responsibility for the quality of all aspects of the production process was shifted to the shop floor, technology enhanced direct quality control, and an independent quality control department reporting to the European headquarters was created. To reduce costs, all operators were expected to report any mistake they noticed by others upstream, so that it could be fixed during the production process rather than afterwards. To increase teams' sense of responsibility for good quality, the production process was discursively reconfigured as a chain of supplier-client relations. Production and quality data on each section and across shifts were discussed every morning among supervisors and the production manager, exposing poorly performing sections, teams, and operators.

"Unable to Work": Diversity as Labor's Incapacity to Work and Generate Value

Within the extremely demanding lean production system, specific socio-demographic groups of workers were often spoken about by referring to their lack of skills and inability to properly function in the factory. In these negative constructions, physical characteristics were highlighted:

> [Who can do what job] has to do with strength. Not with thinking . . . strength and height. [Workers have to be] quite strong. Like here with the doors, I have women that could do [the jobs], Susan, she would probably be able to learn. And if I start looking, perhaps another two out of the 18 [women] I have. The rest I don't think would, because they don't have the strength. . . . You have to pull hard, that's why. There are also men you can't put on that job, who would not be able to learn. [. . .] The handiness [counts], too. . . . You put somebody on a new job and after two days they can do it, they are handy. Others come back to me and say: "My shoulder hurts, my wrist. . . ." (Male supervisor, middle aged, local background)[1]

In this excerpt women are portrayed as lacking, as a whole, the physical characteristics necessary to carry out the jobs in this section of the line. Although exceptionally strong or handy women can actually do "heavy" jobs and frail or unhandy men cannot, this supervisor clearly associates physical inability with being a woman. The association is so strong that in the factory the term "women's jobs" was used to refer to the few jobs that were "easy" and "light" enough to be carried out by smaller, more lightly built operators—mostly women

but also some men—or by operators "weakened" by age or impairment.

While women represented the largest group of "unable" operators, it was operators with permanent physical impairments whom my informants talked about in the most problematic way:

> Medically impaired people, that is for us really a problem. There are people you can only give a couple of jobs to, you have to let them work less. We have one for instance who has four impairments. He can only replace the batteries of the lift trucks. You can't give him any other job. We take the impairment into consideration, we select a job and discuss it with him. Another has back problems, has been operated, then he cannot lift heavy stuff. It can be for years. . . . Some people cannot work in too bright light, they can't work on the computer the whole day. Others cannot work shifts, they have problems with their bio-rhythm, they get ulcers. So we try not to give them the night shift. (Male supervisor, Ukrainian background)

The physical inability to carry out many factory jobs had particularly negative implications in the lean factory where workers were expected to be flexible and carry out multiple jobs to maximize their own productivity. Flexibility broadened not only the physical but also the mental and relational skills required from all workers. As a result, even when physically healthy, workers over 45 years of age were considered unable to learn new jobs and adapt to new teams to optimally function in the factory:

> People who have worked long here, they are left alone. They say: "Look, the youth you still can use, they can adapt." (Male supervisor, middle aged, local background, emphasis added)

This widespread understanding was reflected in an agreement between the company and the trade unions that workers above 45 be excluded from the requirement to learn two additional jobs.

In a productive system structured around teams in which workers needed to intensively communicate, those who did not speak Dutch were also seen as a problem:

> Everything is more based on teamwork, you depend more on each other, and have to communicate. If you don't know the language you cannot communicate and don't know what your colleague or boss wants. It's a handicap. (Older male HR manager, local background)

Such problems were acute during peak production times, when temporary operators were hired, a large number of whom were first-generation migrants.

Although differences were mostly associated with inability, in a few cases top and line managers mentioned specific positive competences of particular socio-demographic groups. For instance, women were considered better than men at precision jobs, women and the elderly were thought to temper young male operators' aggressiveness, stimulating cooperation, discipline, and productivity, and ethnic minority workers' cultures were seen as contributing to a good climate on the shop floor. Yet these advantages could hardly compensate for the serious problems "different" workers posed to organizing work within lean production. Indeed, the idea of diversity as lack of ability and flexibility was widely shared in the factory. Many male operators told me that the jobs on their station were not suitable for (most) women, the elderly, and the disabled. Female operators themselves, management, the medical staff, and even trade union representatives made similar statements.

The common productive logic shaping the understanding of diversity as inability is well illustrated by a supervisor's answer to my question of how many "impaired" operators he had on his line:

I have one that is pregnant . . . Caroline, who's now mounting panels, has an impairment in her knees. . . . Abdel in his shoulders, Star in her back . . . Guerrini, has no physical impairment but is limited because of his age, B has been having pain in his knees lately, has no permanent impairment, but suffers from pain in his knees . . . Sarah has a hip prosthesis, she can't work on the line, Susan V. has arthritis in her shoulder . . . Marta has problems with her height, because she is very small . . . Morales here has problems with his shoulder and his wrist . . . he can do that job but I can't give him a heavier gun . . . S. has a problem with stress, when I arrived here, he had been on sick leave for a year . . . plus he is missing a piece of his forefinger on his right hand, so he can't do fine work . . . on that job, he has been OK, but if I give him another . . . Johnny goes every month to the hospital to get an injection in his back, otherwise he goes crazy from the pain . . . Eric has a problem in his shoulders, cannot work above shoulder height. These are all permanent medical impairments . . . Then I have Laura with her hearing problems, she cannot work in noisy

environments [because of her hearing device] . . . some people have been here for long, never any problem, and all of a sudden they come up to me: chrome and nickel, allergy. I have to give them another job. I think I've gone through all. How many are they? 10, 12? It's a third of my line, I can give a limited amount of jobs to. (Male supervisor, middle aged, local background)

Tellingly, this respondent mentioned not only official impairments, as I had expected, but also any other "differences" which he had to take into account when assigning work: pregnancy, bodily traits, psychological problems, and allergies. As a supervisor whose main task was to match people to jobs they could carry out, he conceived impairment broadly, as anything—including any identity—limiting one's ability to work. This explicitly instrumental understanding of his (diverse) personnel is inherent to his position as a line manager, for whom labor needs in the first place to produce. Interestingly, he seemed to genuinely care for his people, and enjoyed a good reputation among his staff.

The umbrella term "diversity" was less frequent on the shop floor, where people tended to talk about one or more specific socio-demographic identities. It was used more by the HR personnel, from top management to administrative clerks. However, across the organization, all categories of informants associated differences to some extent with one and the same logic of production. Consider the HR manager's description of the personnel composition:

Eighteen percent of our people do not have the Belgian nationality and about 25% have foreign origins. [. . .] We have about 10% women. We have about 2% with a serious handicap, people for whom we have to look for a suitable job or for whom we have to adapt existing norms. [. . .] If you ask me if there are Catholics or Protestants, I don't know. *It's not important to us, for diversity. As far as we are concerned, it's not directly related to doing the jobs.* (Older male HR manager, local background; emphasis added)

Or the definition of diversity given by an HR clerk in the factory:

I would like to express [diversity] in negative terms: [the challenge is] to organize your teamwork despite your diversity. *Despite the hindrances caused by diversity: language problems, man/woman, ethnic minorities, physical disabilities, things like that. . . .* (Older male HR clerk in the factory, local background; emphasis added)

Both interviewees clearly conceptualize diversity instrumentally, in terms of the work a diverse workforce is expected to carry out in the factory by virtue of their position as labor within the relations of production.

Whereas the business case for diversity commonly links diversity to organizations' financial performance—the bottom line—at CarCo diversity was discursively related to the specific performance of selected groups in the production system. Only one of my informants related it to the generation of economic value. Explaining CarCo's weak competitive position in the automobile market, he told me:

> Why don't you make a car for which men and women can do the jobs? Then you have easier jobs for everybody. We now put the dashboard in. Every shift we have 12 people that have to crawl in the vehicle to hang all kinds of things to it. Why don't you build the dashboard on a carousel, like before? Cables, heating, steer, you can mount everything into it standing, then you check it, and you take it and fix it with two screws. You only need two men in the car. As simple as that. Every company does this, except us. [. . .] *And then you would have 12 women's jobs instead of men's jobs.* . . . Everybody could do them. Even women could handle a heavy pistol, if you are outside, standing, you can hang it on a balancer, but inside the car you can't. And so you can make a woman's job out of a man's job, or a job for everybody. You have to make the production process in function of the man [*sic*] who has to work, not just to make the car look good. [. . .] And if it's easy, then you can put anybody on the job, *and then it's a cheap car.* (Older male supervisor, local background; emphasis added)

This supervisor's words clearly indicate how diversity operates in the factory, as a "proxy" of the limited capacity of specific segments of labor to generate surplus-value. He suggests introducing a more "diversity-friendly" production system, that is, one made of "women's jobs" that everybody can do, to broaden the pool of suitable workers and, conversely, devalue their work, enforcing class relations more favorable to capital. Different from the classical business case rhetoric, diversity increases the company's competitiveness not by creating additional value through additional competencies but by lowering the cost of labor, labor's wage, making products cheaper.

"Unwilling to Work": Diversity as Labor's Resistance to Exploitation

At CarCo, "different" workers were also constructed as less willing to work. In these cases, informants talked about workers' intentional strategic use of their "difference" to evade ("heavy") work. Disability was by large measure the most mentioned trait, followed by age and gender. A supervisor told me:

> Who has a medical impairment here? . . . take any man on my line right now, he says: "The job that I am doing, I don't want it anymore." He wants to get rid of it, and keeps going to the doctor: "I can't, it hurts here, it hurts there," and he gets a medical impairment. And then we take care of the man. So, what's happening here? The good man who does everything keeps doing his job, and the one who says: "They won't get me, I'll get myself an easy job," that one gets a medical impairment. (Older male supervisor, local background)

He further recollected with nostalgia how, in the past, operators who could not do the job were simply laid off and, as a result, other operators became more "reasonable" in their demands.[2] Different from in the previous cases, disability is clearly constructed here in adversarial terms, as a conscious strategy on the part of workers to resist management. To accommodate disability is presented as giving in to workers' demands, losing control over labor. Ironically, a trade union representative made strikingly similar remarks.

The interviewee further indicates the key role of the medical unit in the struggle between management and labor. Whereas the company doctor and nurses were expected to establish which jobs an individual could legitimately be asked to do based on "objective" medical tests, he suggests that workers could obtain certified impairments by insisting long enough. Along the same lines, the HR clerks in the factory stated:

> Some people think they won't have to work on the line anymore because of the impairment they got certified by the medical unit. A lot of people just try to get a nice job through impairment: "I can't do anything else, I want to do that." The biggest problem is to make those people work again once the impairment is gone. (Older male HR clerk in the factory, local background)

Women were also occasionally presented as taking advantage of their "difference." Sometimes they resisted certain jobs in subtle ways, as is well illustrated by the following:

> We were just talking about a woman in the meeting . . . "I can't do it." You already see it from her body language when she comes in. Some of my colleagues saw her and knew she wouldn't do it [a heavy job]. Now, she still can't do [the job] and they want to give her back to me, but I don't want her. Women take advantage of their position, that's for sure. (Older male supervisor, local background)

In other cases, they openly refused "unsuitable" jobs. For instance, a young female trade union representative recounted the following episode:

> Some time ago there was a girl in the B hall. The team leader told her: "You are here and you want to be treated as an equal, then you also have to do the heavier jobs." She answered to him: "The by-laws state that the employer has to give me work that I can physically do." I find this good, if you put them in their place, they shut up. But not everybody can. I know people who work really hard but don't say anything because they are not like that. It's not fair.

A widespread complaint about women was that they frequently asked to go to the bathroom. This was interpreted as a way to take a break from the line. Little could be done, however, as "women have their periods" and, if the team leader refused to stand in for them, they would not hesitate to stop working and call the unions.

It was, however, young workers who were constructed as the most resistant:

> Motivation is important, showing that you want to do it. Not like the youth that comes in these days. I've seen some, mounting mufflers on the other line, from a temporary work agency . . . [they lasted] four hours. There was a body builder, such arms . . . and he said: "What kind of work is this, I'm going home, I don't do this." And then you have skinny, thin men that want to do it. And they are able to. It depends on how you've been raised, I think. I always had to work hard at home. I was also among the last who had to go to the army. There you also get some character. [. . .] I think you work against yourself if you refuse [to do a job]. You always have to try. (Young male operator, local background)

Young male workers were assumed to possess all the necessary mental and physical skills to function properly in the lean production system, and were therefore expected to be able and willing to do all jobs. As their refusal to carry out jobs or to work could not be attributed to any kind of "difference," it was interpreted as resulting from their generation's careless attitude towards work, not as a form of class struggle. It was therefore unanimously condemned, also by co-workers. This interpretation is particularly illuminating considering that young operators had a particularly weak position within the labor force, as temporary personnel in-sourced through an external work agency. They were expected to quickly learn and perform heavy jobs on a line at full speed yet had no prospect of permanent employment, no matter how well they worked.

In these excerpts, specific socio-demographic groups are constructed by referring to their members' active deployment of their "different" identities as unable to work in order to resist managerial control and exploitation. As the data suggest, precisely because certain socio-demographic identities were constructed as inability, they could be re-appropriated by individual workers to claim "lighter" and "easier" work, breaks, and leaves of absence, in the struggle for less effort for their wages. Young workers, who were considered "able," lacked an identity to legitimate their resistance, and were therefore constructed as the most deviant of all. Diversity as "unwillingness to work" additionally constitutes diversity in negative terms by associating it directly to labor's resistance against capital.

The "Dark Side" of the "Best Case": Sacking Diversity through Outsourcing and Restructuring

The negative constructions of diversity were not only anchored in the underlying class relations, they also informed CarCo's strategic action to reproduce such relations in order to enhance the company's competitiveness and profitability. In the years prior to the field study and the months following it, "easy," lower value-added jobs were outsourced and one-third of the workers were laid off through restructuring. Although these decisions were at first sight unrelated to the company's diversity management, a closer look revealed relationships to the company's understandings of "different" workers as "unable and unwilling" and had particularly harmful implications for "different" workers.

Some years prior to the study, the company had outsourced the production of seat covers and the assembly of smaller parts to sub-contractors located in the proximity of the factory:

> Before, they had more sub-assembly, and that was done by women, on a line. Sub-assembly, assembling the pieces before they got to the line. They made ventilator windows, etc., mostly women. They were lighter jobs. All of that is gone, has disappeared or has been outsourced. We don't hear anything about it anymore. They have tried to get rid of the simplest jobs. What is over then? Normally, you try to keep the work on the vehicle itself, the rest you get rid of, that's for somebody else to do. (Older male supervisor, local background)

Through outsourcing, "marginal" phases of the production process with lower added value were eliminated. Yet, it was precisely these operations "of little value" that were carried out by women and "unable" employees. As a result, the company was left with fewer "easy" jobs for these workers. A trade union representative explained:

> Actually it should be the opposite, we should hire people and give them work [instead of outsourcing]. They [CarCo would] rather outsource to a sheltered workshop [employing slightly mentally disabled workers]. They let them do the pre-assembly. But they don't do it to give work to the disabled. They do it [outsourcing] because it's cheaper. They look at it from the economic point of view, efficiency. They are running a company. But they are not good at diversity of the most impaired [inside the company], as we call them here. [. . .] These individuals are victims of the situation. They have to work in teams and in a team you have to keep up or you are out. They get frustrated; those that get excluded. (Male head trade union representative, local background)

Interestingly, by outsourcing "easier" jobs to a sheltered workshop employing disabled people—an apparently "ethical" policy—the company actually diminished its ability to accommodate its own "disabled" workers. Further, this solution enhanced profitability, as sheltered workshops can supply at competitive prices because they are subsidized by the state. Outsourcing externalized to society the costs of lower productivity by the disabled while keeping the more demanding production processes, which generate higher value added, within CarCo, thus decreasing the company's capacity to provide jobs for its own "different" workers.

Further, some months after the field study, CarCo implemented a major restructuring. The company negotiated with trade unions representing a large majority of the employees three criteria to identify who had to leave in order to minimize involuntary layoffs: a pre-retirement scheme for operators aged 50 or above, a monetary bonus for voluntary leaves based on tenure, and a penalty point system. In Belgium pre-retirement has long been a popular way of restructuring companies avoiding lay-offs. Companies and older employees are aligned, as the former get rid of labor whose knowledge and/or physical ability is considered inadequate, and the latter can stop working earlier in their lives. Indeed, the vast majority of Belgian workers are quite happy to retire if they obtain decent benefits.[3] The bonus system was accepted by the unions, as it left it up to individuals whether to leave or stay. Negotiations instead focused on how much employees should receive.

These two measures were complemented by a penalty point system for achieving the desired number of layoffs. This type of agreement was unprecedented in the country. It was based on individuals' suspensions in the last five years, written warnings in the last 15 years, oral warnings in the last two years, unjustified absences, recurrent sick leaves in the last five years, and, as the last criterion, tenure (National newspaper, 8 December 2003: 14).[4, 5] With this agreement, the trade unions consented to sacking less compliant workers, as identified through these criteria which can be seen as best available "proxies of resistance." Of these criteria, only sick leaves raised heavy criticism. A prominent employment law scholar (National newspaper, 8 December 2003: 14) and the representative of a progressive association of lawyers (Press agency, 11 September 2004, retrieved on the Internet) argued in the media that this criterion was against recent anti-discrimination legislation because it penalized workers on the grounds of their health. A few dozen dismissed employees sued the company on the grounds that the sick leave criterion indirectly discriminated based on age, as older operators with longer years in service run a higher risk of getting ill (National popular newspaper, 19 January 2005, retrieved on the Internet).

As a whole, the agreement showed how restructuring was carried out largely at the expense of two groups of "different" workers: the older and the disabled. CarCo could have easily laid off the operators with the shortest tenure, according to the established principle "last in, first out." Yet it was precisely this criterion that was not considered as an option. A trade union representative stated in the press:

> If you lay off all the youth, you put a mortgage on the whole factory. It makes no sense to save jobs now if you have to shut down later on. (National newspaper, 8 December 2003: 14)

The need to keep younger workers was particularly pressing, as the average age of the permanent worker population was increasing due to the halt in hiring in the last years and the policy of addressing peaks in production with temporary employees. The trade unions were clearly co-opted into laying off the least compliant and the least productive groups within labor in the hope to save the most productive core, those who were most likely to meet the increasing demands in terms of productivity, flexibility, and quality. They defended the penalty system as the least of all evils, praising its objectivity and transparency. The elimination of "easy" jobs with low value added through outsourcing and the elimination of "different" workers through restructuring clearly connect the negative constructions of diversity to the company's broader business strategy. It unveils an alternative, "dark" business case of diversity behind the "best" case.

Diversity and Class: Reflections on the CarCo Case

Attempting to get a more fine-grained understanding of the instrumental nature of diversity denounced by the critical literature, the study proposed to analyze this notion from a class perspective. Class is suitable to theoretically underpin the "instrumental" nature of diversity in organizations because it highlights the instrumental nature of labor—including of its diversity—in its relation to capital. It therefore represents a master matrix of power onto which other social identities are anchored in work settings. Based on the empirical case just described, the study shows how the discursive construction of diversity at once reflected existing class relations between capital and labor and was implicated in their material reproduction.

At CarCo, female, disabled, and older workers' "different" identities were discursively constructed in two highly problematic ways. Against the common rhetoric of the business case of diversity, these workers were constituted as less able, less flexible, and less valuable labor on the one hand and as less compliant labor on the other. Both discursive constructions clearly reflect the instrumental relation between a socio-demographically heterogeneous labor force and capital, for which such labor is in the first place a resource to be exploited through the labor process. These constructions of "different" labor as inherently less exploitable further informed class relations. Indeed, to enhance the company's profitability and competitiveness, CarCo attempted to increase the surplus-value extraction from labor by eliminating older and less healthy workers in restructuring and outsourcing low value-added segments of the production process that could be carried out by female, older, and disabled workers.

These findings are in line with the extant critical research showing how certain workers are discursively constituted through social identities such as gender, race/ethnicity, age, etc. in negative, instrumental terms as having inferior or no skills and being less valuable labor carrying out less valuable work (cf. Cockburn 1985; M. W. Wright 2001; Zanoni and Janssens 2004). The study, however, expands the literature by theorizing how such instrumental discursive constructions are entangled with the material reproduction of class relations. Namely, class dynamics are played out along multiple socio-demographic identity lines by defining labor through such identities, inscribing them in the capitalist mode of production. Through such inscription, they are rendered intelligible in terms of their (lack of) potential to yield surplus-value for capital (cf. Bernans 2002; Zanoni and Janssens 2004), and thus indissolubly linked to economic value. Such inscription legitimizes managerial action upon a diverse labor force aimed at maximizing surplus-value, in the logic of class relations structuring organizations (Noon 2007; Squires 2006).

Starting from the key idea that relations between capital and labor are structurally tense due to the indeterminacy of labor (Smith 2006), the CarCo case appears to indicate that discursive constructions of socio-demographic identities operate as proxies of the (lower) labor potential of specific socio-demographic groups within the workforce, reducing the indeterminacy of their labor for both parties. Especially for line managers, identities determined labor by postulating that workers belonging to certain groups would not be able to make the effort necessary to function in lean production, constituting them as "unable," and thus less desirable and less valuable, labor. These negative constructions were, however, widely shared by other company actors including trade union representatives, white collar employees, HR managers and even operators, independent of their socio-demographic profile. Their plausibility rested on the association of identities with skills required by a production system which—everybody knew—imposed ever higher demands on labor. In this sense, diversity appears to effectively serve CarCo's exploitation.

Nonetheless, the construction of diversity as "unwillingness to work" also indicates that once differences are intelligible through the relations of production, they are not only deployable by management to better control labor but can also be potentially re-appropriated by labor to resist such control. Indeed, according to many of my informants, some "different" workers also actively appropriated their negative identity as "unable" to claim jobs commensurate to their allegedly lower ability, to which they are entitled by Belgian labor legislation, thereby individually resisting exploitation. This class struggle is not collectively fought by the trade unions but rather by individual workers at the company doctor's office (cf. Holmqvist 2009). Whether an individual claims less demanding work because of his or her limited ability or as a way to resist exploitation remains necessarily an open question, as identities do not completely resolve the indeterminacy of labor at the individual level. Yet such individual resistance strategies appear likely to be effective in an institutional context characterized by advanced legislation protecting workers from arbitrary demands and dismissal by management and in which trade unions are present to enforce its implementation.

Yet it is precisely this highly protective institutional context for labor that helps explain why the company resorted to structural measures to increase its profitability. Outsourcing and restructuring enacted class relations more favorable to capital by eliminating, respectively, the less flexible and less productive groups—that is, "different" groups—and the lower value-added production processes that were carried out by them. Future diversity research might consider further examination of how identities and diversity are related not only as innovative ways to control but also as ways to resist control (Dick and Hyde 2006; Van Laer and Janssens 2010; Zanoni and Janssens 2007), and how such class dynamics are related to specific institutional contexts in which they are embedded. While the idea that differences can be used to better exploit is widely accepted, the converse possibility, that differences might be better used to resist exploitation, has been less investigated.

The industrial relations literature has traditionally held that highlighting differences within the labor force divides it, harming its capacity to resist (Edwards 1979; Harvey 1993; Hyman 1994; Selmi and McUsic 2002). However, some Marxist scholars in the field of geography have embraced diversity suggesting that today, to be effective, the struggles of a diverse labor force should be conducted beyond the workplace, through alliances with a variety of social actors in the wider community including community organizations, contractors, clients, the media, and the political world (Gibson-Graham, Resnik, and Wolf 2000; Wills 2008). While such an approach is plausible in deunionized service industries in highly liberal economies such as the ones studied in this literature, it seems far from the CarCo case, where diversity appears to be anchored in "older"-type class relations, still characterized by protective legislation and a strong union, despite clear market pressures on the global automobile sector. Within the managerial literature on diversity, the CarCo case is instructive because it sheds light on the problematic qualification of an organization as a "best case" of diversity. Various diversity management initiatives testified to the company's goodwill concerning diversity. Indeed, the company had a good reputation as a diversity-friendly employer and a corporate citizen. For instance, the ethnic composition of the workforce reflected the region's population, and inter-ethnic relations were relatively unproblematic. However, a deeper analysis of the company's strategic actions to ensure its competitiveness and profitability showed how they disproportionately targeted workers that were considered less productive precisely by virtue of their "difference." These findings highlight the limitations of so-called "best practices" which ameliorate specific groups' positions in the organization yet do so in ways that leave existing relations between capital and labor unquestioned. As labor is expected in the first place to generate value for the company, diversity is welcomed and even celebrated only if it is functional for (or at least compatible with) generating such value. When this fundamental condition ceases to be met, even "best cases" are likely to reveal unexpected "dark sides."

Conclusion

In this chapter, I have proposed to critically analyze diversity in an automobile company by re-conceptualizing the notion of diversity through class. I have argued that, once diversity is understood as a set of socio-demographic identities inscribed within class relations, it is no longer a simple, under-theorized, container concept functional for management goals. Rather, it becomes an analytical tool for better understanding how inequality is produced and maintained in contemporary organizations. Inequality emerges from class relations, the exploitative relation of capital to labor, whereby labor is socially constructed as made up of individuals with distinct socio-demographic identities, reflecting unequal potential to produce economic value and to be exploited. While I do not claim an ontological primacy of class over other identity axes, I argue that class relations fundamentally structure contemporary organizations, providing in these contexts a matrix of power onto which other identities are grafted. In this perspective, diversity does not simply intersect with class, but is contingent upon it for its very meaning within the organizational context. There exists no diversity, that is, no socio-demographic identity with an economic value tag attached to it, outside the logic of capitalist organizing.

The analysis of the CarCo case illustrates that diversity, as an umbrella concept under which many identities are subsumed, can be critically re-appropriated to designate the same exploitative rationale informing the meaning of a variety of "different" identities in a workplace. The case further suggests that, precisely by virtue of its inscription in class relations, the notion of diversity potentially carries within it its own contradiction the possibility of re-appropriation by individual workers to contest their own exploitation, although such resistance might in turn trigger more antagonistic strategies by capital, along the very logic of class relations.

Notes

1. All names used in the article are fictitious.
2. It is unclear whether this representation of past employment relations is accurate. The company was highly unionized from its beginnings, excluding the possibility of systematic arbitrary lay-offs by management. No other informant mentioned such a possibility, although many referred to the military style that reigned on the shop floor in the past.
3. The societal costs of pre-retirement are, however, enormous, as an ever bigger share of the population grows older and the average professionally active life is among the shortest in the world (European Industrial Relations On-line 2001).
4. Of the 2,900 operators who left the company, about 1,200 pre-retired, nearly 1,000 "voluntarily" left (yet some did so anticipating they would be laid off based on the penalty point system), and 750 were actually laid off based on their penalty points.
5. Names and exact publication dates of the newspapers have been omitted to protect the anonymity of the company.

References

Acker, J. 2006. *Class Questions: Feminist Answers.* Lanham, MD: Rowman and Littlefield.

Adib, A., and Guerrier, Y. 2003. "The Interlocking of Gender with Nationality, Race, Ethnicity and Class: The Narratives of Women in Hotel Work." *Gender Work and Organization* 10(4): 413–432.

Anthias, F. 2001. "The Material and the Symbolic in Theorizing Social Stratification: Issues of Gender, Ethnicity and Class." *British Journal of Sociology* 52(3): 367–390.

Barker, J. R. 1993. "Tightening the Iron Cage: Concertive Control in Self Managing Teams." *Administrative Science Quarterly* 38(3): 408–437.

Bernans, D. 2002. "Merely Economic? Surplus Extraction, Maldistribution, and Misrecognition." *Rethinking Marxism* 14(1): 49–66.

Boogaard, B., and Roggeband, C. 2010. "Paradoxes of Intersectionality: Theorizing Inequality in the Dutch Police Force through Structure and Agency." *Organization* 17(1): 53–75.

Bourdieu, P. 1984. *Distinction: A Social Critique of the Judgement of Taste.* London: Routledge.

Braverman, H. 1974. *Labor and Monopoly Capital: The Degradation of Work in the Twentieth Century.* New York: Monthly Review Press.

Butler, J. 1998. "Merely Cultural." *New Left Review* 227 (January/February): 33–44.

Cockburn, C. 1985. *Machinery of Dominance: Women, Men and Technical Know-how.* London: Pluto.

Collins, P. H. 1986. "Learning from the Outsider within: The Sociological Significance of Black Feminist Thought." *Social Problems* 33(6): S14–S32.

Crenshaw, K., Gotanda, N., Peller, G., and Kendall, T. 1995. *Critical Race Theory: The Key Writings that Formed the Movement.* New York: New Press.

Delbridge, R. 1995. "Surviving JIT: Control and Resistance in a Japanese Transplant." *Journal of Management Studies* 32(6): 803–817.

Dick, P., and Hyde, R. 2006. "Consent as Resistance, Resistance as Consent: Re-reading Part-Time Professionals' Acceptance of Their Marginal Positions." *Gender, Work and Organization* 13(6): 543–564.

Edwards, R. 1979. *Contested Terrain: The Transformation of the Workplace in the Twentieth Century.* London: Heinemann.

Eisenstein, Z. 1977. "Constructing a Theory of Capitalist Patriarchy and Socialist Feminism." *Critical Sociology* 7(3): 3–16.

Engels, F. [1884] 1972. *The Origin of the Family: Private Property and the State.* New York: Pathfinder Press.

European Industrial Relations On-line. 2001. *Employment in Europe (2001) Report Highlights Improved Labour Market Performance, 09.* http://www.eurofound.europa.eu/eiro/2001/09/study/tn0109184s.htm (accessed December 2008).

Fraser, N. 1998. "Heterosexism, Misrecognition and Capitalism: A Response to Judith Butler." *New Left Review* 228 (March/April): 140–149.

Gibson-Graham, J. K., Resnik, S. A., and Wolf, R. D., eds. 2000. *Class and Its Others.* Minneapolis: University of Minnesota Press.

Gimenez, M. 1978. "Structural Marxism on 'The Woman Question.'" *Science in Society* 42(3): 301–323.

Graham, L. 1994. "How Does the Japanese Model Transfer to the United States?" In *Global Japanization? The Transnational Transformation of the Labour Process* (ed. T. Elger and C. Smith), 123–151. London: Routledge.

Harding, S., ed. 2004. *The Feminist Standpoint Theory Reader: Intellectual and Political Controversies.* New York: Routledge.

Hartmann, H. 1981. "The Unhappy Marriage of Marxism and Feminism: Towards a More Progressive Union." In *The Unhappy Marriage of Marxism and Feminism* (ed. L. Sergent), 1–41. London: Pluto.

Harvey, D. 1993. "Class Relations, Social Justice, and the Politics of Difference." In *Place and the Politics of Identity* (ed. M. Keith and S. Pile), 41–66. London: Routledge.

Hill Collins, P. 2000. *Black Feminist Thought: Knowledge, Consciousness, and the Politics of Empowerment.* New York: Routledge.

Holmqvist, M. 2009. "Medicalization of Unemployment: Individualizing Social Issues as Personal Problems in the Swedish Welfare State." *Work, Employment and Society* 23(3): 405–421.

Holvino, E. 2010. "Intersections: The Simultaneity of Race, Gender and Class in Organization Studies." *Gender, Work and Organization* 17(3): 248–277.

Hyman, R. 1994. "Changing Trade Union Identities and Strategies," in R. Hyman and A. Ferner (eds) *New Frontiers in European Industrial Relations,* pp. 108–139. Oxford: Blackwell.

Janssens, M., and Zanoni, P. 2005. "Many Diversities for Many Services: Theorizing Diversity (Management) in Service Companies." *Human Relations* 58(3): 311–340.

Janssens, M., and Zanoni, P. 2008. "What Makes an Organization Inclusive? Organizational Practices Favoring the Relational Inclusion of Ethnic Minorities in Operative Jobs." Paper presented at the 21st IACM Conference, Chicago, IL, July 3–6.

McCall, L. 2005. "The Complexity of Intersectionality." *Signs* 30: 1771–1802.

McDowell, L. 2008. "Thinking Through Work: Complex Inequalities, Constructions of Difference and Trans-National Migrants." *Progress in Human Geography* 32(4): 491–507.

Marx, K. 1976. *Capital. Volume 1.* London: Penguin Books.

Miltenburg, J. 1989. "Level Schedules for Mixed-Model Assembly Lines in Just-in-Time Production Systems." *Management Science* 35(2): 192–207.

Minow, M. 1997. *Not Only for Myself: Identity, Politics and the Law.* New York: New Press.

Nkomo, S. 1992. "The Emperor Has No Clothes: Rewriting 'Race into Organizations.'" *Academy of Management Review* 17(3): 487–513.

Noon, N. 2007. "The Fatal Flaws of Diversity and the Business Case for Ethnic Minorities." *Work, Employment and Society* 21(4): 773–784.

Resnick, S., and Wolff, R. 2003. "The Diversity of Class Analyses: A Critique of Erik Olin Wright and Beyond." *Critical Sociology* 29:7–27.

Scully, M. A., and Blake-Beard, S. 2006. "Locating Class in Organizational Diversity Work: Class as Structure, Style and Process." In *Handbook of Workplace Diversity* (ed. A. M. Konrad, P. Prasad, and J. K. Pringle). London: Sage. pp. 431–454.

Selmi, M., and McUsic, M. 2002. "Difference and Solidarity: Unions in a Postmodern Age." In *Labour Law in an Era of Globalization: Transformative Practices and Possibilities* (ed. J. Conaghan, R. M. Fischl, and K. Klare), pp. 429–446. Oxford: Oxford University Press.

Sewell, G. 1998. "The Discipline of Teams: The Control of Team-Based Industrial Work Through Electronic and Peer Surveillance." *Administrative Science Quarterly* 43(2): 397–428.

Smith, C. 2006. "The Double Indeterminacy of Labour Power: Labour Effort and Labour Mobility." *Work, Employment and Society* 20(2): 389–402.

Squires, J. 2006. "Equality and Diversity Policy Frames: Intersectionality and Diversity Management." Paper presented at the Conference Revisiting Governance from Feminist and Queer Perspectives, AHRC Research Centre for Law, Gender and Sexuality, University of Kent, UK, June 29.

Thompson. P. 1983. *The Nature of Work: An Introduction to Debates on the Labour Process.* Houndsmill: MacMillan.

Tsai, L.-H. 1995. "Mixed-Model Sequencing to Minimize Utility Work and the Risk of Conveyor Stoppage." *Management Science* 41(3): 485–495.

Van Laer, K., and Janssens, M. 2010. "Diverse Resistance to Diversity Discourses: Minority Professionals' Engagement with Discourses in the Flemish Workplace."

Paper presented at the second Equal Is Not Enough conference, Antwerp, Belgium, December 1–3.

Wills, J. 2008. "Making Class Politics Possible: Organizing Contract Cleaners in London." *International Journal of Urban and Regional Research* 32(2): 305–323.

Wright, E. O. 1997. *Class Counts.* Cambridge: Cambridge University Press.

Wright, M. W. 2001. "Desire and the Prosthetics of Supervision: A Case of Maquiladora Flexibility." *Cultural Anthropology* 16(3): 354–373.

Young, I. 1980. "Socialist Feminism and the Limits of Dualist Systems Theory." *Socialist Review* 50–51: 169–188.

Yuval-Davis, N. (2006) "Intersectionality and Feminist Politics." *European Journal of Women's Studies* 13(3): 193–209.

Zanoni, P., and Janssens, M. 2004. "Deconstructing Difference: The Rhetorics of HR Managers' Diversity Discourses." *Organization Studies* 25(1): 55–74.

Zanoni, P., and Janssens, M. 2007. "Minority Employees Engaging with (Diversity) Management: An Analysis of Control, Agency, and Micro-Emancipation." *Journal of Management Studies* 44(8): 1371–1397.

Questions

1. Describe CarCo. What was "diversity?" How extensive were CarCo's policies regarding "diversity?" What did they look like? What was TQM? What about "commitment?" How did TQM relate to CarCo's approach to diversity? How did outsourcing and restructuring influence CarCo's commitment and approach to diversity?

2. Whom did people see as problematic at CarCo? Why? What were "diversity" and "difference" really code for at CarCo? Who exactly are they different from? In other words, who was seen as normative and unproblematic? What constituted "difficult" work at CarCo? What was considered "easy" work? Why were these conceptualizations problematic, from Zanoni's perspective? Do you agree? What criteria should we use to define which jobs or tasks are most "valuable?"

3. Zanoni argues that class relations *structured* how management employed diversity at CarCo. That is, in the chicken or egg scenario, class relations came first; diversity was a tool for controlling and exploiting workers. (Workers, then, in turn, adopted diversity as a way to reinforce or resist exploitative working conditions.) How so? Are there other institutional contexts or dimensions of racial, gender, or disability inequalities that make them "come first" in a sense? Restructuring especially exposed the underlying capitalist assumptions about productivity and value. How was restructuring typically done, and how was it done at CarCo? What was so problematic about it, according to Zanoni? Is this also problematic? What are alternative ways of thinking about class relations that aren't based on assumptions of instrumentality and efficiency or aren't exploitive of workers?

4. Some "diverse" workers reportedly also took on the perspective that they were less capable. Why? How could they resist doing so? Historically, how have oppressed groups resisted othering which positions them as lesser than? Which ways of resisting have been most effective? How so? Why?

5. What is the typical business case for diversity? What are alternative ways of thinking about diversity? How might diversity be used to resist being controlled in workplaces? What about in other settings, such as classrooms, religious institutions, or families? Look at several lists of the best companies for promoting diversity, including DiversityInc's Top 50 List, *Forbes's* list of best companies for women and minorities, Black Enterprise's list, and the *New York Times'* list of "leading in diversity." Who does Catalyst (catalyst.org) highlight? How is diversity defined in each list/review? Is that what our goal should be? What programs or approaches are touted as the most effective? What are the "best practices" for achieving diversity? Do these approaches undercut the use of diversity to exploit workers? Are there better ways?

II

The Racial Formation of American Indians: Negotiating Legitimate Identities within Tribal and Federal Law

EVA MARIE GARROUTTE

In Part I, Michael Schwalbe argued for thinking about race as a verb—racializing—rather than a noun—a static, clearly demarcated group of people. Thinking of races as groups is problematic for many reasons: The boundaries are unclear and always changing, people cross over them, and some people do not fit into any grouping. To racialize is to create the boundaries between groups of people. Racializing exists to order interactions and distribute resources in shorthand ways that don't rely on individualized knowledge of people. Thinking of race as a verb highlights its socially constructed nature and pushes us to consider who makes the boundaries and to what consequence.

Michael Omi and Howard Winant's (1994) racial formation theory offers one way to think about racialization. According to Omi and Winant (1994, 55), racial formation is the "socio-historical process by which racial categories are created, inhabited, transformed, and destroyed." Their work traces the historical racial projects of the second half of the twentieth century, highlighting especially the role of social policy in creating racial groups and boundaries. They argue that white racial rule in the United States was formerly a matter of force, but racial formation has transformed it to domination through coercion. That is, whites now rule by getting the racially oppressed themselves to buy in to the very racialization—the policies and practices—which oppresses them.

Excerpted from Garroutte, Eva Marie. 2001. "The Racial Formation of American Indians: Negotiating Legitimate Identities within Tribal and Federal Law." *The American Indian Quarterly* 25:224–239. © University of Nebraska Press – Journals.

The piece that follows illustrates the importance of the law in defining racial and ethnic groupings. It also raises complicated issues about how we should think about categorical boundaries and who should have the power to classify. Enshrined in trade agreements, land settlements, censuses, and various acts, the U.S. federal government has devised complex, ad hoc, politically motivated ways of defining who is and isn't Indian. Tribes, however, are sovereign entities which define Indianness using their own local standards. The process is complicated and sometimes fraught given the assortment of criteria used to define people as Indian or members of tribes, including blood quantum, relation to people on historical rolls of Indians, and residence on reservations, among others. What's more, Garroutte demonstrates how intermarriage, historical resistance to being formally listed as Indian, and competing interests create uneven and even contradictory identification systems. Given the complexity of racialization, some students may come to question the wisdom of classifying people at all.

Much is on the line for identifying as Indian, however. As Garroutte makes clear, many legitimate and life-sustaining material resources are granted only to Indians or members of individual tribes. Tribe members, for example, may have a legal right to income earned on tribal lands or access to living on tribal lands. They may also be protected by the Indian Child Welfare Act, Native American Grave Protection and Repatriation Act, and Indian Arts and Crafts Act, legislation passed to protect Indian rights trampled on previously by ethnocentric social welfare workers, overzealous law enforcement, culturally insensitive museums, and non-Indian artists coopting Indian labels to turn a profit. On a social psychological level, identifying as Indian provides legitimacy and authenticity to individuals.

Reference

Omi, Michael, and Howard Winant. 1994. *Racial Formation in the United States: From the 1960s to the 1990s.* New York: Routledge.

Tribal Legal Definitions

There are a large number of legal rules defining American Indian identity, and they are formulated and applied by different actors for different purposes. I begin with the ones that tribes use to determine their citizenship. Many people are surprised to discover that each tribe sets its own legal criteria for citizenship. They imagine that the U.S. government controls such aspects of tribal lives. In reality, tribes typically have the right to create their own legal definitions of identity and to do so in any way they choose. Indeed, this prerogative is commonly viewed legislatively as one of the most fundamental powers of an Indian tribe.[1]

The most common tribal requirement for determining citizenship revolves around "blood quantum" or degree of Indian ancestry. About two-thirds of all federally recognized tribes of the coterminous United States specify a minimum blood quantum in their legal citizenship criteria, with one-quarter blood degree being the most frequent minimum requirement.[2]

Degree of blood is calculated on the basis of the immediacy of one's genetic relationship to ancestors whose bloodlines were (supposedly) unmixed. The initial calculation often begins with a "base roll," a listing of tribal membership and blood quanta in some particular year.[3] These base rolls make possible very elaborate definitions of identity. They allow one to reckon that the offspring of, say, a full-blood Navajo mother and a white father is one-half Navajo. If that half Navajo child in turn produced progeny with a Hopi person of one-quarter blood degree, those progeny would be judged to be one-quarter Navajo and one-eighth Hopi. Alternatively, they could also be said to have "three-eighths general Indian blood." Certain tribes require not only that citizens possess tribal ancestry but also that this ancestry comes from a *particular* parent. Thus, the Santa Clara Pueblo (New Mexico) will not enroll children in the tribe without paternal descent, and the Seneca Tribe (New York) requires maternal descent.

Such modern definitions of identity based on blood quantum closely reflect nineteenth- and early twentieth-century theories of race introduced into indigenous cultures by Euro-Americans. These understood blood as quite literally the vehicle for the transmission of cultural characteristics: "'Half-breeds' by this logic could be expected to behave in 'half-civilized,' that is, partially assimilated, ways while retaining one half of their traditional culture, accounting for their marginal status in both societies."[4] Given this standard of identification, full-bloods tended to be seen as the "really real," the quintessential Indians, while others were (and often continue to be) viewed as Indians in diminishing degrees.[5]

These theories of race articulated closely with political goals characteristic of the dominant American society. The original stated intention of blood quantum distinctions was to determine the point at which the various responsibilities of that dominant society to Indian peoples ended. The ultimate and explicit federal intention was to use the blood quantum standard as a means to liquidate tribal lands and to eliminate government trust responsibility to tribes along with entitlement programs, treaty rights, and reservations.[6] Indians would eventually, through intermarriage combined with the mechanism of blood quantum calculations, become citizens indistinguishable from all other citizens.

A significant number of tribes—almost one-third of those populating the lower forty-eight states—have rejected specific blood quantum requirements for determining tribal citizenship. They often require, instead, that any new enrollee be simply a lineal (direct) descendant of another tribal member. They may also invoke additional or alternative criteria. For instance, the Tohono O'Odham (Arizona) consider residency definitive, automatically admitting to citizenship all children born to parents living on the reservation. The Swinomish (Washington) take careful stock of various indicators of community participation, ignoring blood quantum, while the Lower Sioux Indian Community (Minnesota) requires a vote of the tribal council. In still other tribes, community recognition or parental enrollment may also be a means to or a prerequisite for enrollment, and a few tribes only accept applicants whose parents submit the necessary paperwork within a limited time after their child's birth. Some tribes also require members to fulfill certain minimal duties, such as maintaining annual contact with the tribal council, in order to maintain their citizenship in good standing.[7]

Tribal Identity Negotiations: Consequences

Tribes, in short, possess the power to define their citizenship through self-generated legal definitions, and they do so in many different ways. Legal definitions regulate the right to vote in tribal elections, to hold tribal office, and generally to participate in the political, and sometimes the cultural, life of the tribe. One's ability to satisfy legal definitions of identification may also determine one's right to share in certain tribal revenues (such as income generated by tribally controlled businesses). Perhaps most significantly, it may determine the right to live on a reservation or to inherit land interests thereon.

As this list suggests, failure to negotiate an identity as a "real" Indian within the legal definition of one's tribe can lead to some dire outcomes for individual people. For instance, legal criteria can tear apart families by pushing certain members off the reservation while allowing others to stay. Thus, in 1997 an article in *Indian Country Today* described the following family scenario: "Mr. Montoya has lived at Santa Clara Pueblo, his mother's home, his whole life. He raised his four children at the pueblo and now has grandchildren there."[8] But Mr. Montoya cannot be enrolled at Santa Clara (New Mexico) because, since 1939, the pueblo has operated by a tribal law that allows for enrollment only on the basis of paternal descent—and his father was not from Santa Clara but, rather, from the nearby Isleta Pueblo. Montoya has inherited rights to his mother's property in Santa Clara, but his ability to enforce those rights remains uncertain.

Families in Montoya's situation sometimes cannot tolerate the tenuousness of their position and choose to abandon the pueblo, their relatives, and their intimate participation in the traditional, tribal culture wherein they were born and raised. But family dissolution "by legal definition" has elsewhere occurred by force. It has occurred to the extent that mixed-race children have been actively expelled from the reservation, even in cases in which the children had been living there under the care of an enrolled relative.

Such an event occurred on the Onondaga Reservation in the recent past. The Onondaga, by a law that reverses the practice of the Santa Clara Pueblo, are matrilineal, enrolling children *only* if their mothers are tribal citizens. In 1974, the tribal council ordered all noncitizens to leave the reservation or face ejection. This order included even noncitizen spouses, who were mostly women, and the children born to Onondaga men by such women. The Onondaga men could stay—but only if they chose to live apart from their wives and children. The national journal of Native news and issues, *Akwesasne Notes*, reported that the rationale behind the expulsion was that, over a period of years, a large number of non-Indians had moved onto Onondaga land and the council feared that the federal government might consequently dissolve the reservation.[9] Most individuals affected by the ruling left peaceably; others had to be forcibly removed. One family burned down its home before leaving.

Legal definitions, then, allow tribes to determine their citizenship as they choose. This determination allows them to delimit the distribution of certain important resources, such as reservation land, tribal monies, political privileges, and the like. But this is hardly the end of the story of legal definitions of identity.

Federal Legal Definitions

Although tribes possess the right to formulate legal definitions for the purpose of delimiting their citizenship, the federal government has many purposes for which it, too, must distinguish Indians from non-Indians, and it uses its own, separate legal definition for doing so. More precisely, it uses a whole array of legal definitions. Because the U.S. Constitution uses the word "Indian" in two places but defines it nowhere, Congress has made its own definitions on an ad hoc basis.[10] A 1978 congressional survey discovered no less than thirty-three separate definitions of "Indians" in use in different pieces of federal legislation.[11] These may or may not correspond with those any given tribe uses to determine its citizenship.

Thus, most federal legal definitions of Indian identity specify a particular minimum blood quantum—frequently one-quarter but sometimes one-half—and others do not. Some require or accept tribal citizenship as a criterion of federal identification, and others do not. Some require reservation residency or ownership of land held in trust by the government, and others do not. Many other laws affecting Indians specify no definition of identity, such that the *courts* must determine to whom the laws apply. Because of the wide variation in federal legal identity definitions, and their frequent departure from the various tribal ones, many individuals who are recognized by their tribes as tribal citizens are nevertheless considered non-Indian for some or all governmental purposes. The converse can be true as well.

Federal Identity Negotiations: Consequences

There are a variety of contexts in which federal legal definitions of identity become important. The matter of economic resource distribution—involving access to various social services, monetary awards, and opportunities—will probably come immediately to the minds of many readers. The particular legal situation of Indian people and its attendant opportunities and responsibilities are the result of historic negotiations between tribes and the federal government, in which the latter agreed to compensate tribes in various ways for the large amounts of land tribes surrendered, often by force. Benefits available to those who can satisfy federal definitions of Indian identity are administered through a variety of agencies, including the Bureau of Indian Affairs, the Indian Health Service, the Department of Agriculture, the Office of Elementary and Secondary Education, and the Department of Labor, to name a few.[12]

Legal definitions also affect specific economic rights deriving from treaties or agreements that some (not all) tribes made with the federal government. These may include such rights as the use of particular geographic areas for hunting, harvesting, fishing, or trapping, as well as certain water use rights.[13] Those legally defined as Indians are also sometimes exempted from certain requirements related to state licensure and state (but not federal) income and property taxation.[14]

Legal definitions also determine the applicability of a number of protections available to individual Indians from the federal government. Notable among these are an Indian parent's rights under the Indian Child Welfare Act of 1978 (25 U.S.C. 1901 et seq.). Before the passage of this act, as many as 25 percent to 35 percent of Indian children in some states were being removed from their homes and placed in the care of non-Indians through such means as adoption and foster care. Many commentators have suggested that a number of Indian families lost their children less because they were genuinely unsuitable parents and more because they refused to abandon traditional cultural values in favor of those enforced by the essentially white, middle-class, social service bureaucracy.[15] For instance, it is a rather common custom in many Indian cultures to share child-rearing responsibilities among various members of the extended family, with the outcome that children do not necessarily live with their biological parents. It has been a common complaint among Indian families that Social Services representatives have automatically assumed, in such cases, that a child suffers parental "neglect" and have used this reasoning as an excuse to initiate foster care placement.

The Indian Child Welfare Act was passed in order to stem the wholesale transfer of children out of their families, tribes, and cultures. It requires that, when Indian children must be removed from their homes, efforts be made to place them with another family member or at least with another Indian family rather than a non-Indian one. The law allows Indian people a means to protect the integrity of their family units and to ensure some cultural continuity for children.

Just as importantly, federally specified legal definitions provide for certain religious freedoms. For one thing, they allow Indian people to seek protection from prosecution for the possession of specific ceremonial objects, otherwise restricted by law. (For instance, many Indian people own eagle feathers that they use in prayer and ceremonies, although non-Indians are not permitted to possess any part of this endangered species. Similarly, Indian members of the Native American Church ingest peyote, legally classified as a hallucinogen, as a sacramental substance in closely controlled worship settings. Non-Indians are forbidden to possess it.) Since the passage of the Native American Graves Protection and Repatriation Act of 1990, federal legal definitions also allow Indian people to claim sacred ceremonial objects, as well as to receive and rebury the remains of their ancestral dead, if these are being held in federally funded museums for display or study (as they very frequently are).

Federal legal definitions of Indian identity can even affect some individuals' ability to pursue their livelihood. A particularly controversial protection that has recently become available to those legally defined as Indians revolves around the Indian Arts and Crafts Act of 1990. Arguments for this legislation started from the recognition that many buyers consider artwork more desirable and valuable if it is created by an Indian person. They proceeded to the observation that a great deal of art was therefore being falsely labeled as Indian-made. The same arguments then concluded that such misrepresentations were seriously reducing the revenues of artists who were, in fact, Indian.[16]

The Indian Arts and Crafts Act forbids any artist who is not a citizen of a federally or state-acknowledged tribe from marketing work as "Indian produced." Penalties for violation of the act include large fines and imprisonment. Certain galleries and organizations have also voluntarily chosen to restrict exhibitions and art

commissions to people who can demonstrate that they are Indians by reference to formal, legal criteria.[17]

Identity and Legitimacy

All the legal rights and protections sketched thus far offer their significant advantages only to those who are able to make claims to Indianness that are formally judged as legitimate within tribal or federal definitions of identity. However, many people cannot manage to pass successfully through one or the other of these definitions. (As noted before, there is no guarantee that those definitions correspond.) By what process is the legitimacy of claims to Indian identity asserted and evaluated within definitions of law? Who is able to negotiate a legal identity, and who is not? How is it that people with seemingly identical characteristics may meet with very different outcomes within the process of racial formation set out in legal definitions? The answers to such questions are frequently quite astonishing.

Let us begin with a consideration of the criterion of blood quantum. Some people of American Indian ancestry find their identity claims challenged because their blood quanta are judged too low, by one standard or another. The question of how much "blood" is "enough" for an individual to call him- or herself Indian is hotly contested in Indian country—and well beyond. As sociologist Eugeen Roosens writes,

> There is . . . [a] principle about which the whites and the Indians are in agreement. . . . [P]eople with more Indian blood . . . also have more rights to inherit what their ancestors, the former Indians, have left behind. In addition, full blood Indians are more authentic than half-breeds. By being pure, they have more right to respect. They are, in all aspects of their being, more *integral*.[18]

Degree of biological ancestry can take on such a tremendous significance in tribal contexts that it literally overwhelms all other considerations of identity (especially when it is constructed as "pure"). As Cherokee legal scholar G. William Rice points out, "Most [people] would recognize the full-blood Indian who was enrolled in a federally recognized tribe as an Indian, even if the individual was adopted at birth by a non-Indian family and had never set foot in Indian country nor met another Indian."[19]

In this, American Indian claims to identity are judged very differently under the law than the claims of other racial groups have been, even into the present day. We see this most clearly if we consider the striking difference in the way that the American popular and legal imaginations work to assign individuals to the racial category of "Indian" as opposed to the racial category "Black." As a variety of researchers have observed, social and legal attributions of Black identity have often focused on the "one-drop rule" or rule of "hypodescent."[20]

In the movie *Raintree Country*, Liz Taylor's character articulates this rule in crassly explicit terms. The worst thing that can happen to a person, she drawls, is "havin' a little Negra blood in ya'—just one little teensy drop and the person's all Negra." Various states have been meticulous in defining exactly how much blood constitutes a "drop," some setting it at one-eighth degree African ancestry, and some setting it much lower.

Racial classification on the basis of the rule of hypodescent has had serious consequences for individuals defined thereby as Black. For instance, in Mississippi in 1948, a young man named Davis Knight was tried for violating antimiscegenation statutes. He responded that he was quite unaware that he possessed any Black ancestry, which in any case amounted to less than one-sixteenth. The courts convicted him anyway and sentenced him to five years in jail. "Blood" was "blood," whether anyone, including the accused himself, was aware of it or not.

A similar legal definition of identity held sway for Blacks in the United States for many years after the 1940s. For instance, up until 1970, Louisiana state law defined as Black anyone possessing "a trace of Black ancestry." The legislature formally revised its definition of racial identity in that year, declaring that only those possessing more than one-thirty-second degree "Negro blood" were to be considered Black.[21] Only in 1985 did it grant parents the right to define, as they choose, the race of their children on their birth certificates. All this presents a striking contrast to the circumstances of American Indians. Far from being held to a one-drop rule, Indians are generally required—both by law and by popular opinion—to establish rather high blood quanta in order for their claims to racial identity to be accepted as legitimate, the individual's own opinion not at all withstanding. Although people must show only the slightest trace of "Black blood" to be *forced* (with or without their consent) into the category "African American," modern American Indians must formally produce strong evidence of often rather *substantial* amounts of "Indian blood" to be allowed entry into the corresponding racial category. The regnant racial definitions applied to Indians are simply quite different than those that have applied (and continue to apply) to Blacks. Modern Americans, as Native American studies professor Jack Forbes puts the matter, "are *always finding 'Blacks'* (even if they look rather un-African), and . . . *are always losing 'Indians.'*"[22]

Another group of people who may find the legitimacy of their racial identities challenged or denied comprises individuals of tribally mixed ancestry. This can be true even for those whose total American Indian blood quanta are relatively high. The reader will remember that the majority of tribes make documentation of a minimum blood quantum—often one-fourth degree Indian blood—part of their legal definitions of identity and that the federal government does the same for at least some of its various purposes. In light of this requirement, consider the hypothetical case of a child possessing one-half Indian ancestry and one-half white ancestry, meaning that he or she has one parent who is exclusively white and one parent who is exclusively Indian. This child's identity claim is likely to get a green light from both the federal government and the tribe—so long as his or her Indian ancestry comes from a single tribe. But compare these potential fortunes with those of another child whose half-Indian heritage derives from *several different* tribes. Let us say that this second child, in addition to his or her one-half white ancestry, is also one-eighth Sisseton Dakota, one-eighth Cheyenne, one-eighth Assiniboine, and one-eighth Sicangu Lakota. This child is, like the first child, one-half Indian. But each tribe of his or her ancestry requires its citizens to document a one-quarter blood degree, *from that tribe only.* From the perspective of each individual tribe, this child possesses only one-eighth tribal blood and is therefore ineligible for citizenship. As far as the several tribes are concerned, he or she is simply non-Indian within their legal definitions of identity.

Some people of Indian ancestry fall afoul, in legal definitions of identity, of still another potential snare. This entanglement has to do with one's ability to establish relationship to a historic Indian community in the way that many legal definitions require. As previously noted, individuals seeking tribal or federal identification as Indian must typically establish that one, or more, of their ancestors appears on one of the tribe's base rolls.

Unfortunately, many people who clearly conform to any other definition of Indian identity do not have ancestors who appear on the base rolls, for a multitude of reasons. Historians agree that the process by which many tribal rolls were initially compiled was almost unbelievably complicated. In the compilation of some tribal rolls, including the Dawes Rolls (1899–1906), from which all of today's enrolled Oklahoma Cherokees (and various other tribes) must show descent, the process that registrants endured took so long that a significant number of them died before the paperwork was completed. This meant that their descendants would be forever barred from becoming tribal citizens.

Even when applicants did manage to live long enough to complete the entire process of enrollment, they frequently found themselves denied. Dawes commissioners enrolled only a small fraction of all those who applied, and they readily agreed that they had denied many people of indubitably tribal ancestry.[23]

Other Indian people of the period actively resisted their registration on the Dawes Rolls, either individually or collectively. For instance, among Oklahoma Creeks, Cherokees, Chickasaws, and Choctaws in the late nineteenth and early twentieth centuries, conservative traditionalists or "irreconcilables" fought a hard fight against registration with the Dawes Commission. The reason was that the Dawes Roll was the explicit first step in what President Theodore Roosevelt had rapturously declared (in his first annual address to Congress in 1901) would be "a mighty, pulverizing engine to break up the tribal mass."[24] The effort, in a nutshell, was to destroy indigenous cultures by destroying their foundation—their collective ownership of land—and to integrate the Indians thus "liberated" into the dominant American culture. It was to allow for Indians to be remade into individual private owners of small farms who would quickly become independent of government attention and expenditures.

Probably no one could have foreseen all of the specific, catastrophic results that would befall tribes with the destruction of the old, traditional system of land tenure. The irreconcilables, however, at least intuited the outlines of the coming disaster. In the words of historian Angie Debo, they "clung to the old order with the stubbornness of despair."[25] In many tribes opposition to allotment ran high. In some, leaders arose who used all their resources, from cunning to force, to discourage their fellows' enrollment and subsequent allotment.[26]

Government patience with such conservative obduracy soon wore thin, and the more influential and uncooperative leaders and their families were hunted out and forcibly enrolled. (Cherokee leader Redbird Smith consented to his own enrollment only after he was finally jailed for his refusal.) However, others who shared his sentiments did manage to elude capture altogether and were never entered onto the census documents used today as the base rolls for many tribes.

The stories of Redbird Smith, and others like him, are narratives of a determined and principled resistance to a monumental step in the process of the Indians' forced acculturation to the dominant American culture. Yet the descendants of those traditionalists who succeeded in escaping census enumeration find themselves worse off, in the modern legal context, for their forebears' success in the fight to maintain cultural integrity. By the criteria their tribes have now established, they can never become enrolled citizens. This fact frequently affects, in turn, their ability to satisfy federal definitions.[27]

All of the foregoing demonstrates that there are great numbers of peculiarities of exclusion spawned by legal definitions of identity. The reverse side of this observation, however, is that a number of people who may have *no* ancestral connections to tribes have been and are defined as Indian in the legal sense alone. In some places and times, for instance, non-Indian spouses of Indian people have been allowed to become legal citizens of Indian nations. Among several Oklahoma tribes, certain African American slaves, formerly owned by Indian people, were likewise made, by due legal process following the Civil War, into tribal citizens even in the absence of any Indian ancestry.[28] And, where census registration implied eligibility for distribution of tribal lands, as it did in Oklahoma, it was not uncommon for individuals with no Indian ancestry, but with active homesteading ambitions and perhaps unscrupulous lawyers in tow, to seek to acquire places on the rolls through dishonest means. Thousands of them succeeded.[29] In so doing, they earned for themselves the name of "five-dollar Indians," presumably in reference to the amount required to bribe the census enumerator.

Finally, this discussion of the oddities that legal definitions of identity have created would not be complete without the acknowledgment that it is not only non-Indian people who have made their way on to the tribal census lists and thus "become" Indian, in the legal sense. Nonexistent people sometimes did, as well. An amusing example comes from the 1885 census of the Sicangu Lakota (South Dakota). As historian Thomas Biolsi records, census takers at the Rosebud Agency "recorded some remarkable English translations of Lakota names."[30]

Nestled in among the common and dignified appellations—Black Elk, Walking Bull, Dull Knife, and others—are personal names of a more colorful class: Bad Cunt, Dirty Prick, Shit Head. "What happened," Biolsi notes, "is not difficult to unravel: Lakota people were filing past the census enumerator, and then getting back in line—or lending their babies to people in line—to be enumerated a second time using fictitious and rather imaginative names."[31] Because this particular census was being taken for the purpose of distributing rations, the ploy was one aimed at the very practical goal of enhancing survival—but the Lakota apparently felt that even such serious work need not be undertaken without humor.

For the purposes of the present discussion, I should note that at least some of the historic oddities of Indian census rolls have continued to create more of the same—forever. That is, while the nonexistent Indians of Rosebud clearly could not have produced children, the living, breathing, "five-dollar Indians" who bought their way onto the census rolls in Oklahoma and other states certainly could. It is impossible to estimate the number of modern-day descendants of those numerous non-Indian "Indians," but one might suppose that it could be fairly large. It seems probable that at least some descendants have maintained tribal enrollment and the privileges attendant on a legally legitimated identity, even while many people of actual Indian descent were and are unable to acquire the same.

In conclusion, the example of Indian identity illustrates the complex and often mystifying nature of racial formation processes as they apply to American Indians. "Indianness" emerges out of complex negotiations that occur within the context of specifiable legal definitions of identity. There are many ways to gain and to lose it that may have little to do with the qualities that most people assume to be of central importance in determining racial identity. At the same time, achieving an Indian identity that satisfies various legal criteria (or failing to do so) has serious consequences. The specific

elements of the racial formation process for Indian people make Native Americans' experience unique among those of modern-day U.S. racial groups.

Notes

1. This tribal right was determined in the 1905 court case *Waldron v. United States* (143 F. 413, C.C.D.S.D., 1905) and later clarified in a celebrated lawsuit, *Martinez v. Santa Clara Pueblo* (540 F.2d 1039, 10th Cir. 1976). However, as with nearly every other rule in Indian country, there are exceptions. A handful of tribes *are* federally required to hold to specific criteria in defining tribal membership—for instance, by maintaining a specific blood quantum standard for citizenship. In most legal discussions, the right to determine citizenship is closely tied to the concept of tribal sovereignty. See Sharon O'Brien, *American Indian Tribal Governments* (Norman: University of Oklahoma Press, 1989); Charles F. Wilkinson, *American Indians, Time, and the Law: Native Societies in a Modern Constitutional Democracy* (New Haven, CT: Yale University Press, 1987).

2. Russell Thornton surveyed 302 of the 317 tribes in the lower forty-eight states that enjoyed federal acknowledgment in 1997. He found that 204 tribes had some minimum blood quantum requirement, while the remaining ninety-eight had none; see Thornton, "Tribal Membership Requirements and the Demography of 'Old' and 'New' Native Americans," *Population Research and Policy Review* 16 (1997): 37.

3. Although a few tribes have no written records of citizenship even today—some of the Pueblos, for instance, depend on their oral traditions—the majority of tribes maintain written membership documents, which are called "tribal rolls"; see Russell Thornton, *American Indian Holocaust and Survival: A Population History* (Norman: University of Oklahoma Press, 1987), 190. The roll chosen as definitive for later citizenship determinations is known as the "base roll." The General Allotment Act of 1887 provided for the creation of some base rolls, but most were compiled in response to the Indian Reorganization Act of 1934. Tribes continued to create membership listings that they use as base rolls after 1934 as well. In some cases, tribes created their base rolls only a few years ago. This is true, for instance, with the Passamoquoddy (Maine), who (having only enjoyed federal acknowledgment as a tribe for two decades) use a 1990 census for their base roll.

4. C. Matthew Snipp, "Who Are American Indians? Some Observations about the Perils and Pitfalls of

Data for Race and Ethnicity," *Population Research and Policy Review* 5 (1986): 249.

5. For an excellent discussion of the evolution, over several centuries, of ideas about blood relationship among European and Euro-American peoples and transference of these ideas into American Indian tribal populations, see Melissa L. Myer, "American Indian Blood Quantum Requirements: Blood Is Thicker than Family," pp. 231–249 in Valerie J. Matsumoto and Blake Allmendiger, eds., *Over the Edge: Remapping the American West* (Berkeley: University of California Press, 1999).

6. Thomas Biolsi, "The Birth of the Reservation: Making the Modern Individual among the Lakota," *American Ethnologist* 22, no. 1 (February 1995): 28–49; Patricia Limerick, The *Legacy of Conquest: The Unbroken Past of the American West* (New York: W. W. Norton, 1988).

7. To view a variety of tribal constitutions and their citizenship requirements, see http://thorpe.ou.edu/.

8. "Mixed Marriages Present Some Property Problems," *Indian Country Today* (May 26–June 2, 1997): d10.

9. *Akwesasne Notes* 6 (Autumn 1974): 32.

10. The two mentions of "Indians" in the Constitution appear in passages regarding the regulation of commerce and the taking of a federal census. The word *tribe* also appears once in the Constitution, in the Commerce Clause.

11. Sharon O'Brien, "Tribes and Indians: With Whom Does the United States Maintain a Relationship?" *Notre Dame Law Review* 66 (1991): 1481.

12. These agencies administer resources and programs in areas such as education, health, social services, tribal governance and administration, law enforcement, nutrition, resource management, tribal economic development, employment, and the like. The most recently published source describing various programs and the requirements for participation is Roger Walk, *Federal Assistance to Native Americans: A Report Prepared for the Senate Select Committee on Indian Affairs of the U.S. Senate* (Washington DC: U.S. Government Printing Office, 1991).

13. For a discussion of the history of American Indian hunting, fishing, and water rights, see Wilcomb E. Washburn, *Red Man's Land/White Man's Law: A Study of the Past and Present Status of the American Indian* (New York: Charles Scribner's Sons, 1971).

14. Non-Indian students in my classes sometimes tell me that Indians also regularly receive such windfalls as free cars and monthly checks from the government strictly because of their race. It is my sad duty to puncture this fantasy. The common belief that Indians receive "free money" probably stems from the fact that the government holds land in trust for certain tribes. As part of its trust responsibility, it may then lease that land, collect the revenue, and distribute it to the tribal members. Thus, some Indians do receive government checks, but these do not represent some kind of bread from heaven; they are simply the profits derived from lands that the Native Americans own. For details on the special, political-economic relationship of Indians to the federal government in relation to taxation and licensure, see Gary D. Sandefur, "Economic Development and Employment Opportunities for American Indians," in Donald E. Green and Thomas V. Tonneson, eds., *American Indians: Social Justice and Public Policy, Ethnicity and Public Policy Series,* vol. 9 (Milwaukee: University of Wisconsin System Institute on Race and Ethnicity, 1991).

15. Suzan Shown Harjo, "The American Indian Experience," in Harriet Pipes McAdoo, ed., *Family Ethnicity: Strength in Diversity* (Newbury Park, CA: Sage, 1993); R. B. Jones, "The Indian Child Welfare Act: The Need for a Separate Law," http://www.americanbar.org/content/newsletter/publications/gp_solo_magazine_home/gp_solo_magazine_index/indianchildwelfareact.html (accessed September 18, 2015).

16. To be specific, the Commerce Department estimated in 1985 that specious "Indian art" imported from foreign countries created $40 million to $80 million in lost income, or 10 percent to 20 percent of annual Indian art sales, for genuine Indian artists every year (H.R. 101-400, 101st Cong., 1st Sess., Congressional Record [1990]: 4–5).

17. An excellent, detailed discussion of this legislation appears in Gail K. Sheffield, *The Arbitrary Indian: The Indian Arts and Crafts Act of 1990* (Norman: University of Oklahoma Press, 1997), 30–31. The Indian Arts and Crafts Act's specification that there are two types of Indian tribes—the federally acknowledged and the state acknowledged—raises another point significant to the present discussion. Although this article discusses identity definitions as they concern individuals, definitions also concern entire groups. Both federal and state governments formally classify certain groups as "acknowledged" Indian tribes and invest them with specific rights and responsibilities not shared by other groups. While the accompaniments of the extension of state acknowledgment to a tribe are highly variable (and sometimes trivial), the consequences of federal

acknowledgment are always profound. By acknowl-edging a group of claimants as an Indian tribe, the fed-eral government extends "government-to-government" relations to it. It legally constitutes that tribal group as a sovereign power and as a "domestic dependent nation," as determined in court cases including *Cherokee Nation v. Georgia* (1831) and (even more importantly) *Worcester v. Georgia* (1832). These are extremely power-ful statuses. In fact, the legal case *Native American Church v. Navajo Tribal Council* (1959) made clear that federally acknowledged tribes enjoy a governmental status *higher* than that of states. For a more detailed discussion of legal cases pertaining to tribal sover-eignty, see O'Brien, *American Indian Tribal Govern-ments* (cited in note 1).

18. Eugeen E. Roosens, *Creating Ethnicity: The Process of Ethnogenesis* (Newbury Park, CA: Sage, 1989), 41–42. Roosens is discussing the situation of Canadian Indi-ans, but the same remarks apply to American Indians.

19. G. William Rice, "There and Back Again—An Indian Hobbit's Holiday: Indians Teaching Indian Law," *New Mexico Law Review* 26, no. 2 (Spring 1996): 176.

20. Naomi Zack, "Mixed Black and White Race and Public Policy," *Hypatia* 10, no. 1 (Winter 1995): 120–132.

21. F. James Davis, *Who Is Black? One Nation's Definition* (University Park: Pennsylvania State University Press, 1991).

22. Jack D. Forbes, "The Manipulation of Race, Caste, and Identity: Classifying Afroamericans, Native Ameri-cans and Red-Black People," *Journal of Ethnic Studies* 17, no. 4 (1990): 24.

23. Kent Carter, "Deciding Who Can Be Cherokee: Enroll-ment Records of the Dawes Commission," *Chronicles of Oklahoma* 69, no. 2 (Summer 1991): 174–205.

24. Theodore Roosevelt, *The Works of Theodore Roosevelt*, vol. 15: *State Papers as Governor and President, 1899–1909* (New York: Scribner's Sons, 1926), 129. Contrast Roosevelt's optimism about allotment with the opinion of U.S. Commissioner of Indian Affairs John Collier, who would later call it "the greatest single practical evil" ever perpetrated on American Indians (quoted in Fergus Bordewich, *Killing the White Man's Indian* [New York: Doubleday, 1996], 124).

25. Angie Debo, *And Still the Waters Run: The Betrayal of the Five Civilized Tribes* (Princeton, NJ: Princeton University Press, 1972), 53.

26. In Oklahoma, the Creeks were especially resistant. Under the leadership of Chitto Harjo, or "Crazy Snake," their full bloods set up their own government and council in 1901. They also appointed a cadre of law en-forcement officers known as "light-horsemen" to deal with tribal citizens who had accepted allotments and to give warning to those who might be considering a simi-lar action. The light horsemen roamed the countryside, confiscating enrollment papers and sometimes arrest-ing and whipping their possessors. After being arrested by federal marshals and found guilty of such activities, Chitto Harjo and his followers continued to defy allot-ment through legal means, hiring lawyers and sending lobbyists to Washington. The Oklahoma Cherokees used their own strategies, often under the guidance of traditionalist leader Redbird Smith. When field parties from the Dawes Commission "came to a full blood set-tlement, they found amusements planned in remote places to call the Indians away. When they tried to secure the names [of Cherokees eligible for allotment] from their neighbors, witnesses were threatened with bodily harm" (Debo, *And Still the Waters Run*, 45). For further discussion of tribal resistance to allotment, see D. S. Otis, *The Dawes Act and the Allotment of Indian Lands* (Norman: University of Oklahoma Press, 1973), 40–46.

27. Modern tribes do realize that some of their proper members are being excluded from legal citizenship, and most have created a mechanism for dealing with this reality. Many tribal constitutions allow for legally "adopting" individuals who do not meet formally specified identity criteria. The adoption provision, sometimes called "selective enrollment," allows for a "safety net" to protect persons judged by some criteria to have a claim on tribal citizenship but who, for what-ever reason, cannot satisfy the usual requirements. Isleta Pueblo (New Mexico), for example, allows for the adoption of individuals with one-half Indian blood from other tribes besides its own but forbids the adoption of non-Indians, while some tribal constitu-tions even provide for the adoption of non-Indians (O'Brien, *American Indian Tribal Governments*, 175 [cited in note 1]). In practice, however, adoptions tend to be rather rare and to be limited to certain categories of people—members' spouses, reservation residents, children who meet a blood quantum requirement but whose parents are not enrolled, and so on. And in most cases adoption is only partial salvation. Adopted individuals may not enjoy full privileges in the tribe, such as voting rights or the ability to pass tribal citi-zenship to offspring. Perhaps even more significantly, the federal government refuses to recognize as Indian

anyone who cannot demonstrate at least *some* blood connection to a tribe, for any purposes, even if the tribe agrees to enroll that person; see Stephen L. Pevar, *The Rights of Indians and Tribes: The Basic ACLU Guide to Indian and Tribal Rights*, 2nd ed. (Carbondale: Southern Illinois University Press, 1992), 13. See further *U.S. v. Rogers* (45 U.S. 566 [1846]) and *State v. Attebery* (519 P.2d 53 [Ariz. 1974]). Thus, even with the "safety net" of tribal adoption in place, many people still cannot achieve a legitimated Indian identity within all of the legal definitions that are likely to be important to them.

28. Modern descendants of such individuals—referred to then and now as "freed-men"—often continue to maintain documentation of tribal affiliation. Presently, they do not qualify for social service benefits, mineral rights, and other benefits that sometimes accrue to those who are tribal citizens by blood. This state of affairs could conceivably change, however. Since 1996, two groups of African American freedmen have been engaged in legal struggles with the Seminole Nation (Oklahoma). A central issue has been their right to share in a $56 million settlement that the tribe received in a land claims case. In 2000, the tribe stripped the Black Seminoles of their tribal membership. The Department of the Interior, however, declared the action illegal. As of this writing, the final outcome of the dispute is uncertain. See Herb Frazier, "Black Seminoles Seek $100m on Retribution from Government," *Charleston Post and Courier*, December 3, 1999: 1; William Glaberson, "Who Is a Seminole, and Who Gets to Decide?" *New York Times*, January 29, 2001: A1, A14.

29. Debo, *And Still the Waters Run,* 38.

30. Biolsi, "The Birth of the Reservation" (cited in note 6).

31. Biolsi, "The Birth of the Reservation," 28.

Questions

1. What is at stake when being legally identified as Indian or not? Who gets to decide who is Indian? Has it always been that way? What criteria do people use? Where did blood-quantum definitions of Indian identity come from? What role did science play in these definitions? What role did politics play? How are blood-quantum definitions applied to Indians different from hypodescent definitions applied to Black Americans? Does the U.S. federal government use the same criteria for determining "Indianness" as the tribes do? Why or why not?

2. What factors complicate the identification of someone as a member of a particular tribe? Why did some people resist listing in the Dawes Roll? How did the government respond to this resistance? What are the twisted consequences for people now? How did non-Indians manipulate the census taking to their advantage? Given the messy nature of legally defining Indian identity, why not get rid of the labels altogether? Is having "no label" an effective response to inequality? What would most likely happen?

3. What federal legislative acts have been enacted to counteract abuse of Indian people's rights? What is the Indian Child Welfare Act of 1978? Why was it enacted? This act has received considerable attention over the last several years, thanks to the 2013 Supreme Court case *Adoptive Couple v. Baby Girl.* You can read a synopsis of the case involving the custody dispute of "Baby Veronica" between a non-Indian adopting couple, Melanie and Matt Capobianco, and her Cherokee father Dusten Brown on the National Indian Child Welfare Association website (www.nicwa.org) or scotusblog.com. You can also listen to the coverage of the case by Nina Totenberg, NPR's legal affairs correspondent (http://www.npr.org/2013/07/24/205224853/s-c-court-orders-baby-veronica-adoption-finalized). What issues were in dispute in the case? What role did the Indian Child Welfare Act play in the case? How did the Supreme Court rule? Do some research on the Supreme Court justices. Are any Indian? Did their Indian statuses affect their ruling? How can one tell? Cases involving children's welfare are extremely emotionally fraught. How do courts decide what's in the best interest of children? What cases have cited *Adoptive Couple v. Baby Girl* since the 2013 Supreme Court ruling? Have they upheld or undercut the Indian Child Welfare Act? What is at stake in these cases?

12

The Girl Hunt: Urban Nightlife and the Performance of Masculinity as Collective Action

DAVID GRAZIAN

On the first day of class, Teresa Ruiz, a newly minted Ph.D. in her twenties, approaches the classroom as she has so many times before. But rather than heading to the chalkboard and computer set up in front, she walks past the early arrivers and seats herself in the row second from the back. She is dressed how she always is on the first day: slacks, button-down shirt, tweed jacket with brown leather patches on the elbow, attaché in hand. She waits as the room fills. It's the first day of Introduction to Sociology.

After five minutes pass, the students become uncomfortable. They start asking each other where the professor is. They check their registration materials to see if they have the right room. Some joke about leaving. Others sit in awkward silence, pretending to be busy with their phones. Then a student turns around, notices Dr. Ruiz's elbow patches and says, "Are you the professor?" Dr. Ruiz gets up, walks to the front of the room, and begins class by asking, "You all are seasoned students. You've been to the first day many, many times before. Why did you wait for me?"

Classrooms are ritualistic sites where professors and students perform status-infused acts for each other. Professors broadcast their authority to students by embodying the image of a professor, standing in the front of the room, commanding everyone's attention, responding to "Dr." or "Professor," leading class discussions, manipulating their voices and mannerisms to highlight important points, holding chalk, distributing syllabi, calling on students, and the like. Reading these cues, students read the professor as "expert" and authority in the room, and they know then how to interact with her. Likewise, students give off impressions of themselves to professors. Sitting in the "magic T" zone, leaning forward, making eye contact, taking copious notes, and asking thoughtful questions project an image of "good student." We hold each other accountable for performing these acts by behaving awkwardly when someone fails to do so, passing judgments about each other's competence, turning a blind eye to the power dynamics at play, and telling other students to be quiet while the professor talks.

Just as *professor* and *student* were performances in the opening vignette, West and Zimmerman (1987) argued that gender is something we *do*, not something we *are*. That is, gender is a performance we take on using our bodies, comportment, styles, and interactions. We act out gender (masculinity through dominance; femininity through deference) to an audience who reads our performance and assesses its credibility. People hold us accountable for doing the performance appropriately. Thus, when we fail to do gender well, we face consequences.

Excerpted from Grazian, David. 2007. "The Girl Hunt: Urban Nightlife and the Performance of Masculinity as Collective Activity." *Symbolic Interaction* 30:221–243. 2007. Society for the Study of Symbolic Interaction.

In the piece that follows, Grazian studies how heterosexual college men objectify women and reinforce male superiority through the "girl hunt," a series of interaction rituals in which men prepare for and go out in the city. They perform masculinity through hyping the myth of the pickup, pregaming, girl hunting, and playing the wingman. As Grazian shows, these performances are collective: engaged in and encouraged by other men so as to create solidarity with other each other and police the boundaries between men and women and among more and less desirable men. Systems of inequality cannot exist without people holding each other accountable to reinforcing boundaries between groups, both subtly and overtly (Hollander 2013; Schwalbe 2008). Questioning someone's loyalty, calling names, and threatening violence against transgressors all push people to go along to get along. They also fire a warning shot to observers: Don't even think about stepping out of line because there will be consequences for you, too. Accountability in the girl hunt is collective and subtle but also compelling—so much so that the men seem to participate eagerly and even live vicariously through each other's success at the game.

Gender boundaries and the status differences between student and professor are just a few of the inequality divides people police through their interactional performances and accountability (see "Doing Difference" by West and Fenstermaker 1995). We signify our class status through the respect we command from others, the cars we drive, even the words we use to describe upholstery. (Watch PBS's *People Like Us* at http://video.pbs.org/program/people-us/.) We signify our ability status by holding doors for people. But it is others holding us accountable to these performances—policing us—which invests us in doing them—and the inequality systems maintained through them.

References

Hollander, Jocelyn A. 2013. "'I Demand More of People': Accountability, Interaction, and Gender Change." *Gender & Society* 27(1): 5–29.

Schwalbe, Michael. 2008. *Rigging the Game: How Inequality Is Reproduced in Everyday Life.* New York: Oxford University Press.

West, Candace, and Sarah Fenstermaker. 1995. "Doing Difference." *Gender & Society* 9(1): 8–37.

West, Candace, and Don H. Zimmerman. 1987. "Doing Gender." *Gender & Society* 1(2): 125–151.

The Performance of Masculinity as Collective Activity

According to the symbolic interactionist perspective, masculinity represents a range of dramaturgical performances individuals exhibit through face-to-face interaction (Goffman 1959, 1977; West and Zimmerman 1987). Like femininity, masculinity is not innate but an accomplishment of human behavior that appears natural because gendered individuals adhere to an institutionalized set of myths they learn through everyday interactions and encounters, and thus accept as social reality (Goffman 1977; West and Zimmerman 1987). Throughout their formative years and beyond, young men are encouraged by their parents, teachers, coaches, and peers to adopt a socially constructed vision of manhood, a set of cultural beliefs that prescribe what men ought to be like: physically strong, powerful, independent, self-confident, efficacious, dominant, active, persistent, responsible, dependable,

aggressive, courageous, and sexually potent (Donaldson 1993; Messner 2002; Mishkind et al. 1986). In the fantasies of many boys and men alike, a relentless competitive spirit, distant emotional detachment, and an insatiable heterosexual desire, all commonly (but not exclusively) displayed by the sexual objectification of women (Bird 1996), characterize idealized masculinity.

Essentialist visions of masculinity obscure how both women and men resist, challenge, and renegotiate the meanings surrounding masculinity and femininity in their everyday lives (Chapkis 1986; Connell 1987, 1992, 1993, 1995; Connell and Messerschmidt 2005; Donaldson 1993; Hollander 2002). The inevitable disconnect between dominant expectations of normative masculinity, on the one hand, and actualized efforts at what West and Zimmerman (1987) refer to as "doing gender" as a dramaturgical performance, on the other, presents a challenging problem for men, particularly because "the number of men rigorously practicing the hegemonic pattern in its entirety may be quite small" (Connell 1995, 79). It is an especially acute dilemma for young men of college age (18 to 25) who . . . display many of the physical traits of early adulthood along with the emotional immaturity, diminutive body image, and sexual insecurities of late adolescence (Mishkind et al. 1986).

The competitive ritual of *girl hunting* epitomizes this dilemma, as heterosexual adolescent males aggressively seek out female sexual partners in dance clubs, cocktail lounges, and other public arenas of commercialized entertainment in the city at night. . . . In contrast to occupational and educational domains in which masculine power can be signaled by professional success and intellectual superiority, sexual prowess is a primary signifier of masculinity in the context of urban nightlife.[1] Indeed, the importance placed on competitive "scoring" (Messner 2002) among men in the highly gendered universe of cocktail lounges and singles bars should not be underestimated.

However, a wealth of data suggests that, contrary to representations of urban nightlife in popular culture, . . . rumors of the proverbial one-night stand have been greatly exaggerated (Williams 2005). . . . Findings from the Chicago Health and Social Life Survey demonstrate that, across a variety of city neighborhood types, typically less than one-fifth of heterosexual adults aged 18 to 59 report having met their most recent sexual partner in a bar, nightclub, or dance club (Mahay and Laumann 2004: 74).[2]

Moreover, the efficacy of girl hunting is constrained by women's ability to resist unwanted sexual advances in public, as well as to initiate their own searches for desirable sex partners. Whereas the ideological basis of girl hunting stresses vulnerability, weakness, and submissiveness as conventional markers of femininity, young women commonly challenge these stereotypes by articulating their own physical strength, emotional self-reliance, and quick wit during face-to-face encounters with men (Duneier and Molotch 1999; Hollander 2002; Paules 1991; Snow, Robinson, and McCall 1991).

For all these reasons, girl hunting would not seem to serve as an especially efficacious strategy for locating sexual partners. . . . But if this is the case, then why do adolescent men persist in hassling women in public through aggressive sexual advances and pickup attempts (Duneier and Molotch 1999; Snow et al. 1991; Whyte 1988), particularly when their chances of meeting sex partners in this manner are so slim?

I argue that framing the question in this manner misrepresents the actual sociological behavior represented by the girl hunt, particularly since adolescent males do not necessarily engage in girl hunting to generate sexual relationships, even on a drunken short-term basis. Instead, three counterintuitive attributes characterize the girl hunt. First, the girl hunt is as much *ritualistic and performative* as it is utilitarian—it is a social drama through which young men perform their interpretations of manhood. Second, as demonstrated by prior studies (Martin and Hummer 1989; Polk 1994; Sanday 1990; Thorne and Luria 1986), girl hunting is not always a purely heterosexual pursuit but can also take the form of an inherently *homosocial* activity. Here, one's male peers are the intended audience for competitive games of sexual reputation and peer status, public displays of situational dominance and rule transgression, and in-group rituals of solidarity and loyalty. Finally, the emotional effort and logistical deftness required by rituals of sexual pursuit (and by extension the public performance of masculinity itself) encourage some young men to seek out safety in numbers by participating in the girl hunt as a kind of *collective* activity, in which they enjoy the social and psychological resources generated by group cohesion and dramaturgical teamwork (Goffman 1959). Although tales of sexual adventure traditionally feature a single male hero, such as Casanova, the performance of heterosexual conquest more often resembles the exploits of the dashing Christian de Neuvillette and his better-spoken coconspirator Cyrano de Bergerac (Rostand 2010). By aligning themselves with similarly oriented accomplices, many young men convince themselves of the importance and efficacy of the girl hunt (despite its poor track record), summon the courage to pursue their female targets (however clumsily), and assist one another in "mobilizing masculinity" (Martin 2001) through a collective performance of gender and heterosexuality.

Methods and Data

I draw on firsthand narrative accounts provided by 243 heterosexual male college students attending the University of Pennsylvania, an Ivy League research university situated in Philadelphia. . . . The study was conducted at Penn among all students enrolled in one of two semester terms of a sociology course on media and popular culture taught by me during the 2003–2004 academic year.[3] Respondents were directed to explore Philadelphia's downtown nightlife by attending at least one nightlife entertainment venue (i.e., restaurant, café, dance club, sports bar, cocktail lounge) located in Philadelphia's Center City district for the duration of a few evening hours' time. They were encouraged to select familiar sites where they would feel both comfortable and safe and were permitted to choose whether to conduct their outing alone or with one or more friends, relatives, intimates, or acquaintances of either gender.

Upon the conclusion of their evening, students were instructed to document their experiences in detailed narrative accounts. . . . After submitting their typed narrative accounts electronically to a team of research assistants (who in turn read them to ensure that each adhered to proper standards of protocol), the respondents' names were removed from their submissions to protect their anonymity. These accounts were then forwarded to me; I assigned them individual case numbers and systematically coded and analyzed them separately on the basis of gender.[4] An initial read-through of accounts submitted by my male respondents revealed recurring commonalities, including a pronounced goal of seeking out young women as potential sexual and romantic partners, and an ambitiously strategic orientation toward this end. Subsequent coding of these accounts highlighted the importance of collective behavior (including the ritualistic consumption of alcohol), a codependent reliance on one's peer group, and the deployment of team-oriented strategies deemed necessary for approaching women in public.[5]

The original sample of 243 heterosexual male students consists of 21.4 percent ($n = 52$) freshmen, 36.6 percent ($n = 89$) sophomores, 21.8 percent ($n = 53$) juniors, and 20.2 percent ($n = 49$) seniors. Participants ranged from 18 to 24 years of age, with a mean age of 19.9 years. Reflecting the privileged social status of Ivy League university students, the racial and ethnic makeup of the sample is as follows: 78.2 percent ($n = 190$) white, 11.5 percent ($n = 28$) Asian, 4.5 percent ($n = 11$) non-Hispanic Black, 2.9 percent ($n = 7$) Hispanic, and 2.9 percent ($n = 7$) mixed race/other.[6] Recent available statistics . . . estimate the proportion of minority students at the University of Pennsylvania at 17 percent Asian, 6 percent Black, and 5 percent Hispanic. In terms of residence prior to college, nearly three-fourths (70 percent) of the sample lived in suburban areas, while about one-fourth hailed from urban environments (26.3 percent) and the rest from rural areas (3.7 percent).

Likewise, nearly three-fourths of the sample (70.4 percent) resided in the northeastern United States, with the rest closely divided among the Midwest (5.3 percent), South (9.1 percent), West (10.7 percent), and eight countries outside the United States (3.7 percent).[7]

Studying College Men

These accounts represent about one-fifth of those submitted by my 243 heterosexual male respondents. While this subgroup comprises a substantial portion of the sample, the findings it suggests by no means represent the behaviors of *all* my students, and this should not be surprising. As Connell (1995), Messner (2002), and others argue, the dominance of hegemonic masculinity is often sustained by the aggressive actions of a minority within a context of normative complicity by a more or less "silent majority" of men who nevertheless benefit from the subordination and sexual objectification of women. Insofar as the ritual of the girl hunt symbolizes a celebrated form of hegemonic masculinity, it is therefore imperative that we examine how it is practiced in the context of everyday life, even if its proponents and their activities represent only one of many possibilities within the constellation of masculine performances and sexual identities available to men. As Connell and Messerschmidt (2005: 850) observe, hegemonic masculinities are "to a significant degree constituted in men's interaction with women." Accordingly, examining how girl hunting is accomplished can help clarify how group interactions link gender ideologies to everyday social behavior.

To ensure informants' anonymity and confidentiality, I have assigned pseudonyms to all persons. However, I have identified all respondents by their reported age, school year, and racial and ethnic background.

The Girl Hunt and the Myth of the Pickup

As I stated previously, it is statistically uncommon for men to successfully attract and "pick up" female sexual partners in bars and nightclubs. However, as suggested by a wide selection of mass media—from erotic films to hardcore pornography—heterosexual young men nevertheless sustain fantasies of successfully negotiating chance sexual encounters with anonymous strangers in urban public spaces (Bech 1998), especially dance clubs, music venues, singles bars, cocktail lounges, and other nightlife settings. According to Aaron, a 21-year-old mixed-race junior:

> I am currently in a very awkward, sticky, complicated and bizarre relationship with a young lady here at Penn, where things are pretty open right now, hopefully to be sorted out during the summer when we both have more time. So my mentality right now is to go to the club with my best bud and seek out the ladies for a night of great music, adventure and female company off of the grounds of campus.

Young men reproduce these normative expectations of masculine sexual prowess—what I call *the myth of the pickup*—collectively through homosocial group interaction. According to Brian, a 19-year-old Cuban sophomore:

> Whether I would get any girl's phone number or not, the main purpose for going out was to try to get with hot girls. That was our goal every night we went out to frat parties on campus, and we all knew it, even though we seldom mention that aspect of going out. *It was implicitly known that tonight, and every night out, was a girl hunt.* Tonight, we were taking that goal to Philadelphia's nightlife. In the meanwhile, we would have fun drinking, dancing, and joking around. (emphasis added)

For Brian and his friends, the "girl hunt" articulates a shared orientation toward public interaction in which the group collectively negotiates the city at night. The heterosexual desire among men for a plurality of women (hot *girls*, as it were) operates at the individual and group level. As in game hunting, young men frequently evaluate their erotic prestige in terms of their raw number of sexual conquests, like so many notches on a belt. Whereas traditional norms of feminine desire privilege the search for a singular and specified romantic interest (Prince Charming, Mr. Right, or his less attractive cousin, Mr. Right Now), heterosexual male fantasies idealize the pleasures of an endless abundance and variety of anonymous yet willing female sex partners (Kimmel and Plante 2002).

Despite convincing evidence to the contrary (Laumann et al. 2004), these sexual fantasies seem deceptively realizable in the context of urban nightlife. To many urban denizens, the city and its never-ending flow of anonymous visitors suggests a sexualized marketplace governed by transactional relations and expectations of personal noncommitment (Bech 1998), particularly in downtown entertainment zones where nightclubs, bars, and cocktail lounges are concentrated. The density of urban nightlife districts and their tightly packed venues only intensifies the pervasive yet improbable male fantasy of successfully attracting an imaginary surplus of amorous single women.

Adolescent men strengthen their belief in this fantasy of the sexual availability of women in the city—the myth of the pickup—through collective reinforcement in their conversations in the hours leading up to the girl hunt. While hyping their sexual prowess to the group, male peers collectively legitimize the myth of the pickup and increase its power as a model for normative masculine behavior. According to Dipak, an 18-year-old Indian freshman:

> I finished up laboratory work at 5:00 pm and walked to my dormitory, eagerly waiting to "hit up a club" that night. . . . I went to eat with my three closest friends at [a campus dining hall]. We acted like high school freshmen about to go to our first mixer. We kept hyping up the night and saying we were going to meet and dance with many girls. Two of my friends even bet with each other over who can procure the most phone numbers from girls that night. Essentially, the main topic of discussion during dinner was the night yet to come.

Competitive sex talk is common in male homosocial environments (Bird 1996) and often acts as a catalyst for sexual pursuit among groups of adolescent and young adult males. For example, in his ethnographic work on Philadelphia's Black inner-city neighborhoods, Anderson (1999) documents how sex codes among youth evolve in a context of peer pressure in which young Black males "run their game" by women as a means of pursuing in-group status. Moreover, this type of one-upmanship heightens existing heterosexual fantasies and the myth of the pickup while creating a largely unrealistic set of sexual and gender expectations for young men seeking in-group status among their peers. In doing so, competitive sexual boasting may have the effect of momentarily energizing group participants. However, in the long run it is eventually likely to deflate the confidence of those who inevitably continue to fall short of such exaggerated expectations and who consequently experience the shame of a spoiled masculine identity (Goffman 1963).

Preparing for the Girl Hunt through Collective Ritual

Armed with their inflated expectations of the nightlife of the city and its opportunities for sexual conquest, young men at Penn prepare for the girl hunt by crafting a specifically gendered and class-conscious nocturnal self (Grazian 2003)—a presentation of masculinity that relies on prevailing fashion cues and upper-class taste emulation. According to Edward, a 20-year-old white sophomore, these decisions are made strategically:

> I hadn't hooked up with a girl in a couple weeks and I needed to break my slump (the next girl you hook up with is commonly referred to as a "slump-bust" in my social circle). So I was willing to dress in whatever manner would facilitate in hooking up.

Among young college men, especially those living in communal residential settings (i.e., campus dormitories and fraternities), these preparations for public interaction serve as *collective rituals of confidence building*—shared activities that generate group solidarity and cohesion while elevating the personal resolve and self-assuredness of individual participants mobilizing for the girl hunt. Frank, a 19-year-old white sophomore, describes the first of these rituals:

> As I began observing both myself and my friends tonight, I noticed that there is a distinct pre-going-out ritual that takes place. I began the night by blasting my collection of rap music as loud as possible, as I tried to overcome the similar sounds resonating from my roommate's room. Martin seemed to play his music in order to build his confidence. It appears that the entire ritual is simply there to build up one's confidence, to make one more adept at picking up the opposite sex.

Frank explains this preparatory ritual in terms of its collective nature, as friends recount tall tales that celebrate character traits commonly associated with traditional conceptions of masculinity, such as boldness and aggression. Against a soundtrack of rap music—a genre known for its misogynistic lyrics and male-specific themes, including heterosexual boasting, emotional detachment, and masculine superiority (McLeod 1999)—these shared ritual moments of homosociality are a means of generating group resolve and bolstering the self-confidence of each participant. Again, according to Frank:

Everyone erupted into stories explaining their "high-roller status." Martin recounted how he spent nine hundred dollars in Miami one weekend, while Lance brought up his cousins who spent twenty-five hundred dollars with ease one night at a Las Vegas bachelor party. Again, all of these stories acted as a confidence booster for the night ahead.

Perhaps unsurprisingly, this constant competitive jockeying and one-upmanship so common in male-dominated settings (Martin 2001) often extends to the sexual objectification of women. While getting dressed among friends in preparation for a trip to a local strip club, Gregory, a 20-year-old white sophomore, reports on the banter: "We should all dress rich and stuff, so we can get us some hookers!" Like aggressive locker-room boasting, young male peers bond over competitive sex talk by laughing about real and make-believe sexual exploits and misadventures (Bird 1996). This joking strengthens male group intimacy and collective heterosexual identity and normalizes gender differences by reinforcing dominant myths about the social roles of men and women (Lyman 1987).

After engaging in private talk among roommates and close friends, young men (as well as women) commonly participate in a more public collective ritual known among American college students as "pregaming." As Harry, an 18-year-old white freshman, explains,

> Pregaming consists of drinking with your "boys" so that you don't have to purchase as many drinks while you are out to feel the desired buzz. On top of being cost efficient, the actual event of pregaming can get any group ready and excited to go out.

The ritualistic use of alcohol is normative on college campuses, particularly for men (Martin and Hummer 1989), and students largely describe pregaming as an economical and efficient way to get drunk before going out into the city. This is especially the case for underage students who may be denied access to downtown nightspots. However, it also seems clear that pregaming is a bonding ritual that fosters social cohesion and builds confidence among young men in anticipation of the challenges that accompany the girl hunt. According to Joey, an 18-year-old white freshman:

> My thoughts turn to this girl, Jessica. . . . I was thinking about whether or not we might hook up tonight. . . . As

I turn to face the door to 301, I feel the handle, and it is shaking from the music and dancing going on in the room. I open the door and see all my best friends just dancing together. . . . I quickly rush into the center of the circle and start doing my "J-walk," which I have perfected over the years. My friends love it and begin to chant, "Go Joey—it's your birthday." I'm feeling connected with my friends and just know that we're about to have a great night. . . . Girls keep coming in and out of the door, but no one really pays close attention to them. Just as the "pregame" was getting to its ultimate height, each boy had his arms around each other jumping in unison, to a great hip-hop song by Biggie Smalls. One of the girls went over to the stereo and turned the power off. We yelled at her to turn it back on, but the mood was already lost and we decided it was time to head out.

In this example, Joey's confidence is boosted by the camaraderie he experiences in a male-bonding ritual in which women—supposedly the agreed-upon raison d'être for the evening—are ignored or, when they make their presence known, scolded. As these young men dance arm-in-arm with one another, they generate the collective effervescence and sense of social connectedness necessary to plunge into the nightlife of the city. As such, pregaming fulfills the same function as the last-minute huddle (with all hands in the middle) does for an athletic team (Messner 2002).[8] It is perhaps ironic that Joey's ritual of "having fun with my boys" prepares him for the girl hunt (or more specifically in his case, an opportunity to "hook up" with Jessica) even as it requires those boys to exclude their female classmates. At the same time, this men-only dance serves the same function as the girl hunt: It allows its participants to expressively perform hegemonic masculinity through an aggressive display of collective identification. In this sense the pregame resembles other campus rituals of male socialization and boundary maintenance, particularly those associated with fraternity life and violence against women (Boswell and Spade 1996; Martin and Hummer 1989; Sanday 1990).

During similar collective rituals leading up to the girl hunt, young men boost each other's confidence in their abilities of sexual persuasion by watching films about male heterosexual exploits in urban nightlife, such as Doug Liman's *Swingers* (1996), which chronicles the storied escapades of two best friends, Mike and Trent. According to Kevin, an 18-year-old white freshman:

> I knew that [my friend] Darryl needed to calm down if he wanted any chance of a second date. At about 8:15 pm, I sat him down and showed him (in my opinion, the movie that every man should see at least once—I've seen it six times)—*Swingers*. . . . Darryl immediately related to Mike's character, the self-conscious but funny gentleman who is still on the rebound from a long-term relationship. At the same time, he took Trent's words for scripture (as I planned): "There's nothing wrong with showing the beautiful babies that you're money and that you want to party." His mind was clearly eased at the thought of his being considered "money." Instead of being too concerned with not screwing up and seeming "weird or desperate," Darryl now felt like he was in control. The three of us each went to our own rooms to get ready.

This collective attention to popular cultural texts helps peer groups generate common cultural references, private jokes, and speech norms as well as build in-group cohesion (Eliasoph and Lichterman 2003; Fine 1977; Swidler 2001). In this case, globally distributed mass-media texts (i.e., films, music recordings and videos, television programs, computer games, comic books) supply audiences with a familiar set of shared discursive strategies and symbolic resources that influence daily social behavior pertaining to gender and sexual expression at a more localized level (Connell and Messerschmidt 2005; Swidler 2001). Similar to the immersion in rap music, the incorporation of collective film viewing into the pregame ritual promotes male group solidarity. But in addition to generating a sense of collective energy, it provides a set of cultural frames useful for making sense of the girl hunt, just as Sanday (1990: 129) documents how fraternity brothers habitually watch pornographic films together in their preparations for late-night parties. Of course, *Swingers* represents much tamer fare: yet, like pornography, the film encourages the development of a hypermasculine identity while supplying young men with scripts for upcoming social interactions with women, reducing women to infantile objects of sexual desire ("beautiful babies"), generating collective excitement for the girl hunt, and giving young men the self-confidence necessary for competing in such a contest.

Girl Hunting and the Collective Performance of Masculinity

Finally, once the locus of action moves to a more public venue such as a bar or nightclub, the much-anticipated "girl hunt" itself proceeds as a strategic display of masculinity best performed with a suitable game partner. According to Christopher, a 22-year-old white senior, he and his cousin Darren "go out together a lot. We enjoy each other's company and we seem to work well together when trying to meet women." Reporting on his evening at a local dance club, Lawrence, a 21-year-old white junior, illustrates how the girl hunt itself operates as collective activity:

> We walk around the bar area as we finish [our drinks]. After we are done, we walk down to the regular part of the club. We make the rounds around the dance floor checking out the girls. . . . We walk up to the glassed dance room and go in, but leave shortly because it is really hot and there weren't many prospects.

Lawrence and his friends display their elaborated performance of masculinity by making their rounds together as a pack in search of a suitable feminine target. Perhaps it is not surprising that the collective nature of their pursuit should also continue *after* such a prize has been located:

> This is where the night gets really interesting. We walk back down to the main dance floor and stand on the outside looking at what's going on and I see a really good-looking girl behind us standing on the other side of the wall with three friends. After pointing her out to my friends, I decide that I'm going to make the big move and talk to her. So I turn around and ask her to dance. She accepts and walks over. My friends are loving this, so they go off to the side and watch. . . .
>
> After dancing for a little while she brings me over to her friends and introduces me. They tell me that they are all freshman at [a local college], and we go through the whole small talk thing again. I bring her over to my two boys who are still getting a kick out of the whole situation. . . . My boys tell me about some of the girls they have seen and talked to, and they inform me that they recognized some girls from Penn walking around the club.

Why do Lawrence and his dance partner both introduce each other to their friends? Lawrence seems to gain almost as much pleasure from his *friends'* excitement as

from his own exploits, just as they are "loving" the vicarious thrill of watching their comrade succeed in commanding the young woman's attention, as if their own masculinity is validated by his success.

In this instance, arousal is not merely individual but represents a collectively shared experience as well (Thorne and Luria 1986: 181). For these young men the performance of masculinity does not necessarily require successfully meeting a potential sex partner as long as one enthusiastically participates in the ritual *motions* of the girl hunt in the company of men. When Lawrence brings over his new female friend, he does so to celebrate his victory with his buddies, and in return, they appear gratified by their *own* small victory by association. (And while Lawrence celebrates with them, perhaps he alleviates some of the pressure of actually conversing with her.)

Along these lines, the collective quality of the girl hunt makes each male participant accountable to the group as well as to himself. In this manner, young single men will goad each other on to persist in the hunt, deriding those who turn away potential pickups. Michael, a 19-year-old white junior, reports on his evening out at McFadden's, an Irish-themed sports bar and nightclub:

> My friend Buddy beckoned to me from the dance floor. Not knowing what he wanted, I snaked my way through the crowd to join him. As I approached him, a girl several years my senior smiled at me. She looked like she wanted to start a conversation, but waited for me to initiate. Not particularly interested in her and with my friend waiting, I awkwardly moved past with what I am sure was a weird smile on my face. *Buddy had seen this entire exchange and said he was disappointed in me for not trying to hit on her.* (emphasis added)

Through their homosocial encounters, young men make one another accountable for their interactions with women, and their vigilance increases the chances that over time these men will eventually comply with the set of practices that sustain the ideals of hegemonic masculinity, *even in instances when such men disagree with those expectations* (Connell 1995; Demetriou 2001).

As Christopher remarked previously on his relationship with his cousin, the collective aspects of the girl hunt also highlight the efficacy of conspiring with peers to meet women: "We go out together a lot. We enjoy each other's company and we seem to work well together when trying to meet women." In the language of the confidence game, men eagerly serve as each other's shills (Goffman 1959; Grazian 2004; Maurer 1940) and sometimes get roped into the role unwittingly with varying degrees of success. Michael continues in his report by describing Buddy's exploits:

Buddy, a 25-year-old University of Pennsylvania alumnus, is the kind of guy who is not afraid to flirt with as many girls as possible. Tonight he was putting his charm to good use, dancing with any girl who would give him the time of day. I realized he had called me over for the purpose of finding a girl for me. Turning to the girl nearest him on the dance floor he said to her, "This is my friend Michael. He's a little shy." Waiting for him to introduce me to her, I realized after a moment that he didn't know these girls either. His introduction was actually one of the cheesiest pickup lines I had ever heard used that wasn't the punch line to a joke. I introduced myself to the girl whose name I found out was Rebecca, a 24-year-old professional from South Philly. I talked to her for a few minutes and admitted my true age to her; surprisingly, she didn't blow me off too quickly, but her interest was definitely in Buddy rather than me at that point. Deciding to leave the two of them to get better acquainted, I excused myself to the bar to get a second beer.

In this instance, Michael politely disengages from the interaction without challenging the ideological basis of the girl hunt itself. Rather, his passive performance amounts to what Connell (1995) refers to as "complicit masculinity," insofar as Michael is able to support his friend's interaction and thus benefit from the "patriarchal dividend" (acceptance within a male homosocial group and the status associated with such membership) gained from the promotion of the ideals of hegemonic masculinity as represented by the girl hunt (also see Demetriou 2001).

Among young people, the role of the passive accomplice is commonly referred to in contemporary parlance as a *wingman*. Popularized by the 1986 film *Top Gun*, the term literally refers to the backup fighter pilots who protect the head of a military flying formation by positioning themselves outside and behind (or on the wing of) the lead aircraft to engage enemy fire when necessary. In recent years, the term has been appropriated to refer to an accomplice who assists a designated leading man in meeting eligible single women, often at costs to his own

ability to do the same. In male-oriented popular culture, the wingman has become institutionalized in men's magazines ("*Maxim*'s Wingman Training Manual" 2003), literature documenting young men's real-and-imagined sex lives (i.e., Max 2006; Strauss 2005), and how-to manuals with such dubiously promising titles as *The Guide to Picking Up Girls*. This last text provides a vulgar description of the colloquialism:

Everyone knows what a wingman must do. Your wingman must take the extra girl for you if there are two girls and you want to talk to one of them. The wingman must lay rap on your girl's friend as long as you rap with your girl. It does not matter that the girl's friend may be very ugly. The wingman must do his job at any cost. He must be able to pull his own weight and back you up. Otherwise, your girl may get pulled away by her friend whom your wingman has failed to entertain. (Fischbarg 2002: 36)

In public rituals of courtship, the wingman serves multiple purposes: he provides validation of a leading man's trustworthiness, eases the interaction between a single male friend and a larger group of women, serves as a source of distraction for the friend or friends of a more desirable target of affection, can be called on to confirm the wild (and frequently misleading) claims of his partner, and, perhaps most important, helps motivate his friends by building up their confidence. Indeed, men describe the role of the wingman in terms of loyalty, personal responsibility, and dependability, traits commonly associated with masculinity (Martin and Hummer 1989; Mishkind et al. 1986). According to Nicholas, an 18-year-old white freshman:

As we were beginning to mobilize ourselves and move towards the dance floor, James noticed Rachel, a girl he knew from Penn who he often told me about as a potential girlfriend. Considering James was seemingly into this girl, Dan and I decided to be good wingmen and entertain Rachel's friend, Sarah.

Hegemonic masculinity is not only expressed by competitiveness but camaraderie as well, and many young men will take their role as a wingman quite seriously and at a personal cost to their relationships with female friends. According to Peter, a 20-year-old white sophomore:

"It sounds like a fun evening," I said to Kyle, "but I promised Elizabeth I would go to her date party." I don't like to break commitments. On the other hand,

I didn't want to leave Kyle to fend for himself at this club. . . . Kyle is the type of person who likes to pick girls up at clubs. If I were to come see him, I would want to meet other people as well. Having Elizabeth around would not only prevent me from meeting (or even just talking to) other girls, but it would also force Kyle into a situation of having no "wing man."

In the end, Peter takes Elizabeth to a nightclub where, although he *himself* will not be able to meet available women, he will at least be able to assist Kyle in meeting them:

Behind Kyle, a very attractive girl smiles at me. Yes! Oh, wait. Damnit, Elizabeth's here. . . . "Hey, Kyle," I whisper to him. "That girl behind you just smiled at you. Go talk to her." Perhaps Kyle will have some luck with her. He turns around, takes her by the hand, and begins dancing with her. She looks over at me and smiles again, and I smile back. I don't think Elizabeth noticed. I would have rather been in Kyle's position, but I was happy for him, and I was dancing with Elizabeth, so I was satisfied for the moment.

By the end of the night, as he and Kyle chat in a taxi on the way back to campus, Peter learns that he was instrumental in securing his friend's success in an additional way:

"So what ever happened with you and that girl?" I ask. "I hooked up with her. Apparently she's a senior." I ask if she knew he was a freshman. "Oh, yeah. She asked how old you were, though. I said you were a junior. I had to make one of us look older."

Peter's willingness to serve as a wingman demonstrates his complicity in sustaining the ideals of hegemonic masculinity, which therefore allows him to benefit from the resulting "patriarchal dividends"—acceptance as a member of his male homosocial friendship network and its attendant prestige—even when he himself does not personally seek out the sexual rewards of the girl hunt.

In addition, the peer group provides a readily available audience that can provide emotional comfort to all group members, as well as bear witness to any individual successes that might occur. As demonstrated by the preceding examples, young men deeply value the erotic prestige they receive from their conspiratorial peers upon succeeding in the girl hunt. According to Zach, a 20-year-old white sophomore:

About ten minutes later, probably around 2:15 am, we split up into cabs again, with the guys in one and the girls in another. . . . This time in the cab, all the guys want to talk about is me hooking up on the dance floor. It turns out that they saw the whole thing. I am not embarrassed; in fact I am proud of myself.

As an audience, the group can collectively validate the experience of any of its members and can also internalize an individual's success as a shared victory. Since, in a certain sense, a successful sexual interaction must be recognized by one's peers to gain status as an in-group "social fact," the group can transform a private moment into a celebrated public event—thereby making it "count" for the male participant and his cohorts.

Of course, as argued here and elsewhere (Laumann et al. 1994) and demonstrated by the sample analyzed here, turning a heterosexual public encounter with a stranger into an immediately consummated sexual episode is a statistical rarity, especially when compared with the overwhelming degree of time, money, effort, and emotion that young men invest in such an enterprise. But if we focus on the *primary* goal of the girl hunt—the performance of normative masculinity—then it becomes clear that the collectivity of the endeavor allows peer group members to successfully enact traditional gender roles even when they ultimately fail at the sexual pursuit itself. Again, the performance of masculinity does not necessarily require *success* at picking up women, just so long as one participates in the endeavor enthusiastically in the company of men.

For instance, Sam, a 22-year-old Black senior, observes how one such peer group takes pleasure in one of their member's public rejection at the hands of an unimpressed woman:

By this time it was around 1:30 am, and the party was almost over. . . . I saw a lot of the guys had their cell phones out while they were talking to the women. I figured the guys were trying to get phone numbers from the girls. So as I walked past one of the guys, I heard him ask a girl for her number. But she just laughed and walked away. That was real funny especially since his friends saw what happened and proceeded to laugh as well.

As young men discover, contrary to popular myths about femininity, it is increasingly uncommon for women to act passively during sexually charged confrontations, even those that may be physically precarious. In such situations, women often resist and challenge the advances of strange men in public through polite refusal or the expression of humor, moral outrage, outright rejection, or physical retaliation (Berk 1977; Hollander 2002; Snow et al. 1991).

Nevertheless, one participant's botched attempt at an ill-conceived pickup can solidify the male group's bonds as much as a successful one. According to Brian, the aforementioned 19-year-old Cuban sophomore:

> We had been in the club for a little more than half an hour, when the four of us were standing at the perimeter of the main crowd in the dancing room. It was then when Marvin finished his second Corona and by his body gestures, he let it be known that he was drunk enough and was pumped up to start dancing. He started dancing behind a girl who was dancing in a circle with a few other girls. Then the girl turned around and said "Excuse me!" Henry and I saw what happened. We laughed so hard and made so much fun of him for the rest of the night. I do not think any of us has ever been turned away so directly and harshly as that time.

In this instance, Marvin's abruptly concluded encounter with an unwilling female participant turns into a humorous episode for the rest of his peer group, leaving his performance of masculinity bruised yet intact. Indeed, in his gracelessness Marvin displays an enthusiastic male heterosexuality as emphasized by his drunken attempts to court an unsuspecting target before a complicit audience of his male peers. And as witnesses to his awkward sexual advance, Brian and Henry take pleasure in the incident, as it not only raises *their* relative standing within the group in comparison with Marvin but can also serve as a narrative focus for future "signifying" episodes (or ceremonial exchanges of insults) and other rituals of solidarity characteristic of joking relationships among male adolescents (Lyman 1987: 155). Meanwhile, these young men can bask in their collective failure to attract a woman without ever actually challenging the basis of the girl hunt itself: the performance of adolescent masculinity.

In the end, young men may enjoy this performance of masculinity—the hunt itself—even more than the potential romantic or sexual rewards they hope to gain by its successful execution. In his reflections on a missed opportunity to procure the phone number of a law student, Christopher, the aforementioned 22-year-old senior, admits as much: "There's something about the chase that I really like. Maybe

I subconsciously neglected to get her number. I am tempted to think that I like the idea of being on the look out for her better than the idea of calling her to go out for coffee." While Christopher's excuse may certainly function as a compensatory face-saving strategy employed in the aftermath of another lonely night (Berk 1977), it might also indicate a possible acceptance of the limits of the girl hunt despite its potential opportunities for male bonding and the public display of adolescent masculinity.

Discussion

A consistent thread in symbolic interactionism concerns how structures of inequality are constituted and reproduced through recurrent patterns of ordinary social interaction. According to Collins (1981: 987–988), the very foundations of the macrosocial world and its institutions can be reduced to the agglomeration of everyday face-to-face encounters conducted among humans over time. As he argues, "Strictly speaking, there is no such thing as a 'state,' an 'economy,' a 'culture,' a 'social class.' There are only collections of individual people acting in particular kinds of microsituations." Schwalbe et al. (2000) emphasize how the repetition of "generic processes" such as oppressive othering, identity work, boundary maintenance, and emotion management all contribute to the reproduction of inequality through their frequent deployment in varied social contexts.

Taken in this way, the "girl hunt" is shorthand for a composite of multiple types of collectively initiated interaction rituals capable of reproducing social inequality on the basis of gender. Group-based efforts at "mobilizing masculinity" (Martin 2001) during the pregame, and "girl watching" (Quinn 2002) in the context of nightclub interaction, operate as processes that fabricate gender difference and male superiority while transforming women into targets of the collective male gaze and objects of sexual desire. By engaging in the "mutually supportive facework" provided by wingmen, would-be suitors reproduce myths of male dominance by cooperatively creating nocturnal selves that "foster impressions of competence and trustworthiness" through strategies of impression management, deception, and guile (Schwalbe et al. 2000: 424). Of course, these generic processes occur not merely in a vacuum but within a social setting in which the regularity of sexist banter and asymmetric courtship rituals encourage the replication of such behaviors, along with the continually renewed ideologies of feminine subordination they promote.

But at the same time, it is equally noteworthy that the girl hunt promotes social inequality and subordinate behavior *among men.* Among participants in the girl hunt, the most dominant men enjoy a disproportionate degree of social prestige relative to their competitors, as is the case in other sexual contests (Wright 1995). Competitive sex talk among adolescent peers in the hours leading up to the girl hunt create an unrealistic set of sexual expectations for impressionable young men, particularly those who already suffer from anxiety over their body image and sexual development (Mishkind et al. 1986). Meanwhile, the repetition of collective rituals of masculine identification successfully conditions young men to suppress empathy for females targeted by the girl hunt, just as the training regimes of military and police units serve to diminish feelings of inhibition and fear among cadets (Schwalbe et al. 2000: 437). As illustrated in the last section, male peers often rely on the cultural scripts associated with girl hunting to hassle one another to perform masculinity by behaving in ways that seem to counter their actual sexual desires. In the end, the interaction rituals associated with the girl hunt reproduce structures of inequality *within* as well as *across* the socially constructed gender divide between women and men. . . .

Notes

1. Other such signifiers include physical dominance and assertiveness relative to other men, skill at competitive bar games, and a high tolerance for alcohol.

2. According to the Chicago Health and Social Life Survey, the exception to this statistic is the Mexican community area called "Westside," in which 23 percent of women (but only 19 percent of men) reported having met their most recent partner at a bar, dance club, or nightclub (Mahay and Laumann 2004: 81).

3. For inclusion in the sample generated for this article, male students either voluntarily self-identified as heterosexual or else were coded as such from their written narrative accounts (i.e., referenced a female sex partner or generalized heterosexual desire). While it is certainly possible that those coded as heterosexual may *also* engage in homosexual or bisexual practices, this did not preclude them from inclusion in the sample, given the nature of the research question. . . .

4. All names were removed to ensure the anonymity and confidentiality of the participants. However, students were asked to supply basic demographic information (including gender, age, year of school, residence, racial and ethnic origin, and sexual orientation [optional]) to be used as a reference during coding and analysis, which was conducted with the help of NVivo, a qualitative data software package.

5. Of course, since these reports account for only one evening's worth of behavior and experience, I cannot validate whether they accurately characterize the lifestyles of my individual respondents, although peer-led focus groups later conducted among a smaller sample of 30 male respondents uncovered similar findings.

6. Nearly 40 percent of the Asian students in the sample are of Indian descent. While my data analysis did uncover very small differences in consumption patterns among my sample on the basis of race and ethnicity, I could not detect notable differences relevant to the arguments presented in this chapter. Nevertheless, for the edification of the reader I identify the ethnoracial background of all participants cited in the rest of the chapter.

7. Students residing in Philadelphia prior to attending the University of Pennsylvania comprise 8.2 percent of the entire sample, while 22.2 percent hail from within the Commonwealth of Pennsylvania. Of those students from outside the Northeast, a disproportionate number resided in the populous states of California and Florida prior to college. The numbers are rounded off.

8. In this context, the male ritual of jumping in unison to loud music bears a close resemblance to the "circle dance" initiated by fraternity brothers immediately prior to an alleged incident of gang rape, as described in Sanday 1990.

References

Anderson, Elijah. 1999. *Code of the Street: Decency, Violence, and the Moral Life of the Inner City.* New York: Norton.

Bech, Henning. 1998. "Citysex: Representing Lust in Public." *Theory, Culture & Society* 15(3–4): 215–241.

Berk, Bernard. 1977. "Face-Saving at the Singles Dance." *Social Problems* 24(5): 530–544.

Bird, Sharon R. 1996. "Welcome to the Men's Club: Homosociality and the Maintenance of Hegemonic Masculinity." *Gender & Society* 10(2): 120–132.

Boswell, A. Ayres, and Joan Z. Spade. 1996. "Fraternities and Collegiate Rape Culture: Why Are Some Fraternities More Dangerous Places for Women?" *Gender & Society* 10(2): 133–147.

Chapkis, Wendy. 1986. *Beauty Secrets: Women and the Politics of Appearance.* Boston: South End.

Collins, Randall. 1981. "On the Microfoundations of Macrosociology." *American Journal of Sociology* 86(5): 984–1014.

Connell, R. W. 1987. *Gender and Power: Society, the Person, and Sexual Politics.* Stanford, CA: Stanford University Press.

Connell, R. W. 1992. "A Very Straight Gay: Masculinity, Homosexual Experience, and the Dynamics of Gender." *American Sociological Review* 57(6): 735–751.

Connell, R. W. 1993. "The Big Picture: Masculinities in Recent World History." *Theory and Society* 22(5): 597–623.

Connell, R. W. 1995. *Masculinities.* Berkeley: University of California Press.

Connell, R. W., and James W. Messerschmidt. 2005. "Hegemonic Masculinity: Rethinking the Concept." *Gender & Society* 19(6): 829–859.

Demetriou, Demetrakis Z. 2001. "Connell's Concept of Hegemonic Masculinity: A Critique." *Theory and Society* 30(3): 337–361.

Donaldson, Mike. 1993. "What Is Hegemonic Masculinity?" *Theory and Society* 22(5): 643–657.

Duneier, Mitchell, and Harvey Molotch. 1999. "Talking City Trouble: Interactional Vandalism, Social Inequality, and the 'Urban Interaction Problem.'" *American Journal of Sociology* 104(5): 1263–1295.

Eliasoph, Nina, and Paul Lichterman. 2003. "Culture in Interaction." *American Journal of Sociology* 108(4): 735–794.

Fine, Gary Alan. 1977. "Popular Culture and Social Interaction: Production, Consumption, and Usage." *Journal of Popular Culture* 11(2): 453–456.

Fischbarg, Gabe. 2002. *The Guide to Picking Up Girls.* New York: Plume.

Goffman, Erving. 1959. *The Presentation of Self in Everyday Life.* Garden City, NY: Anchor Books.

Goffman, Erving. 1961. *Asylums: Essays on the Social Situation of Mental Patients and Other Inmates.* New York: Anchor.

Grazian, David. 2003. *Blue Chicago: The Search for Authenticity in Urban Blues Clubs.* Chicago: University of Chicago Press.

Grazian, David. 2004. "The Production of Popular Music as a Confidence Game: The Case of the Chicago Blues." *Qualitative Sociology* 27(2): 137–158.

Hollander, Jocelyn A. 2002. "Resisting Vulnerability: The Social Reconstruction of Gender in Interaction." *Social Problems* 49(4): 474–496.

Kimmel, Michael S., and Rebecca F. Plante. 2002. "The Gender of Desire: The Sexual Fantasies of Women and Men." *Advances in Gender Research* 6:55–77.

Laumann, Edward O., John H. Gagnon, Robert T. Michael, and Stuart Michaels. 1994. *The Social Organization of Sexuality: Sexual Practices in the United States.* Chicago: University of Chicago Press.

Laumann, Edward O., Stephen Ellingson, Jenna Mahay, Anthony Paik, and Yoosik Youm, eds. 2004. *The Sexual Organization of the City.* Chicago: University of Chicago Press.

Lyman, Peter. 1987. "The Fraternal Bond as a Joking Relationship: A Case Study of the Role of Sexist Jokes in Male Group Bonding." In *Changing Men: New Directions in Research on Men and Masculinity* (ed. M. S. Kimmel). Newbury Park, CA: Sage. pp. 148–163.

Mahay, Jenna, and Edward O. Laumann. 2004. "Neighborhoods as Sex Markets." In *The Sexual Organization of the City* (ed. E. O. Laumann, S. Ellingson, J. Mahay, A. Paik, and Y. Youm). Chicago: University of Chicago Press. pp. 69–92.

Martin, Patricia Yancey. 2001. "'Mobilizing Masculinities': Women's Experiences of Men at Work." *Organization* 8(4): 587–618.

Martin, Patricia Yancey, and Robert A. Hummer. 1989. "Fraternities and Rape on Campus." *Gender & Society* 3(4): 457–473.

Maurer, David W. 1940. *The Big Con: The Story of the Confidence Man.* New York: Bobbs-Merrill.

Max, Tucker. 2006. *I Hope They Serve Beer in Hell.* New York: Citadel.

"*Maxim's* Wingman Training Manual." 2003. *Maxim*, May.

McLeod, Kembrew. 1999. "Authenticity within Hip-Hop and Other Cultures Threatened with Assimilation." *Journal of Communication* 49(4): 134–150.

Messner, Michael A. 2002. *Taking the Field: Women, Men, and Sports.* Minneapolis: University of Minnesota Press.

Mishkind, Marc, Judith Rodin, Lisa R. Silberstein, and Ruth H. Striegel-Moore. 1986. "The Embodiment of Masculinity." *American Behavioral Scientist* 29(5): 545–562.

Paules, Greta Foff. 1991. *Dishing It Out: Power and Resistance among Waitresses in a New Jersey Restaurant.* Philadelphia, PA: Temple University Press.

Polk, Kenneth. 1994. "Masculinity, Honor, and Confrontational Homicide." In *Just Boys Doing Business? Men, Masculinities, and Crime* (ed. T. Newburn and E. A. Stanko). London: Routledge. pp. 166–188.

Quinn, Beth A. 2002. "Sexual Harassment and Masculinity: The Power and Meaning of 'Girl Watching.'" *Gender & Society* 16(3): 386–402.

Rostand, Edmond. 2010. "Cyrano de Bergerac." *Holmi* 11:1429–1437.

Sanday, Peggy Reeves. 1990. *Fraternity Gang Rape: Sex, Brotherhood, and Privilege on Campus*. New York: New York University Press.

Schwalbe, Michael, Sandra Goodwin, Daphne Holden, Douglas Schrock, Shealy Thompson, and Michele Wolkomir. 2000. "Generic Processes in the Reproduction of Inequality: An Interactionist Analysis." *Social Forces* 79(2): 419–452.

Snow, David A., Cherylon Robinson, and Patricia L. McCall. 1991. "'Cooling Out' Men in Singles Bars and Nightclubs: Observations on the Interpersonal Survival Strategies of Women in Public Places." *Journal of Contemporary Ethnography* 19(4): 423–449.

Strauss, Neil. 2005. *The Game: Penetrating the Secret Society of Pickup Artists*. New York: Regan Books.

Swidler, Ann. 2001. *Talk of Love: How Culture Matters*. Chicago: University of Chicago Press.

Thorne, Barrie, and Zella Luria. 1986. "Sexuality and Gender in Children's Daily Worlds." *Social Problems* 33(3): 176–190.

West, Candace, and Don H. Zimmerman. 1987. "Doing Gender." *Gender & Society* 1(2): 125–151.

Whyte, William H. 1988. *City: Rediscovering the Center*. New York: Doubleday.

Williams, Alex. 2005. "Casual Relationships, Yes. Casual Sex, Not Really." *New York Times*, April 3, pp. 1, 12.

Wright, Robert. 1995. *The Moral Animal: Evolutionary Psychology and Everyday Life*. New York: Vintage.

Questions

1. What makes nightspots unique social settings? How are expectations for behavior different there from other settings, such as school or work? If girl hunting isn't an efficacious way to initiate sexual encounters with women, why do men do it?

2. From a symbolic interactionist perspective, going out is a performance. What does this mean? What does performance have to do with manhood and social class? How did men prepare for an evening of girl hunting? What is pregaming, and why do men do it? What other rituals helped men build their confidence for a night out? What cultural tools (e.g., movies) did they use to do so? How did they use them?

3. Joey offers a description of pregaming in which men dance around with each other and cheer each other on. How did men respond to women in the setting? Why did men respond that way if the point is to girl hunt? Is girl hunting an individual action or a collective one? Why? Who is the audience for men's performance? Heterosexual women? Men? Both? What does a wingman do? In what ways is the wingman complicit in the girl hunt, even if he isn't hitting on women himself? How does the girl hunt reinforce men's power and authority? What other bonding and performance rituals do people in dominant groups perform with and for each other?

4. Is there a female equivalent to girl hunting? If so, does it work the same way? If not, why not? What role did power play in girl hunting? How does girl hunting reinforce inequality between women and men? Among men? Would girls engaging in boy hunting have the same consequences for inequality? How do women police gender boundaries? Is policing of boundaries qualitatively different for people from subordinated groups? Different in form? Effect?

5. Why do the men (and the author) say *girl* hunting and not *woman* hunting or *lady* hunting? How does the term "girl" police women and position men as a group as higher status and deserving of power? Is this true when women call each other "girl"?

6. What role does alcohol play in male domination? In preparing men to dominate? What other cultural tools do people in dominant groups use to ease their ability to dominate or dull their ability to relate to other people?

13

Creating Model Consumers: Producing Ethnicity, Race, and Class in Asian American Advertising

SHALINI SHANKAR

In 2014 Ebola ravaged West Africa. Ebola is a particularly cruel disease. It is passed by bodily fluids when patients are symptomatic; when loved ones comfort the sick or prepare bodies for burial, they are most susceptible to infection. Containing the disease requires early intervention, following strict medical protocols that isolate the sick from the non-sick, and extensive decontamination procedures. (See Doctors without Borders' Ebola page for more information, or you can see a *60 Minutes* video inside a treatment hospital at *http://www.cbsnews.com/videos/60-minutes-gets-inside-look-at-a-liberian-hospital-treating-ebola/*.)

Doctors without Borders (officially Médecins Sans Frontières or MSF), a humanitarian medical aid organization which won the Nobel Peace Prize in 1999, is on the front lines treating patients. In 2014, a collective of African musicians collaborated on a song titled "Africa Stop Ebola," the profits from which benefited MSF. The song, whose chorus calls Ebola "invisible enemy," encourages people that doctors will help them and gives hope that they will beat Ebola and overcome the disease. It also provides basic medical advice about not touching others if someone is sick. The song deflects stigma by insisting that the cured are not contagious. The artists sing in numerous West African languages, French, and English.

Around the same time, a group called Band Aid 30, led by Bob Geldof and comprised of mostly British singers, released "Do They Know It's Christmas?" The song, timed with the 30th anniversary of the original song that benefited famine relief in Ethiopia, raised funds to combat Ebola (we could not locate the specific recipient). The video of the song opens with a dark scene of two fully gowned doctors laying a blanket over a partially undressed African woman whom they then carry out by the hands and feet. The following scenes cut between artists of various colors, ages, and genres crooning to let the apparently unaware know that it *is* Christmas. Fuse ODG, a prominent English performer of Ghanaian descent, turned down Band Aid's request to participate in making the song, explaining that he was "shocked and appalled" by the lyrics, which he (ODG 2014) viewed as negatively and inaccurately portraying Africa. He decried the lack of dignity provided to the dead in the video. "I, like many others, am sick of the whole concept of Africa—a resource-rich continent with unbridled potential—always being seen as diseased, infested, and poverty-stricken," he wrote in *The Guardian* (ODG 2014).

The two songs and videos offer a striking contrast in how pop culture employs multiculturalism to motivate consumption in the name of a social cause. One is bright, hopeful, instructive, calling for trust in doctors and unity to overcome disease. The other is dark, fearful, calling for teaching Africans about the truth of Christmas. In one, West Africans are subjective: They are actors who should take precautions and partner with doctors to protect themselves and each other. They fight the disease to overcome it. In the other, they are objects: themselves helpless and unaware of Christmas but the object of prayer, touch, and outreach. While both songs play up and on plurality and community, Band Aid's song and video reinforce the colonial relationship between Europe and Africa and the notion of the first world as saviors through science, medicine, and consumption.

In the following piece, Shalini Shankar uses "metaproduction" to study multiculturalism and consumption. Using ethnographic research of advertising executives, Shankar provides a critical analysis of the portrayal of Asian Americans in advertisements designed to appeal to them while retaining the universality of general-market branding. Advertisers repackage the "model minority stereotype" into the "model consumer." Executives use language and imagery to appeal to small segments of Asian American consumers in self-aware ways that conscientiously counteract stereotypes of Asian Americans. Nonetheless, in doing so, they racialize Asian Americans in classed ways that make the vast majority of Asian Americans and global capitalism invisible.

Shankar's work also draws our attention to the importance of analyzing consumption, particularly as embedded in global capitalism, as a display of social status and as a potential mechanism for social change. "Buy, buy" and "spend, spend" seem to be preferred solutions to global problems, be they disease, terrorist attacks, teetering markets, or racial stereotypes. Can consumption patterns reflect real social changes? And can we buy and consume our way to a better world?

Reference

ODG, Fuse. 2014. "Why I Had to Turn Down Band Aid." *The Guardian*, November 19. http://www.theguardian .com/commentisfree/2014/nov/19/turn-down-band-aid-bob-geldof-africa-fuse-odg (accessed December 5, 2014).

Fortune, wealth, luck, you know, those are all common themes. You know, I could go to a marketer [and] he may not know the Asian American market well. I could say to him, "You know, Chinese love the color red and the number eight and the number nine and gold, and so here's our ad." And the client would think, "Oh wow! I'm really touching this Asian American market now, because I've got all the cues that resonate with them, right? You know, I got the red, I got the dragon, I got the eight, I got the nine." And then when I see it, it's just this cliché thing, you know? It doesn't say anything to me.

—Steve, account executive, Asian Collaboration Advertising and Marketing Agency, New York

Sitting in his modern, minimalist, loft-style office on Madison Avenue, Steve conveyed a central tension in the creation and development of advertising aimed at Asian American audiences. He and his client bring conflicting notions to bear on the creative process, in that each believes a different set of signs will be most appealing to

Asian audiences in the United States. According to Steve's performance of his client, the latter is drawn to signifiers that are neither American nor Asian American per se; they are perhaps best understood as icons that signify Asia in the broad U.S. imagination. Although icons such as dragons and numerology certainly could conjure images of Asia for Asian Americans more particularly, Steve indicates that he, like his audiences, would find them simplistic and ineffective. Executives like Steve pride themselves on avoiding icons that might diminish the complex subjectivity of Asians in the United States. They approach their creative work on a "meta" level that reveals their knowledge of broader historical and cultural narratives about Asian Americans, their familiarity with language varieties and uses of speech, and their ability to create indexes for different Asian ethnic groups. All the while, they aim to please clients who expect to maintain brand identity and to see evidence of Asian American language and culture that will reach this emerging market.

In this chapter, I examine the ideological underpinnings of racial and ethnic formation while also foregrounding the processes and practices of media production. . . . [M]etaproduction offers a way to understand how Asian American–niche advertising executives transform census and marketing data into representations suitable for commercial consumption by populating them with indexes of ethnicity and class. Executives' goal in this media production is to compel corporate clients wishing to reach this niche market to look beyond iconic signs that conjure Asia in mainstream U.S. culture and to opt instead for those signs that index ways of being Asian American. . . . One outcome I trace here is a shift in the perception of Asian Americans from model minority producers in the U.S. economy to sophisticated, upwardly mobile model minority consumers.

I analyze discussions among "creatives" who are responsible for generating concepts, original artwork, and writing copy for ads; agency executives' interactions with clients, those corporate entities who commission advertising; and the activities of other industry personnel, including account executives who oversee the entire process, producers responsible for casting, directing, and postproduction of print, TV, radio, and Internet ads, and media buyers who place ads in various media. . . .

Creating the Genre of Asian American Advertising

Executives aspire to reach Asian American consumers through specialized communications that transform general market brand identities into ethnically and racially specific communications for Asians in the United States. Ethnographic studies of advertising have illustrated the localized ways in which this industry does not simply reflect existing values but actively formulates and creates them (Mazzerella 2003; Miller 1997). Likewise, executives make the category of "Asian American" and the five most profitable ethnic groups it encompasses—Chinese, Korean, Vietnamese, Filipino, and South Asian—meaningful and recognizable among themselves, their clients, and their audiences. Understanding regional ideologies, values, and norms specific to a target audience is paramount to effectively constructing consumers and markets (Davila 2001; Foster 2007; Kemper 2001; Malefyt and Moeran 2003; Moeran 1996a). Asian American executives make ads that are "in-language," meaning they include an Asian language or Asian variety of English, and "in-culture," meaning they include nonlinguistic signs that represent one or more Asian American ethnic groups.

Metaproduction is a process of material and linguistic signification that uses values already deemed "meta" in some sense, specifically, those that are metacultural and metalinguistic. As an analytic, metaproduction connects microlevel cultural and linguistic signification with broader categories of brand identity and racial meaning. Metaproduction here attends not only to the deployment of linguistic and material signs in advertisements but also to the political economy that underpins Asian American advertising production. In industry parlance, the term category "niche market" includes agencies that create and produce advertising and marketing for specific segments of the U.S. population.

Advertising agencies that cater exclusively to the Asian American market emerged in the mid-1980s and are concentrated in New York, Los Angeles, and San Francisco. These ten or so major agencies offer a range of services that include producing advertisements for print (ethnic newspapers and magazines), television (local access cable and satellite channels), the Web, and social media platforms (Twitter and smartphone applications). Additionally, they prepare direct marketing and e-mail blasts (commonly known as junk mail and spam, respectively) as well as community-level event sponsorship and public relations. Goods and services categories such as automotive, telecommunications, liquor, insurance, banking, casinos, and fast food have been especially invested in marketing directly to Asian American consumers. The majority of executives working at these agencies are themselves first- or second-generation Asian Americans, and many are fluent in one of the languages used for writing advertising copy (Hindi, Korean, Mandarin, Tagalog, or Vietnamese). This ethnolinguistic heritage forms a major part of the expertise these advertising executives project, a point I develop in greater detail elsewhere (Shankar 2015).

The two case studies discussed herein are based on observations and audio recordings I collected during four months of research conducted in 2009 at "Asian Ads." Asian Ads is a 75-person pan-Asian advertising agency that was cofounded in 1986 by three first-generation Chinese Americans and is currently owned by one of them. On a daily basis, I observed and audio-recorded creative brainstorms, account status meetings, production activities, client calls, and industry events. This work was part of a multiyear, multisite research project I began in 2008 that includes fieldwork in Asian American ad agencies and their industry events and more limited fieldwork in general market agencies. . . . I used the Asian American Advertising Association's website to contact major agencies in New York, Los Angeles, and San Francisco. Eight of the leading Asian American agencies were exceedingly gracious in inviting "the professor" to visit them and conduct interviews. At some, my visit was brief, involving an extended interview with a single representative and viewing an "agency reel" of the firm's best work. At others, I spent several days observing meetings and production sessions and interviewing numerous executives. New York City–based Asian Ads allowed me to conduct longer-term fieldwork and to audio-record meetings. . . . As a South Asian American conversant who is literate in Hindi, I best understood communications made for this audience but closely followed all accounts I was permitted to observe.

"Allied Country Dividend" Print Ad

In a print ad campaign for Allied Country Insurance and Financial Services (hereafter, AC), the client asked Asian Ads to produce versions of a general market ad for the Chinese, Korean, and South Asian American market "segments," as they are called in this industry. Asian Ads had an excellent relationship with AC, which regularly commissioned ads and even sent representatives to the annual Asian American Advertising Federation conference to demonstrate its investment in Asian American marketing. In some AC campaigns, those on the account team had been given free rein to generate original concepts for the layout, message, and style of the ad,

provided they maintain brand identity—an evaluation reserved for the client. For this campaign, however, AC had requested Asian Ads to make versions of a general market print ad for each segment. Once the account supervisor received the agency brief from the client (see Brief 1), head of creative An Rong delegated the job to three members of his department. On this job, Jun Yi, a first-generation Taiwanese American man, Esther, a 1.5-generation Chinese American woman, and Andrew, a first-generation Filipino American man, worked together on a creative brainstorm. Presenting the "concept" of the ad, or what would be communicated, was an important step in the Asian Ads creative process. After creatives Esther and Jun Yi worked independently to generate ideas, they met with copywriter Andrew to discuss them. The team convened in a casual meeting area in the front of the office, their ideas and sentences punctuated by the chimes of approaching elevators, which opened directly into the loft-style office.

In their meeting, the team searched for the most relevant ways to represent Chinese American ethnicity while also preserving the message of the general market [ostensibly covering all groups in the U.S.; GM] print ad. They began by distilling the key messages of the GM ad and considering how they might tailor them for Chinese Americans. The broader aim was to generate creative concepts that could later be adapted for Korean and South Asian American segments, but the work at hand was to create a winning Chinese American version of what the client called the "dividend ad." The

BRIEF 1   Allied Country Dividend Brief

	Creative Agency Brief[1]
Client	Allied Country
Agency	Asian Ads, New York, NY
Brand managers	Mike and Janet
Project	Dividend Ad: In-language, in-culture print ad for Chinese, Korean, and South Asian American segments.
Overview	This is a campaign for financial services that emphasizes monetary dividends.
Objective	We want to increase brand presence among target segments so that they use Allied Country for their financial service needs.
Target audience	Primary target will be men, 35–64-year-olds, with household incomes of $80k+.
Reasons to believe and buy	Allied Country is a trusted company that can help build and plan your financial future.

very notion of "dividends" signals a level of financial security and well-being that might be a distant memory for many Americans in the current economic climate, but the task was to present this idea as a natural and unquestioned part of everyday Chinese American life. Both Jun Yi and Esther had studied the GM print ad, which featured a cheerful white father and son dressed in matching white oxford shirts and rolled-up khakis, walking on a log of driftwood at the beach with their arms outstretched for balance. They brought several hand-sketched concepts that conveyed the main themes they associated with the notion of "dividend," including security, prosperity, and empowerment. Each concept also featured a round visual element that would allow for the incorporation of AC's circular logo—an innovative flourish that the clients loved in Asian Ads' previous work.

At this stage of the metaproduction process, Esther and Jun Yi presented concepts that reflected the themes of the GM ad in ways that would resonate with Chinese Americans. For instance, "risk and reward" was represented in one image by a rock climber ascending a cliff, a large circular knot holding him steady, and in another by whitewater rafters in circular rafts holding their paddles triumphantly up in the air, signaling their safety. Another theme, "skill and accomplishment," was conveyed by two ice skaters "making a figure eight on the ice and signifying infinite peace of mind," Esther explained. Jun Yi added to this category by offering sketches of a father teaching his son how to hit a golf ball out of a sand trap, a hand holding Chinese exercise balls against pressure points to build strength, and a gymnast balancing on a beam and exhibiting agility. A third set of images that directly addressed the theme "benefit" included a child eating an ice cream cone, a woman in a difficult yoga pose, and a father and son peering into a bird's nest filled with three small eggs. The team agreed that all of these had strong potential and that it was time to call in creative director An Rong to narrow down the list.

As in other metacultural and metalinguistic assessments, evaluation and judgment constitute an integral part of metaproduction. In this case, a critical discussion ensued about which ads would have the greatest resonance with a Chinese American audience. Andrew, the copywriter, reminded the team that they needed to find a concept that "works across different Asian segments and conveys security without signaling insecurity." As they waited for An Rong, Esther cycled through the short list of concepts by embodying a Chinese American consumer and voicing engagements with each creative idea. She mused, "The rock presents risk, but the knot is security, so I choose [AC]." . . . The team offered critical feedback to one another about select concepts, such as the ice cream and yoga, which showed end results but not how one could achieve them. Esther asserted that the idea of yoga could work for all three segments, but Jun Yi countered that it was irrelevant to financial services and did not address the notion of "dividend." When creative director An Rong finally arrived, he preempted Esther and Jun Yi's presentation with his own reading of the general market ad, which he called "the sea." Remarking that the sea is dangerous and unstable, but one can still enjoy it, he strategized, "We need to show some unpredictable environment but the family still enjoying it." The quizzical expressions on Esther's and Jun Yi's faces suggested that their reading of the GM ad had been somewhat different than that of their creative director, but they nonetheless proceeded with the presentation. After taking in the concepts, An Rong was sharp and focused in his critique. Arguing that rock climbing offered little cultural insight, he challenged, "Is this in-culture? Why not just use the general market ad?" Jun Yi conceded that it did not have any apparent significance for Chinese American audiences and, unlike the GM ad, it did not meld notions of family and security. They all agreed, however, that golf would provide an ideal concept because of its popularity among Chinese and Korean Americans.

The team faced the task of obtaining client approval for two print ad concepts on their short list. On a conference call with AC, account executive Sunil began by priming his client: "They are gonna sell their concept to you today, if you will buy it!" Asian Ads cycled through the concepts the team had sent to AC in advance, beginning with the golf idea. The client swiftly and politely declined, explaining that it had already been done too many times in AC's GM ads. A wave of disappointment was palpable in the Asian Ads conference room, especially as the team had found this message to be particularly apt for Chinese American and Korean American audiences. The bird nest concept, however, seemed to hold the client's imagination longer, and Jun Yi seized the opportunity to narrate the concept's indexical value: "All their hard work for the family, for their loved ones, the bird nest is protection. First-generation immigrants want to make a good future for their children. The father and son look at the bird nest, and [AC] gives you the benefit and strength to protect your family." Approval of a second concept followed the client's acceptance of the bird nest concept: The team agreed to the client's recommendation to use a graphic design program to modify the general market "sea" ad by splicing Asian American faces onto it. In conjunction with the Chinese copy, the client thought the visual would suffice, and the ad could be produced on schedule and within budget.

In this campaign, executives chose signs to represent Chinese Americans in sophisticated, cosmopolitan ways that also convey the essence of the AC brand. Like the general market ad that features a middle-class man who is able to reap the benefit of financial dividends by spending leisure time with his son at the beach, the nest signifies a lifestyle in which Asian Americans already flush with capital would be well advised to manage this wealth effectively. Similar to the now–Chinese American father walking with his son on the beach in oxford shirts and rolled-up khaki pants, the Chinese American father who takes time to explore the wonders of nature with his son is pleased with the boy's reaction to the perfect robin's eggs they find. Also notable in this case . . . is the partial success of the agency's creative strategies. For instance, the client rejected the golf concept on the grounds that it had already been used in the GM ads. The need for differentiation in the Asian American ads, then, is reflected both in the inclusion of individuals who index particular Asian American ethnic groups—in this case, Chinese Americans—and in scenarios that will resonate with the ads' audiences. Although the rejection of the golf ad was something of a setback, the polysemy of the bird's nest allowed for multiple indexical readings.

The Genre of Asian American Advertising

The AC case illustrates several processes, including the emergence of Asian American advertising as a genre. If one considers both general market advertising in the United States and Chinese advertising in China as genres with conventional characteristics and features that resonate, to an extent, with Chinese Americans, then Asian American advertising targeting that group fills an intertextual gap; that is, it emerges between these two well-defined genres and draws from them to produce a third. Intertextuality, a process by which elements from one

text are referenced in another in ways that index the former and may be resignified as a result, contributes to the creation of genre in this way: "By choosing to make certain features explicit (and particularly by foregrounding some elements through repetition and metapragmatic framing), producers of discourse actively (re) construct and reconfigure genres" (Bauman and Briggs 1992: 584). Producers of Asian American advertising, likewise, select and showcase features from advertising genres in Asian countries, the United States, and other relevant sources.

Conventions and content from general market advertising cannot be altogether overlooked, as brand identity must be preserved across genres. Chinese representations of family, security, and financial planning are signified in ways that dovetail with AC's general market brand identity. Recall the rejection, for instance, of the golf idea that Asian Ads thought would work well for Chinese Americans but that AC thought had already become overdone in its general market campaigns. Creating representations that are in-culture, as An Rong pointed out, in this case led to the use of certain ethnically marked signs, such as Chinese American actors and Mandarin text. It also meant re-creating genre features from the general market campaign, such as fathers and sons exploring nature. In other executions for AC, Asian Ads created far more marked indexes of ethnicity, such as a traditional Indian wedding scene and a jade pendant handed down between generations of women. In those ads, as in the AC ad, the genre of Asian American advertising is most effective when executives are able to find the right indexical references to convey general market brand identity.

The use of ethnically marked signs, as in advertising elsewhere (see Bhatia 1992; Piller 2001), is indeed an important way in which the genre of Asian American advertising is distinguishable from general market advertising. Arlene Davila (2001) skillfully demonstrates how Latino executives downplay key ethnonational and linguistic differences in favor of a more uniform cultural and linguistic identity, and she makes a compelling case for the remaking of the Latino for marketing and consumption. In her research and mine, clients value the inclusion of recognizable emblems of ethnicity in ads because it enables them to justify spending advertising dollars to reach niche audiences, but executives note the shortcomings in this approach. Steve put it to me like this: "How can you touch them in this 'Asian' way, but be relevant, not cliché, and not overdone?" The AC ad offers an example of how this process worked smoothly for the most part and demonstrates how the client, like the customer, is always right. Even though executives would prefer to stay with their creative strategies, they change course as a matter of survival.

. . . Assessments about culture, language, and what constitutes ethnicity are articulated, and choices are made about the efficacy of representations. . . . [T]he messages produced fall somewhere on a continuum between essentialist and antiessentialist representations. In the AC case, creativity and originality that are prized in general market advertising are openly curtailed by constraints imposed by clients with limited advertising budgets and established brand identities. The ads should exhibit the right sensibilities—material and linguistic—of Asian American culture and language but also the correct brand message, one that correlates with the general market brand identity. To produce the genre of Asian American advertising, then, executives deentextualize and reentextualize elements from genres of general market and Asian advertising.

Executives additionally define the genre of Asian American advertising through their promotion of it as a vital and effective way to reach Asian American consumers. For instance, many were quick to explain to clients, and to me, that ads created for audiences in Asia do not resonate with Asian audiences in the United States, even though they may feature faces, voices, and ways of speaking and interacting that index a degree of familiarity. They also pointed out that general market ads lack the cultural and linguistic markers that are signature elements of Asian American niche advertising and are, accordingly, less effective forms of communication. On the one hand, this disposition is typical of agency executives who want to convince their corporate clients that only specialized communication will effectively reach consumers (see Mazzerella 2003; Miller 1997 for similar arguments). On the other hand, the link between racialized representation and consumerism is so fundamental to niche marketing that there is something substantive to be learned from the process of creating a marketable semiotic link between ideas, texts, and the Asian American consumer's wallet. The Chinese American case I discuss here, as well as the South Asian American case I discuss next, further

contribute to the emergence and definition of the Asian American genre in advertising.

Creating Model Consumers

Ad executives do not simply use racialized identities but actively create them through the process of making advertising. If, in fact, "we do not yet know all that is involved in the essentialization process whereby such a metadiscursive category—a category of contingently achieved role inhabitance—is projected onto the world" (Silverstein and Urban 1996, 8), then metaproduction can contribute to understanding how this essentialization is accomplished. What is at stake, then, is the "continual back and forth interplay between the metadiscursive category and the actual instances of discourse that are used to categorize and interpret it" (Silverstein and Urban 1996, 8). As a fairly new category that has been featured in media since the mid-1960s, Asian American advertising is playing the double role of inhabiting the category as well as projecting it into society. Executives use earlier discourses of racialized capitalism along with current ideologies of neoliberalism to shape representations of the Asian American consumer. Numerous insights have been offered about the rise of neoliberalism and its attendant cultural shifts (see di Leonardo 2008; Goldberg 2009; Harvey 2005); here I am most concerned with the remaking of public discourse that results from the production of racial representation. In neoliberal discourse, meanings of race and ethnicity that are rooted in political economy are recoded simply as "differences" that can be considered equal (Comaroff and Comaroff 2001). Neoliberalism especially idealizes the notion that individuals can thrive in capitalism without state assistance and that market deregulation creates opportunities for unlimited financial growth and accumulation (Harvey 2005).

Neoliberalism is a contemporary logic in a racialized capitalism that has long positioned Asian Americans as ideal, especially compared to other racial minorities. Introduced in 1966 by the *New York Times* and *U.S. News and World Report,* the model minority stereotype portrayed Asian Americans as self-sufficient, good citizens at a time when the state was looking to cut social services overall. Asian Americans were lauded as productive members of U.S. society, whereas other minority populations, especially African Americans, were unfavorably depicted for their reliance on state welfare (Kim 1999; Prashad 2000). Attributes such as strong familial ties, educational attainment, good citizenship, and economic mobility meld easily with market research and with executives' use of 2000 and 2010 census data to show that Asian Americans have the highest per capita income, are a rapidly growing population with spending power in the billions, and have been less affected by the economic downturn than the average American. In other words, they are ideal consumers to target through specialized advertising. Account supervisor Suzie, a first-generation Chinese American woman at a New York City agency, underscores the importance of contemporary Asian American representations that reflect these ideologies:

> Our clients always want us to have cultural nuances in the ads, but we don't want to do it too much. You want to think about your audience as modern customers that are really in sync with today's appeal and today's look. You don't really want to put too much of these so-called cultural nuances in there, but rather, something that speaks to the family, because Asians are very family-centric and they really focus on their kids' education. It could still be very modern and not outdated. We don't want to seem outdated.

Suzie's comments, like Steve's, suggest the existence of competing representations based on different signs that ad executives and clients each promote for different purposes. To best reach their Asian American audiences, executives avoid obvious icons of Asia, what Suzie calls "so-called cultural nuances," such as numerology or Chinese characters, that might index outdated notions of what it means to be Chinese in China as well as in the United States. By contrast, the model minority stereotype offers the potential to provide a modern narrative from which to create indexical signs that valorize family and education. . . . [T]he nest egg featured in the ad fits perfectly with the neoliberal ideology of self-sufficiency and financial wherewithal. Likewise, the sea ad also indexes class mobility and leisure through its tasteful depiction of beach activity. These representations reinforce the model minority stereotype while they also affirm the current success of Asian Americans. As refined, cultured individuals who are connected to nature and the corporate world, these Asian Americans are able to enjoy upper-middle-class life in ways that still prioritize family. These are not huddled masses of immigrants simply yearning for a better life; rather,

they are middle-class professionals who are being shown the value of financial planning. Ad executives expect their clients to appreciate the complex subjectivities indexed through these signs, but clients can counter with their own signs of what they believe will work better.

The Deluxis "Winter Sales Event" Print Ad

Creating a South Asian American print ad for the "Deluxis Winter Sales Event" should have been a fairly smooth process, considering that the Asian Ads team had done a number of well-received Deluxis ads for Chinese American and South Asian American audiences. Asian Ads had been working with Deluxis for about a year and a half and was very familiar with the luxury automaker's brand identity and style of advertising. Asian Ads worked in tandem with Latino and African American agencies to promote Deluxis cars to a broad multicultural market. For the winter sales event, each multicultural agency was asked to create in-culture and in-language copy for a print ad sent by Deluxis's general market agency—a glamour shot of two silver cars on an icy surface in front of a bright blue sky, large snowflakes, and trees with ice-coated fronds (see Brief 2). The GM ad read, "This holiday season, celebrate two decades of inspired performance," and the multicultural agencies were asked to keep this message as consistent as possible in their in-language versions. Of the three versions Asian Ads was commissioned to make—Chinese Mandarin, Chinese Cantonese, and South Asian—I focus on the third, both because I understand Hindi and because it was the most contentious. The executives on the account included creative Stanley, a first-generation Chinese American man; account executive Joyce, a first-generation Chinese American woman; and freelance copywriter Jayshree, a South Asian American woman who had previously worked on Deluxis ads. The account team also asked Priya, a South Asian American account executive, to assist because Asian Ads did not then have a creative from this ethnic group.

Because the visuals were predetermined, the team focused on writing copy . . . that would work well with the featured imagery. Jayshree admitted to me that it was a formidable challenge to find suitable terms for certain concepts and words in the GM ad, including snowflakes and a winter "holiday season." Of course, many South Asian Americans had experienced winter in the United

BRIEF 2   Deluxis Winter Sales Event Brief

	Creative Agency Brief
Client	Deluxis Automobiles
Agency	Asian Ads, New York, NY
Brand managers	Mike and Josie
Project	Winter Sales Event: In-language, in-culture print ad for South Asian American segment.
Overview	This is a campaign for the December holiday sales event.
Objective	We want our South Asian American consumers to buy a Deluxis car during a season they may not associate with holidays or car buying.
Target audience	Primary target will be 35–59-year-old men, with total household incomes of $100k+. The audience is familiar with the luxury car market and may already own one.
Reasons to believe and buy	Deluxis is a high-performing luxury automobile. We want them to know about our new financing options and cash back incentives.

States, but snowflakes are not a preferred indexical sign for this audience. Moreover, the December holiday season is not one that most Hindu or Muslim South Asian Americans associate with celebration in South Asia. Nonetheless, some culturally relevant sign was required to compel this group to embrace the consumerism of the Judeo-Christian holidays. On Monday of the week the ad copy was to be submitted to the client, Jayshree remarked to account executive Sunil and me that the Deluxis copy had "vexed her all weekend." She explained that car companies rely on their winter sales events and that a seasonal promotion was a perfectly natural idea for Deluxis but that she was having trouble generating a catchy phrase that closely resembled the GM copy and that also had the right cultural resonance. Her copy, "*Dhoom machao, jashn manao! Yeh hai* two decades of inspired performance," which she translated as "Have a blast, celebrate! This is (here's to) two decades of inspired performance," was sent to the client for review.

In a conference call with the client, the indexical meanings of this utterance came under intense scrutiny and debate. About 28 minutes into the call, when the client had already approved the Latino concept as well as the two Chinese concepts, he voiced hesitation and concern about the English back translation of the South Asian American copy. In the following excerpt, Stanley, the creative, has just finished reading the transliterated Hindi copy for Mike, the client, and after a sizable

pause, Mike responds. Priya, the only Hindi speaker on the call, attempts to address Mike's concerns.[2]

Excerpt: "Have a blast!"

1   Mike: Okay, so the: have a blast, celebration, is that,

2   what is the context in which that term would typically

3   be used?

4   (Team looks to Priya, who takes it as a cue to speak)

5   Priya: Um, typically for Indians, celebration and

6   festivity is larger than life, it means a punch line.

7   So "Dhoom machao! Jashn manao!" it's not as if you're

8   **going partying** and you're saying "Have a blast!"

9   It's more the background for have a blast, it's more

10   celebration, festivity. It's an expression, it's an

11   emotion, it's larger than life, happy. Being Indian

12   myself, I relate. When I read the line, I relate to it very

13   well. I think it is happy. It's happy thoughts, and

14   you read the line, and you immediately connect it

15   to what the message is, even in the body copy.

16   Mike: So it's basically saying "celebrate this, this event"

17   cele[brate, come celebrate with us]

18   Priya: yes, right. Yes, celebrate the winter sales event.

19 Be a part of it, have a blast.

20 Mike: And this is kind of arguing with that, but
    I guess

21 I shouldn't.

22 Many: ((Laughter))

23 Mike: My question is more content as I don't
    really

24 understand, the content feels a little over the top.

25 (Team looks to Priya again)

26 Priya: It's actually not **too** over the top. The
    actual

27 general market headline is "This holiday season,

28 celebrate two decades of inspired performance."

29 The Indian line is actually very similar to that,
    in fact

30 it's almost the same, it's just a little happier.
    Indians

31 are a little, it's a very common expression,

32 many Bollywood movies have this expression,
    it's

33 actually very common. I mean I—even in India

34 you see this line very commonly used, so I don't

35 think it's **very** over the top.

In this excerpt, Mike and the Asian Ads team introduce different indexical values for "Dhoom machao, jashn manao!" Even though Mike politely prefaces his disapproval with "and this is kind of arguing with that, but I guess I shouldn't" (lines 20–21), he nonetheless cannot reconcile the back translation of "Have a blast!" with the Deluxis brand identity and calls it "a little over the top" (line 24). In response, Priya defends the phrase's relevance and offers a justification for the choice. As a smart young executive with a newly minted marketing degree from a prestigious U.S. university, Priya seems to understand that what Mike is getting at is context: Is the phrase in question too irreverent or déclassé for this luxury brand? She attempts to clarify the connotations of the phrase in lines 5–15, though in doing so betrays her recent college graduate status: "It's not as if you're going partying and you're saying 'Have a blast'. . . it's more celebration, festivity." Additionally, she makes linkages with Bollywood and downplays the idea that the phrase is "over the top," but Mike remains skeptical. The call ended with Mike indicating that he will again consult his Indian American colleagues at Deluxis (who work in information technology, not marketing) to see

how they respond to the copy. Asian Ads was soon notified that the client's colleagues did not respond favorably and that revised copy was required as soon as possible.

In this instance of metaproduction, Asian Ads' message was deemed potentially incongruous with the Deluxis brand and the identity of the intended consumer. Asif Agha's (1998, 2007) extensive investigations of the ways in which people make sense of speakers' identities offer another way to consider this outcome. He asserts, "Since our ideas about the identities of others are ideas about pragmatic phenomena, they are in principle metapragmatic constructs. In particular, such ideas are metapragmatic stereotypes about pragmatic phenomena" (Agha 1998, 151). As values that are openly reportable, contestable, and consciously grasped, metapragmatic stereotypes of Asian American speakers are used to imagine audiences. What the average consumer sounds like and how he or she would respond to the talk of others are at stake here. Even though the Asian Ads team did not perceive a disconnect between their message and the brand identity, the client did. So did Sunil, the other Hindi speaker in the office. After learning that the client had rejected the team's idea, he joked quietly with Priya and me that for the summer sales event, "Jashn manao!" should be reworded "Garmi banao!"—"Make heat!"—which, of course, would be even more inappropriate for Deluxis because of its lewd connotations.

The case was particularly vexing for Jayshree because the client loved the copy she had written for earlier ads. For instance, in an ad for the G-series sedan fall sales event, the client had approved the playful phrase "G is for *josh.*" A Hindi–Urdu speaker reading this ad may appreciate the clever play on the phoneme /j/ and its bivalent meaning in both English and Hindi. In the ad, the English *G* refers to the featured sedan model, and the same phoneme begins the word *josh*, which means "excitement." In this successful use of a metalinguistic sign, the second-order indexical value connotes sophistication and literacy. The intended consumer is not only wealthy enough to purchase a luxury sedan but is also educated enough to be lured in by the wordplay in the ad. The message is refined, and the consumer is expected to be the same. To get to this place in the winter sales event, Jayshree offered a new version in which she removed "dhoom machao" and retooled the rest of the copy to read "Jashn manao! This is two decades of inspired performance," and translated it as

"Celebrate! This is two decades of inspired performance." She also offered a second option, both of which were sent to the client for review.

During the next conference call, the Asian Ads team and client were finally able to agree on a metalinguistic sign that offered pleasing indexical meanings to both parties. Stanley described revisions made to the first option, "jashn manao," and then moved on to the second: "Additionally we also came up with **another** option, which if we pair with the visual, this would be an elegant visual, and that line reads '*Is haseen mausam,* celebrate two decades of inspired performance.' The back translation is 'This beautiful, festive season, celebrate two decades of inspired performance.' And also with this I think we feel like we captured the [Deluxis] brand."

Stanley underscored those qualities indexed by the new copy and linked them to the visuals and the Deluxis brand identity. His use of the adjectives *elegant* and *beautiful* stands in stark contrast to "have a blast." To a Hindi–Urdu speaker, the poetic value of "Is haseen mausam" is indisputable. *Haseen* is an Urdu word conveying stunning beauty, and *mausam* is a word for weather with positive connotations of harvest, fertility, and traditional celebration. Both work well with the notion of a well-educated, wealthy, and discerning South Asian American consumer. The client ultimately approved this copy, and the Asian Ads team was pleased with and relieved by the outcome.

In this example of metaproduction, executives and clients clashed over the metapragmatic meaning of signs. Asian Ads considered the phrase "Dhoom machao, jashn manao!" to be an apt signifier of the wealth and refinement connoted by a luxury car. Hindi–Urdu speakers might positively associate it with weddings, lively festivals such as *holi,* in which colored powder is thrown on passersby, or even the short-lived Disney Channel India children's show whose title bears part of the phrase *(Dhoom Machao!).* But in this instance, the client countered with its own second-order indexical meaning based on the English back translation and internal opinions to which the Asian Ads team was not privy.

Noteworthy here is the process by which the genre of Asian American advertising is created through the continuity it forms with ongoing representations of Asian Americans as model minorities. Richard Bauman and Charles L. Briggs note the "leakiness" and contingency of genre and argue, "Some elements of contextualization

creep in, fashioning indexical connections to the ongoing discourse, social interaction, broader social relations, and the particular historical juncture(s) at which the discourse is produced and received" (1992, 585). In keeping with the elegant, refined identity of Deluxis, the Hindi phrase ultimately chosen offers second-order indexical values of education and sophistication. As Stanley's comments suggest, these are attributes of the modern identities the team wished to portray. Moreover, the ad offers new indexical meanings about seasons and holidays that are distinctly South Asian American.

The genre of Asian American advertising thus comprises the numerous campaigns and ads aimed at specific ethnic groups within the larger category. Here, the Deluxis ad offers a media-based representation of the ethnic group South Asian American as wealthy luxury-automobile drivers. The final copy the client chose is arguably the more refined of the two options presented and indexes a more prestigious consumer. Likewise, the AC ad presents Chinese Americans as cultured, wealthy consumers. Taken together, these ads, along with scores of other campaigns, reflect the emergence of the genre of Asian American advertising as well as the racialization of Asian Americans.

Linking Metaproduction and Racialization

. . . The work of Asian American ad executives raises questions of where Asian Americans fit in the sliding scale of U.S. racialization and what to make of the broader political-economic framework that governs ethnic advertising production. By observing their open discussions of negative stereotypes in agencies, at their annual conference, and in casual conversation, I came to believe that many who work in niche advertising are acutely aware of mass-mediated stereotypes of Asian Americans and the role advertising has played in perpetuating them. They are not only proud of the work they do but also see it as a counterpoint to past and current racist imagery of Asian Americans. For instance, during the early twentieth century, xenophobic sentiment crystallized in an ideology referred to as the "yellow peril" that at once characterized Asian Americans as dangerous invaders who required containment and as licentious, amoral, and infantile individuals in need of patriarchal control (Okihiro 1994). "Orientals," as they were called, were depicted on business or "trade" cards and their representations thus circulated through this mass-produced form of advertising

(Matsukawa 2002; Metrick-Chen 2007). These earlier racializations underlay Asian exclusion acts and anti-Asian sentiment, ranging from anticitizenship and antimiscegenation laws to the World War II internment of Japanese Americans, and they continued to contribute to subsequent waves of hostility due to U.S. military conflict in Korea, Vietnam, and, most recently, the Middle East and Pakistan in a post–9/11 era.

The representations executives produce . . . enable them to circulate a more modern and complex Asian American subjectivity than that tied to the anti-immigrant sentiment prevalent in previous generations of ads as well as in some contemporary general market advertising. Their work certainly differs from mainstream advertisements that have been critiqued for racist imagery that furthers xenophobic and anti-immigrant sentiment (Chávez 2001; Steele 2000), especially general market advertising that still features racist representations of Asian Americans (see Kim and Chung 2005; Knobloch-Westerwick and Coates 2006; Ono and Pham 2009). Just as in other studies that have demonstrated advertising to be an effective arena for cultural production that challenges dominant social meanings (Moeran 1996b), here metaproduction plays an important role in remaking the racial category of Asian American by countering simplistic racializations.

Through the genre of Asian American advertising, executives remake core elements of the model minority stereotype into contemporary narratives of the economic solvency championed by neoliberalism to depict Asian Americans as refined professionals with sophisticated identities and tastes (see Shankar 2013, 2015). The hardworking Asian American model minority producer, a staple of capitalist rhetoric and public policy since its 1960s introduction, emerges in a new form as the sophisticated model minority consumer. Executives use census and market research data to illustrate Asian Americans' high per capita income and willingness to spend money. The newly minted version of the model Asian American enables ad executives to enter the marketplace of multicultural advertising and work alongside agencies that target the Latino and Black markets in the United States. In this sense, neoliberal logics make this version of the Asian American appear new for marketing purposes, but it can also be considered another version of the same model minority stereotype that emerged from racialized capitalism.

In attempting to counter negative general market representations of Asian Americans while also reaching target audiences, Asian American advertising is delimiting this category to include a far more elite subsection of the population than the original model minority stereotype. In her astute analysis of the myriad gaps and erasures in the creation of the Latino category for advertising and marketing, Davila (2001) demonstrates how ethnonational history, varieties of Spanish, postcolonial histories, and numerous other inequalities are subsumed to make "Latinos Inc." Inasmuch as executives might like to make an analogous Asian Americans Inc., this unified category does not allow them to emphasize the very cultural and linguistic specificities that they must stress to reach individual Asian American ethnic groups. Apart from the occasional public-service ads for health issues or the U.S. Census, for instance, it is rarely beneficial for them to combine Chinese, Korean, South Asian, Filipino, and Vietnamese American populations under a single cultural and linguistic rubric. Language differences are a concern even within ethnic groups, as South Asian Americans may speak one of 15 major languages and Chinese Americans may have strong ties to either Mandarin or Cantonese. Because the range of nations encompassed in the category "Asian" is so wide, and because different languages are needed for each, executives and their clients know that Asian American marketing almost always involves making several versions of an ad, each in-culture or in-language for a particular ethnic group. Despite admitting the impossibility of subsuming all of these specificities into a larger group, executives know that to win accounts alongside Latino and African American niche agencies, they have to convince clients that the category of Asian American, despite its myriad differences, is viable.

Executives capitalize on depicting immigrants of Asian descent as good citizens and good consumers by focusing on family, consumption, and other favorable attributes, but these emergent racial and ethnic definitions are detached from the politics of globalization that engender their conception. The complexity of the ever-shifting geopolitical relationship the United States has with different Asian nations is exactly what this type of advertising (and, to be fair, advertising anywhere) wants to sidestep altogether, and neoliberal discourses of individual economic success enable them to do this with considerable ease. Indeed, everyday realities of outsourcing jobs and production to Asia, the rising dominance of China and India in the global economy, and other indicators that draw attention to the powerful production capabilities of Asia, and, by extension, many members of its diasporas, are here dramatically downplayed.

In niche advertising, only the five most profitable Asian American ethnic groups are included; others are excluded either because they are too small, such as Pacific Islanders, or because they are considered too assimilated, as in the case of Japanese Americans. Even within the five major groups, populations that are currently targets of political and social tension, including Muslims in a post–9/11 United States, tend to be avoided (see also Rana 2011). Working-class Asian Americans who may not be succeeding economically or socially or are otherwise not performing up to model minority expectations also fall through the cracks of this racial refashioning process. Of course, this "spin" is what disengages these representations from the political economy that underpins them, as Davila (2008) argues in the case of the "whitewashing" that occurs with Latinos. A significant point of contrast to note here between Latinos and Asian Americans is that the model minority stereotype seems to have addressed the issue of "whitewashing" already. Indeed, the notion of Asian Americans as "part of a solution," as Vijay Prashad (2000) puts it, has prevailed in popular media (see also Jun 2011; Lee 1997; Tuan 1998). In these ways, niche advertising is creating a racialized identity for Asian Americans that is distinct from that of white Americans but nonetheless positions them as good racial minorities and, of course, as good consumers.

Acknowledgments

Research featured in this chapter was funded by the National Science Foundation Cultural Anthropology Program (grant 0924472) and Northwestern University.

Notes

1. The briefs that appear in this chapter are simulations of the originals, per the terms of my nondisclosure agreement with the agency.
2. Transcription key: "[]" = overlap; "**bold**" = speaker emphasis; "?" = rising intonation.

References

Agha, Asif. 1998. "Stereotypes and Registers of Honorific Language." *Language in Society* 27:151–193.

Agha, Asif. 2007. *Language and Social Relations.* New York: Cambridge University Press.

Bauman, Richard, and Charles L. Briggs. 1992. "Genre, Intertextuality, and Social Power." In *Language, Culture, and Society* (ed. Ben G. Blount), 567–591. New York: Waveland.

Bhatia, T. K. 1992. "Discourse Functions and the Pragmatics of Mixing: Advertising across Cultures." *World Englishes* 11(1): 195–215.

Chávez, Leo. 2001 *Covering Immigration: Popular Images and the Politics of the Nation.* Berkeley: University of California Press.

Comaroff, John L., and Jean Comaroff 2001. "First Thoughts on a Second Coming." In *Millennial Capitalism and the Culture of Neoliberalism* (ed. Jean Comaroff and John Comaroff), 1–58. Durham, NC: Duke University Press.

Davila, Arlene. 2001. *Latinos Inc.: The Marketing and Making of a People.* Berkeley: University of California Press.

Davila, Arlene. 2008. *Latino Spin: Public Image and the Whitewashing of Race.* New York: New York University Press.

di Leonardo, Micaela. 2008. "Introduction: New Global and American Landscapes of Inequality." In *Landscapes of Inequality: Neoliberalism and the Erosion of Democracy in America* (ed. Jane Collins, Micaela di Leonardo, and Brett Williams), 3–20. Santa Fe, NM: School for Advanced Research Press.

Foster, Robert. 2007. "The Work of the New Economy: Consumers, Brands, and Value Creation." *Cultural Anthropology* 22(4): 707–731.

Goldberg, David. 2009. *The Threat of Race: Reflections on Racial Neoliberalism.* Malden, MA: Blackwell.

Harvey, David. 2005. *A Brief History of Neoliberalism.* New York: Oxford University Press.

Jun, Helen. 2011. *Race for Citizenship: Black Orientalism and Asian Uplift from Pre-Emancipation to Neoliberal America.* New York: New York University Press.

Kemper, Steven. 2001. *Buying and Believing: Sri Lankan Advertising and Consumers in a Transnational World.* Chicago: University of Chicago Press.

Kim, Claire. 1999. "The Racial Triangulation of Model Minorities." *Politics and Society* 27(1): 105–138.

Kim, Minjeong, and Angie Chung. 2005. "Consuming Orientalism: Images of Asian/American Women in Multicultural Advertising." *Qualitative Sociology* 28(1): 67–91.

Knobloch-Westerwick, Silvia, and Brendon Coates. 2006. "Minority Models in Advertisements in Magazines Popular with Minorities." *Journalism and Mass Communication Quarterly* 83(3): 596–614.

Lee, Benjamin. 1997. *Talking Heads: Language, Metalanguage, and the Semiotics of Subjectivity.* Durham, NC: Duke University Press.

Malefyt, Timothy, and Brian Moeran, eds. 2003. *Advertising Cultures.* Oxford: Berg.

Matsukawa, Yuko. 2002. "Representing the Oriental in Nineteenth-Century Trade Cards." In *Re-Collecting Early Asian America: Essays in Cultural History* (ed. Josephine Lee, Imogene Lim, and Yuko Matsukawa), 200–217. Philadelphia, PA: Temple University Press.

Mazzerella, William. 2003. *Shoveling Smoke: Advertising and Globalization in Contemporary India.* Durham, NC: Duke University Press.

Metrick-Chen, Lenore. 2007. "The Chinese in the American Imagination: 19th Century Trade Card Images." *Visual Anthropology Review* 23(2):115–136.

Miller, Daniel. 1997. *Capitalism: An Ethnographic Approach.* London: Berg.

Moeran, Brian. 1996a. *A Japanese Advertising Agency: An Anthropology of Media and Markets.* Honolulu: University of Hawai'i Press.

Moeran, Brian. 1996b. "The Orient Strikes Back: Advertising and Imaging in Japan." *Theory, Culture, and Society* 13(3): 77–112.

Okihiro, Gary. 1994. *Margins and Mainstreams: Asians in American History and Culture.* Seattle: University of Washington Press.

Ono, Kent A., and Vincent N. Pham. 2009. *Asian Americans and the Media.* Cambridge: Polity.

Piller, Ingrid. 2001. "Identity Constructions in Multilingual Advertising." *Language in Society* 30:153–186.

Prashad, Vijay. 2000. *The Karma of Brown Folk.* Minneapolis: University of Minnesota Press.

Rana, Junaid. 2011. *Terrifying Muslims: Race and Labor in the South Asian Diaspora.* Durham, NC: Duke University Press.

Shankar, Shalini. 2013. "Racial Naturalization, Advertising, and Model Consumers for a New Millennium." *Journal of Asian American Studies* 16(2): 159–188.

Shankar, Shalini. 2015. *Advertising Diversity: Ad Agencies and the Creation of Asian American Consumers.* Durham, NC: Duke University Press.

Silverstein, Michael, and Greg Urban. 1996. "The Natural History of Discourse." In *The Natural Histories of Discourse* (ed. Michael Silverstein and Greg Urban), 1–17. Chicago: University of Chicago Press.

Steele, Jeffrey. 2000. "Reduced to Images: American Indians in Nineteenth-Century Advertising." In *The Gender and Consumer Culture Reader* (ed. Jennifer R. Scanlon), 109–128. New York: New York University Press.

Tuan, Mia. 1998. *Forever Foreigners or Honorary Whites? The Asian Ethnic Experience Today.* New Brunswick, NJ: Rutgers University Press.

Questions

1. What is consumption? What role does consumption play in the U.S. economy? What is the connection between consumption, racializing and gendering? How is the global economy gendered and racialized?

2. What are the demographics of the executives in this study? What are they tasked with doing? To whom are they selling? Who is the researcher? How did the researcher's background and skills influence the study?

3. What does Shankar mean by "metaproduction?" What are the "yellow peril" and orientalism? What is the model minority stereotype? What is harmful about each? Who is included and excluded from these stereotypes?

4. Were ad executives cognizant of stereotypes about Asian Americans? How did their awareness influence their approach to advertising? How did the ad creatives transform the model minority into a model consumer in their campaigns? How did they use language to do so? Imagery?

5. What objections to potential ads did people raise? Why? How are consumption and advertising inflecting race and ethnicity with class-based meanings? How are ads "whitewashed"?

6. Asian spa items, Asian-scripted tattoos, and depictions of dragons on clothing are examples of how Americans consume Orientalism as an object. Where else do you see the consumption of Orientalism? What meanings are people signifying to others when they wear or modify their bodies with Orientalism? How are these meanings related to larger social systems of inequality?

7. The Internet has changed advertising and the dissemination of information quite radically. Marketing companies track your activity online and then target ads at you based on your search history, interests, and friendship groups. How else is advertising different in new media? Do some research to find the most successful integrated or social media ad campaigns of the year. (Check out *Forbes'* list of most unforgettable ads, for example.) Or, watch the Super Bowl and its ads. What makes for successful ad campaigns? How are race, ethnicity, nativity, and gender stereotypes used or challenged in these campaigns? What role does multiculturalism play? How are these campaigns the same as or different from those described by Shankar? Now, look at your own social media accounts and the ads targeted at you. What sorts of products are marketed toward you? Do these ads use multiculturalism or Orientalism? How so? How is "coolness" conveyed and sold to you? In what ways are these ads targeted?

8. Pick one of the advertisements analyzed in the chapter or in the preceding question. Reconceptualize it to disrupt racial stereotypes. What pictures would you use? Copy? Music? Images? Is it possible to market something using multiculturalism without reinforcing racism? How, or why not?

9. Can consumption lead to social change? What kinds? For whom? Who is left behind? Are there other limits on making change by purchasing products and services?

14

Discrimination in a Low-Wage Labor Market: A Field Experiment

DEVAH PAGER, BRUCE WESTERN, AND BART BONIKOWSKI

Discrimination is perhaps the most easily recognizable form of boundary policing. Discrimination is when people afford opportunities to members of the dominant group or exclude people from subordinate groups from the same opportunities. You may see some forms of discrimination as legitimate if not the just consequence of meritocracy. For example, employers may prefer workers with particular certifications or direct experience when picking someone to hire. Social scientists refer to these education and skill qualifications as "human capital." Discriminating based on human capital is legitimate because people expect opportunities and pay to be commensurate with their qualifications and performance. Equal pay for equal work. Unequal pay requires unequal work.

When opportunity and pay fall along categorical lines (e.g., race) but do not match up to human capital, discrimination lacks legitimacy within a meritocratic system. Title VII of the Civil Rights Act of 1964 prohibited discrimination in employment based on race, color, religion, sex, and national origin. It specifically outlawed discriminatory practices in hiring, firing, and compensation. Yet observing discrimination is more difficult than ever. Discrimination can result from overt racial hostility, which is easy to measure if employers admit to it. More often, however, discrimination is rooted in other, more subtle and difficult-to-measure sources: unconscious biases, group members' affinity for others like themselves, a desire to protect the dominant group's access to resources, homogeneous social networks, or bias against a subordinate group's "cultural capital" (interactional styles).

Devah Pager, Bruce Western, and Bart Bonikowski designed a clever field experiment to observe discrimination directly. In their approach, known as an audit study, they match white, Black, and Latino men on human capital, appearance, and cultural capital. Then, they send each group of trained testers to apply for the same real entry-level positions in New York City. (They also assign a criminal record to some whites.) The authors track whether or not a potential employer calls back or offers a job to each potential worker. They compare the positive responses to Black and Latino workers to whites with and without a criminal record to determine if employers discriminate based on race.

What Pager, Western, and Bonikowski found was startling and is evidence of the continuing importance of racialization in the United States. Whites and Latinos were significantly more likely than Blacks to receive a positive response from employers, and equally qualified Black men would have to search for a job *twice* as long as whites in order to receive a callback or job offer. Moreover, employers responded equally positively to Blacks with *no* criminal record and whites *with* one.

The researchers took their analysis a step further: They had the job applicants take extensive field notes to document their interactions with potential employers. These extra data allowed the researchers to compare and contrast how employers responded to the different applicants and what sorts of jobs they offered. Field notes revealed nuanced ways of discriminating that were unidentifiable by the audit alone. First, employers categorically excluded Black applicants from the get-go, telling them but not the others that a job was filled or that references needed to be checked before proceeding. In one example of this during the study, an employer turned all three applicants away but then called the white and Latino applicants back inside and offered them a job.

More extensive contact with interviewers allowed employers to get to know applicants better and thus make more nuanced but less biased judgments. Yet employers discriminated at this point in a second way: by shifting standards, or interpreting the applicants' qualifications in racialized ways. For instance, lack of experience was disqualifying for Black applicants but not for whites or Latinos. Employers also gave white felons the benefit of the doubt, but did not do the same for Blacks without a criminal record.

Finally, employers channeled workers into race-coded jobs. They channeled Black workers away from sales and service positions and into behind-the-scenes jobs. These findings show that employers treated white workers as better suited for interacting with customers and for jobs with more responsibility.

Despite the end of *de jure* discrimination 50 years ago, *de facto* discrimination is alive and well. Moreover, three processes identified in this chapter—categorical exclusion, shifting standards, and channeling workers—show how discrimination both employs and reinforces tired racial/ethnic boundaries.

Does employer discrimination continue to affect labor market outcomes for minority workers? Clear answers are elusive because discrimination is hard to measure. Without observing actual hiring decisions, it is difficult to assess exactly how and under what conditions race shapes employer behavior. We address this issue with a field experiment that allows direct observation of employer decision making. By presenting equally qualified applicants who differ only by race or ethnicity, we can observe the degree to which racial considerations affect real hiring decisions. Furthermore, we move beyond experimental estimates of discrimination to explore the processes by which discrimination occurs.

Examining the interactions between job seekers and employers, we gain new insights into how race influences employers' perceptions of job candidate quality and desirability. Studying the multifaceted character of discrimination highlights the range of decisions that collectively reduce opportunities for minority candidates.

CONCEPTUALIZING DISCRIMINATION

Empirical studies often portray discrimination as a single decision. Research on employment disparities, for example, considers the role of discrimination at the point of initial hire; research on pay disparities considers discrimination at the point of wage-setting decisions. In reality, discrimination may occur at multiple decision points across the employment relationship. In this way, even relatively small episodes of discrimination—when experienced at multiple intervals or across multiple contexts—can have substantial effects on aggregate outcomes.

Depictions of discriminators also often portray the labor market as divided neatly between employers with a "taste for discrimination" and those who are indifferent to race (Becker 1957). Consequently, it is suggested, job seekers can avoid discrimination by sorting themselves into sectors of the labor market where discrimination is less likely to occur (Heckman 1998, 103). . . . According to this conceptualization of labor market discrimination, racial preferences or biases are fixed and concentrated among a specific subset of employers.

Other evidence challenges this tidy distinction between employers who do and do not discriminate. Alternative formulations of labor market discrimination encourage us to view the process as more interactive, contextual, and widespread. Theories of both statistical discrimination and stereotypes view race as a heuristic employers use to evaluate job applicants about whom little is known. Here, group-based generalizations provide guidance about the expected profile of individuals from a given group and facilitate decision making when information or time are scarce (Aigner and Cain 1977; Fiske 1998). Heuristics of this kind are pervasive (and often unconscious). Their effects may vary depending on the availability of and attention to person-specific information (such as that conveyed through application materials or in an interview) that may interact with and potentially override initial expectations.

A long line of social psychological research investigates how stereotypes give way to individualizing information, as well as the conditions under which stereotypes demonstrate a stubborn resistance to change (Bodenhausen 1988; Fiske 1998; Trope and Thomson 1997).[1] This research suggests that salient personalizing information can quickly counteract stereotyped expectations; however, in evaluating difficult-to-observe or ambiguously relevant characteristics, or when decision makers have competing demands on their attention, stereotypes often filter information in ways that preserve expectations (Darley and Gross 1983; Dovidio and Gaertner 2000; Gilbert and Hixon 1991). In these cases of decision making under uncertainty, racial preferences or biases are unlikely to be expressed in any static or uniform way but will vary in intensity and consequence depending on other characteristics of the applicant, the employer, and the interaction between the two.

In addition to noting the varying role of race across employment interactions, some research shifts the focus from employer characteristics to the characteristics of the job for which a given worker is being considered. Previous research points to the negative consequences of the changing composition of low-wage jobs for Black men, with the shift from manufacturing to services skewing the distribution of skill demands toward "soft skills," for which Black men are considered lacking (Moss and Tilly 2001). Jobs involving customer service or contact with clients heighten the salience of race because of employers' concerns about the dress and demeanor of young Black men (Moss and Tilly 2001). Jobs at the "back of the house" or those emphasizing manual skills are less likely to activate concerns of this kind. In this scenario, discrimination may begin not at the employer level but at the job level, with Black applicants excluded from some job types and channeled into others. In this case, we would look to variation in discrimination not among employers but among the job openings for which workers are being considered.

THE CHANGING LANDSCAPE OF LOW-WAGE LABOR MARKETS

Economic theory predicts the decline of discrimination through market competition (Becker 1957), but several features of contemporary low-wage labor markets may sustain or renew racialized decision making. Shifts in the composition of both low-wage jobs and workers have potentially created new incentives and opportunities for employers to enact racial preferences in hiring. First, low-wage job growth is concentrated in service industries, in positions that place a heavy emphasis on self-presentation, interaction with customers, and other personality-related attributes (Moss and Tilly 2001).

Second, low-wage labor markets today are characterized by increasing heterogeneity of the urban minority work force, with low-skill Black workers now more likely to compete with other minority groups—in particular, low-skill Latino workers. Interviews with employers in Los Angeles and Chicago suggest consistent preferences for Latinos over Blacks, with Latino workers viewed as more pliant, reliable, and hard-working (Kirschenman and Neckerman 1991; Waldinger and Lichter 2003).

Finally, low-wage labor markets are increasingly supplied by workers with criminal records. Nearly a third of Black men without a college degree have prison records by their mid-30s, adding to employers' reservations about Black male job applicants (Pager 2007; Pettit and Western 2004).

The growing importance of soft skills, ethnic heterogeneity, and job seekers with criminal records suggest the persistence or increasing incidence of discrimination in contemporary low-wage labor markets. Whether based on statistical generalizations or inaccurate stereotypes, preconceived notions about the characteristics or desirability of Black men relative to other applicant types are likely to structure the distribution of opportunity along racial lines.

METHODS FOR STUDYING LABOR MARKET DISCRIMINATION

Racial discrimination in the labor market is typically studied by comparing the wages of whites and minorities, statistically controlling for human capital characteristics. Estimates from a variety of social surveys suggest that the Black-white difference in hourly wages among men usually ranges between about 10 percent and 20 percent (Cancio, Evans, and Maume 1996; Darity and Meyers 1998; Neal and Johnson 1996). Although widely used, this residual method, in which discrimination is defined as the unexplained race difference in wages, is sensitive to the measurement of human capital. Where race differences in human capital are incompletely observed, the effect of discrimination may be overestimated (Farkas and Vicknair 1996; Neal and Johnson 1996).

Residual estimates of discrimination infer employer behavior from data on workers' wages. Field experiments,

by contrast, offer a more direct approach to the measurement of discrimination. This approach, also referred to as an audit methodology, involves the use of matched teams of job applicants—called testers—who apply to real job openings and record responses from employers. Testers are assigned equivalent résumés and are matched on a variety of characteristics like age, education, physical appearance, and interpersonal skills. Because Black and white testers are sent to the same firms, and testers are matched on a wide variety of characteristics, much of the unexplained variation that confounds residual estimates of discrimination is experimentally controlled.

The current study updates and extends earlier research in several ways. First, we focus directly on the question of racial discrimination, in both conceptualization and design. This emphasis allows us to situate our research within ongoing debates about discrimination and to provide a rigorous design for detecting racial discrimination. Second, we move beyond standard two-race models of discrimination by including matched Black, white, and Latino job seekers, reflecting the racial heterogeneity of large urban labor markets. To our knowledge, this is the first study of its kind to simultaneously examine the employment experiences of three racial/ethnic groups. Third, to help calibrate the magnitude of racial preferences, we compare applicants affected by varying forms of stigma; specifically, we compare minority applicants with white applicants just released from prison. [T]he present analysis provides a direct test by comparing the outcomes of minority and ex-offender applicants who visit the same employers. Finally, we extend our analysis from the quantitative evidence of differential treatment to a rich set of qualitative data that allow for an exploration of the process of discrimination. Drawing from the testers' extensive field notes that describe their interactions with employers, we provide a unique window into the range of employer responses that characterize discrimination in contemporary low-wage labor markets.

RESEARCH DESIGN AND METHODS

The New York City Hiring Discrimination Study sent matched teams of testers to apply for 340 real entry-level jobs throughout New York City over nine months in 2004. The testers were well-spoken, clean-cut young men, ages 22 to 26. Most were college-educated, between 5 feet 10 inches and 6 feet in height, and recruited in and around New York City. They were matched on the basis of their verbal skills, interactional styles (level of eye contact, demeanor, and verbosity), and physical attractiveness. Testers were assigned fictitious résumés indicating identical educational attainment and comparable qualities of high school, work experience (quantity and kind), and neighborhood of residence. Résumés were prepared in different fonts and formats and randomly varied across testers, with each résumé used by testers from each race group. Testers presented themselves as high school graduates with steady work experience in entry-level jobs. Finally, the testers passed a common training program to ensure uniform behavior in job interviews. While in the field, the testers dressed similarly and communicated with teammates by cell phone to anticipate unusual interview situations.

We fielded two teams that each included a white, Latino, and Black tester. To help ensure comparability, the Latino testers spoke in unaccented English, were U.S. citizens of Puerto Rican descent, and, like the other testers, claimed no Spanish language ability. The first team tests a standard racial hierarchy, with the white tester serving as a benchmark against which to measure variation in racial and ethnic discrimination. To calibrate the magnitude of racial stigma, the second team compares Black and Latino testers with a white tester with a criminal record. The criminal record was typically disclosed in answer to the standard question on employment applications, "Have you ever been convicted of a crime? If yes, please explain." We instructed testers to reveal, when asked, that they had recently been released from prison after serving 18 months for a drug felony (possession with intent to distribute, cocaine). In addition, following Pager (2003), the white tester's criminal record was also signaled on the résumé by listing work experience at a state prison and by listing a parole officer as a reference.

For both teams, we sampled employers from job listings for entry-level positions, defined as jobs requiring little previous experience and no more than a high school degree. Job titles included restaurant jobs, retail sales, warehouse workers, couriers, telemarketers, customer service positions, clerical workers, stockers, movers, delivery drivers, and a wide range of other low-wage positions. Each week, we randomly drew job listings from the classified sections of the *New York Times, Daily News, New York Post, Village Voice*, and the online service *Craigslist*. The broad range of job listings allowed for extensive coverage of the entry-level labor market in New York. From the available population of job listings, we took a simple random sample of advertisements each week. Testers in each team applied to each job within a 24-hour period, randomly varying the order of the applicants.

Our dependent variable records any positive response in which a tester was either offered a job or called back for a second interview. We recorded callbacks using voicemail boxes set up for each tester. We have a matched triplet, and information from all three testers should ideally contribute to an inference about a contrast between any two. Ghosh and colleagues (2000) suggest that matched pairs can be fit with a hierarchical logistic regression with a random effect for each pair. We generalize their approach to our matched triplets, fitting a random effect for each employer.

THE PROBLEMS OF MATCHING

The quality of audit results depends on the comparability of the testers. Because race cannot be experimentally assigned, researchers must rely on effective selection and matching to construct audit teams in which all relevant characteristics of testers are similar—something that may leave substantial room for bias.

Because we rely on in-person audits for our study of low-wage labor markets, the effective matching of testers is a key concern.[2] We reviewed more than 300 applicants to identify our final team of 10 testers.[3] Successful applicants were subject to two lengthy screening interviews and a written test, a far more probing job selection process than the testers encountered in their fieldwork.[4] Each tester passed a standard training period, was required to dress uniformly, and was subject to periodic spot checks for quality control.[5]

[I]f a Black tester expects to be treated poorly by employers, he may appear more withdrawn, nervous, or defensive in interactions. The nature of the interaction may create a self-fulfilling prophecy, in which the tester experiences poor outcomes for reasons unrelated to his race (Steele and Aronsen 1995). We assess these tester effects by analyzing the degree to which personal contact between testers and employers is associated with widening racial disparities. Overall, we find no evidence that testers' interpersonal styles or expectations are associated with increasing discrimination; if anything, personal contact appears to weaken the effect of race.

By using "callbacks" as one of our key dependent variables, we include cases that represent an employer's first pass at applicant screening.[6] Indeed, recent surveys suggest that employers interview an average of six to eight applicants for each entry-level job opening (Pager 2007). If race represents only a minor concern for employers, we would expect all members of our audit team to make it through the first cut. If race figures prominently in the first round of review, we can infer that this characteristic has been invoked as more than a mere tie-breaker. In these cases, the evidence of race-based decision making is quite strong.

EXPERIMENTAL RESULTS

The primary results from the field experiment focus on the proportion of applications submitted by testers that elicited either a callback or a job offer from employers, by race of the applicant. Our first team assesses the effects of race discrimination by comparing the outcomes of equally qualified white, Latino, and Black applicants. Figure 1a reports positive response rates for each racial/ethnic group. In applications to 171 employers, the white tester received a callback or job offer 31.0 percent of the time, compared with a positive response rate of 25.2 percent for Latinos and 15.2 percent for Blacks. These results show a clear racial hierarchy, with whites in the lead, followed by Latinos, and Blacks trailing behind.

Figure 1b shows the contrasts between the three race groups. Once we adjust for employer and tester effects, the confidence interval for the white-Latino ratio of 1.23 includes one.[7] By contrast, the white-Black ratio of 2.04 is substantively large and statistically significant. The positive response rate for Blacks is also significantly lower than the rate for Latinos. The points in the figure show the cross-validation results obtained by sequentially dropping cases associated with each individual tester. All ratios remain consistently greater than one, indicating that employers treat Blacks less positively regardless of which testers are applying for jobs. Overall, these results indicate that, relative to equally qualified Blacks, employers significantly prefer white and Latino job applicants. The findings suggest that a Black applicant has to search twice as long as an equally qualified white applicant before receiving a callback or job offer from an employer.

The results from this first comparison indicate employers' strong racial preferences, but the magnitude of this preference remains somewhat abstract. To calibrate the effects of race against another stigmatized category, the ex-offender, we repeated the experiment, this time assigning a criminal record to the white tester. Figure 2a shows the percentage of positive responses—job offers or callbacks—received by each tester. In this experiment, whites with criminal records obtained positive responses in 17.2 percent of 169 job applications, compared with 15.4 percent for Latinos and 13.0 percent for Blacks.[8] The white testers' racial advantage narrows substantially in this comparison; yet the white applicant with a criminal

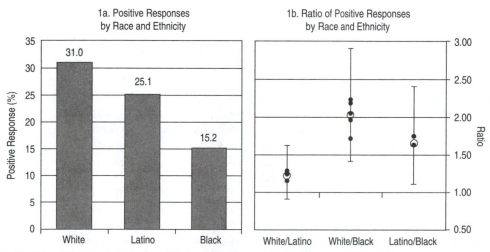

1a. Positive Responses by Race and Ethnicity

1b. Ratio of Positive Responses by Race and Ethnicity

Figure 1 Positive Response Rates and Paired Comparisons by Race and Ethnicity.

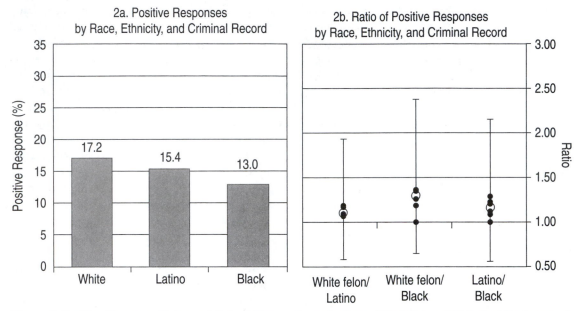

Figure 2 Positive Response Rates and Paired Comparisons by Race, Ethnicity, and Criminal Background.
Notes: Positive responses refer to callbacks or job offers. Hollow circles in Figure 2b indicate point estimates of the ratio. Solid circles indicate ratios obtained by sequentially dropping testers from the analysis. We estimated 95 percent confidence intervals from a hierarchical logistic regression with employer and tester random effects. Number of employers = 169.

record still does just as well as, if not better than, than his minority counterparts with no criminal background.

Figure 2b shows that the white-Latino ratio is close to one and the confidence interval overlaps one by a large margin. The white-Black ratio is now a statistically insignificant 1.32, compared with a significant ratio of 2.04 when the white tester had a clean record. As in the previous experiment, Latinos were preferred to Blacks, but here the difference is not significant. As before, the cross-validation treatment effects, obtained by dropping employers associated with one particular tester, are all close to one. These results indicate that, regardless of which testers were sent into the field, employers differentiated little among the three applicant groups. The comparison of a white felon with Black and Latino applicants with clean backgrounds provides a vivid calibration of the effects of race on hiring decisions. While ex-offenders are disadvantaged in the labor market relative to applicants with no criminal background, the stigma of a felony conviction appears to be no greater than that of minority status. Replicating earlier results from Milwaukee (Pager 2003), these findings suggest

that New York employers view minority applicants as essentially equivalent to whites just out of prison. . . .

Race at Work: An Examination of Interactions between Applicants and Employers

The strong evidence of hiring discrimination from the field experiment provides a clear measure of the continuing significance of race in employer decision making. These numbers, however, tell us little about the process by which race comes to matter. Fortunately, the in-person design of the experiment allows us to further supplement the experimental findings with qualitative evidence from testers' field notes that report their interactions in job interviews. These detailed narratives describe employers' deliberations and suggest some of the ways race comes into play during employment interactions.

Our analysis examines cases in which testers had sufficient interaction with employers for content coding. Consistent with the notion that contemporary forms of discrimination are largely subtle and covert, many cases contain little that would lead us to anticipate the differential treatment that followed. Of those that do, however, we observe several consistent patterns in employers' responses. In particular, three categories of behavior stand out, which we refer to here as: categorical exclusion, shifting standards, and race-coded job channeling. The first type of behavior, categorical exclusion, is characterized by an immediate or automatic rejection of the Black (or minority) candidate in favor of a white applicant. Occurring early in the application process, these decisions involve little negotiated interaction but appear to reflect a fairly rigid application of employers' racial preferences or beliefs. A second category of behavior, shifting standards, reflects a more dynamic process of decision making. Here we observe cases in which employers' evaluations of applicants appear actively shaped or constructed through a racial lens, with similar qualifications or deficits taking on varying relevance depending on an applicant's race. Finally, a third category of behavior moves beyond the hiring decision to a focus on job placement. Race-based job channeling represents a process by which minority applicants are steered toward particular job types, often those characterized by greater physical demands and reduced customer contact.

By observing the interactions that characterize each of these behavior types, we gain a rare glimpse into the processes by which discrimination takes place. At the same time, we emphasize that this discussion is intended as a descriptive exercise rather than a formal causal analysis. Indeed, the categories we identify are not mutually exclusive; some of the same processes may be operating simultaneously, with employers' shifting evaluations of applicant skills leading to different patterns of job channeling, or assumptions about the appropriate race of the incumbent of a particular position leading to forms of categorical exclusion. Likewise, this typology cannot account for all of the differential treatment we observe—at least half of the employer decisions were made on the basis of little or no personal contact between applicant and employer, leaving the nature of the decision entirely unobserved.

Categorical Exclusion

Few interactions between our testers and employers revealed signs of racial animus or hostility toward minority applicants. At the same time, a close comparison of test partners' experiences shows a number of cases in which race appears to be the sole or primary criterion for

an employer's decision. With little negotiation or deliberation over the selection decision, these employers' decisions seem to reflect a preexisting judgment regarding the adequacy or desirability of a minority candidate. The uncompromising nature of the employer's decision can be characterized as a form of categorical exclusion.

A clear-cut case of categorical exclusion was provided when all three testers applied for a warehouse worker position and received a perfunctory decision. Zuri, one of our Black testers, reported: "The original woman who had herded us in told us that when we finished filling out the application we could leave because 'there's no interview today, guys!' . . . When I made it across the street to the bus stop . . . the woman who had collected our completed applications pointed in the direction of Simon, Josue, and myself [the three test partners] motioning for us to return. All three of us went over. . . . She looked at me and told me she 'needed to speak to these two' and that I could go back." Zuri returned to the bus stop, while his white and Latino test partners were both asked to come back at 5 p.m. that day to start work. Simon, the white tester, reported, "She said she told the other people that we needed to sign something—that that's why she called us over—so as not to let them know she was hiring us. She seemed pretty concerned with not letting anyone else know."

In this context, with no interview and virtually no direct contact with the employer, we observe a decision that appears to be based on little other than race. The job is a manual position for which Zuri is at least as able, yet he is readily passed over in favor of his white and Latino counterparts.

This case is unusual in that three testers were rarely present at a given location at the same time. More often, we found evidence of differential treatment only after comparing the testers' reports side by side. Here again, we observed several hiring decisions in which race appeared to be the sole or primary source of differentiation. In one example, the three testers inquired about a sales position at a retail clothing store. Joe, one of our Black testers, reported that, "[the employer] said the position was just filled and that she would be calling people in for an interview if the person doesn't work out." Josue, his Latino test partner, was told something very similar: "She informed me that the position was already filled, but did not know if the hired employee would work out. She told me to leave my résumé with her." By contrast, Simon, their white test partner, who applied last, had a notably different experience: "I asked what the hiring process was—if they're taking applications now, interviewing, etc. She looked at my application. 'You can start immediately?' Yes. 'Can you start tomorrow?' Yes. '10 a.m.' She was very friendly and introduced me to another woman (white, 28) at the cash register who will be training me."

A similar case arose a few weeks later at an electronics store. Joe, the Black tester, was allowed to complete an application but was told that his references would have to be checked before he could be interviewed. Meanwhile, Simon and Josue, his white and Latino partners, applied shortly afterward and were interviewed on the spot. Joe's references were never called, while Simon received a callback two days later offering him the job.

When evaluated individually, these interactions do not indicate racial prejudice or discrimination. Side by side, however, we see that minority applicants encounter barriers not present for the white applicant, with employers citing excuses for putting off the Black or minority candidate (e.g., "the job has already been filled" or "we'd have to check your references before we can proceed") that appear not to apply for the white applicant. To be sure, certain cases may capture random error— perhaps a position became available between the testers' visits, or an employer was otherwise preoccupied when one applicant arrived but not another, leading to the employer's differential response. Still, the consistency of the pattern in these data suggests that random error is unlikely to be a dominant factor. Indeed, of the 171 tests conducted by the first team (no criminal background), white testers were singled out for callbacks or job offers 15 times, whereas there was only a single case in which a Black tester received a positive response when his white or Latino partner did not.[9]

These cases of categorical exclusion, although directly observed in only a small number of audits (5 of the 47 cases of differential treatment across the two teams), reveal one form of discrimination in which racial considerations appear relatively fixed and unyielding.[10] Before Black (or minority) candidates have the chance to demonstrate their qualifications, they are weeded out on the basis of a single categorical distinction. Categorical exclusion represents one important form of discrimination. While these rather abrupt interactions reveal little about the underlying motivation that drives employers'

decisions, they do demonstrate the sometimes rigid barriers facing minority job seekers. In these cases, Black (or minority) applicants are discouraged or dismissed at the outset of the employment process, leaving little opportunity for a more nuanced review.

Shifting Standards

Making it past the initial point of contact was not the only hurdle facing minority applicants. Indeed, among those who recorded more extensive interaction with employers, we observe a complex set of racial dynamics at work. On the one hand, personal contact with employers was associated with significantly improved outcomes for all testers and a narrowing of the racial gap. The testers' interpersonal skills seemed to reduce the influence of racial bias, or at least did not exacerbate it. Yet, even in the context of this more personalized review, we see evidence of subtle bias in the evaluation of applicant qualifications. In particular, a number of cases reveal how testers' "objective" qualifications appear to be reinterpreted through the lens of race. Although testers' résumés were matched on education and work experience, some employers seemed to weigh qualifications differently depending on the applicant's race. In the following interactions, we see evidence that the same deficiencies of skill or experience appear to be more disqualifying for the minority job seekers (N = 11).

In one case, Joe, a Black tester, was not allowed to apply for a sales position due to his lack of direct experience. He reported, "[The employer] handed me back my résumé and told me they didn't have any positions to offer me . . . that I needed a couple years of experience." The employer voiced similar concerns with Josue and Kevin, Joe's Latino and white partners. Josue wrote, "After a few minutes of waiting . . . I met with [the employer] who looked over my résumé. He said that he was a little worried that I would not be able to do the work." Kevin reported an even stronger reaction: "[The employer] looked at my résumé and said, 'There is absolutely nothing here that qualifies you for this position.'" Yet, despite their evident lack of qualifications, Kevin and Josue were offered the sales job and asked to come back the next morning. In interactions with all three testers, the employer clearly expressed his concern over the applicants' lack of relevant work experience. This lack of experience was not grounds for disqualification for the white and Latino candidates, whereas the Black applicant was readily dismissed.

When applying for a job as a line cook at a midlevel Manhattan restaurant, the three testers encountered similar concerns about their lack of relevant experience. Josue, the Latino tester, reported, "[The employer] then asked me if I had any prior kitchen or cooking experience. I told him that I did not really have any, but that I worked alongside cooks at [my prior job as a server]. He then asked me if I had any 'knife' experience and I told him no. . . . He told me he would give me a try and wanted to know if I was available this coming Sunday at 2 p.m." Simon, his white test partner, was also invited to come back for a trial period. By contrast, Joe, the Black tester, found that "they are only looking for experienced line cooks." Joe wrote, "I started to try and convince him to give me a chance but he cut me off and said I didn't qualify." None of the testers had direct experience with kitchen work, but the white and Latino applicants were viewed as viable prospects while the Black applicant was rejected because he lacked experience.

In other cases, employers perceived real skill or experience differences among applicants despite the fact that the testers' résumés were designed to convey identical qualifications. In one example, the testers applied for a job at a moving company. Joe, the Black applicant, spoke with the employer about his prior experience as a stockperson at a moving truck company, but "[the employer] told me that he couldn't use me because he is looking for someone with moving experience." Josue, his Latino partner, presented his experience as a stocker at a delivery company and reported a similar reaction, "He then told me that since I have no experience . . . there is nothing he could do for me." Simon, their white test partner, presented identical qualifications, but the employer responded more favorably: "'To be honest, we're looking for someone with specific moving experience. But because you've worked for [a storage company], that has a little to do with moving.' He wanted me to come in tomorrow between 10 and 11." The employer is consistent in his preference for workers with relevant prior experience, but he is willing to apply a more flexible, inclusive standard in evaluating the experience of the white candidate than in the case of the minority applicants. Employers' shifting standards, offering more latitude to marginally skilled white applicants than to similarly qualified minorities, suggest that even the evaluation of "objective" information can be affected by underlying racial considerations.

Even in cases where the white tester presented as a felon, we see some evidence that this applicant was afforded the benefit of the doubt in ways that his minority counterparts were not. In applying at an auto dealership, for example, the three testers met with very different reactions. Joe, the Black tester, was informed at the outset that the only available positions were for people with direct auto sales experience. When Josue, his Latino partner, applied, the lack of direct auto sales experience was less of a problem. Josue reported, "He asked me if I had any customer service experience and I said not really. . . . He then told me that he wanted to get rid of a few bad apples who were not performing well. He asked me when I could start." Josue was told to wait for a callback on Monday. When the employer interviewed Keith, their white ex-felon test partner, he gave him a stern lecture regarding his criminal background. The employer warned, "I have no problem with your conviction, it doesn't bother me. But if I find out money is missing or you're not clean or not showing up on time I have no problem ending the relationship." Despite the employer's concerns, Keith was offered the job on the spot. The benefit of the doubt conferred by whiteness persists here, even in the context of a white applicant just released from prison.

A pattern in these interactions, when compared side by side, is the use of double standards—seeking higher qualifications from Blacks than non-Blacks, or viewing whites as more qualified than minorities who present equivalent résumés. Recent research emphasizes employers' use of race as a proxy for difficult-to-observe productivity characteristics (Moss and Tilly 2001; Waldinger and Lichter 2003). Where we have detailed field notes on job interviews, the interactions we observe suggest that employers also use race in interpreting and weighing observable skill characteristics. Standards appear to shift as employers evaluate various applicants' qualifications differently depending on their race or ethnicity (see also Biernat and Kobrynowicz 1997; Yarkin, Town, and Wallston 1982).

Race-Coded Job Channeling

The first two categories of differential treatment focus on the decision to hire. Beyond this binary decision, employers also face decisions about where to place a worker within the organizational hierarchy. Here, at the point of job placement, we observe a third category of differential treatment. In our review of the testers' experiences, we noticed that applicants were sometimes encouraged to apply for different jobs than the ones initially advertised or about which they had inquired. In many cases, these instances of channeling suggest a race-coding of job types, whereby employers prefer whites for certain positions and minorities for others. In one case, Zuri, a Black tester, applied for a sales position at a lighting store that had a sign in the front window stating "Salesperson Wanted." Zuri described the following interaction: "When she asked what position I was looking for I said I was open, but that since they were looking for a salesperson I would be interested in that. She smiled, put her head in her hand and her elbow on the table and said, 'I need a stock boy. Can you do stock boy?'" Zuri's white and Latino test partners, by contrast, were each able to apply for the advertised sales position.

Another Black tester, Joe, was similarly channeled out of a customer service position in his application to a Japanese restaurant. Joe reported, "I told her I was there to apply for the waiter position and she told me that there were no server positions. I told her it was advertised in the paper, and she said there must have been a mistake. She said all she had available was a busboy position. I told her since there was no waiter position, I would apply for the busboy." Later that day, Kevin, his white test partner, was hired for the server position on the spot.

We also observed channeling of the Latino testers. Josue's field notes of an audit at a clothing retailer begin by describing the "young white 20-something women running the place." One of the women interviewed him, asked about past work experience, and asked which job he was applying for. "I told her 'sales associate,'" Josue reported, and he presented a résumé on which the most recent job listed was as a sales assistant at a sporting goods store. "She then told me that there was a stock position and asked if I would be interested in that." Josue was offered the stocker job and asked to start the next day.

In many cases, these instances of channeling are coded as "positive responses" in the initial analyses. While our key concern is about access to employment of any kind, this general focus masks another form of racial bias at work. A closer analysis of the testers' experiences suggests that decisions about job placement, like hiring more generally, often follow a racial logic. We coded all instances of job channeling across both our teams and counted 53 cases (compared with 172 positive responses). By comparing the original job title to the suggested job type, we then categorized these cases as downward channeling, upward channeling, lateral channeling, or unknown. We define downward channeling as (1) a move from a job involving contact with customers to a job without (e.g., from server to busboy), (2) a move from a white-collar position to a manual position (e.g., from sales to stocker), or (3) a move in which hierarchy is clear (e.g., from supervisor to line worker). We define upward channeling as a move in the opposite direction. We focus on these two types of channeling for our current analysis. After eliminating cases in which all testers within a team were similarly channeled, we have 23 additional cases of differential treatment that were not recorded by our initial measurement of job offers and callbacks.

Like hiring criteria, job placement is also patterned by race (see Table 1). Black applicants were channeled into lower positions in nine cases, Latinos were channeled down in five cases, and whites experienced downward channeling in only one case. Many of these cases were restaurant jobs in which the tester applied for a position as a server but was steered to a job as a busboy or dishwasher. In almost all cases, the original position required extensive customer contact while the suggested position did not (e.g., salesperson to stocker). Testers were sometimes guided into lower positions because their résumés indicated limited work experience, but racial differences in channeling suggest that insufficient work experience was more penalizing for minorities than for whites. The one case of downward channeling among white applicants involved a tester presenting with a criminal background.

In fact, whites were more often channeled up than down. In at least six cases, white testers were encouraged to apply for jobs that were of a higher-level or required more customer contact than the initial position they inquired about. In one case, the white tester was even encouraged to apply for a supervisory position, despite limited work experience. Kevin reported: "[The employer] then asked me if I had any experience in construction. I told him I did not. He asked if I would be okay working with people that have thick accents like his. I told him that was fine. He then told me that he wanted me to be his new company supervisor."

Employers appear to have strong views about what kind of person is appropriate for what kind of job, based on either their own assumptions of worker competence or assumptions about what their clients expect or prefer in the appearance of those serving them. Consistent with testers' field notes, employers appear to apply more stringent hiring criteria to minority workers, preferring whites for jobs that require greater skill or responsibility. In addition, minorities are disproportionately channeled out of customer service positions, consistent with other research in which employers view minority applicants as lacking communication skills or as otherwise discomfiting for customers. Although our testers presented highly effective styles of interpersonal communication, the cursory review process for these jobs often leaves group membership more salient than any individuating characteristics.

The three types of differential treatment we observe illustrate how employers enact their racial preferences in the hiring process. Rather than outward hostility or racial animus, we see more subtle forms of discouragement or rejection. At multiple points in the hiring process, Black (or Latino) applicants face additional hurdles or barriers that reduce their chances of employment and affect the quality of jobs for which they are considered. Figure 3 illustrates the processes identified in the preceding discussion. At each of the three decision points, we see pathways deflected by various forms of racial bias. Subtle differences in employers' responses—often imperceptible to the applicants themselves—produce a pattern of outcomes systematically affected by race.

Complementing the quantitative indicators of differential treatment, these qualitative observations provide a rare window into the processes by which discrimination occurs. The three categories of differential treatment observed in these data point to the range of experiences that constitute discrimination in the employment process.[11] In a small number of cases, minority testers were disqualified early on in decisions that appear to reflect employers' fairly rigid preferences. These instances of categorical exclusion represent one of the most extreme forms of discrimination, wherein minority applicants have little opportunity to overcome employers' potential concerns. By contrast, a larger number of interactions suggest a more complicated set of negotiations at play. In evaluating applicant qualifications, minority applicants, and Black men in particular, appear

Table 1 Job Channeling by Race.

Original Job Title	Suggested Job
Blacks Channeled Down	
Server	Busser
Counter person	Dishwasher/porter
Server	Busboy
Assistant manager	Entry fast-food position
Server	Busboy/runner
Retail sales	Maintenance
Counter person	Delivery
Sales	Stockboy
Sales	Not specified[a]
Latinos Channeled Down	
Server	Runner
Sales	Stock
Steam cleaning	Exterminator
Counter person	Delivery
Sales	Stock person
Whites Channeled Down	
Server	Busboy
Latinos Channeled Up	
Carwash attendant	Manager
Warehouse worker	Computer/office
Whites Channeled Up	
Line cook	Waitstaff
Mover	Office/telesales
Dishwasher	Waitstaff
Driver	Auto detailing
Kitchen job	"Front of the house" job
Receptionist	Company supervisor

Note: This table includes all cases of upward and downward channeling, except when all testers on a team were channeled similarly.
[a]Employer told tester that "sales might not be right for you."

to be held to a higher standard than their white counterparts. Black men are disqualified more readily, or hired more reluctantly, than their white partners with identical skills and experience. Furthermore, racialized assessments of applicant quality and "fit" affect not only the decision to hire but also decisions about job

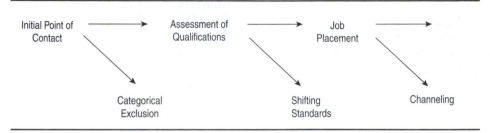

Figure 3 Discrimination at Three Decision Points.

placement, with minority applicants more often channeled into positions involving less skill or customer contact. Together, these experiences illustrate how racial disadvantage is dynamically constructed and reinforced, with the assessment of applicant qualifications and suitability subject to interpretation and bias. While not an exhaustive catalogue of discrimination experiences, the fact that these dynamics are observed in natural settings (with little prompting) attests to their relative frequency and regularity. Our testers' experiences suggest how race shapes employers' evaluations in subtle but systematic ways, with important implications for structuring opportunity along racial lines.

Discussion

Sending trained testers with equivalent résumés to apply for entry-level jobs reveals clear evidence of discrimination among low-wage employers in New York City. Blacks were only half as likely to receive a callback or job offer relative to equally qualified whites; moreover, Black and Latino applicants with clean backgrounds fared no better than a white applicant just released from prison. The magnitude of these racial disparities provides vivid evidence of the continuing significance of race in contemporary low-wage labor markets. There is a racial hierarchy among young men favoring whites, then Latinos, and finally Blacks as the candidates of last resort.

The episodes of discrimination recorded in this study were seldom characterized by overt racism or hostility. In fact, our testers rarely perceived any signs of clear prejudice. It was only through side-by-side comparisons of our testers' experiences that patterns of subtle but consistent differential treatment were revealed. Minority applicants were disqualified more readily and hired more reluctantly than their white partners with identical skills

and experience. Additionally, Black and Latino applicants were routinely channeled into positions requiring less customer contact and more manual work than their white counterparts. In interactions between applicants and employers, we see a small number of cases that reflect employers' seemingly rigid racial preferences. More often, differential treatment emerged in the social interaction of the job interview. Employers appeared to see more potential in the stated qualifications of white applicants, and they more commonly viewed white applicants as a better fit for more desirable jobs.

Our findings of discrimination are particularly striking because the testers in this study represent a best-case scenario for low-wage job seekers. The testers were college-educated young men with effective styles of self-presentation. Although posing as high school graduates with more limited skills, these young men stood well above the typical applicant for these low-wage jobs. The effects of race among individuals with fewer hard and soft skill advantages may well be larger than those estimated here.

Notes

1. Theories of statistical discrimination also predict employer responsiveness to individual characteristics (e.g., Altonji and Pierret 2001; Oettinger 1996; cf. Pager and Karafin 2009).

2. In-person audits also allow for the inclusion of a wide range of entry-level job types (which often require in-person applications); they provide a clear method for signaling race, without concerns over the class connotations of racially distinctive names (Fryer and Levitt 2004); and they allow us to gather both quantitative and qualitative data, with information on whether an applicant receives the job as well as how he is treated during the interview process.

3. These 300 applicants were prescreened for appropriate age, race, ethnicity, and gender.

4. Indeed, as an employer herself, the researcher must identify subtle cues about applicants that indicate their ability to perform. Whether or not these cues are explicit, conscious, or measurable, they are present in a researcher's evaluation of tester candidates, just as they are in employers' evaluations of entry-level job applicants. Like employers, researchers are affected by both objective and subjective/subconscious indicators of applicant quality in their selection and matching of testers in ways that should ultimately improve the nuanced calibration of test partners.

5. In addition to on-site supervision at the start and finish of each day of fieldwork, on several occasions we "tested the testers." For example, we hid video cameras in the offices of confederate employers, which allowed us to monitor testers' compliance with the audit protocol as well as to use the tapes as a training tool to better synchronize test partners' performance (not counted among results).

6. Positive responses recorded in this study were fairly evenly split between callbacks and job offers. Employers who made offers on the spot were typically hiring more than one applicant, thus similarly avoiding a situation in which a forced-choice becomes necessary. In fact, rates of job offers were more evenly distributed by race relative to callbacks.

7. In a model pooling cases from the two teams, with main effects for team and criminal background, the white-Latino gap becomes statistically significant. The generality of this result certainly deserves more study. The Puerto Ricans of New York that our Latino testers represent are a long-standing community of U.S. citizens. In other local labor markets, where markers of citizenship and accent are more prominent sources of difference, evidence of ethnic discrimination may be stronger.

8. The overall rate of positive responses is lower for all testers relative to the results presented in Figure 1. This is likely due to the staggered fielding of teams and resulting differences in the composition of employers audited across the two time periods.

9. In an additional 13 cases, both white and Latino testers received positive responses; in seven cases, the Latino tester alone was selected. . . .

10. The denominator of 47 represents the total number of cases of Black-white differential treatment from the first (N = 28) and second (N = 19) teams. In calculating the numerator, we do not include a number of additional cases of differential treatment resulting from applications in which there was little or no personal contact between testers and the employer (rates of personal contact were similar by race of tester). In such cases, differential treatment may reflect categorical exclusion (based on a visual assessment of the candidate), shifting standards (based on a review of the completed applications), random error, or something else.

11. To be sure, our study captures only a few of the many pathways in the employment process that are potentially affected by racial bias. Beyond our window of observation, the pathways of this diagram would presumably continue along later points in the employment process, including wage-setting decisions, training opportunities, promotion, and termination decisions. This research represents one incremental contribution to understanding—and documenting—the varied decision points that may be affected by race.

References

Aigner, Dennis J., and Glen G. Cain. 1977. "Statistical Theories of Discrimination in Labor Market." *Industrial and Labor Relations Review* 30:749–776.

Altonji, Joseph G., and Charles R. Pierret. 2001. "Employer Learning and Statistical Discrimination." *Journal of Economics* 116:313–350.

Becker, Gary S. 1957. *The Economics of Discrimination.* Chicago, IL: University of Chicago Press.

Biernat, Monica, and Diane D. Kobrynowicz. 1997. "Gender and Race-Based Standards of Competence: Lower Minimum Standards but Higher Ability Standards for Devalued Groups." *Journal of Personality and Social Psychology* 72:544–557.

Bodenhausen, Galen. 1988. "Stereotypic Biases in Social Decision Making and Memory: Testing Process Models of Stereotype Use." *Journal of Personality and Social Psychology* 55(5): 726–737.

Cancio, A. Silvia, T. David Evans, and David J. Maume. 1996. "Reconsidering the Declining Significance of Race: Racial Differences in Early Career Wages." *American Sociological Review* 61:541–556.

Darity, William, Jr., and Samuel L. Meyers. 1998. *Persistent Disparity: Race and Economic Inequality in the United States since 1945.* Cheltenham, UK: Edward Elgar.

Darley, John M., and Paget H. Gross. 1983. "A Hypothesis-Confirming Bias in Labeling Effects." *Journal of Personality and Social Psychology* 44:20–33.

Dobbin, Frank J., J. Meyer Sutton, and W. R. Scott. 1993. "Equal Opportunity Law and the Construction of Internal Labor Markets." *American Journal of Sociology* 99:396–427.

Dovidio, John F., and Samuel L. Gaertner. 2000. "Aversive Racism and Selection Decisions." *Psychological Science* 11:315–319.

Farkas, George, and Keven Vicknair. 1996. "Appropriate Tests of Racial Wage Discrimination Require Controls for Cognitive Skill: Comment on Cancio, Evans, and Maume." *American Sociological Review* 61:557–560.

Fiske, Susan. 1998. "Stereotyping, Prejudice, and Discrimination." In *Handbook of Social Psychology* (ed. Daniel Todd Gilbert, Susan Fiske, and Gardner Lindzey), 357–411. Boston, MA: McGraw-Hill.

Fryer, Ronald G., Jr., and Steven D. Levitt. 2004. "The Causes and Consequences of Distinctively Black Names." *Quarterly Journal of Economics* 119:767–805.

Ghosh, Malay, Chen Ming-Hui, Atalanta Ghosh, and Alan Agresti. 2000. "Hierarchical Bayesian Analysis of Binary Matched Pairs Data." *Statistica Sinica* 10:647–657.

Gilbert, Daniel T., and J. Gregory Hixon. 1991. "The Trouble of Thinking: Activation and Application of Stereotypical Beliefs." *Journal of Personality and Social Psychology* 60(4): 509–517.

Heckman, James J. 1998. "Detecting Discrimination." *Journal of Economic Perspectives* 12:101–116.

Kirschenman, Joleen, and Katherine Neckerman. 1991. "'We'd Love to Hire Them, but. . .': The Meaning of Race for Employers." In *The Urban Underclass* (ed. Christopher Jencks and Paul Peterson), 203–234. Washington, DC: Brookings Institute.

Moss, Philip, and Chris Tilly. 2001. *Stories Employers Tell: Race, Skill, and Hiring in America*. New York: Russell Sage.

Neal, Derek, and William Johnson. 1996. "The Role of Premarket Factors in Black-White Wage Differences." *Journal of Political Economy* 104:869–895.

Oettinger, Gerald S. 1996. "Statistical Discrimination and the Early Career Evolution of the Black-White Wage Gap." *Journal of Labor Economics* 14:52–78.

Pager, Devah. 2003. "The Mark of a Criminal Record." *American Journal of Sociology* 108:937–975.

Pager, Devah. 2007. *Marked: Race, Crime, and Finding Work in an Era of Mass Incarceration*. Chicago, IL: University of Chicago Press.

Pager, Devah, and Diana Karafin. 2009. "Bayesian Bigot? Statistical Discrimination, Stereotypes, and Employer Decision-Making." *Annals of the American Academy of Political and Social Science* 621(1): 70–93.

Pettit, Becky, and Bruce Western. 2004. "Mass Imprisonment and the Life Course: Race and Class Inequality in U.S. Incarceration." *American Sociological Review* 59:151–169.

Steele, Claude M., and Joshua Aronson. 1995. "Stereotype Threat and the Intellectual Test Performance of African Americans." *Journal of Personality and Social Psychology* 69(5): 797–811.

Trope, Yaacov, and Erik P. Thomson. 1997. "Looking for Truth in All the Wrong Places? Asymmetric Search of Individuating Information about Stereotyped Group Members." *Journal of Personality and Social Psychology* 73(2): 229–441.

Waldinger, Roger, and Michael I. Lichter. 2003. *How the Other Half Works: Immigration and the Social Organization of Labor*. Berkeley, CA: University of California Press.

Yarkin, Kerry L., Jerri P. Town, and Barbara S. Wallston. 1982. "Blacks and Women Must Try Harder: Stimulus Person's Race and Sex Attributions of Causality." *Personality and Social Psychology Bulletin* 8:21–24.

Questions

1. What are single-point discrimination, statistical discrimination, and job-level discrimination? Is discrimination the result of employers' racial animosity? If discrimination isn't the result of bad employers, how does it work? What changes in the job market have shaped how employers respond to Black workers?

2. What is the residual method of measuring discrimination? What problems arise from this method? What is the audit study approach? What are the benefits of using an audit study? Does it test discrimination directly? How do you know? What are the limitations? How do the authors carry out the audit study in this reading?

3. What did the audit study reveal? Was there racial discrimination? How did it compare and interact with having a criminal record?

4. Were employers openly hostile? What were the three ways employers discriminated in this study? How pervasive was each? How did the authors study this? What other mechanisms of discrimination may be at work but unobservable? Is there a way to directly observe them? How?

5. The authors only use men as testers. What effect does that have on the research, or in what ways does that bias the research? Should women or transgender people be studied separately? Why or why not?

6. In Pager's previous work (*Marked: Race, Crime, and Finding Work in an Era of Mass Incarceration,* University of Chicago Press, 2008), we learn that many employers do not realize they are discriminating or are even committed to non-discrimination yet still discriminate based on race. How can we address employer discrimination, given that reality?

15

The Power in a Name: Diagnostic Terminology and Diverse Experiences

GEORGIANN DAVIS

As we have seen throughout Part II, social labels carry tremendous power. They influence how people evaluate and treat each other, wittingly or not. They affect how people think about themselves. And they serve as gateways to resources. Medical labels in the form of diagnoses, for example, determine what services, treatments, and medicines insurance companies will cover. The creation of diagnoses and the act of diagnosing itself are social processes. The *Diagnostic and Statistical Manual of Mental Disorders (DSM)* is a catalogue of the symptoms doctors and practitioners use to identify people with mental disorders. Groups of psychiatrists review the science, consult each other, gather feedback from stakeholders, and update the manual occasionally. During the creation of the latest edition, the fifth (*DSM-V*), the American Psychiatric Association posted proposed changes on its website and invited comments from the public. Patients, families, and advocates engaged in activism to shape the diagnostic criteria. Several changes elicited considerable pushback from the public, including the narrowing of the definition of Autism Spectrum Disorder, which advocates and patients feared would reduce people's access to services. Autism Speaks (www.autismspeaks.org), a major advocacy and resource group for autism, maintains a website dedicated to tracking issues related to *DSM-V*. They provide a *DSM-V* Q&A, a survey of lost services, and ways to advocate.

The Internet has made locating and coordinating people affected by medical diagnoses much easier, and family- and patient-groups organize themselves to influence the medical profession in a variety of ways. Families of children with clubfoot, for example, have disseminated information about the success of non-surgical treatment, known as the Ponseti Method, to each other through a Yahoo! group (nosurgeryforclubfoot). Parents have been instrumental in transforming the standard of care away from surgery in the United States and around the world. The Cystic Fibrosis Foundation (www.cff.org) and the Congenital Central Hypoventilation Syndrome Family Network (www.cchsfamilynetwork.org) partner with scientists to conduct medical research to find treatments and cures for deadly conditions. In these cases and many others, patients and families directly influence scientific research agendas.

Patient advocates with intersex traits offer a powerful example of successful activism—against confining labels and surgical modification of babies to fit into a gender binary. In the study presented here, Georgiann Davis examines how people with intersex traits interact with the medical community using the prism of a new medical label "disorders of sex development." Davis finds a complex picture in which people with intersex traits relate to the new term—and the medical profession—by rejecting the label in favor of "intersex," by adopting the label, or by varying their approach. Additionally, people's self-identifications seem to reflect how they relate to their family members and their senses of self. Students of inequality will see how social change is often non-linear and complex. They will also see how individual actions relate to larger social patterns.

In the 1990s, an intersex[1] identity was born as many individuals with intersex traits bonded with one another over their shared medical histories in order to challenge the medicalized (surgical and hormonal) treatment of intersexuality (e.g., Preves 2003; Turner 1999). Intersexuality is defined here as a condition in which one is born with "ambiguous genitalia, sexual organs, or sex chromosomes" that deviate from the "norm" (Preves 2003, p. 2). Historically, medical professionals treated intersexuality by surgically modifying the "abnormality" at birth, or sometime during adolescence, despite the fact that such surgery left many intersexuals emotionally and physically scarred (Preves 2003). This medical treatment, and the publication of provocative feminist critiques of such practices (e.g., Fausto-Sterling 1993; Kessler 1990), paved the way for the formation of intersex support groups and the development of the intersex rights movement (Karkazis 2008; Preves 2003). Turner (1999) even concluded that through the mobilization efforts of the Intersex Society of North America (ISNA), intersexuals managed to move beyond the sex binary and create a "third sex." She stated:

> Embodying what they feel is a failure of medicine to make them what they cannot be in the first place, [intersexuals] envision a wholly new intersection of sex and gender, a kind of "third sex" that evades gender determination yet also somehow solidifies into a category of identity. (Turner 1999, 458)

The medical profession also acknowledged that the birth of a baby with an intersex trait constitutes a "social emergency" (Committee on Genetics [COG] 2000, 138).

In 2006, the American Academy of Pediatrics revised their policy regarding the treatment of intersex infants due to technological advancements and intersex activism, among other factors (Lee et al. 2006). They offered several recommendations including revising "intersex" to the new diagnostic terminology "disorders of sex development" (DSD). Research has already indicated that this recommended terminology was widely accepted throughout the U.S. medical profession as a way for medical professionals to reclaim jurisdiction over intersexuality, which intersex activists were successfully defining as a social, rather than medical, problem (Davis 2011). The introduction of DSD terminology, and its acceptance throughout the global medical community in a relatively short amount of time (Davis 2011; Pasterski, Prentice, and Hughes 2010a, 2010b), left me wondering about the fate of intersex identity.

Although there have been a handful of non-clinician academics who are openly critical of the new DSD nomenclature (e.g., Davidson 2009; Holmes 2009; Karkazis 2008; Reis 2007), it has received scholarly support. Academics Alice Dreger and April Herndon (2009), for instance, acknowledge that "[r]eception of the new terminology has been mixed among people with intersex" (p. 212), yet they embrace the possibility for positive change that DSD terminology could bring to those whose lives are personally affected by intersexuality. They conclude "that [DSD] terminology accords with the experience of many intersex adults and patients; it gives them a term that feels right in that it seems simultaneously to name, scientize, and isolate what it is that has happened" (Dreger and Herndon 2009, 212). In 2008, Ellen Feder and Katrina Karkazis, academics and allies to intersex activists, collaborated together in a paper in which they openly struggled with the new DSD language but were willing to embrace it if it "[would] help to refocus medical care on lifelong health; [and] not only contribute to improving medical care but also to promoting attention to affected individuals' quality of life" (p. 33). Feder (2009) has since advocated for "progressive" DSD language (p. 226). Karkazis, on the other hand, remains skeptical of DSD and has since moved away from it in her work (Karkazis et al. 2012).

However, while many medical experts support DSD nomenclature and several influential scholars of intersex studies remain hopeful in it, little empirical research explores how intersex individuals themselves feel about this terminology. This current empirical research is intended to fill this gap. I begin with a brief overview of the medicalization of intersexuality, focusing specifically on the medical consensus statements intended to guide treatment. I next incorporate sociological theories about naming and medicalized deviance to argue that DSD terminology cannot be ignored by intersex individuals because it was officially introduced by medical professionals, a powerful and institutionalized professional collective with legitimized control and authority over bodies. While this empirical research shows that intersex individuals have diverse opinions about the new DSD terminology, I also argue that DSD nomenclature is invested with a degree of power, given the medicalized context in which it was introduced. Finally, I report on the observed connections between participants' preferred terminology, their self-understandings, and their relationships with family members and medical professionals.

The Medicalization of Intersexuality
Medical Management and Feminist Critiques

Technological advancements in the twentieth century provided medical practitioners with the tools to surgically and hormonally treat individuals who deviated from binary sex. Intersexuals were defined as having "abnormal bodies" that needed medical and surgical attention in order to fit into the sex binary and arguably

ameliorate the stigma and shame associated with not comfortably fitting into the sex categorization system. A substantial body of work across the humanities and social sciences provides critical analyses of this process (e.g., Dreger 1998a, 1998b; Fausto-Sterling 1993, 1996, 2000a; Holmes 2008; Karkazis 2008; Kessler 1990, 1998; Preves 2000, 2002, 2003).

Some feminists were critical of the medical management of intersexuality due to their conceptualization of sex and gender as socially constructed binaries. By arguing for the recognition of five sexes, Fausto-Sterling (1993) attempted to debunk dichotomous notions about sex. Kessler (1998) later critiqued Fausto-Sterling's "Five Sexes" by maintaining that intersexuals should be thought of as evidence of sexual "variability" rather than sexual "ambiguity." According to Kessler (1998), it is neither possible nor logical to maintain the binary sex system when recognizing the existence of multidimensional sexual variability. To categorize intersexuals by attempting to define sex, Kessler maintains, is to perpetuate the validity of the categorization system. In 2000, Fausto-Sterling accepted Kessler's critique, writing that "It would be better for intersexuals and their supporters to turn everyone's focus away from genitals" (Fausto-Sterling 2000b, 22).

By providing analytic ground for activists to challenge the medical profession, feminist writers (e.g., Fausto-Sterling 1993; Kessler 1990) helped spark an intersex rights movement that seemed to begin to change how physicians treat intersexuality. Fausto-Sterling, for instance, is credited with facilitating the formation of the Intersex Society of North America (Chase 1997, 1998a; Fausto-Sterling 2000a, 2000b; Preves 2003). The publication of her 1993 essay, "The Five Sexes," inspired Cheryl Chase, despite her open criticism of the piece, to create the Intersex Society of North America, at one time the world's largest intersex advocacy and support group before it closed its doors in the summer of 2008 (Chase 1997, 1998a, 1998b). In 1997, the American Academy of Pediatrics refused to engage "zealous" intersex activists (Diamond 1997; Fausto-Sterling 2000a, 2000b). However, three years later, Chase delivered a plenary address to the Lawson Wilkins Pediatric Endocrine Society, a group she had once protested against (Karkazis 2008). The American Academy of Pediatrics ultimately acknowledged that the birth of an individual with an intersex trait created a professional "social emergency"

(COG 2000, 138). Shortly thereafter medical professionals instituted guidelines for the treatment of intersexuality, including, but not limited to, taking a more cautious approach to early surgical interventions (COG 2000).

Medical Statements

The 2000 medical guidelines for the treatment of intersex infants recommended that intersex infants "should be referred to as 'your baby' or 'your child'—not 'it,' 'he,' or 'she'" (COG 2000, 138). Early cosmetic surgery, however, remained a treatment option. The guidelines noted that parents should be informed that "abnormal appearance can be corrected and the child raised as a boy or a girl as appropriate" (COG 2000, 138). The guidelines stated that a number of factors should be considered when determining which sex category, or in their language "gender assignment," should be recommended for a given intersex child. Most notably, these factors included "fertility potential" and "capacity for normal sexual function" (COG 2000, 141). Both of these factors are deeply rooted within cissexism[2] and heteronormative ideologies about sexuality that presume sex, gender, and sexuality are all biologically correlated.

In 2006, the American Academy of Pediatrics revised their policy regarding the treatment of intersex individuals. They maintained that their protocol needed revision due to "progress in diagnosis, surgical techniques, understanding psychosocial issues, and recognizing and accepting the place of patient advocacy" (Lee et al. 2006, 488). The timing and extent of this revision could be read as one way in which power operates through the institution of medicine. This particular revision illustrates the power invested in medicine to not only treat but also define and (re)name intersexuality as DSD.

Naming and Medicalized Deviance

A medical condition does not officially exist until after the "abnormality" in question is defined (Conrad 2007; Scott 1990). The process by which an "abnormality" is defined has shifted throughout history. In ancient Greece, medicine was practiced without diagnostic names (Veith 1981). Instead, descriptions of disease were used until eighteenth-century medical professionals turned to a botanical model of classification that linguistically identified, labeled, classified, and named a wide range of medical conditions. This move to naming

diseases was not widely accepted by all medical professionals, yet this "classificatory project" prevailed (Jutel 2009, 280).

It has only been several years since the 2006 consensus statement reclassified intersexuality as DSD, yet evidence suggests that intersexuality has already become an outdated term within medical discourse (Davis 2011; Pasterski et al. 2010a, 2010b). The process of naming ought to concern us because history has shown that there are implications to defining conditions as disorders (e.g., Brown 1990, 1995, 2007; Conrad 2007; Cooksey and Brown 1998; Jutel 2011). Consider, for example, attention deficit hyperactivity disorder (ADHD). Conrad (2007) argued that ADHD diagnosis expanded in the 1990s to include adults who were not previously diagnosed in ways that had a lasting impact on how individuals, after diagnosis, understood and explained their behaviors.

The trajectory of intersex medicalization, and shifts in its naming, is evidence of Conrad and Schneider's (1980) five-stage model of medicalized deviance. Intersexuality was initially viewed as an unfavorable deviation from the sex binary (stage one). Then, with medical advancements, doctors had the tools to identify and describe intersexuality chromosomally (stage two). Soon after, medical professionals started claiming intersex expertise (stage three). What marks the fourth stage in Conrad and Schneider's (1980) model is a battle over diagnoses. The medical profession faced a substantial amount of resistance in this stage from some feminist scholars and intersex activists determined to stop, albeit unsuccessfully, the fifth and final stage, where the condition in question becomes a legally recognized "abnormality," as is evident in the shift to DSD. This raises several important questions. How widespread is DSD terminology among intersex individuals? How do intersex individuals feel about DSD nomenclature? How does this nomenclature relate to identity formation?

Methods

My analysis relies on thirty-seven in-depth interviews conducted throughout the United States with individuals who have intersex traits. As part of my doctoral research, I collected data from October of 2008 to April of 2011 through the now defunct Intersex Society of North America, the Androgen Insensitivity Syndrome Support Group–USA,[3] Accord Alliance, and Organization Intersex

International. I collected over 40 hours of interview data, with each interview ranging from 45 minutes to well over 3 hours. All interviews were audiorecorded and transcribed, and all participants were asked to choose their own pseudonym. In some instances, participants requested that I not use a pseudonym, in which case, I honored their request. I conducted all of the interviews face-to-face in order to gain informants' trust and establish a level of comfort only possible in person. Before the start of data collection, ethics approval was obtained from the University of Illinois at Chicago.

As a feminist with an intersex condition, my lived familiarity with intersexuality has shaped this project from conceptualization to data collection and analysis. However, throughout each stage, I have stayed true to standpoint epistemology, an epistemology that takes into account a variety of experiences—including the experiences of the researcher—when asking, addressing, and evaluating a particular research question and its findings (Sprague 2005). Standpoint epistemology allows us to frame research questions from our own standpoint or the standpoint of others. It grounds interpretation in experience, and through this process allows for research that challenges dominant standpoints. As Koyama and Weasel (2002) document, most of what we know about intersexuality has been presented by non-intersex academics and clinicians, and while unquestionably valuable as pieces of the conversation, their scholarship does not make up the entire puzzle. Intersexuality needs to be analyzed from more diverse standpoints, especially those who are personally impacted.

Findings

All of my participants were familiar with DSD terminology. However, it was not similarly received by all, as some were opposed to it, others supported it, and a few were indifferent to it. Still, everyone seemed to have to acknowledge and engage with this terminology. This potentially forceful situation might explain why I observed some polarization between participants who were dissatisfied with DSD terminology and participants who welcomed it. While there were several who stood on the outside of what appears to be a polarization, by neither embracing nor rejecting the DSD terminology, they too were familiar with the term. As I describe herein, this terminology preference, or lack thereof, was frequently related to how participants understood themselves and how they described their relationships with family and medical professionals.

"Who Wants To Be a Fucking Disorder? . . . I Don't"

In the late 1990s, individuals with intersex traits reportedly embraced intersexuality and claimed it as an identity (see Turner 1999). Thus, I was not surprised to hear a substantial number of my participants speak negatively about DSD terminology. Jeanne, for example, explained to me that "disorders of sex development is such a mouthful . . . and it is kind of a cold word . . . intersex . . . I identify with it." When I asked Pidgeon[4] what she prefers to call her condition, she enthusiastically replied, "hermaphrodite or intersex . . . I feel like the language shift to DSD makes no sense to me . . . I don't feel it was necessary." Millarca expressed similar discontent with DSD language. With passion she stated that "DSD is not . . . is not something a lot of people want to identify with . . . nobody wants to be a disorder . . . who wants to be a fucking disorder? . . . I don't."

Participants who tended to be dissatisfied with the new nomenclature also seemed to differently understand and form their identities. For example, Stevie, who embraced intersex language, said:

> Ultimately when we look in the mirror . . . and we're like either shocked by oh my god I need some lipstick . . . or oh my god I want to toughen up . . . look more macho or butch . . . we basically are responding to the inner conversation in our mind's eye of what we want to see . . . how we want to appear . . . how we want to be perceived.

Stevie explained gender as a performance that she could alter with lipstick, for example, should she desire. Pidgeon similarly understood gender: "[P]lay with your gender if you want . . . you can do whatever you want! . . . Check out all avenues of sexuality and gender and have fun with it."

Many of the participants who were dissatisfied with DSD terminology also described fractured familial and medical relationships. For example, Stevie was estranged from her parents throughout her twenties and thirties due to how her parents attempted to police the formation of her non-normative gender identity. Stevie said:

> My mother wanted to get me involved in social philanthropic things that would model . . . what a woman in

society does. . . . [For example,] there was a modeling component to [an organization my mother got me involved in] . . . a "modellette program" . . . basically had beauty and poise training . . . [My parents] knew they had a task to try to bring about a certain result . . . to raise this child as a girl.

Recently, Stevie became reacquainted with her father, a reunion that happened only after her mother's death. When I asked Pidgeon, who claimed an intersex identity, to describe how her parents attempted to influence her identity formation, she replied:

> I think a lot of times, our parents are so scared that the doctors made the wrong decision and we're going to veer off to this other gender world . . . so they kind of police it. My parents didn't technically tell me all the time that "you're a girl and you're going to be a girl" but I'm sure it was always playing in the background of decision-making.

When I asked Millarca how her parents responded to her activism and comfort claiming an intersex identity in public settings, she replied:

> My family was ashamed. They thought that I shouldn't talk about things in the family outside of the family. So they didn't want to hear or watch the documentary or the show or anything . . . [Today, my relationship with family is] the same. It's still strange. We don't really associate very often . . . it's been like that most of my life. It's not like this just because I'm intersex, it's everything, like intersex, being gay, being into leather and S&M, and just not conforming to their politics.

Participants who expressed dissatisfaction with DSD nomenclature also commonly described troubled relationships with medical professionals. Millarca, for instance, stated, "I don't trust doctors." Ann was concerned that her sexuality would be a problem for her endocrinologist. She recalled, "I remember him asking me if I was . . . after the surgeries were done . . . if I was dating boys . . . in my mind . . . the right thing would be to say 'yes, I am' . . . I remember thinking that I should just tell him that I am even though I was not." Many of the older participants who claimed an intersex identity also refused to defer to the prestige and authority society grants medical professionals. Chris said:

> I just find [genetic experts] . . . dogmatic . . . they have it all figured out . . . and that doesn't sound like science to

me. . . . Just because they have a doctor in front of their name . . . when I was younger . . . I was a lot more respectful of that.

Most of the participants who spoke critically of DSD terminology were heavily involved in 1990s intersex activism, a period characterized by intersex activists protesting against medical professionals. Many were also still involved in activism in the form of appearing on television shows and in documentary films. It was therefore not a surprise to hear many of those involved with intersex activism to voice strong opposition to terminology formally introduced by medical professionals. This historical and contemporary activism might also explain how many participants' positive self-understandings were coupled with criticism of medical professionals. Furthermore, involvement in intersex activism might explain why many of them shared stories of troubled relationships with their families to whom being an activist may be a shameful and public choice whereas a medical condition may be something one is born with and can be hidden from public view.

"Oh Get the Fuck over It"

For every two participants who passionately expressed dissatisfaction about DSD terminology, there was one who intensely welcomed it. Jane, for example, did not understand why others so adamantly resisted DSD language. She felt the terminology could be a route for productive conversations with medical professionals. She explained:

> I can be on the outside of the room arguing about terminology and if I embrace [DSD] and the door opens and let's have a real good substantive conversation because we are talking about the same thing . . . you can call me frog. I don't give a crap what you call me as long as we're moving forward advocating for families and advocating for small children that don't have a voice . . . so, when people want to argue till the cows come home that "*disorder is such an ugly word*" and "*we're not disorders . . . we're not disordered*" . . . oh get the fuck over it.

Tara also expressed support for DSD terminology over intersexuality, although without Jane's focus on strategy for change. She said, "Hermaphroditism and all those kinds of ones . . . I am not a fan of obviously." Marilyn explained that intersex terminology "bothered [her] a little bit because it was just a little bit too political." Karen touched on this political tension when I asked her about her terminology preference. She considered intersex as "bad because it describes a possible third sex or worse . . . a limbo state between them and I don't think humans are in limbo."

There was also a tendency for participants who embraced the new nomenclature to report less positive sense of self. In Tara's own words:

> After I found out that I technically am a genetic male . . . when I wear a baseball hat or something I kinda look in the mirror and I'm like, do I look like a dude? . . . Some women obviously look like women.

Tara was concerned that gender was biologically correlated to sex rather than something we perform. This understanding of gender leaves individuals feeling "abnormal," possibly reflecting their sense of self as "disordered." Marilyn similarly shared a less positive sense of self:

> When I was growing up, I was having a hard time feeling very feminine because I wasn't developing. . . . I didn't feel like a complete woman.

While Marilyn went on to explain that her feelings of not being "a complete woman" were lessening as she got older, she still concluded, "I still don't feel like a complete woman."

Though it was common for participants who embraced DSD terminology to report a less positive sense of self, I also regularly heard them describe positive relationships with family and medical professionals. For example, Liz, who did not claim an intersex identity, said that her mother, "was supportive . . . she was just supportive . . . it was very good. She went through all the steps with me . . . took me to doctors and stuff. Very simple." Vanessa similarly shared that her parents "always have been supportive of [her] . . . and [tried] to make [her] a happy person." As with Liz, Vanessa did not particularly care for intersex terminology. She explained, "intersex rubs me the wrong way . . . I'm comfortable . . . with disorder of sex development. It's the development of your sex in utero . . . I think it explains . . . something that happened versus something that you chose." Interestingly, Vanessa was also careful to explain that the support she desired from her parents was an ongoing process: "I would say they're supportive. I think my dad is becoming increasingly so . . . I think my mom is still turning the other way and

keeping her distance on this. She'll say, 'I'm here for you if you wanna talk,' but then if I wanna talk, she's sort of busy. . . . That's sort of what goes on with her."

Many participants who accepted DSD terminology had similar positive relationships with medical professionals. Liz explained that, "[A doctor] cleared everything up. . . . I saw a couple of other doctors [in my city] that also cleared everything up." Tara similarly had positive experiences with medical professionals. She elaborated:

> [My diagnosis] was straight forward. . . . The doctor was . . . really nice about it . . . supportive . . . summed it up like . . . you basically are born like a woman that had a hysterectomy . . . you just have to take estrogen to help with your bones . . . we're gonna remove your gonads.

Karen at one time had less positive relationships with medical professionals, but reported that this has shifted. She explained, "I've been treated like shit by doctors for a very long period of time [but] not currently." When I asked her what had changed, she said she started approaching doctors with what she needed without disrespecting them. She explained:

> I said, "This is what I want. This is how I want to be handled. This is what I want you to do. I don't want you to stop being a doctor and not tell me the things I need to know, but I've been lied to in the past and I've been treated terribly and treated like a lab rat, and that's not going to happen here." So he agreed and that's that.

Many of the participants who supported the medical profession's DSD terminology were never involved in intersex activism, nor did they have any interest in constructing an intersex identity. Instead, they welcomed DSD language because it conceptualized intersexuality as a medical, rather than social, condition. This could explain why these participants described having mostly positive relationships with medical professionals. It also might account for why many shared stories of parental support, as they conceptualized their condition as a medical problem that one was born with rather than an identity one has chosen. However, the medical conceptualization of intersexuality as a disorder might also explain why participants commonly described less positive understandings of the self.

"Use Whatever Term Suits . . ."

Although many of my participants held strong views on the medical profession's DSD development terminology, there were a minority of others who were non-committal to either intersex or DSD language and/or felt individuals should have the right to choose whatever terminology they preferred. Even though Cheryl Chase, the founder of the former Intersex Society of North America, advocated for DSD terminology in the medical context—for which she hoped it would replace hermaphrodite language—by "engineer[ing] the entire thing . . . getting the language changed into [the consensus statement] by working through allies," the term belongs to the medical profession who officially introduced it. While Chase encouraged DSD terminology, she also supported the preferences of others:

> I think people should use whatever term suits them. I think in a medical context, "intersex" is really counterproductive. It isn't a diagnosis. . . . It's totalizing, and the way in which it's totalizing causes doctors to be so freaked about it that they're going to lie. If that's the word that they get to use, they're not gonna use it, they're gonna lie about it. And we know that lies create shame.

Maria explained, "I have mixed feelings . . . for technical reasons, I think DSD is appropriate. But as an activist, intersex really highlights . . . it really is different . . . it's just not some disorder." Mariela hadn't "put much thought into" terminology. She went on to say that she preferred, "Either one, really. It's another label."

Participants who were non-committal to the terminology seemed to adhere to diverse understandings of the self. On one hand, Mariela expressed concern about her feminine identity. She explained, "I'm still really self-conscious about my body . . . and I'm worried about falling in love and when to disclose." Skywalker had similar concerns, although her concerns improved after she became partnered. She explained, "I'm enough of a woman that he doesn't care and that's enough for us." On the other hand, Maria had a more positive self-understanding which came from her critique of the sex binary which she concluded was an "oversimplification." Emily also had a more positive self-understanding, for she saw the self as something capable of change. She used to think of herself "as definitely more masculine" but that shifted as people started pointing out that she had "a lot of feminine qualities." When I asked her where these qualities came from, she said, ". . . socialization . . . friends, family, watching the movies."

While I did not observe a clear pattern of self-understanding among those who were non-committal to terminology, there was a tendency in the interviews for those who were open to both terminologies to describe positive relationships with their parents. For example, Skywalker "talk[s] to [her] mom a fair amount" about her condition and in return receives lots of supportive Internet information from her mom's WebMD searches. Emily described her relationship with her parents as "good" and went on to say that her parents are people she "get[s] along with." Jenna had a similarly positive relationship with her parents. She explained, "My parents were like as long as [I'm] happy, that's all that matters."

Differences among those who were non-committal to terminology once again appeared when they described their relationships with medical professionals. For instance, Emily explained that she was "distrusting" of medical professionals. She also went on to say that she takes whatever they say "with a grain of salt." While Skywalker had a similar troubled relationship with doctors who encouraged her to "lose weight" and "let [her] hair grow out" to adopt a female identity and attract men, others who were indifferent about the terminology had more positive relationships with medical professionals much like those who embraced DSD language. Mariela described doctors as "very supportive . . . they did what they could, it was just me that didn't want to deal with it." Mariela did not claim an intersex identity nor did she exclusively prefer DSD language. Instead, she preferred "Either one, really." Kelly similarly expressed, "I have a very good relationship with my primary care physician."

Participants who were indifferent about the medicalized DSD terminology seem to be capable of diminishing at least some of the institutional power embedded within the diagnostic nomenclature. By not strictly adopting one label over another, they could use whichever term they find more effective in any given setting and at any given time. For instance, one could use the power of the intersex label to construct a more positive self-identity if one begins to feel "abnormal." When one communicates with medical professionals and/or family members about their struggles with intersexuality, one could perhaps rely on DSD terminology and its construction of intersexuality as a medical problem to fulfil certain relational needs. There should be nothing inherently challenging about floating between intersex and DSD language. However, such flexibility might be challenged by those who are passionate about terminology, which includes some intersex people and some medical professionals alike.

Discussion

DSD terminology is not uniformly accepted by those whose bodies the terminology describes. Yet, all of my participants were familiar with it lending to the medical profession's power to name and introduce new terminology in ways that could not be avoided. While research participants held diverse views about this new terminology, they were all familiar with it, indicating how prevalent and unavoidable DSD has become. What also emerged from the interviews were patterns between how participants felt about DSD terminology and understandings of the self. Additionally, the terminology preference participants expressed was regularly aligned with how they described their family and medical relationships. Participants who were inclined to oppose DSD terminology commonly described more positive conceptualizations of the self, yet they also spoke of troubled relationships with family members and medical professionals. Participants who tended to embrace DSD terminology generally described positive relationships with their families and medical professionals, yet it was not uncommon for them to also express feelings of "abnormality." Although in the minority, there were a few participants who were indifferent to the new terminology, and/or felt people should have the ability to choose their own terminology without their choice being politicized.

What my analysis suggests is that medicalized power-to-define operates through DSD terminology. No matter how opposed one is to this terminology, it must be engaged with. The same is not true with intersex terminology that 1990s intersex activists successfully reclaimed and defined as a social, rather than medical, problem. Very few medical professionals continue to use intersex terminology (Davis 2011; Pasterski et al. 2010a, 2010b). While DSD terminology might allow collaboration with medical professionals, it might also heighten the struggles and difficulties around self-understanding that some participants in my study expressed. Participants who were inclined to hold on to intersex terminology, expressing strong opposition to DSD language, regularly shared stories of struggles, but

their struggles did not seem oriented toward the self. Rather, their struggles were commonly described in terms of fractured family and medical relationships, likely heightened by their history with intersex activism. Although it might be beneficial to hold on to intersex language, which is consistent with claiming intersex as an identity, perhaps the best approach is to straddle the terminological options and not be exclusively tied to either label. This approach could allow individuals to strategically employ whichever terminology they assume to be most productive in any given situation. It also suggests that there does not need to be a permanent preference in terminology. However, to float between labels for strategic purposes, one needs to acknowledge that a medical condition is only as real as its definition (Conrad 2007; Scott 1990). Perhaps, the medicalized institutional power expressed through diagnostic naming can be diminished when diagnostic labels are approached as socially constructed phenomena employed or withheld for strategic purposes.

The participants who passionately prefer one term over another seem to be in a verbal battle with one another rather than with the medical profession who officially introduced the terminology. Those who are indifferent about the terminology may have escaped the war for now, but unless more people meet them in the middle, I imagine they are going to have to pick a side sooner or later. Regardless of where one falls on this naming issue, there is evidence here that diagnostic terminology is powerful because it originates in the medical profession, and in the case of DSD, is not uniformly accepted by those it describes. Given the five-stage model of medicalized deviance (Conrad and Schneider 1980), the naming situation described here is particular because it seems to be evidence of a sixth stage where there is a battle happening among intersexuals themselves and not exclusively between those with intersex traits and those who have the institutional power to officially define nomenclature. As long as there are sides for intersex people to fall on, this turf war over naming will likely continue in ways that constrains progress toward ending the shame and stigma wrapped up in the intersex diagnosis.

Notes

1. I use the language of "intersex" and "intersexuality" throughout this chapter as opposed to "disorders of

sex development" for three reasons. First, due to the greater visibility such words have had in academic publications, across disciplines, over the newer DSD terminology, I found it was necessary to continue to reach a broader audience. Second, recent publications in the medical sciences have, for the most part, abandoned "intersex" language despite the fact that not all individuals with such conditions prefer DSD terminology (see Pasterski et al. 2010a, 2010b). Third, and the main reason for my choice in terminology, as an individual with an intersex trait, I prefer intersex language over DSD nomenclature.

2. Cissexism is the belief that gender is authentic only when it is neatly aligned with sex and sexuality.

3. AISSG-USA now goes by AIS-DSD Support Group. Available at: http://www.aisdsd.org/

4. Participant has indicated preference for this spelling of the chosen pseudonym. In an earlier publication, the pseudonym was spelled Pigeon (see Davis 2011).

References

Brown, Phil. 1990. The Name Game: Towards a Sociology of Diagnosis. *The Journal of Mind and Behavior* 11(3/4): 385–406.

Brown, Phil. 1995. Naming and Framing: The Social Construction of Diagnosis and Illness. *Journal of Health and Social Behavior* 35:34–52.

Brown, Phil. 2007. *Toxic Exposures: Contested Illnesses and the Environmental Health Movement.* New York: Columbia University Press.

Chase, Cheryl. 1997. Making Media: An Intersex Perspective. *Images* Fall: 22–25.

Chase, Cheryl. 1998a. Hermaphrodites with Attitude: Mapping the Emergence of Intersex Political Activism. *GLQ: A Journal of Lesbian and Gay Studies* 4(2): 189–211.

Chase, Cheryl. 1998b. Surgical Progress Is Not the Answer to Intersexuality. *Journal of Clinical Ethics* 9(4): 385–392.

Committee on Genetics: Section on Endocrinology and Section on Urology. 2000. Evaluation of the Newborn with Developmental Anomalies of the External Genitalia. *Pediatrics* 106:138–142.

Conrad, Peter. 2007. *The Medicalization of Society: On the Transformation of Society.* Baltimore, MD: Johns Hopkins University Press.

Conrad, Peter, and Joseph W. Schneider. 1980. *Deviance and Medicalization: From Badness to Sickness.* St. Louis, MO: The C. V. Mosby Company.

Cooksey, Elizabeth. C., and Phil Brown. 1998. Spinning on Its Axes: DSM and the Social Construction of Psychiatric Diagnosis. *International Journal of Health Services* 28(3): 525–554.

Davidson, Robert J. 2009. DSD Debates: Social Movement Organizations' Framing Disputes Surrounding the Term "Disorders of Sex Development." *Liminalis—Journal for Sex/Gender Emancipation and Resistance* 3: 60–80.

Davis, Georgiann 2011. "'DSD Is a Perfectly Fine Term': Reasserting Medical Authority through a Shift in Intersex Terminology." In *Sociology of Diagnosis* (ed. P. J. McGann and David J. Hutson), 155–182. West Yorkshire: Emerald.

Diamond, Milton. 1997. Management of Intersexuality: Guidelines for Dealing with Persons of Ambiguous Genitalia. *Archives of Pediatric Adolescent Medicine* 151(October): 1046–1050.

Dreger, Alice Domurat. 1998a. Ambiguous Sex—Or Ambivalent Medicine? Ethical Issues in the Treatment of Intersexuality. *Hastings Center Report* 28(3): 24–35.

Dreger, Alice Domurat. 1998b. *Hermaphrodites and the Medical Intervention of Sex.* Cambridge, MA: Harvard University Press.

Dreger, Alice Domurat, and April M. Herndon. 2009. Progress and Politics in the Intersex Rights Movement: Feminist Theory in Action. *GLQ: A Journal of Lesbian and Gay Studies* 15(2): 199–224.

Fausto-Sterling, Anne. 1993. The Five Sexes: Why Male and Female Are Not Enough. *The Sciences* 33(2): 20–25.

Fausto-Sterling, Anne. 1996. How to Build a Man. In *Science and Homosexualities* (ed. V. A. Rosario), 219–225. New York: Routledge.

Fausto-Sterling, Anne. 2000a. *Sexing the Body: Gender Politics and the Construction of Sexuality.* New York: Basic Books.

Fausto-Sterling, Anne. 2000b. The Five Sexes, Revisited. *The Sciences* 40(4): 18–23.

Feder, Ellen, and Katrina Karkazis. 2008. What's in a Name? The Controversy over Disorders of Sex Development. *Hastings Center Report* 38(5): 33–36.

Feder, Ellen K. 2009. Imperatives of Normality: From "Intersex" to "Disorders of Sex Development." *GLQ: A Journal of Lesbian and Gay Studies* 15(2): 225–247.

Holmes, Morgan. 2008. *Intersex: A Perilous Difference.* Selinsgrove, PA: Susquehanna University Press.

Holmes, Morgan. (Ed.). 2009. *Critical Intersex.* Farnham: Ashgate.

Jutel, Annemarie. 2009. Sociology of Diagnosis: A Preliminary Review. *Sociology of Health and Illness* 31(2): 278–299.

Jutel, Annemarie. 2011. *Putting a Name to It: Diagnosis in Contemporary Society.* Baltimore, MD: Johns Hopkins University Press.

Karkazis, Katrina. 2008. *Fixing Sex: Intersex, Medical Authority, and Lived Experience*. Durham, NC: Duke University Press.

Karkazis, Katrina, Rebecca Jordan-Young, Georgiann Davis, and Silvia Camporesi. 2012. Out of Bounds? A Critique of the New Policies on Hyperandrogenism in Elite Female Athletes. *American Journal of Bioethics* 12(7): 3–16.

Kessler, Suzanne J. 1990. The Medical Construction of Gender: Case Management of Intersexed Infants. *Signs* 16(1): 3–26.

Kessler, Suzanne J. 1998. *Lessons from the Intersexed*. New Brunswick, NJ: Rutgers University Press.

Koyama, Emi, and Lisa Weasel. 2002. From Social Construction to Social Justice: Transforming How We Teach about Intersexuality. *Women's Studies Quarterly* 30(3/4): 169–178.

Lee, Peter A., Christopher P. Houk, S. Faisal Ahmed, and Ieuan A. Hughes. 2006. Consensus Statement on Management of Intersex Disorders. *Pediatrics* 118(2): e488–e500.

Pasterski, Vickie, P. Prentice, and Ieuan A. Hughes. 2010a. Consequences of the Chicago Consensus on Disorders of Sex Development (DSD): Current Practices in Europe. *Archives of Disease in Childhood* 95:618–623.

Pasterski, Vickie, P. Prentice, and Ieuan A. Hughes. 2010b. Impact of the Consensus Statement and the New DSD Classification System. *Best Practice and Research Clinical Endocrinology and Metabolism* 24:187–195.

Preves, Sharon. 2000. Negotiating the Constraints of Gender Binarism: Intersexuals' Challenge to Gender Categorization. *Current Sociology* 48(3): 27–50.

Preves, Sharon. 2002. Sexing the Intersexed: An Analysis of Sociocultural Responses to Intersexuality. *Signs* 27(2): 523–556.

Preves, Sharon. 2003. *Intersex and Identity: The Contested Self*. New Brunswick, NJ: Rutgers University Press.

Reis, Elizabeth. 2007. Divergence of Disorder? The Politics of Naming Intersex. *Perspectives in Biology and Medicine* 50(4): 535–543.

Scott, Wilbur J. 1990. PTSD in DSM-III: A Case in the Politics of Diagnosis and Disease. *Social Problems* 37(3): 294–310.

Sprague, Joey. 2005. *Feminist Methodologies for Critical Researchers: Bridging Differences*. Lanham, MD: Rowman and Littlefield.

Turner, Stephanie S. 1999. Intersex Identities: Locating New Intersections of Sex and Gender. *Gender and Society* 13(4): 457–479.

Veith, I. 1981. Historical Reflections on the Changing Concepts of Disease. In *Concepts of Health and Disease: Interdisciplinary Perspectives* (ed. A. L. Caplan, H. T. Engelhardt, and J. J. McCartney), 221–230. Reading, MA: Addison-Wesley.

Questions

1. What does the author mean by "medicalization" of people who are intersex? How have feminist researchers and intersex individuals challenged the medical profession's approach to people's bodies? What resources have they used to change the medical treatment of people with intersex traits?

2. What terms are used to describe people with sex variability? Where did DSD come from? Why do so many reject DSD terminology, even though it is new and increasingly adopted by medical professionals? Others are fine with DSD terminology. What is their understanding? Why would people who more readily adopt DSD nomenclature have better relationships with their families and medical professionals? Is it the term itself that leads to those relationships, or is there a broader social circumstance that is associated with both DSD terminology and those more positive relationships? What are the ramifications of selecting DSD versus intersex or another term for accessing medical care?

3. What is the relationship between sex and gender, according to sociologists? How does sex diversity fit into this schema? In what ways does intersexuality disrupt the gender order? How does having a social constructionist or performative understanding of gender influence people's senses of self?

4. Examine the resources available to families of children born with intersex traits at Accord Alliance (http://www.accordalliance.org/) and Organization Intersex International (http://oiiinternational .com/). What challenges do families with children with intersex traits face? What are the social

origins of those challenges? Should intersexuality be "treated?" If so, when? If not, why not? Who should decide? How has the standard of care for intersex babies changed over time? What is the United Nations' position? At whom is intersex advocacy directed right now? What shape is it taking?

5. What can we learn about how social change happens from the example of intersexuality advocates? What are potential costs to the self and relationships of activism? How can people protect themselves from those costs?

16

Explaining and Eliminating Racial Profiling

DONALD TOMASKOVIC-DEVEY AND PATRICIA WARREN

Widespread protests erupted in 2014 after white police officers killed unarmed Black men and boys during police stops. In two especially high-profile cases—of officer Darren Wilson shooting Michael Brown in Ferguson, Missouri, and officer Daniel Pantaleo holding Eric Garner in a chokehold while he gasped, "I can't breathe," in New York City (the latter was videotaped)—grand juries chose not to indict the officers. Protestors decried the use of deadly force against Black boys and men even for minor offenses (Garner, for example, was suspected of selling cigarettes illegally), a biased system that failed to hold police accountable, and white officers' over-policing of Black neighborhoods and activities, among other injustices. Students across the country rallied, holding signs that read "Black Lives Matter," and staged "die ins."

In their analysis of racial profiling in policing presented here, Donald Tomaskovic-Devey and Patricia Warren describe three ways that racial stereotypes translate into discriminatory behavior among police. First, formal rules codify targeting Blacks or Latinos. Drug policies and official trainings have taught officers to suspect Blacks and Latinos and to seek them out as potential criminals. "Stop, Question, and Frisk," a signature public safety program of Mayor Michael Bloomberg in New York City, led to hundreds of thousands of stops, most of the targets of whom were Black. According to the calculations by the New York Civil Liberties Union of publicly available data, in 2013 (the latest year with complete data) 56 percent of the total 191,558 stops were of Blacks, 29 percent of Latinos, and 10 percent of whites (NYCLU 2014). Support Our Law Enforcement and Safe Neighborhoods Acts (Arizona Senate Bill 1070), a 2010 act intended "to discourage and deter the unlawful entry and presence of aliens and

Excerpted from Tomaskovic-Devey, Donald and Patricia Warren. 2009. "Explaining and Eliminating Racial Profiling." *Contexts* 8:34–39. © SAGE PUBLICATIONS INC., JOURNALS.

economic activity by persons unlawfully present in the United States," call on officers to verify the immigration status of people they suspect of being in the United States illegally during "lawful stop, detention or arrest" (as modified by Arizona House Bill 2162). It also "allows a law enforcement officer, without a warrant, to arrest a person if the officer has probable cause to believe that the person has committed any public offense that makes the person removable from the U.S.," according to the Fact Sheet for S.B. 1070.

Second, routine patrols of high-crime areas, when they are also neighborhoods of color, lead to more contact between police and citizens. Targeting Black businesses, Black neighborhoods, or Black-typed crime (e.g., those involving crack) is another way that policy produces racial bias.

Third, unconscious biases that are ingrained in officers' minds cloud their perceptions of Black citizens and their actions. Especially when police do neighborhood patrols and have a high degree of discretion, officers' perceptions of who is dangerous influence their stops.

Despite the pervasiveness and insidious nature of racial bias, however, Tomaskovic-Devey and Warren's research shows that there is plenty to do about it. In their "driving while Black study," North Carolina highway patrol was four times as likely to search Black drivers as whites—yet those drivers were 33 percent less likely to be found with contraband. Collecting data on race for each police stop, analyzing the data for bias, and holding people accountable quickly and substantially reduced racial profiling. Lawsuits by civil rights organizations can also reduce discrimination. Exposure to non-stereotypic individuals and education can reduce hidden biases.

References

NYCLU (New York Civil Liberties Union). 2014. "Stop-and-Frisk Data." *NYCLU*. http://www.nyclu.org/content/stop-and-frisk-data (accessed December 12, 2014).

Support Our Law Enforcement and Safe Neighborhoods Act. 2010. Arizona Senate Bill 1070.

2010. Arizona House Bill 2162.

Fact Sheet for S.B. 1070. 2010. Arizona State Senate. http://www.azleg.gov/legtext/49leg/2r/summary/s.1070pshs.doc.htm (accessed December 12, 2014).

The emancipation of slaves is a century-and-a-half in America's past. Many would consider it ancient history. Even the 1964 Civil Rights Act and the 1965 Voting Rights Act, which challenged the de facto racial apartheid of the post–Civil War period, are now 50 years old.

But even in the face of such well-established laws, racial inequalities in education, housing, employment, and law enforcement remain widespread in the United States.

Many Americans think these racial patterns stem primarily from individual prejudices or even racist attitudes. However, sociological research shows that discrimination is more often the result of organizational practices that have unintentional racial effects or are based on cognitive biases linked to social stereotypes.

Racial profiling—stopping or searching cars and drivers based primarily on race, rather than any suspicion or observed violation of the law—is particularly problematic because it's a form of discrimination enacted and organized by federal and local governments.

In our research we've found that sometimes formal, institutionalized rules within law enforcement agencies encourage racial profiling. Routine patrol patterns and responses to calls for service, too, can produce racially biased policing. And, unconscious biases among individual police officers can encourage them to perceive some drivers as more threatening than others (of course, overt racism, although not widespread, among some police officers also contributes to racial profiling).

Racially biased policing is particularly troubling for police-community relations, as it unintentionally contributes to the mistrust of police in minority neighborhoods. But, the same politics and organizational practices that produce racial profiling can be the tools communities use to confront and eliminate it.

Profiling and Its Problems

The modern story of racially biased policing begins with the Drug Enforcement Agency's (DEA) Operation Pipeline, which starting in 1984 trained 25,000 state and local police officers in 48 states to recognize, stop, and search potential drug couriers. Part of that training included considering the suspects' race.

Jurisdictions developed a variety of profiles in response to Operation Pipeline. For example, in Eagle County, Colorado, the sheriff's office profiled drug couriers as those who had fast-food wrappers strewn in their cars, out-of-state license plates, and dark skin, according to the book *Good Cop, Bad Cop* by Milton Heumann and Lance Cassak (2003). As well, those authors wrote, Delaware's drug courier profile commonly targeted young minority men carrying pagers or wearing gold jewelry. And according to the American Civil Liberties Union (Harris 1999), the Florida Highway Patrol's profile included rental cars, scrupulous obedience to traffic laws, drivers wearing lots of gold or who don't "fit" the vehicle, and ethnic groups associated with the drug trade (meaning African Americans and Latinos).

In the 1990s, civil rights organizations challenged the use of racial profiles during routine traffic stops, calling them a form of discrimination. In response, the U.S. Department of Justice argued that using race as an explicit profile produced more efficient crime control than random stops (Engel, Calnon, and Bernard 2002). Over the past decade, however, basic social science research has called this claim into question (Lundman and Kaufman 2003, Warren et al. 2006).

The key indicator of efficiency in police searches is the percent that result in the discovery of something illegal. Recent research has shown repeatedly that increasing the number of stops and searches among minorities doesn't lead to more drug seizures than are found in routine traffic stops and searches among white drivers (Antonelli, 1996; Kociewiewski, 2002; Lamberth, 1996). In fact, the rates of contraband found in profiling-based drug searches of minorities are typically lower, suggesting that racial profiling decreases police efficiency.

In addition to it being an inefficient police practice, Operation Pipeline violated the assumption of equal protection under the law guaranteed through civil rights laws as well as the 14th Amendment to the U.S. Constitution. It meant, in other words, that just as police forces across the country were learning to curb the egregious civil rights violations of the twentieth century, the federal government began training state and local police to target Black and brown drivers for minor traffic violations in hopes of finding more severe criminal offending. The cruel irony is that it was exactly this type of flagrant, state-sanctioned racism that the civil rights movement was so successful at outlawing barely a decade earlier.

Following notorious cases of violence against minorities perpetrated by police officers, such as the video-taped beating of Rodney King in Los Angeles in 1991 and the shooting of Amadou Diallo in New York in 1999, racially biased policing rose quickly on the national civil rights agenda. By the late 1990s, challenges to racial profiling became a key political goal in the more general movement for racial justice.

The National Association for the Advancement of Colored People (NAACP) and the American Civil Liberties Union (ACLU) brought lawsuits against law enforcement agencies across the United States for targeting minority drivers. As a result, many states passed legislation that banned the use of racial profiles and then required officers to record the race of drivers stopped in order to monitor and sanction those who were violating citizens' civil rights.

Today, many jurisdictions continue to collect information on the race composition of vehicle stops and searches to monitor and discourage racially biased policing. In places like New Jersey and North Carolina, where the national politics challenging racial profiling were reinforced by local efforts to monitor and sanction police, racial disparities in highway patrol stops and searches have declined.

Our analysis of searches by the North Carolina Highway Patrol shows that these civil rights–based challenges, both national and local, quickly changed police behavior. In 1997, before racial profiling had come under attack, Black drivers were four times as likely as white drivers to be subjected to a search by the North Carolina Highway Patrol. Confirming that the high rate of searches represented racial profiling, Black drivers were 33 percent less likely to be found with contraband compared to white drivers. The next year, as the national and local politics of racial profiling accelerated, searches of Black drivers plummeted in North Carolina. By 2000, racial disparities in searches had been cut in half and the recovery of contraband no longer differed by race, suggesting that officers were no longer racially biased in their decisions to search cars.

This isn't to suggest that lawyers' and activists' complaints have stopped profiling everywhere. For example, Missouri, which has been collecting data since 2000, still has large race disparities in searching practices among its police officers. The most recent data (for 2007) show that Blacks were 78 percent more likely than whites to be searched. Hispanics were 118 percent more likely than whites to be searched. Compared to searches of white drivers, contraband was found 25 percent less often among Black drivers and 38 percent less often among Hispanic drivers.

How Bias Is Produced

Many police–citizen encounters aren't discretionary; therefore, even if an officer harbors racial prejudice it won't influence the decision to stop a car. For example, highway patrol officers, concerned with traffic flow and public safety, spend a good deal of their time stopping speeders based on radar readings—they often don't even know the race of the driver until after they pull over the car. Still, a number of other factors can produce high rates of racially biased stops. The first has to do with police patrol patterns, which tend to vary widely by neighborhood.

Not unreasonably, communities suffering from higher rates of crime are often patrolled more aggressively than others. Because minorities more often live in these neighborhoods, the routine deployment of police in an effort to increase public safety will produce more police–citizen contacts and thus a higher rate of stops in those neighborhoods.

A recent study in Charlotte, North Carolina, confirmed that much of the race disparity in vehicle stops there can be explained in terms of patrol patterns and calls for service. Another recent study of pedestrian stops in New York yielded similar conclusions—but further estimated that police patrol patterns alone led to African American pedestrians being stopped at three times the rate of whites. (And, similar to the study of racial profiling of North Carolina motorists, contraband was recovered from white New Yorkers at twice the rate of African Americans.)

Police patrol patterns are, in fact, sometimes more obviously racially motivated. Targeting Black bars, rather than white country clubs, for Saturday-night random alcohol checks has this character. This also happens when police stop minority drivers for being in white neighborhoods. This "out-of-place policing" is often a routine police practice, but it can also arise from calls for service from white households suspicious of minorities in their otherwise segregated neighborhoods. In our conversations with African American drivers, many were quite conscious of the risk they took when walking or driving in white neighborhoods.

"My son . . . was working at the country club. . . . He missed the bus and he said he was walking out Queens Road. After a while all the lights came popping on in every house. He guessed they called and . . . the police came and they questioned him, they wanted to know why was he walking through Queens Road [at] that time of day," one black respondent we talked to said.

The "wars" on drugs and crime of the 1980s and 1990s encouraged law enforcement to police minority neighborhoods aggressively and thus contributed significantly to these problematic patterns. In focus groups with African American drivers in North Carolina, we heard that many were well aware of these patterns and their sources. "I think sometimes they target . . . depending on where you live. I think if you live in a side of town . . . with maybe a lot of crime or maybe break-ins or drugs, . . . I think you are a target there," one respondent noted.

These stories are mirrored in data on police stops in a midsize Midwestern city reported in figure 2. Here, the fewer minorities there are in a neighborhood, the more often African Americans are stopped. In the whitest neighborhoods, African American drivers were stopped at three times the rate you'd expect given how many of them are on the road. In minority communities, minority drivers were still stopped disproportionally, but at rates much closer to their population as drivers in the neighborhood.

This isn't to say that all racial inequities in policing originate with the rules organizations follow. Racial attitudes and biases among police officers are still a source of racial disparity in police vehicle stops. But even this is a more complicated story than personal prejudice and old-fashioned bigotry.

Bias among Individual Officers

The two most common sources of individual bias are conscious prejudice and unconscious cognitive bias.

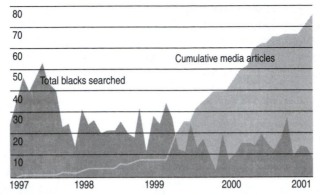

Figure 1 Black Searches and Media Coverage of Racial Profiling in North Carolina.

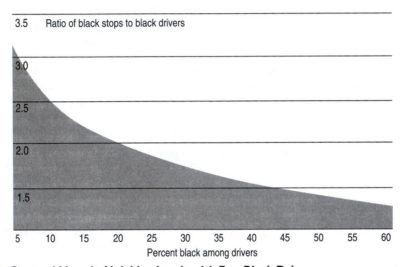

Figure 2 Blacks Stopped More in Neighborhoods with Few Black Drivers.

Conscious prejudice is typically, but incorrectly, thought of as the most common source of individuals' racist behavior. While some individual police officers, just like some employers or real estate agents, may be old-fashioned bigots, this isn't a widespread source of racial bias in police stops. Not only is prejudice against African Americans on the decline in the United States, but most police forces prohibit this kind of racism and reprimand or punish such officers when it's discovered. In these cases, in fact, organizational mechanisms prevent, or at least reduce, bigoted behavior.

Most social psychologists agree, however, that implicit biases against minorities are widespread in the population. While only about 10 percent of the white population will admit they have explicitly racist attitudes, more than three-fourths display implicit anti-Black bias.

Studies of social cognition (or, how people think) show that people simplify and manage information by organizing it into social categories. By focusing on obvious status characteristics such as sex, race, or age, all of us tend to categorize ourselves and others into groups. Once people are racially categorized, stereotypes automatically, and often unconsciously, become activated and influence behavior. Given pervasive media images of African American men as dangerous and threatening (see figure 1), it shouldn't be surprising that when officers make decisions about whom to pull over or whom to search, unconscious bias may encourage them to focus more often on minorities.

These kinds of biases come into play especially for local police who, in contrast to highway patrol officers, do much more low-speed, routine patrolling of neighborhoods and business districts and thus have more discretion in making decisions about whom to stop.

In our research in North Carolina, for example, we found that while highway patrol officers weren't more likely to stop African American drivers than white drivers, local police stopped African Americans 70 percent more often than white drivers, even after statistically adjusting for driving behavior. Local officers were also more likely to stop men, younger drivers, and drivers in older cars, confirming that this process was largely about unconscious bias rather than explicit racial profiles. Race, gender, age, class biases, and stereotypes about perceived dangerousness seem to explain this pattern of local police vehicle stops.

Strategies for Change

Unconscious biases are particularly difficult for an organization to address because offending individuals are typically unaware of them, and when confronted they may deny any racist intent.

There is increasing evidence that even deep-seated stereotypes and unconscious biases can be eroded through both education and exposure to minorities who don't fit common stereotypes, and that they can be contained when people are held accountable for their decisions. Indeed, it appears that acts of racial discrimination (as opposed to just prejudicial attitudes or beliefs) can be stopped through managerial authority, and prejudice itself seems to be reduced through both education and exposure to minorities.

For example, a 2006 study by sociologists Alexandra Kalev, Frank Dobbin, and Erin Kelly of race and gender employment bias in the private sector found that holding management accountable for equal employment opportunities is particularly efficient for reducing race and gender biases. Thus, the active monitoring and managing of police officers based on racial composition of their stops and searches holds much promise for mitigating this "invisible" prejudice.

Citizen and police review boards can play proactive and reactive roles in monitoring both individual police behavior as well as problematic organizational practices. Local police forces can use data they collect on racial disparity in police stops to identify problematic organizational behaviors such as intensively policing minority neighborhoods, targeting minorities in white neighborhoods, and racial profiling in searches.

Aggressive enforcement of civil rights laws will also play a key role in encouraging local police chiefs and employers to continue to monitor and address prejudice and discrimination inside their organizations. This is an area where the federal government has a clear role to play. Filing lawsuits against cities and states with persistent patterns of racially biased policing—whether based on the defense of segregated white neighborhoods or the routine patrolling of crime "hot spots"— would send a message to all police forces that the routine harassment of minority citizens is unacceptable in the United States.

Justice in the Obama Era

Given the crucial role the federal justice department has played in both creating and confronting racial profiling, one may have wondered whether the election of President Barack Obama would have had consequences for racially biased policing.

Obama certainly has personal reasons to challenge racist practices. And given the success of his presidential campaign, it would have seemed he had the political capital to address racial issues in a way and to an extent unlike any of his predecessors.

At the same time, Obama vowed to continue to fight a war on terrorism, a war often understood and explicitly defined in religious and ethnic terms. In some ways, the threat of terrorism has replaced the threat of African Americans in the U.S. political lexicon. There's evidence as well that politicians, both Democrat and Republican, have increased their verbal attacks on illegal immigrants and in doing so may be providing a fertile ground for new rounds of profiling against Hispanics in this country. So, while the racial profiling of African Americans as explicit national policy was unlikely in the Obama Administration, other groups have not been so lucky.

Americans committed to racial justice and equality will likely take this as a cautionary tale. They likely hoped the Obama Administration would decide to take a national leadership role in ending racial profiling. But as sociologists we hope any administration won't make the all too common mistake of assuming racial profiling is primarily the result of racial prejudice or even the more widespread psychology of unconscious bias.

References

Antonelli, Kris. 1996. "Profiles Lose Favor in Drug Interdiction: Legal Challenges Say Checklists Target Racial Groups." *The Baltimore Sun,* December 10, 1B.

Harris, David A. 1999. "Driving While Black: Racial Profiling on Our Nation's Highways." American Civil Liberties Union. https://www.aclu.org/report/driving-while-black-racial-profiling-our-nations-highways. Accessed on September 18, 2015.

Engel, Robin Shepard, Jennifer M. Calnon, and Thomas J. Bernard. 2002. "Theory and Racial Profiling: Shortcomings and Future Directions in Research." *Justice Quarterly* 19:249–273.

Heumann, Milton, and Lance Cassak. 2003. *Good Cop, Bad Cop: Racial Profiling and Competing Views of Justice.* New York: Peter Lang Publishing.

Lundman, Richard J., and Robert L. Kaufman. 2003. "Driving While Black and Male: Effects of Race, Ethnicity, and Gender on Citizen Self-Reports of Traffic Stops and Police Actions." *Criminology* 41(1): 195–220.

Kociewiewski, David. 2002. "Study Suggests Racial Gap in Speeding in New Jersey." *New York Times,* March 21, B1.

Kalev, Alexandra, Frank Dobbin, and Erin Kelly. 2006. "Best Practices or Best Guesses? Assessing the Efficacy of Corporate Affirmative Action and Diversity Polices," *American Sociological Review* 71:598–617.

Lamberth, John. 1996. *A Report to the ACLU.* New York: American Civil Liberties Union.

Warren, Patricia, Donald Tomaskovic-Devey, William Smith, Matthew Zingraff, and Marcinda Mason. 2006. "Driving While Black: Bias Processes and Racial Disparity in Police Stops." *Criminology* 44: 709–738.

Questions

1. Pretend for a moment that you are a consultant brought in to your local police department. They want to know if there is racial bias occurring. What are the potential sources of bias? How could you go about finding out if people are biased and discriminatory? What sort of data would you need? What sort of remedies would you recommend police agencies take? What about officers themselves?

2. Some people believe that collecting data on race, sex, sexual orientation, and disability reifies the social categories and therefore maintains systems of inequality. Does their argument have merit? Is this an effective social change mechanism? If government agencies or social scientists did not collect data on these characteristics, would it reduce inequality? Why or why not?

C. Data Analysis Exercise: Is Racism Dead?

This exercise presents data from the General Social Survey (GSS). The GSS is a national attitudinal survey that has been conducted since 1972 to analyze trends in people's attitudes across time (Davis and Smith 2005). You will analyze trends in people's attitudes towards Blacks in the United States. People were asked to respond to the following questions, "On the average, Blacks have worse jobs, income, and housing than white people. Do you think these differences are: "Mainly due to discrimination" (yes/no), "Because most Blacks just don't have the motivation or will power to pull themselves out of poverty?" (yes/no) "Because most Blacks have less in-born ability to learn?" or "Because most Blacks don't have the chance for education that it takes to rise out of poverty?" Table 1 shows the percentage of whites, Blacks, and Hispanics who responded yes. Use the Table to answer the following questions.

Table 1 Percentage Saying "Yes" to Each Item Explaining the Black/White SES Gap for Selected Years (1977–2004 GSS)

| | | Race/Ethnicity | | | | | |
| | | Non-Hispanic White | | African American | | Hispanic | |
NORC Item	Year	Percent	(N)	Percent	(N)	Percent	(N)
"less in-born *ability*"	1977	26.2	(1,229)	—	—	—	—
	1985–89	20.7	(3,937)	15.8	(538)	17.3	(220)
	1990–94	15.1	(4,215)	12.2	(632)	11.5	(243)
	1996–98	9.9	(2,845)	9.8	(510)	10.8	(203)
	2000–04	10.3	(2,651)	13.9	(526)	15.4	(240)
"lack of *motivation or will power*"	1977	66.2	(1,217)	—	—	—	—
	1985–89	62.4	(3,908)	35.9	(518)	55.7	(221)
	1990–94	58.3	(4,101)	37.7	(621)	54.9	(233)
	1996–98	49.4	(2,728)	40.0	(492)	54.4	(195)
	2000–04	50.0	(2,545)	44.9	(515)	50.6	(240)
"lack of chance for *education*"	1977	50.9	(1,245)	—	—	—	—
	1985–89	51.8	(3,991)	67.8	(534)	56.1	(223)
	1990–94	51.3	(4,221)	65.9	(637)	47.2	(246)
	1996–98	43.7	(2,840)	55.1	(510)	43.9	(198)
	2000–04	43.2	(2,632)	54.0	(525)	42.8	(241)
"due to *discrimination*"	1977	40.9	(1,236)	—	—	—	—
	1985–89	39.2	(3,938)	76.6	(518)	60.6	(226)
	1990–94	35.8	(4,154)	79.6	(626)	49.8	(243)
	1996–98	33.0	(2,788)	63.8	(489)	48.2	(199)
	2000–04	31.0	(2,603)	60.7	(506)	40.7	(234)

Data from: Hunt, Matthew O. 2007. "African American, Hispanic, and White Beliefs about Black/White Inequality, 1977–2004." *American Sociological Review* 72(3): 390–415.

Questions:

1. How do the survey questions suggest very different causes of inequality? What broader ideologies do they reflect? Is attributing racial differences to will power a new form of racism? Use readings from this section to support your answer.

2. How have people's responses changed across time? What do most whites attribute racial differences

to? Most Blacks? Most people who are neither white nor Black?

3. How do the white, Black, and Hispanics answers compare to one another? Whose attitudes are most alike? Whose are different? Whose attitudes have been converging across time? What do you think can explain these differences? Are they what you expected?

4. Is racism by individuals dead or has it taken on a new flavor?

References

Davis, James A. and Tom W. Smith. 2005. *General Social Surveys, 1972–2004: Cumulative Codebook,* Chicago, IL: University of Chicago National Opinion Research Center.

Hunt, Matthew O. 2007. "African American, Hispanic, and White Beliefs about Black/White Inequality, 1977–2004." *American Sociological Review* 72(3): 390–415.

D. Data Analysis Exercise: When Do Women Have Orgasms?

In the chapter by Grazian, you read about a "girl hunt." In this data analysis exercise, you will continue to explore the relationship between gender and hooking up, delving deeper into the ways in which gender inequality structures sexual satisfaction. Armstrong, England, and Fogarty (2012) analyzed data from the Online College Social Life survey from 21 colleges and universities in the United States. Figure 1 focuses on 6,591 college women who had reported having had sex. The survey asked college women about the nature of their relationship with

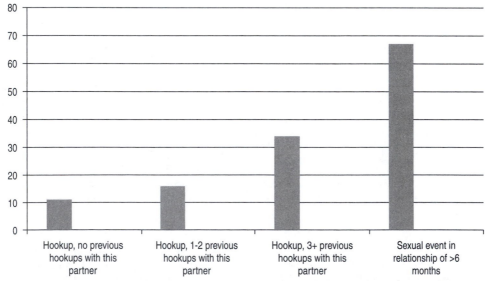

Figure 1 Percentage of Women Who Reported Having an Orgasm by Relationship to Partner.
Source: Armstrong, Elizabeth, Paula England, and Alison C. K. Fogarty. 2012. "Accounting for Women's Orgasm and Sexual Enjoyment in College Hookups and Relationships." *American Sociological Review* 77(3): 435–462.

their sexual partner and whether or not they reported having an orgasm. Figure 1 shows their findings.

Questions:

1. How likely are women to have orgasms when they are hooking up with someone for the first time? What about for women in long-term relationships? What is the nature of the relationship between relationship type and likelihood of having orgasms? Is this what you expected? Why or why not?

2. Armstrong et al. (2012) supplemented the survey data with qualitative interviews with men and women. Both men and women stated that they did not expect women to have an orgasm or for men to care whether or not the woman has an orgasm when hooking up for the first time. For example, one man said, "With my partner now, now that I'm in a relationship, I think [her orgasms are] actually pretty important. More important than I think the hookup because you have more invested in that person. *You*

know, when you have sex, it's more a reciprocal thing" (Armstrong et al. 2012, 457). The statement suggests that hook-up sex is not reciprocal in nature, and thus is a selfish act. However, women did not express the idea that hookups could be selfish. They were more likely to respond that they felt uncomfortable expecting or asking men to do things that would give them pleasure when having sex for the first time. How do the college students' understanding of hookups and orgasms reflect a larger pattern of gender inequality?

3. How do these findings about hookups and orgasms relate to the chapter by David Grazian about the "girl hunt?"

Reference

Armstrong, Elizabeth, Paula England, and Alison C. K. Fogarty. 2012. "Accounting for Women's Orgasm and Sexual Enjoyment in College Hookups and Relationships." *American Sociological Review* 77(3): 435–462.

E. Data Analysis Exercise: Is Smoking a Social Class Marker?

Sociologists have long debated how to think about social class: as categories of people based on who owns property and businesses versus those who work (Marx and Engels 1978); as categories of people with more or less buying power and status (Weber 1978); or as a verb, as controlling economic resources (Schwalbe 2008). This data analysis exercise explores the symbolic boundaries of social class through the lens of smoking.

1. What social class do you consider yourself to be part of? When you classified yourself, what did you use to differentiate one class from another? How did you learn to think of social class in this way? Whose version of class did you use?

2. In Part II, we learned that classifying people based on social class (largely considered an achieved status) is different from classifying people based on race or gender (ascribed statuses). How so?

3. People often buy products and use them in ways that signify to others that they are part of a particular group. People may even try to "look the part" of another social class in order to pass. Watch the video clip from PBS's *People Like Us* at http://www.cnam .com/people-like-us/about/index.html. What social markers did people use to distinguish themselves from each other and signify that they are part of a particular social class?

4. In 2012, 18.1 percent of American adults were current smokers, according to the Center for Disease Control. That represents about 42.1 million Americans. Figure 1 shows the rates of daily smoking by the amount of cigarettes per day, between 2005 and 2010. What changes to people's smoking habits occurred during that time period? What has caused the changes in people's smoking habits?

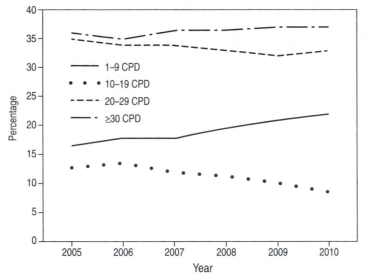

Figure 1 Percentage of Daily Smokers Aged ≥18 Years, by Number of Cigarettes Smoked Per Day (CPD) and Year—National Health Interview Survey, United States, 2005–2010.
Source: Centers for Disease Control and Prevention. 2011. "Vital Signs: Current Cigarette Smoking Among Adults Aged ≥ 18 Years—United States, 2005–2010." Atlanta. http://www.cdc.gov/mmwr/preview/mmwrhtml/mm6035a5.htm?s_cid=mm6035a5_w#fig1 (accessed January 5, 2015).

5. Despite the changes in people's smoking habits, some groups of Americans are more likely to smoke than others. Look at Figures 2 through 4. Who is the most likely to smoke? Least likely? How is smoking related to notions of being educated and cultured and manhood? How is smoking related to workplace stress?

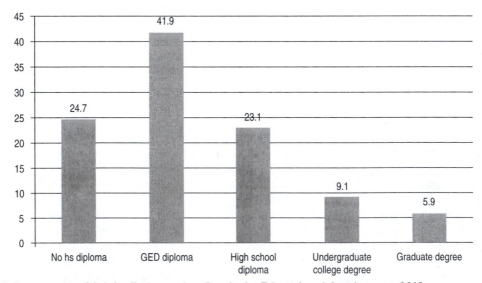

Figure 2 Percentage of Adults Estimated to Smoke by Educational Attainment, 2012.
Source: Centers for Disease Control and Prevention. 2014. "Adult Cigarette Smoking in the United States: Current Estimates." Atlanta. http://www.cdc.gov/tobacco/data_statistics/fact_sheets/adult_data/cig_smoking/index.htm (accessed January 5, 2015).

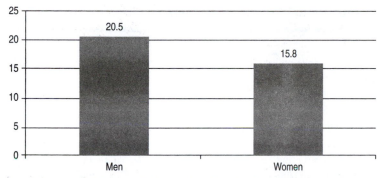

Figure 3 Percentage of Men and Women Estimated to Smoke, 2012.
Source: Centers for Disease Control and Prevention. 2014. "Adult Cigarette Smoking in the United States: Current Estimates."
Atlanta. http://www.cdc.gov/tobacco/data_statistics/fact_sheets/adult_data/cig_smoking/index.htm (accessed January 5, 2015).

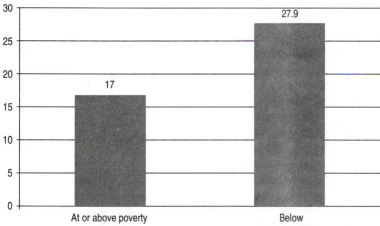

Figure 4 Percentage of Adults Estimated to Smoke by Poverty Status, 2012.
Source: Centers for Disease Control and Prevention. 2014. "Adult Cigarette Smoking in the United States: Current Estimates."
Atlanta. http://www.cdc.gov/tobacco/data_statistics/fact_sheets/adult_data/cig_smoking/index.htm (accessed January 5, 2015).

6. According to the CDC's analysis of the 2010 National Health Interview Survey, the vast majority of smokers want to quit (68.8 percent), and over half (52.4 percent) had tried to quit during the past year. What social and medical resources do people with more education and above the poverty level have to quit smoking? What cultural ideas about self-control, autonomy, and health consciousness are implicated in smoking and successfully quitting?

References

Marx, Karl, and Frederick Engels. 1978. "Manifesto of the Communist Party." In *The Marx-Engels Reader* (ed. Robert C. Tucker), 473–491. New York: W. W. Norton & Company.

Schwalbe, Michael. 2008. *Rigging the Game: How Inequality Is Reproduced in Everyday Life.* New York: Oxford University Press.

Weber, Max. 1978. *Economy and Society: An Outline of Interpretive Sociology.* Berkeley: University of California Press.

Projects and Resources to Make a Difference

Here are some projects you may do to make a difference:

Project 1. American Indian identity and art today. Many media depictions of American Indians, first peoples, and Native Americans portray them as a people of the past, ignoring the rich culture among different peoples today. Explore what it means to be Native American or American Indian today or how people express their identities through art. What are the tribes in your area? Who are prominent artists or folk artists? Do some research on their art by talking to the artists and visiting where their art is made or displayed. How are identities expressed through the art? Visit the National Museum of the American Indian in Washington, D.C., or visit their website. Examine the contemporary and modern art collections. How are artists expressing identity through their art today? How can you support these artists?

Project 2. Screening of the film *Intersexion* on campus. *Intersexion* is a film about the lived experience of intersectionality. Host a screening on your campus and a discussion to follow. After the discussion, break participants into groups and brainstorm concrete ways that your campus can work to disrupt the sex/gender binary. Together as a group, prioritize one or two and devise a plan and timetable to address them on your campus.

Project 3. Challenging racial profiling. Are data on race and police stops collected in your area and state? Are these data publicly available? Does the police department use them internally to monitor racial profiling? Find out. If data are not collected, figure out who the major stakeholders are to get data collected so that the racialization can be monitored. What community organizations are already working on racial profiling as an issue? Partner with them to address the data issue or another pressing race and incarceration issue in your area.

Additional Resources:

- For resources on intersexuality see Accord Alliance, an organization that educates parents and medical professionals about intersexuality. They provide a handbook for individuals who are intersex and their families, and advocacy materials: http://www.accordalliance.org/. Organization Intersex International provides resource and advocacy materials at http://oii-usa.org/. AIS-DSD Support Group (www.aisdsd.org) provides peer support, education, and advocacy. For an accessible overview of sex development and related conditions see Toronto's Sick Kids website at http://www.sickkids.ca/ and search for "sex development."

- The Sentencing Project (www.sentencingproject.org) provides research and advocacy materials regarding racial disparities in the criminal justice system and the mass incarceration of Black men. The American Civil Liberties Union has a campaign against racial profiling in policing (https://www.aclu.org/racial-justice/racial-profiling).

- For egalitarian/gender-bending toys and media for children, see the website of Peggy Orenstein, author of *Cinderella Ate My Daughter* (New York: Harper, 2012), at http://peggyorenstein.com/resources.html. Let Toys Be Toys (http://www.lettoysbetoys.org.uk/) offers practical advice for challenging gender stereotypes and complaining to toy companies.

- The Center for a New American Dream (http://www.newdream.org/) offers resources for reducing consumption and consumerism.

How Do Dominant Groups Get and Hoard Resources?

Charles Tilly (1998) referred to inequalities as categorical and durable. Similar to what we have learned so far, inequalities are created through socially constructed categories. Socially constructed categorical inequalities help us understand how social constructionism and intersectionality work together in the reproduction of inequality. We invent categories of people (by race, gender, class, etc.) and the boundaries separating them. These categories, to Tilly, are problem-solving distinctions that help people control access to resources. In short, categories, which are social constructions and are intersecting, help people gain and keep resources. For Tilly there are several key mechanisms through which inequalities become durable, lasting inequalities.

Part III follows Tilly's influential work and examines the how dominant group members get and hoard resources through three social processes. First, dominant groups exploit subordinates. Exploitation is a process in which dominant groups draw significantly

increased returns by coordinating the effort of subordinates whom they exclude from the full value added by that effort. This exploitation can result in profit, but it can also lead to political, social, or emotional rewards for dominants. This leads to the second process, exclusion. Dominant groups, in Tilly's words, "hoard opportunities," meaning they control access to resources. This control is exercised in several ways, including discrimination and people holding subordinate groups to cultural standards of the dominant group. Third, dominant group members even threaten and enact violence to control subordinate members' access to resources. Resources can include a healthy work environment and even food and water.

The social change readings present laws, law enforcement, food justice activism, and unionization as potential agents of resistance and change. In the data analysis exercises on women's representation among political officials, workplace deaths, and residential segregation, students apply their understanding of exploitation, exclusion, and violence to new areas. Taken as a whole, Part III shows how dominant groups come to control and even monopolize valued resources.

Specifically, in Part III we will learn that:

- *Inequality is reproduced on a macro scale through globalization.* We live in a global economy with trade agreements between nation-states—and global corporations which have more wealth and resources than most countries. In this global world, laborers migrate and immigrate to places with increasing demands for their labor.

- *Inequality is reproduced through the control of resources, but resources do not just include money or power. Resources include natural resources.* Certainly people control access to housing resources, education, and employment, but powerful people can also control access to natural resources such as water and food.

- *Inequality is reproduced on a very personal scale—inequality is embodied.* People are commodities, meaning their bodies and labor can become objectified and sold. Bodies can also be controlled through school uniform policies, displacement and housing discrimination, and abuse, sexualization, and sexual harassment.

- *The reproduction of inequality can be extreme and involve hostile forms of control, including physical assault, displacement, and even death.* As suggested in the last item, we may often think of the reproduction of inequality occurring through unfortunate events such as not being hired for a job because of employment discrimination. However, the readings in this section describe how the reproduction of inequality can be hostile. Subordinates, coworkers, and clients verbally and physically harass women, and men who are not traditionally masculine, at work. Undocumented workers are at great risk to suffer abuse from employers and co-workers. Neighbors create hostile living conditions and use hate-filled language to intimidate people into moving. Even worse, governments collude with rebel groups, using racist language to control access to water and food and commit genocide through displacing families and violent attacks.

Reference

Tilly, Charles. 1998. *Durable Inequality*. Berkeley: University of California Press.

The Globalization of Care Work: Neoliberal Economic Restructuring and Migration Policy

JOYA MISRA, JONATHAN WOODRING, AND SABINE N. MERZ

Neoliberal ideology emerged decades ago and was the cornerstone of the Reagan (United States) and Thatcher (United Kingdom) administrations in the 1980s. This ideology includes the belief in deregulated markets and businesses, suggesting that a "free market" will spark economic growth. This ideology has also resulted in the defunding of social services and the weakening of welfare states based on a revision of liberal individualist ideology that emphasizes "individual responsibility." Economic growth and responsibility seem honorable things to endorse, but this ideology has been consequential in the reproduction of inequality.

In this reading, the authors examine how ideology and policy have influenced the globalization of care work. Through their study of migration patterns, they show how policies in both the sending and receiving countries are largely shaped by care work demands due to women entering the workforce. To care financially for their families, Moroccan and Polish women temporarily migrate to do domestic work for families in France and Germany. Processes of uneven global development and immigration policies, or the lack of policies, are largely constraining and exploitative of women doing care work.

In the past decade, significant scholarly research has focused on the "globalization of care work," or how care has been distributed and redistributed in an international system where immigrant workers provide care in wealthier countries (Anderson 1997; Chang 2000; Constable 1997; Ehrenreich and Hochschild 2003; Glenn 1986, 1992; Heyzer and Wee 1994; Hondagneu-Sotelo 2000; Misra and Merz 2007; Momsen 1999; Romero 1992). Much of this research highlights the interconnectedness of the global political economy via analyses of the experiences of immigrant women workers and their domestic employers.

In this chapter, we shift the focus to the level of policy to argue that policies have created and reinforced the redistribution and internationalization of care work. In particular, we ask *how neoliberal economic restructuring, in the guise of structural adjustment policies, welfare state restructuring, and immigration and emigration policies, has helped give shape to the "international division of reproductive labor."* While gendered processes such as care work have too often been relegated to the periphery in scholarly debates, they are central to an understanding of the working of the global economy (Misra 2000; Pyle 2001; Pyle and Ward 2003; Salih 2001). We place the gendered international division of reproductive labor into perspective as part of the global political economy.

The Globalization of Care Work

Capitalism has always relied on a certain gendered division of labor, where women play a major role in

Excerpted from Misra, Joya, Jonathan Woodring, and Sabine N. Merz. 2006. "The Globalization of Care Work: Neoliberal Economic Restructuring and Migration Policy." *Globalizations* 3:317–332. Copyright © 2006 Routledge.

subsidizing the economy through their reproductive labor. While care work has often been carried out in the context of gender relations in the household, the structures of class, race/ethnicity, and nationality also are implicated in shaping care work. It is increasingly apparent that care work is also distributed in an international system where poor immigrant women workers provide care work for more well-to-do families in wealthier countries (Phizacklea 2003; Misra and Merz 2007; Young 2000). This is the trend we seek to explore.

Care work demands have heightened in wealthier countries due primarily to the shift to a postindustrial economy. Immigration patterns also now assume a postindustrial character where the service economy is dominant and regimes of flexible accumulation are the norm (Wallace 2002). This shift in the pattern of capitalist development has increased women's participation in the paid labor market, and demographic shifts, such as the aging of the population, have also contributed to women becoming a larger and larger share of immigrant workers (Anderson 1997; OECD 2001; Sassen 2003). While, for many years, men were more likely to emigrate for work and could expect well-regulated jobs that were in the industrial sector, in this postindustrial era current trends emphasize informal jobs in service work and care work that are directed at women immigrants (Hondagneu-Sotelo 2000; Wichterich 2000). Women now make up more than half of all immigration flows, and in certain countries (such as Indonesia, the Philippines, and Sri Lanka) they strongly predominate (Anderson 1997; Ehrenreich and Hochschild 2003; OECD 2001; Sassen 2003; Wichterich 2000). As Momsen (1999) notes, in many cases these women immigrants are "invisible" statistically, because they work in jobs that are not recorded by censuses or recognized as contributing to the national economy.

While the trend of immigrant women providing care for wealthier families is not new, the increasing deepening of political-economic, technological, and cultural-legal connections among states and societies has resulted in an intensification of these processes, drawing in more and more immigrant women workers from around the globe and changing the patterns of care work. Immigration patterns have substantially changed as workers become more mobile and flexible. Immigrant women workers are now responsible for significant amounts of care work in North America, Europe, East Asia, Australia, the Middle East, and other regions (Pyle 2001; Pyle and Ward 2003). Care workers are also now

more likely to emigrate only temporarily in order to support their families at home (Hondagneu-Sotelo 2000; Rerrich 2002). These workers send their earnings home, helping to guarantee a smooth flow of currency for their home countries (Bakan and Stasiulis 1996) or temporary immigrants, with only temporary work permits, but many immigrant care workers are not recognized as legal workers (Heyzer 1994; Pyle and Ward 2003).

Immigration and Emigration in a Capitalist World-Economy

Capitalist development creates high-paying professional jobs in wealthy nations and a higher demand for low-wage service workers (Sassen-Koob 1984). With the move towards "flexible specialization," employment relations take on a more informal nature, relying on decentralized, flexible workforces who are willing to work with few if any protections and benefits (International Labour Office 2002). As informal employment relations are legitimized in previously formal sectors, so too does this informality penetrate the economy as a whole. In this context, immigration patterns are shaped in large part by global capitalist development. Immigrant women workers are both displaced from former modes of employment and drawn to meet the service needs generated by global capital expansion.

However, immigration is shaped not only by the global economy. State policies—in both sending and receiving countries—play a central role in determining immigration patterns (Heisler 1985; Rystad 1992). Receiving and sending countries develop a variety of policies, though these are embedded in multilateral agreements (for example, with the International Labour Organization) and bilateral agreements between countries (Heisler 1985). Such policies are affected by a variety of social actors—including workers, capitalists, ethnic organizations, humanitarian groups, and state actors. These polices help explain immigration trends and patterns since migration choices are shaped by their institutional context—including labor market and immigration policies and their implementations, as well as international legislation (Rystad 1992). For example, both sending and receiving countries may be most interested in maintaining patterns of temporary migration, as opposed to permanent resettlement. Such patterns ensure remittances and transfers of emigrants to sending countries, while limiting the long-term responsibilities for receiving countries.

Immigration policies also contribute to the exploitation of immigrant women workers. For example, countries often do not give work visas or work permits for certain types of work—such as care work—even when they recognize that many immigrants illegally take such positions (Hess 2002). This gendered practice pushes many documented immigrants into undocumented, unprotected, and poorly paid jobs (Smet 2000).

For care workers, immigration policies, and sometimes the lack of policies, have dire consequences for these workers. Since states generally do not recognize the importance of care work (in part because care workers are generally women) to the economy, work permits for care workers are generally very constrained. These policies render many immigrant women workers largely undocumented and dangerously vulnerable due to a lack of political recourse against their employers (Anderson 1997; Heyzer and Wee 1994). As Anderson (1997, p. 37) notes, "The need for this kind of [caring] labour is not properly reflected in immigration and employment policies, making domestic workers who are already vulnerable to abuse and exploitation even more dependent on their employers by denying them an independent immigration status—or any legal immigration status at all."

Neoliberalism and the Changing Distribution of Care Work

Over the last several decades, neoliberalism has become the predominant economic approach shaping policies worldwide. Neoliberal perspectives argue that economic growth occurs most when the market is least constrained by state protections. Economic growth should occur when labor markers are deregulated, and when the state rescinds social safety nets and protections. Without the presence of state interference, the market should work more effectively.

Neoliberalism affects the international division of care by shaping the contexts and polices of the countries both sending and receiving immigrant care workers. As part of the withdrawal of the state support for care, care work has been passed back into the private sphere, where women are expected to subsidize the economy with their caring work (Wichterich 2000). Economic restructuring around the globe has placed greater pressure on women to meet their families' care needs, while absolving the state of responsibility for playing a larger role in meeting care needs. This is not to say that neoliberalism has magically forced economic restructuring throughout the world—state actors (as well as actors within nongovernmental organizations) use neoliberal ideologies to justify lowering state costs for care; this is a political strategy that simply draws on an economic ideology.

Neoliberalism is the predominant economic ideology embedded in the structural adjustment policies imposed on developing countries by international lending agencies such as the International Monetary Fund and the World Bank. In these settings, neoliberalism has not only emphasized family responsibility for any care needs but has also dictated a deregulation of labor markets, which results in the lowering of wages and the elimination of health and safety standards. These stressful financial conditions mean that more workers also immigrate to wealthier countries in hopes of greater economic opportunity (Chang 2000; Heyzer 1994; Momsen 1999).

While neoliberal ideologies have not decimated the social welfare policies of wealthier nations, they have encouraged a greater emphasis on market-based solutions and a rolling back on the state's role in care provision (Della Sala 2002; Morgan 2002). Welfare state restructuring has led to a decline in both social spending and social care services (Daly and Lewis 1998). States have increasingly privatized care (sending care provision to private, nonprofit, and voluntary sectors) while also marketizing state provision of care (contracting out services and care provisions and withdrawing state support from certain provisions) (Knijn 2000). For example, while many welfare states formerly provided and subsidized high-quality elder care and childcare, over the last decade the trend has been for states to simply subsidize care that families find and negotiate or entirely withdraw from care provision (Jenson and Sineau 2001). Rather than providing services and care through the public sector, which may increase budgetary pressures on states, the state encourages the development of low-wage private sector services, which leads to higher levels of wage inequality (Pierson 2001).

At the same time, neoliberalism has also weakened worker protections and wages, so that middle-and working-class families are caught in a constant struggle to support themselves. Hiring low-wage care work allows more highly educated women to enter the workforce and substantially increase the household income. By relying on a flexible and cheap labor force of immigrant women workers, reproduction in wealthy countries is then carried out despite the rollback in state provision of social services (Momsen 1999). As welfare state provision of care recedes and families increasingly face economic struggles, there is a strong demand for low-wage immigrant care workers, who may have few other employment opportunities due to their immigration status (Chang 2000; Hondagneu-Sotelo 2000; Misra and Merz 2007; Momsen 1999; Young 2000).

Of course, the demand for care workers in wealthy nations results from additional demographic changes (Pierson 2001). As middle-class white women gain greater access to paid employment, low-wage workers replace the caretaking and housekeeping tasks these women previously provided (Bakan and Stasiulis 1996; United Nations 2005). Rising divorce rates and lower marriage rates have also created more lone-parent families, who need additional levels of care support, while rapid increases in the elderly population in need of care create greater demands for care.

From the perspective of the sending countries, faced with the powerful pressures of neoliberalism on their economies, more and more workers consider immigration as a means to supporting their families. Indeed, the economic pull created by neoliberal strategies is a central reason for the emigration of immigrant workers. Neoliberal structural adjustment includes: privatizing, limiting, or cutting social welfare programs on health, education, and welfare; privatizing state enterprises and cutting subsidies on products and services; limiting labor market policies such as wage minimums and curtailing wages more generally; liberalizing imports and easing restrictions on foreign investment; and devaluing the currency in order to make export prices more competitive (Bakan and Stasiulis 1996; Bello 2000; Laurell 2000).

Although these policies were put into place in order to promote economic growth, they have led to increasing levels of poverty and income inequality. Sassen (2003) notes that among the costs of these programs are higher unemployment levels, fewer firms focused on providing goods oriented toward the local economy, and a very heavy burden of government debt. Mounting government debt has subsequently resulted in cutbacks in health services, education, and childcare, all of which have led to women's increased responsibility for caregiving. As a result, increasing numbers of women have looked for income-generating strategies, including

informal sector and subsistence work, and emigration both within and across countries (Dewan 1999; Laurell 2000; Sassen 2003). Indeed, remittances from immigrant workers play a key role in helping national economies service their growing debts (Bakan and Stasiulis 1996; Sassen 2003).

Therefore, neoliberal strategies have contributed to care crises across the globe, while simultaneously creating a situation in which more women workers in poorer countries use the strategy of immigration in order to meet their families' financial needs. Rather than states taking responsibility for aiding families, neoliberal strategies have led to an international division of care work that places the burden for care on the least powerful (immigrant women workers).

Comparative Case Studies

We examine the economic contexts and policies in four countries over the last 15 years. We accomplish this by examining welfare state restructuring and immigration policies in France and Germany; and structural adjustments and emigration policies in Morocco and Poland. Examining two dyads of cases is critical for our understanding of the international division of care. While neoliberal strategies shape all countries, differences in institutional contexts mean that these strategies play out differently in different countries. Context matters. Examining two dyads of countries helps specify how policies are shaping the international division of care.

We chose to focus on two fairly similar European receiving countries (Germany and France), and then examine immigrant care workers from more significantly different sending countries (Poland and Morocco). Germany and France are two of the largest and most influential countries in Europe, and are the two European Community countries with the largest numbers of non-European Community immigrant workers (OECD 2004). In addition, Germany and France have taken somewhat different approaches to immigration, labor market policy, and welfare state provision, making a comparison between these receiving contexts fruitful. At the same time, Moroccans are currently the largest group of immigrants flowing into France. Police workers are among the largest group of immigrant flowing into Germany, surpassed only by Yugoslavia (OECD 2003). Poland and Morocco also face significantly different economic pressures, and have adopted different states to coping with these pressures, making a comparison here useful. Finally, these countries are indicative of the pressures Western Europe now faces from the East (Poland) and the South (Morocco). We believe that analyzing these two sets of countries helps provide greater evidence that neoliberalism drives much of the international division of reproductive labor.

Economic Restructuring and Emigration in Poland and Morocco

Poland

Poland was among the healthiest of the Eastern European economies in transition, with fairly strong growth, around 5 percent for the 1990s, which has slowed dramatically since the turn of the century (to only 1.4 percent in 2002) (World Bank 2004b). In 2002, the gross national income per capita was $4,970 (World Bank 2004a). Economic restructuring has meant that Poland has focused on developing its service sector and allowed the previously strong agricultural and manufacturing sectors to weaken. Given the end of state socialism, such restructuring has meant that previously state-owned businesses have become privatized, and many social service programs have been cut.

This shift away from state-owned businesses, along with the development of a service sector, has meant that unemployment runs very high in both the short and long term, particularly among older workers from the weakened agricultural and manufacturing sectors. Unemployment stands at about 18 percent for men and at almost 20 percent for women and is growing, while long-term unemployment is higher than in most of the world (OECD 2003). Women are only slightly less likely to be working than men. Unemployment and poverty are particularly high in rural areas.

Within this context, migration has been a central strategy for workers to pursue. The vast majority of Polish immigrants—80 percent—migrate to Germany, in part due to proximity, but also as a result of long-standing migration patterns, including large numbers of ethnic German Polish citizens who migrated to Germany for decades before the end of state socialism. While Polish emigration policy used to discourage and limit migration, Poland now attempts to shape emigration by encouraging short-term migration. As a result, Polish workers are more likely to emigrate for very short

periods—more than 60 percent of Polish emigrants are abroad for less than one year. This is in part due to bilateral agreements and contracts. For example, Polish workers may come over to Germany for three months as "seasonal workers," for up to eighteen months as "guest workers," or for up to three years as "contract workers." In addition, many Polish care workers work in Germany briefly on tourist visas. A significant portion of the Polish population reports that irregular short-term migration for working abroad is a main source of their income. However, data on remittances from immigrants suggest that fewer workers remit money; most simply bring their earnings back into the country when they return, in part because many are working illegally on tourist visas (International Monetary Fund [IMF] 2002; United Nations Development Programme [UNDP] 2002).

Morocco

Morocco has a fairly weak economy, with growth rates of about 3 percent since the beginning of the 1990s, with somewhat higher but variable growth since the late 1990s (World Bank 2004a). Morocco is considerably poorer than Poland, with a gross national income per capita of only $1,170, although it is more successful than many African countries. The Moroccan economy relies heavily on agriculture. Structural adjustment prescriptions of the World Bank have led to fundamental reforms in agricultural and rural policy, including subsidies, significantly decreasing government spending, and increasing privatization. In addition, structural adjustment has included significant tax cuts (World Bank 2005).

Structural adjustment has coincided with higher levels of poverty, particularly in rural areas, as well as lower levels of education and declining measures of good health. Poverty has jumped significantly over the past 15 years, in part as a result of the loss of government subsidies. Poverty is very high among Moroccan women, as well as among those living in rural areas (World Bank 2005). Unemployment is particularly high—at 20 percent, among the highest in the world. In Morocco, women are significantly less likely to be working than men, and have unemployment rates above 25 percent (Agénor and Aynaoui 2003). Young workers have particularly high unemployment rates, above 30 percent in most parts of the country. Unemployment is also surprisingly high for highly educated workers.

More than half of the unemployed at any given time are young men and women who are looking for their first job. Over the last decade, unemployment rates have decreased in rural areas, but greatly increased in urban areas (Agénor and Aynaoui 2003).

Given these levels of unemployment, it is not surprising that migration is quite high, totaling over 25,000 people every year. Moroccan migrants work primarily in France, Belgium, and the Netherlands. As a former protectorate of France (from 1912 through 1956), Morocco continues to have strong ties to France, and many Moroccans speak French. Emigration policy calls for a lowering of emigration, particularly among the highly educated youth; at the same time, there have been no real moves to attempt to lower emigration. Migration policy also nominally addresses the problem of illegal immigration, particularly in concert with the French state. Yet, Morocco strongly supports the principle of "free movement" between countries, and garners significant benefits from the high levels of migration. Although Moroccan women emigrate for a variety of reasons—including economic opportunities and political concerns—they often emigrate as part of "family reunification" plans, although, because family reunification requires a certain level of resources, many women instead come over on tourist visas and stay illegally (Killian 2005). Although Moroccan women migrants do not necessarily work in the labor force, many of those that do work as domestic workers (Killian 2005; Salih 2001).

Morocco is among a handful of countries receiving the highest levels of remittances worldwide. While most remittance data grossly underestimates the amount of remittances, Morocco's remittances now compose over 10 percent of the gross domestic product (UNDP 2002; World Bank 2004b). Banks in Morocco are set up to offer joint accounts between remitters and recipients, and low-fee wire transfers. These remittances make emigration a fairly attractive option, particularly insofar as Moroccan emigrants continue to remit significant portions of their income.

Economic Restructuring and Immigration in Germany and France

Germany

Welfare state restructuring in Germany began as a result of deindustrialization and high unemployment,

exacerbated by reunification. Since the German welfare state has been largely financed through social insurance tied to employment, unemployment has created a substantial fiscal crisis in the welfare state. German welfare state restructuring has centered around tightening eligibility requirements and cost-shifting, such as changing the contribution rates for social insurance schemes, usually at a cost to beneficiaries (Aust, Bönker, and Wollmann 2002).

What is surprising about the German case is that restructuring appears to have actually *expanded* care provision. Legislation now provides for long-term care insurance, as well as a caregivers' allowance. There has also been a much needed expansion of childcare. While for decades West Germany relied primarily on unpaid, family-based care for both the elderly and children, recent legislation appears to support a mix of paid and unpaid care. The restructuring to provide additional care exists in part in order to draw German women into the labor market more effectively. Deindustrialization has led to the loss of many jobs, primarily among men. The growth of the service sector, on the other hand, provides more jobs for women. In order to limit the effects of high unemployment, German women have been brought into the labor market as flexible workers meant to subsidize the ailing welfare state. There has been a marked transformation from a male-breadwinner model to a one in which women work—albeit primarily part-time (Daly and Rake 2003; Young 2000).

These changes are complicated in their repercussions. Men's high-paid manufacturing jobs have turned into women's low-paid service jobs, and families do not necessarily have the same level of resources with this shift. Restructuring has also imposed greater financial burdens on the tax contributions made by workers, and has also replaced earlier, more expansive social assistance safety nets with flat-rate, fairly limited services. The German welfare state now provides a wider range of basic services, and fewer comprehensive services. Restructuring has led then, in some ways, to a less responsive welfare state. At the same time, the government has pulled back from evaluating quality of care.

While the German government has extended certain social care programs, including allowances and subsidies for care providers, much of the care, particularly elder care, is done by immigrant workers. German care workers prefer to work in the more highly paid and well-regulated institutionalized sector. Yet, institutionalized care is more expensive for the German government. For legal workers, the German government has since 1997 provided service checks, which allow tax rebates for families employing domestic workers for more than 10 hours a week. Yet very few people have used this system, in part because it requires employers to make contributions to the social insurance program (Smet 2000).

Polish women make up a large proportion of these care workers, and many of these workers are not legal immigrants (more Polish women than men live in Germany). Immigration has long been an issue in Germany, which has had among the highest rates of immigration along with the strictest immigration and naturalization laws in Europe (Liebig 2004). During the 1990s, Germany finally moved away from earlier laws that limited citizenship primarily to ethnic Germans, excluding even those from other ethnic backgrounds who were born in Germany (Schmidtke 2001). While few immigrants and children of immigrants have attained citizenship, legally there are now opportunities to attain citizenship through residence; more immigrants receive a special status based on residence (Schmidtke 2001). In addition, after many years of significant inequality, in 1990 Germany gave immigrants equal rights and access to the welfare state.

German policy attempts to lower immigration rates through a number of means, particularly limiting long-term residency only to highly skilled workers. Even so, immigrants are more likely to be employed in jobs that are characterized by poor working conditions. Germany has a number of bilateral agreements with various countries, including Poland, setting up temporary visas for temporary workers, from three months to three years. Prior to 1990, informal channels existed between German employers and Polish seasonal workers. While illegal before 1990, these networks were legitimized in 1990 through the passage of the bilateral agreement on seasonal employment between the two nations. While the bilateral agreement establishes various temporary work programs, it also facilitates illegal immigration and the informal economy (Wallace 2002).

However, until 2001, care workers were not given work permits. Germany now provides some work permits for "household help," due to the intercession of government leaders who argued that the system of elder care would break down without the permits (Meier-Braun

2002). These permits allow care workers from Poland, Slovakia, Slovenia, the Czech Republic, and Hungary to work in Germany for up to three years. Employers must qualify to employ these domestic workers, and they must be receiving long-term care insurance benefits for a relative in the household (OECD 2004). Work permits are not provided for care workers doing primarily domestic work or childcare. In addition, permits are not allowed for nurses or home care employees, but only to less well-paid "household helpers," in order to limit any impact of issuing these work permits to German nationals. However, the lack of a real mechanism for enforcement of this provision makes the law malleable and blurs the boundaries between the legal and the illegal. Employers are legally bound to pay German-level wages, but those willing to do the care work are often vulnerable women workers who will accept informal employment relations as they themselves are illegal immigrants. Therefore, despite the permit system, many more thousands of care workers continue to enter Germany illegally, often on three-month tourist visas. Care work, because of its high potential to be informal, is also among the easiest types of work for immigrant women without work permits to get.

Therefore, restructuring in Germany has led to additional support for care, in part in order to draw women into the workforce, though in less well-paid service sector jobs. This higher labor force participation of women coupled with an increase in the elderly population has led to higher demand for care workers. German immigration policy has responded, allowing a certain number of permits for eldercare workers for families receiving benefits through the long-term care insurance program. Yet, rather than emphasizing quality of care, German immigration policy limits these work permits to the low-paid "household helpers" (although in many cases these workers actually have higher levels of certification). As a United Nations (2005, p. 121) report notes, "Though legally employed and paid at German rates, the state stipulates that these carers cannot compete against German-trained homecare employees and that their permit must be for 'household assistant' . . . they have in effect sanctioned deskilling." In addition, German policy does not extend permits to other types of care workers. These policies help maintain a cheap system of care for the German state by relying upon Polish immigrant women caregivers.

France

French welfare state restructuring has followed a different pattern. During the 1980s, the French welfare state expanded the social safety net for the poor. More importantly, the French state has focused on pursuing active labor market policies. Restructuring has centered on creating new employment through welfare policy (Mandin and Palier 2002). Care for both children and the elderly has been increasingly privatized, not simply to cut government costs but also to create jobs. In other words, welfare state restructuring has individualized care as a strategy to reduce unemployment (Daly 2001; Morgan 2002).

Restructuring has, then, meant a shift away from some forms of institutional care—for example, for the elderly and children under three years of age. There is now more of a mix between formal and informal care, and direct payments for those caring for children and the elderly at home. As a result, France has also seen a strong increase in private care, with annual expenditures devoted to these arrangements increasing significantly. Since 1993, the state subsidizes care through a tax rebate, while also making the administration of care fairly easy with a voucher system that alleviates the need for families to calculate contributions to the social security system for their workers (and encourages families to register employees) (Morgan 2002; Smet 2000). Upper-middle-class families, with the resources to help supplement the fairly low levels of direct payments the state provides to private caregivers, have benefitted from this arrangement. These families are also able to use individualized care.

The consequences of restructuring have been more problematic for poor, working-class, and lower-middle-class families, and for many caregivers. For example, the French crèche system has for decades provided excellent high-quality care for children under the age of three on a sliding-scale basis. With the increased push toward marketization, wealthier families choose instead to hire private minders for their children. As higher-income families opt out, their higher fees are gone, and their political backing for crèche is weakened. As a result, families who need crèche find it much more difficult to find a place. Class distinctions, once mitigated through state care provisions, have become increasingly visible as care becomes further privatized (Andall 2000). This strategy of transferring care labor to immigrant workers is a viable alternative only for families with larger incomes. At the same time, care workers themselves receive lower wages and benefits than when employed in high-quality public care provision. Many now work under the table, even with the voucher system in place.

While the French state has not pulled back on welfare spending, it has instead shifted its role from a provider to a financer of care, in part as a means to creating more care jobs, but with a number of problematic repercussions for care workers and families with fewer resources. French immigration policy focuses on limiting the flow of immigrants, while also integrating immigrants into France. France signed its first bilateral agreement with Morocco in 1963, which has been amended twice to introduce short-term and long-term visas for Moroccan workers in France, and French workers in Morocco. These agreements primarily aim to ensure that France receives the supply of labor while discouraging illegal immigration, although it also provides for certain rights and provisions for Moroccan workers (De Lary 2004). French policy primarily limits immigration (particularly for North African Muslims) by restricting work permits and making it difficult for immigrants to attain citizenship. In addition, French policy focuses on stopping illegal immigration, primarily through detaining and deporting foreigners (Lloyd 2003). Harsh laws, such as laws that require African nationals to provide proof of adequate funds in order to stay in the country, have been put into place and then later repealed (Killian 2005). The French government has also granted a number of amnesties in which illegal immigrants have been granted visas (Lloyd 2003). The French government has drawn some criticisms for the contradictions in these policies.

Temporary work permits tend to go to highly educated workers; however, less well-educated workers can receive seasonal work permits for agricultural labor. Moroccans compose the highest number of legal seasonal immigrant workers, although many more work illegally in France (OECD 2004). Women often enter France through "family reunification" strategies, since it can be more difficult for women to receive work permits (Djaiz et al. 2002; Lloyd 2003). Moroccan women also enter illegally on tourist visas.

France does not issue work permits for domestic workers; however, perhaps more than 50 percent of immigrant women in France work as domestic workers

(RESPECT 2000; Weinert 1991). This work is highly exploitative, particularly when unregulated (Killian 2005; Mozère et al. 2001). French employers can attempt to legalize domestic workers by claiming an inability to find legal employees. In addition, France has among the best labor regulations governing (legal) domestic workers in Europe (Blackett 1998). However, little incentive exists for employers to legalize workers, which can be a difficult and arduous process and almost always means that employers must pay higher wages and taxes, reduce their employees' work hours, and provide vacation leave (average wages for legal workers are still lower than average wages in other sectors) (Blackett 1998; Mozère et al. 2001; Weinert 1991).

Restructuring in France has led to an increased need for care workers, primarily for families that can afford to hire individualized care, but immigration policy does not recognize this increased demand. This may be in part because of contradictions in the policies—the French state sees privatization and marketization of care as an employment creation strategy, but few French nationals are interested in the jobs this strategy creates. In addition, if immigration policy changed to make it easier for care workers to attain work permits, families would need to pay higher wages and benefits to care workers, which may make it more difficult for families to afford private caregivers. In essence, French policies work in concert to create an inequitable system from which wealthier families profit, but from which care workers and lower income families lose.

Conclusions

These cases provide evidence for taking the context into account in considering how the international division of caring labor is created and reinforced by explicit and implicit state policies. There are tremendous inequalities—by gender, class, race, ethnicity, and nationality—in how care work is done (Misra and Merz 2007). Yet, it is overly simplistic to blame these inequalities simply on the exploitations of workers by employers. Complicit in this system are domestic political institutions, operating in a capitalist world economy, which benefit from the labor subsidies of immigrant women care workers.

States are complex institutions. There is no omnipotent state actor, actively creating a set of mutually reinforcing and logically consistent policies. Rather than being a monolithic actor, the state is divided in multiple ways and enmeshed in exchanges with many different actors and spheres. In addition, the dynamic natures of policymaking and policy enforcement, as well as the dynamic nature of society as a whole, mean that different policies may both reinforce and contradict one another.

However, we believe that the states have drawn on the ideology of neoliberalism—with its emphasis on the primacy of the market—to shape economic restructuring and migration in these two dyads in ways that have led to an intensification in the globalization of care and supported the inequalities inherent in the globalization of care. Polish and Moroccan workers migrate in response to high levels of poverty and unemployment created by neoliberal structural adjustment, even though structural adjustment and migration policies have played out rather differently in these two contexts. Neoliberal economic restructuring in France and Germany, although very different in form, leads to higher levels of demand for immigrant caregivers. There have been some policy responses to these needs. While French families who employ in-home carers receive tax reductions and benefit from simplified administrative procedures, many still do not register care workers, and many immigrant care workers remain undocumented. While German immigration policies now recognize the need for eldercare workers, they authorize hiring immigrant care workers only in jobs defined as low-skilled. Even where policies recognize the demand for care work, they do so inequitably. One explanation for this is that the contradictory policies in receiving countries help guarantee a cheap supply of labor. By exploring economic restructuring and immigration in this integrated fashion, we hope to have drawn attention to both the contradictions and the consistencies in state policies, and the ways that policies may be working to support a redistribution of care that relies upon the economic exploitation of immigrant women workers.

References

Agénor, Pierre-Richard, and Karim El Aynaoui. 2003. "Labor Market Policies and Unemployment in Morocco." http://www.worldbank.org/wbiep/macro-program/agenor/pdfs/Immpa-Morocco.pdf (accessed January 15, 2004).

Andall, Jacqueline. 2000. Gender, Migration, and Domestic Service: The Politics of Black Women in Italy. Burlington, VT: Ashgate.

Anderson, Bridget. 1997. "Servants and Slaves: Europe's Domestic Workers." *Race + Class* 39(1): 37–49.

Aust, Andreas, Frank Bönker, and Hellmut Wollmann. 2002. "Welfare State Reform in Germany from 1982 to the Present." Welfare Reform and Management of Societal Change Report. http://s3.amazonaws.com/zanran_storage/www.kent.ac.uk/ContentPages/3151869.pdf (accessed March 1, 2004).

Bakan, Abigail, and Daiva K. Stasiulis. 1995. "Making the Match: Domestic Placement Agencies and the Racialization of Women's Household Work." *Signs* 20:303–335.

_____. 1996. "Structural Adjustment, Citizenship, and Foreign Domestic Labour: The Canadian Case." In *Rethinking Restructuring: Gender and Change in Canada* (ed. Isabella Bakker), 217–242. Toronto: University of Toronto Press.

Bello, Walden. 2000. "Building an Iron Cage: The Bretton Woods Institutions, the WTO, and the South." In *Views from the South* (ed. Sarah Anderson), 54–90. Chicago: Food First.

Blackett, Adelle. 1998. "Making Domestic Work Visible: The Case for Specific Regulation."

Labour Law and Labour Relations Programme. Geneva: International Labour Office.

Chang, Grace. 2000. *Disposable Domestics: Immigrant Women Workers in the Global Economy*. Boston: South End Press.

Constable, Nicole. 1997. *Maid to Order in Hong Kong: Stories of Filipina Workers*. Ithaca, NY: Cornell University Press.

Daly, Mary. 2001. "Care Policies in Western Europe." In *Care Work: The Quest for Security* (ed. Mary Daly), 33–55. Geneva: International Labour Office.

Daly, Mary, and Jane Lewis. 1998. "Introduction: Conceptualizing Social Care in the Context of Welfare State Restructuring." In *Gender, Social Care, and Welfare State Restructuring* (ed. Jane Lewis), 1–24. Aldershot: Ashgate.

Daly, Mary, and Katherine Rake. 2003. *Gender and the Welfare State: Care, Work and Welfare in Europe and the USA*. London: Polity Press.

De Lary, Henri. 2004. "Bilateral Labor Agreements Concluded by France." In *Migration for Employment: Bilateral Agreements at a Crossroads,* 43–54. Paris: OECD.

Della Sala, Vincent. 2002. "'Modernization' and Welfare State Restructuring in Italy: The Impact on Child Care." In *Child Care Policy at the Crossroads: Gender and Welfare State Restructuring* (ed. Sonya Michel and Rianne Mahon), 171–190. New York: Routledge.

Dewan, Ritu. 1999. "Gender Implications of the 'New' Economic Policy: A Conceptual Overview." *Women's Studies International Forum* 22(4): 425–429.

Djaiz, Samir, Pinar Hükum, Didier Le Saout, and Yalaz Wiem. 2002. "Migrant Women and Business Education: A Contribution to French Economy." *Migration Studies* 104 (January): 1–10.

Ehrenreich, Barbara, and Arlie Russell Hochschild, eds. 2003. *Global Woman: Nannies, Maids, and Sex Workers in the New Economy*. New York: Metropolitan Books.

Glenn, Evelyn Nakano. 1986. *Issei, Nisei, War Bride: Three Generations of Japanese American Women in Domestic Service*. Philadelphia, PA: Temple University Press

_____. 1992. From Servitude to Service Work: Historical Continuities in the Racial Division of Paid Reproductive Labor. *Signs* 18:1–43.

Heisler, Barbara Schmitter. 1985. "Sending Countries and the Politics of Emigration and Destination." *International Migration Review* 19:469–484.

Hess, Sabine. 2002. "Au Pairs Informalisierte as Domestic Workers: Flexibility and Ethnicization of Supply Work." In *Global Market Household* (ed. Claudia Gather, Birgit Geissler, and Maria S. Rerrich), 103–119. Münster: Westfälisches Steamboat.

Heyzer, Noeleen. 1994. "Introduction: Creating Responsive Policies for Migrant Women Domestic Workers." In *The Trade in Domestic Workers: Causes, Mechanisms and Consequences of International Migration* (ed. Noeleen Heyzer, Gerrtje Lycklama a Nijeholt, and Nedra Weerakoon), xv–xxx. London: Zed Books.

Heyzer, Noeleen, and Vivienne Wee. 1994. "Domestic Workers in Transient Overseas Employment: Who Benefits, Who Profits." In *The Trade in Domestic Workers: Causes, Mechanisms, and Consequences of International Migration* (ed. Noeleen Heyzer, Gerrtje Lycklama a Nijeholt, and Nedra Weerakoon), 31–101. London: Zed Books.

Hondagneu-Sotelo, Pierette. 2000. "The International Division of Caring and Cleaning Work." In *Care Work: Gender, Labor, and the Welfare State* (ed. Madonna Harrington Meyer), 149–162. New York: Routledge.

International Monetary Fund. 2002. *Balance of Payment Statistics*. Washington, D.C.: International Monetary Fund Publication Services.

International Labour Office. 2002. *Women and Men in the Informal Economy: A Statistical Picture*. Geneva: International Labour Office.

Jenson, Jane, and Mariette Sineau. 2001. "New Contexts, New Policies." In *Who Cares? Women's Work, Childcare, and Welfare State Redesign* (ed. Jane Jenson and Mariette Sineau), 19–55. Toronto: University of Toronto Press.

Killian, Caitlin. 2005. *Gender, Culture, and Identity: North African Women in France*. Unpublished Manuscript, Drew University, Madison, NJ.

Knijn, Trudie. 2000. "Marketization and the Struggling Logics of (Home) Care in the Netherlands." In *Care Work: Gender, Labor, and the Welfare State* (ed. Madonna Harrington Meyer), 232–248. New York: Routledge.

Laurell, Asa Cristina. 2000. "Structural Adjustment and the Globalization of Policy in Latin America." *International Society* 15:306–325.

Liebig, Thomas. 2004. "Recruitment of Foreign Labor in Germany and Switzerland." In *Migration For Employment: Bilateral Agreements at a Crossroads*, 157–186. Paris: Organisation for Economic Co-operation and Development.

Lloyd, Cathie. 2003. "Women Migrants and Political Activism in France." In *Gender and Ethnicity in Contemporary Europe* (ed. Jacqueline Andall), 97–116. Oxford: Bath.

Mandin, Lou, and Bruno Palier. 2002. "Welfare Reform in France, 1985–2002." Welfare Reform and Management of Societal Change Report. http://www.kent.ac.uk/wramsoc/workingpapers/index.htm (accessed March 1, 2004).

Meier-Braun, Karl-Heinz. 2002. *Germany, A Country of Immigration*. Frankfurt: Suhrkamp Verlag.

Misra, Joya. 2000. "Gender and the World System: Engaging the Feminist Literature on Development." In *Cases, Place, and People: World-Systems Studies* (ed. Thomas D. Hall), 105–127. Totawa, NJ: Rowman and Littlefield.

Misra, Joya, and Sabine Merz. 2007. "Neoliberalism, Globalization, and the International Division of Care." In *Wages of Empire: Globalization, State Transformations, and Women's Poverty* (ed. Amalia Cabezas, Ellen Reese, and Marguerite Waller), 113–126. Boulder, CO: Paradigm Press.

Momsen, Janet Henshall. 1999. "Maids on the Move: Victim or Victor?" In *Gender, Migration, and Domestic Service* (ed. Janet Henshall Momsen), 1–20. New York: Routledge.

Morgan, Kimberly. 2002. "Does Anyone Have a 'Libre Choix'? Subversive Liberalism and the Politics of French Child Care Policy." In *Child Care Policy at the Crossroads: Gender and Welfare State Restructuring* (ed. Sonya Michel and Rianne Mahon), 143–167. New York: Routledge.

Mozère, Liane, Hervé Maury, Yankel Fijalkow, Viviane Dahan, and Caroline Lenhart. 2001. "Petites métiers urbains au féminin ou comment échapper à la précarisation." *Migration et Etudes* 101 (September-October): 1–6.

Organisation for Economic Co-operation and Development (OECD). 2001. *OECD Employment Outlook*. Paris: OECD.

OECD. 2003. *Trends in International Migration*. Paris: OECD.

OECD. 2004. *Trends in International Migration*. Paris: OECD.

Phizacklea, Annie. 2003. "Gendered Actors in Migration." In *Gender and Ethnicity in Contemporary Europe* (ed. Jacqueline Andall), 23–37. Oxford: Berg.

Pierson, Paul. 2001. "Post-Industrial Pressures on Mature Welfare States." In *The New Politics of the Welfare State* (ed. Paul Pierson), 80–104. New York: Oxford.

Pyle, Jean. 2001. "Sex, Maids, and Export Processing: Risks and Reasons for Gendered Global Production Networks." *International Journal of Politics, Culture, and Society* 15(1): 55–76.

Pyle, Jean, and Kathryn Ward. 2003. "Recasting Our Understanding of Gender and Work during Global Restructuring." *International Sociology* 18(3): 461–489.

Rerrich, Maria S. 2002. "From Utopia of Equal Distribution Partnership a Reality of the Globalization of Housework." In *Global Market Household* (ed. Claudia Gather, Birgit Geissler, and Maria S. Rerrich), 16–29. Münster: Westfälisches Steamboat.

RESPECT. 2000. "Migrant Domestic Workers in Europe: A Case for Action." www2.ohchr.org/english/bodies/cmw/docs/DGD/**RESPECT**.doc (accessed January 15, 2004).

Romero, Mary. 1992. *Maid in the U.S.A.* New York: Routledge

Rystad, Göran. 1992. "Immigration History and the Future of International Migration." *International Migration Review* 26(4): 1168–1199.

Salih, Ruba. 2001. "Moroccan Migrant Women: Transnationalism, Nation-States, and Gender." *Journal of Ethnic and Migration Studies* 27(4): 655–671.

Sassen-Koob, Saskia. 1984. "Notes on the Incorporation of Third World Women into Wage-Labor through Immigration and Off-Shore Production." *International Migration Review.* 18(4): 1144–1167.

Sassen, Saskia. 2003. "Strategic Instantiations of Gendering in the Global Economy." In *Gender and Immigration: Contemporary Trends* (ed. Pierette Hondagneu-Sotelo), 43–60. Berkeley: University of California Press.

Schmidtke, Oliver. 2001. "Transnational Migration: A Challenge to European Citizenship Regimes." *World Affairs* 164(1): 3–17.

Smet, Miet. 2000. "Report on Regulating Domestic Help in the Informal Sector." European Parliament Session Document.

United Nations Development Programme. 2002. *Human Development Report*. Geneva: United Nations.

United Nations. 2005. *Gender Equality: Striving for Justice in an Unequal World*. Geneva: United Nations.

Wallace, Claire. 2002. "Opening and Closing Borders: Migration and Mobility in East-Central Europe." *Journal of Ethnic and Migration Studies* 28(4): 603–625.

Weinert, Patricia. 1991. "Foreign Female Domestic Workers: HELP WANTED!" World Employment Programme Research Working Paper. Geneva: International Labour Organization.

Wichterich, Christa. 2000. *The Globalized Woman.* New York: Zed Books. World Bank. 2004a. World Development Indicators.

World Bank. 2004b. Global Development Finance.

World Bank. 2005. Morocco Country Assistance Review.

http://datacatalog.worldbank.org/. Posted 2001 (accessed April 27, 2005).

Young, Brigitte. 2000. "The 'Mistress' and the 'Maid' in the Globalized Economy." In *Socialist Register 2001: Working Classes, Global Realities* (ed. Leo Panitch and Colin Lay), 315–327. London: Merlin Press.

Questions

1. Misra and her colleagues focus on the globalization of care work through the contexts of both the sending and the receiving countries. Why is this significant?
2. In what ways are sending countries similar? How are they different? In what ways are receiving countries similar? How are they different?
3. How do development and immigration policies affect care work? What are the consequences for care workers?
4. In what ways is care work exploitive?
5. Who needs to be cared for in the United States? Who does the bulk of the care work? From where do care workers in the United States come? Where do they do this work? What legal protections do care workers have? What social policies influence who does the care work and how? Be specific. Who benefits from the patchwork care work systems in the United States, and in what ways?

18

Bad Attitudes and Good Soldiers: Soft Skills as a Code for Tractability in the Hiring of Immigrant Latina/os over Native Blacks in the Hotel Industry

MARGARET M. ZAMUDIO AND MICHAEL I. LICHTER

Discrimination can be legal or illegal. When employers hire or promote a more skilled worker over another, for example, they are relying on legitimate criteria to discriminate. Too many times, however, employers base hiring and promotion decisions on raced, gendered, and other preferences for particular types of workers. For example, employers may take rare experiences with a few workers' productivity

Excerpted from Zamudio, Margaret M. and Michael I. Lichter. 2009. "Bad Attitudes and Good Soldiers: Soft Skills as a Code for Tractability in the Hiring of Immigrant Latina/os over Native Blacks in the Hotel Industry." *Social Problems* 55(4):571–589. Copyright © 2008, Oxford University Press.

and make generalizations to entire categories of workers. They may interpret their positive experiences with a hardworking immigrant employee as a sign that immigrants are harder workers than nonimmigrants. The employer might then develop a preference for immigrant workers and not hire others. Negative experiences might lead to the opposite experience: Bad experiences lead to exclusion of workers with particular ascribed or achieved statuses. Further, what employers consider negative or positive traits might also be filtered through racial, gender, nationalist, and other biases.

Preferences for certain types of workers happen within a larger economic context. The U.S. economy over the last several decades has shifted from producing *things* (the decline in the manufacturing sector) to producing *services* and *experiences* (*the rise of financial services and retail*). The changes in the economy across the twentieth century dramatically altered what jobs were available to workers—and what employers looked for when hiring. Rather than focusing on employees' "hard skills" (e.g., scores on tests, ability to drive a forklift), employers increasingly evaluated employees' "soft skills" (*Moss and Tilly 1996*), or their interactional styles and attitudes. Employers increasingly want workers who can interact with customers smoothly. But evaluating workers' "soft skills" introduces cultural, class, and racial bias into decision making in new, subtle ways. Particularly problematic are employers' views of culturally inflected styles—such as wearing baggy clothing or avoiding eye contact—as evidence of Black and poor workers' "bad attitudes" and "poor people skills." Employers' evaluations of soft skills become tools for excluding those workers from opportunities.

In this study of the hotel industry, Margaret Zamudio and Michael Lichter evaluate the role of bias in employers' assessments of "soft skills" in a new way. Rather than biasing employers *against* Black workers, they show that employers and managers have a preference *for* Latino workers—because they believe they will work harder and with fewer complaints than Black workers. The authors challenge the notion that preferences advantage Latino workers, arguing instead that they become a tool of exploitation. "Complaining" workers are workers that actually are resistant to exploitive working conditions. The authors highlight contradictions in employers' accounts of preferences, especially their preference for "soft skills." Employers' preferences reflect their assessment of which workers they can most easily exploit, and that is no advantage.

Reference

Moss, Philip, and Chris Tilly. 1996. "'Soft' Skills and Race: An Investigation of Black Men's Employment Problems." *Work and Occupations* 23(3): 252–276.

Researchers have, since the early 1990s, begun paying closer attention to managers' perceptions of various groups of native and immigrant workers. This research has documented widespread biases among managers against Black applicants in favor of immigrant Latina/os (Kirschenman and Neckerman 1991; Moss and Tilly 1996; Neckerman and Kirchenman 1991; Waldinger 1996, 1997; Wilson 1996). In the post-civil rights era, where labor market inequality research has largely emphasized the role of post-industrial economic shifts (see, e.g., Wilson 1978, 1987), this research has reinvigorated a focus on discrimination as a central cause in the eroding labor market position of urban Blacks, largely due to the introduction of racial bias during the job interview in a labor market highly dependent on soft skills. Philip Moss and Chris Tilly (1996) define "soft skills" "as skills, abilities, and traits that pertain to personality, attitude, and behavior rather than formal or technical knowledge" (p. 253). While the existing research concludes that the demand for soft skills has engendered various hiring processes that allow for greater discrimination against Blacks, scholars have tended to accept employer motives at face value, and they present soft skills as a legitimate skill requirement for entry-level jobs. In this chapter we challenge the relevancy of soft skills as legitimate skill requirements for entry-level jobs. In fact, our aim is to caution researchers about the coded meanings of this concept and about uncritically classifying employer talk about attitudes and motivation as indicators of soft skills when these preferences appear to speak more to tractability.

Soft Skills

By examining an occupational category where in reality the objective skill requirements to do the job require little soft skills as traditionally defined, we conclude that employers' talk about soft skill requirements raise employer discriminatory race talk to a more sophisticated level. In the new service economy we have an expansion of jobs at the entry level for cashiers, bartenders, waitresses, front desk help, etc., where it makes sense to rate a potential employee on their soft skills. These jobs clearly require that employees work directly with people, communicate effectively, and engage in a level of emotional labor (see, e.g., Hochschild 1983). In these cases, the attributes of gender or a sunny disposition or nurturing affect, for example, is marketed as a skill, and add another level of exploitation to the work (Zamudio 2004). But in the expansive back-of-the-house positions that many of these employers are discussing, these attributes are unnecessary for doing the job. It is simply less relevant for a worker to have a good attitude or sunny disposition or interaction skills for a workday filled with cleaning toilets, laundering towels, and flipping mattresses. Yet, we find that it is exactly these so-called soft skills rather than objective skills that employers emphasize when hiring for these back-of-the-house positions. As we have seen in previous studies of employers, the talk about these skills is charged with references to group differences in terms of race/ethnicity and nativity differences, a discussion that is less prevalent at the higher end of the labor market where one would expect a greater need for soft skills (see Thomas 2003).

The unintended consequence of categorizing these attributes as skills is to supply a veneer of legitimacy to the discriminatory strategies of employers. Because these attributes have been accepted as skills, employers can provide a "legitimate" reason for excluding low-skilled native Blacks from the labor market. That they simply lack the skills to do the job can then be echoed by scholars trying to understand the eroding labor position of native Blacks. For example, from Wilson (1996) we learn that "the hard and soft skills among inner-city Blacks that do not match the current needs of the labor market are products of racially segregated communities . . ." (137). Moss and Tilly (1996) state: "three factors underlie negative evaluations of Black men as workers:

racial stereotypes, cultural differences . . . and *actual skill differences*" (270, emphasis added). Employer preference for immigrant Latina/os in back-of-the-house jobs raises another challenge for the treatment of soft skills as skills. For if lack of soft skills determines the eroding labor market position of low-skilled Blacks, would not it also have the same impact on immigrant Latina/os who on average have less education than native Blacks? If immigrant Latina/os, who not only have lower skills on average (Waldinger 1997) but also fail to meet the basic levels of language proficiency necessary for communicating well with others, as many employers complain, or even the shared culture necessary to express one's attitude and motivations, is it possible that soft skills mean something other than the way they have been traditionally defined by scholars and discussed by the employers in these studies?

We can explain the different employment outcomes for native Blacks and immigrant Latina/os in low-end labor markets where employers are allegedly seeking soft skills by examining the ambiguity in what employers are talking about when they say they are looking for good attitudes, interaction skills, and/or motivation. These words describe different things. Surely a good attitude may mean a sunny outlook, a sort of pleasantness. On the other hand, a good attitude may mean someone who accepts the intensification of the labor process without challenging management. Interaction skills refer to the ability to communicate in varied settings, or getting along. But it can also describe an employee's lack of challenge to unfair treatment and work conditions. Motivation may mean the desire to learn new things or it may mean working above and beyond out of fear of losing one's job. Predispositions to pleasantness, cooperativeness, and learning are attributes particular to individuals not groups. Therefore, it would be irrational and particularly costly for employers to engage in statistical discrimination against Blacks in order to maximize the likelihood that they obtain these desired attributes in the workforce. On the other hand, immigrants as a group are more likely than native labor to share certain alternative characteristics captured in attributes employers describe as "attitude," "interaction," and "motivation." For example, the level of political and social vulnerability influences how workers respond to managerial control, and it can create a fear-driven motivation to work above and beyond what is required, an attitude of acceptance, and a restrained interactive approach to exploitive conditions.

Thus, when scholars pinpoint statistical discrimination to explain the labor market difficulties of Blacks, they are partially correct. However, it is not because of real skill differences between native Blacks and immigrant Latina/os. Statistical discrimination allows employers to maximize a particular characteristic of a group in their workforce in order to increase production. We argue that in the case of back-of-the-house jobs, employers seek to maximize vulnerability and minimize resistance. In this sense, statistical discrimination allows for greater productivity, but not for the reasons cited by prior studies of employer attitudes. As employers suggest, they can get more work out of immigrant Latina/os. But this difference in productivity is not a reflection of differences in skills, but rather an expression of social structure that differentiates native and immigrant workers.

Thus, employer descriptions about the desired attributes in their employees do reflect concerns with productivity. But this is a productivity derived from pure exploitation, not one rooted in a skilled workforce as commonly understood. For this reason, we would expect to find the ambiguous discourse of soft skills rather than objective skill requirements in the unskilled labor market segments where employers seek greater control of the labor process. This assumption is consistent with Thomas's (2003) findings that employers' racial biases played less of a role when hiring for skilled positions. At this level, education, not racial perceptions, plays a greater role. In fact, employers use the language of soft skills to express a non-skill difference between immigrant Latina/os and native Blacks that they do not want to discuss openly; immigrants are more vulnerable, more willing to submit to managerial control without complaint, and thus more exploitable.

Skills Study

This chapter draws upon evidence from a study of employers conducted in Los Angeles County, California. Los Angeles provides an ideal setting as it is considered a "multiethnic metros" or "prismatic metropolis" where racial and ethnic groups are broadly and significantly represented (Bobo et al. 2000). This chapter focuses on

40 interviews conducted with a sample of hotel employers in charge of hiring entry-level workers. The majority of the employers interviewed worked in human resources (HR). In the absence of an HR office, generally the hotel manager provided the interview. The hotel industry represents an ideal case for our study because a large proportion of the jobs in the industry are entry-level back-of-the-house jobs. While considered low-skilled, back-of-the-house work by definition rarely requires a public face. , Studying this work, allows us to better scrutinize the meaning of soft skills. In addition, low-skilled back-of-the-house work makes up the largest segment of jobs in the industry with the median education levels of workers at 12 years or less (Waldinger and Lichter 2003).

Back-of-the-House Jobs

The position of housekeeper gives us a good understanding of the type of work that back-of-the-house jobs involve, and allows us to assess soft skills in relation to the job. When describing housekeeping jobs, most managers went straight to the obvious: "cleaning guest rooms," "vacuuming," and "making up rooms." "Making sure guests have all their needs, towels, accessories, and to make them feel at home." Details include "change beds, clean restrooms, dust all furniture," "take note of maintenance needs, make sure all rooms have what they need," and the occasional "deep cleaning" in addition to "daily cleaning of the rooms," but "no furniture moving or mattress flipping." A somewhat subtler responsibility is to "see that everything is consistent with the standards of the hotel."

If the task bundles differ somewhat across establishments, so do the skills managers see as necessary for performing the job. Asked about the most important skill required for the job, managers split into two camps. From a list that included "interaction with customers," "interaction with coworkers," "job-specific skills," and a few additional choices, 46 percent selected "interaction with customers," and 44 percent selected "job-specific skills." For some, job-specific skills were a matter of safety, "so that they do not hurt themselves." For most, however, the housekeeper has to be good at cleaning, "because that's our selling point. They have to do a good job in there, and know what they are doing, or everything else is chaos." Typifying those who selected job-specific skills over interaction skills, the manager of a small, inexpensive downtown hotel asserted that housekeepers must provide "efficient cleaning in a quick and timely manner. It's nice to get along with clients, but if you don't clean the room quickly, you're dead in the water." Emphasizing the bottom line, another observed, "Basically, all hotels offer the same soap, linens, etc., but it's how clean your room is, the extra care given," that gives a hotel a competitive advantage.

Those who put interaction with customers first tended to emphasize organizational ideology, as did this manager: "We are a customer service organization. Hospitality is the most important thing at a hotel." Another noted: "It's the business we're in, taking care of guests, making sure they have good experience and then return. If you have other skills, but can't interact well, that's a problem." Amplifying this point, another manager emphasized that guests "pay the bills. Our business is to serve the guests. We want them to come back. In essence we want to make that guest part of our sales staff. A guest can either make you or break you," and another noted: "That's were we get our repeat business. If they [staff] take care of our guests then they come back." A manager at a large, expensive Westside hotel put it a bit more grandly. To her, the most important skill for housekeepers is:

Hospitality, because that sets the tone for everything else that follows. A hotel, if you look at it, what you have is a museum. If you add people, you have a home. That's where we start. Hospitality: a natural inclination to want to please, help, and serve other people. It's something you can't train someone to be. Either they want to or they don't. [It involves] being able to make eye contact quite naturally, and to give the greeting of the day. That's the standard of the hotel: you make eye contact, smile, and give the greeting of the day. In some hotels, it's acceptable to shuffle by the guest and not say hello, but it's not acceptable here.

Or, as another manager put it: "In the hotel industry we sell service. People come to sleep. So the only thing we can provide them is to come in contact with competent individuals who want to serve them and take care of their needs. A room attendant who does not speak to a guest in hallway after he requests something is not going to [be remembered] in a kindly manner."

Fully 93 percent of the managers said that the job could be done by someone without any prior experience, 64 percent did not require any prior related work experience, and only 25 percent required a year of related work experience. Only 14 percent of the managers said that their hotels required a high school diploma for these positions. One manager told us that "it's not a job that requires much formalized education or training. It doesn't demand much skill. The requirements are only very minimal. It's a hands-on type of position, unskilled."

While managers seemed sure that they could rapidly impart technical skills to any applicant they hired, most felt quite differently about interaction skills. In a refrain heard from many of our respondents, a manager observed: "You can teach technical skills. You cannot teach someone to be pleasant," or as another put it: "We can train them to do technical tasks, but we cannot train a service attitude." A third manager noted: "In the interview, we don't look for good work experience, but for someone who can interact well and can project a good image. Technical skills can be taught. You can't teach people how to get along. In life, you've got it or you don't." This conviction that a "service attitude" is innate and immutable—"you've got it or you don't"—was pervasive.

Despite the emphasis on interaction, managers put surprisingly little importance on the "hard" cognitive skills about which we queried them. None listed reading, writing, or English language ability as the most important skill for the job when we asked for separate ratings of each skill, and these three were the least highly rated in importance. This makes sense in two ways. First, many of the managers had large numbers of limited-English-proficient staff members who, in their minds, were the only workers available for the job. Many customers' concerns and complaints could be handled well with just a few words of English—"hello," "towel," "toilet paper," etc.—with the customer's satisfaction hinging at least as much on the tone of the interaction—polite, subservient—as its content. The employer's failure to note English language ability as a required skill, however, challenges the notion of soft skills as a skill at all. If soft skills capture a worker's ability to interact with customers, at face value a seemingly legitimate requirement for the job, then we would expect the employers to list English as a fundamental skill for the job. But, as we argue herein, it is unlikely that soft skills actually represent a real skill required to do the job. In fact, when we queried another way by asking employers to rate "the most important quality" rather than skill of a worker, fully 44 percent rated "attitude" as the most important quality. Interaction with customers ranked second with 22 percent listing it as the most important quality.

How do hotels find the housekeeping workers with the attributes they seek? Several managers mentioned highly informal screening methods. For example, at one hotel, the staff member who accepts applications from potential employees makes an initial assessment. "We have a smile quotient: Do they smile on their own? It reveals personality. Appearance: Are they clean? If they're unsatisfactory on any factor, they're not considered for the job." On-the-spot assessments are not rare; another manager reported: "When they walk in if they have a good attitude we like them. If they come in with no experience, they come in and if they want to work, we like them. You may think it's crazy but it works. If you came in with a bad attitude, you wouldn't be able to do what you're [going to be] doing."

Most employers appeared to weigh subjective judgments at least as heavily as background factors in making their hiring decisions. The phrase "gut feeling" came up frequently. Managers sometimes described their interviewing process in metaphysical terms; one reported: "We have sixth senses," while another noted: "When our antennae go up, we heed them." One of these managers elaborated: "You can pick up on how a person reacts to a question, the tone of the voice throughout the whole interview process. When you've been doing this for ten years, you should know." One hotel employer reported, "The interview process focuses on chemistry: Is this a good match for me and my other employees?" Another asked, rhetorically: "Do you look me in the eye? That's a big one. I always feel that if a person doesn't look me in the eye, what are they hiding? What are they afraid of?"

The employer interviews in the hotel industry suggest that there has also been an increased emphasis on soft skills in areas such as housekeeping where they traditionally did not matter. While it is clear that the greater reliance on interviews to screen for soft skills has the potential of undermining native Black applicants, it is not clear how this same process favors immigrant Latina/os. Clearly, how well Blacks rate on this skill is easily influenced by employer prejudices and is

subject to employers' own particularistic understandings of "appropriate interaction and conversational style—in short, shared culture" (Neckerman and Kirschenman 1991, 442). However, immigrant Latina/os should not fare any better when soft skills are in demand; and the interview is the prime source of screening, given that immigrant Latina/os are less likely to speak or understand English, an essential interaction skill and central to a shared or common culture, than native Blacks. Employers complained over and over again about the inability of immigrant Latina/os to speak English and communicate with guests. For example, an employer describes the problem she has with the housekeeping staff:

> It's really important for our housekeepers to speak to our guests in English. Our service suffers if they don't understand. Many of the housekeepers have very little English skills. When a guest walks by, the maids turn to look away and avoid making eye contact. The guests interpret this as rudeness. But they look away because they're scared that the guest may need help and will talk to them in English.

The lack of English skills and the housekeepers' avoidance of guest contact is a theme that runs throughout the interviews. Therefore, it is difficult to conclude that the changing skill requirements somehow account for the disadvantaged position of low-skilled native Blacks while providing an advantage for low-skilled immigrant Latina/os. It seems more appropriate to suggest that employers continue to discriminate against native Blacks, but hire immigrant Latina/o applicants for qualities other than skill.

As the following descriptions of employer biases suggest, employers prefer immigrants. But is this predilection rooted in the superior soft skills of the worker or the status of nonnative, noncitizen workers, which captures a sort of vulnerability that employers perceive make workers more controllable? In objective terms, it is difficult to argue that immigrant Latina/os, who often lack fundamental communications skills, somehow possess greater soft skills than native Blacks. The following three sections outline the employers' perceptions of immigrant Latina/o, Black, and native workers as a whole. The subsequent analysis suggests that the bias inherent in screening for soft skills is in fact a bias in favor of workers who are perceived as more vulnerable and therefore more controllable. In this way, nativity is a proxy for degrees of controllability in workers.

Employers' Perceptions of Immigrant Latina/os

Employers generally explained the high and increasing presence of immigrants in their industry in one of two ways: First, it is an industry with low barriers to entry and therefore a good place for immigrants to start. As one manager observed: "Traditionally the hospitality industry attracts immigrants because the skills are those you can acquire while working." Another manager seconded this, adding: "With the majority of them not speaking the language, it's the only place where they can start." Second, natives disdain many of the jobs the industry has to offer, and so hotels need to hire immigrants. "Those [Latina/o immigrants] are the people applying for those jobs," noted one manager: "Other ethnic groups don't apply for them. That flap about immigrants taking jobs from natives I don't buy. . . . Very few Blacks apply for those jobs or any jobs. I don't think they're displacing anyone." Or, as another manager echoed: "You can't get any whites to take this work. Blacks by and large don't like this."

Furthermore, managers typically had words of praise for immigrants, like the following remarks from several different managers: "I'm very happy with their performance. They're very reliable." "They are good workers." "They have great work ethic." "They are very good, very loyal. . . . They succeed and learn the job well." "Their performance is very much higher. . . . They give very good service to the guests. They are usually the employees of the month, the ones doing a very spectacular job." "They're very positive and willing to work."

Other managers were much more restrained in their assessment of immigrant Latina/o workers. Some managers insisted that immigrants were no different from anybody else. Others who had positive things to say about immigrants, particularly Latina/o immigrants, made clear that they did not find them to be innately or culturally superior to native workers. Asked whether the "immigrant work ethic" was responsible for the rapid increases in immigrant employment in Los Angeles over the past decade or so, a hotel employer responded: "No, it's just a matter that they're willing to take lower paying jobs." Another said: "No. It's because they are willing to work, and they can do the kind of work that's available which doesn't require a great deal of skill or much experience. Some of them where they come from really don't have a very good work ethic, back in Mexico. You ever heard of 'I'll do it mañana?'" Another manager scoffed: "My employees have no work ethic. They will do the work. . . . It's hard, dirty work. . . . Immigrants are not willing to work harder, but they are willing to do the work."

Employers' Perceptions of Native Blacks

Consistent with earlier studies on employer attitudes, we found that most of the managers we interviewed held negative attitudes toward native Blacks while applauding the work ethic of Latina/o immigrants. On the whole, managers view Blacks as having an "attitude problem," making them poor substitutes for immigrants with a strong work ethic. "There's [a problem with] the willingness to go beyond the level of service requested, authority figures, generally there's a problem with insubordination. . . . In my personal view, the Latina/o workers work much harder and are less problematic with absenteeism and family problems," reported a manager. Or, as another manager put it:

> If you're talking about service in the hotel industry, you have to have a certain attitude. If you come with a chip on your shoulder, with negativeness, [with a sense that] "I've been a victim," and don't come across as guest oriented and helpful . . . [then] there is an attitude that is there. It's hard to pinpoint, because when you say it, you're accused of being a racist. . . . Whether they are Black men or Black women, they are from this country, and they feel that they haven't been treated well, that slavery has deprived them of rights. So they have that chip [on their shoulder]. . . . In some of my interviews with Latina/os, I'm asking them about their work ethic. I ask, "Is the job a necessity?" and they say, "Yes." And I say, "The work is not easy; are you willing to sweat?" And they say, "Yes." "But you have to sweat with ganas." And they say, "Yes." Because this job requires that you have ganas. I wouldn't approach it that way with Blacks.

In the minds of most managers Blacks often lack the motivation they expect from immigrants, and managers often detect a sense of entitlement in Black job applicants and Black workers. This is an "I'm owed attitude" that managers associate with a demand for justice: "Since I'm Black and have been discriminated against in the past, now you owe me to make up for the past." As a white female manager noted with disapproval, this sense of entitlement has the effect of "putting people on the defensive." On the other hand, Blacks are also faulted for being pessimistic about their job prospects. As a white female HR manager at a large airport hotel told us: "If he thinks he's not going to get the job because he is Black or that he should get the job because he is Black, I'm not going to hire him. He's got a bad attitude. In the end, to believe that you're not going to get the job because you're Black, then you portray that attitude, and you don't get the job, [it's a] self-fulfilling prophecy. Young Black males who do not portray that attitude succeed."

Employers' Perceptions of Natives in General

It is evident that employers see Blacks as a less compliant labor force than immigrants. Yet, digging a little deeper, it is also evident that employers' views of Blacks are not just racial views. Asked to compare native Blacks with Latina/o immigrants, a manager in one of the area's most exclusive hotels responded: "I would not group the Blacks with Hispanics, I would group them with whites. They [whites] don't have a very high work ethic either." Along the same lines, another employer opined: "Realistically a guy who hops the border is willing to bust his butt.... Most of the Hispanics and Asians have a solid work ethic. Can't say that for the natives in this country." However, as the managers themselves readily admit, the hotel jobs for which they hire are often dirty, they entail physically demanding, mentally numbing tasks performed under the critical eye of a supervisor, they require polite deference to customers and managers, and they pay very little. These are hardly conditions that would inspire many natives of whatever stripe to hard work—something that managers sometimes conceded, if obliquely, like this one: "Immigrants never even find out what America is about. They are happy making $5 an hour." In fact, employer discourse suggests that they are looking for something other than "Americanness."

When employers spoke about Latina/os, they always referred to immigrants unless specifically asked about native Latina/os. When specifically asked about Latina/os who were raised in the United States, opinions were divided, with some praising them as hard workers ("They're pretty industrious. We've hired several children of employees and they tend to have a good work ethic. Probably because their fathers are cracking a whip over them"), and some noting their value as bilingual workers able to communicate with both workers and customers. Despite nearly equal representation in the industry, negative comments about native Latina/os were much rarer than negative comments about native Blacks. Still, a substantial minority of the managers criticized native Latina/os for being too American. For example, one employer observed: "They traditionally fall into the American work ethic and have the kind of expectations that we would expect from any American born worker. They're more educated, and they have more tools at their disposal." Another employer volunteered that "They're not as loyal. They have the ability to move up and do more. Their longevity is less. They have more knowledge of resources available to them." Another employer characterized native-born Latina/os as, like Blacks, having "a chip on their shoulder too. They think they're better than their parents because they went to school."

Settled immigrants who acquire "more tools" or "knowledge of resources available to them," also provoked criticism from employers. When immigrants assert their rights, they are also considered to be lagging in their work ethic. For example, an employer reported that although "85 to 90 percent of my experience [with immigrants] has been positive and favorable," the rest are "these people who feel like the work is too hard, that they shouldn't have to do this kind of thing. They're the ones who go out and get the union, thinking it's going to be better. Their personal aim is to destroy the employer or to make life miserable for them."

Managerial Control and the Preference for Immigrant Workers

According to economist Richard Edwards (1979), once a manager hires workers and purchases their labor power, "it is true *without limit* that the more work he can wring out of the labor power he has purchased, the more goods will be produced; and they will be produced without any increased wage costs" (p. 12). The challenge to the manager is how to control the workers in such a way as to "wring" the maximum amount of work from them. "Here, 'control' is defined as the ability of capitalists and/or managers to obtain desired work behavior from workers. Such ability exists in greater or lesser degrees, depending upon the relative strength of workers and their bosses" (Edwards 1979:17). Hotels are service-producing organizations, many employing tens or hundreds of workers. Each day, the typical mid-sized or large hotel has dozens of workers on site making beds, toting bags, changing light bulbs, folding laundry, parking cars, washing dishes, waiting tables, answering telephones, registering guests, soliciting sales, balancing the books, and more. In hotels, as in other capitalist enterprises, a hierarchy of upper managers, departmental managers, and front line supervisors exercise control as they coordinate, direct, evaluate, and discipline these workers.

Control was a major issue for the hotel employers we interviewed, many of whom spoke of increased pressures to get more out of their workers. As costs and competition have climbed, the entire industry has been under increased pressure to contain costs. Given the labor intensity of the industry, this has translated into an impetus to rationalize and intensify the work process—to work "smarter and harder," in lay terms. For example, an employer reported that "because of economic conditions we have situations where we need to get rooms done efficiently. We realigned the schedule last month. Housekeepers need to take two minutes less to clean a room. We eliminated a half hour of unproductive time that way. . . ." As staffing decreased, the manager noted, the average load for housekeepers increased from 15 a day to 17, "which is a lot."

Maintaining worker cooperation and compliance while raising job requirements and keeping wages flat cannot be easy, even in a slack labor market. Since the success of the hotel depends in large part on the quality of service employees' work, and since meeting budgetary targets depends on the workers keeping "up to speed," it should be clear that ensuring obedience to authority is a central managerial mission. Thus, it's not surprising that in employers' talk about the immigrant "work ethic," what they praised most was a willingness to submit to managerial authority without protest. Explaining employer preference for immigrants, a manager admitted: "I have to say that employers tend to think that they'll be good workers and keep quiet. . . . People think that way. Hire them and there won't be no problems." A manager at a downtown establishment concurred, saying: "My experience is that most Latina/os have a much better work ethic than the whites and

Blacks I've employed here. . . . There is less complaining. I more or less tell them what has to be done and they do it in a rather happy manner." A Beverly Hills employer stated, "Hispanic workers are willing to go out of the way and put in that extra effort for you. Whereas not just Blacks, but generally anybody born in the United States, I've never really viewed as [having a] work ethic. Immigrants are willing to do more work for me as part of some general work ethic. . . . I get more compliance out of immigrant workers to work harder, to work overtime."

Employers appeared to be quite aware of "the relative strength of workers," which they took to be tied to the level of degradation and desperation they faced in their home countries. Several of the employers explicitly related the willingness of immigrants to work hard in unrewarding jobs to the hardships they faced in their home countries and the difficulties they experienced in coming to the United States and finding work. One of our respondents at a run-down downtown hotel wryly listed "the qualifications for the job" as being "to walk 4,000 miles, sleep under the weeds, be humiliated and beaten down, and, if you're a woman, 'put out' every three miles. If you have done this then you're probably qualified." When a Latina/o manager was asked why he felt immigrants made up such a large segment of their labor force, he responded: "My bottom gut answer is that they'll accept any condition to work, to make money, to feed their families." Another employer agreed. "It's basic need. They will accept low wages with little opportunity for growth positions." Another employer said: "Immigrants are very reliable and dedicated to their job. The company is aware of this. The company openly welcomes all people of different origins. They're low-paying jobs, which immigrants will accept because they're willing to take anything." Another employer reported that without immigrants "we would probably have to hire more individuals to do the same amount of work. Generally you'll find that immigrants would do one and a half times the work." One employer remarked: "You tend to find immigrants work a bit harder for the simple reason that they have more strings attached to their lives. Either they are sending money back home, or they're here to make as much money with the dream of going back home. It's not easy to be a minority under any circumstance. You sometimes have to prove yourself, and work even harder than the next person to keep what you have. For those reasons their work ethic tends to be better."

In any event, although a handful of employers cited willingness to work for low wages as an important determinant of the general preference for immigrant workers—for example, "It's cheaper to hire someone from someplace else. They're cheap labor."—this was not the main message we heard. Instead, the main issue for employers when distinguishing among workers was not the hard skills or credentials they brought to the job, not the wages they demanded, but the degree to which workers acknowledged managerial authority—the degree to which managers could exercise control.

The routine of screening for soft skills employers define as work ethic, attitude, willingness, and so on serves to justify the exclusion of native Blacks, and probably of native workers in general. But, as the preceding analysis suggests, these so-called skills merely represent the extent to which workers will submit to exploitative work conditions. Like English workers of the nineteenth century, Americans have normative standards defining what the old slogan "A Fair Day's Wages for a Fair Day's Work" means. In a labor surplus environment, native workers may have little choice but to apply for entry-level hotel jobs, but they cannot be expected to accept what they reasonably regard as highly exploitative conditions with enthusiasm and without complaint. Lackluster performance is a traditional form of resistance (Kelley 1996), an assertion of their right to work in a dignified manner.

Conclusion

In line with the findings from previous studies on employer attitudes, employers in the Los Angeles hotel industry prefer immigrant Latina/o workers over native Black workers for entry-level positions. At first, one might conclude that this preference is due to employer perceptions that immigrant Latina/os have a superior work ethic and a positive attitude. In the more forthright interviews with employers, they often reveal that immigrant Latina/o workers are "willing" to do more and, in fact, are easier to control. In contrast, employers cast native Black workers as problematic. They depict native Black workers as projecting a bad attitude, carrying a chip on their shoulder, being uncooperative and uncommunicative, in sum, as lacking soft skills. The data also suggest that the perception of particular

groups lacking a work ethic extends to native whites and native Latina/os.

We argue, however, that the emphasis on the intangible skills that researchers often refer to as soft skills and employers call attitude, interaction skills, and work ethic as a job requirement for low-skilled entry-level jobs is, in practice, a shorthand for finding workers who are perceived as more controllable. Formally defined, soft skills suggest cultural competency and ability to interact with others. Employers offer little evidence that immigrant Latina/o workers are more likely than native Black workers to possess the level of soft skills required for entry-level unskilled positions. Moreover, the fact that employers never selected English language skills as one of the most important requirements for the entry-level hotel maid job suggests that communication skills were in fact not central to the position.

Our research suggests that social scientists should be careful in accepting employer talk about attitudes, motivation, and work ethic as indicators of soft skills. We are not suggesting that employers are mistaken about the differences in the amount of work they are able to extract from immigrant Latina/o versus native Black workers. Rather we are arguing that it is incorrect to interpret these differences as due to differences in soft skills or work ethic. While employers say they are looking for happy, hard working, communicative team players for entry-level positions, the conditions of the job and the expectations they have of immigrant Latina/o workers indicate they are more concerned with selecting workers they perceive to be receptive to tight managerial control and the intensification of the labor process.

References

Bobo, Lawrence D., Melvin L. Oliver, James H. Johnson, Jr., and Abel Valenzuela. 2000. "Analyzing Inequality in Los Angeles" In *Prismatic Metropolis: Inequality in Los Angeles* (ed. Lawrence D. Bobo, Melvin L. Oliver, James H. Johnson, Jr., and Abel Valenzuela), 3–51. New York: Russell Sage Foundation.

Edwards, Richard. 1979. *Contested Terrain: The Transformation of the Workplace in the Twentieth Century*. New York: Basic Books.

Hochschild, Arlie Russell. 1983. *The Managed Heart: Commercialization of Human Feeling*. Los Angeles: University of California Press.

Kelley, Robin D. G. 1996. *Race Rebels: Culture, Politics, and the Black Working Class*. New York: Free Press.

Kirschenman, Joleen, and Kathryn M. Neckerman. 1991. "'We'd Love to Hire Them, But . . .': The Meaning of Race for Employers." In *The Urban Underclass* (ed. C. Jencks and P. E. Peterson), 203–232. Washington, DC: The Brookings Institution.

Moss, Philip, and Chris Tilly. 1996. "'Soft' Skills and Race: An Investigation of Black Men's Employment Problems." *Work and Occupations* 23:252–276.

Neckerman, Kathryn M., and Joleen Kirschenman. 1991. "Hiring Strategies, Racial Bias, and Inner-City Workers." *Social Problems* 38: 433–447.

Thomas, Ward. 2003. "The Meaning of Race to Employers: A Dynamic Qualitative Perspective." *The Sociological Quarterly* 44: 227–242.

Waldinger, Roger. 1996. "Who Cleans the Rooms? Who Washes the Dishes? Black/Immigrant Job Competition Reassessed." In *Immigrants and Immigration Policy: Individual Skills, Family Ties, and Group Identities*, vol. 79: *Contemporary Studies in Economic and Financial Analysis* (ed. H. O. Duleep and P. V. Wunnava), 265–288. Greenwich, CT: JAI Press.

Waldinger, Roger. 1997. "Black/Immigrant Competition Re-Assessed: New Evidence From Los Angeles." *Sociological Perspectives* 40:365–386.

Waldinger, Roger, and Michael I. Lichter. 2003. *How the Other Half Works: Immigrants and the Social Organization of Labor*. Berkeley: University of California Press.

Wilson, William Julius. 1978. *The Declining Significance of Race*. Chicago: University of Chicago Press.

Wilson, William Julius. 1987. *The Truly Disadvantaged: The Inner City, the Underclass, and Public Policy*. Chicago: The University of Chicago Press.

Wilson, William Julius. 1996. *When Work Disappears: The World of the New Urban Poor*. New York: Alfred A. Knopf.

Zamudio, Margaret M. 2004. "Alienation and Resistance: New Possibilities for Working-Class Formation." *Social Justice* 31(3): 60–76.

Questions

1. What stereotypes do the managers have about Black workers? What stereotypes do they have about Latino/a workers?

2. What is meant by "soft skills"? How do employers use this language, and what contradictions do the authors note?

3. How are soft skills related to perceptions of work by race and nativity? How are soft skills related to the job of hotel housekeeping?

4. What contradictions do the authors find in their discussion of race, soft skills, and housekeeping? What are the consequences, especially concerning exploitation, for Latina workers in this study?

5. How might the findings in this study relate to other industries? How might stereotypes and discourse be used as tools to exploit workers, even when it appears as a good thing on the surface level? How might the stereotypes and discourse vary depending on the race, gender, and nationality of the worker?

6. Consider your own work history. What soft skills were central to the job, and what role did they play in your hiring and/or promotion? Are soft skills legitimate criteria for judging workers? Why or why not? If you see them as legitimate, how can employers balance their desire to have smooth customer–worker interactions with their legal and moral obligation not to discriminate?

19

New Commodities, New Consumers: Selling Blackness in a Global Marketplace

PATRICIA HILL COLLINS

Patricia Hill Collins is perhaps best known for her work on standpoint theory and intersectionality. These concepts are related and, in short, mean we each view the world through our social location as a person with, among other things, a race, a gender, and a class. We view the world differently because we experience it differently. Throughout her work, Collins always calls attention to how historical, economic, and social factors combine to influence how we experience the world today. In this chapter, Collins retains these foci and highlights the role of consumption.

Juliet Schor (1998) argues that during the 1920s consumerism became a national phenomenon in the United States. By this she means that discretionary spending became widespread. As production processes shifted, people other than the rich were able to purchase products. Media and technological developments have led to an environment where advertisements for merchandise bombard us on a regular basis. TV commercials, magazine advertisements, billboards, and social media give us messages that our lives will be better if we buy particular things. Further technological advances lead consumers to buy newer versions of products, even if previous versions still operate. People evaluate others based on the types of brands they wear, their style of clothes, and what type of cell phones they have. We have developed into a consumer society where advertising and spending have become normative and, while everywhere, often times invisible. This consumer ideology has developed alongside the creation and perpetuation of different forms of inequality.

In this piece, Collins challenges the reader to examine exploitation through the lens of consumption within a globalized capitalist marketplace. Collins shows how prison culture and Black sexuality are exploited to sell young, poor American Black women's and men's bodies and culture around the world, including to U.S. Black young people themselves. Using the example of Nelly's "Pimp Juice," Collins argues that our analysis of capitalism should be expanded to include both the consumer and the consumed.

Reference

Schor, Juliet B. 1998. *The Overspent American*. New York: University of California Press.

It's just me against the world, baby, me against the world.
I got nothin' to lose—it's just me against the world.

—TUPAC SHAKUR

In the eyes of many Americans, African American youth such as hip hop legend Tupac Shakur constitute a threatening and unwanted population. No longer needed for cheap, unskilled labor in fields and factories, poor and working-class Black youth find few job opportunities in the large, urban metropolitan areas where most now reside. Legal and undocumented immigrants now do the dirty work in the hotels, laundries, restaurants, and construction sites of a growing service economy. Warehoused in inner city ghettos that now comprise the new unit of racial segregation, poor Black youth face declining opportunities and an increasingly punitive social welfare state. Because African American youth possess citizenship rights, social welfare programs legally can no longer operate in racially discriminatory ways. Yet, rather than providing African American youth with educational opportunities, elites chose instead to attack the social welfare state that ensured benefits for everyone. Fiscal conservatives have cut funding for public schools, public housing, public health clinics, and public transportation that would enable poor and working-class Black youth to get to burgeoning jobs in the suburbs. Hiding behind a rhetoric of color-blindness, elites claim that these policies lack racial intentionality (Bonilla-Silva, 2003). Yet when it comes to who is affected by these policies, African American youth constitute a sizable segment of the "truly disadvantaged" (Wilson, 1987). No wonder Tupac Shakur laments, "It's just me against the world, baby, me against the world. I got nothin' to lose—it's just me against the world."

Philosopher Cornel West posits that this attitude of "having nothing to lose" reflects a growing sense of nihilism among urban Black American youth and argues that this form of hopelessness constitutes a greater danger to African Americans than that faced by any previous generation (West, 1993). But are African American youth as nihilistic as West suggests? In her study of pregnant, low-income Black adolescent girls, sociologist Wendy Luttrell finds only optimism. Luttrell's subjects were fully aware of how society looked down upon them and, in response, saw their unborn children as sources of hope. Historian

Robin D. G. Kelley also presents a less fatalistic view. Tracing the history of how Black male youth in postindustrial Los Angeles used gangsta rap to criticize police brutality, Kelley suggests that African American youth negotiated new strategies for grappling with the contradictions of a declining economy (Kelley, 1994, 183–227). Recognizing that Black culture was a marketable commodity, they put it up for sale, selling an essentialized Black culture that white youth could emulate yet never own. Their message was clear—"the world may be against us, but we are here and we intend to get paid."

With few exceptions, current literature on globalization fails to explain the experiences of contemporary African American youth with the new racialized social class formations of globalization. Instead, African American youth are often conceptualized as a marginalized, powerless, and passive population within macroeconomic policies of globalization. They serve as examples of an economic analysis that only rarely examines intersections of class and race. In contrast, I suggest that because African American youth are in the belly of the beast of the sole remaining world superpower, they present an important local location for examining new configurations of social class that is refracted through the lens of race, gender, age, and sexuality. Stated differently, because they are centrally located within the United States, Black American youth constitute one important population of social actors who negotiate the contradictions of a racialized globalization as well as the new social class relations that characterize it.

This chapter asks, what might the placement of poor and working-class African American youth in the global political economy, both as recipients of social outcomes of globalization as well as social agents who respond to those outcomes, tell us about the new racialized class formations of globalization? Conversely, what light might the experiences of poor and working-class African American women and men shed on new global forms of racism? These are very large questions, and I briefly explore them by sketching out a two-part argument. First, I investigate how ideas of consumption, commodification, and control situate Black youth within a global political economy. I suggest that shifting the focus of class analysis from production to consumption provides a better understanding of Black youth. Second, I develop a framework for understanding the commodification of Black bodies that ties this process more closely to social class relations. In particular, I use the status of African American youth to explore how the literal and figurative commodification of Blackness fosters new strategies of control. I examine the sex work industry, to illustrate the interconnections among consumption, commodification, and control. I conclude the chapter with a brief discussion of the implications of my arguments.

New Commodities: Advanced Capitalism And Black Body Politics

Because contemporary theories of social class emphasize production, they do not adequately address the realities of poor and working-class African American youth within the global capitalist political economy. Within American sociology, most approaches to African American social class structures focus on jobs, labor market placement, and wage inequalities. For example, in his excellent analysis of the increasing intersection of ghetto and prison within contemporary African American civil society, Loïc Wacquant identifies four peculiar racial institutions (slavery, Jim Crow, ghetto, the hyperghetto and prison) and uses the form of labor required by each historical formation to develop his argument about the core of the economy and dominant social type (Wacquant, 2001, 98–103). Similarly, William Julius Wilson's important work on contemporary Black urban poverty sees the absence of good-paying jobs as the major problem facing Black youth (Wilson, 1987, 1996). Wacquant and Wilson point to labor markets and unemployment to explain the poverty status of poor and working-class Black youth, thus illustrating the contributions of focusing on production.

Complementing the traditional focus on production with greater attention to the growing significance of consumption within global capitalism provides new directions for understanding the experiences of African American youth. African American youth are a hot commodity in the contemporary global marketplace and global media. Their images have catalyzed new consumer markets for products and services. The music of hip hop culture, for example, follows its rhythm and blues predecessor as a so-called crossover genre that is very popular with whites and other cultural groups across the globe. Circulated through film, television, music, news, and advertising, mass media constructs and sells a commodified Black culture from ideas about

class, gender, and age. Through a wide array of genres ranging from talk shows to feature-length films, television situation comedies to CDs, and video rentals to cable television, the images produced and circulated within this area all aim to entertain and amuse a highly segmented consumer market. This market is increasingly global and subject to the contradictions of global marketplace phenomena.

One implication of the significance of consumption for understanding social class relations of Black youth concerns the constant need to stimulate consumer markets. Contemporary capitalism relies not just on cutting the costs attached to production, but also on stimulating consumer demand. Just as sustaining relations of production requires a steady supply of people to do the work, sustaining relations of consumption needs ever-expanding consumer markets. Moreover, just as people do not naturally work and must be encouraged or compelled to do so, people do not engage in excess consumption without prompting. In this context, advertising constitutes an important site that creates demand for commodities of all sorts. Marketing and advertising often create demand for things that formerly were not seen as commodities (e.g., the rapid growth of the bottled water industry), as well as for intangible entities that seem difficult to commodify. In this regard, the rapid growth of mass media and new informational technologies has catalyzed a demand for Black culture as a commodity.

Under this ever-expanding impetus to create new consumer markets, nothing is exempt from commodification and sale, including the pain that African American youth experience with poverty and powerlessness. Nowhere is this more evident than in the contradictions of rap. As Cornel West points out, "the irony in our present moment is that just as young Black men are murdered, maimed and imprisoned in record numbers, their styles have become disproportionately influential in shaping popular culture" (West, 1993). In this context, rap becomes the only place where Black youth have a public voice, yet it is a public voice that is commodified and contained by what hip hop producers think will sell. Despite these marketplace limitations, rap remains a potential site of contestation, a place where African American youth can rebel against the police brutality, lack of jobs, and other social issues that confront them (Kelley, 1994). Thus, work on the culture industry illustrates how images of Black culture function to catalyze consumption.

The actual bodies of young African Americans may also be commodified as part of a new Black body politics. Here, the literature on gender and globalization, especially the sex industry, is helpful in understanding how a new Black body politics might operate within relations of consumption. Situating feminist analyses of body politics within relations of production and consumption that characterize contemporary globalization provides new avenues for understanding commodification and the emergence of a new Black body politics. For Marx, all workers under capitalism are alienated; they are objectified as they sell their labor power to employers for a wage in order to survive. For women, especially those in racial/ethnic groups as well as in industrializing and developing countries alike, good jobs are more difficult to find. Under these circumstances, some women do not sell their bodily labor to produce a commodity. Instead, their bodies become commodities. In a global context, as newly industrializing countries struggle to find commodity niches in the global economy, they frequently find the best niches taken. Consequently, in some countries sex tourism becomes a significant market fostering national economic development and international capital accumulation (Wonders and Michalowski, 2001).

This new gender scholarship offers a new framework for analyzing a new Black body politics that African American youth confront under conditions of globalization. In the United States, African Americans also find the good jobs taken and confront a similar issue of the pressures to commodify their bodies, especially if those bodies are young. More importantly, this impetus to commodify Black bodies is not new. Chattel slavery in the American South prior to and during the formation of the American nation-state clearly treated the bodies of people of African descent as commodities. Objectifying Black bodies enabled slave traders and slave owners to turn Black people's bodies into commodities. Slavers assigned monetary value to Black people's bodies, and then traded Black bodies as commodities on the open market.

Some scholars on race have taken a closer look at how the institution of chattel slavery accomplished this process of objectification, commodification, and exploitation. Literary critic Hortense Spillers suggests that

relations of slavery and colonialism transformed understandings of Black people's bodies. Spillers identifies how "captive bodies," namely, the bodies of enslaved Africans, were severed from their agency, a use of violence that eliminated gender: "Their New World, Diasporic plight marked *a theft of the body*—a willful and violent . . . severing of the captive body from its motive will, its active desire" (Spillers, 2000, 160). This theft of the body severed it from its own agency and thus formed the moment of objectification. Spillers suggests that this new objectified body became a canvas for racist discourse: "These indecipherable markings on the captive body render a kind of hieroglyphics of the flesh whose severe disjunctures come to be hidden to the cultural seeing by skin color" (Spillers, 2000, 61). Once objectified and marked in this fashion, slave owners and slave traders treated Black bodies as commodities that can be traded, bought, and sold on the open market.

Because bodies are not simply raced but also gendered, this new Black body politics takes gender-specific forms. In particular, beginning in the 1980s, the bodies of young Black men became increasingly appropriated by the prison system. Typically, these alarming rates of incarceration have been interpreted as central to new mechanisms of social control (Collins, 2004, 215–246). The discipline of young African American men that lands so many in prison seems woven into the fabric of everyday life. Within large urban areas, gangs, ghettos, public schools, public housing, and prison work together in a quasi-seamless fashion. Prisons and ghettos gain meaning from one another, and both shape new racial formations within American society (Wacquant, 2001). On one level, the growth of the punishment industry constitutes an effective political response to this puzzle of idleness among young Black men as well as an effective mechanism for curtailing their citizenship rights. If there are no jobs, one can hardly make them go to them. Racial profiling and locking up men seemed designed to discipline them into not challenging a system that treated them as throwaways. The issue of felon disenfranchisement speaks to this need to discipline Black men through the prison system. In the early 2000s, 48 states in the United States had felon disenfranchisement laws. Under felon disenfranchisement laws, criminal offenders typically forfeit voting rights as a collateral consequence of their felony convictions. These laws appear to be race neutral, yet because young Black men are disproportionately incarcerated, these laws have a racially disparate impact on this group. In a comprehensive study of these laws, Behrens and Uggen conclude:

> Our key finding can be summarized concisely and forcefully: the racial composition of state prisons is firmly associated with the adoption of state felon disenfranchisement laws. States with greater nonwhite prison populations have been more likely to ban convicted felons from voting than states with proportionately fewer nonwhites in the criminal justice system. (Behrens and Uggen, 2003, 596)

Yet the growth of the punishment industry also illustrates how Black male bodies are objectified, commodified, and incorporated in service to maintaining prisons as consumer markets. In essence, Black men's commodified bodies become used as raw materials for the growing prison industry. It is very simple—no prisoners means no jobs for all of the ancillary industries that service this growth industry. Because prisons express little interest in rehabilitating prisoners, they need a steady supply of bodies. In this way, prisons made use of the bodies of unemployed, unskilled young Black men, the virtually indistinguishable young Black men who populate corners of American cities.

The vast majority of young Black people who are incarcerated by the punishment industry are male, yet it is important to remember that disproportionately high numbers of young Black women are also incarcerated and thus are subject to this form of commodification. Moreover, young Black women may also encounter an additional bodily commodification of their sexuality. The majority of sex workers may be female, obscuring the minority of males who also perform sex work as well as the objectification and commodification of Black male bodies within mass media as an important component of the sex work industry. In essence, the bodies and images of young African Americans constitute new commodities that are central to global relations of consumption, not marginalized within them.

New Consumers: Sex Work and Hip Hop Capitalism

Here, I want to take a closer look at this process by exploring how sexuality has grown in importance in the commodification of the bodies and images of Black American youth and how this sex work in turn articulates with Black agency in responding to advanced capitalism. In essence, Black youth are now caught up in a burgeoning sex work industry, one that is far broader than commercial sex work as depicted in the media. Young African Americans participate in the sex work industry, not primarily as commercial workers as is popularly imagined, but rather as representations of commodified Black sexuality as well as potential new consumer markets eager to consume their own images.

Racialized images of pimps and prostitutes may be the commercial sex workers who are most visible in the relations of production, yet the industry itself is much broader. A broader definition of sex work suggests how the sex work industry has been a crucial part of the expansion of consumer markets. The sex work industry encompasses a set of social practices, many of which may not immediately be recognizable as sex work, as well as a constellation of representations that create demand for sexual services, attach value to such services, identify sexual commodities with race, gender, and age-specific individuals, and rules that regulate this increasingly important consumer market. Feminists argue that class, race, ethnicity, age, and citizenship categories work to position women differently within the global sex work industry. By far, international trafficking of women and girls for purposes of prostitution has received the lion's share of attention. Here, race, ethnicity, and age shape the commodification of women's bodies to determine the value placed on categories of sex workers. The discussions of global prostitution and trafficking of women highlight the exploitation of large numbers of women, yet it is difficult to locate young African American women and the sex work of young Black men within this literature. In particular, women who are not engaged in visible sex work or who do not show up on crime statistics on sex workers are often considered outside the realm of sex work.

Here, I want to pursue a different argument, namely, the case that sex work is permeating the very fabric of African American communities in ways that resemble how sex work has changed the societies of developing countries. In essence, poor and working-class African American youth increasingly encounter few opportunities for jobs in urban neighborhoods while the mass marketing of sexuality permeates consumer markets. In this sense, their situation resembles that of Black youth globally who confront similar pressures in response to globalization. At the same time, the situation of African American youth is unique in that the sexualized images that they encounter are of themselves. In essence, their own bodies often serve as symbols of this sexualized culture, placing African American youth in the peculiar position claiming and rejecting themselves. How might this happen?

From the Bahamas to Cuba, Caribbean societies that depend heavily on tourism recognize how important sex work can be for local economies (Alexander, 1997). These societies recognize how sex work has been reconfigured within their domestic borders, especially following the Structural Adjustment Policies of the 1980s (Emeagwali, 1995). Building on this literature, I investigate how reconfiguration of the sex work industry within the United States has shaped the domestic relations within African American communities generally and for poor and working-class African American youth in particular.

Nigeria, the most populous nation state on the African continent, provides an important case for building such an analysis. Reporting on patterns of trafficking in Italy, Eshohe Aghatise describes differential mechanisms used to traffic women from Eastern Europe and Nigeria as well as the differential value placed on women within Italian sex markets. The trafficking of Nigerian women and young girls into Italy for prostitution began in the 1980s in response to Nigeria's economic problems caused by structural adjustment policies of the International Monetary Fund (IMF) (Emeagwali, 1995). As Aghatise points out:

> [W]omen and girls started leaving Nigeria for Europe on promises of fantastic well-paying jobs to be obtained in factories, offices, and farms. They arrived in Italy only to find themselves lured into prostitution and sold into sexual slavery to pay off debts, which they were told they incurred in being "helped" to come to Europe. (Aghatise, 2004, 1129)

Trafficking of girls and women is a problem, yet an additional issue concerns the use of girls within domestic sex work markets. In a rare analysis of how sex work is organized within a Black society, Bamgbose examines emerging patterns of adolescent prostitution in Nigeria. As she bluntly claims, "the truth is that in Nigeria,

cultural values have broken down" (Bamgbose, 2002: 569). Bamgbose describes how the global sex industry now penetrates into Nigerian society:

> Adolescent prostitution is now out in the open in Nigeria after decades of what has amounted to a cross-cultural conspiracy of silence . . . it has assumed the proportion of a multibillion-dollar industry with adolescents being sold and traded like other mass-produced goods. It is no longer restricted to certain parts of the world; it has penetrated into Nigerian society and is now a thriving business in most Nigerian cities. (Bamgbose, 2002, 571)

Because the men who patronize the sex industry prefer younger sex workers, young women more often service clientele, with older women working as madams who procure the adolescent sex workers. Offering a rare insight into adolescent sex work within an African society, Bamgbose describes how the domestic Nigerian sex work industry operates, one divided into a continuum of activities of the "Sugar Daddy Syndrome," "night brides," "floating prostitutes," "call girls," and finally, trafficking. Under the Sugar Daddy Syndrome, young girls patronize men, usually older in age, for sexual pleasure. Such older men, who are wealthy, are usually referred to as "sugar daddies" or "man friends." They are the favorites of adolescent girls who seek financial and material support in return for their services. The duration of this relationship lasts longer than a one-night stand, and the economic power wielded by such older and wealthy men, irrespective of educational status, puts the young girls involved in a particularly vulnerable position (Bamgbose, 2002, 572–573).

"Night brides" and "floating prostitutes" solicit their clients on the streets of major cities. They differ, however, in several ways. "Night brides" consist of young girls who search for customers on the street for a night of dating. They give preference to foreigners who are able to pay in foreign currency. One important aspect is that some are involved in sex work as a full-time activity, whereas others use it as part-time work. "Many of the part-timers are students in secondary schools and universities who combine prostitution with schooling. They need the money to pay fees or acquire material things, such as clothes and shoes" (Bamgbose, 2002, 573). In contrast to these girls who search for dates for one evening, "floating prostitutes" solicit business during the day and most closely resemble Western notions of streetwalkers. Older men sexually abuse many of these girls in exchange for small amounts of money or gifts, which some hand over to their families. In contrast, college students in the sex work industry were more likely to work as "call girls." In such cases, male or female pimps get in contact with already known and available girls whenever there is a demand for them.

The parallels between Nigerian responses to the IMF's structural adjustment policies and the reactions of poor and working-class African Americans to the social welfare policies of the Reagan/Bush administrations during this same period (1980–2005) are striking. With no jobs for its large youth population, poor Nigerian families learned to look the other way when traffickers commodified and exported its girls and women for the international sex industry and/or when girls saw domestic sex work as their only option. They learned to accommodate a changing set of social norms that pushed young girls toward sex work, for some for reasons of basic survival, yet for others as part of the costs of upward social mobility. Poor and working-class African American girls seemingly confront a similar set of challenges in the context of a different set of circumstances. In this regard, the continuum of sex work from sugar daddies, night brides, floating prostitutes, call girls, and trafficked women also applies, yet in a different constellation that reflects the political and economic situation of African Americans as well as cultural values of American society.

Two important features may shape young African American women's participation in the sex work industry. For one, because African American girls are American citizens, they cannot be as easily trafficked as other groups of poor women who lack U.S. citizenship. Girls are typically trafficked into the United States, not out of it. African American girls do enjoy some protections from these forms of exploitation, yet expanding the definition of sex work itself suggests that their patterns of participation have changed. For another, commercial sex work is not always a steady activity, but may occur simultaneously with other forms of income-generating work. In the global context, women sex workers also engage in domestic service, informal commercial trading, market-vending, shining shoes, or office work (Kempadoo and Doezama, 1998, 3). In a similar fashion, African American girls may have multiple sources of income, one of which is sex work. The "night brides"

and "call girls" of Nigeria may find a domestic counterpart among Black American adolescent girls, yet this activity would not be labeled "sex work," nor would it be seen as prostitution. Restricting the concept of sex work and prostitute to the image of the streetwalker thus obscures the various ways that young Black women's bodies and images are commodified and then circulated within the sex work industry.

"Sugar daddy" and "night bride" sex work may be taking on new life in the context of shrinking economic opportunities. Take, for example, the sexual histories of young, Southern, rural poor Black women. Some women start having sex at very young ages, almost always with older men, and find that they have little ability to persuade their partners to use condoms (Sack, 2001). An informal sex-for-money situation exists, where nothing is negotiated up front. Rather, unstated assumptions, where women who engage in casual sex with men expect to be rewarded with a little financial help, perhaps in paying the rent, or in buying groceries, hold sway. From the outside, these behaviors may seem to be morally lax, yet the impoverished Black women engaged in sex-for-money relationships desperately need the money, especially if they have elderly parents or dependent children (Sack, 2001). This informal sex-for-money situation is sex work. As Kempadoo points out, "in most cases, sex work is not for individual wealth but for family well-being or survival" (Kempadoo and Doezama, 1998, 4).

The consequences of this sex-for-material-goods situation can be tragic. The pressures for young Black women to engage in sex work have affected the rapid growth of HIV/AIDS among poor Black women in the Mississippi Delta and across the rural South. Between 1990 and 2000, Southern states with large African American populations experienced a dramatic increase in HIV infections among African American women. For example, in Mississippi, 28.5 percent of those reporting new HIV infections in 2000 were Black women, up from 13 percent in 1990. In Alabama, the number rose to 31 percent, from 13 percent, whereas in North Carolina, it rose to 27 percent, from 18 percent (Sack, 2001). Most of the women contracted HIV through heterosexual contact, and most found out that they were HIV positive when they became pregnant.

These examples suggest that many young African American women resign themselves to commodifying their bodies as a necessary source of income. They may not be streetwalkers in the traditional sense, but they also view commodified Black sexuality as the commodity of value that they can exchange. These relations also become difficult to disrupt in the context of a powerful mass media that defines and sells images of sexualized Black women as one icon of seemingly authentic Black culture. Young African American women encounter a set of representations that naturalizes and normalizes social relations of sex work.

Black male involvement in the sex work industry may not involve the direct exploitation of Black men's bodies as much as the objectification and commodification of sexualized Black male images within hip hop culture. The prevalence of representations of Black men as pimps speaks to this image of Black men as sexual hustlers who use their sexual prowess to exploit women, both Black and white. Ushered in by a series of films in the "Blaxploitation" era, the ubiquitous Black pimp seems here to stay. Kept alive through HBO-produced quasi-documentaries such as *Pimps Up, Hos Down*, African American men feature prominently in mass media. Despite these media constructions, actual pimps see themselves more as businessmen than as sexual predators. For example, the men interviewed in the documentary *American Pimp* all discuss the skills involved in being a successful pimp. One went so far as to claim that only African American men made really good pimps. Thus, the controlling image of the Black pimp combines all of the elements of the more generic hustler, namely, engaging in illegal activity, using women for economic gain, and refusing to work.

Representations of Black women and men as prostitutes and pimps permeate music videos, film, and television. In the context of a powerful global mass media, Black men's bodies are increasingly objectified within popular culture in ways that resemble the treatment of all women. Violence and sexuality sell, and associating Black men with both is virtually sure to please. Yet the real struggle is less about the content of Black male and Black female images and more about the treatment of Black people's bodies as valuable commodities within advertising and entertainment. Because this new constellation of images participates in commodified global capitalism, in all cases, representations of Black people's

bodies are tied to structures of profitability. Athletes and criminals alike are profitable, not for the vast majority of African American men but for the people who own the teams, control the media, provide food, clothing, and telephone services to the prisons, and who consume seemingly endless images of pimps, hustlers, rapists, and felons. What is different, however, is how these images of authentic Blackness generate additional consumer markets beyond the selling of these specific examples of cultural production.

Recognizing the value of commodified Black culture, many African American rap stars have started their own record labels, clothing companies, and, more recently, sports drink divisions. Their desire lies in sharing the profits of a huge global consumer market of youth who purchase the rap CDs, sports drinks, gym shoes, and clothing lines of hip hop culture. Take, for example, the 2003 release of Pimp Juice, a new sports beverage that was lauded by Vibe magazine as the best energy drink. Despite Pimp Juice's claims that it provides vitamins and that its 10 percent apple juice content makes it healthy, the yellow and white design of its can resembles beer cans. Initially, Pimp Juice was marketed within African American neighborhoods, yet by 2004 Pimp Juice was disseminated by 60 distributors in the United States, in 32 states and in 81 markets. According to its distributor, because Pimp Juice is flying off the shelves in the United Kingdom, the Caribbean Islands, and Mexico, the distributor aims to sell the product in Australia, Japan, China, and Israel. The irony of this particular product is that Nelly, the rap star whose song titled "Pimp Juice" helped resurrect the popularity of the concept of the pimp, also owns the company that distributes Pimp Juice.

The lyrics of Nelly's song "Pimp Juice" make it clear what pimp juice really is and who it is for. Nelly opens his song by boasting that because his woman only wants him for his "pimp juice," he needs to "cut her loose." He then moves on to describe the power seats, leather, and sunroof of his pimp-mobile. When "hoes see it," according to Nelly, they "can't believe it." Nelly knows their game and puts them out, telling them to dust their shoes off so as not to touch his rug. For those who still don't get it, Nelly ends his song with a rousing definition of pimp juice: "your pimp juice is anything, attract the opposite sex, it could be money, fame, or straight intellect." Always an equal-opportunity kind of guy, Nelly proclaims, "bitches got the pimp juice too, come to think about it dirty, they got more than we do." By itself, the song "Pimp Juice" is just a song. Yet when coupled with the music video of Nelly representing a pimp and mass marketing campaigns that put cans of actual Pimp Juice in corner stores for young African Americans to see and buy, the circle is complete.

Implications

African American youths' encounters with Pimp Juice comprise the case examined here, yet the new commodities and new consumer markets in this example point to much larger issues. The hip hop capitalism of Nelly's brilliant marketing of "Pimp Juice" illustrates how sexualized understandings of Black women's and men's bodies and culture become marketed and put up for sale in the global marketplace. It also focuses on new consumers of bodies and images, in particular, how Black people become target audiences for their own degradation (e.g., the case of Pimp Juice) as well as Nelly's plans to go global with this popular product. When it comes to the commodification of Black bodies, few African Americans celebrate the criminal justice system. At the same time, when it comes to the commodification of images associated with prison culture as well as an array of products that signal a seemingly authentic Black culture, Blacks are well represented among the consumers of these images.

This chapter points to the need to develop new frameworks for studying how non-immigrant or native populations fare under advanced capitalism. When it comes to race, globalization literature typically focuses on immigrant experiences catalyzed by transnational labor markets. The new racial/ethnic communities within the United States, Canada, the United Kingdom, France, the Netherlands, and similar white societies garner the bulk of attention, with the core issue being the ability of such groups to assimilate into the host country. Whether voluntary immigrants or desperate refugees, the process of immigration signals leaving behind the unknown for the promise of an unknown and often hoped-for better future. Yet how might we understand racial/ethnic populations with lengthy histories within the borders of advanced industrial societies? Poor and working-class African American youth,

for example, are stuck in hyperghettos with nowhere to go. In this regard, African American youth share much with indigenous populations such as Native Americans, the Maori of New Zealand, and the Aboriginal peoples of Australia who faced conquest and genocide within their white settler societies and/or ethnic nation states. At the same time, because contemporary inner city African American youth are typically a third- and fourth-generation urban population, they share space with the very same new immigrant groups of color for whom America still represents new hope. In essence, this focus on African American youth and similar populations may shed light on what is in store for other groups who find themselves structurally irrelevant in their newly claimed societies. When Tupac Shakur and others of his generation say, "It's just me against the world, baby, me against the world. I got nothin' to lose—it's just me against the world," perhaps we should put down our cans of Pimp Juice and listen.

References

Aghatise, Esohe. 2004. "Trafficking for Prostitution in Italy." *Violence Against Women* 10(10): 1126–1155.

Alexander, M. Jacqui. 1997. "Erotic Autonomy as a Politics of Decolonization: An Anatomy of Feminist and State Practice in the Bahamas Tourist Industry." In *Feminist Genealogies, Colonial Legacies, Democratic Futures* (ed. M. Jacqui Alexander and Chandra Talpade Mohanty), 63–100. New York: Routledge.

Bamgbose, Oluyemisi. 2002. "Teenage Prostitution and the Future of the Female Adolescent in Nigeria." *International Journal of Offender Therapy and Comparative Criminology* 46(5): 569–585.

Behrens, Angela and Christopher Uggen. 2003. "Ballot Manipulation and the 'Menace of Negro Domination:' Racial Threat and Felon Disenfranchisement in the United States, 1850–2001." *American Journal of Sociology* 109(3): 559–605.

Bonilla-Silva, E. 2003. *Racism without Racists: Color-Blind Racism and the Persistence of Racial Inequality in the United States.* Lanham, MD: Rowman & Littlefield.

Collins, Patricia H. 2004. *Black Sexual Politics: African Americans, Gender, and the New Racism.* New York: Routledge.

Emeagwali, Gloria T. 1995. *Women Pay the Price: Structural Adjustment in Africa and the Caribbean.* Trenton, NJ: Africa World Press.

Kelley, Robin D. G. 1994. *Race Rebels: Culture, Politics, and the Black Working Class.* New York: Free Press.

Kempadoo, Kamala and Jo Doezema. 1998. *Global Sex Workers: Rights, Resistance, and Redefinition.* New York: Routledge, 1998.

Sack, Kevin 2001. "AIDS Epidemic Takes Toll on Black Women." *New York Times,* July 3. http://www.nytimes.com/2001/07/03/health/03AIDS.html (accessed September 2, 2015).

Spillers, Hortense J. 2000. "Mama's Baby, Papa's Maybe: An American Grammar Book." In *The Black Feminist Reader* (ed. Joy James and Tracy D. Sharpley-Whiting), 57–87. Malden, MA: Blackwell.

Wacquant, Loïc. 2001. "Deadly Symbiosis: When Ghetto and Prison Meet and Mesh." *Punishment & Society* 3(1): 95–134.

West, Cornel. 1993. *Race Matters.* Boston, MA: Beacon Press.

Wilson, William J. 1987. *The Truly Disadvantaged: The Inner City, the Underclass, and Public Policy.* Chicago: University of Chicago Press.

Wilson, William J. 1996. *When Work Disappears: The World of the New Urban Poor.* New York: Knopf.

Wonders, Nancy A. and Raymond Michalowski. 2001. "Bodies, Borders, and Sex Tourism in a Globalized World: A Tale of Two Cities—Amsterdam and Havana." *Social Problems* 48(4): 545–571.

Questions

1. What does Collins mean by commodities? How is "Blackness" a commodity in the global marketplace?

2. How is exploitation related to commodities and consumption? What role does the body play? Specifically, what do we learn about the consumption and exploitation of Black sexuality and bodies as commodities?

3. What examples does Collins give about the commodification of Black sexuality? In what ways is this commodification exploitative?

4. Patricia Hill Collins is well respected as a pioneering scholar of "intersectionality." How is this approach to theory and understanding the social world reflected in this reading? How would her analysis look different if it wasn't intersectional?

5. What role does the consumer have in the exploitation of others? In what ways can consumers challenge and resist reproducing inequality?

6. Perhaps you have lived or traveled in another country. Where? Did people consume American pop culture? What? How? What about hip-hop specifically? Do some research to examine which pop or hip-hop songs have been at the top of music or video charts of a southern African country, an eastern African country, and a western African country. What images of Black men and Black women were people consuming specifically? How has the globalization of media complicated people's consumption patterns and thus notions of race, nativity, gender, and sexuality? What new images of Black and brown bodies are Americans consuming? How?

20

The Complexities and Processes of Racial Housing Discrimination

VINCENT J. ROSCIGNO, DIANA L. KARAFIN, AND GRIFF TESTER

Since the middle of the twentieth century, racial integration has been the law of the land. In 1954, *Brown v. the Board of Education of Topeka* declared "separate but equal" educational facilities unconstitutional, overturning the standard set in 1896 in *Plessy v. Ferguson*. In 1968, the Fair Housing Act (Title VIII of the Civil Rights Act of 1968) outlawed discrimination based on race, color, national origin, religion, sex, familial status, or disability when selling, renting, or financing housing. This legislative action was designed to correct the racist and class-based housing discrimination epitomized by "redlining," the federal policy of underwriting home mortgages to whites in white neighborhoods. Redlining incentivized segregated living and subsidized white family wealth across three generations at the expense of Black families (Oliver and Shapiro 2006).

Yet in the twenty-first century, white and Black families especially still live in different neighborhoods. Residential racial segregation persists and in some areas remains incredibly high. The dissimilarity index is a common measure of segregation across an area. It ranges from zero to 100 with zero meaning the area is fully integrated and 100 meaning it is totally segregated. According to Census Scope data (Frey and Myers 2015), the Cleveland-Lorain-Elyria, Ohio, area has an alarming Black-white dissimilarity index of 79.7. Another interpretation is that almost 80 percent of these populations would have to move to fully integrate. In short, we are isolated by race despite supposedly living in a post-racial society. How does this continue to happen?

Drawing on Ohio Civil Rights Commission data, this study answers this question in part by showing how dominant groups secure resources through exclusionary and nonexclusionary practices. The authors uncover two general processes through the example of how racial discrimination in housing happens. Exclusionary discrimination includes outright refusal to rent or sell to people of color, false representation of housing availability, unfair financing practices, requiring differential qualifications to rent, and refusal to provide insurance. Nonexclusionary discrimination occurs through harassment, intimidation, and unfair terms and conditions when someone already lives somewhere. The study demonstrates how dominant group members use a variety of tools to distance themselves from subordinates, or ghettoize them, which results in people living in racially segregated neighborhoods.

Excerpted from Roscigno, Vincent J., Diana L. Karafin, and Griff Tester. 2009. "The Complexities and Processes of Racial Housing Discrimination." *Social Problems* 56:49–69. Copyright © 2009, Oxford University Press.

References

Frey, William H., and Dowell Myers. 2015. "Cleveland-Lorain-Elyria, OH, Segregation: Dissimilarity Indices."
    Census 2000 and Social Science Data Analysis Network. *Census Scope*, U.S. Census Bureau. http://www
    .censusscope.org/us/m1680/chart_dissimilarity.html (accessed January 13, 2015).
Oliver, Melvin L., and Thomas M. Shapiro. 2006. *Black Wealth, White Wealth: A New Perspective on Racial
    Inequality*. New York: Taylor & Francis,.

Black-white inequality remains a lingering social problem in the United States, and this is partly reflected in the housing arena (Charles 2003; Massey and Denton 1993). Several explanations for ongoing segregation have been posited, ranging from persistent economic disparities to race-specific housing preferences. The most convincing analytical evidence, however, points to the prevalence of discrimination in housing markets. Central here are audit analyses—analyses that have effectively delineated minority vulnerability and gatekeeper discretion in enacting housing exclusion (Massey and Lundy 2001; Yinger 1995).

Following background discussion pertaining to racial discrimination in housing and what audit analyses have revealed, we embed our focus on discriminatory processes in classic socio-logical concerns pertaining to social closure, power and status, and the interactional foundations of inequality. The aim, in both conception and analyses, is to address the call for "mechanism-oriented" analyses of stratification and its origins (Reskin 2000) by highlighting the multiple processes of housing discrimination that contribute to inequitable outcomes—a call that has been clearly echoed in recent overviews of the housing inequality literature (e.g., see especially Charles 2003; Massey 2005; Ondrich, Ross, and Yinger 2003).

Drawing on unique quantitative and qualitative data, comprised of over 750 verified housing discrimination cases, we ask how the discrimination revealed in these data aligns with the results of housing audits. Are there particular vulnerabilities among victims in terms of race, gender, and/or familial status, and who are most often the agents of discrimination? And finally, how do processes of exclusionary and nonexclusionary housing discrimination play out in real residential settings and what are the implications for victims? We conclude by discussing the implications of our analyses for the housing literature and more general conceptions of social stratification, interaction, and status-based social closure.

Racial Housing Discrimination in the United States

The latest U.S. Census reveals that Blacks, compared to Hispanics and Asians, continue to experience relatively high levels of residential segregation. According to Camille Zubrinsky Charles (2003), Black-white segregation is extreme in 29 of the 50 largest metropolitan areas of the United States, while remaining areas have seen little to no change over the last two decades. Though Hispanic and Asian segregation rates continue to rise, Black segregation remains disproportionately higher (Charles 2003).

How does one make sense of high and persistent segregation levels, even 40 years after passage of the Fair Housing Act? The most compelling evidence, derived from historical case analyses of residential turnover and contemporary audit designs, points to discrimination. Douglas Massey and Nancy Denton (1993), credited with bringing racial residential segregation to the forefront of scholarly debates surrounding the plight of the Black urban underclass with their publication *American Apartheid*, certainly concur that discriminatory action is to blame. They describe the maintenance of the Black ghetto through purposeful discrimination toward Blacks by individuals, organizations, public policy, the real estate industry, and various lending institutions (see also Farley and Frey 1994). Similarly notable are Kevin Gotham's (2002) analyses of neighborhood racial transition in the 1950s through 1970s and Edward Orser's (1994) analyses of Baltimore from 1955 through 1965. In addition, Arnold Hirsch's (1998) historical analysis of Chicago's South Side demonstrates the role of political elites, including government agencies and local businesses, in resisting the in-migration of Blacks from the South from 1940 through 1960. Indeed, and historically speaking, organized resistance has often been shaped by homeowner's associations, tenants' councils, and parent-teacher groups, as well as city coder enforcement agencies, real estate companies, and public school officials (Seligman 2005).

Consistent with case-specific historical treatments are the results of contemporary housing audits. Housing audit (or racial testing) studies have been used for some time by fair housing groups as a systematic means of uncovering actual discrimination. Characterized by two racially distinct, though similarly situated, individuals (one minority and one white), testers are sent into similar circumstances in the housing market. With efforts to control for social and human capital characteristics, such tests have served as an effective way to uncover discrimination and, thus, violations of the law. Although the intent is typically to provide a legal foundation for discrimination suits, audits can provide excellent quantitative and qualitative information on discriminatory practices—practices that are, by their nature, difficult to observe (Yinger 1995).

Beginning in 1977, HUD launched the Housing Market Practices Survey (HMPS), which conducted 3,264 tests in 40 metropolitan areas. The study provided evidence of significant discrimination against African Americans in sales and rental markets. The results of HMPS played a role in the passage of the 1988 amendment to the Fair Housing Act and demonstrated the need for a second national study (The Housing Discrimination Study) which was launched in 1989 and covered 25 metropolitan areas. A comparison of the two nationwide studies demonstrated that discrimination had not decreased between 1977 and 1989 (Yinger 1995). Initial analyses from the most recent nationwide HUD audit indicate that African Americans and Hispanics continue to face significant discriminatory barriers when searching for a home to rent or buy. Rates of overall discrimination may have decreased somewhat between 1989 and 2000, with the exception of racial steering of African Americans and limitations in the financing opportunities and access to rental units for Hispanics (Ross and Turner 2005).

As noted by Massey (2005), interpreting any declines as straightforward "decreases in housing discrimination" is potentially problematic insomuch as such audit testing can only gauge housing *exclusion*. Audits do not and cannot capture what we refer to in this chapter as nonexclusionary forms of housing discrimination—forms that entail harassment and differential treatment *once an individual is housed*. It may very well be the case that prevailing forms of housing discrimination may simply be shifting over time and that housing discrimination has consequently become a "moving target" as realtors, landlords, and others have become more astute to exclusion and its illegalities. Declines may also be a function of changes in state and federal policy that affect the number of complaints filed and/or processed, changes in the overall political climate of the United States, or budget and funding cuts that have impacted fair housing enforcing agencies.

Processes and Dimensions of Housing Discrimination

A focus on both exclusionary and nonexclusionary forms of racial discrimination, and the status-based and interactional processes involved, helps advance our understanding of this particular form of inequality while also informing broader sociological conceptions surrounding the microinteractional foundations of group disadvantage. By exclusionary, we are referring to *actions and practices that exclude an individual or family from obtaining the housing of their choosing*. Nonexclusionary discrimination, in contrast, refers to *discriminatory actions and practices that occur within an already established housing arrangement, most often entailing racial harassment, differential treatment of tenants, or disparate application of contractual terms and conditions of residency*. Our intent in delineating between the two is not to construct a mutually exclusive typology. Indeed, periodically they are mutually reinforcing—a point we return to in our conclusion. Rather, empirically disentangling the two offers insight into the heterogeneity of discriminatory processes, actors implicated, and vulnerabilities and consequences for victims.

Our analytic interest in *processes* of discrimination is consistent with classical theory pertaining to "social closure" and the ways in which it may be activated in the course of interaction. Social closure—a term utilized by Weber to denote the process or processes by which actors seek to maximize advantage by restricting access and privileges to others—often occurs through institutional exclusion and dominant group positioning. It also comes about, consciously and unconsciously, within the context of everyday interaction—interaction that, through language, symbolic acts, and/or physical control or force, has as its aim status-hierarchy preservation and the various advantages/disadvantages that hierarchy affords (Roscigno 2007).

As an orienting lens through which to study inequality, social closure directs us toward an in-depth understanding of the processes through which stratification hierarchies, including those pertaining to race and housing, are both defined and maintained. Especially central are status and power and the ways in which they (1) shape vulnerabilities to inequality and, in our case, discrimination, and (2) are enacted by gatekeepers (i.e., realtors, landlords, banks, etc.) within the course of interaction—gatekeepers who may have *status-based power* derived from their race (and gender) but, perhaps more notably, *position-based power* derived from their location within an institution or organization

Status and power differentials are arguably central to understanding *who the perpetrators are* and *how the discrimination is enacted*. Mortgage brokers, for instance, with significant institutional (or position-based) power, can shape exclusion in profound ways for minority groups whether or not minority group members are aware of such effects. Residential neighbors, in contrast, who may have status-based power derived from their race, can harass and intimidate Black tenants despite a lack of institutionalized exclusionary power. Although such action may not be systematic or aggregate in its consequences, it will nevertheless hold important implications for the day-to-day experiences and social-psychological well-being of minorities in their current residential contexts. Residential landlords are likely an interesting case in point, with some institutional power to exclude. Yet, they may also attempt to reify the prevailing racial hierarchy and draw from status-based power when engaging in nonexclusionary forms of discrimination (i.e., differential treatment or harassment)—a point on which our analyses concur.

Racially discriminatory action is, of course, officially constrained by both law and organizational mandates. Yet, it would be naïve to assume that there is not significant discretion even in the most formalized, bureaucratic environments, or that informal subcultures do not play a role in shaping either individual behavior or the impact of diversity policies (in this regard, also see Coleman 2006; Kalev, Dobbin, and Kelly Dobbin 2006). Indeed, gate keeping actors likely exert flexibility in defining, rather informally, what attributes would make the best client or resident. Moreover, they often have the power to ignore or invoke formal procedures and rules—procedures and rules that are arguably neutral but that may, in fact, be discriminatorily applied or used in targeted, detrimental ways toward a particular group

(Roscigno 2007; Roscigno, Garcia, and Bobbitt-Zeher 2007). Our analyses speak to these very possibilities.

Data

Data were obtained from the Ohio Civil Rights Commission (OCRC). We include as the main sampling frame all cases of racial discrimination in housing filed in the state for the period of 1988 through 2003. The OCRC is mandated to enforce civil rights laws pertaining to employment, housing, credit, and places of public accommodation. The OCRC maintains a data set of basic case information for each instance of housing discrimination filed at any of the six regional offices located throughout Ohio. Ohio's law prohibiting housing discrimination (O.C.R.C. 4112) is "substantially equivalent" to federal laws (Title VIII of the Civil Rights Act of 1968) and, because of this, the OCRC has had, since 1988, a work-share agreement with the U.S. Department of Housing and Urban Development (HUD). As a result of this agreement, and after investigation, OCRC determinations are adopted and enforced by HUD. Thus, these data provide a rich body of discrimination suits from a state that, given the overlap with federal law, the heterogeneity in housing and neighborhood types, degree of urbanicity, and significant minority composition in quite large cities (i.e., Cincinnati, Akron, Cleveland, Toledo, Dayton, Columbus), is a reasonably generalizable case in point.

Such case data, rarely used in research beyond aggregate descriptive patterns of case filings, reflect instances whereby an individual, family, or group had the knowledge that their rights may have been violated and that their grievances might be addressed through a formal political agency. As such, levels of actual discrimination throughout the state during the 15-year time period, though not our particular focus, are unquestionably underestimated (Galster 1987). There are numerous, unreported acts of race discrimination in housing every year—unreported due to lack of knowledge of one's rights, fear of retaliation, or lack of knowledge that certain behaviors are, in fact, discriminatory under the law.

Over the 15-year time period, approximately 2,176 cases of racial discrimination in housing were filed. Of these, 757 or approximately 35 percent were verified by the Civil Rights Commission. Table 1 reports breakdowns of all 2,176 cases alongside the subset of those

Table 1   Cases of Racial Housing Discrimination

	All Cases Filed		Verified Cases	
	N	%	N	%
Black females	1,110	51	431	57
Black males	631	29	220	29
White females	152	7	30	4
White males	152	7	8	1
Other females	44	2	38	5
Other males	87	4	30	4
Total	2,176	100	757	100

verified. Given the somewhat limited population of Asians, Hispanics, and other race/ethnic minorities within these cases and in the state of Ohio more generally, these groups are combined into the category of "other."

Notably, the distributional patterns are relatively parallel between all cases and those verified, with African American men and women making up the preponderance of those filing. Also noteworthy is lower overall verification of white cases—an artifact perhaps of the seriousness with which OCRC takes white claims, but much more likely (given neutral investigative criteria) the consequence of limited evidence and frivolous "reverse discrimination" claims.

Exclusion and Housing Discrimination

As noted earlier, African Americans are by far the most impacted by exclusion. African American women, men, and households represent 90 percent of these cases. This is particularly noteworthy, given that African Americans constitute only about 18 percent of the entire population of the state. Consistent with Massey and Lundy's (2001) finding, derived from a housing search telephone audit, African American women appear to be especially vulnerable, representing 55 percent of the total number. African American males constitute 22 percent and other minorities represent 8 percent, while whites represent just 2 percent.

One benefit of having access to case-specific data is that it allows for deeper inspection of the processes involved, including statements from witnesses and defense statements from perpetrators. It is clear that the majority of cases of exclusionary discrimination (82 percent) entail various forms of outright exclusion,

such as a direct refusal to rent or even negotiate a rental with a prospective tenant (70 percent), refusal to sell or negotiate the sale of a property (6 percent), or the false denial or representation of apartments or homes actually available for rent or sale (6 percent). Outright exclusion is sometimes characterized by the use of overt racial slurs and verbal refusal to rent out an apartment, yet more often consists of subtle actions, such as lying about apartment availability, or relaying differential standards for rental qualification that immediately disqualifies certain individuals.

An additional 17 percent of exclusionary cases are characterized by discriminatory terms and conditions pertaining to the rental or sale of a home, in which the final outcome is a denial of access. Such discrimination, which prevents minority home seekers from obtaining housing, includes: unfair financing or loan qualifications or terms (6 percent), steering or restricting the choices of home seekers (1 percent), differential terms and conditions to qualify to rent a home (8 percent), and refusing to provide insurance, which prevents the acquisition of a home (2 percent). Perpetrators typically utilize legitimate-appearing processes to exclude minorities from gaining access to housing. Applicants, for instance, may go through several steps of the rental or sales process—steps auditors are often unable to take because of their fictitious role as a potential renter/buyer—and spend significant time and resources with the hopes of gaining housing. Yet, they are participating in a false process, tainted with discriminatory practices and conditions that ultimately result in exclusion. Discriminatory advertising is represented in 1 percent of exclusionary cases. Notable is the fact that most cases of exclusion, approximately 84.5 percent, are in rental compared to housing sales.

We speculated earlier that the principal perpetrators of exclusion would largely be institutional actors—actors with positional power to impede or outright exclude. Notably, landlords and owners are most likely to exclude individuals from housing, comprising 84 percent of the cases. Other actors or institutions responsible for exclusion include real estate agents or institutions (6 percent), banking/lending agents or institutions (4 percent), and insurance agents or institutions (4 percent). Whereas owners and landlords tend to exclude outright, banks are largely implicated in exclusion by refusal to provide loans. For their part, insurance agents can reject applications for homeowner's insurance, while realtors in our data either steer or refuse service to potential African American clients. City and metropolitan housing authorities are the perpetrator in only 2 percent of cases. Neighbors, who have no real institutional power to exclude, are predictably absent.

Our qualitative immersion reveals that the overrepresentation of African American women among victims of exclusionary discrimination is, to a considerable extent, a function of the intersections of familial status, race, and sex. Take, for instance, the case of Susan, an African American female with children. She entered the office of a small apartment complex to inquire about an available apartment, and was told that she had too many kids and to "get your Black ass out." The following is taken from her deposition with the attorney general.

Q: Tell me about your efforts to look for another place to live.
A: Every time I tried to find a place, they would tell me I had too many children.

Q: Okay.
A: And that being a single mother and having all those children I was not accepted anywhere.

Q: What type of place were you looking to move to?
A: A three-bedroom home or apartment or whatever, in a decent area for what income I could afford to pay. (After saying she was told by a person on the phone that they would not rent to her.)

Q: Okay, what was your reaction after hearing that news?
A: I got off the phone and I cried to my mom because I couldn't find a home for my children. I was afraid I was going to end up homeless with four children, all because of my husband beating me up. I'm—nobody would take me because I didn't have a husband.

In this case, Susan was repeatedly denied the opportunity to rent an apartment when prospective landlords learned that she had children. She had reasonable hope that she would find a place "in a decent area for what income I could afford to pay," yet was still illegally denied access as a result of her status as an African

American mother with "too many children." This was all the more troublesome given her efforts to escape an abusive situation. The tremendous stress and psychological turmoil she experienced as a result of this process is evident in her stated fear of becoming homeless.

Discriminatory exclusion on the basis of familial status—the presence of children under 18 years of age—is related to stereotypes about single women, especially single African American mothers, and may be impacting the larger patterns we find in these data. Indeed, a significant amount of case materials reveal a similar tendency. For example, in one case, a sales agent asked an African American woman with children if she "was going to operate a day care center from her home," despite the fact that the woman had never operated a day care center before and said nothing to infer she would if the apartment was rented to her. In other cases, the roots of exclusion and its relation to family status are explicit:

Anna Miller, a Black female with children, was told by the landlord that he would not rent to her because "there were too many in my family." When Anna asked if her race had anything to do with his decision the landlord became belligerent. . . .

A witness in this particular case, who is also a Black female with one child, testified that when she asked the landlord if she could have pets he said no. When she asked the landlord why, he told her that she had "no business taking care of pets when she had her hands full taking care of her child." The case investigator interviewed other residents and found that white tenants with children were permitted to have pets. Margaret Sims, a white female tenant, told the investigator that it was her fault that the landlord did not rent to Anna Miller because she (Sims) had asked him "not to rent the downstairs unit to anymore niggers" because the Black family that lived there previously "were terrible." The landlord told Margaret Sims that he "would do his best to find her a good neighbor." Here, the landlord is certainly the culpable party, although a white neighbor is also partially to blame. Additionally, although Anna appeared to suspect that her race was a factor in the landlord's decision from the initial interaction, it was evidence garnered after this interaction, during the investigation, from residents and the landlord himself that made it clear that race was a factor in the decision. In fact, considering that the landlord initially said he would not rent to Anna because the number of children in her family (which is also illegal) and that there were African Americans living in the rental complex, some prospective tenants may not have thought that their race was a factor from such an initial interaction with the landlord.

Exclusion of African Americans occurs not only in rental markets, but also in sales markets, as is evidenced by 14 percent of the cases. Here, the perpetrator is more often than not an agent within a real estate, insurance, or banking/lending institution. Although such discrimination tends to be characterized by subtle and difficult-to-detect processes, such as application of differential criteria to qualify for loans or for a low interest rate, more blatant actions are also evident. Take, for instance, the case of Patricia, an African American female attempting to purchase a home. When initially meeting with her realtor to discuss qualifying for an apartment, the realtor "asked me what made me think I could afford a home costing $190,000." When Patricia complained to the company, she was assigned a new agent, who asked her similar questions. Patricia then directly complained to the new agent that such behavior was inappropriate, yet was told, "It's you people who get on my nerves." The investigation revealed that white housing seekers were not subjected to such rude, blatant questions in their intake meetings.

In a similar case, Terry, an African American male, made a $239,000 offer on a house. That same day, after Terry's offer was received, the white seller accepted a $4,000 lower offer from a white family. During the investigation, the seller told the OCRC that she "seriously doubted [Terry's] ability to obtain financing."

African American couples are clearly vulnerable to exclusionary treatment as well. Michael and Tyree, for instance, were continually asked to verify their income and the source of their income because the lending agent stated that he had to "make sure that their money was not made illegally or from drugs." Like the prior cases discussed, the lending agent here delayed the application process by subjecting the couple to more stringent screening standards than similarly situated white loan applicants, due to stereotypes about their race. The dearth of qualitative case materials, including but not limited to the examples reported here, demonstrate delays in the loan application process—delays resulting in the loss of loan closing "specials" and lower interest rates. Case material also demonstrates that some lenders target African American borrowers with teaser rates

that allow people on fixed incomes to borrow more money than they can afford to pay back.

A somewhat unexpected dynamic of housing exclusion that emerged is the denial of housing to interracial couples. Indeed, immersion into the case material wherein the charging party is either white or African American revealed that discrimination sometimes centers on disapproval of interracial coupling. Desmond, an African American male, for instance, suggests that:

> I was approved to rent on February 22, 1996 a two-bedroom apartment. However, when management found out that Teresa Landon, [white] female, was moving in with me we were both denied occupancy. We were denied occupancy due to being perceived as an interracial couple.

The investigation revealed that Teresa and her children had been living with a different person at the same complex for four months (a [white] male), with the landlord's knowledge, without being on the lease. However, when the manager learned Teresa would be moving in with Desmond, the landlord required that her name be placed on the lease and that she apply for rental. After claiming that Teresa did not qualify to rent the apartment, both Desmond and Teresa were denied rental. What is particularly interesting here is that the African American charging party (Desmond) was not excluded until after the initial interaction with management, when he was identified as part of an interracial couple. Also notable is the subtle and legitimate-appearing means by which the discrimination was carried out (i.e., claiming that Teresa did not qualify to rent the apartment). The investigation, however, revealed that this standard of qualification was not utilized for other white tenants in the complex.

Importantly, and relative to what audits might reveal, other prospective tenants in our case materials were excluded from housing *after* their initial interactions with landlords. For example, a few days after Robert and Hazel, an African American couple, were told that they had gotten the apartment they had applied for, the landlord called back to inform them that they could not move in because he found another tenant with a better income. The tenant who actually obtained the apartment was white, and the investigation revealed that Robert and Hazel's income was more than enough to cover the monthly rent. Similarly, after being told she could move into the apartment and paying the rental deposit, Norma, an African American, was told by the landlord that he could not let her move in because a friend of the family wanted the apartment. As Norma stated and the OCRC verified, the "for rent" sign remained in the window of the apartment long after she was informed she could not move in. During the investigation, the landlord told the OCRC investigator that the friend of the family who expressed interest in the apartment changed his mind and that he did not think to contact Norma.

Exclusionary discrimination remains an important part of contemporary stratification, with implications for housing segregation patterns highlighted in much prior work. African American women seem to be especially vulnerable in the arena of housing searches due to their sex and especially their familial status—statuses that may be providing institutional actors, such as landlords, with shorthand information that can be enacted in discriminatory ways. Whether directed toward African American mothers, African Americans generally, or interracial couples, the qualitative material on exclusion also reveals that the costs of exclusion do not revolve solely around housing access.

Nonexclusionary Discrimination

Racial discrimination discourages attempts to garner housing, often resulting in insult and distress for victims. Such distress is perhaps even more evident in instances of nonexclusionary discrimination, wherein an individual, couple, or family who are already housed experience ongoing differential treatment, harassment, and intimidation. Such discrimination is especially problematic given that the residential victim is often legally bound to a rental agreement or lease, and is often in direct interactional contact with the perpetrator on an ongoing basis, especially in the case of neighbors and landlords. Given what would arguably be significant implications for minority victims' overall sense of safety and well-being, it is surprising that so little attention has centered explicitly on this type of discrimination.

Whereas exclusionary cases are characterized largely by outright processes of exclusion, nonexclusionary cases entail unfair or differential terms, treatment, and conditions. Indeed, 84 percent of nonexclusionary cases involve the application of discriminatory terms and conditions *within the current residential setting of the victim.* The majority of these cases, 52 percent, involve terms, conditions, and privileges relating to a current rental arrangement. Examples include differential enforcement of pet policies within a rental complex, unfairly raising the rent of a select group of tenants, or only allowing certain tenants privileges (e.g., using the pool after hours, having parties, etc.). Thirteen percent of terms-and-conditions cases involve failure to provide equal access to services and facilities. This is typically characterized by purposeful neglect of service needs, such as refusing to fix a leaking bathtub or broken water heater.

An additional 16 percent of terms and conditions encompass discriminatory financing, loans, and appraisals of one's current property, while 3 percent involve inequitable failure to provide homeowner's insurance. In these cases, perpetrators often utilize subtle, financially lucrative tactics that take advantage of minority homeowners in predominantly African American neighborhoods. Finally, and certainly noteworthy, 16 percent of nonexclusionary cases in our data reflect the direct use of harassment, intimidation, and coercion toward Blacks and other minorities. Examples include the ongoing use of racial slurs toward Black residents in an apartment complex, or personal racial threats of violence, rape, or even death. Certainly illegal, this form of discrimination creates a racially tainted environment that victims are forced to navigate, and sometimes on a daily basis.

Who is doing the discriminating? As with exclusionary forms of discrimination, landlords and owners are the largest group of perpetrators represented. Notably, though, they are responsible for 17 percent less of these discriminatory actions relative to exclusion. Through coercion or intimidation, neighbors represent 3 percent of the perpetrators of non-exclusionary discrimination cases. Interestingly, actors embedded in more formal institutions, such as banks or insurance agencies, also appear in these cases. Banking and insurance institutions are the perpetrator 16 and 7 percent of the time, respectively. Qualitative materials suggest that such institutions engage in differential and/or unfavorable terms and conditions in the refinancing of an individual's current home, or the refusal to provide or renew homeowner's insurance for individuals living in predominantly African American neighborhoods. Hence, while these victims are not directly excluded from housing, they often suffer financial loss and/or excessive anxiety and stress as a result of illegal actions of the perpetrator. Finally, city or metropolitan housing authorities and real estate companies represent 5 and 3 percent of cases, respectively.

Qualitative immersion offers some insight into the patterns identified previously, and especially the nature of nonexclusionary discrimination and its social-psychological consequences. Nonexclusionary housing discrimination takes many forms, ranging from racial slurs to responding differently or more quickly to whites who report maintenance problems. And, as denoted by the example that follows, the same individual may experience multiple types of such discriminatory treatment. Alvin, an African American male, claimed he had been subjected to housing discrimination by the owner of the boarding house in which he lived. Specifically, he noted how the owner of the house raised his rent, but not the rent of white tenants.

> Since my first day at [respondent's facility] I have been subject to racial slurs and different rules not imposed on other white tenants. . . . Gordon said he was raising my rent because I was the only one who cooked, and this was causing the electric bill to go up. I informed Gordon that the electric was going up because other white tenants were using space saver heaters. Gordon said, "You lying nigger." After I could not use the cooking facility, Gordon gave me permission to cook on a grill. I came home and discovered that Steve (a white manager) threw my grill away. Steve has been known on numerous occasions to refer to me as "nigger."

The evidence collected by the civil rights investigator substantiated the charging party's claim. Indeed, after interviewing the manager, the investigator notes that, "The manager admits to using derogatory racial slurs while in the complainant's presence, but he claims that he used such words 'in fun,' and that he did not mean it derogatorily." In addition, numerous witnesses provided statements stating that Alvin, the only Black resident, was treated differently than other residents and that white residents who interacted with Alvin were also sometimes treated differently. One witness commented that the owner told him that, "we get this nigger out of here and we'll be back to an all-white building." Thus, although Alvin successfully acquired housing at a point in the past, the antagonistic racial slurs and differential

treatment he was subjected to within this setting resulted in a less than ideal, safe, or secure situation. Undoubtedly, the impact of this experience on the victim's sense of well-being and security is as consequential as, if not more than, that which might have been caused had he been excluded from the housing initially.

The breadth of discriminatory processes is no less extensive in nonexclusionary cases. Bertha and Howard, an African American couple renting an apartment in one of the state's largest cities, filed a charge of discrimination based on repeated harassment from their neighbor who also happened to be the complex's rental agent. They describe what occurred, as well as their interpretation of it as being racially motivated.

> Since October, we have been subject to ongoing harassment from our next door neighbor and rental agent Julia Reynolds. An example of this harassment includes Ms. Reynolds placing trash on our property. We have complained about this harassment to Brian Anderson, Ms. Reynold's supervisor; however, no action has been taken to address our concerns. The neighbor who lives on the other side of Ms. Reynolds is white and has not been subject to such harassment.

A neutral investigation by the Civil Rights Commission found probable cause that the harassment experienced by Bertha and Howard was racially motivated. Though one might conclude this to be a less severe case of discrimination, the mental anxiety, stress, and compromised aesthetic enjoyment of their property over a long period of time, in this case by a neighbor, was quite consequential for this couple. Bertha and Howard paid their rent on time each month and were entitled to the same privileges and standards of treatment as other tenants.

Many cases of nonexclusionary discrimination do take on an even more severe form, such as intimidation and physical threat. Such was the experience of Alicia, an African American mother renting an apartment in a large complex. After several altercations, the boyfriend of her white neighbor (Betty) made several threats. According to the qualitative material and investigative documents:

> Brian Stanley, who is Betty's boyfriend and who is moving on to the property, has harassed Complainant and has threatened to kill Complainant, Complainant's boyfriend, and their "Nigger" baby because of their

allegations against Betty. The property manager, Jason Short, has been aware of the harassment and threats since April, and is still allowing Brian Stanley to move on to the property. Jason Short is good friends with Betty.

Though not all cases are this extreme, the powerlessness and lack of ability to get help from individuals who hold authority (i.e., the landlord/manager) is common among nonexclusionary discrimination cases. In fact, in many of the cases, if the harassment does not cease, the victim must either move (exclude themselves) or seek outside assistance (i.e., from the Civil Rights Commission, an attorney, or a fair housing group). For example, Sandy, a [white] female states:

> . . . that she and her children, four white and one biracial, have been subjected to harassment, racial slurs, and physical confrontations by other, [white] residents. Sandy states that the landlord has failed to take any action to stop the harassment. Evidence indicates that Sandy, her children, and other African American residents and their children were subjected to a racially charged, tainted environment.

Cases such as these suggest quite clearly that conceptualization of housing discrimination need to be broadened to include discriminatory acts that occur within residential settings. In many cases minorities may gain access to housing, yet their daily experiences are far from comfortable. Clearly, housing discrimination is a multi-dimensional phenomenon characterized by dynamic and interactional processes between multiple actors. Moreover, while certainly a large portion of discriminatory actions are aimed at institutional exclusion altogether, others seem more geared toward preserving status and maintaining racial hierarchy.

Our findings highlight aggregate patterns pertaining to both victims and perpetrators, and reveal the sometimes complex, sometimes explicit, and sometimes more subtle forms of racial discrimination that minorities are likely to encounter. African American women are most likely to face both exclusionary and nonexclusionary types of housing discrimination—a pattern we interpret as a function of several factors, including their gender and class status as well as their status as mothers. It is no doubt the case that stereotypical notions of the single Black mother are playing a part in these relations, shaping landlords' willingness to rent, banks' willingness to provide mortgages, and neighbors' levels of civility. Alongside African American women, African American men, families, and even interracial couples face discrimination that is both exclusive in nature and aimed at differential treatment, harassment, and intimidation.

Findings pertaining to exclusion speak to, and indeed are consistent with, the large body of audit research on housing discrimination. At the same time, however, our findings demonstrate that discriminatory forms uncovered by audit methods are present at *multiple* stages of the rental and sales process. Furthermore, our data highlight the actual experiences of minority tenants as they navigate the sales and rental markets—experiences of discrimination that were investigated and verified by civil rights investigators and usually confirmed by witnesses. Findings on exclusion also reveal the ways in which less or more proximate institutional actors play a role. Landlords and owners of housing units are on the front line, accounting for over 80 percent of all exclusionary discrimination cases in our data. We expect that this is actually an overestimate, given that discriminatory actions in lending and insurance are more covert in nature and possibly even unintended. Nevertheless, the institutional power of landlords and owners—power to allow access or not—combined with the face-to-face interactions they have with prospective tenants, sets up the most prevalent situation in which discrimination is both explicit and experienced by minorities. The consequences, as witnessed in some of the exemplary material reported, include exclusion (and the associated costs in resources and delayed time to securing housing), but also stress, anxiety, anger, and despair.

Less often directly studied are forms of discrimination that occur once minorities are actually housed, something we have referred to in this chapter as nonexclusionary discrimination. Such discrimination entails, most generally, differential treatment, harassment, and intimidation and has as its explicit intent the expression of intolerance, the reification of status on a social-interactional level, and even psychological and physical intimidation. Neighbors play a part, as revealed in our examples of biracial couples and families with biracial children, wherein the victims were harassed, threatened, and in some cases eventually evicted from their dwellings.

Interestingly, and somewhat contrary to what we expected, institutional actors (i.e., again, disproportionately landlords) continue to play a quite obvious role in nonexclusionary forms, most often by denying equal treatment to minority persons who are already residing in housing units. While we are not suggesting that nonexclusionary forms of discrimination are necessarily "new," this form of discrimination may become more prevalent as awareness and enforcement increases about what Massey (2005) calls "the classic discriminatory mechanisms" (i.e., exclusion) (p. 149). Housing providers, out of fear of prosecution, may provide minorities access to housing, but that does not necessarily mean that they will be treated fairly. Furthermore, exposure to harassment and intimidation in and around the home or neighborhood on a daily basis may impact minority preferences over time, as the literature on transitioning neighborhoods and neighborhood preferences highlights (for a helpful discussion and overview of this process, see Yinger 1995). The interaction between experiences with discrimination and minority preferences, and the relationship between the two with aggregate patterns of segregation, may only be fully disentangled if scholars incorporate nonexclusionary forms of discrimination into their conceptualizations and research agendas.

Housing discrimination continues to be a social problem in the United States for racial minorities, although the processes of inequality and closure we have highlighted are not merely characteristic of housing. As many of our qualitative materials attest, gatekeeping actors exercise considerable discretion in their decision making, and invoke a relatively flexible set of filters when determining institutional access. Such discretion is also activated in day-to-day treatment and monitoring. This is no less true of other institutional arenas, such as employment, where minorities as well as women face numerous inequalities pertaining to both access (e.g., hiring and firing) and mobility and harassment (e.g., Huffman and Cohen 2004; McBrier and Wilson 2004; Padavic and Reskin 2002; Pager 2003). Discretion, even within bureaucratic or legal bounds, is part and parcel of stratification maintenance, creation, and challenge. As the qualitative materials so poignantly suggest, human beings actively engage in reifying inequality, and victims of inequality are much more than mere recipients of differential treatment. Victims,

instead, often go through a series of steps to try to counter the inequality they are experiencing, including negotiation, avoidance, confrontation, and, in the case of filing a discrimination suit, politically and legally fighting what is unjust.

References

Charles, Camille Zubrinsky. 2003. "The Dynamics of Racial Residential Segregation." *Annual Review of Sociology* 29:167–207.

Coleman, James William. 2006. *The Criminal Elite: Understanding White-Collar Crime.* 6th ed. New York: Worth Publishers.

Farley, Reynolds, and William H. Frey. 1994. "Changes in the Segregation of Whites from Blacks during the 1980s: Small Steps toward a More Integrated Society." *American Sociological Review* 59:23–45.

Galster, George C. 1987. "The Ecology of Racial Discrimination in Housing." *Urban Affairs Quarterly* 23:84–107.

Gotham, Kevin F. 2002. "Beyond Invasion and Succession: School Segregation, Real Estate Blockbusting, and the Political Economy of Neighborhood Transition." *City and Community* 1(1):83–111.

Hirsch, Arnold R. 1998. *Making the Second Ghetto: Race and Housing in Chicago 1940–1960.* Chicago: University of Chicago Press.

Huffman, Matthew L., and Philip N. Cohen. 2004. "Race Wage Inequality: Job Segregation and Devaluation Across U.S. Labor Markets." *American Journal of Sociology* 109:902–936.

Kalev, Alexandra, Frank Dobbin, and Erin Kelly. 2006. "Best Practices or Best Guesses? Assessing the Efficacy of Corporate Affirmative Action and Diversity Policies." *American Sociological Review* 71:589–617.

Massey, Douglas. 2005. "Racial Discrimination in Housing: A Moving Target." *Social Problems* 52:148–151.

Massey, Douglas, and Garvey Lundy. 2001. "Use of Black English and Racial Discrimination in Urban Housing Markets: New Methods and Findings." *Urban Affairs Review* 36(4):452–469.

Massey, Douglas S., and Nancy Denton. 1993. *American Apartheid.* Cambridge, MA: Harvard University Press.

McBrier, Debra Branch, and George Wilson. 2004. "Going Down?: Race and Downward Occupational Mobility for White Collar Workers in the 1990s." *Work and Occupations* 31:283–322.

Ondrich, Jan, Stephen Ross, and John Yinger. 2003. "Now You See It, Now You Don't: Why Do Real Estate Agents

Withhold Available Housing to Black Customers?" *Review of Economics and Statistics* 85:854–873.

Orser, W. Edward. 1994. *Blockbusting in Baltimore: The Edmondson Village Story.* Lexington: University of Kentucky Press.

Padavic, Irene, and Barbara Reskin. 2002. *Women and Men at Work.* Thousand Oaks, CA: Pine Forge Press.

Pager, Devah. 2003. "The Mark of a Criminal Record." *American Journal of Sociology* 108:937–975.

Reskin, Barbara F. 2000. "The Proximate Causes of Discrimination." *Contemporary Sociology* 29:319–329.

Roscigno, Vincent J. 2007. *The Face of Discrimination: How Race and Gender Impact Work and Home Lives.* Lanham, MD: Rowman and Littlefield.

Roscigno, Vincent J., Lisette Garcia, and Donna Bobbitt-Zeher. 2007. "Social Closure and Processes of Race/Sex Employment Discrimination." *Annals of the American Academy of Political and Social Sciences* 609:16–48.

Ross, Stephen L., and Margery A. Turner. 2005. "Housing Discrimination in Metropolitan America: Explaining Changes between 1989 and 2000." *Social Problems* 52:152–180.

Seligman, Amanda I. 2005. *Block by Block: Neighborhoods and Public Policy on Chicago's West Side.* Chicago: University of Chicago Press.

Yinger, John Milton. 1995. *Closed Doors, Opportunities Lost: The Continuing Costs of Housing Discrimination.* New York: Russell Sage Foundation.

Questions

1. Roscigno and colleagues examine the processes of racial housing discrimination and note the importance of examining both exclusionary and nonexclusionary processes. What examples do the authors give of exclusionary processes? What are nonexclusionary processes?

2. Why is it important to study both exclusionary and nonexclusionary processes? Are these processes mutually exclusive, or do they often happen simultaneously?

3. What are the implications for these forms of discrimination for the people who experience them (both the discriminators and those whom are discriminated against)?

4. Both the introduction to this reading and the reading focus on Ohio. Is Ohio a unique case? How might these forms of discrimination occur in other places? What evidence would suggest that they do? Don't?

5. What are the consequences of housing discrimination for other forms of inequality?

6. Income and wealth inequality in the United States is growing. That is, the gap between the rich and the poor is getting wider. At the same time, class-based housing segregation is on the rise so that fewer and fewer people in the United States live in class-integrated neighborhoods. Rather, poor people increasingly live surrounded by other poor people. Alternatively, wealthy people increasingly live next to wealthy neighbors. What are the implications of increasing class inequality *and* class segregation for taxes and the provision of services, such as education, emergency services, and road repair? For politics? For people's perceptions of the class structure in the United States? Historically, what has happened politically and socially during periods of heightened inequality? Are we headed in the same direction? Why or why not?

21

"Tuck In That Shirt!" Race, Class, Gender, and Discipline in an Urban School

EDWARD W. MORRIS

Fifteen years ago, Barry Glassner (1999) wrote about the "culture of fear" in the United States. According to Glassner, the media exaggerate and sensationalize events. In turn, this creates a panic and fear among viewers. Politicians even utilize these techniques in their campaigns to get votes. For instance, a politician might demonstrate that he or she is "tough on crime" by showing that the opponent is supposedly not. This tactic continues even though crime rates are at an all-time low in the United States. One specific fear Glassner focused on in his book was the fear of Black men. He called the chapter "How We Perpetuate Prejudice without Even Trying." In it, he highlights how media portrayals of Black men as violent fuel whites' fears of victimization even though it is statistically extremely unlikely that a white person would be victimized by someone of a different race, much less specifically a Black man. We continue to see these portrayals in crime fiction television shows and local news coverage. The perception of Black men as troublesome raises the question: If Black bodies are the problem, what is the solution?

For many people in positions of authority, the solution is hyper-regulation of Black people on the streets, in stores, and even, as Morris shows us here, in schools. Morris' study of an urban middle school examines how school officials surveilled and disciplined students differently at the intersection of race, class, and gender. Officials interpreted students' dress and manners in ways that reflected their preconceived notions about how subordinated people and bodies needed reform. Disciplining these students into conforming to the styles of the dominant group undercut students' academic performance and bred confusion and resentment. This study demonstrates how associating highly valued characteristics with the dominant group becomes a mechanism for excluding subordinates from opportunities.

Reference

Glassner, Barry. (1999). *The Culture of Fear: Why Americans Are Afraid of the Wrong Things.* New York: Basic Books.

Virtually every day that I conducted research at Matthews Middle School, a predominately minority, urban school, I heard an adult admonishing a student, "Tuck in that shirt!" The prevalence of this phrase represents the connections among dress, behavior, and discipline that composed a primary but unofficial emphasis at the school. In this chapter I incorporate the theoretical concepts of cultural capital and bodily discipline to analyze this concern with student dress and comportment. I show how educators identified students deemed

Excerpted from Morris, Edward W. 2005. "'Tuck in that Shirt!' Race, Class, Gender, and Discipline in an Urban School." *Sociological Perspectives* 48:25–48. Copyright © 2005, ©SAGE Publications.

deficient in cultural capital, especially regarding manners and dress, and attempted to reform these perceived deficiencies through regulating their bodies. This process differed by race, class, and gender as interconnected, rather than distinct, concepts. Perceptions of race, class, and gender guided educators' assumptions of which students lacked cultural capital and which students required disciplinary reform. Although many school officials viewed this discipline as a way of teaching valuable social skills, it appeared instead to reinforce race, class, and gender stereotypes and had the potential to alienate many students from schooling.

Background

One of the most enduring perspectives on social inequality in education has been reproduction theory. This theory, broadly defined, argues that schools tend to reproduce and even exaggerate inequalities of race, class, and gender (e.g., Bourdieu and Passeron 1977; Bowles and Gintis 1976; Willis 1977). Recent research on reproduction stresses the relationship of bodily display and behavior to inequalities in schooling. One line of this research shows that forms of cultural capital, including styles of dress and behavior, influence student success. Another line of research examines how schools discipline, control, and shape students' bodily activity.

Pierre Bourdieu developed one of the most popular versions of reproduction theory. According to Bourdieu (1977, 1984), social status in various fields, or social settings, is strongly tied to certain cultural tastes, skills, preferences, and knowledge, which he terms "cultural capital." People who possess cultural capital understand and appreciate the cultural norms held by those with societal power and have a greater ability to obtain this power themselves. According to Bourdieu, people tend to have differing abilities to understand such norms, or differing amounts of cultural capital, depending on their class position growing up. Research in education has confirmed Bourdieu's version of reproduction theory, especially in demonstrating how various forms of cultural capital result in school success (e.g., Farkas 1996; Lareau 1987; Lareau and Horvat 1999; Lewis 2003; Roscigno and Ainsworth-Darnell 1999; for a review, see Lamont and Lareau 1988).

Here I propose that clothing styles and manners can function as very important and visible aspects of cultural capital. It is often repeated, for instance, that to succeed in the white-collar business world one must learn to "dress for success"—wear appropriate attire to convey the impression of neatness, order, and ambition. In this case, occupational success relates strongly to a particular set of cultural norms regarding clothing style. A similar dynamic certainly occurs within schools: Those students whose dress reflects the cultural styles preferred by those in power should be viewed as successful students.

However, many students, especially those who are poor or racial-ethnic minority group members, are often perceived to lack the cultural background and skills (including methods of dress and comportment) that schools reward. Research finds that the cultural styles of poor and racial-ethnic minority students can irritate many educators, which often leads to the alienation and marginalization of these students (Bernstein 1986; Delpit 1995; Farkas 1996; Gilmore 1985; Heath 1983; Ogbu 1978). According to this argument, poor and minority students have obtained certain knowledge, as well as ways of speaking, behaving, and dressing, from their community contexts.

The forms of cultural capital useful in poor and minority communities often become impediments in the school context, hampering these students' access to education. For example, Valenzuela (1999) describes a mismatch between styles of dress in a poor, Latino neighborhood and that neighborhood's high school. A Latina student, Carla, had been scolded by school officials for her "ganglike attire," which they interpreted as conveying opposition to the school. Valenzuela (1999, 83) explains that Carla merely tried to dress like everyone else in her community.

Adult–student conflict over school standards of dress and behavior is exceedingly complex and may reflect a mixture of misunderstandings, as well as a dynamic of control and resistance. If students interpret the school as strict and uncaring, they could use clothing and behavior in ways that purposely oppose its authority. Youth, especially working-class youth, might use certain styles of speech, behavior, and dress to signal their resistance to middle-class norms, which they experience as oppressive (Foley 1990; Hebdige 1979; Willis 1977). Hebdige's (1979) study of British subcultures, for instance, describes clothing as a particularly important form of class-based youth identity, to challenge the "symbolic order" of bourgeois institutions.

A similar form of style-based challenge exists in the contemporary United States with hip-hop fashions such as oversized baggy pants, conspicuous chains and jewelry, and hooded sweatshirts, to name a few. Although sometimes embraced by white and middle-class young people, these styles acquire a threatening tenor of opposition for many when worn by minority youth, especially boys (Anderson 1990; Patillo-McCoy 1999). However, these styles may just reflect a youth identity that includes relatively innocuous resistance to adult, mainstream norms.

The question of control and resistance to clothing styles and manners leads to a second area of research on social reproduction that focuses on discipline. This research examines how schools attempt to mold students, especially those perceived as lacking or resistant in some way, into embodying what school officials consider proper comportment. Schools exercise this goal, according to this perspective, through persistent bodily discipline, or regulation of bodily movements and displays. Foucault ([1977] 1995) argued that modern control is enacted through techniques of surveillance and physical regulation, or "discipline," aimed at the body. Although Foucault focused his analysis on prisons, he claimed that an array of modern institutions, including schools, use similar disciplinary techniques. Subsequent research in education has pursued this claim and documented that schools attempt to discipline students into embodiments of compliance (Ferguson 2000; Martin 1998; McLaren 1986; Noguera 1995). Schools use this discipline to rework the behavior and appearance of students so their bodies display acceptable, normative comportment.

Schools include some aspects of this bodily regulation, such as dress codes, in their overt curricula. However, they teach most lessons about appropriate behavior, such as which students should be quieter and more docile, for instance, in a "hidden curriculum" (Giroux and Purpel 1983; Snyder 1971). The hidden curriculum tacitly teaches students unspoken lessons about their race, class, and gender (Anyon 1980; Orenstein 1994) and often manifests in how schools regulate their students' bodies. In this way schools produce students who not only learn specific subject matter but also learn how to embody raced, classed, and gendered realities.

Several important studies have examined how schools participate in (re)producing gender (e.g., Thorne 1993), race (e.g., Lewis 2003; Olsen 1997), and class (e.g., MacLeod [1987] 1995). Increasingly, studies have also explored the interaction of gender with race and ethnicity in this process (Ferguson 2000; Williams, Alvarez, and Hauck 2002). This literature suggests that race, class, and gender are not inherent characteristics people possess but identities people work to inhabit and re-create (West and Fenstermaker 1995). Coupling the notions of the hidden curriculum and disciplinary control, some research on schools has focused on bodily regulation in the social reproduction process. Martin (1998), for instance, shows how preschools shape the bodily practices of children, producing girls and boys with gender-specific mannerisms. The schools she studied restricted girls' behaviors more than boys' behaviors. Ferguson (2000) considers race and gender simultaneously in her study of disciplinary procedures aimed at Black boys. The school she studied viewed the dress and behavior of Black boys as recalcitrant and oppositional and attempted to exert strict control over them. Ferguson (2000, 72) argues that culturally based assumptions about Black males made these boys appear as "challenging, oppositional bod[ies]," requiring constant surveillance and regulation in dress, behavior, and speech. In this way, schools react to students based on perceptions of race and gender and use these concepts (in interrelated form) as a basis for specific patterns of regulation.

Literature on disciplinary regulation in schools as well as literature using the notion of cultural capital suggest that schools can engender alienation and resistance from students who do not fit school norms. Students whose cultural knowledge and styles do not fit the school model can feel outcast and confused (e.g., Valenzuela's [1999] example of Carla). Similarly, strict social control from school officials can provoke resistance from students, which causes the school to perceive them as deserving even more discipline (McNeil 1986). This cycle often produces disengagement from school. When cultural capital and bodily discipline relate to race, class, and gender (as they invariably do), this can reproduce these inequalities by generating students who feel alienation from school.

I explore the relationship among race, class, gender, bodily display, and discipline in more detail. Using observational and interview data from an urban middle school in Texas, I expand our view of this problem to include the educational experiences of African

American girls, Latino boys, and white and Asian American girls and boys. I examine how educators' assumptions about these students drove the different ways they disciplined their bodies, especially in dress and manners.

Findings

The Importance of Dress at Matthews

Matthews was a public school but required students to wear uniforms based on the school colors—navy blue, red, or white shirts, and navy blue or khaki shorts or pants. Girls could wear navy blue or khaki skirts or skorts (half skirt, half shorts) that fell below the knee. Most sneakers and dress shoes were allowed, except sandals and boots. The school expected students to have their shirts tucked in at all times. According to teachers, the movement for uniforms at Matthews began about eight years before I started my fieldwork. Teachers told me that this was a collaborative effort between parents and the school, and the few parents I spoke with supported the uniforms. Similar to many urban schools, the uniform dress code at Matthews was intended to decrease gang activity (to rid the school of the "flying colors," according to one teacher) and make student poverty less visible. The regulation of the dress code, however, was a constant source of conflict between teachers and students.

Teachers' profound interest in instilling discipline through dress was reflected in their nearly ubiquitous calls to "tuck in that shirt!" This phrase is peppered throughout my field notes, and although adherence to the dress code was not an initial concern of my study, I soon found it emblematic of the school's exhaustive focus on bodily discipline. According to the principal, a survey of teachers conducted by the school just before I arrived found that dress code violations and discipline problems were among the top issues teachers wanted improved. Indeed, like other urban schools that require uniforms, teachers and administrators at Matthews linked the dress code to student discipline and order in general. The school sent an information sheet titled "Standard Mode of Dress" to each student's home. This document states that the purpose of the dress code is to "ensure a safe learning environment" and "promote a climate of effective discipline that does not distract from the educational process." It describes the dress code and emphasizes in bold print that "baggy and over-sized clothing *will not*

be allowed" (original emphasis). Students who deviated from this code, typically those who did not tuck in their shirts, were often spotted by adults and disciplined into compliance.

For many of the educators at the school, policing the dress code extended to an emphasis on teaching students how to dress "well." Many even coupled this interest with genuine, caring concern for student upward mobility in this working-class context. For example, the school held what it called a "dress for success" day, when students were invited to dress as one might for the "business world." Also, many teachers encouraged their students to dress up when giving a presentation in class, and teachers at the school were expected to dress up (often suits and ties for men and dresses and nylons for women), lending a tone of formality to the school. Matthews devoted entire assemblies to instructing students on how to dress properly.

Thus, beyond the uniforms, the school sought to discipline the kids into wearing clothing considered appropriate on nonuniform school days and events. This discipline served as part of a hidden curriculum, emphasizing strict regulation of dress for working-class students whom adults thought did not possess knowledge of "appropriate" manners and clothing. A Black administrator named Ms. Adams, for example, instructed a group of girls, most of whom were Black, in how to dress for one formal event by warning, "Don't come in here with no hoochie-mama dress all tight up on your butt!" (field notes, 4/12/01). I also observed other school officials, all of them African American women, critiquing girls (who were almost always African American as well), for wearing "hoochie-mama" clothing. These adults appeared to identify the styles of Black girls in particular as overly sexual and sought to reform them (see also Collins 1990).

However, concerns over clothing and appearance were not just directed toward girls. Adults also feared that boys, especially Black and Hispanic boys, might wear something considered inappropriate to formal events, such as oversized pants that sagged below the waist. Several African American men and women at the school encouraged boys to dress like "gentlemen," even giving some practical advice such as not wearing white socks with a suit. In this sense, these boys appeared to educators to display "marginalized masculinities," interpreted as overly coarse and aggressive (Connell 1995).

Educators aimed to reform these styles and behaviors into what were perceived to be mainstream masculine forms. School officials viewed the gendered prescription of dress for both girls and boys as a central part of teaching the students appropriate manners. In this process, they distinguished "street" styles, which they deemed brash, from "appropriate," conservative styles of dress and behavior.

Many adults at Matthews saw making students adhere to the dress code and use proper manners as a way to provide them with social skills, including those needed for future employment. This concern is interesting, because research on cultural capital has rarely examined public institutions that attempt to transmit such cultural skills. A second-year African American teacher named Mr. Kyle, for instance, said this:

> They have to learn to follow the rules—like coming to class late, I won't tolerate that. Or tucking in the shirts. . . . [I]t's a rule and you have to learn to follow it. I teach them to say "Yes Sir" and "Ma'am." It's a way to model good behavior, so that way they're not just booksmart— if they go for an interview for a job, they've got to learn how to talk to someone. . . . [I]f you know how to be respectful, you can get a job. (Interview, 3/22/02)

Many adults thought that teaching students "the rules" of dress and manners, including adherence to the dress code, was an important way to prepare students for future success. School officials viewed their discipline of student's bodies, especially in appropriately masculine and feminine ways, as transmitting cultural capital—modeling the type of dress and conduct that could be linked to upward mobility. However, school officials did not appear concerned with the dress and manners of all students in the same way. Disciplinary action differed according to how perceptions of race and class interacted with perceptions of masculinity and femininity.

Acting Like a Young Lady: Race and Perceptions of Femininity

Aside from "Tuck in that shirt!" the most often used phrase that I recorded in my field notes was some variation on "Act like a young lady!" Adults invariably directed this reprimand at African American girls; I never recorded it directed at Latina girls, Asian American girls, or white girls (although members of these

groups did receive other reprimands). Adults occasionally instructed boys (primarily Black boys) in how to act like "gentlemen," but this was far less common and was never used as a reprimand. Teachers and administrators used the phrase "Act like a young lady" to instruct Black girls in how to sit and get up properly, dress appropriately, and speak quietly, as the following excerpt illustrates:

> As the students are working on Texas Assessment of Academic Skills (the state achievement test) worksheets, Brittany, a Black girl wearing dark blue shorts and a white shirt, gets up from her desk to get a tissue. The action seems perfectly innocuous to me, but Ms. Taylor, a black teacher, sees something unacceptable in it. Before Brittany can get to the tissue box, Ms. Taylor makes her go back to her seat, sit down, and then get up "like a young lady." Brittany seems rather confused by this and seems about to protest but eventually obeys with some huffing. She gets up much slower this time and with her legs closer together, looking at Ms. Taylor the whole time for assurance that everything is correct. Ms. Taylor says, "Thank you, Brittany." And Brittany proceeds to get her tissue while still looking rather perplexed. (Field notes, 3/21/01, 1:00)

In a subsequent interview I conducted with Ms. Taylor, a veteran teacher, she explained why she considered it necessary to teach some girls "ladylike" behavior, as she did with Brittany:

> I talk to them about how a lady talks and walks—I used to put books on their heads, so they would learn to stand straight and sit straight, with no slouching. I've had to say things like "Close your legs—ladies don't sit like that." But there is a lack of parental involvement, and they are not taught these things. Some come in here as young ladies already, but some have to learn. (3/27/02)

According to my observations, the girls adults thought needed to learn this lady-like behavior tended to be African American. One first-year teacher, a Black man named Mr. Neal, told me in a conversation that Black girls in particular required instruction in acceptable manners.

> Mr. Neal talks to me about how important he thinks it is for Black, urban youth to learn how to express themselves in acceptable ways, like through video and film. He tells me: "Like the Black girls here—they lack social skills. The way they talk, it's loud and combative. They

grow up in these rough neighborhoods, and that's how they act to survive. We need to teach them more social skills because that's one of the big problems now." (Field notes, 3/6/02)

Mr. Neal's statement echoes Grant's (1984) finding that teachers tend to focus on improving the social skills of Black girls. As he mentions, many teachers, both Black and white, interpreted Black girls as overly "loud" and aggressive. This was one of the main ways adults thought these girls deviated from their model of ideal feminine behavior, and it often stimulated reprimands:

> I am walking outside among the portable buildings that are used as classrooms while the school building is under construction. It is between classes, and the kids are running around to find their friends, and laughing boisterously, as usual. A group of three Black girls runs by Mr. Henry, a Black male teacher, laughing loudly. This upsets him and he scolds them as they leave: "Hey! You need to act like young ladies!" (Field notes, 5/11/01, 10:30)

In this passage, Mr. Henry is offended not only by the volume of the girls' laughter but also by the speed of their movements. He implies through his gendered scolding of this behavior that the girls would conduct themselves in a more acceptable and gender-appropriate manner if they slowed and controlled their bodily movements and spoke quietly. Adults did not often demand that boys (of any racial-ethnic background) exert similar control over themselves. I witnessed no admonitions to "act like young gentlemen!" for example. Thus, similar to Martin (1998), I find that school officials restricted the movements of girls more than boys and encouraged girls to exert greater control over their bodies. Race appeared to shape the perception of femininity. Educators tended to read the behaviors of Black girls as more stereotypically masculine than feminine and attempted to discipline them into exhibiting behavior closer to stereotypical femininity.

Interestingly, however, this concern with the gendered comportment of Black girls did not seem to affect teachers' perceptions of them academically. Although Black girls were frequently disciplined, they were not viewed as particularly "bad." They were overrepresented in pre–Advanced Placement classes, and teachers frequently described them in "regular" classes as among their best students. In fact, stereotypically masculine behavior, such as the boldness many adults interpreted as "loud," often seemed to benefit Black girls in the classroom. As Mr. Wilson, a veteran white teacher, said in describing some of the best students in his class, "The Black girls up there I don't worry about, they can fend for themselves—they're loud, but they're a sharp bunch and do their work" (field notes, 10/3/01). Although many adults viewed training girls to "act like young ladies" as putting them on the path to upward mobility, their discipline of Black girls seemed to curtail some of the very behaviors that led to success in the classroom. Despite adults' good intentions, this disciplinary pattern could actually serve to solidify racial and gender inequality by restricting the classroom input and involvement of Black girls.

Symbolizing Opposition: Race, Masculinity, and Style

In contrast to girls, adults saw many boys at Matthews as "bad" and occasionally threatening. This was particularly true for Latino and African American boys. In my observations, members of these groups were the most likely to "get in trouble." Unlike that for most girls, this discipline often entailed stern reprimands and referrals to the office for punishment. My findings of the negative disciplinary experiences of African American boys match those of Ferguson (2000). However, I found that school officials at Matthews also considered many *Latino* boys equally if not more dangerous and subjected them to constant surveillance and bodily discipline. The discipline directed at Latino boys was strongly mediated by their presentation of self, however, especially through their choice of clothing, hairstyle, and response to authority (Bettie 2000; Goffman 1973; West and Fenstermaker 1995). Teachers interpreted Hispanic students who projected a "street" persona through their dress and behavior as indifferent to school. Markers of this persona included gang-related dress such as colored shoelaces, colored or marked belts, or a white T-shirt or towel slung over a particular shoulder. However, other markers of this street style were less directly related to gang involvement, such as baggy Dickies brand pants, shaved or slicked-back hair, or refusal to keep the shirt tucked in. Many of these markers appeared instead to reflect a working-class identity.

Latino boys provoked fear in many teachers, especially when the boys were suspected of gang involvement.

One white teacher, for example, referred to a group of Hispanic boys she called "gangsters" as "the type that would get back at you" (field notes, 5/13/02). Although many adults and students told me that most kids affiliated with gangs at the school were wannabes rather than full-fledged members, and I never witnessed any gang violence on or near school grounds, teachers viewed any "gang-related" students as potentially dangerous and disciplined them accordingly. Students suspected of being in gangs were almost always Latinos and were monitored closely by adults, especially in terms of their dress.

For example, many school officials interpreted types of clothing as gang related when worn by Latino boys. Ms. McCain, a white fourth-year teacher, expressed this view when asked in an interview how she identified gang members: "Like if one of my Hispanic boys is wearing all blue—blue shirt and blue pants. The Crips, they wear blue rag." Many students, irrespective of race or gender, wore blue clothing at Matthews, occasionally all blue. Yet Ms. McCain implied that she interprets such clothing to indicate gang membership only when worn by Latino boys.

Discipline and surveillance were especially directed at Hispanic boys who projected various elements of a "street" persona. This persona did not necessarily include direct gang markers but almost always included wearing baggy Dickies brand pants. Many Latino and African American boys preferred this brand of pants and shorts and usually wore them oversized and low on their hips. The choice of Dickies by these students suggests a working-class-based, "tough" identity because the brand is primarily marketed as men's blue-collar work clothing (see Hebdige 1979 for a discussion of other styles of clothing and class identity). Many adults at Matthews, such as Ms. Boyd, an African American fifth-year teacher, interpreted Dickies negatively: "You know how they wear these baggy Dickies pants and stuff—you know where that comes from? It's like how they dress in prison. A lot of them see their older brothers or whatever in prison and that's what they pattern themselves after" (field notes, 4/20/01). For Ms. Boyd, Dickies represented oppositional values. Interestingly, I rarely saw white students wearing Dickies, and only a few Asian students wore them. The brand was overwhelmingly preferred by Black and Latino students, usually boys. This parallels Ferguson's (2000) finding

that school officials viewed many Black boys as "bound for jail." My findings from Matthews expand this view to include Hispanic boys and highlight how something as simple as a style of pants can indicate potential criminality when worn by Black or Latino boys.

However, bodily display, especially clothing choice, had a major influence on how educators viewed and treated Latino boys. The few Latino boys who wore Dockers brand pants and dark sneakers or dress shoes and kept their shirts tucked in signaled to teachers that they were good students. One Hispanic student of this type was named Thomas. Thomas projected a middle-class, "school-boy" persona through his Dockers pants, tucked-in shirt, and parted hair (see also Ferguson 2000). Although I heard him called a "little nerd" by some of his classmates, he received positive reactions from teachers in class. Thomas was rambunctious and did have a few referrals to the assistant principal's office. However, these referrals were not for severe and persistent behavior, and teachers did not interpret Thomas's actions as threatening.

I suggest that this dichotomous view stemmed largely from educators' perceptions of social class. Teachers seemed to hold more polarized views of the potential class backgrounds of Latino students than they did for other students. I found that many Latino students at Matthews actively "performed" (Bettie 2000) class identity and membership, especially through their dress. A middle-class performance displayed the students' possession of cultural capital in the form of dress and grooming, indicating a middle-class or upwardly mobile background and mitigating the discipline they received. Although Latino boys in general were viewed as potentially problematic, social class–oriented signals, in the form clothing and manners, could ameliorate the negative perceptions associated with being male and Hispanic.

At the same time, any display of a working-class street style by Latinos could lead educators to perceive them as oppositional. This was true for boys as well as girls but appeared less acute for girls. Latinas who displayed a street style could be disciplined and seen as "bad" but not as dangerous as Latinos who displayed this style. Teachers suggested that although they believed many of the Latinas were connected to gangs, they did not see them as "ringleaders" or instigators of trouble in classrooms, or as overly aggressive. Some teachers even tried to protect Hispanic girls from boys they suspected of gang activity. Mr. Wilson told me, for example, that he tried to separate the Hispanic boys and girls in one of his classes because he thought that the girls "wanted to do their work:" "I try to give them as much positive reinforcement as possible, so they don't get under the influence of those boys" (field notes, 10/3/01). Teachers could view Latinas exhibiting a street style as oppositional, but they did not see this as the tendency for Latinas in general. By contrast, they did view many Latino boys as inclined to opposition and having the potential to influence others in that same way. Thus, race- and class-oriented style did not really compromise femininity for Latinas or lead adults to view them as resistant, but these factors had important implications for perceptions of masculinity for Latino boys.

Impacts of Disciplinary Control

Several scholars suggest that discipline, especially when harsh and controlling, often engenders resistance and alienation (Ferguson 2000; Foucault [1977] 1995; McNeil 1986). When directed at historically marginalized student groups, such discipline may only perpetuate their marginalization and inequality in the educational system. At Matthews, the different ways in which students and teachers interpreted discipline in dress and manners provides insight into how this discipline might actually reproduce educational inequalities.

Although most teachers at Matthews favored strict discipline in dress and manners, a few did not. A white teacher named Ms. Scott, for example, said this when I asked why she thought so many adults insisted on making the students tuck in their shirts: "Because it's an easy battle. You might not be able to get them to sit in their seat and do their work, but you can make them tuck their shirt in. It's an easy way for teachers to assert their authority over the kids and make it look like they have control" (field notes, 2/1/02). Ms. Scott implied that teachers who did not have enough control over their students to make them do schoolwork could project a facade of control through the regulation of student clothing. Similarly, some teachers I observed also made their students tuck in their shirts before going to lunch while ignoring untucked shirts in their own classrooms. These findings emphasize how important teachers considered the visibility of student compliance with clothing rules and echo Foucault's ([1977] 1995, 187)

assertions that "in discipline it is the subjects that have to be seen. Their visibility assures the hold of power that is exercised over them." Students displaying tucked-in shirts symbolized and embodied the control and order sought by the school.

In contrast to adults, virtually all the students I talked to at Matthews expressed displeasure with the dress code, especially the policy of keeping shirts tucked in. Most complained that the dress code made them physically uncomfortable and stifled their ability to express creativity. The students most persistently targeted for dress code infractions—Black and Latino boys—appeared most resistant to this policy. For example, I tutored Daniel, a Latino boy, on a persuasive paper he was writing against the school's tucked-in shirt policy. I asked him why he thought adults cared so much about this. He replied, "Because they think it makes us look like we're educated." When I asked him why he opposed that, he thought for a while and finally stated, "Because it doesn't matter what you look like to be educated, it's all up here [points to his head]." In contrast to most adults at Matthews, Daniel viewed regulation in dress and manners as unnecessary and asserted that mental development itself should be the primary form of cultural capital that teachers transmit to students.

Student displeasure with the dress code often translated into resistance. This resistance, especially in the form of untucked shirts and baggy pants worn low on the hips, symbolized defiance of the school for many teachers. According to Mr. Simms, a veteran white teacher, "We've tried to get them to wear pants that fit around their waist, but that hasn't really worked. That baggy style with the pants hanging low came from the Black community and the prisons—they use it as a way to defy authority" (interview, 5/8/02). Mr. Simms, like Ms. Boyd, claimed that the baggy style derived from prison dress. But unlike Ms. Boyd, he also located its origins in "the Black community," specifically connecting it to race. Although Mr. Simms thought this style originated with Black prisoners, in other conversations I had with him he pointed out Latino kids who he said used baggy pants as a mode of defiance. Although white and Asian American students also resisted the dress code, adults interpreted their resistance as benign and harmless. Mr. Simms, along with other school officials, interpreted the race- and class-based "street" styles of

Black and Latino children in particular as purposely oppositional. Many educators seemed to think that purging these styles from the school would also purge the opposition. However, as Valenzuela (1999) reported also, most youth I talked to at Matthews wanted to wear baggy pants and untucked shirts not specifically to oppose the school but because this was normative dress among youth in their neighborhood. The restriction of these styles perplexed many students and led them to see the school as an alien, unfairly punitive institution. Because of its restrictions, the school inadvertently transformed the expression of youth identity, encompassing relatively innocuous stylistic rebelliousness, into a mode of subversive opposition. This, it appeared, only promoted more resistance from many students and did little to bond them to the school.

For example, I tutored an African American boy named Derek, who wore baggy Dickies pants and his hair in cornrows, on a position paper he was writing on school uniforms. Derek, a shy and thoughtful kid, explained to me why he was against the uniform policy during a tutoring session:

> I sit with Derek in the library, and he tells me his reasons why he is against uniforms. As I talk to him, I learn that he feels strongly about this and is not just making up reasons for the exercise. One of his reasons is that the kids already have clothes and buying extra uniform clothes makes it more expensive. Another is that the uniforms create a prisonlike atmosphere in the school. He writes that you could compare the students to prisoners because of the control the school uses with uniforms and timetables: "they [prisoners] wear uniforms, we wear uniforms, they have a certain time to eat, we have a certain time to eat."

I ask Derek to explain his point that the uniforms make kids feel like prisoners. He explains, "It's 'cause like everyone is wearing the same thing like in prison." I ask what specifically is bad about that. He responds, "Because it's like we did something wrong, but we didn't do anything. Prisoners are there because they did something wrong. We're just here to learn, we didn't do anything wrong, but it's like we're being punished." (12/10/01, 9:30)

Whereas adults such as Mr. Simms saw the restriction of certain styles of clothing and behavior as eliminating prisoner-like defiance, Derek interpreted this

discipline as creating a prisonlike atmosphere in the school. Ironically, Mr. Simms and Derek seem to agree in their view that Derek is like a prisoner. However, in Mr. Simms's case, this view stems from a stereotypical assumption that guides disciplinary practice, and in Derek's case, it stems from being a target of this practice. Foucault ([1977] 1995) argues that disciplinary institutions such as schools and prisons intend to produce individuals who internalize discipline and regulate themselves. Similarly, the disciplinary practices aimed at students at Matthews, often based on stereotypical assumptions about their lack of conformity, seemed to produce students who internalized these very assumptions. Because some adults interpreted certain dress and behaviors as oppositional or inadequate and sought to discipline them away, this meant that students subject to this discipline could come to see themselves as oppositional or inadequate.

Conclusion

Schools teach children many lessons. These lessons often transgress the formal elements of overt curricula and instruct children how to speak, what to wear, how to move their bodies, and, ultimately, how to inhabit different race, class, and gender positions. At Matthews, school officials helped implement and regulate dress and manners out of an expressed, genuine desire to help students. Left hidden, however, were the assumptions of which students needed this discipline, and in what form.

I want to highlight two ways in which this study advances our understanding of inequality in education. First, it demonstrates how the production of difference and inequality in schooling takes place not just through gender, or just through race, or just through class, but through all of these at once. Similar to Collins's (1990) concept of a "matrix of domination," race, class, and gender interrelate to profoundly alter one another in guiding expectations and sanctions of young people. My study suggests that race, class, and gender profoundly alter each other in framing perceptions of different students, which translates into different methods of regulating and shaping their behaviors. Examining organizational discipline at these intersections is crucial to developing a more nuanced understanding of the role of schools in producing and reproducing social inequalities.

Adults not only viewed Black boys as dangerously masculine, as Ferguson (2000) finds, but also viewed Black girls as inadequately feminine. This perception of Black girls influenced educators to restrict behaviors perceived as loud and aggressive, even though these very behaviors aided Black girls in the classroom. Although not always producing the intended results, the discipline adults directed at Black girls aimed to mold these energetic girls into models of quiet compliance and deference. In this way, perceptions of race can work through perceptions of masculinity and femininity to guide how adults approach different youths, resulting in different ways that race and gender inequality can manifest in school settings.

For Latinos in this urban, southwestern setting, "brownness" worked somewhat differently when combined with gender and social class perceptions. School officials did not view Latinas as inadequately feminine but did view many Latino boys as potentially aggressively masculine, similar to popular culture characterizations of dangerous Latino masculinity (see Fregoso 1993, 29). Latino boys in this setting endured adult assumptions that because of their race and gender, they had the potential for danger and should be monitored and disciplined accordingly.

Overcoming this assumption required displays of cultural capital from Latino boys in the form of dress and manners not required of other students (especially white and Asian American students, whose race often seemed to represent cultural capital in itself) (see also Lareau and Horvat 1999). Through these displays, Latino boys could signal a middle-class background, which reduced the surveillance and discipline directed at them. By contrast, adults viewed Latinos and Latinas who displayed a non-middle-class "street-based" persona as oppositional. The negative perceptions of this class-based display were especially acute for Latino boys, however. Thus, for Latino boys in particular, adults' perceptions of their class could alter perceptions of their race and masculinity.

When adopted by white and Asian American students, a street-based style elicited some discipline but seemed to be less menacing to educators. In this way, race modified perceptions of class- and gender-based behavior. Even when these students affected a street style almost identical to that of Black and Latino youth, educators typically interpreted white and Asian American boys as harmless and white girls as well mannered. "Whiteness" and "Asianness," although partially qualified by class-based performative display, appeared to indicate docility and normative masculinity and femininity. Educators assumed at the outset that white and Asian American students did not need disciplinary reform, which only solidified their connection to educationally valuable forms of cultural capital in dress and manners. These examples point to the complex ways in which race, class, and gender combined to shape perceptions and regulations of students at Matthews.

Educators' identification of which students lacked cultural capital was greatly influenced by their perceptions of students' race, class, and gender. Students identified as lacking or resistant would never measure up to those whose race and class position suggested the possession of social skills in and of itself. In addition, the methods for transmitting and instilling this form of cultural capital involved persistent bodily discipline, which many students experienced as confusing and alienating. My observations suggest that students targeted for disciplinary reform can internalize the discipline aimed at them, and while for some this may lead to self-regulation and complicity, for others it could produce resistance and disengagement from school.

References

Anderson, Elijah. 1990. *Streetwise: Race, Class, and Change in an Urban Community.* Chicago: University of Chicago Press.

Anyon, Jean. 1980. "Social Class and the Hidden Curriculum of Work." *Journal of Education* 162:67–92.

Bernstein, Basil. 1986. "On Pedagogic Discourse." In *Handbook of Theory and Research for the Sociology of Education* (ed. J. G. Richardson), 205–240. New York: Greenwood Press.

Bettie, Julie. 2000. "Women without Class: *Chicas, Cholas,* Trash, and the Presence/Absence of Class Identity." *Signs* 26:1–35.

Bourdieu, Pierre. 1977. "Cultural Reproduction and Social Reproduction." In *Power and Ideology in Education* (ed. J. Karabel and A. H. Halsey), 487–511. New York: Oxford University Press.

———. 1984. *Distinction: A Social Critique of the Judgment of Taste.* Cambridge, MA: Harvard University Press.

Bourdieu, Pierre, and Jean-Claude Passeron. 1977. *Reproduction in Education, Society, and Culture.* London: Sage.

Bowles, Samuel, and Herbert Gintis. 1976. *Schooling in Capitalist America: Educational Reform and the Contradictions of Economic Life.* New York: Basic Books.

Collins, Patricia Hill. 1990. *Black Feminist Thought: Knowledge, Consciousness, and the Politics of Empowerment.* New York: Routledge.

Connell, R. W. 1995. *Masculinities.* Berkeley: University of California Press.

Delpit, Lisa. 1995. *Other People's Children: Cultural Conflict in the Classroom.* New York: Free Press.

Farkas, George. 1996. *Human Capital or Cultural Capital? Ethnicity and Poverty Groups in an Urban School District.* New York: Aldine de Gruyter.

Ferguson, Ann Arnett. 2000. *Bad Boys: Public Schools in the Making of Black Masculinity.* Ann Arbor: University of Michigan Press.

Foley, Douglas E. 1990. *Learning Capitalist Culture: Deep in the Heart of Tejas.* Philadelphia: University of Pennsylvania Press.

Foucault, Michel. [1977] 1995. *Discipline and Punish.* 2nd ed. (trans. A. Sheridan). New York: Vintage.

Fregoso, Rosa Linda. 1993. *The Bronze Screen: Chicana and Chicano Film Culture.* Minneapolis: University of Minnesota Press.

Gilmore, Perry. 1985. "'Gimme Room': School Resistance, Attitude, and Access to Literacy." *Journal of Education* 167:111–128.

Giroux, Henry, and David Purpel. 1983. *The Hidden Curriculum and Moral Education.* Berkeley, CA: McCutchan.

Goffman, Erving. 1973. *The Presentation of Self in Everyday Life.* New York: Overlook Press.

Grant, Linda. 1984. "Black Females' 'Place' in Desegregated Classrooms." *Sociology of Education* 57:98–111.

Heath, Shirley Brice. 1983. *Ways with Words.* Cambridge: Cambridge University Press.

Hebdige, Dick. 1979. *Subculture: The Meaning of Style.* London: Routledge.

Lamont, Michelle, and Annette Lareau. 1988. "Cultural Capital: Allusions, Gaps, and Glissandos." *Sociological Theory* 6:153–168.

Lareau, Annette. 1987. "Social Class and Family-School Relationships: The Importance of Cultural Capital." *Sociology of Education* 56:73–85.

Lareau, Annette, and Erin McNamara Horvat. 1999. "Moments of Social Inclusion and Exclusion: Race, Class, and Cultural Capital in Family-School Relationships." *Sociology of Education* 72:37–53.

Lewis, Amanda E. 2003. *Race in the Schoolyard: Negotiating the Color Line in Communities and Classrooms.* New Brunswick, NJ: Rutgers University Press.

MacLeod, Jay. [1987] 1995. *Ain't No Makin' It.* 2nd ed. Boulder, CO: Westview Press.

Martin, Karin A. 1998. "Becoming a Gendered Body: Practices of Preschools." *American Sociological Review* 63:494–511.

McLaren, Peter. 1986. *Schooling as a Ritual Performance: Towards a Political Economy of Educational Symbols and Gestures.* London: Routledge and Kegan Paul.

McNeil, Linda M. 1986. *Contradictions of Control: School Structure and School Knowledge.* New York: Routledge.

Noguera, Pedro A. 1995. "Preventing and Producing Violence: A Critical Analysis of Responses to School Violence." *Harvard Educational Review* 65:189–212.

Ogbu, John. 1978. *Minority Education and Caste: The American System in Cross Cultural Perspective.* Orlando, FL: Academic Press.

Olsen, Laurie. 1997. *Made in America: Immigrant Students in Our Public Schools.* New York: New Press.

Orenstein, Peggy. 1994. *School Girls: Young Women, Self-Esteem, and the Confidence Gap.* New York: Doubleday.

Patillo-McCoy, Mary. 1999. *Black Picket Fences: Privilege and Peril among the Black Middle Class.* Chicago: University of Chicago Press.

Roscigno, Vincent J., and James W. Ainsworth-Darnell. 1999. "Race, Cultural Capital, and Educational Resources: Persistent Inequalities and Achievement Returns." *Sociology of Education* 72:158–178.

Snyder, Benson R. 1971. *The Hidden Curriculum.* New York: Knopf.

Thorne, Barry. 1993. *Gender Play: Girls and Boys in School* by Barrie Thorne. New Brunswick, NJ: Rutgers University Press.

Valenzuela, Angela. 1999. *Subtractive Schooling: U.S.-Mexican Youth and the Politics of Caring.* Albany: State University of New York Press.

West, Candace, and Sarah Fenstermaker. 1995. "Doing Difference." *Gender and Society* 9:8–37.

Williams, L. Susan, Sandra D. Alvarez, and Kevin S. Andrade Hauck. 2002. "My Name Is Not Maria: Young Latinas Seeking Home in the Heartland." *Social Problems* 49:563–584.

Willis, Paul. 1977. *Learning to Labor.* New York: Columbia University Press.

Questions

1. How do schools regulate and discipline bodies? Why did this school enact a dress code?
2. What is cultural capital, and how is it related to race, gender, and class inequality?
3. Give specific examples of how school personnel enforced the dress code. How did this vary by the race, gender, and class of the student? How was discipline related to raced, gendered, and classed stereotypes?
4. How did discipline result in exclusion from school? How might varying degrees and forms of discipline be consequential for the students in other ways?
5. Morris, like Collins, calls attention to Black bodies. While Collins focuses on commodification and exploitation, Morris is more attentive to discipline and exclusion. Comparing these two chapters and these processes, what have we learned about the reproduction of racial inequalities, and how are these connected to gender, class, and sexuality?
6. Who else's bodies are hyper-regulated in the United States? In what ways?

22

The Displaced and Dispossessed of Darfur: Explaining the Sources of a Continuing State-Led Genocide

JOHN HAGAN AND JOSHUA KAISER

Sadly, mass killings have taken place throughout history and in every corner of the globe. There is still debate on whether or not some events constitute genocide. At the least, tens of thousands of Native Americans in the United States died in conflicts with colonists. The Indian Removal Act, more commonly known as the "Trail of Tears," forcibly moved Native Americans from the southeastern United States to reservations west of the Mississippi River. More recently, voluntary relocation programs emerged during the 1940s and 1950s (Indian Relocation Act of 1956) with the goal of terminating tribes and getting Native Americans to move to urban areas and assimilate to "American" culture. Yet, these actions are not formally classified as genocide.

The case of Native Americans in the United States highlights the importance of controlling space, forced migration, and the control of food and water resources. The following study also represents a contested "genocide." The authors show how Sudanese political leaders not only enacted elimination of a group of people through mass killings and rapes but also through systematic, state-led attacks on water and food. The result was the displacement of millions of Black Africans.

There is increasing convergence and growing confidence in estimates of the mortality and forced migration associated with the conflict that began in 2003 and is still ongoing in Darfur. The estimates are that from 200,000 to 400,000 Darfurians have died (Degomme and Guha-Sapir 2010; Hagan and Palloni 2006) and that from 2 million to 3 million Darfurians have been involuntarily displaced from their homes (United Nations 2005). The death toll speaks to the issue of the partial *extermination* of groups in Darfur, while the displacement numbers address the prospect of their *elimination* from Darfur (de Waal 2005). The International Criminal Court [ICC] identifies the Black Africans who are the predominant victims of this death and displacement as members of the Zaghawa, Masalit, and the Fur ethnic groups, while this Court identifies the perpetrators as heads of Arab Janjaweed militias and leadership figures in the Government of Sudan, including President Omar al-Bashir and then Deputy Minister Ahmad Harun (Office of the Prosecutor 2008).

The 1948 Genocide Convention defines genocide as "acts committed with intent to destroy, in whole or in part, a national, ethnical, racial or religious group" (United Nations 1948: Article II) including, in addition to killing, "deliberately inflicting on the groups conditions of life calculated to bring about its physical destruction in whole or in part" (United Nations 1948: Article II). This definition identifies both mortality and forced migration—death and displacement—as key elements of extermination and elimination constituting genocide. The inclusion of extermination in the genocide convention definition is an obvious consequence of the context of its drafting in the shadow of the Nazi Holocaust. The further reference to elimination is a potentially farther reaching element of this convention that makes the meaning of genocide relevant to a wider range of conflicts than a singular reference to extermination would allow. The element of elimination expands the meaning of genocide beyond immediate wholesale killing to include the intentional creation of physical and social conditions leading to the destruction of individual communities, as well as in multiple communities and whole nations.

Even though the ICC Chief Prosecutor, Luis Moreno-Ocampo, resisted until 2008 calling Darfur genocide, he nonetheless had already remarked that "this strategy has been seen before" (Office of the

Prosecutor 2005, 93). He explained what he meant with an example from the conflict in the former Yugoslavia, noting that,

> In March 1995, President of Srpska Radovan Karadzic . . . issued Directive 7. It specified that the Republika Srpska was to "by planned and well-thought out combat operations, create an unbearable situation of total insecurity with no hope of further survival or life for the inhabitants of Srebrenica." The parallel to Darfur is clear.

The International Criminal Tribunal for the former Yugoslavia (United Nations 2005) had previously found that genocide had occurred in the former Yugoslavian town of Srebrenica in the mid-1990s. This judgment is a precedent for Moreno-Ocampo's analysis by citing both evidence of the selective killing of young adult ("fighting age") men and the forced displacement of women and children, which made it "impossible for the Bosnian Muslim people of Srebrenica to survive" (Office of the Prosecutor 2005). The killing *combined with forced displacement to eliminate* Bosnian Muslims from Srebrenica, ending an era of group life in this community. Prosecutor Moreno-Ocampo did not seek a genocide charge against President Al-Bashir of Sudan for the massive crimes in Darfur until 2008, and the Pre-Trial Chambers of the ICC only finally authorized a warrant for the arrest of Al-Bashir to stand trial for genocide in 2010, more than five years after the crimes took place.

Analysts of genocide in general, as well as public and political discourse, far more often focus on death and extermination than on displacement and elimination, and this has been true in Darfur as well as elsewhere (but see Physicians for Human Rights 2006). De Waal (2005, xix) underlines the particular importance of this point in context of Darfur by noting that

> What is happening in Darfur is not Genocide (capitalized) in this sense of the absolute extermination of a population. It does, however, fit the definition contained in the Genocide Convention, which is much broader and encompasses systematic campaigns against ethnic groups with the intention of eliminating them in whole or in part.

It is important to note that de Waal does not conclude that the ICC should charge President Al-Bashir with genocide; he instead argues that "an effective response to Darfur's crisis will be complicated, comprehensive, and long" (2005, xix).

Explaining State-Led Elimination by Displacement in Darfur

As we have noted, explanations of genocide in general, and specifically of the genocide in Darfur, have focused on death and extermination more than on displacement and elimination. Yet, there is even greater consensus about the massiveness of the numbers of displacements than deaths, and the elimination of Black African group life as it previously existed in Darfur arguably is even more comprehensively imposed by the displacements than by the deaths. Explanations need to take this reality into account.

Explanations of state-led elimination by displacement in Darfur must attend to the motive and intent of the perpetrators and the vulnerability, and especially the food and water insecurity, of the victims. It can be argued that, when it comes to crime, vulnerability is opportunity and that opportunity itself provides the motivation that shapes intent (cf. Gottfredson and Hirschi 1990, 24). The environmental pressures of desertification are an exogenous constant in Darfur, and in this sense it is correct to say that possession of arable land is everything in the Darfur conflict.

Black African groups have long possessed arable farm land in Darfur, but they did not individually or collectively possess sufficient arms or military means to protect their farms and villages, and this vulnerability presented an opportunity for landless Arab groups. While a number of Arab herding groups also have had recognized claims to land in Darfur, several northern Rizeigat groups have not, and these groups are key participants in the Janjaweed militia accused of attacking the Black African farming groups. Libya's Muammar al-Gaddahi helped arm the militias, who were already arming themselves and were fed, uniformed, and further armed by the Sudanese government, which has recruited the militias into the People's Defence Force (PDF).

The intent to take land from Black African farming groups played an explicit part in the mobilization and training of the militias. Musa Hilal asserted that the Black African groups had settled and farmed land that originally belonged to Arab groups. In the context of growing desertification and an increasingly desperate need for grazing land and water, Hilal's claims and ensuing threats

became a salient "crisis framing" of the situation in Darfur (Hagan and Rymond-Richmond 2008).

There are many accounts of how this crisis framing was expressed. A *Washington Post* journalist, Emily Wax (2004), gained access to the training camps and reported that the militia prepared for attacks by singing war songs proclaiming, "We go to the war. We go to defeat the rebels. We are not afraid of war. We are the original people of the area." Samantha Power (2004, 9) reported in the *New Yorker* an interview with a defector who described men in a camp parading around singing songs challenging local Africans with claims that "We are lords of this land. You Blacks do not have any rights here."

The racial characterization of the conflict in Arab-African terms is contested if not controversial, and it is important to emphasize that our focus is on the use of race as a socially constructed motivational tactic in Darfur. De Waal (2005, xiv) emphasizes the contemporary and externally driven origins of this social construction:

> Darfur's Arab-African dichotomy is an ideological construct that has emerged very recently, largely as a result of events outside the region. Arab supremacism in Darfur was born in 1987 along with the region's "Arab Alliance," which owes more to Khartoum and Libya than to any realities in Darfur. This in turn led Fur and Masalit militants to adopt the label "African," emphasizing a common political identity with Southerners and the Nuba.

The tracing of the racialization of the conflict to Khartoum speaks in particular to the issue of state leadership.

Prunier (2005, 162) links the racial motivation and intent in Darfur to its land-based environmental foundation, noting that the 1984 famine sharpened the divide between the nomadic herders and farmers and that now this dichotomy is superimposed on an Arab versus African dichotomy, with state-led agency. He concludes that, "This marked the beginning of years of low-intensity racial conflict and harassment, with the 'Arab' Centre almost automatically siding against the 'African Periphery.'" The Sudanese government defined "Arab" as good, and "African" as bad.

In Darfur, state-authorized agents, such as Ahmad Harun, integrated the local Janjaweed militia with the PDF and local police (Office of the Prosecutor 2007, 40). Locally organized indoctrination included instruction in "us" and "them" distinctions that escalated from demeaning and degrading to dehumanizing characterizations. These included attributions of subordinate, slave, and sub-human statuses. Racial epithets constituted the hooks for the dehumanization leading to elimination and extermination. The dehumanizing logic and intention was clear, for as Dower (1986, 89) brutally explains and our analysis will further assess, "it is . . . easier to kill animals than humans." Of course, not only killing but displacement and elimination are made easier by dehumanization as well.

Our thesis is that the racial epithets heard during attacks in Darfur were transformed into motive and intent and expressed in an eliminationist frenzy to drive the Black African groups in Darfur from their lands. Attackers shouting racial epithets undertook ground assaults on African villages. These epithets in Darfur involve tropes of slavery and sub-humanity:

> They called her Nuba [a derogatory term for Black Africans], dog, sons of dogs, and we
> came to kill you and your kids.
> You donkey, you slave; we must get rid of you.
> You blacks are not human. We can do anything we want to you. You cannot live here.
> We kill our cows when they have black calves—we will kill you too.
> All the people in the village are slaves; you make the area dirty; we are here to clean the area.
> You blacks are like monkeys. You are not human.
> Black prostitute, whore; you are dirty—black.
> We will kill any slaves we find and cut off their heads.
> The government has ordered anyone black to be killed—even the black birds.

These words and phrases shouted by the perpetrators are explicit evidence of dehumanizing motivations and intentions during attacks on Black African villagers. Prunier (2005, 165) captures the significance of this racialization when he concludes that since Darfur had been in a state of protracted racial civil war since the mid-1980s, the tools were readily available; they merely needed to be upgraded. It was done and the rest is history.

Thus, the government of Sudan helped train and joined its forces with the Janjaweed militia in organized attacks on Black African groups. However, it is also essential to understand that the perpetrators took special advantage of the vulnerability and insecurity of the latter groups by systematically attacking their food and water supplies, so that these groups would no longer be able to sustain their lives in their farms and villages. This vulnerability, of course, intensified in the context and against the backdrop of the increasing desertification of Darfur.

De Waal's (2005) classic research on famine previously has revealed the adaptiveness of Black African survival strategies during the mid-1980s in Darfur. One of the most remarkable findings of this work was that members of these groups would store meager amounts of grain and seeds through even the last painful stages of starvation: they would actually die with remaining hidden and unconsumed amounts of grain and seeds. Thus, Darfurians practiced especially well-developed and interdependent coping strategies within their villages that they had learned during droughts and famines. For example, villages would build communal wells that were operated both by hand and with pumps, where they could afford them. There were also private wells, and, in the rainy season, water was also drawn from the *wadis* around which the villages were often built.

Preserving access to food and water as a risk-management strategy of survival was understood as among the highest priorities in these villages, even in the face of death. The Sudanese government and the attacking Arab groups recognized this vulnerability and insecurity, and they targeted food and water supplies with scorched earth tactics aimed at overwhelming these communal survival strategies. They recognized that if they could dislodge and displace villagers from their homes and communities, they would in addition be highly vulnerable to the scorching heat and wind in the desert, and therefore also vulnerable to starvation, dehydration, and disease.

Attacks on food and water supplies were powerful weapons for displacement and genocidal elimination, which underlines the overlapping explanatory importance of famine and genocide to one another. The joined forces of the government and the Janjaweed militias coordinated their attacks not only to kill and rape, but also to systematically burn all homes and crops, steal and kill all livestock, poison and destroy all wells, seek out and destroy all food stores, and uproot and kill all trees.

These were attacks designed to eliminate as well as exterminate Black African groups in Darfur. These attacks might be called famine crimes as well as crimes of genocide (de Waal 2005). De Waal (2005, xii) observes that "Ethnographers of famine and genocide have much to learn from one another. . . . In Darfur today, where much violence is directed at destroying livelihoods . . . the convergence is evident."

Displacement and the Atrocities Documentation Survey

The U.S. State Department's Atrocities Documentation Survey [ADS] (see Howard 2006) was conducted in July and August 2004 in preparation for Colin Powell's testimony before Congress and the UN Security Council. The Survey was conducted in and around the refugee camps in Chad and provides a unique opportunity to study displacement processes in an ongoing genocide. The ADS team proportionately sampled in relation to size and ethnicity within sectors of the camps and informal refugee villages. The survey cost nearly a million dollars to conduct and includes 1,136 respondents. This analysis is based on 932 of these respondents who fled from 22 originating village clusters (henceforth called "villages") that had 15 or more respondents each included in the survey.

A limitation of the ADS for our purposes is that it includes only displaced Darfurians who ultimately fled to Chad. However, we focus on incidents of reported displacement, including displacements prior to fleeing to Chad. As well, population pyramids from displacement camps within Darfur are similar with regard to age and gender to those in Chad. Probably as a result of targeted killing, both Chadian and Darfurian camps have a disproportionate absence of fighting-age men (ages 18–29 years). There are no indications that the Darfur refugees in Chad differ in significant ways from internally displaced Darfurians in the bordering areas.

The average refugee in the sample was 37 years old. The sample was about 60 percent female and 40 percent male, reflecting the reduced representation of fighting-age men. About half were Zaghawa (52 percent), about one fourth Masalit (27 percent), and about one twentieth Fur (5.5 percent), with the remainder from other ethnic groups (14 percent).

The survey was conducted as the second of the two major waves of attacks was abating [and] the survey collected specifically *dated* information about 35 kinds of criminal victimization linked to displacements—including the burning of homes, killings, and attacks on food and water supplies, and . . . the survey included reports of hearing racial epithets during the attacks and information about the attackers, as well as information about rebel activity in the area of the attacks. The attackers were coded as belonging either to government forces or Janjaweed militia by categorization of clothing and equipment reported by interviewees.

It is especially important that the ADS included dated information about the attacks. This allows our analysis to consider the genocide as an unfolding *process*. Genocide is, of course, a dynamic rather than a static phenomenon, even when it occurs in an explosive rather than a more drawn out process, as it has in Darfur.

Findings from Survey Interviews and Proportional Hazard Models

Our analysis is based on estimations of standard semi-parametric hazard models and examples drawn from the survey interviews. Readers will note clearly recurring patterns in the examples we present from the interview narratives. These patterns are reflected and anticipated by the proportional event-history models.

We first examine observed patterns from March 2003 to August 2004 of the risk of being attacked by Government of Sudan [GoS] forces and/or Janjaweed militias. The risk of attack from the GoS troops acting alone by air (i.e., bombing) or by land (i.e., ground assaults) were higher than by the Janjaweed on their own, and these also peaked in the second wave. GoS air attacks often preceded ensuing ground attacks:

> A 71-year-old male Zaghawa living in North Darfur reported that his town had been bombed repeatedly for three months before the day of the attack that led to his displacement. GoS soldiers came to the town market the day before the attack that led to the final displacement. On the day of the attack, GoS planes bombed his village more than 20 times. This day the attack included GoS trucks and Janjaweed on horses. The trucks had mounted machine guns. Many villagers were killed as the attackers shouted "Nuba, Nuba" and "we want to kill the Blacks and take the land." He estimated that the military were driving about 100 trucks and that about 300 Janjaweed were on horses and camels. He fled when the

shooting started and people were falling around him. He broke his hip. The attackers took their cattle, burned the village, and poisoned their wells, with the water changing color and smell. (from survey interviews)

The most significant finding is that the highest risk of attack through both waves and most of the months, and especially during the second wave of attacks, involved the GoS and the Janjaweed acting together, and is consistent with attributing leadership responsibility to the GoS in the genocidal attacks in Darfur. An eyewitness account describing the joint organization of one such attack follows:

A 43-year-old male Masaleit living in a village near Masteri in West Darfur reported an attack in mid-February of 2004. The attack began at about four in the morning and involved about 600 GoS soldiers and militia. An Antinov aircraft circled the area and the soldiers arrived in trucks armed with mounted automatic weapons and on camels and horses. They sprayed bullets across and into the village, killing children, women, men, and elderly persons. While some of the soldiers were shooting, others looted the homes and set fire to the huts. The attackers shouted to one another, "don't leave anything," as they called to each other to loot and burn the huts. His wife and uncle were killed as they tried to run away while carrying a child. His wife was shot in the doorway as she tried to escape. The attackers took all the livestock (camel, sheep, goats, cattle, and horses) and food that they could carry and transport, and then they burned the rest. He tripped and broke his collarbone and lay still pretending to be dead for the three hour duration of the attack. All the wells were poisoned with what smelled to him like DDT. Birds and animals that drank from the wells died. He counted 22 dead bodies after the attack, including seven young girls. A few scattered huts remained after the attack, but when other villagers tried to return a week later, they found that the attackers had returned before them and burned even these. (U.S. Department of State 2004).

We next analyzed patterns from March 2003 to August 2004 involving the hazard of hearing racial epithets during the attacks. These results are consistent with earlier findings that collective racial intent is present almost exclusively when GoS forces attack simultaneously with Janjaweed militia (Hagan and Rymond-Richmond 2008). In these attacks the risks were greater for male and younger refugees, who were probably more

likely to hear and understand the racial epithets because they were more likely to know Arabic (i.e., boys were more likely to be sent to school, especially the Islamic schools).

When the GoS attacked together with the Janjaweed, the risks of hearing racial epithets were much greater, and . . . this risk of racialization was especially high during the second wave of attacks. Several examples from the survey interviews illustrate the context of these joint attacks that featured racial epithets.

A 16-year-old Fur woman in North Darfur reported that the attack began at four in the morning. GoS and Janjaweed attacked together and they began by looting food stores and burning the houses. The attack included one white Antinov airplane and five black helicopters. On the ground, the attackers shouted that "They will destroy all the people with black skin" and that they "want to kill all the Black people and clean the ground." Her brother saw the soldiers pour poison in the wells, and they told him not to drink the water.

A 30-year-old Zaghawa female from North Darfur reported that her village was attacked in the early morning with Antinov planes, helicopters, and soldiers in vehicles. The attackers were in uniforms and were a mix of GoS forces and militia. They looted the homes, set them on fire, and poisoned the wells. The entire village was burned by the bombing and shelling. During the attack a soldier yelled, "You dirty servants, we killed your husbands and should take you to be servants for our wives." They looted the sheep and killed the villagers who protested.

A 61-year-old Masaleit male from a medium-sized town in West Darfur reported an attack from September 2003. He was working on his farm outside of town when he heard shooting. He ran toward his home and was stopped by soldiers. They demanded to know where all the animals were kept and beat him with sticks. The attackers wore military uniforms and arrived in vehicles and on horses and camels. Planes flew overhead. The attackers were shouting "Nuba, Nuba." About 65 people were killed. He was able to hide in the undergrowth of the Wadi. Before the attack, government soldiers were in the town and Janjaweed came during the night on horses. The next day someone went out to draw the water and found that oil had been put in the well. They could not drink the water. His mother was beaten and died of the injuries. After burying her he fled. (U.S. Department of State 2004)

Besides predicting the presence of collective racial intent, the combination of GoS forces and Janjaweed militia are also highly predictive of forced displacement. The results indicate that the risk of displacement was about 110 percent higher when the GoS and Janjaweed joined together in the attacks than when GoS forces attacked alone and about 85 percent higher than when Janjaweed militia attacked alone.

When we include the different tactics involved in the attacks, the effects of the combined GoS and Jajanweed attacks are reduced (but nonetheless significant) because of the relationship between the perpetrating groups and the severity of the attacks. Attacks resulted in displacement about 23 percent more often when they involved burning and destroying homes, about 87 percent more often when they involved killings and missing persons, and about 129 percent more often when they involved the targeting of food and water supplies. Thus, as general explanations of genocide would expect, killings and destruction of homes were significant factors in predicting displacement. Yet, attacks that involved theft or destruction of food supplies, theft or killings of livestock, and poisoning or destruction of water sources were even more influential, as the single, most powerful factor in provoking forced displacement.

Two examples from the survey interviews provide final illustrations of the ways in which the elements of the attacks combined to create a recurring scenario in North and West Darfur villages:

> A 36-year-old Zaghawa male who lived near Kornoi reported GoS bombing along with Janjaweed wearing uniforms attacking on the ground. They said "We came here because we want to kill all the Black people." He said that if he had been close enough to hear more, he probably would have been killed. They took 18 cattle, 24 camels, and about 400 goats. His home was burned to the ground. They took 52 men from the village, forced them to their knees, and executed them, each with a gun in his mouth. The entire village was destroyed. He reported that "We passed through one village where there was nothing left at all. They even ruined the well water because there was something in it that smelled bad and we were told we couldn't drink it."

> A 40-year-old Zaghawa woman who lived near Kornoi reported that the GoS and Militia attacked her village in January of 2004. They killed many people and poisoned the water well. They poisoned the well by

killing a donkey and throwing it and other dead animals into the well. They also took food stocks. They separated the men from the women and killed the men (U.S. Department of State 2004)

There is a recurring pattern to these accounts that is further illustrated in a description by Human Rights Watch (2004, 26) of coordinated, joint GoS-Janjaweed attacks in the Masteri area of West Darfur in January and February 2004. The pattern included coordination of the attacks by time and place, a close working relationship of the GoS and Janjaweed forces, their arrival and departure together, and a recurring pattern that included the killing of fighting-age men and the destruction of food and the poisoning of wells. The attacks around Masteri systematically cleared the Black African settlements and left mostly Arab groups as the remaining presence. GoS planes not only bombed these settlements beforehand, they circled the settlements for days after to make sure the villagers left and did not return. When Human Rights Watch visited the Masteri area after the attacks, "the only civilian life encountered was a terrified group of some fifteen people—men and women, and pitifully thin—who were attempting to reach their former village to dig up buried food stores."

Conclusions

The evidence presented in this chapter is of a pattern of racialized, state-led attacks on food, livestock, and water supplies, indicating the intent by the political leadership of the Government of Sudan to eliminate the collective livelihoods of Black African groups in Darfur. The widespread and systematic poisoning of wells is perhaps the most striking evidence of the intent of jointly attacking GoS and Janjaweed forces to dislodge and displace Black African groups from their villages and farms, but the further evidence of killing, looting, burning, and, more generally, of completely destroying these villages with scorched-earth tactics fills out the picture of the intent to exterminate and eliminate these groups.

Most analyses of the conflict in Darfur have focused on the killings and have involved contentious efforts to establish the level of mortality involved. This work is important and is now producing a convergence regarding the hundreds of thousands of deaths resulting from this conflict. This evidence speaks to the 1948 Genocide Convention's definition of genocide as destruction of protected groups "in whole or in part," and the extent to which this criterion of extermination is met in Darfur. However, the Geneva Convention also emphasizes "deliberately inflicting on a group conditions of life calculated to bring about its physical destruction in whole or in part," which is a criterion of genocide that focuses more on the elimination of protected groups. This criterion addresses the concern in Darfur that, beyond widespread killing, the joint attacks of the GoS forces and Janjaweed militias have used forced migration and displacement as a means of permanently eliminating the Black African groups from their villages and farms in Darfur. The fact that these groups have nearly entirely been removed from their land and have been isolated in displacement and refugee camps for more than five years supports the conclusion that they have been the victims of elimination.

We have already noted parallels between the circumstances of extermination and elimination in Darfur and the earlier prosecution at the International Criminal Tribunal for the former Yugoslavia (ICTY) of genocide in the town of Srebrenica in the former Yugoslavia. The Holocaust and Armenian genocide also provide historical parallels to the situation in Darfur. A report by Physicians for Human Rights (2006, 40) notes that French delegates who contributed to the drafting of the post–World War II Genocide Convention insisted on the inclusion of the provision regarding the creation of conditions that make life unsustainable. They maintained that this was necessary to address circumstances in which members of a group, though not killed immediately, were subjected to conditions calculated to bring about the same result over a prolonged period of time. The French cited as examples the ghettos where Jews were confined in conditions of starvation and illness that led to their extinction in the lead-up to the Holocaust. They also noted actions taken by the Turkish government during World War I to deprive Armenian populations of food during forced marches with the intent to undermine the capacity to sustain group life. Still, this tactic of elimination is underdeveloped in applications of the Genocide Convention and in research on the topic of genocide.

A key challenge in developing the international criminal law and research on the use of elimination strategies is the issue of intent. There is abundant evidence of intent in Darfur, both as understood legally

and social-scientifically, and this is reflected in our analysis of the ADS data. The direct evidence of this intent includes the dehumanizing racial epithets that we find most prominent in the second wave of attacks in Darfur, against protected groups—especially the Fur and Masaleit—and during combined attacks that include both the GoS forces and Janjaweed militias. Both the frequently cited *Akayesu* decision in Rwanda (United Nations 1998) and the *Jelisi* decision in Bosnia (United Nations 1999) emphasize the importance of spoken language as evidence of genocide. The words and phrases used by perpetrators to dehumanize victims play similar roles in research on genocide and hate crimes (Green, McFalls, and Smith 2001; Horowitz 1980 Jenness and Broad 1997). In both kinds of crime, dehumanizing language is an intrinsically important motivational process that diminishes moral and practical constraints on participants and bystanders, as recognized in law and social science research.

There is also strong circumstantial evidence of genocidal intent, which is allowed as proof of specific intent to commit genocide in international law. In the *Jeliisic* case in Bosnia, the court (United Nations 1999) held in an appeal decision that, in the absence of direct explicit evidence, [intent may] be inferred from a number of facts and circumstances, such as general context, the perpetration of other culpable acts systematically directed against the same group, the scale of the atrocities committed, the systematic targeting of victims on account of their membership of a particular group, or the repetition of destructive and discriminatory acts (1995, Point 4).

All of these circumstantial forms of evidence apply in the current case of Darfur, where the attacking and targeted groups, and the scale and repetition of mass atrocities is well documented through our analysis of the ADS, and is corroborated by other research.

After the intervention of the Appeals Chamber of the ICC, the Pre-Trial Chamber (ICC 2010) in July of this year finally reversed an earlier decision and concluded that there were now "reasonable grounds" to approve a warrant for the arrest of President Al-Bashir for trial on charges of genocide. The reasoning of the judges in this decision was based on the kind of elimination argument we have advanced in our analysis of the ADS data. They concluded that "the conditions of life inflicted on the Fur, Masaleit and Zaghawa groups [in Darfur] were calculated to bring about the physical destruction of a part of those ethnic groups" and that "forcible transfer by resettlement by members of other tribes, [was] committed in furtherance of the genocidal policy." The Prosecutor's Office (ICC 2010) maintained a month later that "the information available suggests that genocide continues today."

Although Sudan's government defends its internal displacement camps in humanitarian terms, it is clear that the personal and food insecurity that the government has created in Darfur is the factor that overwhelmingly keeps the displaced persons in the camps. Almost all of the respondents in a follow-up 2009 survey in the Chad refugee camps indicated a desire to return to their land in Darfur, and most indicated that security-related concerns prevented them from doing so. The concerns are explicitly about physical, food, and water security—in other words, the "conditions of life" necessary for survival. The displacement is itself evidence of genocide by elimination.

Evidence of genocide in Darfur continues to mount with report of the mistreatment of persons in the camps in Darfur. Since March 2008, when the ICC issued its first warrant for the arrest of President Al-Bashir, the Sudanese government has followed a policy in Darfur of disrupting the work and expelling the employees of Western humanitarian aid groups. In June of 2009, President Obama's Special Envoy to Sudan, Scott Gration, referred to Darfur as experiencing "the remnants of genocide." The Administration's U.S. Ambassador to the United Nations, Susan Rice, disagreed with this assessment, and President Obama has spoken of Darfur as the scene of "ongoing genocide." Evidence of genocide in Darfur continues to mount with reports of the mistreatment of persons in the camps in Darfur. The United Nations recently reported that constraints on aid organizations were increasing (Osman 2010).

In August of 2010, Sudan reinstated a ban on humanitarian access to Kalma, the largest displacement camp with nearly 100,000 persons in South Darfur. Sudanese government policies pitting groups against one another in camps such as Kalma have provoked violent confrontations between political rivals and forced many displaced persons from their camps. The Human Rights and Advocacy Network for Democracy [HAND] reported that "in addition to the ongoing violence there is severe shortage of food, medicine, potable water and

other essential service in the IDP camps which also played a major role in accelerating the exodus" (2010: 3).

In July 2010, the majority of the persons in Kalma were believed to have fled the camp. The HAND report indicates that some IDP leaders expressed fears that movement of IDPs outside Kalma camp meets an old goal set by GoS to gain full control over the IDP camps in Darfur, split the IDPs on ethnic and political lines, and finally, dismantle the IDP camps all over the region (HAND 2010).

The conditions of displacement in Darfur continue to reflect their origins in the genocidal intentions of the leadership of the Government of Sudan. These intentions are expressed through processes of extermination and elimination which require further combined documentation in research on genocide. Genocide needs to be understood as a process of displacement and elimination that can persist long after the mass killing and extermination that are more commonly regarded as its hallmark.

References

Degomme, Olivier, and Dearati Guha-Sapir. 2010. "Patterns of Mortality Rates in Darfur Conflict." *Lancet* 375:294–300.

De Waal, Alex. 2005. "Preface to 2005 Edition." In *Famine that Kills: Darfur, Sudan, 1984–1985* (ed. Alex de Waal.), vii–xx. New York: Oxford University Press.

Dower, John. 1986. *War without Mercy: Race and Power in the Pacific War.* New York: Pantheon Books.

Gottfredson, Michael, and Travis Hirschi. 1990. *A General Theory of Crime.* Stanford, CA: Stanford University Press.

Green, Donald, Laurence McFalls, and Jennifer Smith. 2001. "Hate Crime: An Emergent Research Agenda." *Annual Review of Sociology* 27:479–504.

Hagan, John, and Alberto Palloni. 2006. "Death in Darfur." *Science* 313:1578–1579.

Hagan, John, and Wenona Rymond-Richmond. 2008. "The Collective Dynamics of Racial Dehumanization and Genocidal Victimization in Darfur." *American Sociological Review* 73:875–902.

HAND. 2010. "Disturbance in Darfur's IDP Camps." *Human Rights and Advocacy Network for Democracy (HAND)*, Geneva, August 13. http://www.david-kilgour.com/2010/Disturbances%20in%20Darfur's%20IDP%20camps.pdf. (accessed September 20, 2015).

Horowitz, Irving Louis. 1980. *Taking Lives: Genocide and State Power.* New Brunswick, NJ: Transaction Books.

Howard, Jonathan. 2006. "Survey Methodology and the Darfur Genocide." In *Genocide in Darfur: Investigating the Atrocities in Sudan* (ed. S. Totten and E. Markusen), 59–74. New York: Routledge.

Human Rights Watch. 2004. "If We Return, We Will Be Killed: Consolidation of Ethnic Cleansing in Darfur, Sudan." *HRW Report*, November: 1-43.

International Criminal Court (ICC). 2010, July 12. "Situation in Darfur, Sudan: In the Case of the Prosecutor v. Omar Hassan Ahmad Al Bashir." Pre-Trial Chamber. The Hague: ICC.

Jenness, Valerie, and Kendal Broad. 1997. *Hate Crimes: New Social Movements and the Politics of Violence.* New York: Aldine de Gruyter.

Office of the Prosecutor. 2005. "Seventh Report of the Prosecutor of the International Criminal Court to the UN Security Council Pursuant to UNSCR 1593 (2005)." The Hague: International Criminal Court.

Office of the Prosecutor. 2007. "Situation in Darfur, The Sudan. Prosecutor's Application under Article 58(7), No. ICC-02/05." The Hague: International Criminal Court.

Office of the Prosecutor. 2008. "Situation in Darfur, The Sudan: Summary of the Case: Prosecutor's Application for Warrant of Arrest under Article 58 against Omar Hassan Ahmad Al Bashir. No. ICC-OTP-20080714." The Hague: International Criminal Court.

Osman, Mohamed. 2010. "Sudan Says Will Deport Foreign NGO Workers." Associated Press, August 19.

Physicians for Human Rights. 2006. *Darfur: Assault on Survival.* Cambridge, MA: Physicians for Human Rights.

Power, Samantha. 2004. "Dying in Darfur." *The New Yorker*, August 30.

Prunier, Gerard. 2005. *Darfur: The Ambiguous Genocide.* Ithaca, NY: Cornell University Press.

United Nations. 1948. Convention on the Prevention and Punishment of the Crime of Genocide, adopted by Resolution 260(II)A of the United Nations General Assembly on 9 December 1948.

United Nations. 1998. *Judgment: The Prosecutor v. Jean-Paul Akayesu*, International Criminal Tribunal Rwanda, Case No. IT-96-T.

United Nations. 1999. *Judgment: The Prosecutor v. Goran Jelisi*, International Criminal Tribunal for the Former Yugoslavia, Case No. IT-95-T.

United Nations. 2005. *Report of the International Commission of Inquiry on Darfur to the United Nations Secretary-General.* Geneva.

U.S. Department of State. 2004. *Document Atrocities in Darfur.* Washington DC: Bureau of Democracy. Human Rights and Labor and Bureau of Intelligence and Research.

Wax, Emily. 2004. "In Sudan: 'A Big Sheik' Roams Free." *Washington Post*, July 18.

Questions

1. The authors argue that we often only think of genocide as mass killing. How do the authors broaden this definition? Why do they argue that it is important to broaden the definition of genocide?

2. Similarly, we often think of enacting violence as being something done with weapons, but the authors argue that controlling access to water and food are also important to consider. In what ways is the environment important in the events happening in Darfur? In what ways is the control of the environment consequential as a weapon of genocide?

3. As the chapter indicates, "The 1948 Genocide Convention defines genocide as 'acts committed with intent to destroy, in whole or in part, a national, ethnical, racial or religious group' (United Nations 1948: Article II)." Why do the authors argue that the atrocities in Darfur constitute genocide? Give specific examples of the argument.

4. What forms of "attack" do the authors examine? How is the government responsible for these attacks? What is the relationship between the government and Janjaweed militias? What are the consequences of them working together?

5. In what ways is inequality reproduced? The authors give several examples of genocide in the chapter, but what other examples can you think of in which large groups of people were displaced? Should those examples be considered genocide?

23

Sexual Harassment, Workplace Authority, and the Paradox of Power

HEATHER McLAUGHLIN, CHRISTOPHER UGGEN, AND AMY BLACKSTONE

According to the Bureau of Labor Statistics (2013), in 2012, 58 percent of women age 16 and older participated in the labor force (70 percent of men did). That is a dramatic increase over two generations of women: in 1950, about one-third of women worked for pay (Bureau of Labor Statistics 2000). Women of color, immigrant women, and poor women have always had higher rates of employment than white, middle-class women. But the mass entrance of middle-class white women into paid employment brought increased scrutiny to women's issues long endemic. Job, occupation, and work segregation inhibit women's pay. Hiring discrimination, men's preferences for other workers like themselves, and making business deals at the bar or on the golf course create "glass ceilings" women struggle to surpass, despite the outlawing of discrimination.

Yet many women are now in positions of authority in workplaces, even if they are underrepresented. The following reading draws our attention to how coworkers and subordinates respond to these women with authority. Do they treat them like other bosses? Is there a backlash of sorts against them?

The reading examines workplace harassment, sex-based and sexual, as an institutionalized mechanism of inequality, just like exploitation and exclusion. The authors find that many women experience sex-based and sexual harassment. Even some men, specifically men who are *not* stereotypically masculine, experience harassment. Further, the authors find that women supervisors are more likely to report harassment and to view the behavior as sexual harassment than are non-supervisors. This study explains why. It demonstrates that co-workers, clients, and supervisors use sex-based and sexual harassment as a tool to discredit women in authority and to gain power when women have power over them.

References

Bureau of Labor Statistics, U.S. Department of Labor. 2000. "Changes in Women's Labor Force Participation in the 20th Century." *The Economics Daily*. http://www.bls.gov/opub/ted/2000/feb/wk3/art03.htm (accessed January 13, 2015).

Bureau of Labor Statistics, U.S. Department of Labor. 2013. "Civilian Labor Force Participation Rates by Age, Sex, Race, and Ethnicity." *December 2013 Monthly Labor Review*. http://www.bls.gov/emp/ep_table_303.htm (accessed January 13, 2015).

The term "sexual harassment" was not coined until the 1970s (Farley 1978), but formal organizational responses have since diffused rapidly (Dobbin and Kelly 2007; Schultz 2003). Today, sexual harassment workshops, policies, and grievance procedures are standard features of the human resources landscape, and a robust scholarly literature ties harassment to gender inequalities (Martin 2003) and other forms of workplace discrimination (Lopez, Hodson, and Roscigno 2009). Power, at work and in the broader society, pervades accounts of harassment in all of these literatures (Berdahl 2007; Rospenda, Richman, and Nawyn 1998; Welsh 1999). Yet, after three decades of scholarship, basic questions about whether and how workplace power affects harassment remain unanswered.

This chapter uses quantitative and qualitative data from the Youth Development Study (YDS) to consider three hypotheses from an integrated feminist model of sexual harassment, testing whether supervisory authority, gender identity, and industry sex composition are linked to experiences of harassment. Using strong statistical controls for individual differences, our quantitative models predict whether respondents report any harassing behaviors, the number of harassing behaviors they report, and whether they subjectively interpret their experiences as harassment. After establishing basic empirical relations using survey data, we analyze qualitative interviews with YDS respondents to delineate and explain the processes underling these relationships. We then situate both sets of results within theories of gender and power and extant research on sexual harassment.

Gender, Sexual Harassment, and Workplace Power

Sexual harassment is classified as a form of sex discrimination under Title VII of the Civil Rights Act of 1964. The U.S. Equal Employment Opportunity commission (EEOC) defines it as "unwelcome sexual advances, requests for sexual favors, and other verbal or physical conduct of a sexual nature" that interferes with one's employment or work performance or creates a "hostile or offensive work environment" (U.S. EEOC 2011). Due, in part, to varying definitions and indicators, prevalence estimates vary dramatically (Welsh 1999), leading many researchers to adopt a strategy of triangulation that considers multiple forms or measures (e.g., Houston and Hwang 1996; Uggen and Blackstone 2004).

Feminist scholarship situates sexual harassment within broader patterns of discrimination, power, and privilege, linking harassment to sex-based inequality (MacKinnon 1979). Quinn's (2002) research on "girl watching," for example, ties patriarchal gender relations to everyday workplace interactions. Quinn argues that other men, rather than women, are often the intended audience of sexist gestures and comments. Although men often view "girl watching" as light-hearted and playful, and seem surprised when women take offense, such activities demonstrate men's power to sexually evaluate women. Similarly, Martin (2001) finds that men "mobilize masculinities" in ways that often exclude and cause harm to women as a group, even when this is not their intention.

Connell's (1987) theory of hegemonic masculinity, which argues that society privileges a single normative ideal of male behavior, provides a broad sociological framework for understanding harassment, gender, and power. Men may be vulnerable to harassment if they are perceived as feminine (DeSouza and Solberg 2004; Waldo, Berdahl, and Fitzgerald 1998), and women may be targeted if they challenge their subordinate position in the gender system. Sexual harassment may thus act as a tool to police appropriate ways of "doing gender" in the workplace and to penalize gender nonconformity (West and Zimmerman 1987).

Research on contrapower harassment suggests that gender, race, and class positions imbue harassers with informal power, even when targets possess greater organizational authority than do their harassers (Rospenda et al. 1998). Women holding authority positions thus offer an intriguing paradox for theory and research on sexual harassment, and scholars have advanced two distinct positions. The first, the vulnerable-victim hypothesis suggests that more vulnerable workers—including women, racial minorities, and those with the most precarious positions and least workplace authority—are subject to greater harassment. The second, the power-threat model, suggests that women who threaten men's dominance are more frequent targets. Although the matter is far from settled, research has found greater support for the paradoxical power-threat model, in which women in authority positions are most likely to face harassment (Chamberlain et al. 2008) and discrimination (Stainback, Ratliff, and Roscigno 2011).

Women supervisors, who hold authority over some men, directly challenge the presumptive superiority of men. Women continue to be underrepresented in positions of authority or relegated to the lower rungs of management (Elliott and Smith 2004; Gorman 2005; Kalev 2009; Reskin 2003; Reskin and McBrier 2000). When women are able to crack the glass ceiling and attain leadership positions, stereotypical gender beliefs about their "natural" abilities continue to shape perceptions of their job performance (Davidson and Cooper 1992; Eagly and Carli 2007). Moreover, while men in traditionally female occupations reap the rewards of a glass escalator to leadership positions (Hultin 2003; Williams 1992), women supervisors are often isolated and seen as undeserving of their positions (Ridgeway and Correll 2004; Ridgeway and Smith-Lovin 1999). In fact, women are unlikely to be promoted to management unless a sizeable proportion of women are already in place, highlighting the difficulty of gaining initial entry to such positions (Cohen, Broschak, and Haveman 1998). Taken together, these processes point to women supervisors as potential targets for harassment.

The idea of masculine overcompensation—in which men react to threats to their manhood by enacting an extreme form of masculinity (Willer 2005)—also helps explain why men may harass women in power. Maass and colleagues (2003), for example, find that male participants in a computer image-sharing task sent more pornographic and offensive images to females identifying as feminists than to females adhering to more traditional gender roles. Along similar lines, Das (2009) concludes that females who are "too assertive" threaten the gender hierarchy and are denigrated through harassment. Correspondingly, De Coster, Estes, and Mueller (1999) find that females with greater tenure, independent of age, are more likely to view sexual harassment as a problem for them at work, concluding that the practice is used instrumentally against powerful females who encroach on male territory. Each of these findings suggests that women supervisors may be more likely than other working women to experience sexual harassment.

It is also possible that supervisors report greater rates of harassment simply because they are more aware of the phenomenon. Supervisors' advanced education and training likely increase their overall legal consciousness and understanding of sexual harassment. As a result, supervisors, who are often responsible for fostering a professional work environment free from harassment and discrimination, may be more likely to recall sexualized workplace interactions and to label such experiences as harassment.

Apart from supervisory authority and expressions of gender, workplace demography also influences harassment experiences. Sexual harassment occurs across a diverse range of job settings (Collinson and Collinson 1996; Dellinger and Williams 2002; Giuffre and Williams 1994), but a large literature debates the importance of numerical sex ratios (Welsh 1999). The weight of the evidence suggests that harassment, of both men and women, most often occurs in male-dominated work settings (Fitzgerald et al. 1997; Mansfield et al. 1991; Rospenda et al. 1998; Uggen and Blackstone 2004). Based on dynamics of sex, gender, and power in the workplace, we form three primary hypotheses:

Hypothesis 1: Females holding workplace authority positions (i.e., females who supervise others) are more likely to experience sexual harassment than are females who do not hold such positions.

Hypothesis 2: Gender nonconformity (i.e., more feminine behavior for males and less feminine behavior for females) is associated with an increased risk of sexual harassment.

Hypothesis 3: Sexual harassment will be greater in industries and occupations characterized by a higher proportion of male workers.

After testing these hypotheses in our quantitative analyses, we turn to qualitative interview data to understand the underlying process behind these patterns. By probing the experiences of our survey participants, we are better able to explain why and how gender, sex, and power shape harassment experiences and workplace interactions more broadly.

Data, Measures, and Methodology

We analyze longitudinal data from the Youth Development Study (Mortimer 2003). The study began in 1988, when participants were ninth graders in St. Paul, Minnesota, public schools. The sample consists of 1,010 youth, who have since been surveyed regularly. For this chapter, we analyze the 2003 and 2004 surveys, when participants were approximately 29 and 30 years old. Survey retention was 73 percent in 2004, and our analytic sample ($N = 522$) consists of all working participants who responded to sexual harassment items in both waves.

Relative to surveys, however, qualitative research is often "better suited to discovering how the meaning of sexual behaviors varies in different organizational contexts" (Dellinger and Williams 2002, 244). Dellinger and Williams (2002), for example, powerfully contrast the "locker room" culture of a male pornographic magazine with the "dorm room" atmosphere of a feminist magazine, showing how organizational culture shapes workers' definitions of harassment. Our survey results reveal patterns of association, but they cannot speak directly to the more subtle and specific mechanisms linking group membership to opportunities and outcomes (Gross 2009; Reskin 2003). We therefore also conducted interviews with 33 YDS respondents (14 men and 19 women) to more closely examine the processes linking power and gender and to better contextualize harassment experiences. Of the interviewees, all but seven identified as white, most self-identified as straight, and they reported a range of supervisory and nonsupervisory jobs. We asked interview participants a series of open-ended questions about their work histories and interactions, inviting them to share what they felt was most important based on our interest in harassment, workplace problems, and workplace sexuality. All interview participants' names are pseudonyms.

Survey Predictors of Sexual Harassment

Over one-third of our sample reported at least one behavioral indicator of harassment in 2004, yet only 7 percent subjectively reported experiencing sexual harassment (11 percent of females but only 1 percent of males). Consistent with our first hypothesis, supervisory authority has significantly different effects for males and females.

We find mixed support for our second hypothesis regarding gender conformity. More feminine females are less likely to report harassment. The effect of femininity and its interaction with sex is less robust than the effect of authority position and its interaction with sex.

Industry sex ratio, however, emerges as a significant predictor of subjective harassment, lending support to our third hypothesis. Industry sex composition is also a significant predictor of the number of harassing behaviors. These findings may reflect, in part, the different nature of harassing behaviors in male-dominated work settings. As suggested by our interview data, behaviors such as suggestive stories or inappropriate comments about women's bodies may be interpreted as more menacing, malicious, or degrading at jobsites where women are socially and numerically isolated. Just as industry sex ratio is predictive only of subjective harassment, it is also plausible that when women are surrounded by men, they may interpret behaviors differently and be more likely to label sexualized behaviors as harassment than will women in more gender-balanced settings.

Moving to individual characteristics, we observe little difference in the likelihood of reporting any harassing behaviors by race, although the rate of harassment among whites is lower than for persons of color. In separate analyses, we examined how sex, supervisory authority, and race intersect to shape harassment experiences. Among white females, 47 percent of supervisors and 20 percent of non-supervisors reported at least one harassing behavior. Workplace power does not significantly increase the odds of harassment for females of color, but it does not serve as a protective factor either: 43 percent of supervisors and 45 percent of non-supervisors experienced harassing behaviors. We observe no significant differences among males. These results suggest that harassment is not a unidimensional experience, shaped by just one aspect of a person's identity. Instead, as demonstrated by intersectionality scholars such as Crenshaw (1991) and Collins (2004), these dimensions operate simultaneously to produce inequalities.

Why and How Authority, Gender, and Composition Matter

Our quantitative analyses establish the basic empirical relations, but we turn to qualitative interviews with YDS participants to delineate why and how these relations matter. To learn more about the processes connecting gender and power, we present respondents' accounts of harassment in the context of our three hypotheses: (1) experiences of women in positions of authority; (2) experiences of workers who do not conform to culturally dominant expectations of gender; and (3) patterns of harassment in male-dominated industries and occupations.

Women in Authority

Consistent with our quantitative analyses, the women we interviewed provided concrete examples of how their supervisory status led to harassment. Marie, a project manager on a construction site, felt she was targeted because she worked as a supervisor in a male-dominated industry. She told us she needed to tolerate some harassment to keep her job and maintain working relationships with colleagues: "If you wanted to leave, sure, you could file a claim or do whatever . . . but if you want to stay at the job . . . you kind of feel like you have to put up with [it]."

Several women told us that men questioned their ability to effectively supervise others, and Marie was no exception. One older subcontractor explicitly told her, "This isn't the job for a woman." Having just walked him through the requirements of some complex paperwork, Marie said, "I think he just thought I was being a nag and that I didn't know what I was doing." Later in the interview, she said, "*Just being a female in management is difficult, and guys don't like it*—especially the guys that work in the field. They think that women should be secretaries" (emphasis added). Marie's experiences echo findings by previous researchers (e.g., Eisenberg 2001; Quinn 2002) that men's harassment of women has more to do with keeping women "in their place" and marking their own turf than with sexual attraction or arousal.

Holly, the first woman in upper management at her manufacturing firm, also heard derogatory remarks from men at work. Her subordinates sometimes joked, "If we had somebody with balls in this position we'd be getting things done." Holly was sexually harassed by a client at a company dinner, being groped throughout the evening by the vice president of an influential firm. She explained, "I didn't know who this guy was, I had no idea. I'm just sittin' next to him and I'm the only girl at the table. . . . And he'd put his arm around me and pull me towards him and, kind of uncomfortable, and I'd push away. And he kept saying . . . 'Oh, I love her. She's beautiful.'" Holly continued, "He just kept going on and touching me and put his hand on [my] leg very forcefully and then he was playing the game of trying to unhook the bra with two fingers, which he did after I tried to get up and get away."

If Holly had not been a supervisor, she would not have been invited to this evening event. Management positions in many manufacturing industries continue to be dominated by men (Hultin 2003; Williams 1992), and supervisors like Holly are often the only women in the room. Holly explained how she was targeted because "*I was the only girl there. There were no other girls.* Like I said, there's a female in management in customer service

but there's always been a girl in management in customer service. But many of the positions above that, which are directly below our owner, *there's not been a woman in any of those positions in eons*" (emphasis added).

Holly suggested her isolation as a woman in management may have been a key mechanism linking her supervisory status to her harassment. Her story also shows how hegemonic masculinity operates through collective practice (Connell 1987; Martin 2006; see also Pascoe 2007 on compulsive heterosexuality). Although her co-workers noticed the harassment, it went on for hours before anyone took action to stop it. Even after others stepped in, it was only to encourage Holly, and not her harasser, to leave the event:

Somebody from our company noticed that [the client] had his hands all over my lap and [my co-worker] goes, "Where are his hands?" and I go, I was sitting like this [shows her legs crossed tightly] and I go, "Exactly where you think they are." And I pushed [the client] away and so that's when [my co-worker] realized and motioned and said, "I want the bill. We're outta here."

Although Holly left after their bill arrived, the men (including the co-worker who intervened) stayed behind for drinks at the bar. No one other than Holly directly confronted her harasser that evening. Several colleagues made it clear *to Holly* that they did not condone the client's behavior, but they did not speak out against it. Instead, they privately and individually took her aside and urged her to leave. To the extent that they played the role of protectors, Holly's colleagues further undermined her authority.

Several other participants told us of contrapower harassment from subordinates and clients that similarly undermined their authority. Jordan, a police officer, was subverted by another officer when they were dispatched to a loud party. Her colleague was demeaning to women in addressing the young men at the party: "Kinda talking bad about women, you know, referring to them as broads . . . and here I'm the only woman, I'm a cop, and it's like you know, you're not really giving these college kids any reason to show me any respect." Other participants witnessed or experienced contrapower sexual harassment against women in diverse work settings. Jerry, a correctional officer, told us how prisoners would stand naked at the front of their cells and masturbate in front of women officers. Cam told us that when he worked as a youth counselor, a teen ejaculated in a condom and then threw it at a woman counselor who "cried a lot and she quit the job." Similar experiences were reported by Janice, a high school teacher who was targeted by a student, and by Nate, who told us of a woman produce manager targeted by a delivery person.

Both interview and survey data suggest that experiences of harassment are far more varied than the "typical harassment scenario" of a male boss and a female subordinate. Although data on harassers are notoriously difficult to obtain and analyze, our surveys provide some insight into the relative power of both parties in the harassment dyad. To illustrate, Figure 1 reports the number of YDS survey respondents who experienced "staring or leering" by a supervisor, co-worker (of equal or subordinate status), or customers or clients. The most common scenario involved male harassers and female targets, followed by male harassers and male targets. The figure also reports the percentage of supervisors, co-workers, and clients within each harasser/target dyad, although we caution that percentages are based on a small number of cases (as indicated on the

y-axis). In all scenarios, staring and leering by co-workers and clients, rather than supervisors, make up the great majority of these accounts. This general pattern holds across most of the other harassing behaviors, although frequencies vary widely.

In supplementary analyses (see Table S4 of the online supplement), female supervisors are consistently more likely than female non-supervisors to experience harassing behaviors, whether from male or female supervisors, co-workers, or clients. This difference is especially pronounced for harassment by male co-workers ($p < .05$). Male supervisors, in contrast, are no more or less likely to experience harassment than are other male workers. Different dynamics could be driving the behavior of various categories of harassers, depending on their structural location relative to female supervisors. Nevertheless, women in authority appear to elicit a power-threat response—especially from below, but perhaps more generally as well. The same forces that exclude women from management positions continue to operate even after women obtain supervisory authority.

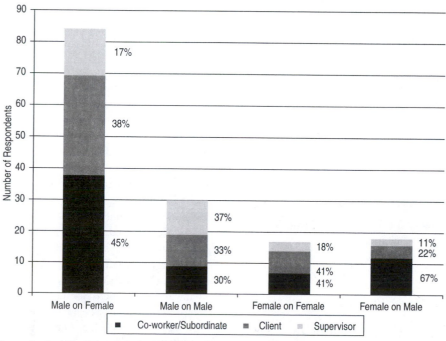

Figure 1 Characteristics of Harassers and Targets for Staring or Leering Item.
Note: Because workers may experience harassment from multiple parties, some reported multiple scenarios for each behavior.

Sexual Orientation and Expressions of Femininity

Results suggest a less consistent link between gender nonconformity and the three harassment outcomes. This provides partial support for Connell's theory of hegemonic masculinity, which emphasizes the significance of gender performance and the negative sanctions elicited by departures from gender expectations. As Marie's experience on the construction site, Jordan's work in law enforcement, and the following interviews with male participants demonstrate, sexual harassment often occurs in group settings where "boys will be boys" and workers are targeted for gender nonconformity.

Seth, a journalist who rated himself as more feminine than most other male respondents on our survey, described a "news guy" who targeted him for not behaving more aggressively. He also recalled a restaurant job where sexist comments were part of everyday interaction: "I can remember [the owner] kind of ribbing men, gay men that were working there, in sort of a patronizing way. . . . With men his attitude was sort of manifest as a sort of dominance thing." Similarly, Cam told us of a co-worker harassed "because of the way he moves, the way he dress [sic], they call him [a] faggot, and they spit on him, they manipulate him."

Dan, who also reported being more feminine, was taunted about his sexuality by co-workers at a post office. Although he identified as heterosexual, they would say "'you're gay' and stuff like that." When sexual material came through the mail, his co-workers would make inappropriate comments and "they'd cut photos of some of the post office guys and put the heads on the bodies of models and stuff like that." Dan told us about a co-worker who was targeted because "he had tendencies, and I think they kind of focused on him because they thought 'okay, you like men.'" Dan was unaware of this worker's sexual orientation, but he told us his co-worker was "more feminine" and isolated because he "hung out with women more than men."

Men's collective practice of masculinity similarly undermined women's authority during Lisa's time working in an advertising agency. Like the fictitious ad agency portrayed on the television series *Mad Men*, "the boys" would exclude women from creative decisions, "drink the afternoon away," and visit strip clubs after hours, leaving the lion's share of the day-to-day work for women staff members. When an "obviously gay" temp worker arrived at the agency, he was immediately labeled as an outsider. The top three men at the firm were taken aback by the worker's arrival, and Lisa could tell they were thinking, "Oh my god! There's a gay man in my office!" She added, "I had seen those guys drunk so many times and they were so macho and so misogynistic that I didn't doubt for one *second* that they'd take him out and beat him up. I thought they were *fully* capable of doing that." Later, Lisa's boss told her, "That guy—get him outta here or someone's gonna break his legs." Lisa explained the situation to the temp worker, who later sued the company for wrongful termination. After the case was settled, Lisa believed she was held responsible for the lawsuit. She described how "my responsibilities slowly eked away from me. . . . Number one, I'm sure some of it was, well, we just can't trust her."

These accounts reveal how putatively "effeminate" men, those perceived to be somehow weak in character or womanlike in their presentation of self (Hennen 2001), are targeted in some work settings. Gender and sexuality were often erroneously conflated in these reports; men were identified as gay simply because of their gender performance. Research on the multiple masculinities enacted by gay men (Connell 1992; Hennen 2008) calls such assumptions into question, of course, as do broader critiques of heterosexuality as an institution (e.g., Ingraham 2008). More generally, our participants' accounts comport with those of previous research (Quinn 2002; Tallichet 1995). Social isolation and what Lisa called a "macho and misogynistic" workplace culture serve as key mechanisms connecting gender performance and harassment—concerns we discuss next in reference to our third hypothesis.

Male-Dominated Professions and Occupations

Earlier, we found only mixed support for our third hypothesis regarding differences across occupational and industrial sectors. Females in predominantly male industries reported significantly greater subjective harassment, with industry composition also approaching significance in the behavioral count models. Although occupational variables are not predictive in the [quantitative analysis], we observe somewhat more harassment in service work for males and in technical and craft occupations for females.

As Dellinger and Williams (2002) suggest, qualitative work is well suited for analyzing how the meaning of sexual behaviors varies in different organizational contexts. Like Tallichet's (1995) study of coal miners, our interviews show how some men use harassment and discrimination to diminish women employed in masculine occupations. For example, Jordan experienced gender-based discrimination before officially beginning her security job. A co-worker refused to issue her a uniform, saying, "There's no way they hired you for security." Despite this early setback, Jordan eventually became a police officer, describing a work environment that "non-police personnel would maybe consider inappropriate. You know everybody probably sees on TV how a lot of the jokes and a lot of the way police officers act can be real callous and can be offensive. . . . There's probably a lot of sexual joking." Jordan encountered co-workers who believed women did not belong in law enforcement. This led to serious and potentially life-threatening discrimination, when a policewoman did not receive the necessary backup from other officers when she responded to calls for service:

> She'd get a call and nobody would go to assist. . . . There would be a few people that were okay with her or whatever that would come and assist her but you know for the most part nobody would answer up to go and eventually the dispatcher will assign somebody to go.

Other participants shared similar accounts of male-dominated settings, as when Jenna's manager at a gas station made comments about her body, and the same day, a co-worker told a customer, "We'll send Jenna to blow your car." Jenna chose not to confront her co-workers, telling us: *I was the only female there. . . .* So it's kinda like they work on the buddy system, you know? So the more you say the more you get yourself in trouble" (emphasis added). Some women felt that sexual harassment came with the territory; they tolerated such behavior while attempting to prove themselves as women in these fields. Marie, for example, encountered "constant" sexual advances and frequent catcalls, staring, and inappropriate sexual questions while working in construction. She told us, "Knowing I was going to be at a company like that, I kind of expected it."

Some men we interviewed also experienced sexually harassing behavior in male-dominated firms. Rick reported hearing many gay and sex jokes at a printing company. He told us, "I would just sit there and grin but it's just the fact that [the jokes] were so awful that I do remember them." Rick believed the working conditions would have been "less, you know, college dorm room" had women been present. Similarly, John described co-workers' interactions during his military service as "pretty unprofessional" and "inappropriate," adding "you could open up a drawer and there would be a bunch of [Playboy] magazines in there."

Marie, Holly, and other women we interviewed pointed to the particular difficulties they experienced as supervisors in male-dominated industries. In light of these comments, we returned to our survey data to learn how workplace sex composition might affect harassment among supervisors and non-supervisors. Figure 2 shows the proportion of respondents reporting harassment by supervisory status in predominantly male and female industries (with predominance defined as 50 percent or more workers). Our sample contains too few female supervisors in male-dominated industries to detect a significant interaction in the models, but data show a consistent pattern: female supervisors are more likely to experience harassing behaviors in predominantly male industries (58 percent) than in predominantly female industries (42 percent).

Gender, Power, and Beyond

This multimethod analysis offers the strongest evidence to date on the interaction of sex, gender, and power in predicting sexual harassment (Berdahl 2007; Connell 1987; Quinn 2002; Uggen and Blackstone 2004). The vulnerable-victims perspective suggests that authority acts as a protective factor, exempting women from the suggestive gaze or unwelcome touch of co-workers, but we find that supervisory status actually increases women's harassment, in keeping with the power threat perspective. Although other research has suggested this counterintuitive result, this study is the first longitudinal investigation to clearly reveal the pattern.

Could this finding be a product of supervisors' greater sensitivity or legal consciousness? If so, we would expect to have observed stronger effects of supervisory status on subjective harassment than on behavioral indicators. However, female supervisors were more likely to report harassment.

Within the supervisor category, there may be important differences in harassment by level of workplace

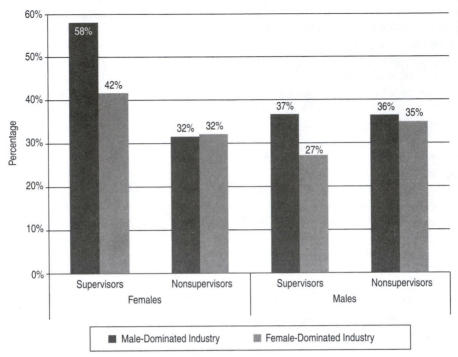

Figure 2 Percentage Reporting any Harassment by Sex, Supervisory Authority, and Industry Sex Ratio.

authority. For example, women in upper management, or in organizations with few women in supervisory roles, may experience more harassing behaviors (Cohen et al. 1998). When we distinguished between females who supervised only one to three workers and those who supervised greater numbers, we found larger positive effects of supervisory authority on harassment for females supervising larger numbers of workers.

Regardless of organizational rank, sexual harassment objectifies workers and reduces women to sexual objects in ways that "may trump a woman's formal organizational power" (Quinn 2002, 392). Indeed, our qualitative interviews help to explain *why* women in authority positions are targeted for harassment. Women supervisors repeatedly spoke about feeling isolated and of harassment by co-workers and subordinates directed toward putting them "in their place." Still, they tolerated such harassment to keep their jobs. Social isolation may also represent an important mechanism linking expressions of gender and industry sex ratios to harassment, in keeping with our second and third hypotheses. Whether attempting to prove they could lead a team of workers or

prove themselves as women in masculine fields, women's isolation in these positions repeatedly left them vulnerable to harassment. Women supervisors were told "this is no place for women," and men and women who diverged even slightly from rigid gender expectations elicited taunts and more menacing responses.

Sexual harassment policies are put in place to protect workers, but organizational practice is often misaligned with formal policies or grievance procedures, calling into question fundamental assumptions many sociologists make regarding organizational constraint and agency (Roscigno 2011). Take, for instance, the sexual harassment of Holly at a company dinner. Her co-workers' concern led to *her* removal from the situation rather than the punishment of her harasser. Her colleagues ended Holly's harassment, but they did so in a way that would not jeopardize their profitable business relationship with the client. Holly's co-workers quickly labeled her harasser as a "bad apple," but the organizational contexts that allowed the harassment and broader gender inequality to occur remained unquestioned.

Many of our interviewees experienced wide-ranging forms of sex-based discrimination as well as sexual harassment. These findings may thus extend more broadly to workplace bullying, intimate partner violence, and other forms of discrimination and harassment. For example, Johnson (1995, 284) identifies "patriarchal terrorism" as a form of intimate partner violence that reflects "patriarchal traditions of men's right to control 'their' women." Similarly, Macmillan and Gartner (1999) direct attention to dyadic power relations, finding that women's employment lowers risks of spousal abuse when their male partners are employed but increases risks when their male partners are unemployed.

Theory and research on gender stratification often make the implicit assumption that problems such as sexual harassment, sex discrimination, and workplace bullying will recede if and when women attain greater power at work. Yet power in the form of supervisory authority also provokes backlash from clients, subordinates, and fellow supervisors. This paradox of power represents a challenge and an opportunity for existing frameworks. Beyond gender, characteristics such as race and class may similarly trump formal organizational authority in determining workplace power. Firms are increasingly adopting policies to increase diversity in management (Kalev, Dobbin, and Kelly 2006), but this study points to a new obstacle for women and, perhaps, racial minorities in leadership positions (but see Hirsh and Lyons 2010).

Although legal and organizational responses to sexual harassment have evolved rapidly in the past three decades, the cultural image of harassers and targets has not kept pace with changing workplace realities. Many still view the typical harassment scenario as one involving a sleazy male boss and a powerless female secretary. As this chapter shows, the reality is far more varied. Moving away from such stereotypes is a critical step for improving organizational policies and training procedures on sexual harassment. Effective training must go beyond male boss/female subordinate role-playing exercises and better reflect the diversity of harassment experiences. Effective grievance procedures must also enable targeted workers to come forward without undermining their own authority. For women who become bosses, their positions create a paradox of power in a gender system that continues to subordinate women. In taking on positions of

authority, they also take on a greater risk of sexual harassment.

References

Berdahl, Jennifer L. 2007. "Harassment Based on Sex: Protecting Social Status in the Context of Gender Hierarchy." *Academy of Management Review* 32:641–658.

Chamberlain, Lindsey Joyce, Martha Crowley, Daniel Tope, and Randy Hodson. 2008. "Sexual Harassment in Organizational Context." *Work and Occupations* 35:262–95.

Cohen, Lisa E., Joseph P. Broschak, and Heather A. Haveman. 1998. "And Then There Were More? The Effect of Organizational Sex Composition on the Hiring and Promotion of Managers." *American Sociological Review* 63:711–727.

Collins, Patricia Hill. 2004. *Black Sexual Politics: African Americans, Gender, and the New Racism.* New York: Routledge.

Collinson, Margaret, and David Collinson. 1996. "'It's Only Dick': The Sexual Harassment of Women Managers in Insurance Sales." *Work, Employment and Society* 10:29–56.

Connell, R. W. 1987. *Gender and Power: Society, the Person, and Sexual Politics.* Stanford, CA: Stanford University Press.

Connell, R. W. 1992. "A Very Straight Gay: Masculinity, Homosexual Experience, and the Dynamics of Gender." *American Sociological Review* 57:735–751.

Crenshaw, Kimberle. 1991. "Mapping the Margins: Intersectionality, Identity Politics, and Violence against Women of Color." *Stanford Law Review* 43:1241–1299.

Das, Aniruddha. 2009. "Sexual Harassment at Work in the United States." *Archives of Sexual Behavior* 38:909–921.

Davidson, Marilyn J., and Cary L. Cooper. 1992. *Shattering the Glass Ceiling: The Woman Manager.* London: Paul Chapman Publishing.

De Coster, Stacy, Sarah Beth Estes, and Charles W. Mueller. 1999. "Routine Activities and Sexual Harassment in the Workplace." *Work and Occupations* 26:21–49.

Dellinger, Kirsten, and Christine L. Williams. 2002. "The Locker Room and the Dorm Room: The Cultural Context of Sexual Harassment in Two Magazine Publishing Organizations." *Social Problems* 49:242–257.

DeSouza, Eros, and Joseph Solberg. 2004. "Women's and Men's Reactions to Man-to-Man Sexual Harassment: Does the Sexual Orientation of the Victim Matter?" *Sex Roles* 50:623–639.

Dobbin, Frank, and Erin L. Kelly. 2007. "How to Stop Harassment: Professional Construction of Legal

Compliance in Organizations." *American Journal of Sociology* 112:1203–1243.

Eagly, Alice H., and Linda L. Carli. 2007. *Through the Labyrinth*. Boston: Harvard Business School Press.

Eisenberg, Susan. 2001. "Marking Gender Boundaries: Porn, Piss, and Power Tools." In *Feminist Frontiers* (ed. L. Richardson, V. Taylor, and N. Whittier), 286–295. New York: McGraw Hill.

Elliott, James R., and Ryan A. Smith. 2004. "Race, Gender, and Workplace Power." *American Sociological Review* 69:365–386.

Farley, Lin. 1978. *Sexual Shakedown: The Sexual Harassment of Women on the Job*. New York: McGraw-Hill.

Fitzgerald, Louise F., Fritz Drasgow, Charles L. Hulin, Michele J. Gefland, and Vicki J. Magley. 1997. "Antecedents and Consequences of Sexual Harassment in Organizations: A Test of an Integrated Model." *Journal of Applied Psychology* 82:578–589.

Giuffre, Patti A., and Christine L. Williams. 1994. "Labeling Sexual Harassment in Restaurants." *Gender and Society* 8:378–401.

Gorman, Elizabeth H. 2005. "Gender Stereotypes, Same-Gender Preferences, and Organizational Variation in the Hiring of Women: Evidence from Law Firms." *American Sociological Review* 70:702–728.

Gross, Neil. 2009. "A Pragmatist Theory of Social Mechanisms." *American Sociological Review* 74:358–379.

Hennen, Peter. 2001. "Powder, Pomp, Power: Toward a Typology and Genealogy of Effeminacies." *Social Thought and Research* 24:121–144.

Hennen, Peter. 2008. *Faeries, Bears, and Leathermen: Men in Community Queering the Masculine*. Chicago: University of Chicago Press.

Hirsh, Elizabeth, and Christopher J. Lyons. 2010. "Perceiving Discrimination on the Job: Legal Consciousness, Workplace Context, and the Construction of Race Discrimination." *Law and Society Review* 44:269–298.

Houston, Sandra, and Naomi Hwang. 1996. "Correlates of the Objective and Subjective Experiences of Sexual Harassment in High School." *Sex Roles* 34:189–204.

Hultin, Mia. 2003. "Some Take the Glass Escalator, Some Hit the Glass Ceiling?" *Work and Occupations* 30:30–61.

Ingraham, Chrys. 2008. *White Weddings: Romancing Heterosexuality in Popular Culture*, 2nd ed. New York: Routledge.

Johnson, Michael P. 1995. "Patriarchal Terrorism and Common Couple Violence: Two Forms of Violence against Women." *Journal of Marriage and the Family* 57:283–294.

Kalev, Alexandra. 2009. "Cracking the Glass Cages? Restructuring and Ascriptive Inequality at Work." *American Journal of Sociology* 114:1591–1643.

Kalev, Alexandra, Frank Dobbin, and Erin Kelly. 2006."Best Practices or Best Guesses? Assessing the Efficacy of Corporate Affirmative Action and Diversity Policies." *American Sociological Review* 71:589–617.

Lopez, Steven H., Randy Hodson, and Vincent J. Roscigno. 2009. "Power, Status, and Abuse at Work: General and Sexual Harassment Compared." *Sociological Quarterly* 50:3–27.

Maass, Anne, Mara Cadinu, Gaia Guarnieri, and Annalisa Grasselli. 2003. "Sexual Harassment Under Social Identity Threat: The Computer Harassment Paradigm." *Journal of Personality and Social Psychology* 85:853–870.

MacKinnon, Catharine A. 1979. *Sexual Harassment of Working Women: A Case of Sex Discrimination*. New Haven, CT: Yale University Press.

Macmillan, Ross, and Rosemary Gartner. 1999. "When She Brings Home the Bacon: Labor-Force Participation and the Risk of Spousal Violence against Women." *Journal of Marriage and the Family* 61:947–958.

Mansfield, Phyllis Kernoff, Patricia Barthalow Koch, Julie Henderson, Judith R. Vicary, Margaret Cohn, and Elaine W. Young. 1991. "The Job Climate for Women in Traditionally Male Blue-Collar Occupations." *Sex Roles* 25:63–79.

Martin, Patricia Yancey. 2001. "'Mobilizing Masculinities': Women's Experiences of Men at Work." *Organization* 8:587–618.

Martin, Patricia Yancey. 2003. "'Said and Done' Versus 'Saying and Doing': Gendering Practices, Practicing Gender at Work." *Gender & Society* 17:342–366.

Martin, Patricia Yancey. 2006. "Practicing Gender at Work: Further Thoughts on Reflexivity." *Gender, Work, and Organization* 13:254–276.

Mortimer, Jeylan T. 2003. *Working and Growing Up in America*. Cambridge, MA: Harvard University Press.

Pascoe, C. J. 2007. *Dude, You're a Fag: Dominance and Masculinity in High School*. Berkeley: University of California Press.

Quinn, Beth A. 2002. "Sexual Harassment and Masculinity: The Power and Meaning of 'Girl Watching.'" *Gender & Society* 16:386–402.

Reskin, Barbara F. 2003. "Including Mechanisms in our Models of Ascriptive Inequality." *American Sociological Review* 68:1–21.

Reskin, Barbara F., and Debra Branch McBrier. 2000. "Why Not Ascription? Organizations' Employment of

Male and Female Managers." *American Sociological Review* 65:210–233.

Ridgeway, Cecilia, and Shelley Correll. 2004. "Unpacking the Gender System: A Theoretical Perspective on Gender Beliefs and Social Relations." *Gender & Society* 18:510–531.

Ridgeway, Cecilia, and Lynn Smith-Lovin. 1999. "The Gender System and Interaction." *Annual Review of Sociology* 25:191–216.

Roscigno, Vincent J. 2011. "Power, Revisited." *Social Forces* 90:349–374.

Rospenda, Kathleen M., Judith A. Richman, and Stephanie J. Nawyn. 1998. "Doing Power: The Confluence of Gender, Race, and Class in Contrapower Sexual Harassment." *Gender & Society* 12:40–60.

Schultz, Vicki. 2003. "The Sanitized Workplace." *Yale Law Journal* 112:2061–2193.

Stainback, Kevin, Thomas N. Ratliff, and Vincent J. Roscigno. 2011. "The Context of Workplace Sex Discrimination: Sex Composition, Workplace Culture, and Relative Power." *Social Forces* 89:1165–1188.

Tallichet, Suzanne E. 1995. "Gendered Relations in the Mines and the Division of Labor Underground." *Gender & Society* 9:697–711.

Uggen, Christopher, and Amy Blackstone. 2004. "Sexual Harassment as a Gendered Expression of Power." *American Sociological Review* 69:64–92.

U.S. Equal Employment Opportunity Commission (U.S. EEOC). 2011. "Sexual Harassment." Washington, DC: U.S. Equal Employment Opportunity Commission. http://www.eeoc.gov/laws/types/sexual_harassment. cfm (accessed November 22, 2011).

Waldo, Craig R., Jennifer L. Berdahl, and Louise F. Fitzgerald. 1998. "Are Men Sexually Harassed? If So, by Whom?" *Law and Human Behavior* 22:59–79.

Welsh, Sandy. 1999. "Gender and Sexual Harassment." *Annual Review of Sociology* 25:169–190.

West, Candace, and Don H. Zimmerman. 1987. "Doing Gender." *Gender & Society* 1:125–151.

Willer, Robb. 2005. *Overdoing Gender: A Test of the Masculine Overcompensation Thesis.* Paper presented at the annual meeting of the American Sociological Association, Philadelphia, PA.

Williams, Christine L. 1992. "The Glass Escalator: Hidden Advantages for Men in the 'Female' Professions." *Social Problems* 39:253–267.

Questions

1. McLaughlin and colleagues note that there is sex-based harassment and sexual harassment. How are these similar, and how are they different? Are they mutually exclusive, or do these processes work more in tandem? Explain.

2. The authors clearly note that sex and gender are separate but related things. Often people demand sex categories to be reflected in stereotypical or expected ways. How is this related to harassment? What do McLaughlin and her colleagues find?

3. It seems reasonable to argue that women and subordinates can "fend off" harassment if they gain more power at work. What do the findings tell us about this argument?

4. While women most often work with other women because of gender-based job segregation, there are certainly women who work in places where most employees are men. Sometimes women even become managers in places where they are among few or no women. What do the authors find in terms of women in these work situations?

5. Often "bullying" and even "harassment" are blown off as non-existent or not serious. How are these examples of enacting violence? How do these processes lead to the reproduction of inequality?

6. What can we do to prevent and mitigate harassment of women and other minority groups in workplaces?

24

Breaking the Food Chains: An Investigation of Food Justice Activism

ALISON HOPE ALKON AND KARI MARIE NORGAARD

Access to safe drinking water, clear air, toxin-free land, and healthy food, even in a country as rich and plush as the United States, is stratified by geographic location, race, and class. Anyone who grew up in an inner city dotted with carry-outs and convenience stores but lacking grocery stores with fresh food can attest to that. So too can those in remote areas of the heartland who are surrounded by corn fields (for animal feed and fuel) but with few farmers' markets.

In the reading about genocide in Darfur, we learned how controlling access to food and water became a means of reproducing inequality with devastating consequences. On the flip side, popular authors such as Michael Pollan (2006) and Eric Schlosser (2012) have argued that food can be a powerful motivation for people to create social change. For example, the film *Food, Inc.* (Kenner and Pearlstein 2008), in which both Pollan and Schlosser appear, in many ways is a challenge to the inequalities present during food production in the United States, an industry highly subsidized through government programs and policies. It demonstrates how industrial agriculture creates unevenly experienced environmental degradation while trying to feed a growing world hungry for cheap food. Despite their appeal, movements concerning food have seen varying success. Nonetheless, within the last few decades we have seen better labeling on food in grocery stores, fast-food chains reporting the nutritional content of their foods, farmers' markets accepting EBT cards (food stamps), and the sprouting of community gardens.

In this reading, we see how institutional racism and racialized geographies in the United States create food deserts where Black farmers and Karuk fisherpeople once produced their own food. Yet farmers and fisherpeople do not take this lying down. This comparative case study examines how the Karuk Tribe of California and a food justice group in Oakland, California, challenge their exclusion from healthy food production and consumption by creating a food market and fighting the licensing of dams on an important river.

References

Kenner, Robert, and Elise Pearlstein. 2008. *Food, Inc.* Film. Los Angeles: Participant Media, Dogwoof Pictures, River Road Entertainment.

Pollan, Michael. 2006. *The Omnivore's Dilemma: A Natural History of Four Meals.* New York: Penguin.

Schlosser, Eric. 2012. *Fast Food Nation: The Dark Side of the All-American Meal.* Boston: Houghton Mifflin Harcourt.

Excerpted from Alkon, Alison Hope and Kari Marie Norgaard. 2009. "Breaking the Food Chains: An Investigation of Food Justice Activism." *Sociological Inquiry* 79:289–305. © 2009 Alpha Kappa Delta.

This chapter examines the concept of food justice through comparative case studies of two racially and spatially distinct Northern California communities. Food justice places the need for food security—access to healthy, affordable, culturally appropriate food—in the contexts of institutional racism, racial formation, and racialized geographies. Our analysis highlights the ability of food justice to serve as a theoretical and political bridge between existing work on sustainable agriculture, food insecurity, and environmental justice.

The West Oakland Food Collaborative and the Karuk Tribe of California frame their food insecurity and high rates of diet-related diseases not as the result of poor individual food choices, but from institutionalized racism. We follow how each community highlights the political and economic histories through which their key food producers, African American farmers and Native American fishermen, were denied the land and water necessary for food production. In addition to poverty, the contemporary racialized geographies (Kobayashi and Peake 2000) through which institutional racism shapes the physical landscape prevent many Black and indigenous communities from purchasing the quality of food they once produced. Lack of geographic and economic access confines their choices to processed, fast, and commodity foods. Additionally, Black and Native American communities suffer from elevated rates of diet-related illnesses such as diabetes. Activists in the communities we study pursue food justice through a diverse array of strategies including challenging state policy and the creation of alternative food systems.

From these case studies, we demonstrate that the concept of food justice allows sustainable agriculture scholars to better contend with institutional racism and environmental justice theorists to connect disproportionate access to environmental benefits to social science analyses of race (Pulido 2000). Moreover, it is our hope that the concept of food justice may create political alliances between proponents of the environmental justice and sustainable agriculture movements through an understanding of food access as a product of institutionalized racism.

Ecology and Equity: Building Theoretical Bridges

While environmental justice advocates have long argued that low-income people and people of color suffer disproportionately from the burdens of environmental degradation, recent scholarship has also begun to emphasize the problem of disproportionate access to environmental benefits. Attention to environmental benefits helps the environmental justice movement to solidify its connection to larger democratic projects such as eco-populism (Szasz 1994), ecological democracy (Faber 1998), and just sustainability (Agyeman 2005). The sustainable agriculture movement, on the other hand, focusing primarily on the environmental benefits of fertile soil, clean water, and pesticide-free food, has often ignored the role of race in structuring agriculture in the United States (P. Allen 2004). Although the term "sustainability" includes both ecological protection and social justice by definition, sustainable agriculture activists have primarily aligned themselves with the environmental rather than environmental justice movement (Alkon 2008). Following a brief review of existing literature within sustainable agriculture and environmental justice, we offer two case studies in which activists situate their own lack of food access within historical processes of institutional racism, racial identity formation, and racialized geographies.

Bringing Social Justice Back into Sustainability

The sustainable agriculture movement has traditionally focused on technical solutions to problems of ecologically devastating food production, making use of the work of university extension agents and agroecologists. Social scientists, however, have portrayed an agriculture system embedded in specific, historically produced social relations as responsible for social and environmental problems. Foster and Magdoff (2000) trace social scientists' interest in sustainable agriculture to Marx's use of soil science in illustrating the environmental consequences of agriculture embedded in a capitalist economic system. The increased industrialization and consolidation of agricultural firms occurring since Marx's observations have held dire consequences for the soil and water on which food production depends (Buttel, Larson, and Gillespie 1990).

While scholarly critiques of the sustainable agriculture movement call broadly for more attention to social justice issues, the concept of food justice contextualizes disparate access to healthy food within a broader and more historicized framework of institutional racism. Because of its focus on racialized access to the environmental benefit of healthy food, food justice can link sustainable agriculture to environmental justice theory and practice.

Theorizing Food in Environmental Justice Scholarship

In the last two decades, environmental justice scholars have successfully documented the unequal distribution of environmental toxics through which low-income people and people of color bear the health burdens of environmental degradation (United Church of Christ 1987). These communities have organized numerous campaigns against the companies responsible (B. Allen 2003; Brown and Mikkelsen 1997; Bullard 1990; Sze 2006). Similarities in these cases shed light on an environmental justice frame (Capek 1993) or paradigm (Taylor 1997, 2000), linking distribution of environmental toxins to a culturally resonant (Gamson and Modigliani 1989) civil rights rhetoric.

While the environmental justice movement is best known for protests against site discrimination, many activists adopt a much broader approach. Often grounded in their own experiences as victims of environmental racism, activists have worked toward pollution prevention (Szasz 1994) and the internalization of the costs of production by the companies responsible (Faber 1998) so that no community should suffer the health effects of environmental toxics. Constantly looking to broaden the environmental justice frame through the inclusion of issues generally ignored by what Brulle (2000) terms the "reform" environmental movement, activists have created a complex approach incorporating the many environmental and social justice factors affecting the places where low-income people and people of color live, work, and play (Alston 1991).

Research Approach

Data on the West Oakland Food Collaborative (WOFC) came from three primary sources: participant observation, semi-structured interviews, and a survey of customers at the West Oakland Farmer's Market. During 18 months of participant observation, Alison Hope Alkon took on a variety of roles including regular customer, volunteer gardener, researcher, and observer at the farmers' market, WOFC meetings, and events and activities organized by WOFC member organizations. Copious notes were taken and later coded, allowing patterns to emerge. Eighteen in-depth interviews were conducted with WOFC participants and farmers' market vendors. Interviews lasting approximately one hour were recorded and transcribed. The survey was administered to 100 farmers' market customers over the course of three weeks through a sample of convenience.

Karie Marie Norgaard began her research in 2003 at the request of the Karuk Tribe. Tribal members had been less than successful at articulating their concerns through the Federal Energy Regulatory Commission process on the relicensing of the Klamath River Hydroproject. The tribe sought to seek greater scientific backing for their claims. Data on the Karuk case study are drawn from four main sources: archival material, indepth interviews with Karuk tribal members, Karuk medical records, and the 2005 Karuk Health and Fish Consumption Survey. The 2005 Karuk Health and Fish Consumption Survey was distributed to adult tribal members within the ancestral territory in the spring of 2005. The survey had a response rate of 38 percent, a total of 90 individuals. Additional medical data have been obtained from relevant federal, state, and county records (Norgaard 2005).

Both researchers recognize the particular tensions that can arise in relationships between white researchers and communities of color. Alkon worked diligently with several individuals active in the West Oakland Food Collaborative to ensure that the community would benefit from her research. To this end, she has edited grant applications for several WOFC member organizations and hired a research assistant who was raised in West Oakland to aid in the distribution of surveys. Research on the Karuk tribe sought to achieve goals specified by tribal members that would correspond to the tribe's existing political needs. All aspects of the research process (interviews, survey design, and implementation) were carried out under direction of or by tribal members themselves.

Culture and Agriculture: The West Oakland Food Collaborative

In an old, partially refurbished Victorian home in West Oakland, now home to the Prescott Joseph Community Center, a group of activists sit around a long wood table discussing projects and strategies for the procurement of food justice. While the group is by no means entirely African American, discussions of institutional racism and inequality pervade many aspects of their work. Among other projects, those attending WOFC meetings run school and community gardens, cooking programs, and food distribution efforts focused on supplying healthy food to this low-income, predominantly African American neighborhood. The most prominent example of the WOFC's work is a weekly farmers' market through which African American farmers and home-based business people sell organic produce, flowers, homemade jams, sweets, and beauty products. Farmers' markets are most commonly associated with the sustainable agriculture movement's promotion of small, local farmers. This market, however, emphasizes antiracism. Indeed, one market vendor described the market's primary purpose as "empowering Black people."

Although the produce featured at the market is much less expensive than in wealthier neighborhoods, it struggles to attract customers unaccustomed to this kind of shopping. While the market is extremely small, it is a lively place. Customers and vendors, the majority of whom know each other by name, catch up on the week's events while shopping for the week's provisions. The farmers' market celebrates African American culture through the products featured (such as black-eyed peas, greens, and yams), the music played (mostly soul and funk), and the special events celebrated (such as Black History Month and Juneteenth). The radical potential of merging racial identity formation with sustainable agriculture is recognized by one market farmer, who claims "this market fights the systems that are in place to keep down sharecroppers like my father and grandfather." Like other environmental justice efforts, the WOFC emphasizes racism and inequality, connecting environmental issues to the lived experiences of low-income people and people of color (Bullard 1990; Novotny 2000).

One of the most egregious instances of racism highlighted by the farmers' market is the discrimination experienced by African American farmers. In the words of one vendor, the West Oakland Farmer's Market is different from others because "we have Black farmers . . . you don't see a lot of Black farmers." WOFC members attribute the historic decline of Black farmers nationwide to the United States Department of Agriculture (USDA)'s denial of loans, subsidies, and other support that enabled white farmers to transition to mechanized agriculture (Gilbert, Sharp, and Felin 2002). In 1997, the USDA settled a class-action lawsuit on this issue, though Black farmers and their descendants have reported difficulties claiming their portion of the settlement (Wood and Gilbert 2000). Discrimination against Black farmers created an agricultural sector dominated by whites and deprived African Americans of a source of wealth and access to economic and environmental benefits.

The goal of the West Oakland Farmer's Market is, in the words of one prominent WOFC member, "to connect Black farmers to the Black community." This view is reflected by the market's customers; a majority of those surveyed (52 percent) claim that support for Black farmers is their most important reason for market attendance. Several surveys also included responses to open-ended requests for additional information with comments reflecting this theme, such as "my consciousness about the plight of Black farmers has grown." These responses suggest that the concept of food justice might productively connect access to environmental benefits to theories of racial identity formation (Omi and Winant 1989).

Not only have African Americans been stripped of their abilities to produce healthy, culturally appropriate food, they are also unable to purchase similar items. WOFC members, along with food justice activists in many parts of the United States, popularize the term "food desert" in order to describe the lack of locally available healthy food (Wrigley, Margetts, and Whelan 2002). Many scholars have observed a positive correlation between the existence of grocery stores and income (Chung and Myers 1999) and a negative one between grocery stores and the percentage of African American residents (Morland et al. 2002).

One WOFC participant, currently organizing to open a worker-owned grocery store, describes the obstacles residents face in obtaining fresh food:

> West Oakland has 40,000 people and only one grocery store. [The many] corner stores sell generic canned goods. You have that option and then the fast food chains is the other option. So what people have the option to buy is putting more and more chemicals and additives and hormones and all of these things into their bodies.

With nearly 1.5 times as many corner liquor stores as the city average (California Alcoholic Beverage Control [CABC] 2006) as well as an abundance of fast food establishments, West Oakland is typical of low-income, African American food deserts in other cities (Block, Scribner, and DeSalvo 2004; LaVeist and Wallace 2000). WOFC members describe the process through which large grocery stores closed urban locations in favor of suburban ones as "supermarket redlining," likening it to racist lending policies and further linking their own work to a broad and historicized antiracist resistance. Through food justice activism, WOFC members link their own food insecurity to institutional racism and its historic and present-day effects on the built environment (Kobayashi and Peake 2000; Massey and Denton 1998). Not surprisingly, residents of this food desert experience high rates of diet-related health problems such as diabetes. WOFC members racialize and politicize diabetes in much the same way that environmental justice activists portray asthma (Sze 2006). In the words of one food justice activist, who recently relocated to Oakland and became involved in many of the WOFC's projects, "diabetes kills more people in our communities than crack!" (Lappe and Terry 2006). In Alameda County, African Americans are twice as likely as other racial groups to suffer from diabetes (CDC 2002).

WOFC members link these health disparities to the lack of locally available healthy food. According to one market farmer, a son of Arkansas sharecroppers who has extensive training in herbal and Chinese medicine: "I've seen the African American people's health declining. It's not having access to healthy food, to a good lifestyle." Another vendor describes how the WOFC's projects provide that access:

> It's the whole process of learning how to grow things and reclaim [public] space and to live sustainable and healthy [lives]. And what it means to understand that, okay, you're prone [to] diabetes. [How do you] counteract that? 'Cause that's a huge thing in West Oakland, and [the WOFC has] things that help you live a more sustainable life knowing that you're prone to diabetes.

The WOFC deploys an analysis that attributes high rates of diabetes to food insecurity, which in turn results from institutional racism.

Because this analysis ties a place-based instance of environmental injustice to a more systemic and historicized understanding of racism, the WOFC's solution focuses on local food and local economics rather than attempts to attract corporate economic development. In the words of one farmers' market vendor: "I don't want Safeway or Albertsons. They abandoned the inner city. They sell poison. They pay crap wages. Independent business is the most important thing." Instead of chain grocery stores, the WOFC emphasizes "community self-sufficiency" and the ability of marginalized communities to provide, at least partially, for themselves. One WOFC participant describes the goal of her activism in the following way:

> [It's about] building a community that takes care of each other's needs. And we can self sustain outside of the dominant system. . . . We want to buy and sell from each other . . . in a way that helps us sustain our neighborhoods or our communities. That's different than consuming in a way that sustains a mega business that's separate and distinct from us.

The WOFC's projects aim to address the needs of low-income, predominantly African American, West Oakland residents through the development of local food and local economic systems.

The West Oakland Food Collaborative's food justice activism combines antiracism with the creation of a local food system. For this reason, their case offers important insights on the development of an environmental justice approach to food and its consequences for theorizing and achieving environmental justice and sustainable agriculture.

Battling Corporate River Management on the Klamath

In the Northern part of the state, the Karuk Tribe of California has mobilized its demand for food justice by lobbying the federal government to block the relicensing of four dams on the Klamath River. These dams prevent the Karuk tribe from sustaining themselves on their traditional foods, which include salmon, lamprey, steelhead, and sturgeon (Norgaard 2005). In addition to lobbying, tribal members have engaged in a variety of protest strategies including working with commercial fishermen and environmental organizations to achieve greater visibility; pleading their case at meetings of the dam's multinational corporate owners, directors, and shareholders; and participating in numerous regional protest activities.

The Klamath River dams disconnect the Karuk from their food sources in several ways. The dams degrade water quality by creating standing water where blue green algae blooms deplete oxygen and create toxic conditions downstream. Levels of the liver toxin mycrocystin were the highest recorded of any water body in the United States and 4,000 times the World Health Organization (WHO) safety limit in 2005 (Karuk Tribe of California 2006). The dams lack fish ladders or other features that would allow the passage of native salmon. When the lowest dam was built, Spring Chinook Salmon lost access to 90 percent of their spawning habitat. Around this time, most Karuk families reported the loss of these fish as a significant food source.

One tribal member describes the devastating effect of the dams on the Karuk food system as follows:

> A healthy riverine system has a profound effect on the people on the river. I have six children. If every one of those kids went down and fished and caught a good healthy limit . . . you could pretty much fill a freezer and have nice good fish all the way through the year. But now, without a healthy riverine system, the economy down here on the lower river is pretty much devastated. All the fishing community is devastated by the unhealthy riverine system. (Ron Reed, Traditional Karuk Fisherman)

The dams and their ensuing environmental degradation have wreaked havoc on the food needs of the tribe.

The Karuk tribe articulates their right to traditional foods not only as an issue of food insecurity but of food justice. They locate their current food needs in the history of genocide, lack of land rights, and forced assimilation that have so devastated this and other Native American communities. These processes have prevented tribal members from carrying out land management techniques necessary to food attainment.

This tragic history provides context to understand the ability of the federal government to license a dam to a multinational corporation within Karuk territory. It is the dams themselves, however, that have had the most sweeping and immediate effect on Karuk food access. Until recently, Karuk people have experienced relatively high rates of subsistence living. Elder tribal members recall their first visit to the grocery store:

> I can remember first going to the store with mom when I was about in the fifth and sixth grade and going in

there and it was so strange to buy, you know, get stuff out of the store. Especially cans of vegetables, like green beans and stuff; Mom used to can all that. And bread. I was about 6 years old when I saw my first loaf of bread in the store. That was really quite a change, I'll tell you. (Blanche Moore, Karuk Tribal Member)

Traditional fish consumption for Karuk people is estimated at 450 pounds per person per year, more than a pound per day (Hewes 1973). Up until the 1980s many Karuk people, especially those from traditional families, ate salmon up to three times per day when the fish were running. Karuk survival has been directly linked to this important environmental resource.

When the dams were built, the Karuk tribe was stripped of access to much of its traditional food as well as the ability to manage the river ecosystem. In contrast to the traditional diet, present-day Karuk people consume less than 5 pounds of salmon per person per year. Self-report data from the 2005 Karuk Health and Fish Consumption Survey indicate that over 80 percent of households were unable to gather adequate amounts of eel, salmon, or sturgeon to fulfill their family needs (Norgaard 2005). As of 2006, so few fish existed that even ceremonial salmon consumption is now limited.

Like West Oakland residents, members of the Karuk tribe cannot purchase the food they once procured through a direct relationship with the nonhuman environment. Most Karuk do not believe in buying or selling salmon. Even if tribal members were willing to buy salmon, replacing subsistence fishing with store-bought salmon would be prohibitively expensive. Replacement cost analysis conducted in the spring of 2005 puts the cost of purchasing salmon at over $4,000 per tribal member per year (Stercho 2005). In the communities within the ancestral territory, this amount would represent over half of the average per capita annual income. While the Karuk are denied access to an environmental benefit because of institutional racism, they cannot replace that benefit through purchase because of poverty.

As in West Oakland, healthy, culturally appropriate food is not available within a convenient distance to tribal members. Tribal members must drive up to 40 miles each way to acquire commodity foods and up to 80 miles each way to shop at supermarkets. According to a nutritional analysis of the local store, it is nearly impossible to access fresh, healthy food on a limited budget:

> The local grocery store in Orleans is lacking in variety and quality of fresh produce and other food products. . . . In addition, the prices are high, making it financially difficult for a family to get adequate nutrition. The yearly median Karuk tribal income is $13,000 or $270 per week. Yet the average cost for a two-person family to eat healthy foods, based on the prices of foods available at the local grocery store in Orleans, is estimated at approximately $150 per week. Note that this represents 55 percent of the income of an average family for the week! (Jennifer Jackson, 2005, 11)

Tribal members link the lack of access to traditional foods to the need for government food assistance:

> Instead of having healthy food to eat—fish—we are relegated to eating commodity foods that the government gives out. That's our subsidy: high starch foods, things that aren't so healthy that the Karuk people are pretty much forced to eat. (Ron Reed, Traditional Karuk Fisherman)

Self-report data from the Karuk Health and Fish Consumption Survey indicate that 20 percent of Karuk people consume commodity foods. Commodity foods tend to be low in essential nutrients and high in complex carbohydrates and fat (Jackson 2005).

Because of the greatly reduced ability of tribal members to provide healthy food to their community, the Karuk experience extremely high rates of hunger and disease. Recent data from University of California at Los Angeles (UCLA)'s California Health Interview Survey (Diamant et al. 2005) show that Native people have the highest rates of both food insecurity (37.2%) and hunger (16.9%) in California (Harrison et al. 2002). The estimated diabetes rate for the Karuk Tribe is 21 percent, approximately four times the U.S. average of 4.9 percent. The estimated rate of heart disease for the Karuk Tribe is 39.6 percent, three times the U.S. average (Norgaard 2005).

Diabetes is described as a new disease among this population and is the consequence of drastic lifestyle and cultural changes (Joe and Young 1993). Tribal members account for both the severity and the sudden onset of diet-related health problems:

> Our people never used to be fat. Our people never used to have these health problems that we are encountering today. Diabetes is probably the biggest one but not the only one. The ramifications of the food that we eat and the lives that we live. High blood pressure is another one. I have high blood pressure. My mother had diabetes. I'm borderline, I'm pretty sure. You can certainly tell that our people never used to be fat. Now you can't hardly find a skinny person around. (David Arwood, Traditional Karuk Fisherman)

Tribal members posit this dramatic shift as a consequence of their denied access to salmon and other traditional foods.

The Karuk tribe is the first in the nation to deploy the concept of food justice in order to link declining salmon populations caused by the dams with high incidences of diabetes and other diet-related diseases. The tribe frames declined river health and the ensuing loss of salmon as a direct result of institutional racism. The Karuk have been stripped of access to an important resource as well as the ability to manage their ancestral land. Because of cost and distance, the tribe cannot purchase what it once produced. Tribe members must rely on locally available unhealthy alternatives and commodity foods—or, in too many cases, go without. Because of this process of denied access to traditional or replacement foods, diabetes researcher Kue Young (1997, 164) writes that the "resolution of the major health problems of Native Americans requires redressing the underlying social, cultural and political causes of those problems." In other words, food access must be connected to the historical process of institutional racism that created food insecurity. Tribal activists make this connection through the concept of food justice.

Conclusion: Political Implications and Alliance Building

Members of the West Oakland Food Collaborative and the Karuk Tribe clearly share similar experiences. Through access to land and water, Black farmers and Karuk fishermen once provided the bulk of their community's food needs. Today, West Oakland residents and Karuk tribal members live in food deserts. They cannot purchase what they once produced on their own. Activists link this lack of food access to their community's elevated rates of diabetes and other diet-related illnesses. Furthermore, both groups frame their grassroots struggles for food justice as attempts to reclaim their ability to produce and consume food.

We use these case studies to demonstrate how the concept of food justice can help the sustainable agriculture movement to better attend to issues of equity, and the environmental justice movement to articulate sustainable alternatives. Moreover, it is our hope that the concept of food justice may create political alliances between the two movements. These theoretical and practical alliances depend on a broader understanding of how racial and economic inequality affect the production and consumption of food, a project we will continue to develop in a forthcoming anthology called *The Food Justice Reader*.

Theoretically, food justice links food insecurity to institutional racism and racialized geography, reshaping thinking within the fields of sustainable agriculture and environmental justice. Scholars and activists in the sustainable agriculture movement have done well to challenge the corporate control of food production systems and identify resulting impacts to the long-term viability of soils and surrounding ecosystems. As food is increasingly controlled by large corporations, ecosystems suffer and communities have less control over local foods. Yet sustainable agriculture scholars and activists have not yet understood the ways that race shapes a community's ability to produce and consume food.

Moreover, a food justice framework links food access to broader questions of power and political efficacy. While many sustainable agriculture advocates and scholars implicitly assume that all communities have the ability to choose ecologically produced food, the concept of food justice can help to illuminate the race and class privilege masked by this approach. Access to healthy food is shaped not only by the economic ability to purchase it, but also by the historical processes through which race has come to affect who lives where and who has access to what kinds of services. Because it highlights institutional racism and racialized geographies, food justice may therefore encourage the sustainable agriculture movement to embrace a more meaningful approach to social justice.

Beyond naming food access as a dimension of environmental inequality, we hope the concept of food justice will contribute to environmental justice work in the following ways. In articulating a demand for access to healthy food, these cases contribute to the developing focus on racially stratified access to environmental benefits within environmental justice. Unfortunately, it is not only the extent of environmental degradation that has intensified in the past half century, but also the degree of social inequality. For this reason it will become more and more important for the environmental justice movement to place attention on access to environmental benefits. Additionally, because food is often central to communities' collective cultural identities, the concept of food justice can illuminate links between environmental justice activism and the process of racial identity formation. These dimensions address both Pellow's (2004) call for scholarly attention to process and history and Pulido's (2000) injunction to connect environmental justice to social science analyses of race.

References

Agyeman, Julian. 2005. *Sustainable Communities and the Challenge of Environmental Justice.* Cambridge, MA: MIT Press.

Alkon, Alison Hope. 2008. "Paradise or Pavement: The Social Construction of the Environment in Two Urban Farmers' Markets." *Local Environment: The Journal of Justice and Sustainability* 13(3): 271–89.

Allen, Barbara. 2003. *Uneasy Alchemy: Citizens and Experts in Louisiana's Chemical Corridor Disputes.* Cambridge, MA: MIT Press.

Allen, Patricia. 2004. *Together at the Table: Sustainability and Sustenance in the American Agrifoods Movement.* University Park: Pennsylvania State University Press.

Alston, Dana. 1991. "*Taking Back Our Lives: A Report to the Panos Institute on Environment, Community Development and Race in the United States.*" Washington, DC: Panos Institute.

Block, Jason P., Richard A. Scribner, and Karen B. DeSalvo. 2004. "Fast Food, Race/Ethnicity, and Income: A Geographic Analysis." *American Journal of Preventative Medicine* 27:211–217.

Brown, Phil, and Edwin J. Mikkelsen. 1997. *No Safe Place.* Berkeley, CA: University of California Press.

Brulle, Robert J. 2000. *Agency, Democracy, and Nature: The U.S. Environmental Movement from a Critical Theory Perspective.* Cambridge, MA: MIT Press.

Bullard, Robert. 1990. *Dumping in Dixie.* Boulder, CO: Westview Press.

Buttel, Fred, Olaf F. Larson, and Gilbert W. Gillespie, Jr. 1990. *The Sociology of Agriculture.* New York: Greenwood Press.

California Alcoholic Beverage Control (CABC). 2006. "Fact Sheet: Oakland Alcohol Retailers." http://www.urbanstrategies.org/programs/csj/AlRetail.html (accessed April 3, 2006).

Capek, Stella. 1993. "The 'Environmental Justice' Frame: A Conceptual Discussion and an Application." *Social Problems* 40:5–24.

Centers for Disease Control and Prevention (CDC). 2002. "National Diabetes Fact Sheet." http://www.cdc.gov/diabetes/pubs/pdf/ndfs_2011.pdf (accessed September 20, 2015).

Chung C., and S. L. Myers. 1999. "Do the Poor Pay More for Food? An Analysis of Grocery Store Availability and Food Price Disparities." *Journal of Consumer Affairs* 33:276–296.

Diamant, Alison L, Susan H. Babey, E. Richard Brown, and Theresa A. Hastert. 2005. "Diabetes on the Rise in California." UCLA Center for Health Policy Research. http://www.ncbi.nlm.nih.gov/pubmed/16397965 (accessed March 31, 2008).

Faber, Daniel. 1998. *The Struggle for Ecological Democracy: Environmental Justice Movements in the United States.* New York: Guilford Press.

Foster, John Bellamy, and Fred Magdoff. 2000. "Liebig, Marx and the Depletion of Soil Fertility: Relevance for Today's Agriculture." In *Hungry for Profit: The Agribusiness Threat to Farmers, Food, and the Environment* (ed. Fred Magdoff, John Bellamy Foster, and Fred Buttel), 43–60. New York: Monthly Review Press.

Gamson, William A., and Andre Modigliani. 1989. "Media Discourse and Public Opinion on Nuclear Power: A Constructionist Approach." *American Journal of Sociology* 95:1–37.

Gilbert, Jess, Gwen Sharp, and Sindy M. Felin. 2002. "The Loss and Persistence of Black-Owned Farms and Farmland: A Review of the Research Literature and Its Implications." *Southern Rural Sociology* 18:1–30.

Harrison, Gail, Charles A. DiSogra, George Manolo-LeClair, Jennifer Aguayo, and Wei Yen. 2002. "Over 2.2 Million Low Income Californian Adults are Food-Insecure, 658,000 Suffer Hunger." UCLA Center for Health Policy Research. http://healthpolicy.ucla.edu/publications/search/pages/detail.aspx?PubID=360 (accessed March 31, 2009).

Hewes, Gordon W. 1973. "Indian Fisheries Productivity in Pre-Contact Times in the Pacific Salmon Area." *Northwest Anthropological Research Notes* 7(3): 133–55.

Jackson, Jennifer. 2005. "Nutritional Analysis of Traditional and Present Foods of the Karuk People and Development of Public Outreach Materials." Orleans, CA: Karuk Tribe of California.

Joe, Jennie, and Robert Young. 1993. *Diabetes as a Disease of Civilization: The Impact of Cultural Change on Indigenous People.* New York: Walter de Gruyter and Co.

Karuk Tribe of California. 2006. "Toxic Algae Threaten Human Health in PacifiCorp's Klamath Reservoirs Blooms Worse than Last Year, Little Response from Company or County." Press release. http://karuk.us/press/06-08-08 toxic reservoirs.pdf (accessed March 31, 2009).

Kobayashi, Audrey, and Linda Peake. 2000. "Racism Out of Place: Thoughts on Whiteness and Antiracist Geography for the New Millennium." *Annals of the Association of American Geographers* 90(2): 392–403.

Lappe, Anna, and Bryant Terry. 2006. *Grub: Ideas for an Urban Organic Kitchen.* New York: Tarcher.

LaVeist T., and J. Wallace. 2000. "Health Risk and Inequitable Distribution of Liquor Stores in African American Neighborhoods." *Social Science and Medicine* 51:613–617.

Massey, Douglas, and Nancy Denton. 1998. *American Apartheid: Segregation and the Making of the American Underclass.* Cambridge, MA: Harvard University Press.

Morland, Kimberly, S. Wing, A. Deiz Roux, and C. Poole. 2002. "Neighborhood Characteristics Associated with the Location of Food Stores and Food Service Places." *American Journal of Preventive Medicine* 22:23–29.

Norgaard, Kari Marie. (2005) "The Effects of Altered Diet on the Health of the Karuk People." Report submitted to the Federal Energy Regulatory Commission Docket #P-2082 on behalf of the Karuk Tribe of California.

Novotny, Patrick. 2000. *Where We Live, Work and Play: The Environmental Justice Movement and the Struggle for a New Environmentalism.* Westport, CT: Praeger.

Omi, Michael, and Howard Winant. 1989. *Racial Formation in the United States: From the 1960s to the 1980s.* New York: Routledge.

Pellow, David N. 2004. "The Politics of Illegal Dumping: An Environmental Justice Framework." *Qualitative Sociology* 27:511–525.

Pulido, Laura. 2000. "Rethinking Environmental Racism: White Privilege and Urban Development in Southern California." *Annals of the Association of American Geographers* 90(1): 12–40.

Stercho, Amy. 2005. "The Importance of Place-Based Fisheries to the Karuk Tribe of California: A Socioeconomic Study." Master's thesis, Humboldt State University, Arcata, CA.

Szasz, Andrew. 1994. *Ecopopulism: Toxic Waste and the Movement for Environmental Justice.* Minneapolis: University of Minnesota Press.

Sze, Julie. 2006. *Noxious New York: The Racial Politics of Urban Health and Environmental Justice.* Cambridge, MA: MIT Press.

Taylor, D. 1997. "American Environmentalism: The Role of Race, Class, and Gender in Shaping Activism 1820–1995." *Race, Gender & Class* 5:16–62.

———. 2000. "The Rise of the Environmental Justice Paradigm." *American Behavioral Scientist* 43:508–590.

United Church of Christ. 1987. *Toxic Wastes and Race in the United States: A National Report on the Racial and Socioeconomic Characteristics with Hazardous Waste Sites.* New York: United Church of Christ Commission for Racial Justice.

Wood, Spencer D., and Jess Gilbert. 2000. "Returning African American Farmers to the Land: Recent Trends and a Policy Rationale." *Review of Black Political Economy* 27(4): 43–64.

Wrigley, Neil Ward, B. Margetts, and A. Whelan. 2002. "Assessing the Impact of Improved Retail Access on Diet in a 'Food Desert': A Preliminary Report." *Urban Studies* 39:2061–2082.

Young, Kue. 1997. "Recent Health Trends in the Native American Population." *Population Research and Policy Review* 16:147–167.

Questions

1. What do the authors mean by "institutionalized racism" and "racialized geographies"? Give some examples from this reading and other readings.

2. What is a "food desert"? How does that relate to the reproduction of inequality? How does the West Oakland Food Collaborative challenge and contest this inequality?

3. How has the dam affected the Karuk Tribe's ability to sustain their families? How have they attempted to combat this?

4. In the reading about genocide in Darfur, we learned how controlling access to food and water can have devastating consequences. How is this related to the experiences of people in Oakland and the Karuk Tribe? How do these processes reproduce various inequalities?

5. What other examples can you think of in which the control of food, water, and a healthy environment is related to the reproduction of inequality? For example, where are the energy plants and garbage dumps located in your community? If your community exports garbage, where to? How might this also relate to consumption? What can we, as consumers, do to help challenge these inequalities?

25

Global Corporations, Global Unions

STEPHEN LERNER

The decline of unions poses a unique challenge to workers. Unions fight for worker input in the decision-making processes that determine their wages, benefits, and work conditions. Across the twentieth century, unions lost power through legislative actions that limited their ability to organize, bargain, and collect dues. This disempowerment is epitomized recently in the contentious actions of Governor Scott Walker to restrict public-employee unions from collective bargaining in the first state that allowed them to do so—Wisconsin—and the ensuing massive protests and unsuccessful recall election. Anti-union activism has left its mark. In 2013, just 11.3 percent of U.S. workers were unionized, down from 20.1 percent in 1983, the first year of comparable data (Union Members Summary 2014). Currently, 24 states have right-to-work statutes, which severely limit union activity. We can expect more restrictive legislation as state houses and governor's mansions are increasingly run by anti-union politicians.

Yet in the piece that follows, Lerner is optimistic about challenging injustices through unionization. He offers a new, updated vision for unionizing within the global economy: by targeting global corporations rather than sectors of workers. Global corporations are now larger than nation states. In fact, as Lerner notes, 52 of the top 100 largest economies in the world are global corporations. Faced with this sort of wealth and power, it would be easy to see how people would *not* challenge injustices in these massive corporations. Yet they are. Type "Walmart settlement" into your search engine and you will see that people are, in fact, challenging these powerful corporations. Recently, workers won an $88 million settlement for retaliation, a $188 million settlement for a class action lawsuit over Walmart's refusal to allow legally mandated breaks for workers, and a $21 million settlement for back pay to warehouse workers. There are many, many more. McDonald's workers demanded a living wage and staged strikes. These are just a few examples of workers organizing themselves to challenge inequality. These are just the sorts of workers that Lerner sees as the new frontier for unionization and collective action: service workers in global hubs. As global corporations extend their reach, could they be making themselves more vulnerable to unions?

References

Union Member Summary. 2014. *Economic News Release: Union Members Summary*. Bureau of Labor Statistics, Department of Labor. http://www.bls.gov/news.release/union2.nr0.htm (accessed January 13, 2015).

In November 2006 a group of Latino immigrant janitors won a historic strike in Houston, Texas—doubling their income, gaining health benefits, and securing a union contract for 5,300 workers with the Service Employees International Union (SEIU). At a critical moment in the strike, 1,000 janitors marched on the police station to protest the illegal arrests of two strikers. The next day, when the charges were dropped and the workers were released, a local newspaper reported the crowd's chant as "Arriba Revolución!" The article got it wrong—workers were actually chanting "Arriba La Unión!" But it got the mood right. It looked and felt like a revolution in Houston. Thousands of immigrant workers and their supporters had successfully challenged the corporate power structure and its allies. They stood up to the police, blocked streets, garnered widespread support, and prevailed against enormous odds. To many observers, a union fight in the heart of Texas seemed like a shot in the dark. But to workers toiling in poverty for the wealthiest corporations on earth, Houston was a shot heard around the world.

The SEIU janitors' month-long strike exposed a global economy addicted to cheap labor. Immigrant workers challenged a system that paid them $20 a night to clean toilets and vacuum the offices of global giants like Chevron and Shell Oil. They stood up to the global real estate interests that own and manage the office buildings where they work and the national cleaning companies that stay competitive by paying workers next to nothing.

Supported by activists from religious, civil rights, and community movements, janitors marched through Houston's most exclusive neighborhoods and shopping districts, into the lives of the rich and powerful. These disruptions forced Houston's elite, normally insulated from the workers who keep the city functioning, to face up to the human downside of the low-wage economy. Invoking the legacy of the civil rights movement, more than 80 union janitors and activists from around the country flew to Houston on "freedom flights" to support the strikers. They chained themselves to buildings, blocked streets, and were arrested for nonviolent acts of civil disobedience.

The city's corporate and political establishment tried to thwart the strikers. Twenty years ago they had successfully resisted an SEIU-led organizing drive among the city's janitors. So when workers took to the streets, the gloves came off again. Police helicopters

circled, mounted police moved in, and protesters nursed broken bones in jail, while the district attorney demanded $40 million in combined bond, nearly $900,000 for each person arrested.

If the strike had been only a local affair, the civic elite would probably have won. But the campaign went global, arising in front of properties controlled by the same firms in cities around the world. As the strike spread, janitors in Chicago, New York, Washington, Mexico City, London, Berlin, and other cities honored picket lines or sponsored demonstrations. These protests and the negative publicity they drew put the struggle of 5,000 workers in Texas in the international spotlight. Houston's business leaders intervened to end the dispute, and the workers secured their historic victory. The strike, the tension and passion it generated, and the reaction of the power structure explain why a reporter hearing "Arriba La Unión" thought he heard "Revolución."

Such a victory in anti-union Texas is worth attention. During the past four decades, union membership has steadily shrunk, first in the United States and now increasingly around the world. As unions have declined, we have seen greater inequality, cuts in social welfare benefits, and a redistribution of wealth to giant multinational corporations around the globe. Trade unions, laws, and social policies that benefited workers have been gutted in country after country. Corporations and newly minted private-equity billionaires boast of their ability to operate anywhere in the world without challenges from workers, unions, or governments to their increasing dominance of the global economy.

Given these trends, many observers have written the labor movement's obituary. But the Houston victory and successes by janitors elsewhere around the world signal a new upsurge of labor activism in America and beyond. Contrary to conventional wisdom, the spread of multinational corporations and the increasing concentration of capital have created the conditions that can turn globalization on its head and lift people out of poverty.

A Turning Point

SEIU's Building Services Division, like many U.S. unions, declined dramatically in the 1970s and 1980s. It lost a quarter of its members, work was part-timed, and benefits were cut. Through its Justice for Janitors campaign in the 1980s and 1990s, the SEIU grappled with how to respond to outsourcing within the United States; as large-contract cleaning companies consolidated on a national basis, so too co-workers in far-flung cities consolidated their efforts to win campaigns and contracts. By 2006, the SEIU had figured out how to use this national scope for growth and power, and members around the country used their sway with national employers and building owners to help the Houston janitors win their strike. Cleaners across the globe bore witness to the struggle and put Houston's real estate leaders under an international microscope.

But the conditions that allowed for success in Houston are already changing. Again the ground is shifting under our feet as the service industry and its clients continue to globalize. Just as the SEIU moved from organizing in single buildings to organizing whole cities and extending that strength to new regions like the South, it must respond to these new changes by developing a deeper global strategy. The largest property owners and service contractors are becoming global companies that operate in dozens of countries and employ or control the employment conditions of hundreds of thousands of workers. Simple solidarity will no longer suffice. Without a global union that unites U.S. workers with their counterparts across the world, workers' power to influence these corporations will continue to wane. Such corporations may threaten workers' way of life, but they also present an opportunity.

It is ironic that a great opportunity to organize global unions comes among the poorest, least skilled workers in one of the least organized and wealthiest sectors of the world economy. Contract janitors, security officers, and others who clean, protect, and maintain commercial property (most of them immigrants) perform site-specific work that is local by nature; their jobs cannot be moved from country to country. Workers who follow global capital from country to country in search of jobs have the power to demand and win better working and living standards. It is among the most invisible and seemingly powerless workers—whose labor is nonetheless essential to the economic success of the most powerful corporations—that we can build a global movement to reinvigorate trade unions, stop the race to the bottom, and lift workers out of poverty. Far from an isolated event, the Houston strike demonstrates how the extraordinary reorganization and realignment of the world's economy has opened up the opportunity to unite workers around the globe in a movement to improve their lives by redistributing wealth and power.

Understanding Globalization

The world is tilting away from workers and unions and the traditional ways they have fought for and won justice—away from the power of national governments, national unions, and national solutions developed to facilitate and regulate globalization. It is tilting toward global trade, giant global corporations, global solutions, and toward Asia—especially China and India. We cannot depend on influencing bureaucratic global institutions, like the International Labor Organization, or fighting entities that are ultimately under the control of global corporations, like the World Trade Organization. Workers and their unions need to use their still-formidable power to counter the power of global corporations before the world tilts so far that unions are washed away, impoverishing workers who currently have unions and trapping those who lack them in ever-deeper poverty. The power equation needs to be balanced before democratic institutions are destroyed.

As multinationals have grown, wealth and capital have become increasingly concentrated. Of the 100 largest economies in the world, 52 are not nations—they are global corporations. The top five companies, Wal-Mart, General Motors, Exxon Mobil, Royal Dutch/Shell, and BP, are each financially larger than all but 24 of the world's nations. The problem is not that corporations operate in more than one country—it is that multinational corporations are so powerful they increasingly dominate what happens in whole countries, hemispheres, and the entire globe.

As global corporations grow and state power declines, national unions are shrinking in membership and power (see Figure 1). Union density is down across the globe. Though many countries experienced an increase in unionization during the 1970s and 1980s, density declined in the 1990s. From 1970 to 2000, 17 out of 20 wealthy countries surveyed by the Organisation for Economic Co-operation and Development had a net decline in union density. While the specifics and timing are different in each country, what is remarkable over the last 30 years is the similarity of the results.

No country, no matter how strong its labor movement or progressive its history, is immune to these global trends. Density is starting to decline in Scandinavia,

South Africa, Brazil, and South Korea, countries that until recently had stable or growing labor movements. In France, general strikes and mass worker and student mobilizations have slowed the rollback of workers' rights, but these are defensive strikes by workers desperately trying to maintain standards that those in surrounding countries are losing.

The Antidote: Global Unions

For 150 years the argument for global unions was abstract, theoretical, and ideological: In brief, capitalism is global, therefore worker organizations should be too. However, even though capitalism was global, most employers were not. Theoretically, workers were stronger if united worldwide, but the day-to-day reality of unionized workers enabled them to win through the power of national governments. Unionized workers saw workers in other countries as potential competition for their jobs rather than allies. There was no immediate, compelling reason to act beyond national boundaries.

Now, globalization itself is creating the conditions to organize global unions in the service economy. The infrastructure of the FIRE sector (finance, insurance, and real estate) and the millions of service jobs needed to support it are concentrated in some 40 global cities, while manufacturing and mobile jobs—aided by new technology—are being shifted and dispersed around the globe. Global unions could certainly be formed in manufacturing or other sectors characterized by mobile jobs, but right now the opportunity is greatest in service jobs concentrated in the cities that drive the world economy.

Global cities—like New York, Hong Kong, London, and São Paulo—are economic hubs that rely on service jobs to function. Multinational corporations and their executives increasingly depend on these cities because they physically work, live, and play in them. Deeply embedded in each of these cities are hundreds of thousands of janitors, security guards, maintenance, hotel, airport, and other service workers whose labor is essential and cannot be off-shored. And, unlike the jobs in

Change in union density, 1970-2000

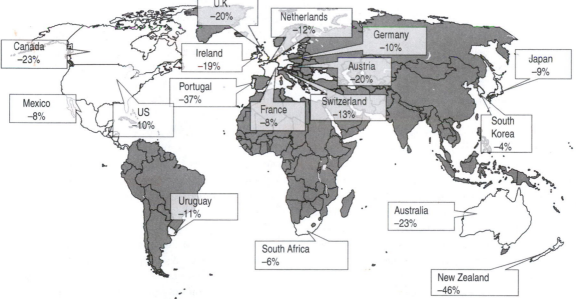

Union decline started and is most pronounced in the United States, where union density overall has dropped to 12 percent. In the private sector, density is now 7 percent, lower than during the Great Depression of the 1930s. The United States is a window into the future for workers and their unions throughout the world: a place where corporations have unfettered power.
Source: SEIU

Figure I Change in Union Density, 1970–2000.

manufacturing and the garment industry, there is no threat of relocation.

The coexistence of immense wealth and low-wage service jobs concentrated in these global economic "engine rooms" dramatically increases the potential power of service workers to build a global movement.

The Houston Victory

Houston's janitors won because the five cleaning contractors that employ them clean more than 70 percent of the office space in the city and operate throughout the United States. Real estate companies like Hines and major tenants like Chevron and Shell operate around the world, allowing union allies to organize actions in places like Mexico City, Moscow, London, and Berlin. The unquenchable thirst of real estate companies for capital to finance their global expansion allowed pension funds like the California Public Employment Retirement fund to intervene, saying that conditions for janitors were both unacceptable and bad for their investment. If Houston's janitors had confronted a local oligarchy of cleaning contractors, building owners, and corporations, they would likely have stood alone and again been crushed.

The union worked among janitors in downtown commercial office buildings in the major northern cities of the United States. But even as the SEIU expanded to organize service workers in other sectors, the gains among janitors were severely threatened by the wave of outsourcing in the 1970s and 1980s.

The union's own structure—dozens of local unions, often competing and undercutting each other in the same city—constrained its ability to fight back, and it needed to build strong local unions that could bargain across a geographic jurisdiction. The SEIU learned the hard way that it could not make gains by organizing building by building; even if a contractor allowed its workers to unionize, the union was likely to be undercut when the contract next went out to bid.

So the SEIU scaled its strategy upward, reckoning that the resources needed to wage a fight in a single building could be more efficiently deployed in winning a contractor's entire portfolio across a city, and by doing this with multiple contractors in a citywide campaign, it could unionize the entire commercial office-cleaning industry. Crucial to this was developing the "trigger": after a contractor agreed to go union, SEIU would not raise wages until a majority of its competitors also went union,

ensuring that no contractor was put at a competitive disadvantage. It began to untangle the complicated relationships between the janitors' direct employers—the contractors—and their secondary employers, the building owners. It also worked to understand the latter's financial, regulatory, political, and operational situation and their key relationships, especially with investors.

The union also learned that the janitors had hidden power: their critical—though invisible—position in the FIRE industry meant they could not be off-shored. As a result, powerful constituencies in these cities rallied to demand justice for janitors in their communities who earned poverty wages while cleaning the offices of multibillion-dollar companies.

These formed the core elements of an integrated strategy that allowed the Justice for Janitors campaign to reestablish or win master agreements for janitors in commercial office markets in the largest U.S. cities, bringing 100,000 new members into the union. In turn that strength allowed the campaign to spread to cities such as Houston, where the same owners operated. Master agreements that included the right to honor picket lines meant that a contractor's unfair labor practices in one city could trigger strike action by SEIU locals in other cities. There is no geographic limit to this strategy—as the key owners and contractors globalize, so do workers. Their victories demonstrate that in many ways multinationals are becoming more—not less—vulnerable as they spread across the globe.

Global Movement

In the face of the ascendancy of neoliberal policies, it may sound preposterous to argue that we are entering a moment of incredible opportunity for workers and their unions. But sometimes an unplanned combination of events may unleash social forces and contradictions that create the possibility—not the guarantee, the possibility—of creating a movement that lets us accomplish things we had never imagined possible. We are now in such a time.

How do we mount a campaign to organize workers into trade unions strong enough to raise wages and unite communities into organizations powerful enough to win decent housing, schools, and medical care? How do we build on the critical lessons and challenges of Houston, where janitors were far stronger than they would have been if they had focused their efforts on one building, company, or group of workers?

Organize Globally

Most trade unions still focus their resources and activity in one country. Despite 100 years of rhetoric about the need for workers to unite across borders, most global work is symbolic solidarity action and not part of a broader strategy. As the economy has become interrelated and global, organizing work must do the same.

Corporations, Not Countries

A campaign to change the world needs to focus on the corporations that increasingly dominate the global economy. To raise wages and living standards, we must force the largest corporations in the world to negotiate a new social compact that addresses human rights and labor rights in enforceable agreements that could lift tens of millions out of poverty. This campaign must be grounded in the work sites of the corporations that drive the economy and the cities in which they are located and from which they get much of their capital.

Unions as well as community, religious, and political leaders need to lead a campaign calling on the 300 largest pension funds in the world to adopt responsible investment policies covering their 6.9 trillion Euros (US$9 trillion) in capital. If corporations want access to the capital in workers' pension funds, they ought to develop responsible policies that govern how workers' money is to be invested and used.

Global Workers, Global Unions, Global Cities

We must create truly global unions, whose mission and focus is on the new global economy, spread across six continents. But they do not need to be in every country or major city in order to have the breadth and reach to tackle the largest global corporations. The challenge of building global unions is not to be everywhere in the world; rather, we need to determine the minimum number of countries and cities in which we must operate in order to exercise maximum power to persuade corporations to adopt a new social compact. This means organizing janitors, security, hotel, airport, and other service workers in some of the 40 or so global cities that are central to the operations of these corporations. Such organization must take place not only in individual work sites, but across cities, corporate groups, and industry sectors to improve immediate conditions and to build a union that organizes not only where workers labor but also in their neighborhoods and communities.

A Moral and Economic Message

It is not enough to organize workers and their workplaces. The campaign needs a powerful message about the immorality of forcing workers to live in poverty amidst incredible wealth. Religious, community, and political leaders need to embrace and help lead the campaign because it highlights the moral issues of poverty, calls the corporations responsible for it to task, and offers solutions that are good for workers and the community as a whole.

There are signs that elements of this campaign are becoming politically fashionable. Public-opinion polls suggest there is significant concern about the growing inequality between rich and poor. In a national Los Angeles Times/Bloomberg poll in December 2006, nearly three-fourths of respondents said they considered the income gap in America to be a serious problem.

To organize successfully at the work site and in communities, immigrants and migrant workers need to be brought out of the shadows of second-class status in the countries where they work. This campaign needs to take the lead in each country, and globally, to defend the rights of immigrant and migrant workers. It must promote laws that give immigrant and migrant workers full legal rights so that they can organize, unite with native-born workers, and help lead this fight.

Disrupting—and Galvanizing—the Global City

It would be naive to imagine that traditional union activity, moral persuasion, and responsible investment policies are enough to change corporate behavior or the world. These are starting points—small steps that allow workers and their allies to win victories, solidify organization, and increase the capacity to challenge corporate power. As activity and tension increase, the global business elite will go back and forth between making minor concessions to placate workers and attacking them at the workplace, in the media, and in political circles. But in the end, we only get real change by executing a two-part strategy: (1) galvanizing workers, community leaders, and the public to lift up our communities and (2) creating a crisis that threatens the existing order.

This is why this moment is so exciting and ripe with opportunity. In the last century industrial workers learned that increasingly coordinated industrial action could cripple national economies, topple governments, and win more just and humane societies. This strategy worked for more than 50 years. But production has been redesigned and shifted across the globe to disperse the power of workers and their unions. The rapid convergence of global corporations and workers in key cities around the world—where corporations are concentrating, not dispersing—has created the conditions and contradictions that allow us to envision how organized service workers can capture the imagination of people in their communities who are disturbed by poverty and income inequality while simultaneously learning how to disrupt the "engine rooms" in cities across the globe and so gain the leverage needed to start to tip the balance of economic power in the world.

Global capitalism operates smoothly in these cities because business leaders from around the world can fly in and out of their airports, stay in their hotels, and travel their streets to offices, banks, finance houses, and stock exchanges. Global cities and the multinational corporations that have centered the economic life of the world in them cannot operate without the global workers, who literally feed, protect, and serve the richest and most powerful corporations and people in the world.

By learning how to disrupt these airports, offices, and hotels, service workers can exert their newly available and previously unimagined power—not for a day, but for weeks and months in an escalating campaign that demands decent wages and living conditions for workers and a stronger, more prosperous future for entire communities and cities. In using this power, they can take the lead in creating a new world where the incredible technological progress, wealth, and economic advances of the global economy lift up the poor, empower the powerless, and inspire all of us to fight for justice.

Starting to Simmer?

In the same year as the Houston janitors' historic strike, the following occurred:

- A month after the Houston strike settlement, immigrant cleaners in London—from South

America, East Asia, and Africa—scored a similar victory. They forced London's largest cleaning contractors to sign union contracts after they occupied the Goldman Sachs building.

- In Australia and New Zealand, janitors marched together in dozens of cities to launch the Clean Start campaign in both countries to negotiate agreements with the real estate industry and cleaning contractors.

- In Miami, Cuban and Haitian janitors at the University of Miami, whose jobs had been outsourced to a private company, struck for nine weeks, went on a 17-day hunger strike, and built a multiracial coalition to win health insurance and a union.

- In the Netherlands, immigrant cleaners in major office buildings and the airport have launched the Ten Euro Campaign, demanding higher pay and greater respect for the country's 200,000 cleaners.

- In South Africa, security guards went back to work after winning a three-month national strike that gained 15,000 new members. Cleaners followed them in a general strike a few months later.

- In Jakarta, security officers occupied the offices of their employer, Group 4 Securicor, the largest private security guard company in the world, settling a year-long strike and winning a rare victory in the Indonesian Supreme Court.

- In Los Angeles, Boston, and Washington, D.C., thousands of mostly African American security officers united and forced building owners and security contractors to accept unionization as part of a campaign that has successfully organized the first new, private-sector industry in the post–World War II era.

- In Germany, Poland, and India, security officers who earn poverty-level wages are starting campaigns to win justice from global security companies.

- In Luxembourg, representatives from security officers' unions in 19 countries joined together and agreed to unite workers in 104 countries in Africa, Asia, Europe, and the Americas in a global campaign to force Group 4 Securicor to respect the human and labor rights of its 400,000 workers in countries around the world.

Recommended Resources

- For more information on global union organizing, see http://www.union-network.org/unipropertyn.nsf. To learn about SEIU, go to www.seiu.org; and to find out more about the corporate accountability campaign on Group 4 Securicor, go to https://corporatewatch.org/ and www.eyeonwackenhut.com

- Dan Clawson. *The Next Upsurge: Labor and the New Social Movements* (Ithaca, NY: Cornell University Press, 2003). A progressive transformation, Clawson believes, will be difficult or impossible without the active involvement of the working class and its collective voice, the labor movement.

- Rick Fantasia and Kim Voss. *Hard Work: Remaking the American Labor Movement* (Berkeley: University of California Press, 2004). Fantasia and Voss examine the decline of the American labor movement and the emergence of a new kind of "social movement unionism" that suggests the potential revival of unionism in the United States.

- Stephen Lerner. "An Immodest Proposal: A New Architecture for the House of Labor." *New Labor Forum* 12, no. 2 (Summer 2003): 7–30; and "A Winning Strategy to Do Justice." *Tikkun* (May/June 2005): 50–51. Drawing lessons from how the SEIU remade itself so that workers could take on big, nonunion employers, Lerner argues that the labor movement's structure, culture, and priorities stand in the way of workers' gains and the need to change.

- Ruth Milkman. *L.A. Story: Immigrant Workers and the Future of the U.S. Labor Movement* (New York: Russell Sage Foundation, 2006). Milkman explains how Los Angeles, once known as a company town hostile to labor, became a hotbed of unionism, and how immigrant service workers emerged as the unlikely leaders in the battle for workers' rights.

- Ruth Milkman and Kim Voss, eds. *Rebuilding Labor: Organizing and Organizers in the New Union Movement* (Ithaca, NY: Cornell University Press, 2004). Milkman and Voss bring together established researchers and a new generation of labor scholars to assess the current state of labor organizing and its relationship to union revitalization.

- Saskia Sassen. *Cities in a World Economy* (Thousand Oaks, CA: Pine Forge Press, 2006). Sassen uses the term "global cities" to capture the growth of service firms under globalization and their concentration in a small number of cities, as well as discussing these firms' increasing dependence on low-paid service workers.

Discussion

1. Describe the events leading up to the successful janitor strike in Houston, Texas. Why was this movement successful? What lessons can we take for future social change?

2. What do we learn about the wealth of global corporations compared to nation states? Why is this important? What are the implications for social change?

3. Several readings in this part have discussed our changing global economy. How do these readings relate to the Lerner reading? What, according to Lerner, are the implications for creating social change for more equitable working conditions?

4. What challenges do unions face? Why does Lerner see global unions as the "antidote"?

5. While it is easy to be pessimistic when learning about so many forms of inequality, Lerner offers many reasons to be optimistic. What are those reasons? What would a global movement look like?

6. How might we apply the model of global unions to address multiple forms of inequality concerning race, gender, class, sexuality, and disability?

F. Data Analysis Exercise: Who Makes the Decisions?

Women's Representation in Politics

What percentage of state executives, state legislators, and members of the U.S. Congress do you think are women? While the women's movement has made substantial gains (e.g., the right to vote, workplace discrimination laws), we know that women have not reached full equality with men. One space where women, especially women of color, are still underrepresented is in U.S. political offices.

The Rutgers Center for American Women and Politics tracks women's representation in politics. Here we provide some of the information documented on their website (see Center for American Women in Politics 2014a, 2015). Use the data provided to answer the following questions.

Part 1.

Figure 1 provides information on all women public officials. The data show trends in representation from the 1950s to 2014.

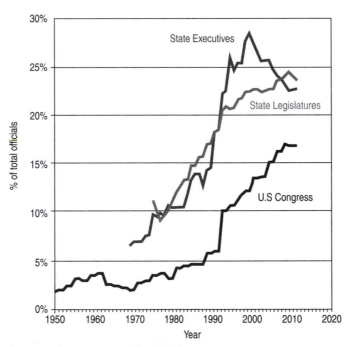

Figure 1 The Percentage of All Officials Who Are Women Across Time.
Source: Center for American Women and Politics, Eagleton Institute of Politics. 2014. "Summary of Women Candidates for Selected Offices 1970–2014" http://www.cawp.rutgers.edu/sites/default/files/resources/can_histsum.pdf (accessed September 12, 2015).

Questions:

1. How has the percentage of women in public office changed across time?
2. How much would women's representation in office have to change to reach the same level of representation as men?

Part 2.

Chart 1 focuses on the percentage of women of color in political offices in 2015. Use the
Information provided in the chart to answer the questions that follow.

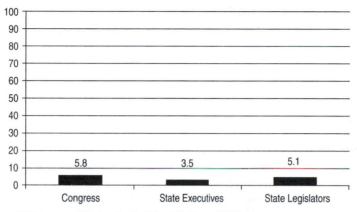

Chart 1 Percentage of Women of Color in Political Office, 2015.
Source: Center for American Women and Politics, Eagleton Institute of Politics. 2014. "Women of Color in Elective Office 2015: Congress, Statewide, State Legislature." http://www.cawp.rutgers.edu/women-color-elective-office-2015 (accessed online September 12, 2015).

Questions:

1. What percentage of people in Congress are women of color? What percentage of state executives are women of color? What percentage of state legislators are women of color? Are these the percentages that you expected? Why or why not?

2. Earlier in the book you learned about the concept of intersectionality. What is meant by intersectionality? How does this chart add to our understanding about the intersections of race and gender among political office holders?

3. What are the broader consequences of women and women of color's underrepresentation in political office? Why?

4. What social factors that you have read about have contributed to the under-representation of all women and especially women of color? What policies or programs do you think would be successful in reducing gender and racial disparity in political office? Why?

References:

Center for American Women and Politics, Eagleton Institute of Politics. 2014. "Women in Elected Office 2014." http://www.cawp.rutgers.edu/sites/default/files/resources/can_histsum.pdf (accessed September 12, 2015).

Center for American Women and Politics, Eagleton Institute of Politics. 2015. "Women of Color in Elective Office 2015: Congress, Statewide, State Legislature." http://www.cawp.rutgers.edu/women-color-elective-office-2015 (accessed September 12, 2015).

G. Data Analysis Exercise: Is Voting a Right?

Felon Disenfranchisement

Whether or not people can vote after committing a felony varies by state. According to a 2014 report by the Sentencing Project, 5.85 million people were unable to vote in 2010 because of felony disenfranchisement laws. In 2015, only Maine and Vermont allow felons the right to vote while they are serving their terms in prison. Fourteen states forbid current inmates the right to vote, 4 states block both inmates and parolees, and 19 states ban

inmates, parolees, and probationers from voting. Finally, 12 states also ban some or all ex-felons from voting who have already served their full term. Use Figure 1 to answer the following questions.

Questions:

1. Looking at Figure 1, how has the number of disenfranchised felons changed from 1960 to 2010?

2. One out of every 13 Black adults is disenfranchised in the United States. This is four times higher than the general adult population. In some states, the rate for Black adults is even higher. To be specific, 23% of Black adults in Florida, 22% of Black adults in Kentucky, and 20% of Black adults in Virginia are disenfranchised. Using reading from previous chapters, discuss how felony disenfranchisement compounds other inequalities faced by Blacks in the United States. How does voter disenfranchisement illustrate cumulative disadvantage?

3. Should all U.S. citizens have the right to vote? Why or why not? What should felony disenfranchise laws be?

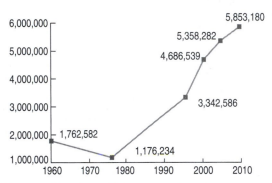

Figure 1   Number of Disenfranchised in the United States 1960–2010.

Source: Chung, Jean. 2013. "Felony Disenfranchisement: A Primer." The Sentencing Project. http://www .sentencingproject.org/detail/publication.cfm?publication_ id=502 (accessed January 3, 2015).

Reference:

Chung, Jean. 2013. "Felony Disenfranchisement: A Primer." The Sentencing Project. http://www.sentencingpro- ject.org/detail/publication.cfm?publication_id=502 (accessed January 3, 2015).

H. Data Analysis Exercise: Do Working-Class Jobs Kill?

This data analysis exercise explores the dangers workers encounter in their workplaces. The Occupational Safety and Health Act of 1970 guaranteed workers safety from known dangers. This act created the Occupational Safety and Health Administration (OSHA; www.osha. gov), which is tasked with creating safety standards, training employers, informing workers, and enforcing regulations. Nonetheless, as we see here, many workers still face health and safety risks in their workplaces.

1. Looking at Chart 1, which private industries had the highest *rates* of workplace injuries and illnesses in 2013? What sort of jobs do people do in that industry? What are work conditions like? How do those work conditions relate to workplace injuries and illnesses?

2. Which industries had the lowest rates? What sorts of work do those workers do?

3. Chart 2 shows the number and rate of workplace fatalities. Which jobs are the deadliest? What sort of

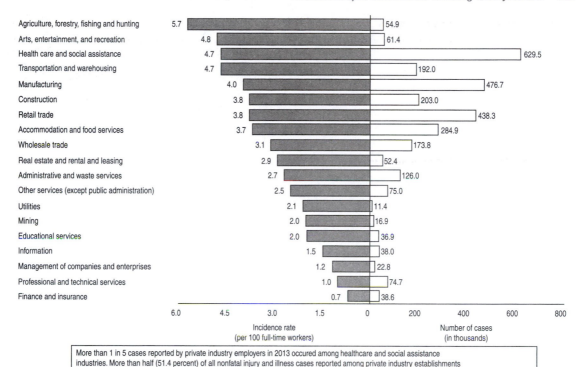

Industry	Incidence rate	Number of cases
Agriculture, forestry, fishing and hunting	5.7	54.9
Arts, entertainment, and recreation	4.8	61.4
Health care and social assistance	4.7	629.5
Transportation and warehousing	4.7	192.0
Manufacturing	4.0	476.7
Construction	3.8	203.0
Retail trade	3.8	438.3
Accommodation and food services	3.7	284.9
Wholesale trade	3.1	173.8
Real estate and rental and leasing	2.9	52.4
Administrative and waste services	2.7	126.0
Other services (except public administration)	2.5	75.0
Utilities	2.1	11.4
Mining	2.0	16.9
Educational services	2.0	36.9
Information	1.5	38.0
Management of companies and enterprises	1.2	22.8
Professional and technical services	1.0	74.7
Finance and insurance	0.7	38.6

Incidence rate (per 100 full-time workers) | Number of cases (in thousands)

More than 1 in 5 cases reported by private industry employers in 2013 occured among healthcare and social assistance industries. More than half (51.4 percent) of all nonfatal injury and illness cases reported among private industry establishments in 2013 occured in three industry sectors alone—health care and social assistance, manufacturing, and retail trade.

Chart 1 Incidence Rates and Numbers of Nonfatal Occupational Injuries and Illnesses by Private Industry Sector, 2013.

Source: U.S. Bureau of Labor Statistics. 2014. "2013 Survey of Occupational Injuries & Illnesses Summary Estimates Charts Package." United States Department of Labor. http://www.bls.gov/iif/oshwc/osh/os/osch0052.pdf (accessed January 2, 2015).

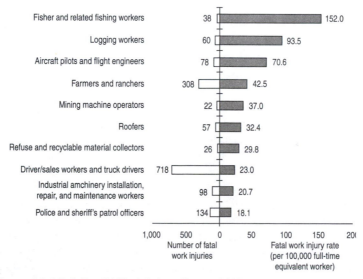

Occupation	Number of fatal work injuries	Fatal work injury rate
Fisher and related fishing workers	38	152.0
Logging workers	60	93.5
Aircraft pilots and flight engineers	78	70.6
Farmers and ranchers	308	42.5
Mining machine operators	22	37.0
Roofers	57	32.4
Refuse and recyclable material collectors	26	29.8
Driver/sales workers and truck drivers	718	23.0
Industrial amchinery installation, repair, and maintenance workers	98	20.7
Police and sheriff's patrol officers	134	18.1

Number of fatal work injuries | Fatal work injury rate (per 100,000 full-time equivalent worker)

Chart 2 Occupations with High Fatal Work Injury Rates, 2010.

Source: U.S. Bureau of Labor Statistics. 2014. "Injuries, Illnesses, and Fatalities." United States Department of Labor. http://www.bls.gov/iif/oshwc/cfoi/worker_memorial.htm (accessed January 2, 2015).

work is relatively safe in the United States? Who—the demographic characteristics—performs that work? Who performs work that is dangerous? What conditions make those jobs so dangerous? What role does unionization play in each industry? What is the pay and prestige of work in these industries? Are people being justly compensated for the risks they face at work?

4. How has the U.S. economy changed over the past 50 years? Which industries have grown and which have shrunk? Where have the jobs associated with declining industries gone? Is someone else doing them? Who? Are those jobs "safe" or "dangerous?" What are the working conditions like? What role does unionization play?

5. Who benefits from the work products or services produced in dangerous industries and jobs?

Projects and Resources to Make a Difference

In this section we read about global economies, commodification, and exploitation. As consumers we may not always think about where things come from, who made them, or their working conditions. However, as our economy has become more interconnected globally, we are more and more likely to find merchandise in our stores that were made in sweatshops. Even our produce can travel as far as from China. In order for people in industrialized nations to buy cheap clothing and electronics, other people are working for less than living wages, experiencing oppressively long work hours and working in dangerous conditions. This is also true of merchandise in college bookstores across North America. If you have a sweatshirt or t-shirt with your college or university's logo on it, it may have been made in a sweatshop.

In order to ensure that their schools did not buy merchandise from sweatshops, student groups have formed on college and university campuses. Students have staged protest events demanding that merchandise with school logos come from companies that pay living wages and provide employees with safe working conditions. As of September 2014, 186 colleges or universities became affiliates of the Worker Rights Consortium, a labor rights organization that monitors working conditions. You can look to see if your school is an affiliate at the Worker Rights Consortium website (http://www.workersrights.org/about/as.asp). Through the Designated Suppliers Programs, schools ensure that their merchandise is made in factories where workers receive living wages and the right to organize. In return, the schools

promise to pay the factories sufficient funds to uphold these conditions. The program has been supported by the Department of Justice.

If your school is not an affiliate of the Worker Rights Consortium, research where they purchase their merchandise. Explore whether or not your school has a student organization focused on workers' rights. Even if your school has adapted fair practices with apparel suppliers, you may also have a student group focused more broadly on workers' rights. One such organization is the United Students Against Sweatshops (USAS) (http://usas.org/). If your organization does not have any student groups, the USAS provides information and suggestions for starting chapters. For example, check out their suggestions for creating and maintaining an effective Facebook page (http://usas.org/organize/resources/facebookguide/).

References

The United States Department of Justice. 2011. "Justice Department Will Not Challenge Worker Rights Consortium's Designated Suppliers Program for Collegiate Apparel." http://www.justice.gov/opa/pr/justice-department-will-not-challenge-worker-rights-consortiums-designated-suppliers-program (accessed January 3, 2015).

United Students Against Sweatshops. "Facebook Guide for USAS Locals." http://usas.org/organize/resources/facebookguide/ (accessed January 3, 2015).

Worker Rights Consortium. "WRC Affiliated Colleges and Universities." http://www.workersrights.org/about/as.asp (accessed January 3, 2015).

How Do Inequalities Become Institutionalized?

We reproduce inequality through tradition, emulation, and adaptation, which we take for granted. Inequalities are difficult to see, either because they are the result of larger, abstract practices or small, daily doings to which we do not pay much attention. Earlier we learned what Berger and Luckmann (1966) describe as the process of social constructionism. They argue further in their classic book, *The Social Construction of Reality*, that social constructions become abstract and taken-for-granted parts of reality. First we form daily habits, which are really just routines to help us solve problems and get things done. Then we give language to describe these habits. These habits and language are often embedded in our institutions and our rules, so we do little to question them. The rules seem legitimate since they come from institutions with

power. We give so little thought to these things that we just go about our day. We have internalized the rules. The process just described is how most people experience their lives within various institutions such as schools and workplaces. Taking this a step further, in Part IV, we will also see how experiences with institutions are intersectional.

Indeed, in Part IV we examine these rather abstract theoretical processes in their concrete, empirical forms. How do inequalities become institutionalized? We will read about three processes through which this happens including bureaucratizing, controlling spaces, and instituting social policy. These processes often seem to take on a life of their own and create what is sometimes called "institutional inertia." You may recognize this more as "tradition" and you may have heard someone say, "We can't change things; we've always done it this way." We do know that traditional ways of doing things are human creations, and in the first section of Part IV we learn how this happens. "Bureaucratizing" is a process in which supervisors and administrators structure how work is done. This labor process—how we do work—is structured to create routinization, remove uncertainty in decision making, and improve efficiency. This process can also have other consequences, which we will read about in the first two readings.

The second section, "Controlling Spaces," is about how people maintain control through social ties, social networks, and spatiality. The two readings in this section focus on global networks because, as we learned in Part III, we live in a global economy. This section examines elites in the global economy as well as the increasing business of reproductive tourism. Both readings highlight how dominant entities control spaces and restrict the access and movement of subordinate ones. The readings in "Instituting Social Policy" focus on how social policies can lessen inequality, but they can also greatly worsen inequalities. The readings in the "Contesting and Changing" section of Part IV demonstrate the effectiveness of various diversity policies on the equity of unpaid work at home. We will also read about how marginalized groups attempt to allay the negative consequences of inequalities through creating safe spaces. In the data analysis exercises, students extend their understanding of institutionalization by examining the wage gap as a by-product of occupational segregation and devaluation, the consequences of taking out student loans, and voter disenfranchisement.

In Part IV, we learn:

- *The reproduction of inequality is spatial in the sense that it varies across time and place.* In this section we will learn how spaces are controlled through the structure of the labor process, through global social networks, through social

policies that prohibit discrimination, through punitive poverty and criminalization policies, and through the creation of safe spaces as means of protection from hostile environments.

- *Social policies vary in how they affect inequality.* Policies meant to reduce inequality vary in how well they do so. We learn that some workplace policies, such as affirmative action or family leave policies, work better than others. Some workplace policies can have positive consequences for equity in families. And unfortunately some groups in hostile places do not have as much power to influence policies as we may hope. Policies, as we learn from Miller, can also create and reproduce inequality.

- *Institutions—including schools and workplaces—are important sites for the reproduction of inequality.* How we structure institutions and their rules and the networks created between them often seem like "business as usual." But these processes are not mystical happenings of the business world. Humans create them—in ways consequential in the reproduction of inequality.

- *Capital is an important component of the reproduction of inequality. Capital comes in several forms.* We might think of capital as money or wealth, but it can also come in other forms. Who we know matters, and that knowledge becomes a resource we call social capital. Levels of education and work experience become resources sociologists call human capital. Finally, while often taken for granted, cultural values placed on dress and behavior can become resources we call cultural capital.

Reference

Berger, Peter L., and Thomas Luckmann. 1966. *The Social Construction of Reality: A Treatise in the Sociology of Knowledge.* New York: Anchor Books.

26

Gender, the Labor Process, and Dignity at Work

MARTHA CROWLEY

Sociology has a rich research tradition in studying work and the labor process. In this tradition, researchers examine how employers structure the various ways in which people do their jobs to control workers and to control the rate of production. This is typically done to maximize efficiency and profit, often with negative consequences for workers.

Another research tradition in sociology studies how work is "gendered." That is, it attempts to understand how we come to see some types of work as men's or women's work. While women have increased their access to jobs once considered men's work, we still find that men and women are highly segregated into different jobs and even different workplaces. Workplace segregation creates a cycle in which many men and women work in different jobs and in different places, which reinforces their expectations that gender is inherently, or somehow biologically, related to how people work. There is little evidence to support this claim. Instead, women and men may work differently because they face different working conditions.

This reading combines both traditions by focusing on how labor processes cultivate worker control in gendered ways. Martha Crowley examines 155 work groups to explore how the labor process is structured differently in jobs that are predominantly held by men compared to jobs predominantly held by women. Specifically she focuses on six traditional mechanisms through which employers control workers: direct supervision, task segmentation, automation, rules, on-the-job training, and participation. The ways employers use these mechanisms are consequential for whether or not workers feel dignity at work. Crowley finds that men most often work in workgroups subjected to "persuasive" control that improves their feelings of autonomy, creativeness, meaning, and satisfaction. In contrast, women's workgroups more often experience "coercive" control through direct supervision that lessens women's feelings of dignity in their work. In short, rather than women and men having essential qualities related to different types of work, they find themselves being treated differently at work.

Gender stratification research has devoted considerable attention to processes underlying wage differentials for women and men. Women suffer economically, for instance, as firms devalue their work and reserve for men positions with authority, high pay, and career advancement potential (Dinovitzer, Reichman, and Sterling 2009; Levanon, England, and Allison 2009; Reskin and Roos 1990; Tomaskovic-Devey 1993). To a lesser extent, this literature also highlights inequality in the work *experience*, particularly with respect to the exercise of discretion and authority on the job (e.g., Cockburn 1983, 1988a; Smith 2002). Women's jobs offer less task variety

Excerpted from Crowley, Martha. 2013. "Gender, the Labor Process and Dignity at Work." *Social Forces* 91(4):1209–1238. Reprinted by permission of Oxford University Press.

and freedom from supervision and opportunity to solve problems, negatively affecting job satisfaction, pride in their work, and perceived sense of control over their lives (Hodson 2001; Ross and Wright 1998). Yet, with the exception of a small number of qualitative case studies, this literature tends not to explore in depth how divergent control structures shape the experience of work in women's and men's jobs, especially with respect to the full range of control techniques used by employers and the simultaneous application of multiple controls.

Research on the labor process is more explicit on control and what it means for workers generally, specifying key modes of control (direct supervision, task segmentation, and rules, for example) and their effects on worker outcomes such as autonomy, alienation, and effort (Burawoy 1979; Edwards 1979; Hodson 1996; Schwalbe 1986). Building on this literature and integrating its Marxist elements with Weberian and Durkheimian perspectives on work and well-being, Randy Hodson's *Dignity at Work* demonstrated that workplace controls vary in the degree to which they allow workers to derive a sense of self-worth and self-respect from their jobs, producing measurable differences in outcomes such as autonomy, creativity, commitment, and effort. Comparative research has demonstrated how complex combinations of multiple control techniques contribute to class variation in workplace dignity (Crowley 2012), but this literature is mostly quiet with respect to gender variation. Do overall approaches to control differ in female and male work groups? What are their implications for workplace dignity? The answers to these questions have important implications for understandings of both gender inequality and the labor process.

Sex Segregation, the Labor Process, and Worker Dignity

Although job desirability reflects a range of considerations, such as pay, scheduling needs, perceived opportunity, and socialization (England 2010; Reskin and Padavic 1994; Webber and Williams 2008), most individuals, regardless of gender, crave the same intrinsic job rewards, including autonomy, interesting tasks, a sense of accomplishment, and the feeling that they are productive, competent, and contributing to the whole (Rowe and Snizek 1995; Tolbert and Moen 1998). These goals and desires are at least as strong for women as for

men (Johnson and Mortimer 2011). Yet research has consistently shown that women's jobs offer less task variety, satisfaction, freedom from direct supervision, and opportunity for problem solving (e.g., Cockburn 1988a; Ross and Wright 1998; Tomaskovic-Devey 1993).

The labor process tradition offers a framework for understanding such inequalities, identifying a range of worker controls embedded in work arrangements and specifying their effects on an array of psychological and behavioral outcomes. Robert Blauner (1964) was among the first to argue that differential exposure to worker controls (including bureaucratic rules and particular technological forms) shape workers' psychological well-being. Subsequent scholarship has called attention to deleterious impacts of these and other constraints, including direct supervision and task segmentation, for psychological and behavioral outcomes and noted the emergence of controls based on alignment of worker and firm interests (most notably, career ladders and participative arrangements) with more beneficial effects (Braverman 1974; Burawoy 1979; Crowley 2012; Edwards 1979; Hodson 1996, 2001).

The literature on workplace sex segregation provides key insights into why women's and men's work experiences may vary as a function of workplace control, highlighting how dominant ideologies, beliefs, and values regarding women's and men's familial responsibilities and orientations (caretaking vs. breadwinning) and masculine/feminine capabilities, identities, and orientations (e.g., feminine deference and vs. masculine aggression) promote men's entry into (and women's exclusion from) jobs offering more advantageous control structures, while channeling women into (and men away from) jobs marked by constraint.

First, firms *exclude* women from jobs associated with skill, autonomy, high pay, and career ladders on the basis of what they are assumed to lack: intelligence, technological skills, physical strength, commitment, ambition, breadwinner status, and emotional fortitude necessary to succeed in a "male" environment and/or advance in career ladders designed for men (Cockburn 1983; Reskin and Padavic 1988; Tomaskovic-Devey and Skaggs 2002; Wright 2001). As Reskin and Roos (1990) explain, organizational gatekeepers' taste for discrimination and use of male sex to proxy skill, commitment, and productivity convert labor queues (employers' rank ordering of preferred workers) into gender queues (preference for men over women), allowing men to monopolize the most lucrative, skill-building, and intrinsically rewarding jobs. Socialized beliefs regarding masculine capabilities and breadwinner orientations also contribute to "supply-side" processes, whereby men seek out jobs consistent with masculine identities and breadwinner roles, scrutinize female "interlopers," and occasionally target them for abuse (Bergmann 2011).

Second, *inclusion* processes steer women into positions reflecting or complementing their external roles. Employers draw upon (and sometimes bend) gender ideologies to support women's concentration in jobs men refuse to take, and they often build gendered expectations of women into work arrangements (Cockburn 1988a; Martin 2003; Raynolds 2001; Salzinger 2003). As Anne Phillips (1983, 102) notes, "It is not just that capitalism needs some skilled and some unskilled workers, and that men have usurped the better jobs for themselves. Rather, jobs are created as masculine and feminine" (see also Skuratowicz and Hunter 2004). Once positions have been established, firms fill them with individuals whose external functions (or stereotypes) correspond to their requirements, often recruiting women for part-time hours, service/deference roles, and routine jobs requiring only speed and dexterity, while reserving for men higher wage positions congruent with their presumed strength, leadership, and breadwinner status (Collinson, Knights, and Collinson 1990; Mills 2003; Williams 2006). These practices are complemented by supply-side processes, including men's avoidance of stereotypically female jobs and women's self-selection into "pink-collar" and part-time jobs compatible with feminine ideals/ caregiving roles (Hartmann 1976; Reskin and Padavic 1994; Webber and Williams 2008).

Third, workers and jobs are subject to *gendering* processes, whereby sex composition influences the nature of work and vice versa. Cynthia Cockburn (1988b, 38) explains: "People have a gender, and their gender rubs off on the jobs they do. These jobs in turn have a gender character which rubs off on the people who do them." Positions filled with women thus come to be regarded as "women's jobs" and workers in them, regardless of their sex, are treated in ways consistent with societal and more local notions of what it means to be a woman (Lee 1998; Muñoz 2008). Consistent with women's subordinate status in society, a sizable female presence is associated with downgrading of worker status, skills, and advancement potential (Davies 1982; Levanon et al. 2009; Tomaskovic-Devey 1993). Female work groups are thus paid less, and often they are patronized or even infantilized, contributing to the use of demeaning and oppressive constraints that in turn reinforce the notion that extensive controls are appropriate and required (Acker and Van Houten 1974; Cockburn 1983, 1988a, 1988b; Coverman 1986; Rogers and Henson 1997).

According to Charles Tilly (1998), these processes have important consequences for the nature of control in jobs occupied by women and men. They reflect and reinforce inequalities found in adjacent institutional and organizational spheres, mapping gender onto crucial intra-organizational boundaries, clustering women in jobs that deny them equitable returns for their contributions and setting up systems of social closure that reserve the most advantageous positions for men. One consequence, he argues, is systematic variation in the discipline/incentive systems found in women's and men's jobs: Female work groups are disproportionately (though not exclusively) located in coercive *drive* systems, where they are subject to closer supervision, more continuous monitoring, and shorter term (often hourly) pay schemes, and men are concentrated in zones of *loyalty*, where they enjoy greater discretion, more freedom from supervision, and lengthier promotion ladders that secure effort via the promise of long-term gain (see also Bielby and Baron 1986; Edwards 1979; Kanter 1977; Reskin and Padavic 1994).

Growing awareness of variations related to labor relations and other contextual influences has prompted more direct investigations of specific controls applied in work settings under study. Recent comparative investigations thus have documented how six key forms of control, addressed next, impact worker dignity (Hodson 2001; Crowley 2012). This more direct approach is particularly salient for understanding workplace gender inequality, since firms sort women and men in the same industry and occupation into different jobs, reserving for men those with greater complexity, freedom from direct supervision, and opportunity for advancement (Bielby and Baron 1986; Tomaskovic-Devey 1993).

Direct Supervision

Direct supervision, the oldest and simplest form of control, is still commonly used to control workers, particularly in the service sector, where firms increasingly enlist customers in monitoring employees (McCammon and Griffin 2000; Williams 2006). Although "facilitative supervision," generally found in the professions, can encourage worker citizenship (Frenkel and Sanders 2007), direct supervision is frequently experienced as demeaning and tends to promote arbitrary decision making and abuse that hamper meaningfulness, satisfaction, cooperation, and effort (Hodson 2001; Rafferty and Restubog 2011). In the service sector, visibility, sexualization of work, and abuse of workers subject to customer control contributes to alienation, burnout, and intent to quit (Deery, Walsh, and Guest 2011; Stein 2007).

Many employers regard women's presumed socialization for deference as incompatible with authority, discretion, and/or aggression expected in management and many professions, but as well suited to coercive controls such as direct supervision (Kanter 1977; Salzinger 2003; Williams 1995). Although many men experience this form of control, firms exhibit a clear tendency to exclude female workers from jobs with significant decision-making authority and actively recruit them into positions that are subject to direct supervision (Cockburn 1983, 1988a; Smith 2002; Tomaskovic-Devey 1993). In manual environments, purposeful replication of external social relations, including patriarchal and familial ties, underscores managerial efforts to capitalize on subservience generalized from other institutional spheres (Lee 1998; Mills 2003; Wolf 1992).

Socialized beliefs regarding female subservience also increases women's exposure to direct supervision via customers, who often serve as proxies for management in service encounters (McCammon and Griffin 2000). Expectations for female subservience, including smiling, taking orders, and submitting to customer abuse are *written into* many service and clerical jobs (Martin 2003). Women's appearance and temperament are thus regarded as uniquely qualifying them for frontline service expectations such as smiling, taking orders, and submitting to customer abuse (Leidner 1991). In contrast, male socialization is regarded as ill fitted to the deference required in many such jobs (Skuratowicz and Hunter 2004), and many men resist even temporary assignment to duties perceived as "women's work" (Nixon 2009; Rogers and Henson 1997; Williams 2006).

Task Segmentation

Task segmentation—the division of more complex functions into subtasks requiring speed and dexterity alone—has long been used to secure effort from employees (Taylor 1947). Narrowing the scope of work activities not only limits opportunity to withhold effort but also severely constrains problem solving, autonomy, meaningfulness, and satisfaction (Braverman 1974; Hodson 1996, 2001). Limited task variation, furthermore, is a key factor in the negative consequences of low-status employment for workers' self-efficacy and self-esteem (Kohn 1976; Ross 2000).

Originally developed for use in manual production, this form of control is found in a broad range of settings, including many of the "pink collar" occupations where women are concentrated (Davies 1982; Kanter 1977). In the manual sector, women are funneled into jobs with task segmentation by managers touting their unique qualifications for the most fragmented assembly roles: their small hands, nimble fingers, high speed, attention to detail and "natural" patience for boring, monotonous tasks (Mills 2003; Salzinger 2003). Socialized beliefs regarding masculine capabilities, identities, and orientations discourage employment of men in such positions (Ong 1987, 152; Wolf 1992, 116; Wright 2001, 361), and some managers punish insubordinate men with temporary assignments to female production lines, where the perceived indignity of task segmentation calls into question their masculinity (Muñoz 2008).

Automation

Scholars have largely rejected Robert Blauner's (1964) contention that technology would liberate workers from alienating work, noting instead that technology bifurcates jobs, deskilling those who operate machines while upgrading skills of those who program or service them (Vallas 1993). "Where the tasks are not just mechanized but truly automated, the worker is reduced to an often-bored observer of a part of the flow of production" (Gamst 1980, 29). Dissatisfaction and meaninglessness often result—especially where automation is combined with task segmentation—in assembly lines, for example (Hodson 1996).

Socialized beliefs regarding masculine capabilities, identities, and orientations promote male monopolies on positions servicing machinery, while females, who are seen as lacking the necessary ambition for techno-logical training, are placed in jobs subject to automation (Hossfield 1990; Lee 1993). In short, "Women may push the buttons, but they may not meddle with the works" (Cockburn 1983, 12). In a Mexican maquiladora, for example, managers fast-tracked men out of machine tending with technical training that served as a "male rite of passage" out of predominantly female assembly roles (Wright 2001, 361).

Rules

Rules pervade work organizations, crossing industrial and occupational divides and controlling workers through symbolism of close attention to their activities and threat of sanctions for noncompliance. Rules generate a great deal of effort among even self-governed professionals and direct almost every aspect of some jobs, scripting interactions with customers and specifying the sequence and pace of food preparation and delivery, for example (Courpasson 2000; Leidner 1991). Rules thus vary a great deal in their effects. They may enhance worker well-being by taking the place of more oppressive forms of constraint; alternatively, they may dictate the method or outcome of work to such a degree that little room for autonomy or creativity remains (Adler and Borys 1996). Where rules are the dominant mode of control, they depress autonomy, creativity, satisfaction, pride, and effort (Hodson 2001).

Although there has been little direct investigation of gender differences in rule-based control, qualitative research on service and manual environments suggests that female work groups are frequently subject to rules not applied to their male coworkers. In many factories, for example, rules that tightly constrain female work groups' movement and social interactions are not applied to male work groups (Lee 1998; Wolf 1992). Frontline service positions where women are often concentrated also entail significant rule-based constraint, as workers receive instruction regarding not only timely and accurate service but also appropriate demeanor, attitude, and appearance (Austrin 1991).

On-the-Job Training

Benchmark labor process theories have long noted a shift away from constraint-based controls such as those listed previously in favor of techniques that secure control by aligning the interests of workers and firms,

especially in predominantly male environments. Although more costly, these methods secure voluntary consent while maintaining the dignity of employees (Friedman 1977; Hodson 1996). On-the-job training, for example, enhances effort and commitment via structured avenues for skill development, earnings growth, and career advancement, especially in manual work (Burawoy 1979; Edwards 1979) and the professions (Greenwood, Deephouse, and Li 2007).

Dominant ideologies about women's and men's familial responsibilities and orientations (caretaking vs. breadwinning) are key factors in women's limited access to these opportunities. Employers equate male sex with capacity for (and interest in) long hours and long-term employment associated with on-the-job training, and they are often reluctant to entrust women, as presumed caregivers, with controls premised on a lengthy time horizon (Tomaskovic-Devey and Skaggs 2002). Stereotypes of women as uncommitted thus become self-fulfilling prophecies as organizational gatekeepers route female applicants into "dead-end" and part-time jobs, where task segmentation, automation, direct supervision and demeaning rules impinge on worker dignity (Marsden, Kalleberg, and Cook 1993; Ong 1987; Ross and Wright 1998; Wolf 1992).

Participation

Participation in workplace decision making through provisions for bounded autonomy over work activities and/or formal solicitation of worker input is a second key means by which to secure voluntary effort from employees. Expanding choices, even within narrowly defined limits, can help firms secure employee effort and even goodwill, enhancing satisfaction, commitment, and effort in part by communicating to workers that the organization values their contributions and cares about their well-being (Burawoy 1979; Hodson 2001). Resistance to participative structures highlighted in some research generally derives from its use in combination with constraint-based controls that undermine these ideals (Vallas 2003).

Similar to their exclusion from opportunities for on-the-job training, women's exposure to participatory control is limited by the industrial, occupational, and job segregation that excludes them from firms and work groups where it is used to garner worker consent (Friedman 1977; see also Tomaskovic-Devey and Skaggs 2002).

Employer stereotypes also play an important role, causing some managers to regard women as lacking interest, ambition, or general fit with the requirements of flexible production (Wright 2001; Zanoni 2011).

Analyzing Control and Gender Inequality in Work Experiences

Research on sex segregation and workplace gender inequality strongly suggests that women's and men's work experiences may vary as a function of control. Male work groups, especially those populated almost entirely by men, are more likely to encounter control structures based on persuasion, while female work groups confront control structures based on constraint. Furthermore, these disparate approaches to control should produce differences in outcomes pertaining to workplace dignity. Coercive control combinations are likely to impinge on worker dignity while persuasive bundles of control should have the reverse effect.

Data and Measures

This study investigates complex combinations of control and their emergent impacts on worker dignity in male and female work groups using data on 155 work groups culled from the population of published, book-length, English-language workplace ethnographies. An electronic and physical search of databases, libraries, and bibliographies yielded approximately 800 ethnographies for potential inclusion in the study, 162 of which contained sufficient information to code organizational and job-related data for at least one clearly identifiable work group (individuals performing the same job in a single organizational setting). A team of four researchers developed the content coding instrument, generating a list of variables and response categories representing core concepts in the workplace literature (organizational attributes, the labor process, workplace social relationships, worker resistance, psychological outcomes, and so on) and revising it following trial codings of eight ethnographies. The data, coding instrument, coding protocol, ethnographic sources, and publications based on these data may be viewed at http://www.sociology.ohio-state.edu/rdh/Workplace-Ethnography-Project.html.

Analytic Strategy and Results

Identity control configurations in work groups with varying percent female, include those with very low (less than 10%), low (10% to 39%), and high (at least 60%) rates of female participation (smaller sample size restricts subdivision of predominantly female work groups). These subsamples (n = 77, 26, and 36, respectively) are useful for investigating how inclusion and gendering processes shape conditions in female work groups, and for illuminating differences in conditions almost exclusively available to men due to processes of social closure (see Bergmann 2011; Tomaskovic-Devey and Skaggs 2002) versus those where women have made greater inroads (see England 2010; Reskin and Roos 1990). I then investigate the distribution of female and male work groups into "coercive" versus "persuasive" control contexts, depending on the balance and presence/absence of controls based on constraint versus alignment of worker and firm interests.

Coercive approaches are those in which a majority of elements represent the presence of constraint or the absence of controls that align worker and firm interests. *Persuasive* approaches are those in which at least half of the components represent an absence of constraint or the presence of controls that align the interests of workers and firms.

Control Typologies in Female and Male Work Groups

Male work groups tended to encounter more persuasive control packages. Of the nine control typologies identified among male work groups with very low (less than 10%) female participation, six are persuasive. Furthermore, the vast majority of the male work groups in this category (53 of 77) were employed in these settings. They included managers, surgeons, engineers, truckers, chefs, and participative assemblers, for example. Only 24 of 77 work groups with very low rates of female participation confronted coercive control typologies; they included assemblers, longshoremen, and miners, among others. A similarly large share of control configurations identified in the remaining male work groups (10% to 39% female) were persuasive, and 19 of the 26 work groups in this category were employed in these settings (they included school administrators, managers, physicians, and firefighters, for example). The seven remaining work groups, including assemblers and meat processors, for example, were employed in work groups confronting coercive control structures.

These figures contrast sharply with those of female work groups. Of the six control types identified among female work groups, four are coercive. Three are composed entirely of attributes denoting presence of constraint or absence of interest-aligning controls, and all four involve direct supervision. Furthermore, 21 of the 36 female work groups encountered one of these four coercive control packages, including nursing aides, maids, frontline fast-food workers, and assemblers, among others. Only two of the six control configurations identified could be classified as persuasive. They were found in jobs such as nursing, waitressing, and sales. Analyses limited to cases conducted in more recent years produced even more marked differences, consistent with diminished reliance on coercion in male but not female work groups. Cases initiated by 1975 ($n = 95$), 1980 ($n = 65$) and 1985 ($n = 47$) revealed rates of coercion in female work groups ranging from 56 percent to 57 percent (compared with 58% in the full sample) and rates ranging from 10 percent to 18 percent in predominantly male work groups (compared with 31% in the full sample).

Coercive and Persuasive Control in Male Work Groups

As expected, coercive control settings have a strong significant and negative effect on every dependent variable in the analysis. None of the persuasive control configurations apparent in these predominantly male work groups involves segmentation. With few exceptions (where effects were in the expected direction but not significant), these configurations allow for greater dignity at work, as indicated by significantly higher levels of autonomy, creativity, meaningfulness, and satisfaction. Relationships with commitment and effort were also evident, but not always significant. Half of the persuasive typologies observed among male work groups were associated with significantly higher rates of commitment, and another half had higher mean scores for effort.

In male work groups with somewhat higher female representation, the effects of coercive control structures were very similar to those identified in male work groups with very low rates of female participation. Interestingly, however, a far lower share of persuasive control structures offered significant benefits for worker dignity. Although they register as persuasive given the overall balance of constraint-based and interest-aligning controls, several entail constraints that erode worker dignity (e.g., supervision, automation, and/or segmentation). Supplementary constraints thus appear to mitigate potential benefits of persuasive controls in these settings.

Coercive Control in Female Work Groups

Sallie Westwood's (1982) participant observation of machine operators (90% of whom were female) in a British clothing factory helps to illustrate how control techniques operate independently and in concert to shape the work experience. The combination of segmentation and automation, for example, removed autonomy and creativity from workers' tasks:

> Each woman was responsible for making up part of a garment—no one made a whole dress, or a whole blouse. Instead, a woman might sew side-seams all day, every day, week in and week out. The work was highly repetitive and, as the women attested, very boring. Changes of style and seasonal variations rang a superficial change in the nature of the work, but whether the cloth was cotton or wool, sewing pieces together was the same. The individual worker had no control over what she would do. (19–20)

The addition of direct supervision and demeaning rules further limited women's autonomy, and their application to female but not male work groups intensified feelings of powerlessness. One worker, Annie, describes how differential treatment of women relative to individuals in predominately male work groups employed in the same firm generated a sense of relative deprivation with respect to autonomy:

> The men get away with murder in this company. Just for example, every night the women leave here one or other of them is checked by security. But the men, they get into their cars and off they go. . . . The men are not supervised like the women. . . . The men in the dyehouse, the cutters and layer-uppers are just doing their own thing most of the time, in my view. (71–72)

Exclusion from opportunities for on-the-job training also precluded women's advancement and confined them to positions subject to coercive control:

> As machinists, the women were expected to clean their machines and to replace the needles should they become blunt or broken—but no more than this. . . . One of the

young supervisors, Carol, was keenly aware of the male monopoly on skill: "They never train the girls for that kind of work. *The men keep it to themselves*." (23, emphasis in original)

What is more, this particular combination of control techniques, particularly segmentation and emphasis on speed in rule-based production targets, has made it difficult for workers to achieve the meaningfulness they might otherwise have derived from their tasks—limiting commitment to the organization. A worker explains:

You can be really good and it makes no difference, it's speed they want. . . . I came here because I used to sew at home . . . and my husband's friend used to say I was really good so I should go to StitchCo because they made quality goods. . . . Then, we used to put our initials on the back of some of the labels because we were proud of our work. Now, I don't even put it on the tag of the work. Because we have to work so quickly the quality is gone. It's the same for the cloth and the cutting, it's rubbish. We make *rubbish* here now and . . . I wonder . . . who buys this stuff. (46–47).

Consistent with understandings of resistance as a means to reclaim dignity denied in formal production arrangements (see Hodson 2001), the women engaged in collective resistance to achieve their aims. For example, when the firm instituted targets the women believed to be unfair, their protest took the form of jobs poorly done. Their collective withdrawal of effort succeeded in securing for the women not only their immediate goal but also greater control over their time.

They consistently and deliberately got the packing wrong and spent their time chatting about the dispute. . . . Later in the week, the [shipment of clothing] came back. Management [temporarily] suspended the [targets] . . . and made an appeal to get the job done as quickly as possible. . . . Amina responded: "Slow down everyone." We all grinned conspiratorially. . . . [T]hey maintained this collectively and individually over the two weeks. . . . The women had fought and won their own time back again. (53–54)

Persuasive Control in Female Work Groups

Female work groups are by no means devoid of intrinsic rewards. Although persuasive controls are observed less

frequently in these settings, they enhance worker dignity where they are applied. For example, the two female work groups enjoyed significantly higher levels of every dependent variable in the analysis. The remaining persuasive approach to control was encountered by just over a third of female work groups. The absence of both segmentation and automation enhances worker dignity, but the absence of career ladders appears to somewhat mitigate the benefits. Although this typology is associated with significantly higher rates of autonomy, creativity, meaningfulness, and satisfaction relative to comparison groups, the differences are smaller in comparison to those found in many predominantly male settings. Furthermore, no benefits are apparent in terms of commitment or effort.

Nurses in Annette Street's (1992) study encountered this persuasive configuration. As the following quote illustrates, the absence of segmentation and automation leaves room for autonomy despite constraints imposed by doctors' orders:

Although much of the nurses' role involves following doctor's orders for the patient, Ann is making independent decisions on the provision of physical care for her patient. . . . The nurse needs to ensure that the patient has adequate air . . . and . . . . [decides] when the patient needs assisted air intake or needs to be weaned off the ventilator. . . . [She] is responsible for the technological interventions and the supervision of drugs and food/drink intake . . . [and] regulates noise and visitors, often a challenging role requiring sensitivity and diplomacy. (185–186)

Although the authority of physicians narrows the scope of their autonomy, nurses are not passive in the face of constraint; they instead exercise creativity within these bounds to ensure the best possible care for their patients. An absence of segmentation and automation is crucial to their efforts. Here, Street (1992) describes a nurse's creative approach to getting the job done:

Bev had set the ventilator to the low level that her experience suggested was appropriate for the patient. A new surgical intern . . . ignored her and . . . set the ventilator to a higher setting . . . remind[ing] her that [this was] "my patient." [Bev] was concerned that the [gentleman] would be rather uncomfortable. . . . [and] decided to go over [the intern's] head. . . . [S]he called the senior anesthetist on another pretext and then casually mentioned:

"We are maintaining the patient on level 10." As she had predicted, the senior doctor replied: "Oh well, we can put him on 4 now, don't you think?". . . When the intern returned and queried the change, she told him that the senior anesthetist had changed the levels when he came into the bay. (234)

Their use of clinical skills to make a difference in the health and experience of patients allows nurses to derive meaning and satisfaction from their jobs:

Nurses recognize the value of their clinical skills, knowledge, experiences, and relationships when they are participating in the process of transformation of a person from illness to health or from illness to death. . . . [N]urses . . . spoke about the satisfaction [they felt] when they were able to recognize a potential difficulty before it was apparent through the regular diagnostic channels . . . or the value of the nurturant activities despite the devaluing of this by a society interested in dramatic cures. (255–256)

Importantly, however, other aspects of the control structure mitigate some of the benefits of persuasive control. Although nurses in Street's study freely offered additional effort in the provision of patient care, they were frustrated with a lack of input into hospital affairs and withdrew both commitment and effort in response to policies they found objectionable—a finding consistent with the absence of any significant positive effect of this configuration on either of these outcomes. For example, they often refused to participate in written record keeping, which they interpreted as administrators' emphasis on recorded rather than actual care. They ignored charts, entered minimal information and either busied themselves with patients or were deliberately absent at the end of their shifts, preferring instead to exchange information verbally upon handover or to ask questions as they arose. In thwarting the organization's efforts in these regards, nurses asserted their claims to dignity at work.

Discussion and Conclusion

In this chapter, I have integrated insights from the workplace gender stratification and labor process literatures, and use content-coded data from workplace ethnographies to investigate control and dignity in female and male work groups. Findings point to substantial gender variation in the nature and degree of workplace control, with significant implications for dignity at work. Male work groups, especially those with very low percent female, tend to encounter persuasive arrangements that enhance worker dignity, while their female counterparts confront more coercive "bundles" of control that erode the foundations of a dignified, meaningful, and productive work life. Reimmersion in the case studies highlights women's use of agency to preserve dignity in the face of constraint.

This study advances the literature theoretically in two key ways. First, it builds on established understandings of workplace gender inequality by exploring hidden disparities in the experience of women's and men's jobs and demonstrating how the organization of work, especially workplace controls, is a fundamental aspect of gender inequality. Prior research on gender stratification has shown that sex segregation has important consequences for tangible outcomes such as authority and wages, but has often been less explicit about variation in the organization of work and control strategies, particularly complex combinations of control generating gender inequalities in the work experience.

Investigating this issue through a labor process lens—especially while attending to complex combinations of control and their effects on worker dignity—sheds light on differences in the content of women's and men's jobs, giving dimension to established awareness that positions set aside for men are more lucrative by demonstrating that they are also more conducive to working with dignity. Although these hidden aspects of inequality are difficult to measure, they are highly important aspects of individuals' lives. This study thus reveals some of the concrete ways that gender is built into organizations and sheds light on important day-to-day activities that constitute and reproduce gender as an institution (see Acker 2006; Martin 2004; Ridgeway 1997).

Second, these findings inform labor process research by highlighting the significance of control combinations and by pointing to work group composition as a key consideration in the organization and experience of work. Scholarship in this tradition has long sought to explain how dominant modes of control change over time, vary across diverse industrial segments, and affect worker sentiments and behavior, especially in manual and mostly male environments (e.g., Burawoy 1979; Edwards 1979; Hodson 1996). This study brings into view the use and effect of control combinations and demonstrates that they are hardly monolithic across status groups. Female work environments are notable for not only their disproportionate constraint but also the prominence of direct supervision—a mode of control long characterized in labor process research as waning over time, but which combines with other constraints to demean and deny opportunity to women. These findings thus bring into sharp relief the need to consider workers' status group membership when applying theories of control.

Admittedly, these data—while ideal for investigating variations across work groups in heterogeneous settings and augmenting both the gender work stratification and labor process literatures—are less helpful in disentangling the mechanisms at play. Some of these are clearly organizational; control structures that isolate workers, routinize their tasks, and dictate the pace of production directly affect levels of autonomy and creativity, for example. Outcomes such as satisfaction, commitment, and effort are likely more relational, although the precise mechanisms need elaboration. How do control arrangements influence interpersonal dynamics at work, and to what degree do these interactions explain effects on worker sentiments and behavior? Do workers confronting oppressive control structures derive less satisfaction from their jobs and withdraw effort in part because they feel bullied, unfairly treated, or disrespected by those around them? Are these processes subject to variations by workers' gender and/or by gender composition of work groups? And do the psychological effects of control affect interactions in other institutional spheres? Do they influence familial relationships, for example, perhaps contributing to interpersonal dynamics that help maintain the "vicious circle" of women's subordination at home and at work (Hartmann 1976)? Answering these questions will help to deepen our understanding of gender disparities in the labor process and may expand the scope of their known effects.

References

Acker, Joan. 2006. "Inequality Regimes: Gender, Class, and Race in Organizations." *Gender & Society* 20: 441–464.

Acker, Joan, and Donald R. Van Houten. 1974. "Differential Recruitment and Control: The Sex Structuring of Organizations." *Administrative Science Quarterly* 19: 152–163.

Adler, Paul S., and Bryan Borys. 1996. "Two Types of Bureaucracy: Enabling and Coercive." *Administrative Science Quarterly* 41:61–89.

Austrin, Terry. 1991. "Flexibility, Surveillance and Hype in New Zealand Financial Retailing." *Work, Employment and Society* 5:201–221.

Bergmann, Barbara R. 2011. "Sex Segregation in the Blue-Collar Occupations: Women's Choices or Unremedied Discrimination?" *Gender & Society* 25:88–93.

Bielby, William T., and Baron, James N. 1986. "Men and Women at Work: Sex Segregation and Statistical Discrimination." *American Journal of Sociology* 91: 759–799.

Blauner, Robert. 1964. *Alienation and Freedom.* Chicago, IL: University of Chicago Press.

Braverman, Harry. 1974. *Labor and Monopoly Capital.* New York: Monthly Review Press.

Burawoy, Michael. 1979. *Manufacturing Consent.* Chicago, IL: University of Chicago Press.

Cockburn, Cynthia. 1983. *Brothers.* London: Pluto Press.

Cockburn, Cynthia. 1988a. *Machinery of Dominance.* Boston, MA: Northeastern University Press.

Cockburn, Cynthia.1988b. "The Gendering of Jobs: Workplace Relations and the Reproduction of Sex Segregation." In *Gender Segregation at Work* (ed. S. Walby), 29–42. Philadelphia, PA: Open University Press.

Collinson, David L., David Knights, and Margaret Collinson. 1990. *Managing to Discriminate.* London: Routledge.

Courpasson, David. 2000. "Managerial Strategies of Domination. Power in Soft Bureaucracies." *Organization Studies* 21:141–161.

Coverman, Shelley. 1986. "Occupational Segmentation and Sex Differences in Earnings." In *Research in Social Stratification and Mobility*, Vol. 5 (ed. R. V. Robinson), 139–172. Greenwich, CT: JAI Press.

Crowley, Martha. 2012. "Control and Dignity in Professional, Manual and Service-Sector Employment." *Organization Studies* 33:1383–1406.

Davies, Margery W. 1982. *Woman's Place Is at the Typewriter.* Philadelphia, PA: Temple University Press.

Deery, Stephen, Janet Walsh, and David Guest. 2011. "Workplace Aggression: The Effects of Harassment on Job Burnout and Turnover Intentions." *Work Employment and Society* 25:742–759.

Dinovitzer, Ronit, Nancy Reichman, and Joyce Sterling. 2009. "The Differential Valuation of Women's Work: A New Look at the Gender Gap in Lawyers' Incomes." *Social Forces* 88:819–864.

Edwards, Richard. 1979. *Contested Terrain.* New York: Basic Books.

England, Paula. 2010. "The Gender Revolution: Uneven and Stalled." *Gender and Society* 24:149–166.

Frenkel, Stephen J., and Karin Sanders. 2007. "Explaining Variations in Co-worker Assistance in Organizations." *Organization Studies* 28:797–823.

Friedman, Andrew L. 1977. *Industry and Labour.* London: Macmillan.

Gamst, Frederick C. 1980. *The Hoghead.* New York: Holt, Rinehart and Winston.

Greenwood, Royston, David L. Deephouse, and Stan Xiao Li. 2007. "Ownership and Performance of Professional Service Firms." *Organization Studies* 28:219–238.

Hartmann, Heidi. 1976. "Capitalism, Patriarchy, and Job Segregation by Sex." *Signs* 1(3:Supplement): 137–169.

Hodson, Randy. 1996. "Dignity in the Workplace under Participative Management: Alienation and Freedom Revisited." *American Sociological Review* 61:719–738.

Hodson, Randy. 2001. *Dignity at Work.* Cambridge, UK: Cambridge University Press.

Hossfield, Karen J. 1990. "'Their Logic Against Them': Contradictions in Sex, Race and Class in Silicon Valley." In *Women Workers and Global Restructuring* (ed. K. Ward), 149–178. Ithaca, NY: ILR Press.

Johnson, Monica Kirkpatric, and Jeylan T. Mortimer. 2011. "Origins and Outcomes of Judgments about Work." *Social Forces* 89:1239–1260.

Kanter, Rosabeth Moss. 1977. *Men and Women of the Corporation.* New York: Basic Books.

Kohn, Melvin L. 1976. "Occupational Structure and Alienation." *American Journal of Sociology* 82:111–130.

Lee, Ching Kwan. 1998. *Gender and the South China Miracle.* Berkeley: University of California Press.

Leidner, Robin. 1991. "Serving Hamburgers and Selling Insurance: Gender, Work and Identity in Interactive Service Jobs." *Gender and Society* 5:154–177.

Levanon, Asaf, Paula England, and Paul Allison. 2009. "Occupational Feminization and Pay: Assessing Causal Dynamics Using 1950–2000 U.S. Census Data." *Social Forces* 88:865–891.

Marsden, Peter, Arne L. Kalleberg, and Cynthia Cook. 1993. "Gender Differences in Organizational Commitment." *Work and Occupations* 20:368–390.

Martin, Patricia Yancy. 2003. "'Said and Done' Versus 'Saying and Doing': Gendering Practices, Practicing Gender at Work." *Gender & Society* 17:342–366.

Martin, Patricia. 2004. "Gender as a Social Institution." *Social Forces* 82:1249–1273.

McCammon, Holly J., and Larry J. Griffin. 2000. "Workers and Their Customers and Clients." *Work and Occupations* 27:278–293.

Mills, Mary Beth. 2003. "Gender and Inequality in the Global Labor Force." *Annual Review of Anthropology* 32:41–62.

Muñoz, Carolina Bank. 2008. *Transnational Tortillas.* Ithaca, NY: ILR Press.

Nixon, Darren. 2009. "'I Can't Put a Smiley Face On': Working-Class Masculinity, Emotional Labour and Service Work in the 'New Economy.'" *Gender, Work and Organization* 16:300–322.

Ong, Aihwa. 1987. *Spirits of Resistance and Capitalist Discipline.* Albany: State University of New York Press.

Phillips, Anne. 1983. "Review of Brothers by Cynthia Cockburn." *Feminist Review* 15:101–104.

Rafferty, Alannah E., and Simon Lloyd D. Restubog. 2011. "The Influence of Abusive Supervisors on Followers' Organizational Citizenship Behaviours: The Hidden Costs of Abusive Supervision." *British Journal of Management* 22:270–285.

Raynolds, Laura T. 2001. "New Plantations, New Workers: Gender and Production Politics in the Dominican Republic." *Gender and Society* 15:7–28.

Reskin, Barbara F., and Irene Padavic. 1988. "Supervisors as Gatekeepers: Male Supervisors' Response to Women's Integration in Plant Jobs." *Social Problems* 35:536–550.

Reskin, Barbara F., and Irene Padavic. 1994. *Women and Men at Work.* Thousand Oaks, CA: Pine Forge Press.

Reskin, Barbara F., and Patricia A. Roos. 1990. *Job Queues, Gender Queues.* Philadelphia, PA: Temple University Press.

Ridgeway, Cecilia L. 1997. "Interaction and the Conservation of Gender Inequality: Considering Employment. *American Sociological Review* 62:218–235.

Rogers, Jackie Krasas, and Kevin D. Henson. 1997. "'Hey, Why Don't You Wear a Shorter Skirt?' Structural Vulnerability and the Organization of Sexual Harassment in Temporary Clerical Employment." *Gender & Society* 11:215–237.

Ross, Catherine E. 2000. "Occupations, Jobs, and the Sense of Control." *Sociological Focus* 33:409–420.

Ross, Catherine E., and Marylyn P. Wright. 1998. "Women's Work, Men's Work, and the Sense of Control." *Work and Occupations* 25:333–355.

Rowe, Reba, and William E. Snizek. 1995. "Gender Differences in Work Values: Perpetuating the Myth." *Work and Occupations* 22:215–299.

Salzinger, Leslie. 2003. *Genders in Production.* Berkeley: University of California Press.

Schwalbe, Michael L. 1986. *The Psychosocial Consequences of Natural and Alienated Labor.* Albany: State University of New York Press.

Skuratowicz, Eva, and Larry W. Hunter. 2004. "Where Do Women's Jobs Come From? Job Resegregation in an American Bank." *Work and Occupations* 31:73–110.

Smith, Ryan A. 2002. "Race, Gender, and Authority in the Workplace: Theory and Research." *Annual Review of Sociology* 28:509–542.

Stein, Mark. 2007. "Toxicity and the Unconscious Experience of the Body at the Employee-Customer Interface." *Organization Studies* 28:1223–1241.

Street, Annette Fay. 1992. *Inside Nursing.* Albany: State University of New York Press.

Taylor, Frederick Winslow. 1947. *Scientific Management.* New York: Harper and Row.

Tilly, Charles. 1998. *Durable Inequality.* Berkeley: University of California Press.

Tolbert, Pamela S., and Phyllis Moen. 1998. "Men's and Women's Definitions of 'Good' Jobs: Similarities and Differences by Age and Across Time." *Work and Occupations* 25:168–194.

Tomaskovic-Devey, Donald. 1993. "The Gender and Race Composition of Jobs and the Male/Female, White Black Pay Gaps." *Social Forces* 72:45–76.

Tomaskovic-Devey, Donald, and Sheryl Skaggs. 2002. "Sex Segregation, Labor Process Organization, and Gender Earnings Inequality." *American Journal of Sociology* 108:102–128.

Vallas, Steven P. 1993. *Power in the Workplace.* Albany: State University of New York Press.

Vallas, Steve P. 2003. "The Adventures of Managerial Hegemony: Teamwork, Ideology, and Worker Resistance." *Social Problems* 50:204–255.

Webber, Gretchen and Christine Williams. 2008. "Mothers in 'Good' and 'Bad' Part-Time Jobs: Different Problems, Same Results." *Gender and Society* 22:752–777.

Westwood, Sallie. 1982. *All Day, Every Day.* London: Pluto Press.

Williams, Christine L. 1995. *Still a Man's World.* Berkeley: University of California Press.

Williams, Christine L. 2006. *Inside Toyland.* Berkeley: University of California Press.

Wolf, Diane Lauren. 1992. *Factory Daughters.* Berkeley: University of California Press.

Wright, Melissa W. 2001. "Desire and the Prosthetics of Supervision: A Case of Maquiladora Flexibility." *Cultural Anthropology* 16:354–373.

Zanoni, Patrizia. 2011. "Diversity in the Lean Automobile Factory: Doing Class through Gender, Disability and Age." *Organizations* 18:105–127.

Questions

1. What does Crowley mean by "dignity at work"? Why is this important for sociologists to study?

2. Crowley shows how the labor process can be controlled in coercive or persuasive ways. What does coercive control look like? Persuasive control?

3. How do these processes of controlling the labor process differ for men and women? What are the implications, according to the author, for various forms of workplace inequality, such as access to management and segregation?

4. While Crowley's focus is on workplaces, how might her findings affect women's and men's lives beyond work? For instance, how might these forms of control in the workplace affect relationships at home? At school? In the community?

27

Paperwork First, Not Work First: How Caseworkers Use Paperwork to Feel Effective

TIFFANY TAYLOR

Existing welfare-to-work programs have changed dramatically in the last few decades. While people often assume that those on welfare take advantage of the system and do nothing for their checks, the reality is far different. Current welfare-to-work programs require clients participate in job-related activities (including job searching and/or working 30 or more hours a week "voluntarily" for an area employer). They are time limited (by the state and federal government) and emphasize sanctioning for any non-compliance with rules. County and state programs report to the federal government in order to keep funding through an expansive amount of paperwork.

In this case study of a county welfare program in rural North Carolina, Tiffany Taylor focuses on how implementing welfare-to-work programs is structured in a way so that caseworkers spend far more time on paperwork than they actually spend assisting program participants to develop skills or find employment. Given the constraints and punitiveness of existing welfare policy, caseworkers use paperwork to feel effective in a job that offers little opportunity to help clients move from welfare to work. Consequentially, caseworkers in this study do very little to help clients gain skills or employment. Nor do they resist or protest problematic aspects of the program. Instead, workers focus on their paperwork so that they can feel good about their work and keep their jobs. This study gives us insight into the role that bureaucracy—in this case, fulfilling bureaucratic requirements—plays in shaping and reproducing inequalities. It also shows us how people's emotions, identities, and financial dependencies create barriers to making change.

Over the past decade, politicians and the press alike have claimed that welfare reform works (Harris and Parisi 2008). Despite these claims, many researchers question the success of welfare reform (Hao and Cherlin 2004; Lichter and Jayakody 2002; Rogers-Dillon 2004). Since 1996, and until the recent recession, many welfare participants in the United States have found some type of employment after leaving welfare. It is not clear how much of this increase in employment is attributable to welfare services or if the employment is stable. Further, welfare participants across the United States have difficulty finding full-time, full-year employment. The jobs available to participants are low-skill, low-wage jobs that offer little to no upward mobility (Butler et al. 2008; Corcoran et al. 2000; Harris and Parisi 2008; Hennessy 2005). The most consistent finding concerning the effects of welfare reform on employment is that the number of families classified as working poor has

Excerpted from Taylor, Tiffany. 2013. "Paperwork First, Not Work First: How Caseworkers Use Paperwork to Feel Effective." *Journal of Sociology and Social Welfare* 40:9–27.

increased dramatically (Lichter and Jayakody, 2002; Corcoran et al., 2000; Hennessy, 2005; O'Connor, 2000). Despite these challenges, welfare agencies argue that they help program participants reach self-sufficiency.

This chapter is a case study of a rural county welfare agency in North Carolina that examines how caseworkers use paperwork as a means to feel effective. While paperwork in social services offices has been taken as a given, how caseworkers use paperwork to feel effective within the constraints of bureaucracy has not been explored. Being good at paperwork allows caseworkers to feel effective within a program that offers them little room to successfully assist clients. Finally, in this chapter, I also answer the call of Lichter and Jayakody (2002) to examine welfare reform in rural areas, which remain under-studied despite their unique, and arguably greater, challenges in comparison to urban areas.

Literature Review

For welfare street-level bureaucrats, the daily work of welfare service provision has changed considerably since the passage of the Personal Responsibility and Work Opportunity Reconciliation Act of 1996 (PRWORA). This reform overhauled Aid to Families with Dependent Children (AFDC), creating Temporary Assistance to Needy Families (TANF) and a complex new set of rules for welfare street-level bureaucrats to follow and enforce (Ridzi 2004, 2009). TANF participants would be required to work, they would have time limits to their assistance, and they would have "family caps" that prohibited additional cash assistance if the program participant became pregnant while receiving cash assistance.

Shortly after PRWORA passed, Hays (2003) studied caseworkers' efforts to deal with this new welfare system that increased the social control aspect of workers' jobs. She found that caseworkers actively resisted these punitive measures and bent the rules to help clients. Several years after Hays' time in the field, welfare was reauthorized and a new requirement increased the number of participants that welfare agencies and caseworkers needed to get into "work-related activities." Some recent research (Handler and Hasenfeld 2007; Ridzi 2004, 2009) suggests that restructuring welfare agencies, ideological buy-in among staff, and the

demanding and competitive performance measures have combined to create a substantial shift in how programs for the poor are implemented. Additional research (Riccucci 2005; Riccucci et al. 2004; Watkins-Hayes 2009) finds more variation in the level of staff buy-in to what Ridzi (2009) terms the "common sense" of welfare reform. By and large, though, caseworkers have little choice but to meet the demands of county, state, and federal performance measures. Further, welfare-to-work remains an ineffective program in helping clients gain steady employment, much less become self-sufficient (Collins and Mayer 2010; Handler and Hasenfeld 2007; Ridzi 2009).

Thirty years ago, Lipsky (1980) argued that caseworkers were too busy doing paperwork to do quality casework. Based on her recent case studies in Massachusetts, Watkins-Hayes (2009) finds that caseworkers get multiple cues that paperwork processing is more important than social work to agencies. My findings are consistent, but I also argue that caseworkers focus on completing paperwork to feel like they are effective in their jobs. Further, caseworkers use the paperwork to protect themselves from being blamed for any wrongdoing. While paperwork is externally required and burdensome to doing effective social work, it also becomes a tool for caseworkers to feel effective in a very constrained and often emotionally draining job.

Location and Methods

Smithgrove County is in eastern North Carolina, where the economy has centered on cotton agriculture and textile manufacturing in the second half of the twentieth century. Several small cities grew from mill towns that textile manufacturers constructed when they sought cheap labor that was socially and geographically isolated (Wood 1986). Wealthy southerners essentially invited these firms to exploit the desperately poor white farmers as mill laborers, while using already exploited Black tenant and sharecropping farmers for their supply of cotton (Tomaskovic-Devey and Roscigno 1996, 1997). This economic development set into motion decades of worker exploitation and poverty (Anderson, Schulman, and Wood, 2000; Wood, 1986). Smithgrove County's racial makeup was attractive to companies at the time, and still today Blacks make up the largest percentage of the population in Smithgrove County (53% compared to White, non-Hispanics at 43% and 4% of the population comprising other racial categories, according to U.S. Census Bureau 2000).

The Bureau of Labor Statistics reports that in 2007 (U.S. Department of Labor 2007) when the data were being collected, Smithgrove County was among 200 U.S. counties with the highest poverty and unemployment. More than a fourth of Smithgrove County's population was living in poverty (more than double the North Carolina average), and more than 9 percent were unemployed (which is much higher than the North Carolina rate of 5.5 percent). These figures simply illustrate that Smithgrove County residents face tough conditions that show little promise of improving. Work opportunities are not plentiful, and most jobs that are currently available offer very low wages.

Smithgrove County and the eastern part of the state never diversified their industrial base. This lack of industrial diversity proved disastrous for the economy by 2000. When the textile and apparel industries moved further south (first to the U.S. Deep South and then to Central America) for cheaper labor, many people in this region were left without jobs (Anderson et al. 2000). In 2007, The Bureau of Labor Statistics (U.S. Department of Labor 2007) reported retail as the largest industry in the county, and the jobs in this sector paid less than $20,000 a year. The county also has a high number of program participants reaching time limits (24 months in North Carolina) because they are not able to find work.

Methods

Data collection for this case study occurred from June 2006 until June 2007. I use several methods in this project, including document analysis, participant observation, and formal and informal interviews. There are a number of benefits to using multiple methods in research. For instance, by interviewing, I learn what caseworkers say they do and how they feel. By observing, I see what caseworkers actually do, including actions that they may take for granted. The various methods, then, serve as a check and balance, improving the reliability and validity of the data and findings (Hammersley and Atkinson 1985; Marshall and Rossman 1998).

The first step in the research was to conduct a thorough review of the policies and procedures relevant to welfare history and policy in the United States, North Carolina, and Smithgrove County. These included training manuals from the job-readiness class, performance reviews, Work First policy manuals, and a variety of forms used by caseworkers and participants on a daily basis. This allowed me to develop an understanding of the historical, social, political, and economic development of Smithgrove County, as well as county, state, and federal welfare policy. This incredible paper trail also raised my awareness of the importance of paperwork for Work First caseworkers, which I discuss in detail later.

Second, I observed as a participant and nonparticipant in a number of settings. These observations included things like shadowing caseworkers as if I were training, such as sitting in on interviews with welfare participants and sitting in the cubicle area observing phone and face-to-face interactions between caseworkers and welfare participants. I also went on home visits to participants' homes, attended the job-readiness class, as well as the regional economic development summit and the quarterly regional workforce and economic development meetings. Additionally, I attended "Success Staffing" meetings, in which Department of Social Services (DSS) workers and their community partners (nonprofit and other government agencies who provide services) met with welfare participants who were in danger of hitting time limits.

Third, I conducted interviews with welfare service providers including caseworkers, line supervisors, the program manager, and area nonprofit workers and managers. I interviewed all thirteen caseworkers working in the Work First program in the county. Of these caseworkers, all were women, five were white and eight were African American. I estimate that six were in their thirties, while the remaining caseworkers were older; their ages ranged from forties up to a few supervisors who were in their sixties. Three of the caseworkers had received cash assistance through the Department of Social Services before becoming caseworkers. An additional caseworker had once received county-coordinated outplacement assistance when the local textile mill closed.

In addition to the caseworkers, I interviewed two employees responsible for interacting primarily with companies, and secondarily with participants, in the county. One of these employees was an African American woman in her thirties whom the DSS employed and paid on a full-time basis. A second liaison was a white woman, also in her thirties, who was employed by the county's Chamber of Commerce, as well as the Department of Social Services. I also formally interviewed three line supervisors as a group and had frequent informal follow-up discussions with them individually. Of these supervisors, two were white and one was African American.

Finally, I interviewed one high-ranking supervisor who oversees Work First programs in the county. This supervisor is a white woman who had worked at the DSS for more than 20 years. She is one of the few workers in this division holding a four-year degree. All the supervisors worked with DSS since before the 1996 welfare reform. All interviews with individuals (in total 19 DSS employees) were semi-structured, using techniques meant to elicit rich stories (Weiss 1994). Interviews lasted from 30 minutes to over two hours, averaging just over an hour. In this chapter, I report how agency workers use paperwork to feel effective in a work environment that is largely structured by achieving statistical measures of success. Second, I explore how workers overcome focus on the paperwork as a source of competence and as a way to show others they are doing their jobs correctly.

Challenges in Getting People to "Work First"

Supervisors argued that the requirement of having half their program participants engaged in work-related activities is impossible to achieve. The state and federal governments have threatened that they will sanction the county if they do not reach their numbers. While this has yet to occur, caseworkers and supervisors have reason to fear sanctions, especially given the tight labor market in Smithgrove County. Despite this, caseworkers embraced the language of "self-sufficiency" and "Work First," and argued that it created a work ethic among otherwise unmotivated participants. Caseworkers and supervisors stated they need to help participants realize that any job is better than welfare. The caseworkers would often say, "It's called Work First, so you need to get to work first" and therefore skill development, education, and many other activities necessary to reach self-sufficiency take a backseat. This consistent message of "self-sufficiency" and going to "work first" to achieve self-sufficiency prompted me to ask caseworkers how they help participants find jobs. The caseworkers' first response was usually that participants must register

with the state employment agency (ESC) through a program called "First Stop."

This program no longer received funding from the state, and several of the supervisors argued that workers at the ESC did not offer enough assistance to participants because of the lack of funding and staff. Kim, a supervisor, expressed her frustrations with the ESC, saying:

> Their money got cut, and their staff, and they just don't want to do the extra stuff. So they have their goals to meet. They have their number crunches they have to have. [. . .] And we have had to put people in there to do it.

The quote illustrates a larger issue of program implementation and the relationships between government agencies. State law requires the ESC to provide a service to Work First participants, but they do not have the funding or staff resources to provide the service. The consequence is that welfare participants who are supposed to move from welfare to work do not get job referrals from the ESC staff. Despite this potential flaw in the policies and rules, caseworkers must still enforce these rules. In fact, caseworkers view themselves as helping participants by referring them to ESC, regardless of whether or not the ESC actually helps the participant. To these caseworkers, the act of referring to another organization is helping, in and of itself.

In addition to registering with First Stop at the ESC, participants must look for jobs (called "job search") on their own for 30 or more hours a week. Caseworkers monitored compliance with this requirement through checking participants' weekly timecards, but did little to help guide this process. Participants manually fill out the hours they participate in "work-related activities" each week using a paper timecard. Manual timecards, according to caseworkers, also create a work-like feeling of responsibility among the participants. Beyond monitoring timecards, caseworkers mandated that participants attend a job-readiness class offered by a local nonprofit. The DSS provides almost all of the funding for the organization offering the class. Participation in this class counts as a work-related activity, which helps the county meet expectations of the state. In the job-readiness class, participants learn to write resumes and learn how to interview for jobs. Unfortunately, this training may not help participants compete for low-wage jobs that often only accept applications, not resumes, and that often do not require formal interviews.

When I asked her what she did to help clients find employment, Kathy, a caseworker, struggled with the question. After some follow-up, she responded, "well, every week Amanda [who works as a liaison between the Chamber of Commerce, the ESC, and the DSS] sends me jobs listed through the ESC. Then I go through and look for ones that match my clients." I asked how she contacted the participants to tell them about the job openings. Kathy replied that she sends them letters in the mail. Caseworkers send all their letters on their designated paperwork day of the week, so it could be days or more than a week before a participant learns of a job opening listed with the state employment agency. In a high unemployment labor market, like in Smithgrove County, job openings are filled quickly.

When I asked Kathy if caseworkers ever contacted participants by telephone to tell them about job openings, she again looked puzzled and replied that she does not call the participants about jobs. It is important to note that she, and all caseworkers, regularly calls participants about completing paperwork. Even one caseworker, Nancy, who takes extra effort to go through the job advertisements in the newspaper on weekends, sends letters with job information to participants on her paperwork day. As a rarity, she does call participants, but only about job fairs. She has never called them about specific job openings.

Once, on a participant home visit, I observed a caseworker give extra effort to help a participant find employment. The participant had a criminal record, and the nature of the charge made it difficult for her to find employment. The caseworker and the participant talked about forms of bonding insurance she may be eligible for and then discussed having the liaison to the Chamber of Commerce assist this participant in finding a job. This conversation was unusual, since this was the only time I witnessed a caseworker and participant interact about something other than updating paperwork or complying with a rule. While caseworkers and managers constantly mentioned the "mutual responsibility" of both participants and the DSS and that "it takes a village," the responsibility of finding a job rested almost solely with the participant and then the caseworker spent her time doing paperwork—documenting the participant's efforts.

Caseworkers estimated they spent 50 to 60 percent of their time doing paperwork. Based on my observations, it would seem these estimates were conservative. Paperwork included sending letters like the ones mentioned previously, but caseworkers also documented conversations, as well as how they spent their time. In this county, caseworkers blocked out one day a week to send letters and catch up on paperwork. Additionally, caseworkers also spent one day every two weeks doing "intake," which means greeting participants and doing the initial eligibility screening interview with someone who usually will become someone else's client. Caseworkers spent the remaining 40 percent, or 16 hours, of the week working with existing participants in their caseload, either face-to-face or, more commonly, on the telephone. Caseworkers in Smithgrove County carried a caseload of approximately 40 to 50 families. If they were to spend 16 hours equally across 40 families, then each family would get only 24 minutes per week of the caseworker's time. What little time caseworkers spent face-to-face or on the telephone was to check that the participant was completing paperwork or following rules, not working with them to find jobs.

In the "interview" process (when the caseworker discussed the application with the potential participant), caseworkers collected information about prior work history and education. The caseworkers then entered this data into the computer. Caseworkers did not ask participants about their job aspirations, or even their skills, in the interviews I observed. Caseworkers never talked with participants about improving skills or receiving training, despite the relevance to participant self-sufficiency. Also, none of the interviews that I observed were completed, since the potential participant did not have all the information necessary to complete the paperwork. Caseworkers do not start processing the application until all the paperwork is completed, which includes the participants providing documentation to prove income, school enrollment, and immunization history, among other things. Having all the paperwork takes precedence over getting the participant started on searching for a job or getting needed assistance.

Social services work is well known for high stress, turnover, and conflict with clients. I was quite surprised that when I asked caseworkers what their main source of frustration was, many caseworkers said it was with completing their paperwork. One caseworker, Nancy, expressed this frustration, saying it would be much easier on caseworkers if participants would just take benefit diversion checks and not go onto the welfare caseload. She then followed this saying, "God forbid if you get sick and you have to be out of work, because your stuff gets behind [. . .] God forbid that we get pulled for something else or called to a meeting. That gets you behind." This frustration in completing paperwork is not surprising, given that paperwork is how caseworkers spend the majority of their time and since, for the caseworkers, completing their paperwork is their main source of success in their jobs.

Caseworkers would often say, "Document, document, document" with a smile. This word had become a mantra for both the supervisors and caseworkers. After hearing this phrase often in my fieldwork, I asked Julie, a caseworker, about it. She responded "Yes, it is like a slogan, 'document, document, document.'" I asked her when she first learned the slogan and she replied, "First day at work. Document, document, document. Document, document, document. Like [Kim, a supervisor], she always has to review everything that I do and she says, 'Did you document? Did you document?'" Julie's repeating of the phrase is reflective of the work environment and socialization. Caseworkers and managers constantly say this phrase, reminding one another of the importance · of documenting everything. Given the repetition of the document mantra and the emphasis on paperwork, I wanted to know why caseworkers thought documenting and completing paperwork were important.

Documenting Accountability and Fairness

Beyond the constant reminders to document, caseworkers argued that documenting everything is important for two reasons. First and foremost, caseworkers were clear that documenting everything provided proof that they had performed their jobs as expected in the event of a hearing or an audit. Second, and related to this, caseworkers argued that documenting and following rules ensured that they had treated clients fairly. Importantly, both reasons were given by all the caseworkers, and they often discussed fairness to clients and covering themselves in overlapping and somewhat confusing ways.

When I asked Alice, a caseworker, about why she thought documenting was important she responded, "Well, it's to, you know, C.Y.A.—cover your ass." Other caseworkers responded similarly, saying it was necessary

to document everything in case the client complained and asked for a hearing. Alice talked further about this, saying that documenting creates a "paper trail" and went on to say, "It helps you keep your job. I'm helping myself and I'm helping the county and I'm helping my co-workers." Notice Alice does not mention that paperwork helps clients, but suggests instead that it is important for covering yourself, keeping your job, and helping the county. Judy elaborated on this idea, saying:

> So it's like a record to show that we did this. We didn't skip this. We went through with this. And sometimes it's a running—it's a running—we have to do a lot of detection, so it lets them know what we are doing. Each time we pick up something or each time we do something, it lets them know that we did all the proper procedures, we explained everything and just chalk it up to that.

Here Judy discussed the importance of keeping a record of what has been done, especially in terms of "detection," which means surveying clients to look for fraudulent behavior. She further elaborates on the extent to which they have to document, saying every time they "pick up" or "do something" they have to document to show they followed "proper procedures."

The caseworkers suggested that it was important to use the paperwork to show that they were doing their jobs correctly, which they argue means they treated a client fairly and followed procedure. When I asked Ann, a caseworker, about the manual and rules, she spoke positively about having a manual, saying, "Well, anything that we need to know, we can pull that manual up and most of the time it's there. And so we don't have to wonder about 'should I do it this way or should I do it that way?'" Ann suggests that having rules and guidelines prevents the worker from having to worry about how something should be done. Also implicit in this statement is that caseworkers wanted to avoid making mistakes and they also wanted to be fair.

Nearly all of the caseworkers and supervisors in Smithgrove County placed a great deal of emphasis on doing a good job and doing it right. Caseworkers did not want to make mistakes in general, and they certainly did not want to make a mistake that might harm a client. Many caseworkers also told me that making a mistake can cost the county money, and they very much wanted to avoid that. In many ways, the caseworkers suggest that being required to document everything and having procedures standardized and routinized helps them treat clients fairly. Documenting everything holds case-workers accountable to treat clients by the rules.

As mentioned earlier, in Smithgrove County, case-workers allocated certain days to do certain tasks. For instance, on a day a caseworker is asked to conduct intake and handle face-to-face interactions with clients, she will see both her clients and clients in other case-workers' caseloads. This division of labor is supposed to make the caseworkers more efficient through having them focus and group similar tasks. Given this labor process, caseworkers need to be able to deal with an-other caseworker's client without interrupting the other caseworker. Nancy explained the importance of docu-menting, given this labor process:

> So that's why it's important. If you're not going to be here, or if your worker's not going to be here a certain day, that you document whatever it is you need for the client to do or whatever in case the client comes in when you're not here.

Alice, another caseworker, also talked about the importance of documenting, given the division of labor:

> We have everything straight and then also to have your co-workers to read behind you because we all the time have to be seeing each other's clients [. . .] you have to cover and it was tough, but we managed. [. . .] Because we are working with everyone.

While caseworkers complained about the amount of duplicate paperwork and the fact that the computers crashed constantly, overall, the paperwork, many argued, helped them in their jobs. Some caseworkers suggested that having the rules and documenting ev-erything holds caseworkers accountable to treat all cli-ents the same, which again, they argued, is the same as treating them fairly. In this sense, standardization means fairness, which means, to them, a lack of dis-crimination. Historically there has been some concern over caseworkers using discretion to illegally discrimi-nate against clients (for detailed analyses of this history see Gordon 1990). The caseworkers seem aware of this criticism and suggest they must consistently document their actions on forms and in the computer databases. Stephanie discussed this, saying:

> You know you have your booklet that you have to do your standard questions, you know. [. . .] When you first

start you feel overwhelmed with the paperwork, but to keep it where more people don't fall through the cracks and not get services they need. Well there's that, I guess, to stop a type of client from getting more than what they need. We've got to have every piece of paper that we do.

This quote from Stephanie illustrates some of the complex feelings about paperwork. First, she discussed the standardization and suggested that caseworkers must always ask the standard questions. Of course, they must then document the answers. Second, she acknowl-edged that the paperwork is overwhelming to a new person, but suggests that learning the paperwork is seen as a big accomplishment. Finally, Stephanie mentioned that paperwork was a means of surveillance to ensure that a client received the appropriate amount of ser-vices. Stephanie's comment also is consistent with the first reason caseworkers give for doing paperwork, which is a way for caseworkers to cover themselves in the event of an audit or hearing. Stephanie continued discussing the importance of paperwork in a way that further shows this overlap in reasoning:

> Umm, it's a point of information, but having that pa-perwork in the books, in the records and a case termi-nates and then she comes back in the next month or 2 or 3 months later, you can kind of, you can kind of glance over the paperwork that she did before, before you go get her and when she says I've never lived outside the state of North Carolina, well when you were here 2 months ago and stated that you had lived in West Virginia and Kentucky, you know. And it kind of helps us to follow the story, umm, and I guess it also has the statement about what they want us to do.

The paper trail here helped Stephanie catch this client's dishonesty. While the bulk of her statement was about catching this client, she later mentions that the paperwork helped caseworkers follow the client's story in a way that helped them know how they could help the client.

Discussion and Conclusions

In this chapter, I have contributed to the research on welfare policy implementation by examining what is often taken for granted—paperwork. My findings illus-trate that caseworkers used paperwork in three main ways: paperwork was a way to feel effective or successful in their jobs; paperwork was a way to show they had followed rules and "covered their asses"; and paperwork was, according to caseworkers, a way to ensure the fair treatment of clients. More broadly, the caseworkers' focus on paperwork highlights their buy-in and compliance with current welfare ideology (Handler and Hasenfeld 2007) and the so-called "common sense" of welfare (Ridzi 2004, 2009).

First, completing paperwork was a way for caseworkers to achieve standard measures of effectiveness and to feel successful in their jobs. A great deal of literature has questioned the effectiveness of current welfare-to-work programs in the United States (e.g., Corcoran et al. 2000; Hennessy 2005; Lichter and Jayakody 2002; O'Connor 2000). There are no clear mechanisms currently in place in the Smithgrove County Work First program that would allow caseworkers to effectively help participants. Even if there were mechanisms, the lack of participant education and skills and the poor local labor market are barriers potentially too large to overcome. Given this, caseworkers turn to the concrete tasks on which supervisors evaluate them: finishing their paperwork on time. While paperwork is frustrating, it is something they can do effectively.

Additionally, caseworkers and managers argued that the paperwork was important to show you were doing your job correctly (cover yourself) and it is important because it holds caseworkers accountable to treating program participants fairly. Lipsky (1980), and later Watkins-Hayes (2009), both describe the conflicting roles of street-level bureaucrats. On the one hand, these workers are expected to help clients, but on the other, they are expected to police the behavior of those they serve. Being somewhat wedged between serving their bureaucracies and their clients creates a dilemma, one that is often solved by focusing on rule-mindedness. In many ways, caseworkers avoid this dilemma through focusing the majority of their time on completing paperwork.

Again, given the lack of mechanisms for helping program participants, caseworkers focus on completing paperwork, arguing that it helps them be fair. No one, however, suggested that the paperwork helps program participants find work or helps them move from welfare to work. The argument that paperwork ensured fairness also seemed a response to arguments of bias or discrimination by caseworkers (see Gordon's 1990 historical work on caseworker bias), something future work should

consider more. While recent work has examined case closure and race (Monnat 2010; Monnat and Bunyan 2008; Schram 2005), it is possible that some caseworkers believe they are resisting bias, which may or may not be the case. In short, the caseworkers in Smithgrove County wanted to treat people fairly and to them, treating everyone the same, in terms of paperwork, meant being fair.

Finally, the caseworkers' focus on paperwork shows their buy-in to welfare ideology (Handler and Hasenfeld 2007) or to the "common sense" of welfare (Ridzi 2004, 2009). The majority of the paperwork is meant to show that the program participant is complying with either parenting guidelines (i.e., vaccinations, school attendance) or work-related participation requirements (i.e., job search and working somewhere under the Work Experience program). The main reason program participants are sanctioned in Smithgrove County is for failure to complete paperwork or document good cause for missing a work- or welfare-office-related appointment. Caseworkers also use paperwork to prove they are following the rules of a punitive welfare ideology (Handler and Hasenfeld 2007; Ridzi 2004, 2009) that encourages caseworkers to constantly surveil program participants in the event that they are engaged in fraudulent activities. None of the documentation actually helps program participants find work.

Paperwork in welfare bureaucracies might never go away and, to some degree, a paper trail is helpful to the program participant in the event that a caseworker does make an error and the participant needs to file a grievance. However, Ridzi (2009) argues that welfare providers could use the massive amounts of paperwork to provide a service to clients instead of using it only for surveillance. Researchers and administrators could track what works and does not work to better inform policy change. This would require minimal structural change to our current system and could uncover best practices or mechanisms for helping clients find good jobs. Creating mechanisms for helping clients find good jobs would not only enhance the well-being of clients, it would likely greatly improve the well-being and job satisfaction of caseworkers.

References

Anderson, Cynthia D., Michael Schulman, and Phillip J. Wood. 2000. "Globalization and Uncertainty: The

Restructuring of Southern Textiles." *Social Problems* 48:478–498.

Butler, Sandra S., Janine Corbett, Crystal Bond, and Chris Hastedt. 2008. "Long-Term TANF Participants and Barriers to Employment: A Qualitative Study in Maine." *Journal of Sociology and Social Welfare* 35(3): 49–69.

Collins, Jane L. and Vicoria Mayer. 2010. *Both Hands Tied: Welfare Reform and the Race to the Bottom of the Low-Wage Labor Market.* Chicago, IL: University of Chicago Press.

Corcoran, Mary, Sandra K. Danziger, Ariel Kalil and Kristin S. Seedfeldt. 2000. "How Welfare Reform Is Affecting Women's Work." *Annual Review of Sociology* 26:241–269.

Gordon, Linda. 1990. *Women, the State, and Welfare.* Madison, WI: University of Wisconsin Press.

Hammersley, Martyn and Paul Atkinson. 1985. *Ethnography: Principles in Practice,* 2nd ed. New York: Routledge.

Handler, Joel and Yeheskel Hasenfeld. 2007. *Blame Welfare, Ignore Poverty and Inequality.* New York: Cambridge University Press.

Hao, Lingxin and Andrew J. Cherlin. 2004. "Welfare Reform and Teenage Pregnancy, Childbirth, and School Dropout." *Journal of Marriage and Family* 66(1): 179–194.

Harris, Deborah A. and Domenico Parisi. 2008. "Welfare and Family Economic Security: Toward a Place-Based Poverty Knowledge." *Journal of Sociology and Social Welfare* 35(3): 97–113.

Hays, Sharon. 2003. *Flat Broke with Children: Women in the Age of Welfare Reform.* New York: Oxford University Press.

Hennessy, Judith. 2005. "Welfare, Work, and Family Well-Being: A Comparative Analysis of Welfare and Employment Status for Single Female-Headed Families Post-TANF." *Sociological Perspectives* 48:77–104.

Lichter, Daniel T. and Rukamalie Jayakody. 2002. "Welfare Reform: How Do We Measure Success?" *Annual Review of Sociology* 28:117–141.

Lipsky, Michael. 1980. *Street-Level Bureaucracy: Dilemmas of the Individual in Public Services.* New York: Russell Sage Foundation.

Marshall, Catherine and Gretchen B. Rossman. 1998. *Designing Qualitative Research,* 3rd ed. Thousand Oaks, CA: Sage Publications.

Monnat, Shannon M. 2010. "The Color of Welfare Sanctioning, Exploring the Individual and Contextual Roles of Race on TANF Case Closures and Benefit Reductions." *The Sociological Quarterly* 51(4): 678–708.

Monnat, Shannon M. and Laura A. Bunyan 2008. "Capitalism and Welfare Reform: Who Really Benefits from Welfare-to-Work Policies?" *Race, Gender and Class* 15(1–2): 115–133.

O'Connor, Alice. 2000. "Poverty Research and Policy for the Post-Welfare Era." *Annual Review of Sociology* 26(1): 547–562.

Riccucci, Norma M. 2005. *How Management Matters: Street-Level Bureaucrats and Welfare Reform.* Washington, DC: Georgetown University Press.

Riccucci, Norma M., Marcia K. Meyers, Irene Lurie, and Jun S. Han. 2004. "The Implementation of Welfare Reform Policy: The Role of Public Managers in Front-Line Practices." *Public Administrative Review* 64(4): 438–448.

Ridzi, Frank. 2004. "Making TANF Work: Organizational Restructuring, Staff Buy-In, and Performance Monitoring in Local Implementation." *Journal of Sociology and Social Welfare* 31(2): 27–48.

Ridzi, Frank. 2009. *Selling Welfare Reform: Work-First and the New Commonsense of Employment.* New York: New York University Press.

Rogers-Dillon, Robin H. 2004. *The Welfare Experiments: Politics and Policy Evaluation.* Stanford, CA: Stanford University Press.

Schram, Sanford F. 2005. "Contextualizing Racial Disparities in American Welfare Reform: Toward a New Poverty Research." *Perspectives on Politics* 3(2): 253–265.

Tomaskovic-Devey, Donald and Vincent J. Roscigno. 1996. "Racial Economic Subordination and White Gain in the U.S. South." *American Sociological Review* 61:565–589.

Tomaskovic-Devey, Donald and Vincent J. Roscigno. 1997. "Uneven Development and Local Inequality in the U.S. South: The Role of Outside Investment, Landed Elites, and Racial Dynamics." *Sociological Forum* 12:565–597.

U.S. Census Bureau. 2000. American FactFinder. <http://factfinder2.census.gov>. (accessed February 12, 2012).

U.S. Department of Labor Bureau of Labor Statistics. 2007. Current Employment Statistics. http://www.bls.gov/ces/. (accessed September 20, 2015).

Watkins-Hayes, Celeste. 2009. *The New Welfare Bureaucrats: Entanglements of Race, Class, and Policy Reform.* Chicago, IL: University of Chicago Press.

Weiss, Robert S. 1994. *Learning from Strangers.* New York: The Free Press.

Wood, Phillip J. 1986. *Southern Capitalism: The Political Economy of North Carolina.* Durham, NC: Duke University Press.

Questions

1. Taylor argues that we often take for granted that some jobs require a lot of paperwork. Why might it be important to study something that seems so mundane and taken for granted by both caseworkers and researchers?

2. How did the author conduct this study? Are there things about how the study was conducted that might be significant? Are there things about *where* the study was conducted that might be significant?

3. What are the challenges to caseworkers being successful? How do caseworkers cope with these challenges?

4. How do the caseworkers' actions relate to broader public opinion and ideologies about welfare and cash assistance?

5. In what other jobs does paperwork play a primary role? What is the relationship to inequality in those jobs? How do people maintain senses of effectiveness in other jobs, even though paperwork and fulfilling bureaucratic requirements don't actually make them effective? Do workplaces encourage creating those feelings of effectiveness through other means? How so? Why? What else distracts us from inequality, and who encourages us to distract ourselves? How?

28

Educational Ties, Social Capital, and the Translocal (Re)Production of MBA Alumni Networks

SARAH HALL

C. Wright Mills' (1956) *The Power Elite* argues that core leaders of the government (politicians and military leaders) and corporations garner substantial control over major policies and social outcomes in the United States and globally. According to Mills, these elite amass such great control that they leave the average citizen with very limited influence over their lives despite the goals of democracy. One way that power elites gain so much power is through strong social ties with other powerful people. The strength and number of these relationships is referred to as "social capital." Mills showed how individuals from elite schools come to network with other elites through various clubs. These strong networks

---

Excerpted from Hall, Sarah. 2011. "Educational Ties, Social Capital and the Translocal (Re)Production of MBA Alumni Networks." *Global Networks* 11:118–138. ©2010 The Author(s) Journal compilation ©2010 Blackwell Publishing Ltd. & Global Networks Partnership.

eventually transcend business networks and become powerful in terms of politics as people learn to capitalize on their relationships. In short, and as many studies have shown since, who we know affects what we know and how we can access and use resources. Similarly, within these clubs and networks, a specific culture is developed, internalized, and quite often taken for granted such that it becomes "cultural capital." This cultural capital, knowledge of norms and customs, can be used to include or exclude people from social groups. Knowing how to talk a certain way, dress a certain way, and even using the correct silverware can be used to show who does—and doesn't—belong to a particular group.

This study examines how U.S. and British business schools concertedly foster international ("translocal") social networks among their MBA alumni. These networks are built through face-to-face contact and also through the use of social media, such as Facebook. Elite MBA programs use these ties to build a sense of reciprocity between the elite schools and alumni by enhancing alumni careers through various events, which in turn shores up alumni giving. Alumni giving and participation in the school later help the school maintain its elite status. For the alumni, they receive innumerable rewards for their association with this elite network throughout their careers. These rewards help elites shape and control the resources of MBA programs as well as global financial services. In short, this study demonstrates how people and organizations cultivate social ties so that they become means for reproducing the social class of the elite.

References

Mills, C. Wright. 1956. *The Power Elite.* New York: Oxford University Press.

Educational background has been widely identified as an important way of securing entry into powerful elite networks. For example, in the United Kingdom, "old boy networks" forged through schooling at a small number of fee-paying schools such as Eton and Harrow and at universities, notably Cambridge and Oxford, were, historically at least, a central way of cementing trust-based relationships within financial services (Cain and Hopkins 2002; Michie 2000). Research has also identified the continued influence of educational background on the hiring practices and gendered nature of recruitment into financial firms (McDowell 1997). Meanwhile, in a seminal study within the sociology of education, Bourdieu (1996) has documented the role of Grandes Écoles in (re)producing and legitimating the French elite. Building on these studies, I focus in this chapter on contemporary Masters of Business Administration (MBA) alumni networks created while studying at leading international business schools. Despite only dating back to the mid-twentieth century, MBA degrees have developed into a valuable credential that individuals turn to in an effort to secure "positional advantage" relative to other individuals within competitive labor markets across a range of economic sectors (Brown and Hesketh 2004; Waters 2009a).

Many argue that the value of MBA degrees stems from the ways they act to "institutionalize" forms of cultural capital (Bourdieu 1986). For example, Sklair (2001) points to the role of an American business school education in fostering a transnational sensibility among members of what he terms the "transnational capitalist class"—a global network made up of individuals working in the upper echelons of transnational corporations and international political bodies (see also Marceau 1989). Such an approach to MBA alumni networks draws attention to their "structural power" (Dicken et al. 2001) within contemporary socio-economic life. Waters (2009b, 115), however, demonstrates that the structural power of educational credentials is at least partly constructed through "geographically embedded social networks (or social capital)." This insight is particularly salient in the case of MBA degrees, for authors commonly cite the networking opportunities created at business schools and membership of the resulting alumni networks as one of the most valuable elements of studying for an MBA degree (Brocklehurst et al. 2007).

The growing number of MBA graduates internationally seems at odds with the existing literature on the reproduction of elite networks, which emphasizes the role of frequent face-to-face interaction in leisure spaces such as sports and private members' clubs (see Beaverstock 2002; Bourdieu 1996; Brayshay, Cleary, and Selwood 2007). Indeed, given that recent estimates suggest that 132,000 individuals graduated with an MBA degree in Europe and the United States in 2006 alone (Brocklehurst et al. 2007), it seems unlikely that such networks can be reproduced solely through frequent face-to-face interaction. The size of MBA networks also raises important questions concerning why such networks are sustained. At one level, the growing number of MBA students provides an enhanced revenue stream for business schools through fees and alumni donations. Yet, at the same time, the expansion in MBA student numbers potentially devalues the credential for graduates as the MBA degree loses its scarcity value, which allows alumni to differentiate themselves from other job seekers (see Waters 2009a).

In the light of these observations, in this chapter I combine work on social capital and personal networks to explore the reproduction of MBA alumni networks in London's financial services district that were created in leading business schools in the United States and United Kingdom. I reveal how individual alumni and development offices in business schools employ a range of technologies such as social networking websites and web-portals to sustain alumni networks through a combination of virtual ties and intense periods of face-to-face interaction—practices that echo work on "network sociality" (Wittel 2001). I argue that the motivation for sustaining such translocal networks lies in the potential for the social and cultural capital of MBA alumni networks to be converted into different types of value ranging from enhanced career progression (in the case of alumni) to increased alumni donations (in the case of business schools).

Social Capital, Network Sociality, and Educational Ties

While the reproduction of MBA alumni networks has received comparatively little academic attention, a significant literature has developed on the relationship between academic credentials and the reproduction of elite networks. The work of Pierre Bourdieu is particularly significant in this respect. Bourdieu (1996) argues that rather than circulating technical know-how among future managerial elites, attaining academic credentials

from particular educational institutions plays a critical role in reproducing elite networks by inculcating individuals into the cultural habits, norms, and social know-how expected of socio-economic elites—what he terms "cultural capital." For Bourdieu (1986), the value of this institutionalized cultural capital lies in the potential for its conversion into economic (monetary) capital through, for example, enhanced career progression.

In the case of elite academic credentials, part of this cultural capital stems from how studying for such credentials positions individuals in potentially powerful social networks beyond graduation. For example, Sklair (2001) identified the networks developed while studying at a small number of American business schools as being an important element in forming transnational elite networks. Work on MBA degrees particularly reflects this. For example, Brocklehurst et al. (2007, 380) argue that:

> When MBA students are asked what benefit they derive from an MBA, they mention the qualification itself, a subsequent improvement in their status, an increase in self-confidence, an induction to a specialized discourse, membership of a network of elite international managers for this they believe they have been carefully selected—but less often than one might expect do they emphasize the acquisition of specific practical skills or techniques.

These examples demonstrate how membership in certain personal networks—or what Bourdieu (1986) terms social capital—is an important element of cultural capital.

In terms of academic credentials, research has shown how people use social capital strategically in relation to educational attainment. More recently, social capital has been identified as important not only in terms of forming part of cultural capital but also in terms of converting the cultural capital institutionalized within academic credentials into economic capital. For example, Waters (2009b) demonstrates how translocal social relations play a critical role in establishing the economic value of an academic credential as employers seek to understand the relative value of international qualifications.

This insight is particularly important for my argument because Waters identifies formal and informal activities undertaken by alumni networks associated with educational institutions as being important in sustaining the value of their associated academic credentials. While we know that alumni networks play an important role in valuing academic credentials over time, we know less about the challenges of reproducing such networks and the motivations that drive individual alumni and alumni associations to overcome them. For example, by definition, members of alumni networks have a shared background and hence personal ties in the networks are likely to be "strongest" in the early years following graduation. As individuals move beyond their common educational background, what started out as a geographically proximate, dense network expands over space as individuals enter labor markets and the ties within the network become potentially "weaker" (Granovetter 1973). Consequently, for alumni networks to survive, the ties within them need constant renewal.

Virtual Educational Ties and Trans-Local Alumni Networks

Wittel (2001, 51) argues that network sociality "consists of fleeting and transient, yet iterative social relations; of ephemeral but intense encounters" and is "not characterized by a separation but a combination of both work and play." Although work on "network sociality" downplays the importance of background in network formation, two insights from work on "network sociality" are valuable when studying alumni networks. First, network sociality emphasizes how intense periods of networking can be temporally constrained rather than necessarily built up over a period of time. Wittel (2001) argues that one also finds intense periods of networking in non-work situations such as parties. These insights are valuable when considering alumni networks because they show how it is possible to reactivate latent educational ties through short periods of intense networking.

Second, research on network sociality illustrates the ways in which personal networks are reproduced and transformed not just through human relations but also through interactions between humans and a range of "technologies" such as transport networks and communication technologies. On first impressions, the importance of virtual technologies such as web-portals and social networking websites echoes what Grabher and Ibert (2006) term "network connectivity." This refers to socially thin networks mediated predominantly

via virtual forms of communication such as online forums and mailing lists. Recent research has pointed to the complex relationship between virtual forums and corporeal interaction by acknowledging that virtual ties can also be important in the reproduction of dense, trust-based relations underpinned by common endeavor and associated forms of reciprocity (see Asheim, Coenen, and Vang 2007; Grabher, Ibert, and Flohr 2008; Maskell, Bathelt, and Malmberg 2006).

Networks are understood as a "topology marked by overlapping near–far relations and organizational connections that are not reducible to scalar spaces" (Amin 2002, 386). In a similar vein, Urry (2002, 266) argues that the combination of virtual and physical interaction means that "co-presence involves nearness and farness, proximity and distance" (see also F. Collins 2009). These insights point to the possibility that educational ties within MBA alumni networks, which are often framed as being powerful transnationally, may be reactivated following graduation through a combination of virtual and corporeal networking activities that are translocal in nature, simultaneously involving different geographical locations (see Smith and Guarnizo 1998).

Methodology

I conducted the research between January 2006 and March 2007 on leading international business schools in the United States and United Kingdom as ranked by *The Financial Times* with an emphasis on finance. I chose MBA alumni networks in investment banking because the financial services sector, and investment banking in particular, is one of the most popular career destinations for MBA graduates. For example, in 2006, 42 percent of MBA graduates from the London Business School went on to work in financial services following graduation. Of those, 23 percent entered investment banking (London Business School 2006). Interviews focused on the role of MBA degrees in an investment banking career and the changing relationship between business schools and financial services, particularly in terms of their alumni.

MBA Alumni Networks and Investment Banking in London's Financial District

The cultural capital associated with holding an MBA degree has historically been most significant in the United States, reflecting its position as the geographic heartland of MBA degrees. However, following the growth of U.S. investment banks in London after the deregulatory changes of "Big Bang" in 1986, entering MBA alumni networks has become increasingly common for investment bankers in the United Kingdom. The technical expertise taught and legitimated via MBA programs, particularly financial economics, initially fueled this growth (Bernstein 1992; Whitley 1986). However, the increasingly sophisticated nature of quantitative finance has resulted in a growing preference for hiring individuals with PhDs in numerate disciplines such as mathematics and physics rather than with the more general management education provided by MBA degrees (Wilmott 2000).

On first impressions, these developments would appear to signal a decline in the importance of MBA programs within investment banking. However, the cultural capital associated with MBA degrees within London's financial district has moved away from enhanced technical competencies to a more explicit focus on the value of being a member of prestigious MBA alumni networks. This perceived "positional advantage" (Brown and Hesketh 2004) associated with holding an MBA degree is particularly apparent in investment banking. Here, until the "credit crunch" began to impact on the profitability of investment banks from August 2007, competition for employment was fierce, with investment banks in London typically limiting their early-career recruitment to a small number of universities (Jones 1998). In this environment, holding an MBA represented one way of gaining employment in such firms, particularly since most banks have a "recruitment process and career trajectory explicitly aimed at MBA graduates" (interview with investment bank human resource manager, August 2006). Moreover, early indications suggest that enrollment in MBA programs has at least been maintained and in some cases has increased in the wake of the global "credit crunch" (Quacquarelli 2008). This reflects the counter-cyclical nature of MBA recruitment associated with previous economic downturns (Dearlove 2008) and points to the continued desire for financiers to enter MBA alumni networks in order to forward their careers, as the following investment banker summarized:

Yes, there are the analytical skills, but to be honest that wasn't at the forefront of my mind [when applying for an MBA degree]. What I was really interested in was having [name of business school] on my CV and the job and career opportunities that would bring—being able to call up people almost literally anywhere in the world [fellow MBA alumni] and be able to chat over ideas with them. (interview, investment bank associate, U.S. MBA, London, September 2006)

At one level, this example echoes work on the "structural power" of MBA alumni networks as individuals use their degrees to secure entry into competitive investment banking labor markets (see, e.g., Sklair 2001). Yet, at another level, it points to the continued value of the social capital of MBA alumni networks as, in the case just mentioned, individuals used such networks to help facilitate the circulation of innovative knowledge within investment banking (on which see Thrift 1994).

However, while membership of MBA alumni networks is potentially valuable for individuals, such networks are not necessarily easily sustained once the shared experience of studying for an MBA ends. As one investment banker explained:

Yes, I'm a [name of business school] alumnus and I feel a degree of commonality with the thousands of other alumni that have passed through [name of business school]. However, in reality I've only kept in contact with a small number of friends. The number of alumni is so huge that it simply isn't possible to maintain meaningful contact. (interview, investment bank vice-president, UK MBA, London, August 2006)

As this example illustrates, on starting their careers in London, graduates typically only maintained regular contact with a small number of fellow students. This points to the dynamic nature of social capital as it moves from formation in business schools to only being partially sustained in London's financial district. While some alumni left their educational ties to develop in this way, my research reveals how it was far more common for both business schools and alumni to reactivate educational ties within MBA alumni networks in order to convert their social and cultural capital into other forms of value. It is to these activities that I now turn.

Business Schools and the Reproduction of MBA Alumni Networks

Leading business schools in the United States and United Kingdom are increasingly focusing on the potential institutional value of their MBA alumni networks, with two aims standing out as being particularly significant. First, MBA alumni networks represent a significant potential source of funding in the form of alumni donations, particularly given the perceived (and in many cases actual) average higher earnings of MBA graduates (McCormack 2007). For example, estimates suggest that 45 percent of MBA graduates in the United States have donated money to the business school at which they studied (Bruce 2007). This reflects the extensive history and significance in terms of resources of philanthropic giving by alumni to U.S. universities more broadly. Indeed, the importance of alumni donations is demonstrated by the renaming of the Chicago Graduate School of Business in November 2008 to the Chicago Booth School of Business in recognition of what it claims to be the largest ever donation to a business school by Chicago GSB alumnus David Booth of $300 million. Alumni donations have not developed at the same rate in the United Kingdom, although British universities are increasingly seeking to develop revenue streams from their alumni in response to funding constraints in the state education system (Fearn 2009; Sutton Trust 2003). To this end, the government launched a "matched funding scheme for voluntary giving" between 2008 and 2011 that enhances donations made to eligible higher education institutions. Within this broader interest in alumni donations, MBA graduates have been heavily targeted because of their relatively high earnings (Shepherd 2007).

Second, business schools use educational ties within their MBA alumni networks as a way of accessing the working practices of their alumni in an effort to enhance their research and teaching activities (Thrift 2005). This has become increasingly important for business schools because in recent years there has been severe criticism of the practical relevance and content of contemporary MBA curricula (see Mintzberg 2004). These critics argue that MBA degrees produce narrowly focused graduates who privilege short-term financial management strategies, notably through a focus on maximizing shareholder value above other corporate aims, such as investment in employees or longer term capital needs (Starkey and Tiratsoo 2007). These criticisms have increased in the wake of the ongoing global financial crisis (see Caulkin 2008). In response, business schools are increasingly seeking to enroll their MBA alumni into their teaching programs and research

activities in an effort to transform business schools into more "dialogical spaces" in which a range of different stakeholders, not limited to academic faculty, contribute to research and teaching activities (Starkey, Hatchuel, and Tempest 2004). Strategies identified as being important in this respect include using links with their alumni to secure placements for their current MBA students, inviting individuals back to give guest lectures, and liaising with alumni in the development of research projects and to secure research access (see Hall 2008). The aim of such activities is to broaden the range of theories taught and researched in business schools as well as to enhance the practical relevance of MBA degrees.

Business Schools, Virtual Networks and the Transformation of Educational Ties

To convert the social and cultural capital of their MBA alumni networks into donations and research and teaching links, business schools focus on providing opportunities for MBA alumni to *reactivate* their educational ties. In doing so, they aim to foster a sense of reciprocity toward the business school among graduates by reminding them of the benefits they have enjoyed as a result of studying for an MBA, such that alumni will be motivated to donate and/or provide research and teaching expertise. Three activities are particularly important in fostering this reciprocity. First, business schools circulate newsletters (in paper form and/or electronically) to their alumni at regular intervals. These publications include details of recent developments within the business school as well as professional and personal updates on MBA alumni. As one U.S. alumni development manager explained in an interview in March 2006, "We aim to provide a mix [in the alumni publications] of both university research news, alumni career achievements, but also personal news—births, deaths, marriages. . . . It's often these personal touches that get people reconnected into the [alumni] network and hence more likely to contribute to our campaigns."

This inclusion of personal alumni news items represents an attempt by business schools to foster a sense of reciprocity among their alumni, as an investment bank associate alumnus with a U.S. MBA described during an interview in London in December 2006: "The newsletters remind you what benefits you got out of the course and that does make me want to give something back. At the moment I've just set up a regular payment, but it's better than nothing."

The second "technology" that business schools use widely to maintain the social capital within MBA alumni networks are password protected dedicated alumni websites (see, e.g., http://www.alumni.hbs.edu/). In many ways, these websites are virtual equivalents of alumni newsletters, providing details of forthcoming alumni events organized by the business school as well as updates of the research and teaching activity of the current business school faculty. However, by allowing alumni to tailor the website to their own particular interests once they have logged in (by, e.g., selecting particular news feeds that relate to their employment sector), business schools aim to increase the likelihood that alumni will reactivate educational ties within their alumni network through forms of relational proximity (Blanc and Sierra 1999). As one investment banker in London described:

> Colleagues here [in an investment bank] were chatting about the web-portal of their business school so I decided to see if mine had one. It did, so I signed up and once I saw a news story about one of my classmates. He was working in London so I contacted him through the portal and we met up and talked work—new deals, possible deals, the power of hedge funds, etc. He mentioned he'd been to a reunion event in London and when the next one came up [in London] I went along partly out of curiosity but also partly to find out how I could use my contacts possibly to switch roles. (investment bank vice president, U.S. MBA, London, March 2006).

As this example demonstrates, the relational proximity reproduced through web-portals involves a combination of virtual ties and face-to-face interaction as suggested by Urry (2002). However, while financiers in London use business school web-portals to reactivate educational ties that enhance their careers, a point I return to in the next section, business schools in the United States and United Kingdom have different aims for such educational ties, as this alumni development manager outlined:

> The great thing about the website is the ways [sic] they can customize it—select news feeds on particular areas of interest and get information on alumni events only in certain parts of the world. The aim is for them to use the website to make the alumni network fit their needs and then of course we hope that if they feel like they are

getting more out of it, they are more likely to contribute to it, in the form of donations etc. (alumni development manager, UK business school, March 2007)

The third way in which business school development offices seek to convert educational ties into alumni donations and research and teaching links is through alumni events such as guest lectures and alumni weekends that are advertised online and in alumni newsletters. Business schools hope that such events will reactivate educational ties by facilitating "network sociality" (Wittel 2001), involving intense periods of face-to-face interaction and networking between alumni in non-work activities. Some of these events are hosted at the organizing business school's campus, a location that clearly has advantages in terms of fostering reciprocity among alumni. However, they are also organized in a number of other major cities, such as London and New York, to facilitate alumni involvement. The emphasis on financial centers such as London reflects both the importance of finance as a career destination for MBA graduates and a desire on the part of business school management to be both discursively and materially close to leading international financial centers (on which see Hall 2008). Hosting events beyond the business school campus is also based on a belief that different working cultures associated with different geographical locations (see Jones 2003) potentially precludes sufficient "common ground" between alumni for effective networking and knowledge circulation to take place.

Taken together, the activities of development offices in business schools in reactivating and maintaining the social capital of MBA alumni networks to extract economic value and research and teaching links from them signals the importance of understanding such networks as translocal in nature, involving both virtual and corporeal educational ties. In particular, the combination of intense face-to-face interaction and ties mediated through virtual forms of communication develops extant literature on the reproduction of elite networks that has tended to stress the importance of corporeal interaction alone.

MBA Alumni and Virtual Educational Ties

In addition to business schools' development offices, individual MBA alumni also aim to extract value from the social capital of MBA alumni networks. This is most noticeable on first entering the work force following graduation, but as their careers progress, investment bankers in London also reactivate their alumni relations, typically when they are seeking a change of career or entering a new area of finance, as one alumnus described:

> I was hired into a fixed income group in London and the head of the group also went to [name of US business school], so he understood where I was coming from. I didn't really think too much about alumni for a while but then I was looking to move to a new bank and was aware that a couple of my business school classmates might be useful contacts, so got back in touch with them at that point. (investment bank vice-president, U.S. MBA, London, September 2006)

MBA alumni working in investment banking in London seek to extract two main types of value from their educational ties. First, the investment bankers I interviewed sought to use their MBA alumni networks to respond to the possibility that "credential inflation" (R. Collins 1979) associated with the rapid growth in the number of MBA graduates globally will devalue their specific MBA degree and hence their employability and career progression (Opengart and Short 2002). To respond to this, they aim to demonstrate the relative superiority of their particular MBA alumni network, demarcated by both business school attended and year of graduation, compared with MBA degrees in general, as an investment bank vice-president with a UK MBA demonstrated during an interview in London in September 2006: "It's clearly in my best interest that [name of business school] degrees are viewed positively by employers, particularly as more and more people complete MBA degrees. Basically, we need it to be clear that there are MBA degrees and there are MBA degrees."

This focus on the *relative* value of different MBA degrees from particular business schools and even particular graduation year groups echoes Bourdieu's (1996) work on processes of specialization in education in which he argues that individuals with access to the necessary resources (typically the middle classes) use specialization in education to reproduce their socioeconomic advantage. This is particularly important in London's financial district because investment banks typically recruit from a relatively small yet common group of international business schools. As such,

many applicants for the same job will have relatively similar academic credentials. In response, and following Waters (2009b), the investment bankers I interviewed frequently relied on personal contacts with others holding the same MBA degree to distinguish between similar candidates when interviewing, as elucidated by one banker: "Sometimes you're looking at essentially identical candidates apart from where they studied and then if someone has some links with that MBA, or knows someone who they worked with who has a degree from the [business] school, that does start to matter" (investment bank president, U.S. MBA, London, November 2006).

Second, investment bankers in London sought to use the social capital within their MBA alumni networks to augment their other personal networks within and beyond London's financial district, echoing Wittel's (2001) work on the strategic use of intense periods of networking for individuals. Social scientists have emphasized the value of such networks to financiers, who use them to keep abreast of industry "buzz" (Storper and Venables 2004) in terms of new innovations, working practices, and job opportunities (see Thrift 1994). The role of educational ties fostered through business schools in the formation and reproduction of such networking practices has, however, been comparatively neglected. My research reveals how investment bankers use latent, translocal educational ties within MBA alumni network membership to deepen existing ties based on a common educational background as well as to foster new geographically local personal network ties. Examples such as the following were indicative:

> Obviously, my MBA colleagues are not always separate from other people I hang out with but having that shared history [from business school] often helps in terms of discussing a particular problem—you are often trained to think in similar ways. But recently I contacted someone I was at business school with but am not in regular contact with because I wanted advice on raising finance and he's in hedge funds now so I wanted to tap into his expertise. (investment bank associate, U.S. MBA, London, December 2006)

This points to the ways in which shared backgrounds created while studying for MBA degrees may be an important element in the social and historical commonality that has been identified as important in facilitating learning and knowledge circulation beyond the case of MBA alumni networks in what Wenger (1998) terms "communities of practice." Moreover, as Grabher and Ibert (2006, 253) note, network ties within such communities "might be formed . . . to circumvent formal organizational arrangements and practices." Echoing this argument, there was widespread cynicism among the investment bankers I interviewed over the activities of business schools in transforming educational ties within MBA alumni networks for their own institutional gains. As one banker remarked, "Why should I go to an alumni event only to be asked to delve into my pocket and make a donation? What's in that for me?" (investment bank vice-president, U.S. MBA, London, March 2006)

MBA Alumni, Virtual Networks, and the (Re)Production of Educational Ties

Like business schools, MBA alumni make significant use of particular technologies as they seek to reproduce educational ties that meet their strategic aims for MBA alumni networks. Of particular importance are online social networking websites such as LinkedIn.com, Naymz.com, and particularly Facebook (see www.facebook.com). Facebook was founded in 2004 as a website for college students in the United States. Over a relatively short period, it has developed significantly, expanding considerably beyond the education sector. Facebook estimates that it had more than 500 million active users in October 2010, defined as members who have used the site in the last 30 days (http://www.facebook.com/press/info.php?statistics). Members provide details about their occupational status as well as publishing their everyday activities to fellow users through using "status updates." This is by no means limited to MBA graduates, though my research revealed the ways in which investment bankers engage with Facebook, as the following response demonstrates:

> I wasn't initially a member and then we had an alumni event and all the photos were circulated via Facebook for members of the [name of business school] network who graduated in 2006 so I joined, and actually I've hooked up with a number of classmates who I'd lost contact with. (investment bank vice-president, U.S. MBA, London, January 2007)

By reproducing educational ties defined by the business school attended and graduation year, online technologies

such as Facebook serve to reproduce *differentiated* educational ties that graduates seek to use to respond to the credential inflation that surrounds MBA degrees. In particular, investment bankers use Facebook instrumentally, carefully managing their online presence to maximize the potential professional value of being a member of a particular MBA year group from a certain business school. Indeed, in addition to differentiating between MBA alumni networks, investment bankers also referred to the rapidly growing popular business literature that aims to educate readers in the use of Facebook for "corporate success" (see, e.g., Alba and Stay 2008), as the following example shows:

> We know from the press that employers look at Facebook. And there are a whole host of resources out there about how to manage your virtual work identity—we even had a seminar about it at work—so I am careful about it. . . . In terms of my MBA, what's good about Facebook is that people see not only that I've got an MBA but where and when I got it and that matters when more and more people have one. I need to stand out. (investment bank associate, UK MBA, London, January 2007)

While the impact of Facebook and other social networking sites in recruitment and promotion decisions clearly deserves further research attention, comments such as this demonstrate how, at the very least, individual financiers in London are using websites such as Facebook to highlight the *specificities* of their MBA alumni network based around their year of graduation and business school attended. This is important for investment bankers because elite labor market intermediaries in London's financial district, such as recruiters, are increasingly using online identities in their shortlisting decisions (Faulconbridge et al. 2009).

Beyond these virtual ties, online social networking sites are also important actors in reproducing educational contacts that can contribute to and enhance face-to-face networks among investment bankers. In this respect, investment bankers use such websites to convert international educational ties based on a common history into geographically proximate ties on which they can draw in their current careers in London by arranging informal networking events that intersect with personal networks beyond those formed at business school. Such practices echo the intense networking associated with "network sociality" (Wittel 2001), as demonstrated in the following example:

> You get notified on Facebook of events organized by your contacts, so I hear about what my fellow classmates are up to now but it extends beyond just MBA people—different groups [of contacts] intersect on Facebook so you are maximizing your exposure to events—even if you don't go, it's a good way of observing what is going on. (investment bank vice-president, U.S. MBA, London, February 2007)

The types of meetings arranged in this way tend to span firm boundaries and include: Facebook organized events in London aimed to help international investment bankers settle into a new city; notification of events hosted by special interest groups for financiers in London, such as the City Women's Networks, which aims to support women working in London (www.citywomen.org); and invitations to research events at business schools, such as the ones the Hedge Fund Centre hosts at the London Business School. As such, while the value alumni seek to extract from their educational ties created while studying for MBA degrees is different from that of business schools, they too rely on a combination of virtual networks and face-to-face interaction that creates translocal MBA alumni networks.

Conclusions

Social scientists have commented widely on the role of educational background in elite network formation (Cain and Hopkins 2002; Sklair 2001). The ongoing reproduction and transformation of these educational ties, however, has received far less attention. In response, in this chapter I have developed recent work on personal networks and social capital to consider how and why the alumni development offices of business schools and individual alumni renew the educational ties within MBA alumni networks created at leading international business schools. My research reveals how business schools are primarily concerned with converting the social capital of MBA alumni networks into sources of alumni donations and closer research and teaching links with contemporary financial services practice. Meanwhile, individual alumni seek to use the social capital of their MBA alumni networks to leverage positional advantage within competitive investment banking labor markets.

Empirically, these findings raise important questions concerning how graduates sustain the reproduction of socio-economic privilege through education (see Bourdieu 1996) beyond graduation and entry into labor markets. In the case of MBA alumni networks, this is significant since certain groups, particularly women, remain under-represented on such courses and in their associated alumni networks (Anderson 2007), a fact that deserves further research attention. Moreover, despite high-profile criticism of the content of MBA programs (Mintzberg 2004), there is evidence that application numbers are increasing as a result of the ongoing turmoil within financial services and the wider global economy that began in the summer of 2007 (Quacquarelli 2008). This suggests that individuals still regard an MBA degree as a valuable credential in enhancing their employability in increasingly uncertain global labor markets. Combining work on social capital and personal networks, my research contributes to two broader debates on transnational elite networks. First, it develops recent work on the spatiality of transnational networks (Featherstone, Phillips, and Waters 2007; Zhou and Tseng 2001). In particular, the case of contemporary MBA alumni networks points to the importance of considering how people use technologies to sustain elite networks alongside face-to-face interaction that has more typically been researched. The intersection between these different kinds of network ties reveals how MBA alumni networks, which are often assumed to be transnational in scope, are better conceptualized as translocal, simultaneously involving a range of different localities from the business school campus to London's financial district within an alumni network that is international in reach.

Recent work has pointed to the role of social capital in processes of valuing credentials, particularly those associated with international educational institutions (Waters 2009b). The case of MBA alumni networks extends this literature by revealing how educational institutions, in addition to individual alumni, seek to extract value from alumni networks. With funding constraints emerging in both the public and private education sectors in the wake of the global financial crisis, and the significant increases in the number of MBA graduates globally, both alumni and educational institutions are likely to explore new ways of converting the social capital of alumni networks into other forms of value.

References

Alba, Jason and Jesse Stay. 2008. *I'm on Facebook—Now What??? How to Get Personal, Business, and Professional Value from Facebook.* Cupertino, CA: Happyabout.info.

Amin, Ash. 2002. "Spatialities of Globalization." *Environment and Planning A* 34:385–399.

Anderson, Linda. 2007. "Still Too Few Women." *Financial Times*, FT Report—Business Education, October 22.

Asheim, Bjørn T., Lars Coenen, and Jan Vang. 2007. "Face-to-Face, Buzz and Knowledge Bases: Sociospatial Implications for Learning, Innovation, and Innovation Policy." *Environment and Planning C: Government and Policy* 25(5): 655–670.

Beaverstock, Jonathan V. 2002. "Transnational Elites in Global Cities: British Expatriates in Singapore's Financial District." *Geoforum* 33(4): 525–538.

Bernstein, Peter. 1992. *Capital Ideas: The Improbable Origins of Modern Wall Street.* New York: Free Press.

Blanc, Hélène and Christophe Sierra. 1999. "The Internationalisation of R&D by Multinationals: A Trade-Off between External and Internal Proximity." *Cambridge Journal of Economics* 23(2): 187–206.

Bourdieu, Pierre. 1986. "The Forms of Capital." In *Handbook of Theory and Research for the Sociology of Education* (ed. John G. Richardson), 241–258. New York: Greenwood Press.

Bourdieu, Pierre. 1996. *The State Nobility: Elite Schools in the Field of Power.* Cambridge: Polity Press.

Brayshay, Mark, Marc Cleary, and John Selwood. 2007. "Social Networks and the Transnational Reach of the Corporate Class in the Early-Twentieth Century." *Journal of Historical Geography* 33(1): 144–167.

Brocklehurst, Michael, Andrew Sturdy, Diana Winstanley, and Michaela Driver. 2007. "Introduction: Whither the MBA? Factions, Fault Lines, and the Future." *Management Learning* 38(4): 379–388.

Brown, Phillip and Anthony Hesketh. 2004. *The Mismanagement of Talent: Employability and Jobs in the Knowledge Economy.* Oxford: Oxford University Press.

Bruce, Grady D. 2007. "Exploring the Likelihood and Reality of MBA Alumni Financial Donations." GMAC Research Report RR-07–12, January.

Burt, Ronald. 1980. "Models of Network Structure." *Annual Review of Sociology* 6:79–141.

Cain, Peter J. and Anthony G. Hopkins. 2002. *British Imperialism 1688–2000.* London: Longman.

Caulkin, Simon. 2008. "When It Came to the Crunch, MBAs Didn't Help." *Observer*, October 26. http://www.guardian.co.uk/business/2008/oct/26/mba-business-education-banking (accessed October 22, 2010).

Collins, Francis Leo. 2009. "Connecting 'Home' with 'Here': Personal Homepages in Everyday Transnational Lives." *Journal of Ethnic and Migration Studies* 35(6): 839–859.

Collins, Randall. 1979. *The Credential Society: An Historical Sociology of Education and Stratification.* New York: Academic Press.

Dearlove, Des. 2008. "Using an MBA to Find the Silver Lining." *The Times*, November 16. http://business.timesonline.co.uk/tol/business/management/mba/article4962408.ece, last accessed October 22, 2010.

Dicken, Peter, Phillip F. Kelly, Kris Olds, and Henry Wai-Chung Yeung. 2001. "Chains and Networks, Territories and Scales: Towards a Relational Framework for Analysing the Global Economy." *Global Networks* 1(2): 89–112.

Faulconbridge, James R., Jonathan V. Beaverstock, Sarah Hall, and Andrew Hewitson. 2009. "The 'War for Talent': The Gatekeeper Role of Executive Search Firms in Elite Labour Markets." *Geoforum* 40(5): 800–808.

Fearn, Hannah. 2009. "Fundraising: How to Get Alumni to Cough Up." *Times Higher Educational Supplement*, August 6. http://www.timeshighereducation.co.uk/story.asp?storycode=407627 (accessed October 22, 2010).

Featherstone, David, Richard Phillips, and Johanna L. Waters. 2007. "Introduction: Spatialities of Transnational Networks." *Global Networks* 7(4): 383–391.

Grabher, Gernot and Oliver Ibert. 2006. "Bad Company? The Ambiguity of Personal Knowledge Networks." *Journal of Economic Geography* 6(3): 251–271.

Grabher, Gernot, Oliver Ibert, and Saskia Flohr. 2008. "The Neglected King: the Customer in the New Knowledge Ecology of Innovation." *Economic Geography* 84(3): 253–280.

Granovetter, Mark S. 1973. "The Strength of Weak Ties." *American Journal of Sociology* 78(6): 1360–1380.

Hall, Sarah. 2008. "Geographies of Business Education: MBA Programmes, Reflexive Business Schools and the Cultural Circuit of Capital." *Transactions of the Institute of British Geographers* 33(1): 27–41.

Jones, Andrew M. 1998. "(Re)Producing Gender Cultures: Theorizing Gender in Investment Banking Recruitment." *Geoforum* 29(4): 451–74.

Jones, Andrew M. 2003. *Management Consultancy and Banking in an Era of Globalization.* Basingstoke: Palgrave MacMillan.

London Business School. 2006. *MBA Employment Report.* London: London Business School.

McCormack, Steve. 2007. "MBA Graduates Can Demand Big Bucks but Salary Is Just One of Many Attractions." *Independent*, June 14. http://www.independent.co.uk/student/postgraduate/mbas-guide/mba-graduates-can-demand-big-bucks-but-salary-is-just-one-of-many-attractions-452991.html (accessed October 22, 2010).

McDowell, Linda. 1997. *Capital Culture: Gender at Work in the City of London*. Oxford: Blackwell.

Marceau, Jane. 1989. *A Family Business? The Making of an International Business Elite*. Cambridge: Cambridge University Press.

Maskell, Peter, Harald Bathelt, and Anders Malmberg. 2006. "Building Global Knowledge Pipelines: The Role of Temporary Clusters." *European Planning Studies* 14(8): 977–1013.

Michie, Ranald, ed. 2000. *The Development of London as a Financial Centre*. London: I. B. Tauris.

Mintzberg, Henry. 2004. *Managers Not MBAs: A Hard Look at the Soft Practice of Managing and Management*. London: Prentice Hall.

Opengart, Rose and Darren C. Short. 2002. "Free Agent Learners: The New Career Model and Its Impact on Human Resource Development." *International Journal of Lifelong Learning* 21(3): 220–233.

Quacquarelli, Nunzio. 2008. "Credit Crunch Refugees Fuel Record Demand for MBAs." *The Times*, November 16. http://business.timesonline.co.uk/tol/business/management/mba/article4962395.ece, (accessed October 22, 2010).

Shepherd, Jessica. 2007. "The Americans Are Coming." *Guardian*, February 20. http://www.guardian.co.uk/education/2007/feb/20/universityfunding.highereducation (accessed October 22, 2010).

Sklair, Leslie. 2001. *The Transnational Capitalist Class*. Oxford: Blackwell.

Smith, Michael P. and Luis E. Guarnizo, eds. 1998. *Transnationalism from Below*. New Brunswick, NJ: Transaction Publishers.

Starkey, Ken and Nick Tiratsoo. 2007. *The Business Schools and the Bottom Line*. Cambridge: Cambridge University Press.

Starkey, Ken, Armand Hatchuel, and Sue Tempest. 2004. "Rethinking the Business School." *Journal of Management Studies* 41(8): 1521–1531.

Storper, Michael and Anthony J. Venables. 2004. "Buzz: Face-to-Face Contact and the Urban Economy." *Journal of Economic Geography* 4(4): 351–370.

Sutton Trust. 2003. "University Endowments—A UK/US Comparison." Discussion paper, May.

Thrift, Nigel. 1994. "On the Social and Cultural Determinants of International Financial Centres: The Case Study of the City of London." In *Money, Power and Space* (ed. Stuart Corbridge, Nigel Thrift, and Ron Martin), 327–355. Oxford: Blackwell.

Thrift, Nigel. 2005. *Knowing Capitalism*. London: Sage.

Urry, John. 2002. "Mobility and Proximity." *Sociology* 36(2): 255–276.

Waters, Johanna L. 2009a. "In Pursuit of Scarcity: Transnational Students, 'Employability,' and the MBA." *Environment and Planning A* 41(8): 1865–1883.

Waters, Johanna L. 2009b. "Transnational Geographies of Academic Distinction: The Role of Social Capital in the Recognition and Evaluation of 'Overseas' Credentials." *Globalisation, Societies and Education* 7(2): 113–29.

Wenger, Etienne. 1998. *Communities of Practice: Learning, Meaning, and Identity*. Cambridge: Cambridge University Press.

Whitley, Richard. 1986. "The Transformation of Business Finance into Financial Economics: The Role of Academic Expansion and Changes in U.S. Capital Markets." *Accounting, Organizations and Society* 11(2): 171–192.

Wilmott, Paul. 2000. "The Use, Misuse and Abuse of Mathematics in Finance." *Philosophical Transactions of the Royal Society A* 358(1765): 63–73.

Wittel, Andreas. 2001. "Toward a Network Sociality." *Theory, Culture and Society* 18(6): 51–76.

Zhou, Yu and Yen-Fen Tseng. 2001. "Regrounding the 'Ungrounded Empires': Localization as the Geographical Catalyst for Transnationalism." *Global Networks* 1(2): 131–153.

Questions

1. What does the author mean by "relational reproduction of networks"? What is significant about examining social networks this way? How might examining social networks in this way uncover ways in which elites control space?

2. Both the elite MBA programs and their alumni gain from alumni networks. What does each stand to gain? Why do they invest so much in maintaining their ties to one another?

3. In what ways are alumni networks reproduced corporeally *and* virtually? How do social media, such as Facebook, matter?

4. How do alumni maintain their privilege? How is the translocal nature of this privilege significant?

5. Outside of alumni networks, what other social groups and organizations act to create social ties for elites? How so? How do they determine membership and maintain exclusivity?

6. How have social media shaped how people create, maintain, and capitalize on social networks? How have companies used them? What are the implications of new social media for how inequalities work?

29

Gendered Geographies of Reproductive Tourism

DAISY DEOMAMPO

As illustrated in Part III, today we live in a global economy, and "women's work" has become commodified. Women can engage in many forms of labor including paid, childcare, and reproductive labor. These forms of labor are not mutually exclusive categories, but instead women often perform both simultaneously. Many women, for example, immigrate to do paid carework for other families' children. Women engaged in this work are in subordinate class, race, and nationality positions relative to the families for which they provide care. Women are also paid for reproductive labor, as women's wombs are increasingly becoming a largely unregulated global commodity (also see Taylor 2011). While there is a new wave of research on surrogacy, we know little about its racialized, gendered, national, and physical capability underpinnings. This reading helps us on that path.

In this study of Indian surrogates, Daisy Deomampo examines how women and their health agencies negotiated space. Deomampo found that while they tried to ensure healthy babies for Western parents, surrogates' mobility was restricted, and they became socially isolated. Expectant parents, on the other hand, enjoyed freedom of motion. This study demonstrates how social and spatial connection and mobility become privileges of the dominant group at the intersection of race, class, gender, ability, and nationality.

References

Taylor, Tiffany. 2011. Re-examining Cultural Contradictions: Mothering Ideology and the Intersections of Class, Gender, and Race. *Sociology Compass* 5(10): 898–907.

Human procreation and childbearing have become global affairs, with increasing numbers of infertile couples and individuals from around the world pursuing surrogacy in India. A particular form of "reproductive tourism," transnational surrogacy allows would-be parents to purchase an egg cell in South Africa, implant the embryo in a womb in India, and bring their baby home to the United States. While processes of human reproduction have become increasingly commodified and disaggregated, a new spatial division of labor has surfaced, as surrogacy requires the assistance of a variety of individuals, from infertility specialists and embryologists, to anonymous and non-anonymous donors, and gestational surrogates and their caretakers. As these reproductive actors come together across space and socioeconomic stratification, how do they experience and comprehend their embodiment of mobility? In this chapter, I examine various reproductive actors' narratives to reveal how notions of space, place, and mobility are implicated in geographical inquiries of reproductive tourism. I focus on the perspectives of commissioning parents and surrogate mothers in order to comprehend how different social groups relate to and experience the differential power relations embedded in reproductive tourism. I engage particularly with the multiple social and spatial boundaries that people will cross—including ethnic, racial, economic, religious, and national—to fulfill their procreative desires. Within this context of globalized reproduction, geographical questions related to space, place, and the body come to the fore, as reproductive tourism highlights important ways that gender, nationality, and kinship link to shifting social and spatial boundaries, as well as particular notions of space and place.

I draw on empirical data from my research with surrogates and commissioning parents in Mumbai, India, to explore the intersections of power within transnational surrogacy through a geographical lens in order to understand how perceptions of mobility and immobility shape their experiences. I contend that examining transnational reproduction within a geographical framework broadens our understanding of stratified reproduction in complex and contradictory ways.

Reproductive tourism, a form of medical tourism, refers to the transnational consumption of assisted reproductive technologies (ARTs). It includes people who travel abroad to procure gametes and embryos, contract with surrogates, and/or obtain services such as in vitro fertilization (IVF), intracytoplasmic sperm injection, artificial insemination, sex selection, and diagnostic tools, including amniocentesis and preimplantation genetic diagnosis (PGD). The providers of these reproductive tissues and services may also undertake reproductive tourism in order to make their bodies "bioavailable" (Cohen 2005).

Patterns of reproductive tourism reveal uneven distributions of assisted conception and related technologies across the globe. Scholars have demonstrated that structural and cultural constraints influence how developing countries assimilate ARTs (Bharadwaj 2006, 2009, forthcoming; Handwerker 2001; Inhorn 2003). While people in high- and middle-income nations tend to have the most access to ARTs, a combination of policy, religious, and cultural values also influence the number of fertility clinics and availability of services (E. F. S. Roberts 2012; Spar 2006).

While assisted reproduction has brought increased freedom and opportunity for some people, making parenthood possible for infertile couples, single men and women, and gay and lesbian couples through artificial insemination, surrogacy, or IVF (Agigian 2004; Layne 1999; Mamo 2007; Ragoné and Twine 2000), advances in reproductive technology, too, have promoted and maintained certain power relations, notions of gender, and particular constructions of the family. Some scholars, for example, argue that these technologies re-essentialize women by reinforcing patriarchal roles and objectifying women's reproductive potential (Rothman 1989). Others reveal how ARTs reinforce the traditional patriarchal family by enabling infertile heterosexual couples to reproduce while many clinics have barred single people, gay or lesbian couples, welfare recipients, and other women who do not conform to patriarchal ideals of motherhood (D. Roberts 1997).

Embedded within reproductive technologies, then, are problems of social inequality. With ongoing advances in reproductive technology, feminist scholars have paid close attention to stratified reproduction and the ways that certain power relations empower some people to nurture and reproduce while disempowering others (Colen 1995; Ginsburg and Rapp 1991; Rapp 2011). Transnational surrogacy in India reflects many of these inequities; in India, as elsewhere, disparities in gender, race, class, and nation place some women's reproductive projects above others' (DasGupta and DasGupta 2010; Pande 2011). Certainly, the global landscape in which surrogacy occurs is highly uneven, offering a powerful exemplar of stratified reproduction.

While there is a growing literature on transnational reproduction around the globe (Bergmann 2011; Inhorn 2010, 2011; Nahman 2008, 2011; Whittaker and Speier 2010), including several special journal issues (Gürtin and Inhorn 2011; Krøløkke, Foss, and Pant 2012), the Indian case represents a critical opportunity to examine how social relationships unfold within the uneven terrain of transnational reproduction. India, a "global hub" of commercial gestational surrogacy, boasts more than 250 IVF clinics and several agencies dedicated to commercial surrogacy, and the Indian Council for Medical Research projects that profits will reach nearly $6 billion in the next few years (Rudrappa 2010). The country has become the "go-to" destination for surrogacy.

In addition, reproductive tourism occurs not only along north–south pathways but also within the global south. While major cities such as Mumbai and Delhi cater to North American, Australian, and European clients, a growing number of IVF/surrogacy clinics in metropolitan cities throughout India cater to regional clientele from Bangladesh and Pakistan, as well as clients from within India, who travel from regions where ART infrastructure remains undeveloped (Kashyap 2011). In my own field research, I found that many Indian fertility clinics cater to clients from African countries such as Tanzania, Nigeria, and Ethiopia who travel to India in search of experienced IVF practitioners and advanced medical facilities that are either unavailable or unaffordable in their home countries. Paradoxically, as ART consumers travel from around the world to access India's flourishing fertility industry, Inhorn has found that many infertile South Asians seek ART services elsewhere, unable to obtain affordable, high-quality services in their own country (Inhorn 2012). These examples of south–south transnational reproduction provide additional case studies through which to think about the complexities of stratified markets of reproductive tourism.

Geographical Approaches

Because reproductive tourism is geographical in nature—that is, occurring in places and involving movements and activities across space and between places—geography is fundamental to the study of transnational reproductive practices. The spatial is a dynamic and ever-shifting social geometry of power and signification whereby global flows and relationships affect different social groups differently. According to Massey (1993), "power-geometry" not only describes who moves and who doesn't but also the power that one holds in relation to the flows and movement. As different social groups have distinct relationships to this mobility, Massey argues, it effectively imprisons some groups. This differential mobility reflects not only an unequal distribution of power but also the power to "weaken the leverage of the already weak" (Massey 1993, 62).

While the confinement of surrogates to maternity homes could be interpreted as a form of "spatial imprisonment," it is also part of the process of place-making. As Harvey argues, "Place, in whatever guise, is like space and time, a social construct. . . . The only interesting question that can then be asked is: by what social process(es) is place constructed?" (Harvey 1996, 293). In the case of reproduction and the globalization of reproductive technologies, the flow of capital circulation influences the construction of the geographical configuration of places; as novel transport, communications systems, and physical infrastructures rework places, new kinds of reproductive networks emerge between high-income countries with capital and low-income nations with "surplus" reproductive labor. Such configurations of labor power shed new light on geographical understandings of place in the current globalized neoliberal economy, where human gametes, surrogates, and other ART procedures can be paid for or arranged with the click of a mouse.

While Harvey provides theoretical underpinnings for understanding place, Chatterjee (1989) introduces a gender framework for analyzing intersections of space, place, gender, and nation. Chatterjee's foundational analysis of the nationalist construction of gender illuminates how Indian surrogates remain trapped in false essentialisms that locate women squarely within the realm of the spiritual, feminine home. Paradoxically, as Indian women traverse material spheres to access the science and technology inherent in gestational surrogacy, they remain fixed in the spiritual sphere of the home, as their reproductive labor is inextricably linked to the inner domain, femininity, and womanhood.

Finally, recent work on waiting and stillness sheds light on the spatio-temporality of mobility as well as immobility, elucidating the nuanced power relations among commissioning parents and surrogates (Bissell and Fuller 2010; Cresswell 2012; Mountz 2011a). While the dynamic of "spatial imprisonment" arguably points to the question of immobility or suspension for surrogates during their pregnancies, the experiences of new parents, too, suggest a spatio-temporality of planning and anticipating, particularly for those who spend weeks and months caring for their babies in India while waiting for health issues to resolve (for prematurely born infants) or for travel documents.

A geographical approach together with feminist scholarship on assisted reproduction explicates the empirical story in this study, which follows surrogates and commissioning parents as they navigate and occupy distinct geographical spaces. Questions about how various reproductive actors negotiate the myriad spaces through which they travel remain. What are the lived experiences of surrogates and intended parents when refracted through the lens of geography? And what does such an analysis reveal about the intersections among space, stratification, and reproduction? I argue that power and mobility play out in complex and contradictory ways, wherein both surrogates and commissioning parents experience moments of movement and mobility interrupted by periods of stillness, immobility, and anticipation. In doing so, this work elucidates how dichotomous portrayals of parents and surrogates as "exploiters and exploited" or "agents and victims" are facile representations of individuals connected through complex transnational processes of reproduction.

Methods

The research described in this chapter is part of a larger study on reproductive tourism in India, where I conducted 13 months of fieldwork between 2008 and 2010. I draw on participant observation at varied sites throughout Mumbai, including infertility clinics, hospitals, intended parents' hotel or apartment accommodations, and surrogate mothers' homes. In addition, I conducted in-depth semi-structured and unstructured interviews with 39 intended parents pursuing gestational surrogacy (representing 26 couples/individuals), 35 Indian surrogate mothers and egg donors, and 21 doctors. Additional participants included traveling egg donors

from South Africa, surrogate brokers and agents, ART legal experts, medical tourism agents, and American adjudicators involved in processing citizenship requests for babies born outside the United States.

The clinics included in this study were self-selected by head doctors and staff who welcomed the presence of a researcher. As Inhorn (2004) has noted, fieldwork in infertility clinics depends heavily on the goodwill of their gatekeepers. Thus, I recruited participants in this study in several ways. Clinic staff initially approached foreign clients as well as Indian women undergoing surrogacy or egg donation to see if they wanted to participate in the study. Following an informed consent procedure, I conducted interviews of approximately one hour with intended parents. I recruited additional participants using the snowball method, following initial contacts made with intended parents. With the assistance of a translator, I conducted interviews in Hindi or Marathi with surrogates, egg donors, and their families, again following an informed consent procedure. The surrogate participants were recruited primarily either at the clinic (through clinic staff) or through the snowball method, and I conducted interviews either in the clinic or at the participants' homes.

Profile of Participants

Of the 39 commissioning parents interviewed in this study, same-sex couples comprised approximately half of the parents interviewed, while heterosexual married couples comprised the remaining half. The majority of commissioning parents hailed from the United States or Australia; other countries of origin include Norway, France, Canada, Israel, and the Netherlands. With the exception of one African American, two Latinos, three Asians, and one of mixed racial background, the parents interviewed identified themselves as white. All parents came from middle- to upper-class socioeconomic backgrounds.

In addition, I interviewed 35 Indian surrogate mothers and egg donors for this study. The women came from primarily low-income families, and most pursued surrogacy as a viable solution to their financial hardships, such as debt or lack of housing. The majority of the women interviewed were married, with the exception of three widows, two divorced women, and one unmarried woman. All of the women had previously given birth, with the exception of one childless woman.

Nearly all of the women identified as housewives, but those who worked outside of the home did domestic work, factory work, or work in the garment industry.

Ethnographic Voices: Surrogates, Movement, and Spatial Imprisonment

I first met Avani in September 2010, at the one-room apartment she occupied with her two children and mother-in-law in suburban Mumbai. Avani sits on the one bed in the modest room so my translator and I can sit on the two plastic chairs she brought in from a neighbor's apartment. In one corner of the bare, rundown room with peeling pink paint are two gas burners and a sink; across the length of the room hangs a clothesline. At the time of our meeting Avani is 25 years old and barely five months pregnant as a surrogate mother for a couple she describes only as "foreign." The surrogacy agency had arranged her move to these temporary accommodations close to the hospital where she will give birth at her doctor's insistence. As the children play on the floor in the corner of the room, Avani tells the story of how she became a surrogate mother.

While Avani's family is originally from Nepal, she was born and raised in an industrial city nearly 40 miles outside Mumbai. Avani tells me that she may have completed first or second standard in school, "which is equal to nothing." She had an arranged marriage in 2000, at the age of 15 to a 20-year-old man. His education, too, was "not much, maybe up to a couple of standards," and while his income is not fixed, he generally earns between US$40 and US$60 per month as a watchman. Avani and her husband have two sons, an eight-year-old and a five-year-old.

Avani first learned about surrogacy less than a year prior to our interview; a friend of hers had previously "gone through the process"—Avani refers to it in a sterile way—and brought Avani to the doctor to learn more about it. Her initial reaction was one of cautious curiosity: "I wanted to see for myself how it happens because it didn't seem real." Assured by the doctor of the safety of surrogacy and compelled by the prospect of earning much needed income for her family—Avani would earn approximately US$4,700 upon delivery of a healthy child—she decided to become a surrogate mother. However, the surrogacy agency required Avani's husband's permission; he had previously refused to allow Avani to get a job as a housecleaner, and he initially refused this, too. After some time, Avani and her doctor convinced

him to agree. Avani prepared herself for the rigorous battery of medical exams, hormone injections, and pills that would prime her body for surrogate pregnancy.

Avani quickly became pregnant, and shortly afterward her doctor ordered her to leave her home and move to new accommodations with her family. During the course of my fieldwork, many doctors assured me that surrogate agencies provide housing solely for the benefit of surrogate mothers and the children they bear. This housing was ostensibly an improvement, and, as the doctors explained to me, surrogate pregnancy is a time of relaxation and repose, as women are not burdened by work or household chores in the arranged housing. I was deeply curious about Avani's experience of the new housing.

As it turned out, Avani lamented her current accommodations and longed to live in her previous home near her extended family:

> Of course I like my place more than this one. Here I'm instructed all the time where to sit and what to do. My husband only comes once or twice a week. He works in my old neighborhood, which is so far from here, so he must stay in our family home. At my place there are so many people living together in my house and every day is nice with them. Here, nobody is around to talk to and there are restrictions on my roaming as well. I get so bored. Our routine is just eating and sleeping. The only work we do is cooking for ourselves.

In my research I found that surrogates' mobility, like Avani's, is quite literally limited. Within the confined spaces of the maternity home, staff members monitor surrogates' nutrition, health, and daily activities, ensuring that surrogates do not engage in any behavior that may harm the fetus. One doctor even admitted that she prefers that surrogates remain indoors at all times, leaving the house only if absolutely necessary. Within these small, one-room flats shared with children or other family members, the surrogates I spoke with shared stories of loneliness and restricted mobility. For Avani, feelings of isolation permeated her surrogacy experience in the apartment: "I live with my mother-in-law and kids but still I feel I'm isolated here. I really don't like to stay without my [extended] family."

Urvashi, six months pregnant at the time of our interview, shared Avani's sense of isolation. She lived in the same apartment building. Throughout our interview, Urvashi spoke quietly yet clearly and sadly, her growing belly visible beneath her floral-patterned *salwar*

kameez and orange *dupatta*. Urvashi married her husband at the age of 15 in an arranged marriage. She had
completed the equivalent of an eighth-grade education
and worked, as she said, "as a housewife only." Her husband's previous job as a watchman earned him a salary
of approximately US$150 per month; however, poor
health forced him to leave his job, and the family has
struggled ever since.

After seeing Urvashi's sister-in-law go through the
process of surrogacy, Urvashi's husband urged her to
consider it, too. However, in contrast to Avani and
many other surrogates I interviewed who needed to
convince their husbands, Urvashi felt uncertain. Yet her
husband, who had been ill and unable to work for several years, was convinced that surrogacy could help
their family's financial situation. Urvashi eventually
agreed, although with some ambivalence. She said, "I
was not ready to do it [surrogacy], but my husband has
not been well for a couple of years and we need money
to treat him. That is the reason I went for the process."

Prior to Urvashi's surrogate pregnancy, her life was
marked by a series of disruptive moves from her native
Nepal. Seeking work and financial stability, Urvashi, her
husband, and their two children migrated to Pune, while
her eldest daughter remained in school in Nepal under
the care of Urvashi's parents. Transience and insecurity
continued to mark their life in Pune, as Urvashi's husband's job lasted only several months; at the same time,
the family found themselves traveling long distances to
the state border between Maharashtra and Gujarat to
secure affordable medicine and health care for her ailing
husband. Once Urvashi decided to pursue surrogacy, the
family again relocated to Mumbai. Six months into her
pregnancy, now 24 and the mother of three daughters,
Urvashi reflected on the difference between her previous
pregnancies and the current surrogate pregnancy: "The
main difference is that I'm not allowed to move around
and work. That is adding pains to me. I definitely like to
go out and have a walk once in a while, but we are not
allowed to do it." Following a wave of movement and
mobility, Urvashi was finally compelled to remain im-
mobile in ways that left her powerless and dispirited.

The narratives of Avani and Urvashi reveal how different bodies are differently privileged in transnational
reproduction. When surrogate mothers are expected to
live separately from their families in unfamiliar neighborhoods, their own desires—to be near loved ones, to
walk around their neighborhoods—are devalued against

the risk of any behavior that may harm the fetus. While
Western intended parents pursuing surrogacy in India
may expect the surrogacy agency to provide housing,
and assume the surrogate will enjoy living in new housing with few work responsibilities, my research revealed
that many women experienced higher levels of stress and
anxiety because of restrictions on their mobility and
separation from their families. Though doctors suggest
that surrogates should move to clinic-appointed housing
in order to avoid the demands of household work and
responsibilities, in doing so they discount the everyday
realities of familial and community support that women
receive at home. In this setting, Avani and Urvashi experience immobility as stressful and isolating, not restful,
as the doctors suggest.

Similarly, in her research in a surrogacy hostel in
the western state of Gujarat, Pande has noted the contradictions that emerge in such closely monitored spaces.
While women have fewer work responsibilities in the
hostel, their daily activities remain tightly controlled,
and women follow a strict daily routine and diet: "Everything works like clockwork," as one surrogate explained
(Pande 2010, 969). Yet, as some women have expressed,
the daily timetable can be monotonous and unpleasant.

To be sure, surrogates do form small communities
in maternity homes with fellow surrogate women, communities that are restrained to a particular place for the
duration of their pregnancies. Particular socioeconomic processes connected to transnational surrogacy
bring about such places and communities and the social
relations within them. Yet, while the distinctive activities of those who dwell there constitute such places,
temporariness and transience also inform them, as surrogates move through them only during their pregnancies. Alliances formed with other surrogates made
Avani's temporary home more bearable, but she planned
to build a home for her family in Nepal. This community is tenuous and temporary, and surrogates return to
their homes and families, who frequently have no
knowledge of the surrogate pregnancy.

Avani's and Urvashi's stories of displacement, spatial imprisonment, and place-making provide important
comparative data for studies of surrogacy in varied locations throughout India. While they lived in adjacent
one-room flats in a shared apartment building, they remained cautious and typically stayed in their homes,
avoiding interaction with other residents of the building.
In contrast, Pande (2010) has shown how the surrogacy

hostel may constitute a gendered space, one that generates emotional attachments and sisterhood among women, and fosters opportunities for resistance and networking. The intensive contact among surrogates in the hostel enables them to share information, grievances, strategies for future employment, and even acts of collective resistance.

However, while communal surrogate housing may be the norm in other parts of India, most Mumbai clinics in which I conducted fieldwork did not arrange housing in shared dormitory-like spaces. Yet, surrogate women who do not live in maternity homes during their pregnancies, too, experience limited mobility. No legislation regulates surrogacy in India, and I encountered a wide range of practices and policies with respect to the treatment, care, and housing of surrogates during their pregnancies. Some clinics simply offered modest stipends for rent and made no arrangements for surrogate accommodations. The mobility of surrogates not bound to live in such housing was far from privileged.

Meera, like many others, became a surrogate and strove for an upwardly mobile future under tenuous circumstances. Meera was 25 at the time of our first meeting. When she was 13, Meera's father became ill, prompting her parents to arrange her marriage with a man 10 years her senior. Meera regretted having to leave school at that time. By the age of 20, Meera had given birth to four daughters and one son and had undergone tubal ligation in order to prevent any further pregnancies.

On learning about surrogacy, Meera was determined to convince a doctor to take her on as a "patient." She admitted to the doctor that she was married, despite the fact that her marriage was always tenuous and fraught with violence and that she was in the midst of a relationship with another man. Meera told the doctor she had only one son and one daughter, not five, because admitting that she was a mother of five would have disqualified her as a potential surrogate due to the Indian Council of Medical Research guideline that a woman may not act as surrogate for more than five births, including her own children. Savvy and strong-willed, Meera viewed surrogacy as a potential windfall that would alleviate her financial insecurity. She seemed willing to do whatever it took to become a surrogate, and she eventually became pregnant with twins for a foreign couple.

Meera's doctor worked with an agency that did not have a fixed policy on housing; some women seemed to move because they wanted to, and others were forced to move to the hospital in order to monitor potential health issues, while most were left to their own devices, often remaining in their own homes. Meera was under constant pressure and had strained relations with her violent husband and in-laws. As she rejected and rebelled against the demands of her family, Meera would often escape to her boyfriend's house. Meera's constant movement made it difficult for Maryam, her caretaker, to contact her when necessary; she would often disappear for days, sometimes weeks, at a time, during her pregnancy.

This freedom of mobility, however, would eventually come to an end when the doctor forced her to remain in the hospital for the remaining four months of her pregnancy, at Maryam's request:

> I told Madam [the doctor] that I'm not ready to take responsibility for her anymore. Admit her in the hospital, otherwise she'll run away again with someone if you keep her in a house with the other surrogates. She is now in the hospital for the rest of her pregnancy and she is not allowed to go out for anything.

This spatial imprisonment at the request of Maryam, herself a former surrogate, reflects the subtle registers on which the relative power over mobility works. In spite of these profound restrictions and surveillance on their movement and mobility at home, in their communities, and in the hospital, movement through Mumbai punctuated Meera's, Avani's, and Urvashi's pregnancies. As Maryam often recounted, her job as an "agent" required her to shepherd women throughout the city, often to different clinics for different procedures within the course of one day. This often entailed long commutes on the local public railway system, because Maryam and most of her patients lived in an industrial city some 40 miles from Mumbai. I sometimes met Maryam and her "patients" during these harried days, and observed the toll these trips took on the women.

I noted, too, how the geographic space of the clinic reflected broader power relations between doctors and surrogates. As infertility clinics in Mumbai are nearly always privately operated, such spaces typically remain exclusive to clients of middle- and upper-class status. Within these same spaces, working-class women are viewed as secondary and out of place. The clinics reflected such inequalities, which manifest in their physical layout and the positioning of different clients of distinct backgrounds throughout. In one clinic, surrogate women recover from certain medical procedures in a storage room that doubles as a makeshift recovery room. The clinics also function as a space in which to reiterate medical authority over any concerns or questions surrogate women may have. Throughout many interviews, women divulged that they rarely posed questions about procedures or medications, nor were they offered the opportunity; they simply received instructions about medical care and medications and were expected to acquiesce to the doctor's demands. The transfer of authoritative knowledge in the clinic and hospital reinforced already existing hierarchies between women and the medical establishment.

Intended Parents, Mobility/Immobility, and Places of Birth

In contrast to surrogates' experiences of spatial imprisonment and restricted mobility, I was struck by the ways in which intended parents moved with comparative comfort throughout their travels. While women such as Meera, Avani, and Urvashi had little say over where and with whom they might live, many intended parents moved with the ease of cosmopolitan travelers whose higher socioeconomic status allowed them the comforts of luxury full-service apartments or five-star hotels. As a researcher, I experienced these disjunctures first-hand, as my interviews allowed me to traverse distinct geographies of class and privilege that would take me at times to luxury hotel suites in Mumbai, and at others to one-room apartments in working-class neighborhoods outside the city.

Yet at the same time, intended parents' sojourns in serviced apartments indicate more than mobility; they also suggest a spatio-temporality of planning, waiting, and anticipating. For instance, Marla and John, an upper-middle-class Norwegian couple, had traveled halfway around the world in order to meet their newborn daughter born via surrogacy. When I first met Marla, a tall, blonde, blue-eyed woman, she was relaxing poolside at a deluxe, five-star hotel in the suburbs of Mumbai in the company of her husband and their newborn baby girl, Ada. It was a warm, humid monsoon afternoon, and Marla and John were clearly in ecstasy caring for Ada, the newest member of their family.

However, once in Mumbai, they found themselves in a liminal state of stillness and anticipation, as they awaited the travel documents that would allow them to return home. Indeed, parents sometimes spent months

in this transient space, waiting for the bureaucratic process of assigning citizenship to unfold. At the time of our interview, Marla and John were approaching their fourth week in Mumbai. As Marla stated, "The woman at the consulate, she is deliberately delaying everything . . . and we are ready to go home. We want to go home to autumn, our family, our friends, and our animals, everything." With the exception of trips to the Norwegian consulate, they rarely ventured outside the comfortable confines of their hotel, and their experience of surrogacy was marked by relative immobility and waiting within spaces of luxury that mark the stark contrast in economic and social status between surrogates and parents. Like Marla, many parents I interviewed who experienced long stays in Mumbai described waiting, liminality, and disruption to their normal, everyday lives. Yet it is worth noting that as Western parents pursued surrogacy as a way to build their families, these moments of disruption also served as opportunities to bond with and care for their children, uninterrupted by the distractions of work and family at home. In contrast, the families of many surrogates, such as those of Avani, Urvashi, and Meera, also experienced disruption and instability, physically separated across space (sometimes across national borders, as in the case of Urvashi and her eldest child) during their surrogate pregnancies.

During these long stays, parents would often reflect on the meaning of "homeland" and "birthplace" for their children. Transnational surrogacy arrangements unquestionably problematize such places for intended parents and their children, as the relationship between homeland and birthplace is no longer distinct. The story of Adam and Ben, 38 and 37 years old, respectively, is instructive. An upper-middle-class couple from Israel, I first met them at their full-service apartment in a wealthy suburb of Mumbai. The couple had previously explored adoption as an option for family building, but gay couples find international adoption almost impossible and Israel has few adoptees available domestically. They eventually decided on surrogacy in India, settling on a clinic in Mumbai that was well known for providing services to gay couples from around the world.

Several weeks prior to our first meeting, Adam and Ben's surrogate, Asha, gave birth via cesarean section to twin girls, Tara and Noelle, who were conceived with the assistance of an anonymous egg donor from South Africa. Throughout the course of our interviews, Adam professed that he viewed the labor of gestation and delivery as stronger and more enduring than the genetic connection that existed between the egg donor and the girls. Despite the genetic material contributed by the young white egg donor and the acknowledgment that Tara and Noelle share more in common with her, in terms of race and class, than with Asha, Adam insisted that Asha and his twin girls had a deeper relationship. He planned to work to reinforce this relationship through efforts to "maintain the Indian element in their identity." "Indian-ness" became something that, in the absence of the Indian "mother" but originating in the girls' birthplace, Adam will build and reinforce over time:

> We will tell them about their histories, their heritage, the stories of how they were conceived, and we're using all the pictures and home movies and stuff, and that is playing up the Indian part very much. They will have pictures of India, they will know about this hotel. They will hear stories of Ganpati and Raksha Bandhan.

As Adam's narrative suggests, understandings about a child's biogenetic origins emerge in tension with a child's right to identity. This identity is viewed as inseparable from his or her "birthplace" in India, the surrogate, and *her* ethnic, cultural, and religious background.

Another expectant parent, Martin, revealed similar sentiments around his child's connection to India. Martin, a 42-year-old from the southern United States, and his partner, Richard, were expecting twins conceived with the eggs of an anonymous Indian donor and Martin's sperm; the resulting embryos were then transferred to the womb of an Indian surrogate. Martin explained that he looked forward to incorporating aspects of Indian culture into their children's lives:

> I'm very open to the idea of it [Indian culture] being a part of the child's life. . . . Certainly, if the child is very interested in their heritage, I could see us returning to India. We are actually planning on giving the children Sanskrit names. So we've picked out two sets of girl names and two sets of boy names that are derived from Sanskrit. I think it's important. For whatever reason, this is the path that our lives have taken us on and I think we need to be respectful of where this became a reality.

For Martin, the journey of building a family through surrogacy in India mobilizes new geographic imaginations that construct and rely on the notion of return. India becomes imagined as a place of origin: origins of family, conception, birth, and heritage.

It, too, becomes a place to which parents imagine a geographic return, in order to shed light on their children's site of origin (despite the very transnational nature of their conception). This was true for both Adam and Martin, despite the fact that Adam's children might be phenotypically white, while Martin's might appear more racially ambiguous.

Like Adam and Martin, many parents I spoke with articulated a strong desire to "maintain the Indian element" in their children's identities through naming rituals, accumulation of material goods for the home (such as Indian fabrics, clothes, and decorative tapestries), and, most importantly, stories that reiterate exotic details of Indian social life. Many of my interviews reflected this thread of the conflation of race and the place of nation. Parents of surrogate children conflated the geographic space of India—and the attendant orientalist discourses that construct "Indian-ness" as exotically opposite to Western sensibilities—with the embodiment of the child's identity through its gestation by an Indian surrogate mother in India. Further, such conflations reveal the pedestrian reliance on "multiculturalism" as a universalizing discourse, which ignores the specificity of local contexts. In constructing India as a place of origin and return, parents rely on a geographic imaginary that flattens out the specificity of India's historical and political economic contexts.

Conclusion

Assisted reproductive technologies, reproductive tourism, and the kinds of families they make possible have engendered new social relationships, spaces, and places. Geographical analyses provide a useful tool for elucidating these relationships, as reproductive tourism connects to the spaces and places in which it is created, imagined, perceived, and experienced. Moreover, space is not just an innocent backdrop or stage set in which events occur, but rather a factor in itself that social relations create.

In transnational reproduction, a wide range of social groups and actors create spaces and places that produce certain meanings and values within circuits of tourism production and consumption. While these meanings and values change over time, I have drawn specifically on the narratives of surrogates and intended parents to reveal how relations of power and inequality play out within global reproductive networks as they embody and experience space and mobility in distinct ways. It would be misleading, however, to portray one group with relative power—in this case, commissioning parents from the global north—as always exercising power to constrain the mobility of another, less privileged group, the surrogate mothers. Such dichotomous portrayals obscure the continuum of experiences that reveal how different groups experience mobility and immobility, power and resistance. By highlighting the subtleties of how power operates through space and mobility, we can observe the different registers on which people exercise and are subject to power.

While I have focused on the specific case of transnational surrogacy, the findings of this research can shed light on power and social relationships formed through other "intimate industries" such as medical tourism, international adoption, international marriage brokerages, call centers, and sex, domestic, and care work. While more research is needed in mapping the operation of this power in the context of surrogacy and reproductive tourism, situating geographic spaces and places in specific neoliberal contexts, such a mapping can serve as an important beginning to demystifying and challenging prevailing structures of power.

References

Agigian, Amy. 2004. *Baby Steps: How Lesbian Alternative Insemination Is Changing the World*. Middletown, CT: Wesleyan University Press.

Bergmann, Sven. 2011. "Fertility Tourism: Circumventive Routes that Enable Access to Reproductive Technologies and Substances." *Signs* 36:280–289.

Bharadwaj, Aditya. 2006. "Sacred Conceptions: Clinical Theodicies, Uncertain Science, and Technologies of Procreation in India." *Culture, Medicine, and Psychiatry* 30:451–465.

Bharadwaj, Aditya. 2009. "Assisted Life: The Neoliberal Moral Economy of Embryonic Stem Cells in India." In *Assisting Reproduction, Testing Genes: Global Encounters with New Biotechnologies* (ed. D. Birenbaum-Carmeli and M. C. Inhorn), 239–257. New York: Berghahn.

Bharadwaj, Aditya. Forthcoming. *Conceptions: Infertility and Procreative Modernity in India*. New York: Berghahn.

Bissell, David, and Gillian Fuller, eds. 2010. *Stillness in a Mobile World*. London: Routledge.

Chatterjee, Partha. 1989. "Colonialism, Nationalism, and Colonialized Women: The Contest in India." *American Ethnologist* 16:622–633.

Cohen, Lawrence. 2005. "Operability, Bioavailability, and Exception." In *Global Assemblages: Technology, Politics, and Ethics as Anthropological Problems* (ed. A. Ong and S. Collier), 79–90. Oxford: Blackwell.

Colen, Shellee. 1995. "'Like a Mother to Them': Stratified Reproduction and West Indian Childcare Workers and Employers in New York." In *Conceiving the New World Order* (ed. F. Ginsburg and R. Rapp), 78–102. Berkeley: University of California Press.

Cresswell, Tim. 2012. Mobilities II: Still. *Progress in Human Geography* 36:645–653.

DasGupta, Sayantani, and Shamita Das DasGupta. 2010. "Motherhood Jeopardized: Reproductive Technologies in Indian Communities." In *The Globalization of Motherhood: Deconstructions and Reconstructions of Biology and Care* (ed. W. Chavkin and J. Maher), 131–153. New York: Routledge.

Ginsburg, Faye, and Rayna Rapp. 1991. The Politics of Reproduction. *Annual Review of Anthropology* 20:311–343.

Gürtin, Zeynep B., and Marcia C. Inhorn. 2011. "Introduction: Travelling for Conception and the Global Assisted Reproduction Market." *Reproductive BioMedicine Online* 23:535–537.

Handwerker, Lisa. 2001. "The Politics of Making Modern Babies in China: Reproductive Technologies and the 'New' Eugenics." In *Infertility around the Globe: New Thinking on Childlessness, Gender, and Reproductive Technologies* (ed. M. C. Inhorn and F. Van Balen), 298–314. Berkeley: University of California Press.

Harvey, David. 1996. *Justice, Nature and the Geography of Difference*. Oxford: Blackwell.

Inhorn, Marcia C. 2003. "Global Infertility and the Globalization of the New Reproductive Technologies: Illustrations from Egypt." *Social Science and Medicine* 56:1837–1851.

Inhorn, Marcia C. 2004. "Privacy, Privatization, and the Politics of Patronage: Ethnographic Challenges to Penetrating the Secret World of Middle Eastern, Hospital-Based in Vitro Fertilization." *Social Science and Medicine* 59:2095–2108.

Inhorn, Marcia C. 2010. "Globalization and Gametes: Reproductive 'Tourism,' Islamic Bioethics, and Middle Eastern Modernity." *Anthropology and Medicine* 18:87–103

Inhorn, Marcia C. 2011. "Diasporic Dreaming: Return Reproductive Tourism to the Middle East." *Reproductive BioMedicine Online* 23:582–591.

Inhorn, Marcia C. 2012. "Reproductive Exile in Global Dubai: South Asian Stories." *Cultural Politics* 8:283–306.

Kashyap, Pooja. 2011. "Test-Tube Babies no Real Option in Patna." *Times of India*, October 20.

Krøløkke, Charlotte, Karen A. Foss, and Saumya Pant. 2012. "Fertility Travel: The Commodification of Human Reproduction." *Cultural Politics* 8:273–282.

Layne, Linda. 1999. *Transformative Motherhood: On Giving and Getting in a Consumer Culture*. New York: New York University Press.

Mamo, Laura. 2007. *Queering Reproduction: Achieving Pregnancy in the Age of Technoscience*. Durham, NC: Duke University Press.

Massey, Doreen. 1993. Power-Geometry and a Progressive Sense of Place. In *Mapping the Futures: Local Cultures, Global Change* (ed. J. Bird, B. Curtis, T. Putnam, G. Robertson, and L. Tickner), 59–69. London: Routledge.

Mountz, Alison. 2011a. "Specters at the Port of Entry: Understanding State Mobilities through an Ontology of Exclusion." *Mobilities* 6:317–334.

Nahman, Michal. 2008. "Nodes of Desire: Romanian Egg Sellers, 'Dignity' and Feminist Alliances in Transnational Ova Exchanges." *European Journal of Women's Studies* 15:65–82.

Nahman, Michal. 2011. "Reverse Traffic: Intersecting Inequalities in Human Egg Donation." *Reproductive BioMedicine Online* 23:626–633.

Pande, Amrita. 2010. "Commercial Surrogacy in India: Manufacturing a Perfect Mother-Worker." *Signs* 35: 969–992.

Pande, Amrita. 2011. "Transnational Commercial Surrogacy in India: Gifts for Global Sisters?" *Reproductive BioMedicine Online* 23:618–625.

Ragoné, Helena, and France Widdance Twine, eds. 2000. *Ideologies and Technologies of Motherhood: Race, Class, Sexuality, Nationalism*. New York: Routledge.

Rapp, Rayna. 2011. "Reproductive Entanglements: Body, State and Culture in the Dys/Regulation of Childbearing." *Social Research* 78:693–718.

Roberts, Dorothy. 1997. *Killing the Black Body: Race, Reproduction and the Meaning of Liberty*. New York: Pantheon Books.

Roberts, Elizabeth F. S. 2012. *God's Laboratory: Assisted Reproduction in the Andes*. Berkeley: University of California Press.

Rothman, Barbara Katz. 1989. *Recreating Motherhood*. New York: Norton.

Rudrappa, Sharmila. 2010. "Making India the 'Mother Destination': Outsourcing Labor to Indian Surrogates." *Research in the Sociology of Work* 20:253–285.

Spar, Debora. 2006. *The Baby Business: How Money, Science, and Politics Drive the Commerce of Conception*. Boston: Harvard Business School Press.

Whittaker, Andrea, and Amy Speier. 2010. "'Cycling Overseas': Care, Commodification, and Stratification in Cross-Border Reproductive Travel." *Medical Anthropology* 29:363–383.

Discussion

1. What does Deomampo mean by "gendered geographies"? What does the author mean by "reproductive tourism"? Why, according to the author, is it important to use the "lens of geography"?

2. Why was India an important place to conduct this research? How did the author conduct her study? Describe her participants.

3. What does the author mean by "spatial imprisonment"? How is this significant in understanding how inequality is reproduced through the control of space?

4. Like Hall, Deomampo highlights the importance of transnationality. How is transnationality meaningful in Deomampo's research? What does this research tell us about power and social relationships?

5. The United States is another country where surrogacy is legal and inequality shapes who seeks surrogates and who becomes a surrogate. Read the *New York Times* article by Tamar Lewin titled "Coming to U.S. for Baby, and Womb to Carry It" published on July 5, 2014. How does global inequality shape surrogacy in the United States? How much do surrogates get paid? Calculate how much money would be paid to a surrogate if she received minimum wage for every hour for 8 months. How much do you think a surrogate should be paid or, alternatively, do you believe that any wage would justify surrogacy? Why or why not? After reading Deomampo and the *New York Times* article, what issues complicate surrogacy? (The *New York Times* article can be found at the following link: http://www.nytimes.com/2014/07/06/us/foreign-couples-heading-to-america-for-surrogate-pregnancies.html?_r=1.)

30

A Cripple at a Rich Man's Gate: A Comparison of Disability, Employment, and Anti-Discrimination Law in the United States and Canada

C. G. K. ATKINS

According to the U.S. Bureau of Labor Statistics (2013), in 2013, only 27 percent of individuals age 16 to 64 with a disability were employed. This is less than half the labor force participation of individuals in that same age group who do not have a disability. Additionally, the BLS reports that individuals with disabilities are more likely to work part-time. Individuals with disabilities are more likely to be employed if they have higher levels of education. Similarly, almost twice as many individuals with disabilities (13 percent) are unemployed compared to individuals without disabilities (7 percent). Note that unemployment figures capture individuals actively looking for work but who are unable to find employment. These statistics point to the importance of examining the causes of employment inequality as it relates to disability in particular.

This piece compares antidiscrimination and employment equity laws for people with disabilities in the United States and Canada. The author provides a detailed account of key pieces of legislation, the history of the disability rights movement, and the consequences of legislation in both Canada and the United States. The comparison shows how the environmental emphasis of the U.S. federal Americans with Disabilities Act has been particularly successful at reducing physical obstacles involved with employment, but both Americans and Canadians with disabilities face continued barriers to economic security and employment. The author, a Canadian, then offers possible solutions to lessen discrimination of disabled people in Canada.

Reference

U.S. Department of Labor, Bureau of Labor Statistics. 2013. "Persons with a Disability: Labor Force Characteristics 2013." Available at http://www.bls.gov/news.release/disabl.nr0.htm (accessed January 14, 2015).

Excerpted from Atkins, C. G. K. 2006. "A Cripple at a Rich Man's Gate: A Comparison of Disability, Employment and Anti-discrimination Law in the United States and Canada." *Canadian Journal of Law and Society* 21(2): 87–111. Reprinted with the permission of Cambridge University Press.

This chapter[1] examines the legislative and judicial history of anti-discrimination and employment equity law with regard to persons with disabilities[2] in the United States and Canada. It compares the two countries' approaches to the problem of the disparate treatment of disabled citizens in the workplace, focusing particularly on the effectiveness of legal remedies during the last two decades. It presents a short history of statutes in both national jurisdictions aimed at ameliorating the economic and social disadvantages associated with disability. A comparison of court and tribunal decisions that result from these measures shows that the United States and Canada have distinctly separate judicial responses to anti-discrimination law; however, despite these differences, both disabled Americans and disabled Canadians continue to fare badly economically and in terms of actual numbers in the workforce.

The environmental portion of *The Americans with Disabilities Act (ADA)*[3] has been extremely successful in its requirement that American physical spaces become universally accessible to people with a wide variety of impairments. It is the employment sections of the statute that have been much less successful, with plaintiffs losing the vast majority of court cases that attempt to negotiate individual access to the workplace. Thus, while the United States has done a good job of promoting physical access to get people to work, disabled Americans still face inordinate obstacles in actually securing and maintaining employment. Conversely, Canada has no federal statutes that require environmental accessibility; it does, however, prohibit discrimination on the basis of (perceived or actual) impairment in the *Canadian Charter of Rights and Freedoms*.[4] The provinces and territories all have similar prohibitions embedded in their human rights statutes. Nonetheless, the Canadian physical environment remains markedly inaccessible. Yet, judicial, tribunal, and arbitration decisions in Canada have been far more amenable in disputes about access and employment than their American counterparts. Canadians have taken a more universal approach to disability, treating it as a social phenomenon, rather than a characteristic of individual employees. Consequently, plaintiffs have received far more positive results in Canada than in the United States. Nonetheless, statistics show that the disabled continue to suffer disproportionate disadvantage in the area of employment in both countries.

When disability is viewed as a social issue and a universal remedy or solution is sought, access and anti-discrimination efforts tend to be more successful. The best examples of this can be found in Canadian Supreme Court decisions and in the environmental portions of the *ADA*. When access is particularized, and when individuals with disabilities must negotiate independently for access to the workplace or the environment, access and antidiscrimination efforts fail. In drawing this comparison, this chapter postulates that the successes in both jurisdictions can be attributed to a *universal* approach to the problem of disability and, further, that the failures in both the United States and Canada can be attributed to placing an obligation on disabled individuals to negotiate access singly and in isolation. For the most part, Canadian legislators have disregarded the need for overarching laws that require universal accessibility.[5] This means that disabled Canadians must negotiate accessibility on their own, resulting in a largely inaccessible social and physical Canadian environment. Gaining access to housing, transportation, education, and retail and public spaces remains a fundamental problem for disabled Canadians. American judges' insistence on scrutinizing the nature of plaintiffs' individual impairments means that disabled Americans are often barred from seeking workplace accommodations and thus become disqualified for jobs.

With the exception of the province of Ontario, Canada has yet to pass any substantive legislation that deals explicitly with the disparate treatment of persons with disabilities. It is thus in a position to try to craft truly effective statutes. Given that legislation and/or judicial decisions that reflect social modeling of disability and focus on making requirements that can be *universally* applied are the most successful in achieving access for persons with disabilities, any Canadian legislation that deals with this issue should embody the spirit of these effective legal forms. Consequently, Canadian legislators should craft laws that require universal accessibility in the manner of the environment portions of the United States' *ADA* and in the manner of most Canadian judicial decisions.

Moreover, these laws should demand that workplaces, regardless of the presence, population, or types of disabilities in their workforces, be universally accessible. These requirements would be enacted in much the same manner that occupational health and safety laws have been integrated into the workplace. And, making communities and workplaces widely and universally accessible would *not* preclude persons with disabilities from being able to negotiate customized access to physical and workplace environments. It seems reasonable that existing adaptations could be tweaked to accommodate individual needs and encourage greater social and economic independence. And, while businesses may protest that modifying job sites carries too heavy a financial burden, similar objections occurred when occupational health and safety laws were first introduced a century ago, but businesses nonetheless adapted and continued to prosper despite the presence of these statutes and the ongoing requirement to maintain and update equipment and safety features.

Finding the political will to reduce physical, social, and economic barriers for citizens with disabilities will require that Canadian legislators create laws that make both public and private spaces universally accessible. Additionally, Canada needs to compel employers to create and sustain universally accessible workplaces, regardless of the number or presence of disabled employees. Such an approach would have economic and social benefits for the community as a whole, by integrating and empowering individuals who are normally dependent on the state or care-providers to mediate their social, political, and economic needs. Moreover, the creation and adoption of such universal measures will have other, less obvious social benefits that will ameliorate the lives of those who regarded themselves as able-bodied.[6]

History of the Disability Rights Movement

In 1948 the United Nations (UN) enacted the *Universal Declaration of Human Rights*,[7] globalizing the liberal concepts of individual freedom and autonomy. Although the entitlement to "rights and freedoms" does not explicitly include people with disabilities, the original decree's intent was universal in its scope, and one could argue that persons with disabilities are included in the "other status" of article 2. However, it is notable that the proclamation nowhere articulates protections and/or rights for a class of individuals who might be discriminated against on the basis of an actual or perceived mental or physical impairment. Against the backdrop of the genocides and destruction of the Second World War, the UN's focus on the tendency of the characteristics of

race, gender, class, religion, and political affiliation to provoke discrimination is understandable. But, as evidenced by its language, there is an absence of any recognition of disabled people's particular vulnerability to oppression and discrimination. UN representatives seem either oblivious to or unconcerned by the fact that the technology that Nazi Germany developed for the eradication of "undesirable" social castes was, in fact, perfected during the euthanization of mentally, physically, and psychiatrically disabled Germans who were seen by Hitler (and some physician groups) as unproductive burdens on the state.[8] Nonetheless, as a result of the large number of people disabled during the war, a new sociomedical, postwar movement—rehabilitation— attempted to reintegrate impaired individuals into peacetime society. However, these individuals were viewed as defective and in need of normalizing psychologically and physically, regardless of the origin of their impairment. Through effective lobbying, medical and social resources in countries such the United States, England, and Canada were allocated to promote the health of the nation by curing disabled people of their abnormalities. The "whole man theory" of rehabilitation psychologized people with disabilities, claiming that they were essentially neurotic and needed to be encouraged to mentally overcome their physical impairments.[9]

In the 1970s, views of disability began to change. The civil rights movements of the 1960s not only spawned racial, sexual, and gender consciousness but also a burgeoning pressure from people with disabilities to gain greater access to their communities. The passage in the United States of the *Rehabilitation Act of 1973*[10]— in response to the creation of a whole new generation of disabled veterans from the conflict in Vietnam—was a harbinger of this change. In 1975, the United Nations signed the *Declaration of the Rights of Disabled Persons*,[11] which explicitly evoked the 1948 declaration's commitment to justice, stating that "disabled persons have the same civil and political rights as other human beings." However, the document also acknowledged that member states might not uphold disabled people's rights because "certain countries, at their present stage of development, can devote only limited efforts to this end."[12] States would have to commit substantial finances to secure disabled persons' social and political participation. Apparently, the UN saw the required economic investment as too burdensome for some nations.

Representatives believed that the political rights of disabled persons were costly. Nonetheless, individual states passed (and continue to pass) resolutions that assert these rights within their own jurisdictions. The United States' *ADA* of 1990 is perhaps the most far-reaching and ambitious of these and serves as a model for other jurisdictions which hope to protect persons with disabilities from discrimination. In 2002, the Disabled People's International met in Japan where delegates strategized about eradicating the "continued exclusion of people with disabilities from the mainstream development process" and urged governments to actively integrate disabled citizens. Almost 30 years after the United Nations' declaration on the rights of persons with disabilities and a full decade after the passage of the United States' *ADA*, the question that begs answering is whether in fact these pieces of human rights legislation have been effective in garnering access and protections for disabled individuals in the workplace.

The United States: Statutes and Disability and Employment

The *ADA* of 1990 has been hailed as the greatest piece of human rights legislation in American history (and perhaps internationally) since the *Civil Rights Act* of 1964.[13] It explicitly endorses equal opportunities for individuals with disabilities. It states that:

> Individuals with disabilities are a discrete and insular minority who have faced restrictions and limitations, subjected to a history of purposeful unequal treatment and, relegated to a position of political powerlessness in our society, based on characteristics that are beyond the control of such individuals and resulting from stereotypic assumptions not truly indicative of the individual ability of such individuals to participate in, and contribute to, society; . . .[14]

The drafting legislators recognized that, until this Act, individuals with disabilities had no effective legal recourse against discrimination in American society. While the Act overtly combats discriminatory practices, it is not a social welfare document. In averring the inalienability of civil rights for the disabled, Congress acknowledged that American society was structurally discriminatory and provided the means by which these architectural and systemic injustices could be remedied.

The Act tackles two main problems, (1) environmental barriers and (2) impediments to employment, and it imposes on employers a "duty to accommodate" disabled employees.

Overall, the drafters of the *ADA* sought to provide disabled Americans with more than adequate safeguards against discrimination; they also endeavored to create an American community that was universally accessible to individuals with a wide variety and degree of impairments. True to the liberal traditions of American politics, the framers wrote that "the continuing existence of unfair and unnecessary discrimination and prejudice denies people with disabilities the opportunity to compete on an equal basis [. . .] and costs the United States billions of dollars in unnecessary expenses resulting from dependency and non-productivity."[15] The *ADA* thus reverses earlier principles of rehabilitation in federal legislation which focused on individuals' inability to successfully adapt and, instead, focuses on modifying the physical, social, and economic environment. In endowing and reaffirming rights, congressional representatives hoped to create a situation in which disabled people could fend for themselves. Politically, the support for civil liberties for disabled Americans becomes a means by which the state can eventually withdraw its ongoing financial and administrative support of the disabled. The law endorses the creation of a nation in which those who have historically been dependent on others (and the state) for their economic, physical, and social well-being can become notionally and actually "equal" and "independent" citizens—free to look after themselves, pursue their own interests, and thereby sustain themselves financially.

Canada: Statutes and Disability and Employment

Canada's legislative history with regard to people with disabilities is less dense and younger than that of the United States. The federal Department of Justice itemizes only a few pieces of legislation prior to the enactment of the *Canadian Charter of Rights and Freedoms* in 1982.[16] While Canadians may well have subscribed to similar constructions of the disabled person as their American colleagues, few of these attitudes were formalized in law (except perhaps in social welfare portions of legislation devoted to looking after veteran's affairs).

In response to the *Charter*, each province and territory has adopted its own version of a bill of rights that articulates civil freedoms in each jurisdiction. These attend to relations between private individuals and enterprises. Provincial human rights commissions adjudicate complaints of discrimination involving individual parties and within the private sector. While all the commissions are empowered to award damages, these are usually not highly remunerative and it is common for respondents/defendants to attend educational, "human rights seminars" as a part of the final decision and settlement. Unlike similar cases in the United States, their aim is to reform discriminatory behaviors through mediation, accommodation, and education and not through punitive damage awards. As well, unlike the *ADA*, these Canadian charters are generalized in their scope. However, while all the human rights codes forbid discrimination in employment on the basis of disability, some provincial statutes are much more detailed and include a clear duty to accommodate persons with disabilities, while still others have put affirmative action programs into place.[17] As an example, the Ontario Human Rights Commission states:

> The duty to accommodate persons with disabilities means accommodation must be provided in a manner that most respects the dignity of the person, if to do so does not create undue hardship. Dignity includes consideration of how accommodation is provided and the individual's own participation in the process.[18]

Here, like the drafters of the *ADA*, Ontario is concerned with causing undue hardship to those who must accommodate persons with disabilities. Nonetheless, the province stipulates that ". . . the person responsible for accommodation would be required to establish that the costs, which remain after steps are taken to recover costs, will alter the essential nature or substantially affect the viability of the enterprise."[19] And even when a person or business can prove undue hardship, the Ontario commission requires that less costly means of accommodation be explored. More importantly, proving undue hardship does *not* necessarily relieve the respondent of a duty to accommodate—instead, a human rights commission will seek to mitigate this hardship and thus encourage workplace accommodation for the disabled employee nonetheless.

In 2001, provincial legislators passed the *Ontarians with Disabilities Act* (ODA).[20] At the time, it seemed as though Canada might be forging new statutory ground with regard to operationalizing the rights of disabled persons. The intent was to institute an act that had similar protections to those guaranteed by the *ADA* in the United States. But political negotiations and concessions diluted some of its original terms, which meant that disabled activists were almost immediately critical of its provisions. They outlined various weaknesses, such as: (1) it only addressed the public but not the private sector in its scope; (2) it permitted too many exemptions, allowing institutions to escape requirements for accommodation and universal access; (3) it lacked a timeline for instituting the changes it mandated and; (4) it did not provide any monetary incentives or grants to finance modifications and renovations to improve access.[21] But in 2005, the government responded to these criticisms by amending the Act. The changes were aimed at "developing, implementing and enforcing accessibility standards in order to achieve accessibility for Ontarians with disabilities with respect to goods, services, facilities, accommodation, employment, buildings, structures and premises on or before January 1, 2025."[22] These standards were created and will be maintained with ongoing consultation with the disabled community. And, specifying standards will make the enforcement of the *ODA* much more possible. A recent search of Ontario court and tribunal records reveals no cases which make specific reference to the *ODA* in its revised form and so it is unclear to what extent the new standards have altered the public sector they sought to change.

A Theorized Comparison of the United States and Canada on Employment and Disability

In comparing the United States and Canada, it is apparent that the statutory fabric of each country is quite different when dealing with issues of disability and employment. Liberal theories of the individual tend to infiltrate American law and American courts' interpretations of law. Canada has a legal and political persona that exhibits both liberal and non-liberal traits. Given Canada's more socialist nature, it is paradoxical that it is the United States that has passed seemingly more revolutionary legislation in terms of encouraging disabled people's participation in the overall community. The comparison of the two countries raises a series of questions. Why does Canada, with a state-subsidized, universal health insurance system, lack a universal disability insurance scheme which guarantees individuals access to their communities and to employment? Why do the United States, which generally reject universal models, enact a sweeping piece of legislation (i.e., the *ADA*) that creates universal accessibility in the social and physical environment and negotiates accommodation in the workplace? Finally, why has the presence of laws in both countries, which aim at increasing the participation of disabled adults in the workforce, failed so badly in terms of actual numbers?[23]

Paradoxically, American liberalism has consistently defeated any political drive for a universal health system, yet at the same time it is this liberalism that encouraged the passage of the *Americans with Disabilities Act*. Perhaps, legislators' awareness of the lack of social welfare support in the United States and their heightened sensitivity to discriminatory practices—brought about by a variety of civil rights movements, including the disabled rights movement—together forged the political will to try to create a level playing-field of opportunity and competition for disabled Americans. The *ADA* focuses on equality, not on social welfare. It aims at a climate in which persons with disabilities have an equality of physical and economic access to the American marketplace. A political spirit of individual rights thus produced an Act which, in its most successful aspects, envisions a universally accessible society.

With Canada's contrasting affection for social welfare programs, universal healthcare, and newly minted individual rights, it is surprising that disabled Canadians do not fare better. Politically, Canadians pay more attention to the equality of result rather than the equality of opportunity. Most people feel that the country's guarantee of universal access to healthcare is a defining national trait. Both provincial and federal governments are keenly aware that they must not appear to dismantle this system even as they modify it. For the most part, Canadians comfortably assume that when they become ill, the government-sponsored system will look after them. Consequently, they tend to extrapolate that the government will again look after them when they become disabled—which is unfortunately not the case.[24] And, while the medical system continues to provide care, accessible housing and accessible transportation either do not exist or are severely limited. (Throughout

the last 15 years, all levels of government have withdrawn from a variety of social services—funding, transportation, and vocational programs oriented toward the disabled have all but disappeared.) Consequently, a misguided confidence in government social welfare means that there is little or no popular, political will which recognizes that the needs and rights of Canadians with disabilities are not being met. The presumption is that the government looks after disabled Canadians because being disabled is equated with being ill. What they do not realize is that government policy makes a clear distinction between disability and illness—the state provides hospitals but not necessarily accessible housing.

Regardless of their differences, a comparison of the economic status of disabled Americans and disabled Canadians reveals that minority civil rights legislation has failed disabled citizens. While Canadian judges act with a holistic approach, Canadian policies simply do not. Canadians with disabilities need legislation that parallels the environmental sections of the *ADA*, which have a universalistic approach to disability and the environment. Without proper transportation, the reduction of physical barriers, and the modification of both private and public premises, human rights legislation will have little effect on disabled Canadians' access to the workplace. In the United States, Americans with disabilities have a universally accessible environment. Each individual does not have to negotiate his or her way into a building, gaining appropriate accommodations such as Braille elevator buttons, ramps, and handrails only if they can prove that they are "limited substantially" by their blindness, paraplegia, or arthritis. A full spectrum of accommodations greets all Americans regardless of disability. It is when each individual must seek his or her unique employment accommodations that the American statute breaks down and individuals cannot negotiate employment and gain economic independence.

A Possible Canadian Solution to Discrimination against the Disabled

Canadians should learn from both the successes and failings of the *ADA*, as well as note the holistic approach of their own Supreme Court. As a country, we need to adopt a similar environmental formula to that of the Americans, requiring that all buildings, transportation, public offices, businesses, housing, and educational institutions have universal accommodations. This would give Canadians with disabilities a much needed liberty to move and act freely in Canadian society. As a political community, Canada needs to take responsibility for facilitating the removal of environmental and attitudinal barriers which currently prevent disabled persons from experiencing the true extent of their equal, social, and political membership. Doing so would be in keeping with a national, sociopolitical culture which values and encourages diversity, equality, and non-discrimination.[25]

Following upon this logic of universal access, if Canadian jurisdictions enact specific laws regarding employment, they should mandate that *all* employers have universal accommodations in place *regardless* of the presence of people with impairments. Undoubtedly, business will complain of financial hardship, and disabled activists might argue that the individuality and uniqueness of impairments would make this impossible. However, in my conception, there is no reason that individuals could not continue to negotiate the fine-tuning of their accommodation needs with a universal system in place. As for the burden of costs, the U.S. Department of Labor estimates that the average cost of workplace accommodations is US$600.[26] Similar efforts in Canada should be no more expensive. Moreover, the government already demands through occupational safety laws that employers provide safe working conditions irrespective of expense. Historically, employers argued that occupational safety statutes were prohibitively expensive when first enacted, but the economy seems to have successfully weathered their imposition. In the same way, Canadian governments should impose a burden of universal accessibility on the workplace. Over the years, specific equipment will have to be updated, modified, or replaced, but this remains true of most capital expenditures that business currently support (e.g., computers, copy machines, office furniture), and this turnover would simply be imbedded in the costs of conducting business. Businesses would be accessible to not only potentially disabled employees, but also disabled clients and disabled consumers as well. Moreover, because many people often find ramps, grab bars, and other modifications unsightly, the presence of universally accessible workplaces would assist in changing attitudes of fellow workers and employers. Canadians would become habituated to environmental and

workplace accommodations, rendering them less stigmatized. Further, the public might even discover unforeseen advantages associated with universal adaptations (e.g., ease of entering premises with wheeled bags, carts, and buggies; finding innovative uses for video and audio software; enjoying more spacious and better lit environments). Such mandatory changes would thus enable Canadians with disabilities not only physically but socially, politically, and financially. Making universal environments more common in Canada might also encourage a bit more awareness and activism within its citizenry. Canadians might *cease* seeing "disabled people" simply as "sick people" and thus entitled to more than the "care" provisions of the medical and social welfare systems. Finally, the successful inclusion and integration of disabled persons in Canada's social and economic life can only contribute to the overall welfare of the community as a whole—a justification that might not appeal to the rugged individualism of American politics but one with which Canadians are familiar and which they might find persuasive.

Notes

1. The title refers to the New Testament story of Lazarus; a crippled beggar who lay and died outside a rich man's gate, he then ascended to heaven whereas the rich man, upon his death, descended to hell (Luke 16:19–26).

2. While the term "persons with disabilities" is the most accurate description of individuals who have physical, mental or emotional impairments who confront social and environmental barriers, I employ "disabled persons" or "disabled individual" to signify the same category of people. I realize that while these terms are not the best, I use them as a stylistic tool, in order to guard my prose from sounding redundant.

3. *Americans with Disabilities Act*, 42 U.S.C. §12204 (1990) [*ADA*].

4. *Canadian Charter of Rights and Freedoms*, Part I of the *Constitution Act*, 1982, being Schedule B to the *Canada Act* 1982 (U.K.) 1982, c. 11 [*Charter*].

5. As of 2006, the federal New Democratic Party (NDP) has shown some interest in a bill which would enforce accessibility nationally. Peter Julian, an NDP M.P. from British Columbia, has drafted a "National Persons with Disabilities Act," to be put forward as a private member's bill.

6. An example of a beneficial side effect of accessibility is the fact that accessible ramps benefit individuals with

wheeled suitcases, carts and strollers, as well as those who use wheelchairs. I mention some of these less obvious advantages in the final section of this chapter.

7. *Universal Declaration of Human Rights,* GA Res. 217(III), UN GAOR, 3d Sess., Supp. No. 13, UN Doc. A/810 (1948) 71 [*Universal Declaration*].

8. For more on the role that medicalized killing of the disabled played in the development of gas chamber technology of the Nazi concentration camps, see Robert Jay Lifton, *The Nazi Doctors: Medical Killing and the Psychology of Genocide* (New York: Basic Books, 1986).

9. See Ruth O'Brien, *Crippled Justice: The History of Modern Disability Policy in the Workplace* (Chicago: University of Chicago Press, 2001), 86 [*Crippled Justice*].

10. *Rehabilitation Act of 1973,* Pub. L. No. 93–112, §504, 87 Stat. at 355 [*Rehabilitation Act*].

11. G.A. Res. 3447 (XXX), 30 U.N. GAOR Supp. (No. 34), U.N. Doc. A/10034 (1975).

12. Ibid., 88.

13. See *Civil Rights Act of 1964,* P.L. 88–353, 78 Stat. 241 (1964).

14. See *ADA, supra* note 3.

15. See *ADA, supra* note 3, §12101.

16. The only legislation that the federal Department of Justice departmental web site notes, prior to the adoption of human rights statutes, is the enactment and repeal of the province of Alberta's sterilization laws in 1948 and 1972, respectively, and Ontario's Blind Person Right's Act in 1970. See Department of Justice Canada, http://canada.justice.gc.ca/en/.

17. Given the constraints of this chapter, I do not itemize each province's and territory's specific human rights legislation; instead I choose here to focus on specifics of some provinces. My conclusions can be extrapolated, with some variation, to other provincial jurisdictions. In the area of human rights statutes, this cross-jurisdictional correspondence is largely the result of the constitutional entrenchment of the *Charter*.

18. See Ontario Human Rights Commission, "Policy Guidelines on Disability and the Duty to Accommodate," November 23, 2000, http://www.ohrc.on.ca/en/policy-and-guidelines-disability-and-duty-accommodate (p. 12).

19. Ibid., 37.

20. *Accessibility for Ontarians with Disabilities Act,* S.O. 2005, c. 11 [*ODA*].

21. In the United States, the *ADA* had been originally and similarly attacked for its lack of financial assistance. Ultimately, this had not weakened the effectiveness of the environmental portions of the Act, nor had this been the difficulty with employment provisions, but Canadian activists nonetheless believed this to be a significant weakness of the Ontario legislation.

22. See *ODA, supra* note 34.

23. See *On Target, supra* note 57 at 5, 7, 9. By extrapolating from statistics on the types of disability exhibited in the Canadian workforce, it seems that less than 9.4 percent of the working population is disabled. Further, "the rate of non-participation is over twice as high for people without disabilities." The U.S. Census Bureau compiled data using the Survey of Income and Program Participation (SIPP) showing that despite the *ADA*'s passage the percent of disabled people in the workforce remained relatively stable during the 1990s. See *Current Population Reports, supra* note 52.

24. In numerous discussions I've had with my Canadian and American peers, they almost always express disbelief that the government does not subsidize disabled people more fully in Canada. They erroneously presume that given the state provides universal health insurance, it provides universal access to equipment, transportation, housing, and benefits. In fact, programs and policies to assist the disabled with the accessibility costs are severely limited and vary from region to region.

25. The constraints of implementing this national sociopolitical culture of diversity and nondiscrimination, particularly with regard to disability, were captured in a recent Supreme Court case. In 2002, the B.C. Supreme Court held that the province's denial of treatment to autistic children contravened the equality rights laid out in section 15 of the *Charter*. Canada's Supreme Court later overturned this decision concluding that the government in British Columbia had not discriminated against the plaintiff in denying payment for a newly emergent therapy for autism, nor had it violated the *Canada Health Act* because the statute does "not promise that any Canadian will receive funding for all medically required treatment." See *Auton (Guardian ad litem of) v. British Columbia (Attorney General),* [2002] B.C.J. No. 2258; [2004] 3 S.C.R. 657.

26. See Job Accommmodation Network (a service of the Office of Disability Employment Policy, U.S. Department of Labor) fact sheet: https://askjan.org/media/lowcosthighimpact.html

Questions

1. What is the ADA? What did it do? What does the author mean when referring to the "environmental portion of the ADA"? How has it been successful?
2. The author compares the United States and Canada on laws concerning disability and employment. What ideological and political difference might account for differences in the laws?
3. The author, a Canadian, makes an argument for how Canada might improve their efforts to prevent employment discrimination based on disability. What are the recommendations? How can the United States use law to improve employment prospects for people with disabilities?
4. Since the publication of this chapter, the Patient Protection and Affordable Care Act 2010 (usually referred to as "Obamacare" or the Affordable Care Act) was passed in the United States. But it was not passed without considerable debate; and while the act has resulted in millions of people having health insurance, government involvement in creating accessible health care continues to be a contentious issue for many in the United States. Based on the author's discussion of the United States and Canada, what might this change in U.S. healthcare policy mean for disability and discrimination at work?

31

Race, Hyper-Incarceration, and U.S. Poverty Policy in Historic Perspective

REUBEN JONATHAN MILLER

In the 1980s, the war on drugs was in full swing. Nancy Reagan indoctrinated schoolchildren to "just say no," and DARE brought police officers into the classroom to teach substance abuse prevention. In 1986, Representative James Wright Jr., a Democrat from Texas, introduced the Anti-Drug Abuse Act of 1986, which Reagan signed in October of that year. Among other things, the act created criminal penalties for simple possession of a controlled substance, established minimum mandatory sentences, and designated designer drugs similar to but not listed as schedule I substances to be treated as such. Nonetheless, within a decade, the crack epidemic ravaged inner cities. And "get tough" legislation, along with hyper-surveillance of Black communities and other racialized practices within the criminal

---

Excerpted from Miller, Reuben Jonathan. 2013. "Race, Hyper-Incarceration, and US Poverty Policy in Historic Perspective." *Sociology Compass* 7:573–589. © 2013 John Wiley & Sons Ltd.

justice system, led to a massive increase in incarceration in the United States. As we see in this reading, at a time when crime in the United States was dropping, incarceration increased sevenfold.

Mass incarceration from the 1980s through today, moreover, has had devastating consequences for communities of color. As Reuben Jonathan Miller explains, mass incarceration is really a story of race and class inequality. Men of color and women of color are disproportionately incarcerated at disgraceful levels. Young Black men without a high school education face an astounding 58.9 percent risk of being incarcerated by their mid-thirties (Pettit and Western 2004). The same cohort of white men face just an 11.2 percent risk. As Pettit and Western (2004) demonstrate, going to jail is a more common life experience for many Black men than going to college or joining the military.

Miller demonstrates how racialized mass incarceration is the byproduct of a long history of race- and class-based policies aimed to discipline and regulate poor people of color in general and Black families and workers in particular. Miller puts forth that social welfare policies designed to intervene in Black families and crime control measures aimed at punishing low-level offender Blacks today have their origins in the Victorian era and southern reconstruction poverty management strategies. By detailing these connections, Miller demonstrates how social policy in effect punishes people because of their race.

References

Anti-Drug Abuse Act of 1986. H.R. 5484. Available at https://www.govtrack.us/congress/bills/99/hr5729#overview (accessed on January 13, 2015).

Pettit, Becky, and Bruce Western. 2004. "Mass Imprisonment and the Life Course: Race and Class Inequality in U.S. Incarceration." *American Sociological Review* 69(2): 151–169.

From Marx's attempts to detangle the paradox of the political economy to Weber's bleak characterization of bureaucratic rationality sociologists have long examined the contradictions of democratic governance and the punishing capacities of state institutions. This is especially true of the modern welfare state. The welfare state has been characterized as a regulatory apparatus employed to legitimate the contradictions of modern political economies and a disciplinary mode of social control, fostering the expansion of precarious labor in times of prosperity, while diminishing working class solidarity during times of political unrest (Piven and Cloward 1993). It has been implicated in bureaucratic processes of racial stratification, instantiating the stigma of dependence while ossifying the social standing of racialized groups (Lieberman 1998; Gilens 1999). More recently, sociologists have examined the contributions of social welfare policy to the dramatic, racially targeted expansion of the U.S. prison system (Beckett and Western 2001; Wacquant 2009).

In this chapter, I bring the literature on welfare reform into discussion with scholarship on race, crime control, and social welfare policy. I trace the genesis of hyper-incarceration (Wacquant 2001)—the targeted policing, arrest, and imprisonment of low-income, predominantly Black inner city men—and the moral suasion imposed on the recipients of traditional social welfare services to the poverty management strategies of the Victorian era and the southern reconstruction period. I highlight public and scholarly discourses used to construct the impoverished, inner city Black family as the target of criminal justice and social welfare intervention, show the ways in which policy decisions contribute to the punishment of race across historical domains, and discuss how the United States has been reconfigured to facilitate these trends. Doing so demonstrates the long-standing collusion between welfare state and criminal justice actors, highlights the significance of race in the development of social policy, and exhibits the importance of social policy decision making for contemporary race and ethnic relations.

Hyper-Incarceration: A Brief Primer

In just under 20 years, the U.S. prison demographic shifted from two-thirds white to over two-thirds non-white (Wacquant, 2001). African Americans, who have historically comprised just over 12 percent of the U.S. population, now represent nearly half of all persons held under lock and key (Maurer 2006). At the same time, the number of prisoners increased sevenfold between 1980 and 2010, reaching a figure that exceeded 2.3 million at the height of incarceration during this recent and historic prison boom. Nearly half of all arrests over the last several decades have been for formal drug charges (upwards of 80 percent in some municipalities according to Lurigio et al. 2010), with almost two-thirds of all new arrests composed of Black men, most of whom were convicted for low-level drug offenses (Alexander 2009). To further complicate matters, released prisoners returning to their home communities and the prisoner reentry organizations that serve them are overwhelmingly concentrated in low-income communities of color (R. Miller 2014). As a result, more than half of the prisoners from the country's most populous urban regions are policed, arrested, returned, and provided services to rehabilitate them all within the very low-income neighborhoods they call home (R. Miller 2014; Peck and Theodore 2009), raising important questions about the concentration of social disadvantage and the containment of unskilled Black laborers (Wacquant 2009).

Scholars have designated the historic prison expansion project and the overwhelming focus of criminal justice intervention within racialized districts of urban disadvantage (Sampson and Loeffler, 2010) "mass incarceration" (Western 2006), the "culture of control" (Garland 2001), "racialized mass incarceration" (BoBo and Thompson 2010), and the "New Jim Crow" (Alexander 2009). Noting the selective targeting of the criminal justice system and the concentration of criminal justice interventions within low-income communities, sociologist Loïc Wacquant designates the era of prison expansion "hyper-incarceration."

It is important to note that the dramatic increase in the size and scope of the U.S. prison system was coupled with an equally historic retrenchment of the social safety net, ushering in what scholars have described as the "punitive turn" in social welfare and criminal justice policy. Building on groundwork laid during the Reagan administration, Congress passed the Personal Responsibility and Work Opportunities Reconciliation Act of 1996 (PRWORA), making good on President William Jefferson Clinton's promise to "end welfare as we know it." Through the advent of new modes of surveillance, draconian eligibility criteria, the sanctioning

of non-traditional family forms, and the enforcement of stringent work requirements, this new legislation moved many dependent poor families off the "dole" as evidenced by the nearly 65 percent drop in the welfare caseload in just under a decade and onto the rolls of the low-wage labor market. PRWORA has had considerable fallout for the racialized targets of urban poverty policy. With fewer benefits and unsustainable wages, scholars have argued that welfare reform helped concretize the positions of the raced targets of social policy within the lower reaches of a deindustrialized economy (Peck 2010; Piven and Cloward [1971] 1993; Wacquant 2009).

The austere turn in social welfare policy and the punitive turn in criminal justice administration have been considered characteristic of U.S.-style neoliberalism— the dominant policy regime in the United States for more than three decades. Neoliberalism has been defined as a set of clustered social and economic policies that privilege market deregulation and limited state intervention, and a logic pervading social, political, and economic discourses, the definition of social problems, and the development of social policy (Harcourt 2011; Harvey 2007; Peck 2010; Wacquant 2012a, 2012b). Following this logic, both PRWORA and mass incarceration are considered emblematic of neoliberal social and economic policy. Both followed a considerable retraction of the social state. In criminal justice, scholars suggest that the state's commitment to rehabilitate prisoners through education and social programs was unseated by commitments to deter crime and incapacitate ex-offenders (Feeley and Simon 1992; Garland 2001; Wacquant 2009). Rehabilitation has, however, endured in modified forms (Phelps 2011) ranging from the therapeutic interventions available within prisons and courts (Fox 1999) to the fragmented constellation of prisoner reentry services operating within prisoners' respective receiving communities (Peck and Theodore 2009; Haney 2010). Despite this, scholars widely agree that the political logics animating criminal justice administration shifted from a rehabilitative to a more punitive orientation.

On the welfare front, cash benefits were significantly decreased, and welfare programs increasingly focused on behavioral modification and the veneration of work, making the poor rather than the states responsible for the mitigation of their own social problems. Thus, punishment scholars have labeled this historic moment an era of neoliberal penality, where social marginality is managed in punitive ways through welfare state and criminal justice institutions (Beckett and Western 2001; Harcourt 2011; Wacquant 2009). A cursory examination of the demographic profiles of the prison and public welfare clientele makes this readily apparent. Blacks and Latinos represent disproportionately large shares of both the prison population and the public welfare caseload, with nearly identical rates of unemployment, negative mental health outcomes, and poverty—more than half of each institution's population lives at or below just half of the U.S. poverty line (Wacquant 2009).

The prison boom has made the United States the world leader in the global "race to incarcerate," with more people under state supervision than in any other country in the history of the world (Maurer 2006; Wacquant 2009). At the same time, welfare reform has added many poor families to the ranks of the working poor, contributing to record disparities in income, wealth, educational achievement, and mental and physiological health outcomes (Nkansah-Amankra, Agbanu, and Miller 2013).

Despite these trends, it is important to note "that the techniques of poverty management and even the disproportionate arrest and imprisonment of minority populations do not make neoliberal approaches to manage the urban poor unique" (Wacquant, 2012b). Rather, these techniques find their roots in colonial discourses on dependence, deviance, and the dangers of pauperism, the once-thought-to-be-outdated modes of racial control, and the selective enforcement of vagrancy convictions in the postbellum south. These techniques and the political logics that guide them were updated during the various "wars" on urban disadvantage: the "War on Poverty," the "War on Drugs," and what historian Michal Katz (2001) has labeled the "War on Dependence." Thus, the disproportionate arrest, sentencing, and incarceration of African Americans particularly, along with the project of responsibilization rolled out under the banner of U.S. neoliberalism more specifically, articulates with longstanding policies and political discourses targeting Black pauperism, Black crime, and Black dependence on the state, which reached their zenith in the regressive 1990s. These practices and the punitive trends they inspire are documented in classical sociological works (see particularly Du Bois [1899] 1995) but have been overlooked in the extant literature on punishment and social welfare provision.

Black Dependence and the Danger of the Dole

Scholars have analyzed the significance of U.S. race and ethnic relations in the development and administration of the welfare state (Neubeck and Casenave 2001; Lieberman 1998; Quadagno 1994). The history of social provision makes the significance of race, perhaps, most apparent. More than a century before the passage of New Deal policies, political discourses about poverty, dependence, and race culminated in profound ways, leading to the ratification of the New Poor Law Act and the concurrent passage of the Total Emancipation Act of 1834 (O'Connell 2009, 2010). The act abolished slavery in Britain and its colonies but did not extend freedom to all slaves. In the United States, economists of the Victorian era had already vigorously debated the role of slavery as a "barrier to the natural motive to labor" (Martin 2008; O'Connell, 2009). Freed slaves, White abolitionists, and members of the Black resistance movements in Europe and the United States struggled for abolition, while at the same time labor reformers operating in the interest of working class whites advocated for labor rights and a sustainable wage. While labor activists openly complained of harsh workplace conditions and worker exploitation by land-owning industrial and agricultural capitalists, activists and labor reformers contended that slaves in the United States were better off than many of their constituents. Access to poor relief was rigidly policed, drawing racial lines where intuitive labor coalitions may have ordinarily formed (Du Bois [1935] 1999; O'Connell 2009).

Prior to the onset of the Civil War, welfare discourses linked the fate of the slave, the freedman, and the pauper (O'Connell 2009). Poverty experts from various fields compared the living conditions and "natural inclinations" of each population, marshaling statistical analyses and the latest social scientific techniques to determine their "readiness for economic freedom" (Martin 2008; O'Connell 2009). Invoking slaves "natural characteristics," Poor Law reformers contended that poor relief fostered a "slave mentality" among the white working class. Receipt of the "dole" was thought to "entitle men to all a slave's security for subsistence without his liabilities to punishment" (Kern 1998, 428, as quoted in O'Connell 2009), foreshadowing critiques of the "nanny state" and the "entitlement society" that would animate political discourses for nearly two centuries. At the same time, slaveholders invoked discourses from the Poor Law debates to support their contention that slaves were incapable of self-reliance and would instead end up on the incapacitating "dole" if granted freedom. Thus, the racist trope of Black dependence was used to delay freedom (and later the franchise) for Blacks, while delaying labor rights and the emergence of a formal welfare state, which arguably would have largely benefited poor white workers (Quadagno 1994). These developments have had notable consequences for the development of social welfare policy and shaped punishment and corrections in important ways.

Constructing the Black Vagrant

W. E. B. Du Bois was among the first scholars to explore the relationship between social welfare policy, race, and punishment during the postbellum period. In his seminal work, *Black Reconstruction in America, 1860–1880,* Du Bois ([1935] 1999) advanced a classical Marxist framework to understand the fates of the white and Black southern proletariat, the benefits reaped by southern states during reconstruction, and the eventual retrenchment of the Black freedman's newly acquired rights through the emergence of restrictive Black Codes and the repressive Jim Crow regime that followed. More importantly for this analysis, Du Bois underscored the importance of the advent of the U.S. Bureau of Refugees, Freedmen, and Abandoned Lands (The Freedman's Bureau), one of the first federally administered social welfare organizations in U.S. history, in the day-to-day lives of the Black southern proletariat (Du Bois [1935] 1999; Goldberg 2008).

The Freedman's Bureau was established in 1865 just months before the close of the Civil War. It provided emergency food, housing, clothing, and healthcare for refugees, former slaves, and poor whites in need. Amid resistance from the unseated white aristocracy, the Bureau established a system of free public education, increased healthcare access through the establishment of free public health clinics, and provided employment assistance for freed Blacks and their poor white, southern counterparts (Du Bois [1935] 1999; Goldberg 2008). These initiatives were federally funded, departing from the locally funded and administered system of poor

relief that existed prior to the Civil War. Along with the provision of what would now be termed public welfare, the Bureau mitigated labor disputes between white planters and Black farmers and assisted Black Civil War veterans who were systematically excluded from veterans pensions (Du Bois [1935] 1999; Goldberg 2008; Taylor 2009).

With more than 5 percent of the total African American population volunteering for combat during the Civil War, the special status afforded veterans due to high public regard for soldiers, and the generosity of Civil War pensions, which lifted many white families out of poverty during the period, hopes for reaching social and economic parity were high (Du Bois [1935] 1999; Goldberg 2008; U.S. Census Bureau 1860). Unfortunately for freedmen, their hopes for parity would be dashed. Hollandsworth (2008) found that there were significant barriers to Black participation in Civil War pensions.

With the systematic exclusion of Black veterans from pension benefits, the Bureau was able to fill crucial gaps in services for disabled would-be pensioners, taking an active role in the negotiation of labor contracts and legal matters for Black veterans and their families (Goldberg 2008). Despite these seemingly progressive policies, the Bureau's work stigmatized its largely Black client base through policies that further inculcated negative Black stereotypes. The redistributive nature of the Bureau's policies and the racial stigma of its client base fueled considerable resistance from unseated southern democrats and republican detractors alike who called for an end to the "failed experiment" just a few years after it was established. In addition, the Bureau struggled to shake the stigma of Black dependence and the general fear of Black pauperism, causing it to embrace a focus on contract labor that derailed a burgeoning spirit of Black entrepreneurship (Du Bois [1935] 1999; Farmer-Kaiser 2004).

Welfare and Punishment in the Postbellum South

The most salient function of the Bureau for contemporary social welfare policy was its promotion of low-wage labor. Due to the ongoing discourse around the nature of race and poverty, along with the supposed incapacitating character of the dole, eligibility for assistance was based on the willingness of former slaves to accept the "most visible and immediate" employment available (Du Bois [1935] 1999, as quoted in Taylor 2009). Freedmen, denied entry to the labor market along with agricultural entrepreneurship in the postbellum south, were forced to engage in sharecropping relationships on the plantations from which they were emancipated. Refusal to work, inability to cover debts incurred under the peonage system, changing jobs, or committing the slightest breach of contract were grounds for prosecution under southern vagrancy laws. Conviction as a vagrant meant lengthy terms of imprisonment under the chain gangs and convict leasing system. As a result, by the end of the nineteenth century, Blacks comprised more than 90 percent of the convict leasing system in a still agricultural but industrializing South (Gorman 1997). During this time, the southern prison system underwent a rapid, racially targeted expansion. Prisoners were sentenced at younger ages for longer periods of time and in exponentially greater volume. Georgia saw a tenfold increase in its prison population between 1865 and 1890. At the same time, Mississippi's prison population quadrupled, while Alabama's more than tripled (Mancini 1978), but these phenomena were not new. Noting racial disproportionality in the U.S. prison system, Beaumont et al. (1833) wrote: "We see that there is in prison, in the five states, 1 colored person out of 4 prisoners. In 1830, there was (in the same states) 1 free colored person out of 30 inhabitants."

Along with imprisonment, poor relief was used as a way to maintain racial and ethnic domination while ossifying the racial hierarchy (O'Connell 2009). As noted, poor relief was administered along racial lines in part to discourage working class solidarity. The construction of the Black vagrant in the public policy and scholarly discourses of the time also substantiated claims about the danger of Black dependence, and the "natural inclinations" of Black workers (and by extension their families), and discouraged the administration of the "dole" to lift poor Blacks out of poverty. The most "available and immediate" work was instead venerated as the antidote to Black poverty in the postbellum period, even when those working conditions were predatory. Thus, the administration of social welfare policy had not only stratifying effects, contributing to the very conditions of generational poverty they sought to avoid, and a general lack of cohesion among the southern proletariat through the inculcation of racial

animus via bureaucratic processes, hardening the racial hierarchy among poor workers, but also classifying effects as well, contributing to the ways in which racial categories were understood (see Wacquant 2012a).

Du Bois penned *Black Reconstruction* in the year congress passed the Social Security Act of 1935. A surface reading of this work reveals social policy and criminal justice administration as a unified mechanism of social control. A careful reading demonstrates the longstanding collusion between social welfare and criminal justice institutions in the production and maintenance of racialized ways of being in the social world. A critical reading highlights the need for an interactional and intersectional exploration of the experience of social policy as the experiences of freed slaves were mitigated by various axes of difference (including gender, region, and local sociopolitical factors). Du Bois, for example, noted but inadequately explored the significant differences in the experiences of poor whites, confederate soldiers, women, and youth from those of freedmen (Farmer-Kaiser 2004; Goldberg 2008). *Black Reconstruction* was among the first works to link social welfare administration, race, and the criminal justice system, laying the groundwork for a productive line of inquiry that would not resurface for nearly half a century.

The Freedman's Bureau closed its doors after just seven years of operation. Its short and overlooked history is significant, not only to the formal emergence of the welfare state but also to the shape of contemporary poverty policy in the United States. Its promotion of low-wage work (sharecropping), use of punishment to modify behavior (vagrancy convictions), and the target population of its interventions (Black freedmen and their families) would foreshadow the shape of social welfare policy, debates about the efficacy of urban policy expenditures, and concerns about the welfare dependence of what would come to be termed the "urban underclass," contributing to the shape of future public policy discourses in important ways that resonated throughout the regressive 1990s and beyond.

From the Urban Poor to the Underclass

The deep collusion between institutions of punishment and social welfare provision extend well beyond the postbellum South. Evidence of contemporary links between these twin institutions of control and social production can be found in the administration of criminal justice historically and contemporarily. By 1870, "moral regeneration" was established as the primary function of imprisonment in the United States through the drafting of the Declaration of Principles (Western 2006). Prison officials tasked with detaining prisoners were also charged with their rehabilitation. This was to be done through a system of religious ritual, moral suasion, and employment occurring inside prisons (Foucault 1977) and within community-based organizations known as prisoner aid societies. Thus, society and the very communities that prisoners came from were deemed responsible for ensuring ex-offenders were successfully integrated into their respective communities, had sufficient work opportunities to support their families, and were given an opportunity to contribute to society in productive ways. To accomplish this, prisoner aid societies were expected to work alongside probation officers, an occupational category overwhelmingly staffed by social workers and seminary graduates. Rehabilitation was understood as a process through which prisoners were resocialized, acclimating them to the worlds of work through prison labor, work release programs, and the moralizing effects of participation in the various organizations of civil society. Labor was not only central to the reform project but also the establishment of employment was itself a formal condition of parole (Simon 1993). This clustering of criminal justice policy initiatives has been aptly designated penal welfarism by sociologist David Garland (2001) due to its emphasis on prisoner rehabilitation through welfarist policies.

Rehabilitation was considered to be the modus operandi of the U.S. prison system for more than a century. Law and society scholars have, however, noted that punishment strategies vary considerably by region. Using Arizona as a case study, Mona Lynch (2009) suggests that the rehabilitative ideal did not have the same kinds of institutional roots in the "new sunbelt" as it did in the industrial North. Perkinson (2009) argues that the recent prison boom can be viewed as more or less a southern story. Southern prisons, particularly in states like Texas, never embraced rehabilitation, have among the harshest sanctions in the nation, and have played an important but underanalyzed role in the historic expansion of U.S. prisons. Following this logic, Eason (2012) suggests that the administration of criminal justice policies was significantly different in the South than in the North with fewer rehabilitative

programs, more stringent sanctions, and harsher punishments for offenders.

In the North, several factors coalesced to unseat penal welfarism. Discriminatory employment practices made formal employment harder to acquire for former prisoners as northern prisons began to hold greater numbers of minorities caught up in the sweep of law-and-order policies (Simon 1993). Thus, as northern prisons "blackened," the acquisition of employment was no longer viewed as feasible. As a result, employment was no longer a formal requirement of parole, contributing to the erosion of support for the rehabilitative ideal.

On the welfare front, public policy discourse concerning the plight of the urban poor took on a decidedly racialized tone in the wake of the progressive 1960s (Quadagno 1994). The hard-fought extension of welfare benefits to the Black working class would mark a tipping point in poverty policy and public approval of welfare state expenditures (Katz 2001; Quadagno 1994). A series of Supreme Court victories guaranteed unprecedented access for poor Black families to social safety-net programs, due process in welfare hearings, and benefit administration. As a result, the Black population on welfare expanded by 333 percent between 1950 and 1970. In addition, the "illegitimacy rate" increased, with Black families representing a third of all "illegitimate" families receiving ADC benefits by 1960 (Katz 2001, 7). Thus, the protest movements of the 1960s brought renewed attention to the social condition of the Black family, launching a cottage industry of urban poverty scholarship seeking to analyze the experiences of what would be later deemed the "urban underclass."

Black Dependence, Black Disorganization, Black Deviance

Initially arguing that social disorganization, deviance, and oppositional adaptation were the rational outgrowth of racism and economic exclusion, works by scholars like Oscar Lewis (1966), Daniel Patrick Moynihan (1965), and Michael Harrington (1962) were co-opted by policymakers seeking to minimize the footprint of the federal government in the lives of the urban poor. Their assertions about Black family deviance substantiated pathological theories already resonant in conservative think tanks and public policy circles (Wacquant 2009). Pathological culture rather than the social ecology of the Black family was seen as the root cause of generational poverty and increased rates of crime. Poor people's values and cultural practices were believed to isolate them from "mainstream," white, middle-class society (Kelly, 1997). Policymakers therefore sought to target the values of the urban poor and shift their cultural practices toward the values of "mainstream" Americans. Subsequently, "treatment" for Black dependence and "non-traditional" family configurations became the interventions of choice (Schram et al. 2010; Schram et al. 2009; Geva 2011).

Despite resistance from prominent academics contending what some scholars deemed "dysfunctional patterns of behavior," survival strategies were employed to mitigate the structural dilemmas Black families faced (Hannerz 1969; Leibow 1967; Stack 1974). A spike in crime occurred in the 1970s, which was conflated with the civil unrest of the Black protest movements of the 1960s (Maurer 2006). A consensus emerged among prominent academics and policymakers alike that the United States' efforts to alleviate poverty and the rehabilitative endeavors of social service programming simply did not work (Martinson 1974; J. G. Miller 1989; Quadagno 1994). While there were important distinctions between welfare and criminal justice discourses, their similarities were striking. Each presented social welfare programs as ineffective and potentially harmful (Murray, 1984). Each reasserted the locus of criminality and the origins of criminal activities within cultural rather than ecological contexts (Wilson and Herrnstein 1985). Each suggested that the emphasis on rehabilitation and other forms of social support were costly, inefficient, and potentially dangerous (Wilson 1975). Finally, reminiscent of assertions from the Victorian "poverty experts" and public intellectuals of the postbellum era, each instantiated long-standing tropes linking intergenerational welfare dependence and crime to the pathology of the Black family (Kelly 1997; Muhammad 2010).

Neoliberal Penalty and the Stratifying Effects of Social Policy

Policy experts called for a "new paternalism" to manage urban poverty (Mead 1997; Soss, Fording, and Schram 2011) and hastened the adoption of "get tough" policies extending to criminal justice and social welfare. With the locus of welfare dependence and criminality established within individual and cultural pathology, state interventions were designed to target the decision making and culturally learned proclivities of the urban underclass. Much like initiatives in the postbellum South, the series of policies that followed led to a historic expansion in the rate and number of prisoners, making the United States the global leader in the "race to incarcerate" (Maurer 2006). The "War on Poverty" was thus unseated by the "War on Drugs," and rehabilitation by mandatory minimum sentencing, "zero tolerance policing," and other "get tough" policies to deter crime and incapacitate offenders.

On the welfare front, anti-poverty programs were themselves blamed for the emergence of the underclass, which was imagined as dependent and hyper-violent urban residents on whom social spending produced little fruit (R. Miller 2014). The 1996 passage of PRWORA marked the transformation of the federally administered, overwhelmingly unpopular public welfare entitlement Aid to Dependent Families with Children (AFCD) into the locally administered block grant Temporary Assistance to Needy Families (TANF). Block grants consist of funding for federal programs allocated to states and local governments to use at their discretion. In effect, block grants then transfer authority from the federal to the local level by allowing states to appropriate and spend funds for federally mandated services as they see fit. TANF gave states considerable autonomy in the administration of social welfare services. The passage of PRWORA, for example, was accompanied by the institution of a federally mandated work requirement to receive welfare, a five-year cap on benefits eligibility, and the administration of new modes of surveillance for welfare recipients (Soss et al. 2011). States, however, had considerable autonomy in how they administered these mandates, so long as they reduced the overall welfare caseload. As such, scholars have argued that welfare reformists did not seek to reduce poverty but instead to reduce dependence.

Policymakers on both sides of the aisle trumpeted welfare reform as a success, citing the nearly 65 percent reduction in the welfare case load in just under a decade (Peck 2010). The many families pushed "off the dole" were quickly moved onto the rolls of a flexible labor sector with few benefits and unsustainable wages (Peck 2010; Wacquant 2009). In addition, street level bureaucrats' discretion and authority in the day-to-day lives of welfare recipients increased significantly (Lipski 1980; Watkins-Hayes 2009). New welfare regulations disqualified large swaths of families struggling with generational poverty from the receipt of continuous welfare benefits (Katz 2001), and sanctions targeting single mothers and "dead beat fathers" were used to fleece the welfare rolls. All the while, these strategies were unevenly deployed (Schram et al. 2009), policing and indeed punishing the reproductive behaviors, leisure, and work patterns of single-parent families from the inner city who were likely to be non-white, considered "non-traditional," and poor (Geva 2011; Roberts 1997; Schram et al. 2009; Soss et al. 2011).

Criminal justice policy followed a similar logic. Criminal sanctions were designed and rolled out to address the demand side of drug trafficking, to crack down on "quality of life" infractions of the penal code, and were overwhelmingly focused on the arrest and incarceration of low-level offenders (Wacquant 2009). These strategies have led to the over-incarceration of the urban poor, the homeless, the drug-addicted and the low-level petty offender (Wacquant 2009). These policies swelled the rolls of the U.S. prison system, which increased sevenfold in less than 20 years. As such, the War on Drugs has been described as the most significant driver of incarceration rates in the United States (Alexander 2009; Maurer 2006).

Arguably, these policies target the same populations in similar ways, but with notable distinctions. Wacquant (2009) suggests that criminal justice and social welfare policies represent the right and left hands of an ambidextrous state. The right hand employs the police, courts, prisons, and detention centers to punitively manage unskilled laborers left vulnerable by processes of deindustrialization and labor market exclusion. Imprisonment, in this analytic, is viewed as a degradation ceremony that extends negative social capital to the overrepresented Black and Latino men who cycle in and out of prisons due to the overwhelming concentration of criminal justice intervention in low-income inner city neighborhoods. Conversely, the left hand of the state attempts to mitigate social problems through the provision of goods and services in gendered and similarly punitive ways. Poor women and their children are managed through the stigmatized social programs emblematic of the left hand, such as cash payments through TANF, the receipt of food stamps,

and childcare subsidies. It is important to note that beyond the dimension of social stigma for welfare recipients, there are material consequences for this social arrangement. Eligibility for welfare benefits has been tied to participation in the low-wage labor market, either through workfare arrangements for the women (Peck 2010; Wacquant 2009) or child support enforcement for the men which include the garnishment of wages, tax liens, the revocation of professional licenses, and the looming threat of future imprisonment for non-compliance (Pate 2010). Along with material hardship, these policies have been shown to contribute to confrontational relationships and the dissolution of already fragile family arrangements.

Scholars disagree on the prison's role and consequence. However, there is general agreement that the clientele of the U.S. prison system are overwhelmingly concentrated in low-income communities of color and that the prison, as an institutional arrangement based on policy decision-making, has both classifying and stratifying effects. Today, 60 percent of Black, inner city high school dropouts and 30 percent of those who do graduate will be arrested at some point during their life course (Western 2006). More insidiously, nearly a fourth of all African American children have an incarcerated parent, with the increased incarceration of African American women shown to account for nearly a third of all new foster care placements in the United States (Roberts 2002). Finally, mass incarceration has been shown to not just increase the economic disadvantage of the families affected by it but also to increase the incidence of negative mental health outcomes in mothers and their children as well (Wildeman 2009). Thus, the prison can be understood as a punitive institution with extra penological effects (Wacquant 2009). In the same way, social welfare policy can be seen as a social institution with punitive, disciplinary, and regulatory effects (Piven and Cloward 1993; Soss et al. 2011). Both of these extend disadvantage across a host of social domain and ossify the precarious positions of racialized groups within the social hierarchy.

Conclusions

While the rates of incarceration and the scale of social welfare retrenchment is novel to the current age, there is considerable continuity between old and new crime control and social welfare interventions. The ways in which we currently "govern social marginality" (Beckett and Western 2001) have resonance with long-standing techniques to discipline and regulate Black workers, dating back at least to the postbellum South. Contemporary critiques of the "nanny state" and the "entitlement society" used to limit the extension of benefits to the urban poor, and aversions to the "redistribution of wealth" from the "makers" to the "takers" of the contemporary political economy resonate with assertions from Victorian "poverty experts" about the incapacitating nature of the "dole," postbellum assertions about the readiness of white paupers and Black slaves for "economic freedom," and poverty discourses discouraging state intervention in the lives of the urban poor. In addition, there is significant continuity between the tough-on-crime policies that target petty drug offenders residing in the low-rent, high-unemployment districts of the postindustrial city, and vagrancy convictions of the postbellum South.

Following Wacquant's (2012b) admonition, scholars must "reconnect social and penal policies and treat them as two variants of poverty policy" in order to "grasp the new politics of marginality" (p. 237). This new marginality, according to Beckett and Western (2001), is governed through mass incarceration and public welfare policy, acting as a single (or unified) policy regime. As a remaking of government, rather than another mode of social control, the punishment of poverty (and race) in the neoliberal age has both stratifying and classifying effects (see Wacquant 2012b), situating groups within a social hierarchy and creating new ways of being in the social world. The punishment of race and poverty during the postbellum period, which I argue underscored the ways in which freed slaves were understood and justified the policies of the Freedman's Bureau to discipline Black workers, was achieved through the mitigation and enforcement of labor contracts with southern planters. Sanctions for violations of these contracts included convictions under vagrancy laws, at once swelling the roles of the postbellum criminal justice system while constituting the Black vagrant as dangerous and dependent in the public imagination. During the post-welfare era, this construction justified welfare reform initiatives that valorized work for its disciplinary effects and punitive responses to minor infractions of the penal code. Thus, how we punish and provide for our most vulnerable populations has had important implications for the ways in which we conceptualize the role of the state and the ways in which race, poverty, and criminality are embodied and understood.

References

Alexander, Michelle. 2009. *The New Jim Crow: Mass Incarceration in an Age of Color Blindness.* New York: The New Press.

Beaumont, Gustave de, Francis Lieber and Alexis de Tocqueville. 1833. "On the Penitentiary System in the United States and its Application in France." http://www.archive.org/details/onpenitentiarysyoobeauuoft, (accessed August 6, 2010)

Beckett, Katherine and Bruce Western. 2001. "Governing through Social Marginality: Welfare, Incarceration, and the Transformation of State Policy." *Punishment and Society* 3(1): 43–59.

Bobo, Lawrence D. and Victor Thompson. 2010. "Racialized Mass Incarceration: Poverty, Prejudice, and Punishment." In *Doing Race: 21 Essays for the 21st Century* (ed. Hazel R. Markus and Paula Moya), 322–355. New York: Norton.

Du Bois, William E. B. [1935] 1999. *Black Reconstruction in America, 1860–1880.* Durham, NC: Duke University Press.

Du Bois, William E. B. [1899] 1995. *The Philadelphia Negro: A Social Study.* Philadelphia: University of Pennsylvania Press.

Eason, John M. 2012. "Extending the Hyper Ghetto: Toward a Theory of Punishment, Race, and Rural Disadvantage." *Journal of Poverty: Innovations on Social, Political and Economic Inequalities* 16(4): 274–295.

Farmer-Kaiser, Mary. 2004. "'Are They Not in Some Sorts Vagrants?' Gender and the Efforts of the Freedmen's Bureau to Combat Vagrancy in the Reconstruction South." *Georgia Historical Quarterly* 88(1): 25–49.

Feeley, Malcom M and Jonathan Simon 1992. "The New Penology: Notes on the Emerging Strategy of Corrections and Its Implication." *Criminology* 30(4): 449–474.

Fox, Kathryn J. 1999. "Reproducing Criminal Types: Cognitive Treatment for Violent Offenders in Prison." *Sociological Quarterly* 40(3) 435–453.

Foucault, Michael. 1977. *Discipline and Punish: The Birth of the Prison.* New York: Random House.

Garland, David. 2001. *The Culture of Control: Crime and Social Order in Contemporary Society.* Chicago: University of Chicago Press.

Gilens, Martin. 1999. *Why Americans Hate Welfare: Race, Media, and the Politics of Antipoverty Policy.* Chicago: University of Chicago Press.

Geva, Dorit. 2011. "Not Just Maternalism: Marriage and Fatherhood in American Welfare Policy." *Social Politics* 18(1): 24–51.

Goldberg, Chad A. 2008. *Citizens and Paupers: Relief, Rights, and Race, from the Freedman's Bureau to Workfare.* Chicago: London. University of Chicago Press.

Gorman, Tessa M. 1997. "Back on the Chain Gang: Why the Eighth Amendment and the History of Slavery Proscribe the Resurgence of Chain Gangs." *California Law Review* 85(2): 441–478.

Hannerz, Ulf. 1969. *Soulside.* New York: Columbia University Press.

Haney, Lynne. 2010. *Offending Women: Power, Punishment, and the Regulation of Desire.* Berkeley: University of California Press.

Harcourt, Bernard E. 2011. *Illusion of Free Markets: Punishment and the Illusion of Natural Order.* Chicago, IL: University of Chicago Press.

Harrington, Michael. 1962. *The Other America: Poverty in the United States.* New York: Penguin.

Harvey, David. 2007. *A Brief History of Neoliberalism.* New York: Oxford University Press.

Hollandsworth, James G. 2008. "Black Confederate Pensioners after the Civil War." *Mississippi History Now.* http://mshistory.k12.ms.us/articles/289/black-confederate-pensioners-after-the-civil-war (accessed August 6, 2010).

Katz, Michael B. 2001. *The Price of Citizenship: Redefining the American Welfare State.* University of Pennsylvania Press.

Kelly, Robin D. G. 1997. *Yo Mama's Dysfunktional!: Fighting the Culture Wars in Urban America.* Boston: Beacon Press.

Kern, William S. 1998. "Current Welfare Reform: A Return to the Principles of 1834." *Journal of Economic Issues* 32(2): 427–432.

Lewis, Oscar. 1966. "The Culture of Poverty." *Scientific American* 215:19–25.

Lieberman, Robert C. 1998. *Shifting the Color Line: Race and the American Welfare State.* Cambridge, MA: Harvard University Press.

Liebow, Elliot. 1967. *Tally's Corner: A Study of Street Corner Negro Men.* Boston: Little Brown Company.

Lipski, Michael. 1980. *Street Level Bureaucracy: Dilemmas of the Individual in Public Service.* New York. Russell Sage Foundation.

Lurigio, Arthur, Thomas Lyons, Laura Brookes, and Tim Whitney. 2010. "Illinois Disproportionate Justice Impact Study Commission: Final Report." Center for Health and Justice at TASC on behalf of the Illinois Disproportionate Justice Impact Study Commission. http://www.centerforhealthandjustice.org/DJIS_Full-Report_1229.pdf (accessed March 30, 2011).

Lynch, Mona. 2009. *Sunbelt Justice: Arizona and the Transformation of American Punishment.* Stanford, CA: Stanford University Press.

Mancini, Matthew J. 1978. "Race, Economics, and the Abandonment of Convict Leasing." *Journal of Negro History* 63(4): 339–352.

Martin, Kathleen. 2008. *Hard and Unreal Advice: Mothers, Social Science and the Victorian Poverty Experts.* New York: Palgrave Macmillan.

Martinson, Robert. 1974. "What Works? Questions and Answers about Prison Reform." *Public Interest* 35:22–54.

Maurer, Marc. 2006. *Race to Incarcerate.* New York: The New Press.

Mead, Lawrence M. 1997. *The New Paternalism: Supervisory Approaches to Poverty.* Washington, DC: Brookings Institution Press.

Miller, Jerome G. 1989. "Is It True that Nothing Works?" *Washington Post,* March, 1989. http://www.prisonpolicy.org/scans/rehab.html (accessed February 13, 2011).

Miller, Reuben. 2014. "Strange Affinities: Race, Religion, and the Punishment Entrepreneurs of the U.S. Carceral Field." In *Routledge Handbook on Poverty in the United States* (ed. Stephen Haymes, Reuben Jonathan Miller, and Maria Vidal de Haymes). London: Routledge Press.

Moynihan, Daniel P. 1965. *The Negro Family: The Case for National Action.* Washington, DC: U.S. Department of Labor.

Muhammad, Khalil G. 2010. *The Condemnation of Blackness: Race, Crime, and the Making of Modern Urban America.* Cambridge, MA: Harvard University Press.

Murray, Charles. 1984. *Losing Ground: American Social Policy, 1950–1980.* New York: Harper Collins Publishing.

Neubeck, Kenneth J. and Noel Cazenave. 2001. *Welfare Racism: Playing the Race Card against America's Poor.* New York: Routledge.

Nkansah-Amankra, Stephen, Samuel Agbanu, and Reuban Miller. 2013. "Disparities in Health, Poverty, Incarceration and Social Justice among Racial Groups in the United States: A Critical Review of Evidence of Close Links with Neoliberalism." *International Journal of Health Services* 43(2): 217–240.

O'Connell, Anne. 2009. "Building Their Readiness for Economic 'Freedom': The New Poor Law and Emancipation." *Journal of Sociology and Social Welfare* 36(2): 85–103.

O'Connell, Anne. 2010. "A Genealogy of Poverty: Race and the Technology of Population." *Critical Social Work* 11(2).

Pate, David J. 2010. "Life After PRWORA: The Involvement of African-American Fathers with Welfare-Reliant Children and the Child Support Enforcement System." In *Social Work with African American Males: Health, Mental Health, and Policy* (ed. Waldo Johnson), 61–80. New York: Oxford University Press.

Peck, Jamie. 2010. *Workfare States*. London: Guilford Press.

Peck, Jamie and Nik Theodore. 2009. "Carceral Chicago: Making the Ex-Offender Employability Crisis." *International Journal of Urban and Regional Research* 32(2): 251–281.

Perkinson, Robert. 2009. *Texas Tough: The Rise of America's Prison Empire*. New York: Metropolitan Books.

Phelps, Michelle S. 2011. "Rehabilitation in the Punitive Era: The Gap between Rhetoric and Reality in U.S. Prison Programs." *Law & Society Review* 45(1): 33–68.

Piven, Frances F., and Richard Cloward. 1993. *Regulating the Poor: The Functions of Public Welfare*. New York: Vintage Books.

Quadagno, Jill. 1994. *The Color of Welfare*. New York: Oxford University Press.

Roberts, Dorothy. 1997. *Killing the Black Body: Race, Reproduction, and the Meaning of Liberty*. New York: Vintage.

Roberts, Dorothy. 2002. *Shattered Bonds: The Color of Child Welfare*. New York: Basic Civitas Books.

Sampson, Robert J. and Charles Loeffler. 2010. "Punishment's Place: The Local Concentration of Mass Incarceration." *Daedalus* 139(3):20–31.

Schram, Sanford F., Joe Soss, Richard C. Fording, and Linda Houser. 2010. "The Third Level of U.S. Welfare Reform: Governmentality under Neoliberal Paternalism." *Citizenship Studies* 14(6): 739–754.

Schram, Sanford F., Joe Soss, Richard C. Fording, and Linda Houser. 2009. "Deciding to Discipline: Race, Choice, and Punishment at the Frontlines of Welfare Reform." *American Sociological Review* 74(3): 398–422.

Simon, Jonathan. 1993. *Poor Discipline: Parole and the Social Control of the Underclass, 1890–1990*. Chicago, IL: University of Chicago Press.

Soss, Joe, Richard C. Fording, and Sanford F. Schram. 2011. *Disciplining the Poor: Neoliberal Paternalism and the Persistent Power of Race*. Chicago: University of Chicago Press.

Stack, Carol. 1974. *All Our Kin: Strategy for Survival in a Black Community*. New York: Harper & Row.

Taylor, Keeanga-Yamahtta. 2009. "W. E. B. Du Bois: Black Reconstruction in America." *International Socialist Review* 57.

U.S. Census Bureau. 1860. "Preliminary Report on the 8th Census." http://www2.census.gov/prod2/decennial/documents/1860e-01.pdf (accessed August 7, 2010).

Wacquant, Loïc J. D. 2001. "Class, Race and Hyperincarceration in Revanchist America." *Daedalus* 140(3): 74–90.

Wacquant, Loïc J. D. 2009: *Punishing the Poor: The Neoliberal Government of Social Insecurity*. Durham, NC: Duke University Press.

Watkins-Hayes, Celeste. 2009. *The New Welfare Bureaucrats: Entanglements of Race, Class, and Policy Reform*. Chicago: University of Chicago Press.

Western, Bruce. 2006. *Punishment and Inequality in America*. New York: Russell Sage Foundation.

Wildeman, Christopher. 2009. "Parental Imprisonment, the Prison Boom, and the Concentration of Childhood Disadvantage." *Demography* 46:265–280.

Wilson, James Q. 1975. *Thinking about Crime*. New York: Vintage.

Wilson, James Q. and Richard Herrnstein. 1985. *Crime and Human Nature: The Definitive Study of the Causes of Crime*. New York: Simon and Schuster.

Questions

1. What factors have contributed to the dramatic increases in incarceration over time? Why does the author, and others, call this "hyper-incarceration"?

2. What is neoliberalism? What does the author mean by the "punitive turn" in both criminal justice and welfare policy? How does this "punitive turn" relate to neoliberalism? What are the tangible aspects of neoliberal ideology?

3. What historical events are important for understanding how race has come to matter so much in welfare and criminal justice policy? How is this history significant in today's welfare and criminal justice systems?

4. What are the "stratifying effects of social policy" according to the author? How is "neoliberal penality" an important part of this stratifying effort? What are the implications for the reproduction of inequality?

5. Given the current political environment, what actions can be taken to counteract the regulation of Black and brown bodies through the criminal justice system?

32

Housework and Social Policy

MAKIKO FUWA AND PHILIP N. COHEN

Work policies can have an effect on family lives. Sociologists have known for some time now that work and family are not "separate spheres" but are instead interrelated. Many workers (usually low-paid immigrant women and women of color) work for pay in home settings: domestic workers, childcare workers, home health workers, and housekeepers. Even for those whose work and home are physically separated, the expectations and quality of life in one area affect them in the other, as people strive to "have it all" but lack the support to do so. Moreover, the paid and unpaid work people do can be consequential for feelings of equity, as well as satisfaction. In many families with children, parents struggle to balance work and family; parents can feel overworked or stressed from work "spilling over" into home life and vice versa. Mobile technologies have pressured professionals to work anytime, anywhere. Working-class individuals struggle to find time with their families while balancing multiple jobs to pay the bills.

A major manifestation of the balancing issues is conflict within families over who does what Arlie Hochschild and Anne Machung (1989) labeled "the second shift": housework. In their classic study, they found families arguing and eventually divorcing when women worked for pay but still bore the brunt of household duties. Those who managed to stay together created "myths" that made inequitable distributions of labor seem fair, even when they objectively were not.

Even today, on average, married women do 18 hours of housework a week (Schneider 2011). Their husbands, however, only contribute about 10 hours a week. What's more, Schneider found that not only do women do lots of housework when they are wholly financially dependent upon their husbands, as you may expect in a "traditional family," but women also do considerably more household labor when they earn more than their husbands. Even though women are doing less housework now than ever and men are doing more, families are still struggling to balance competing demands based on outdated notions of womanhood, manhood, and good workers.

The following reading examines a possible way to lessen a major source of family conflict. Makiko Fuwa and Philip Cohen's findings shed light on what policies, and in what contexts, women and men share housework more equitably. This study of 33 countries examines how social policies influence the division of household labor and how families negotiate it. Specifically, how do affirmative action policies and work-family balance policies affect the division of household labor and how much housework men and women perform? Overall, Fuwa and Cohen find that women still do more than half of the housework in all countries. However, the amount does vary, and social policies are quite influential. Latvia

Excerpted from Fuwa, Makiko and Philip N. Cohen. 2007. "Housework and Social Policy." *Social Science Research* 36:512–530. Copyright © 2006 Elsevier Inc.

has the most equal division, while Japan has the most traditional. Policies that reduce gender inequality and work-family conflict lead to the most equal division of household labor. Women's household bargaining power is enhanced by workplace policies geared toward equal access but weakened by more generous family leave policies. These findings have important implications if we hope to live satisfying, balanced lives—and increase equity at home.

References

Hochschild, Arlie, and Anne Machung. 1989. *The Second Shift: Working Parents and the Revolution at Home.* New York: Viking.

Schneider, Daniel. 2011. "Market Earnings and Household Work: New Tests of Gender Performance Theory." *Journal of Marriage and Family* 73(4): 845–860.

Introduction

Recent research on the gender division of household labor has examined how social context affects not only the overall division between men and women but also the dynamics of negotiation between men and women. For example, Batalova and Cohen (2002) showed that countries with more macro-level gender equality also have greater housework equality between husbands and wives, holding constant individual couples' characteristics. However, Fuwa (2004) found that the returns to individual women's assets—especially their employment and egalitarian gender attitudes—were also greater in countries where women hold more power generally.

Researchers have thus situated processes driving gender inequality at the micro level within broader systems of gender inequality at the macro level. But we know little about the mechanisms by which macro-level patterns of gender inequality infiltrate these micro-level negotiations. Thus, Geist (2005) demonstrates that micro-level patterns are associated with broadly defined welfare regimes across 10 countries, but leaves open the question of "more specific causal mechanisms" (2005, 25) to be investigated at the macro level. State policies regarding women's employment and work–family conflicts are a good starting point for such an investigation, given recent research suggesting that such policies have systematic effects on gender inequality at all levels (Esping-Andersen 1999; Gornick and Meyers 2003; O'Connor, Orloff, and Shaver 1999). In this chapter, we use Chang's (2000) policy typology to test whether women's bargaining power over housework is associated with state policies regarding gender inequality in work and families: equality of access for women in the labor market and family and childcare services for dual-earner families.

Social Policy, Labor Market, and the Family

One of the most significant economic and social changes in the last several decades has been the increase in married women's labor force participation (Sayer, Cohen, and Casper 2004). Even though more women are committed to the labor market, they perform the majority of unpaid labor in the United States (Bianchi et al. 2000) as well as across industrialized countries (Batalova and Cohen 2002; Geist 2005), reproducing gender inequality in the family and creating conflict between spouses (Hochschild 1989).Women's family responsibility, in turn, often disrupts their careers, which has a negative impact on their wages later in life (Taniguchi 1999). In response to these conflicts, how to reconcile work and family responsibilities has emerged as a leading social problem (Gornick and Meyers 2003).

Meanwhile, research on the division of household labor has begun to move beyond micro-level analysis based on couples' and individual characteristics such as income, education, and attitudes. This individual-level focus risks assuming that these resources are static in nature, and tends to reify their meaning. For instance, micro-level analysis has shown that spouses with more resources, such as full-time employment and higher incomes, do a smaller share of housework (see Shelton and John 1996 for review). However, since the power of these resources is attributed to individuals, this research does not address how social conditions—and especially state policies—influence the negotiation over housework (Batalova and Cohen 2002; Fuwa 2004; Geist 2005; Kamo 1994).

States have responded to the problem in various ways, explicitly or implicitly. Some countries, such as Sweden, offer family policies such as public childcare to mitigate women's burden (Esping-Andersen 1999). Eastern and Central European countries also provided generous childcare services and parental leave, but these were reduced after the collapse of socialist regimes. Liberal capitalist countries such as the United States, to the extent that they intervene at all, promote women's economic independence through affirmative (positive) action programs and anti-discrimination policy (Chang 2000; O'Connor et al. 1999). Such social policies may influence the impact of women's labor force participation on the division of household labor, by changing the demand for and cost of a certain division of household labor or by promoting egalitarian gender ideology.

Earlier attempts to categorize patterns of state welfare policy focused on the treatment of employment relations. Esping-Andersen (1990), for example, argues that countries differ in their effort to "de-commodify" citizens by providing social security and lessening their dependence on employment. However, feminists faulted this state-market focus for neglecting the family, a prime institution for providing welfare for both workers and their dependents. Since women shoulder the majority of caring work, how states mitigate the gendered division of labor through market regulation and welfare provision affects gender inequality in the family as well as in the labor market (Gornick and Meyers 2003; Lewis 1992; O'Connor et al. 1999; Stier, Lewin-Epstein, and Braun 2001).

In response, Esping-Andersen (1999) argues that social democratic welfare states such as Scandinavian countries have "de-familialized" some reproductive functions such as child care. Providing social services and protection on a universal basis to individuals rather than traditional family units minimizes the risks to individual citizens of either "market-failure" or "family-failure." In contrast, conservative countries such as Germany promote policies that encourage exclusion of married women from the labor market and dependence of wives on their husbands for social security. In these countries, families are expected to shoulder the function of social reproduction. Liberal countries such as the

United States provide only minimal services in the case of market-failure. Since state provision of family services are almost non-existent, American families rely on services in the private sector.

A systematic analysis that incorporates the dynamics of macro-level factors will contribute to a better understanding of couples' division of household labor. Using Chang's (2000) categorization of social policies on women's employment into two aspects—equality of access policies and substantive benefit policies—this project offers empirical tests of these multi-level dynamics. We take advantage of the 2002 International Social Survey Programme data to analyze the association between social policies and the division of household labor in 33 countries.

Ideological Frameworks of Social Policy on Women's Employment

This study conceptualizes state policies as actively creating and reinforcing certain social conditions and gender norms regarding women's roles (Schneider and Ingram 1997). In fact, Treas and Widmer (2000) suggest that "one indicator of the success of state interventions is whether state ideology is internalized by citizens and manifest in public opinion" (1410). Feminist scholars distinguish frameworks for labor market regulation according to their underlying ideologies of women and work (Kessler-Harris 1987; Vogel 1993). Chang (2000) suggests that social policies on women's employment may be decomposed into two aspects: equality of access and substantive benefits policies. This study uses her framework to test the effect of social policies on the division of housework.

Equality of Access Policies

Orloff (1993, p. 318) argues that since many women are excluded from paid labor, "commodification—that is, obtaining a position in the paid labor force—is in fact potentially emancipatory" for women. Equality of access policies encourage women's access to jobs and economic security, thus promoting women's economic independence (Chang 2000; Orloff 1993). State policies also affect ideologies regarding women's employment. Sjöberg (2004) argues that family policies can be seen as normative orders that "structure world views . . . regarding the 'proper' role of women in society and the degree to which the participation of women in the labour market on equal terms with men is seen as something to be desired" (112).

Countries differ in terms of implementing equality of access policies. Liberal countries such as the United States, Canada, and Australia have implemented anti-discrimination and affirmative action policies (O'Connor et al. 1999). Between the 1960s and 1990s, occupational sex segregation in the managerial category was dramatically reduced in the United States and Canada (Chang 2000). The female–male wage ratio for administrative and managerial workers in the United States is the highest among the most developed countries. In the United States, labor market occupational integration is strongly associated with gender earnings equality even for women who work in female-dominated occupations (Cohen and Huffman 2003; Cotter et al. 1997). This means that social policies that encourage occupational integration may be beneficial to all women.

Equality of access policies may enhance women's opportunities as well as their sense of entitlement as workers. Nevertheless, these policies are limited in their effectiveness at reducing gender inequality to the extent that they treat workers as men, presumed not to have family demands on their time. Still, research shows that countries where women have advanced in economic and political areas have a more egalitarian division of housework on average (Batalova and Cohen 2002). Further, the effects of women's resources on the division of housework within couples are greater in these countries (Fuwa 2004).

Substantive Benefit Policies

Substantive benefit policies provide family and childcare services for dual-earner families (Chang 2000). One of the most direct links to the gender division of housework might be through parental leave, which varies considerably in terms of length, levels of wage coverage, and restriction on who is eligible to take leave. For example, while the United States provides only 12 weeks of unpaid parental leave (and that for only some workers), Sweden offers one year of parental leave with 80% wage coverage (plus six months with lesser benefits). Norway also shows a rare case of state intervention in redistributing childcare responsibility to fathers, with a "father's quota" that reserves four weeks of parental leave exclusively for fathers—a policy that led to dramatic increases in the rate at which fathers took parental leave (Bruning and Plantenga 1999). Some

European countries also have the father's quota system, although the length of the leave is usually very short (see Gornick and Meyers 2003, Table 5.3).

Family leave policies, however, often presume women's roles as wives and mothers. The former East Germany, for instance, allotted the "household day" to catch up on household tasks only to women. Although Sweden provides generous parental leave that may be taken by mother or father, most leaves are still taken by mothers, which may encourage prolonged absence from work (Hoem 1995). Thus, parental leave policies are a double-edged sword: While they may mitigate women's family responsibility and encourage job continuity (Ruhm 1998), patriarchal bias in the policy structure and low benefit rates may reinforce gender inequality in the market and in the family (Fagnani 1999). In contrast to public childcare provision for very young children, which helps mothers continue working, parental leave encourages mothers to withdraw from the labor market at least temporarily. Since the 1994 expansion of the child-rearing allowance in France, labor force participation of women with two young children declined from 74 percent in 1994 to 56 percent in 1998 (International Labour Organization, 2005a). Also, nine months of paid leave reduces women's hourly wage by around 3 percent (Ruhm 1998). Thus, where women are expected to withdraw from the labor force when they have young children, their economic assets may be less effective in equalizing the division of household labor.

Integrating Micro-Level Factors in Multi-Level Contexts

As we have seen, the policy environment surrounding couples' division of household labor varies widely across countries. However, the economic analysis of housework has focused on individuals' resources such as employment status and income. Bargaining theory suggests that husband and wife negotiate to reach a household decision agreement based on their individual resources, until disagreement in their preferences reaches a divorce-threat point (McElroy 1990). For example, when wives have full-time employment and high income, these resources are used in the negotiation with their husbands to realize a more egalitarian division of household labor. However, since the divorce threat point can shift depending on women's opportunities outside the marriage, "extra household environment parameters" (McElroy 1990, 1997)—such as social policies that increase the employability of women in the market—may influence the negotiation processes. The effects of such factors are rarely examined explicitly.

Asserting the importance of a multi-level analysis from a sociological perspective, Blumberg (1984) introduced an economic power model that incorporates the effect of macro-level power differences between men and women. She argues that the effect of individual women's resources on the division of household labor is "discounted" by women's macro-level economic dependency on men. This is the finding of Fuwa's (2004) cross-national study of housework, which shows that women's employment and gender ideology have stronger effects on the gender division of household labor in countries where there is less gender inequality in the labor market and political spheres.

However, macro-level economic power is unlikely to be the only structural factor that influences individual women's decision-making processes. Folbre (1994) suggests a more complex model of interest and identity formation, in which individuals are influenced by the structural constraints of asset distribution, political rules, and cultural norms as well as personal preferences. Employed women's negotiation over the division of household labor may be simultaneously affected by material distribution in the labor market, policies that determine who bears the cost of family labor, and cultural norms regarding women's roles. Even personal preferences such as the enjoyment of caring for others—often treated as a matter of "taste"—are shaped in relation to these constraints; and individual choices, in turn, reshape these structures. Thus, structural factors "define identities and interests that specify the context of individual choice" (Folbre 1994, 48).

We argue that social policy is one of the key contextual elements that shape economic power between men and women in the labor market, political rules that reduce or encourage the traditional division of labor, and cultural norms regarding who is responsible for caring for the family. Social policy not only contributes material and ideological support for a certain division of household labor but also affects how well women can use their economic assets in individual negotiations. Geist (2005) finds that housework dynamics vary across social welfare regimes in 10 countries, holding constant variation in couples' individual characteristics. It is possible this effect arises from broad cultural differences across countries, but it may also be that specific policies have more direct effects. Identifying such policies will improve our ability to evaluate social policy for its effects on micro-level gender dynamics. That is the empirical question for this study.

Hypotheses

We examine if the two aspects of social policies—equality of access and substantive benefits—affect the overall division of household labor and the impact of wives' employment and relative earnings on the division of household labor. Based on previous research, we propose four hypotheses, each of which applies net of controls for couple-level characteristics. The first is on the effects of social policies on countries' average division of housework. Equality of access and substantive benefit policies offer different approaches to gender inequality; however, both indicate some governmental commitment to policies that might mitigate the unequal division of household labor. Thus we hypothesize:

H_1: Countries with developed equality of access policies (affirmative action and absence of discriminatory policy) and substantive benefit policies (parental leave and public childcare) have a more egalitarian division of household labor on average.

Because equality of access policies enhance women's opportunity in the labor market and foster a sense of entitlement to work, they may enhance the effects of women's full-time employment and income. Thus, we hypothesize:

H_2: In countries with developed equality of access policies (affirmative action and absence of discriminatory policy), women's full-time employment and higher income have a stronger effect on the gender division of household labor.

Because parental leave policies often encourage women to take time off from employment, the availability of parental leave may reduce the effect of women's resources on a more egalitarian division of housework. We predict:

H_3: In countries with developed parental leave policies, women's full-time employment and higher income have weaker effects on the gender division of household labor.

In contrast, because public childcare helps mothers of young children to continue working, and provides ideological support to a dual-earner model, this policy may encourage women to use their resources for a more egalitarian division of housework. Thus, we hypothesize:

H_4: In countries with developed public childcare policies, women's full-time employment and higher income have stronger effects on the gender division of household labor.

Data, Measures, and Models

To test these hypotheses, we use data from the 2002 International Social Survey Program: Family and Changing Gender Roles III. The data reflect a cross-national collaboration in which independent institutions replicate survey questions in their own countries (Zentralarchiv fur Empirische Sozialforschung 2004). The ISSP 2002 collected data from 34 countries, making it the largest existing cross-national data set on the division of household labor. We use data from Australia, Austria, Brazil, Bulgaria, Chile, Cyprus, Czech Republic, Denmark, Finland, Flanders (Belgium), France, Germany (East and West), Great Britain, Hungary, Ireland, Israel, Japan, Latvia, Mexico, Netherlands, New Zealand, Northern Ireland, Norway, Poland, Portugal, Russia, Slovenia, Slovakian Republic, Spain, Sweden, Switzerland, and the United States. We exclude Philippines and Taiwan because they lack information on key variables. Our sample is restricted to married or cohabiting respondents who are at least 18 years old; data were collected from one member of each household. A total of 23,178 respondents are included in our analysis.

Results

Country-level descriptive statistics are shown in Table 1. On average, the housework hour ratio between husband and wife is most equal in Latvia (0.25); Japan has the most traditional division of household labor (0.79). Consistent with previous cross-national studies (Batalova and Cohen 2002; Geist 2005), women perform more than half of the housework across all countries.

Liberal countries such as Australia and the United States, and Scandinavian countries such as Norway

and Sweden, have implemented affirmative action policy on women's employment and promotion. However, the countries differ in the strength of measures taken and in their attitudes toward affirmative action. Germany uses a quota-like preferential treatment policy in hiring and promoting women in the public sector. Although Australia has implemented one of the most widespread affirmative action plans in the private sector, the Australian government also insists on the principle of equal opportunity and merit in the recruitment processes. (We tested Australia coded as both with and without affirmative action. The results are substantively the same.)

In contrast, none of the former socialist countries in the sample have affirmative action policies. These governments express critical views of affirmative action policies. Slovakia states in its 1998 CEDAW country report: "The equal position of men and women is guaranteed by the Constitution and is reflected in all the laws regulating the political, economical, social and cultural sphere. Slovakia did not need to implement temporary and special measures in order to accelerate the establishment of equal position of women and men" (Slovakia Country Report [Addendum] 1998, 14). However, all of these former socialist countries except Latvia retain at least one piece of sex-discriminatory policy that exclude women from night work, underground jobs, or jobs that involve lifting heavy objects. For example, Bulgaria labor codes retain "'Special protection of women,' which regulates the prohibition of some kinds of work by women that are damaging to their health and maternity functions" (Bulgaria Country Report 1994).

The length of maternity and/or parental leave varies widely by country. Liberal countries such as the United States and New Zealand, as well as Israel and Mexico, have the shortest parental leave (12 weeks). In contrast, Slovakia provides as long as a 3.6 years of parental leave. Most former socialist countries have a parental leave until the child reaches three years old. However, as in Russian case, some of the leaves are restricted to mothers; fathers are allowed to take parental leave only with mothers' written permission (Teplova 2004). In its pro-natal policy, France also has expanded the parental leave during the last decade. Conservative countries such as Austria, Germany, and Spain also have long parental leave policy.

Table 1 Country-level Descriptive Statistics.

Country	N	Wife's Housework Hours	Husband's Housework Hours	Housework Hour Ratio[a]	Affirmative Action	Absence of Discriminatory Policy[b]	Parent Leave (Months)	Public Childcare[c]
Latvia	507	18.4	11.1	0.25	No	3	3.7	0.43
Poland	708	20.7	12.2	0.26	No	1	27.7	0.10
Slovakian Republic	688	22.3	12.1	0.30	No	1	42.3	0.58
Denmark	823	13.1	7.0	0.30	No	3	12.0	0.90
Australia	738	21.5	11.5	0.30	Yes	3	12.0	0.03
Russia	713	26.6	14.2	0.30	No	2	24.4	0.38
Sweden	668	14.1	7.3	0.32	Yes	3	20.0	0.84
USA	574	13.2	6.6	0.33	Yes	3	2.8	0.14
Mexico	734	28.5	14.3	0.33	No	2	2.8	0.40
Finland	760	13.1	6.3	0.35	No	3	36.0	0.48
Czech Republic	729	23.0	10.9	0.36	No	1	36.0	0.40
Bulgaria	579	23.7	11.1	0.36	No	1	36.0	0.39
Great Britain	979	14.2	6.5	0.37	No	3	7.1	0.31
E Germany	252	18.0	7.8	0.39	Yes	2	36.0	0.81
Flanders	739	23.5	9.7	0.42	Yes	2	15.4	0.96
New Zealand	601	15.4	6.3	0.42	No	3	2.8	0.32
Hungary	566	27.8	11.2	0.43	No	1	36.0	0.30
Norway	951	11.6	4.6	0.43	Yes	3	12.0	0.56
Slovenia	693	21.8	7.7	0.48	No	1	12.0	0.64
Netherlands	498	17.0	6.0	0.48	Yes	3	9.7	0.39
Israel	725	17.3	6.0	0.48	Yes	3	2.8	0.75
West Germany	509	21.2	7.3	0.49	Yes	2	36.0	0.31
France	1019	12.4	4.1	0.50	No	1	37.3	0.83
Switzerland	488	21.0	6.6	0.52	No	1	3.7	0.52
Northern Ireland	399	16.6	5.2	0.52	No	3	15.6	0.31
Austria	1068	22.1	6.8	0.53	No	1	27.7	0.36
Brazil	846	34.9	10.5	0.54	No	0	3.9	0.09
Ireland	643	31.4	8.9	0.56	Yes	3	7.4	0.19
Chile	787	37.2	9.9	0.58	No	2	4.1	0.07
Spain	1322	29.5	7.3	0.60	No	1	36.0	0.24
Cyprus	515	17.8	4.4	0.61	No	1	3.7	0.00
Portugal	623	25.4	6.1	0.61	No	1	30.0	0.14
Japan	734	25.9	3.0	0.79	No	2	15.2	0.01

Data sources: Affirmative action policy: Bacchi (1996, 1999); CEDAW country reports (2005); Chalude et al. (1994); Chang (2000); O'Connor et al. (1999); Peters (1999). Absence of discriminatory policy: ILO conventions (International Labour Organization, 2005b). Data as of January 2001. Public childcare for children age under 3: CEDAW country reports (2005), Central Bureau of Statistics (2004), Council of the European Union 7069/04 (2004), Eurydice Data base on Education (2003), Fordor (2004), Gornick and Meyers (2003); Heymann et al. (2004), Kamerman (2000), Dombrovsky (2004), OECD (2001), Petrie et al. (2003), Saxonberg and Siroatka (2004), Teplova (2004); UNESCO (2005). Public childcare for children age 3 or older: Gornick and Meyers (2003) UNESCO (2005) calculated from Statistical Annex Table 3 and 11. Parental leave policies: OECD, 2001, Clearinghouse on International Developments in Child (2005).

[a] The housework hour ratio ranges from −1 when the husband does the all housework to 1 when the wife does the all housework.

[b] Absence of discriminatory policy ranges from 0 when all the discriminatory treaties are present to 3 when none are present.

[c] Public childcare is created by adding the score for public childcare for under 3 years old (0–1) and 3 or older (0–1) and dividing by 2.

In general, Scandinavian countries show high public childcare availability, since in these countries services are mostly provided by government. Liberal countries such as Australia and the United States have low rates in public childcare since private childcare is dominant in these countries. Most former socialist countries, except Poland, still have relatively high public childcare rates after the collapse of the socialist regimes.

Conclusion and Discussion

Using Chang's (2000) concept of social policy on women's employment—equality of access and substantive benefit policies—this study analyzed social policy effects on the division of household labor in 33 countries. We hypothesized that countries with developed equality of access (affirmative action and absence of discriminatory policy) and substantive benefit policies (parental leave and public childcare) have a more egalitarian division of housework on average. The hypothesis is supported with regard to discriminatory policy and parental leave policy, but not for affirmative action and public childcare.

We find that the effect of women's full-time employment on housework is stronger in countries with affirmative action policies, and weaker in those with a longer parental leave policy. The effect of women's higher relative income is stronger in countries without discriminatory policy. However, childcare policy does not have a significant effect on the efficacy of either wives' full-time employment or relative income.

Our results suggest that social policies intended to reduce gender inequality and work–family conflicts can have equalizing effects on the division of household labor between men and women. Thus, removing discriminatory policy and implementing parental leave policies may be conducive to realizing a more equal division of housework, regardless of women's individual characteristics. However, these social policies have different effects on the association between women's individual assets and the division of household labor. On the one hand, equality of access policy brings additional leverage for wives with full-time jobs, perhaps by increasing the value of their employment to their families. On the other hand, parental leave policy may actually weaken the housework bargaining power women get from full-time employment, by helping to maintain women's primary role as mothers even when they are employed.

These findings suggest that those advocating policies to reduce the conflict between work and family responsibility need to be careful not to reinforce traditional gender norms. The introduction of a "father's quota" may be the first step, but the reduction of gender wage differences also may be necessary to encourage fathers to take greater advantage of available leave. Also, we note that although equality of access policies help women to realize a more equal division of housework, these equality of access policies do not address problems of gender-biased expectations in the work environment (Gornick and Meyers 2003). Instead of accepting standards where workers are presumed to be without family responsibilities, future social policies should challenge these norms to create work environments that are more compatible with family life.

This study helps take research on the gender division of household labor further beyond its focus on the balance of individual assets as the determinant of couple dynamics. A broader context of gender inequality is an important factor both for the overall division of housework (Batalova and Cohen 2002) and for realizing the efficacy of women's assets in the negotiations between husbands and wives (Fuwa 2004). However, we have shown that state policies regarding gender inequality and work–family conflict may affect both of these outcomes as well. In so doing, we hope to increase attention among researchers and policymakers to the ways that social policy in these areas shapes the context not only for publicly visible forms of gender inequality, such as workplace discrimination, but also for the more intimate negotiations in households, where gender inequality is reproduced.

References

Batalova, Jeanne A. and Philip N. Cohen. 2002. "Premarital Cohabitation and Housework: Couples in Cross-National Perspective." *Journal of Marriage and Family* 64: 743–755.

Bianchi, Suzanne M., Melissa A. Milkie, Liana C. Sayer, and John P. Robinson. 2000. "Is Anyone Doing The Housework? Trends in the Gender Division of Household Labor." *Social Forces* 79: 191–228.

Bacchi, Carol L. 1996. *The Politics of Affirmative Action: 'Women', Equality and Category Politics*. Thousand Oaks: Sage Publications.

Bacchi, Carol L. 1999. *Women, Policy, and Politics: The Construction of Policy Problems.* Thousand Oaks: Sage Publications. Blumberg, R. L. 1984. "A General Theory of Gender Stratification." *Sociological. Theory* 2: 23–101.

Bruning, Gwennaëleand and Janneke Plantenga. 1999. "Parental Leave and Equal Opportunities: Experiences in Eight European Countries." *Journal of European Social Policy* 9: 195–209.

Bulgaria Country Report [2nd and 3rd Report]. 1994. "Convention on the Elimination of All Forms of Discrimination against Women." http://www.un.org/womenwatch/daw/cedaw/ (accessed May 5, 2005).

CEDAW. 2005. "Convention on the Elimination of All Forms of Discrimination against Women (CEDAW) Country Reports." http://www.un.org/womenwatch/daw/cedaw/reports.htm (accessed January 21, 2005).

Central Bureau of Statistics. 2004. "Statistical Abstract of Israel No. 55." http://www1.cbs.gov.il/reader/shnatonenew.htm (accessed January 25, 2005).

Chalude, Monique, Attie de Jong, and Jacqueline Laufer. 1994. "Implementing Equal Opportunity and Affirmative Action Program in Belgium, France and the Netherlands." In: *Women in Management: Current Research Issues* (ed. Marilyn J. Davidson and Ronald J. Burke), 289–303. London: Paul Chapman Publishing.

Chang, Mariko L. 2000." The Evolution of Sex Segregation Regimes." *American Journal of Sociology* 105:1658–1701.

Clearinghouse on International Developments in Child, Youth and Family Policies at Columbia University. 2005. "Maternity, Paternity, Parental and Family Leave Policies." http://www.childpolicyintl.org/maternity.html (accessed January 21, 2005).

Cohen, Phillip N. and Matt L. Huffman. 2003. "Occupational Segregation and the Devaluation of Women's Work across U.S. Labor Markets." *Social Forces* 81: 881–908.

Cotter, David A., JoAnn DeFiore, Joan M. Hermsen, Brenda M. Kowalewski, and Reeve Vanneman. 1997. "All Women Benefit: The Macro-Level Effect of Occupational Integration on Gender Earnings Equality." *American Sociological Review* 62:714–734.

Council of the European Union 7069/04., 2004. "Joint Employment Report." http://europa.eu.int/comm/employment_social/employment_strategy/employment_en.htm (accessed January 21, 2005).

Dombrovsky, Vyacheslav, 2004. "Latvia: Parental Insurance and Childcare: Statements and Comments." http://peerreview.almp.org/pdf/sweden04/latSWE04.pdf (accessed May 6, 2005).

Esping-Andersen, Gøsta. 1990. *The Three Worlds of Welfare Capitalism.* Cambridge: Polity Press.

Esping-Andersen, Gøsta., 1999. *Social Foundations of Postindustrial Economies.* New York: Oxford University Press.

Eurydice Database on Education. 2003. "Country Flies: Slovakia." http://www.childcareinachaningworld.nl/downloads/country_files_slovakia.pdf (accessed May 6, 2005).

Fagnani, Jeanne. 1999. "Parental Leave in France." In: *Parental Leave: Progress or Pitfall?* (ed. Peter Moss and Fred Deven), 69–83. Brussels: NIDI/CBGS Publications.

Folbre, Nancy. 1994. *Who Pays for the Kids? Gender and the Structures of Constraint.* New York: Routledge.

Fuwa, Makiko. 2004. "Macro-Level Gender Inequality and the Division of Household Labor in 22 Countries." *American Socioligcal Review* 69:751–767.

Geist, Claudia. 2005. "The Welfare States and the Home: Regime Differences in the Domestic Division of Labour." *European Sociological Review* 21:23–41.

Gornick, Janet C. and Marcia K. Meyers. 2003. *Families That Work: Policies for Reconciling Parenthood and Employment.* New York: Russell Sage Foundation.

Heymann, Jody, Alison Earle, Stephanie Simmons, Stephanie M. Breslow, and April Kuehnhoff. 2004. "The Work, Family and Equity Index: Where the United States Stands Globally?" http://www.hsph.harvard.edu/globalworkingfamilies/images/report.pdf (accessed May 6, 2005).

Hochschild, Arlie. 1989. *The Second Shift: Working Parents and the Revolution at Home.* New York: Viking.

Hoem, Britta. 1995. "The Way to the Gender-Segregated Swedish Labour Market." In *Gender and Family Change in Industrialized Countries* (ed. Karen O. Mason, and An-Magritt Jensen, 279–296. Oxford: Clarendon Press.

International Labour Organization. 2005a. "Government Programmes in France—Work and Family." http://www.ilo.org/public/english/employment/gems/eeo/program/france/fami.htm (accessed January 21, 2005).

International Labour Organization. 2005b. "ILO Conventions." http://www.ilo.org/ilolex/english/convdisp1.htm (accessed January 21, 2005).

Kamo, Yoshinori. 1994. "Division of Household Work in the United States and Japan." *Journal of Family Issues* 15:348–378.

Kamerman, Sheila B. 2000. "Early Childhood Education and Care: an Overview of Developments in the OECD Countries." *International Journal of Education Research* 33, 7–29.

Kessler-Harris, Alice. 1987. "The Debate over Equality for Women in the Workplace." In *Families and Work* (ed. Naomi Gerstel and Harriet E. Gross), 141–161. Philadelphia, PA: Temple University Press.

Lewis, Jane. 1992. "Gender and the Development of Welfare Regimes." *Journal of European Social Policy* 2:159–173.

McElroy, Marjorie B. 1990. "The Empirical Content of Nash-Bargained Household Behavior." *Journal of Human Resources.* 25:559–583.

McElroy, Marjorie B. 1997. "The Policy Implications of Family Bargaining and Marriage Markets." In *Intrahousehold Resource Allocation in Developing Countries* (ed. Lawrence Haddad, John Hoddinott, and Harold Alderman), 559–583. Baltimore: Johns Hopkins University Press.

O'Connor, Julia S., Ann S. Orloff, and Sheila Shaver. 1999. *States, Markets, Families: Gender, Liberalism, and Social Policy in Australia, Canada, Great Britain, and the United States.* Cambridge: Cambridge University Press.

OECD. 2001. "OECD Employment Outlook: Balancing Work and Family Life: Helping Parents into Paid Employment." http://www.oecd.org/dataoecd/11/12/2079435.pdf (accessed January 21, 2005)

Orloff, Ann Shola. 1993. "Gender and the social rights of citizenship: The comparative analysis of gender relations and welfare states." *American Sociological Review* 58(3): 303–328.

Peters, Anne. 1999. *Women, Quotas and Constitutions: A Comparative Study of Affirmative Action* for Women under American, German, European Community and International Law. Boston: Kluwer Law International.

Petrie, Pat, Peter Moss, Claire Cameron, Mano Candappa, Susan McQuail, and Ann Mooney. 2003. "Early Years and Childcare International Evidence Project: Provision of Services." http://www.dfes.gov.uk/research/data/uploadfiles/intevpaper2provision.pdf (accessed May 6, 2005)

Ruhm, Christopher J. 1998. "The Economic Consequences of Parental Leave Mandates: Lessons from Europe." *Quarterly Journal of Economics* 113:285–317.

Saxonberg, Steven and Tomas Siroatka. 2004. "The Role of Social Policy in Seeking the Balance between Work and Family after Communism." Paper presented at the International Sociological Association conference, Paris, September, 2–4 2004.

Sayer, Liana C., Phillip N. Cohen, and Lynne M. Casper. 2004. *Women, Men and Work.* The American People Series. New York: Population Reference Bureau & Russell Sage Foundation.

Schneider, Anne L. and Helen Ingram. 1997. *Policy Design for Democracy.* Lawrence: University Press of Kansas.

Shelton, Beth A. and Daphne John. 1996. "The Division of Household Labor." *Annual Review of Sociology* 22:299–322.

Sjöberg, Ola. 2004. "The Role of Family Policy Institutions in Explaining Gender-Role Attitudes: A Comparative Multilevel Analysis of Thirteen Industrialized Countries." *Journal of European Social Policy* 14:107–123.

Slovakia Country Report [addendum]. 1998. "Convention on the Elimination of All Forms of Discrimination against Women." http://daccessdds.un.org/doc/UNDOC/GEN/N98/136/58/IMG/N9813658.pdf?OpenElement (accessed May 5, 2005).

Stier, Haya, Noah Lewin-Epstein, and Michael Braun. 2001. "Welfare Regimes, Family-Supportive Policies, and Women's Employment along the Life-Course." *American Journal of Sociology* 106:1731–1760.

Taniguchi, Hiromi. 1999. "The Timing of Childbearing and Women's Wages." *Journal of Marriage and the Family* 61:1008–1019.

Teplova, Tatyana. 2004. "Social Reforms in Russia: Labour Market Implications." In *"Welfare State Restructuring: Processes and Social Outcomes" RC19 Annual conference.* Paris, September 2–4.

Treas, Judith and Eiuic D. Widmer. 2000. "Married Women's Employment over the Life Course: Attitudes in Cross-National Perspective." *Social Forces* 78, 1409–1436.

UNESCO. 2005. "Global Monitoring Report 2003/4: Early Childhood Care and Education (Statistical Annex)." http://portal.unesco.org/education/en/ev.php-RL_ID=24145&URL_DO=DO_ TOPIC&URL_SECTION=201.html (accessed May 5, 2005)

Vogel, Lise. 1993. *Mothers on the Job: Maternity Policy in the U.S. Workplace.* New Brunswick, NJ: Rutgers University Press.

Zentralarchiv fur Empirische Sozialforschung. 2004. "The International Social Survey Programme." Distributed from the University of Cologne.

Questions

1. What, according to the authors, has been "one of the most significant economic and social changes in the last several decades"? How is this change significant?

2. What is the relationship between women working and housework? What issues does this create in families? How does this relationship vary by country?

3. The authors argue that it is important to understand issues of employment and housework at multiple levels. What do they mean by this? What are the various levels of study here?

4. How does social policy influence the relationship between employment and housework? What are the implications for the reproduction of inequality? What policies are most effective and why?

5. Increasingly, families are headed by single mothers, who may or may not have other adults in the household with whom to negotiate a second shift. How is work–family balance complicated in single-parent households? Who does the housework? What solutions might exist for these families? Alternatively, given the gendered nature of housework, how is work–family balance complicated in households headed by same-sex couples?

33

Safe Spaces: Gay-Straight Alliances in High Schools

TINA FETNER, ATHENA ELAFROS, SANDRA BORTOLIN, AND CORALEE DRECHSLER

Subordinate groups have long faced daily instances of harassment, exclusion, and belittlement in their workplaces, stores, places of worship, and schools. These "microaggressions" create hostile environments where people feel out of place, unwelcome, and mistreated. "Safe spaces" are locations of coping, strength, and activism within mainstream spaces. In safe spaces, marginalized people can gain a stronger sense of collective identity that is needed to deal with the toll of microaggressions and discrimination they routinely experience. They also are important to creating large-scale social movements: They become places for building social solidarity and collective action.

LGBTQ students are perhaps best known for demanding safe spaces in schools. As the authors note, LGBTQ students are more likely than others to face overwhelming hostility at school, including being bullied and harassed. Further, LGBTQ students are also more likely to suffer from depression and commit suicide than their straight peers. Given these realities, they especially need safe spaces in schools so they can find peace, replenishment, and outlets for change.

Excerpted from Fetner, Tina, Athena Elafros, Sandra Bortolin, and Coralee Drechsler. 2012. "Safe Spaces: Gay-Straight Alliances in High Schools." *Canadian Review of Sociology* 49:188–207. ©2012 Canadian Sociological Association/La Société Canadienne de Sociologie.

This interview study of youth in gay-straight alliances, a particular type of safe space, in the United States and Canada demonstrates which alliances are most successful in creating safe contexts, safe relationships, and safe activities. They show how hostile environments push groups underground, including straight-youth-enhanced groups. The authors also show that having groups leads to awareness-raising activities, which is certainly important, but has little effect on policies. Some groups are more inclusive and more active than other groups, which the authors argue is largely shaped by the context in which the group forms. This study pushes readers to consider how they can create effective safe spaces in their own communities.

In activists' circles as in sociology, the concept "safe space" has been applied to all sorts of programs, organizations, and practices. Few studies have specified clearly what safe spaces are and how they support the people who occupy them. We examine one social location typically understood to be a safe space: gay-straight alliance groups in high schools. Using qualitative interviews with young adults in the United States and Canada who have participated in gay-straight alliances, we unpack this complex concept to consider some of the dimensions along which safe spaces might vary. Based on interviews with participants, we derive three interrelated dimensions of safe space: social context, membership, and activity.

The idea of building "safe spaces" for vulnerable groups is a common-sense notion that recognizes the negative consequences of social isolation and marginalization. Among those working with adolescents, the need for safe space for youth is widely recognized (Cruz 2008; Griffin et al. 2004; Lee 2002). While it is common for advocates to claim that safe spaces are necessary both for adolescent development and for activism, some scholars argue that the lack of specificity in this concept undermines researchers' ability to understand the qualities of safe spaces and the mechanisms through which social and cultural supports are passed on to group members (e.g., Polletta 1999). In this chapter, we improve the conceptual clarity of safe spaces through a qualitative analysis of one case: gay-straight alliance groups in high schools.

Gay-straight alliances are a form of social support for lesbian, gay, bisexual, transgender, and questioning (LGBTQ) high-school students that emerged in the late 1980s and early 1990s. These alliances are generally student-run social clubs akin to other high-school social groups, such as drama clubs, math teams, or yearbook clubs. However, the main purposes of gay-straight

alliances are to provide support to LGBTQ students in difficult personal circumstances or in hostile school environments and to advocate for LGBTQ students. Many consider gay-straight alliances to be part of the larger LGBTQ movement (e.g., Cortese 2006; Miceli 2005). Over the last two decades, gay-straight alliances have spread throughout high schools across North America, with the aid of the Internet and several social movement organizations (for a discussion of patterns of emergence, see Fetner and Kush 2008). This type of student group has been touted as a potential haven in a hostile world (e.g., Cortese 2006; Hatzenbuehler 2011). However, little research has explored how students themselves experience these groups and the spaces they create as supportive or safe. Nor have scholars identified the particular aspects or dimensions of social spaces that offer a sense of safety or security.

In sociology, safe spaces have been given deep attention in the literature on social movements and activism. Several terms have been used to capture this concept, such as "free spaces" and "havens," among others. In particular, social movement scholars use these terms to discern the spatial and social requirements for creating, elaborating upon, and maintaining heterodox ideas about social justice, the value of marginalized groups, and the call for social change (Evans and Boyte 1986; Robnett 1997). Safe spaces have been credited with producing radical identities, training movement leaders, and allowing for the development of counterhegemonic ideologies (Morris 1984; Whittier 1995). However, it is not altogether clear what counts as a safe space and whether these spaces always result in activism.

We approach the concept of safe space from a sociological perspective, acknowledging that safe spaces are not likely to be simple or singular in the social world. We interview young adults in Canada and the

United States to discover their experiences of gay-straight alliances as safe spaces, to consider the qualities of safe spaces, and to understand their potential for supporting social change. As we discuss herein, our model contains three dimensions of safe space—context, membership, and activities—which we capture with the following questions: *safe from what? safe for whom?* and *safe for what activities?*

On the one hand, the concept of safe space is too vague. It is applied post hoc to a wide variety of social spaces without consensus as to the qualities that make spaces safe (Polletta 1999). On the other hand, sociologists have claimed that safe spaces are very powerful precursors to mobilization, even going so far as to claim that democratic movements require safe spaces (Evans and Boyte 1986). By considering one type of safe space, the gay-straight alliance, in a wide variety of high schools throughout Canada and the United States, we put forth a conceptual framework that articulates key dimensions of safe spaces without assuming a priori that all these spaces are alike. In doing so, we offer a clear conceptual framework of safe spaces for social movement scholarship and highlight the qualities of gay-straight alliances that make them feel safe to LGBTQ students and their straight-identified allies.

The Need for Safe Spaces in High Schools

High schools can be sites of bullying and abuse for lesbian and gay youth, or for anyone who does not closely conform to traditional gender. Although this may be changing for the better over time, what little data exist on this topic show that antigay harassment is common. For example, the Gay, Lesbian, and Straight Education Network (GLSEN) in the United States ran six surveys on high-school climates between 1999 and 2009. The most recent report indicates that 61 percent of LGBT students feel unsafe and 72 percent hear derogatory remarks, while 85 percent are verbally harassed and 40 percent are physically harassed based on their sexual orientation (Kosciw et al. 2010). In addition, almost 70 percent of U.S. transgender students have been verbally harassed in the previous year. GLSEN also notes that among LGBT students of color, 80 percent were verbally harassed and 60 percent were physically harassed (Diaz and Kosciw 2009). Reports from Canada indicate that the school climate is also hostile. Findings

from Egale Canada's first National Climate Survey on Homophobia include the following:

> Three-quarters of LGBTQ students feel unsafe in at least one place at school, such as change rooms, washrooms, and hallways. Half of straight students agree that at least one part of their school is unsafe for LGBTQ students. (Taylor et al. 2008, 47)

The school climate for transgender students is even more difficult. Based on their recent survey, Egale Canada finds that 95 percent of transgender participants feel that their school is unsafe (Taylor et al. 2008).

Given that LGBTQ youth are at greater risk of a host of social problems, including depression, suicide, dropping out of school, homelessness, and drug use (Birkett, Espelage, and Koenig 2009; Espelage et al. 2008; Hatzenbuehler 2011; Rotheram-Borus, Hunter, and Rosario 1994; Russell 2003), and that these youth are more likely to experience stress, conflict with their families, personal homonegativity, and sexual risk-taking (Carragher and Rivers 2002; Saewyc et al. 2006; Williams et al. 2005), the provision of safe spaces for LGBTQ students in high schools is widely understood to be necessary and urgent (Russell 2003; Szalacha 2003). According to Wells (2006), gay-straight alliances aid in fostering an inclusive learning community that values diversity as essential to the creation of safe schools. Gay-straight alliances are also found to positively affect school experiences even for youth who are not group members (Walls, Kane, and Wisneski 2010).

Thinking about Safe Spaces

For decades, the sociological literature has used the concept "safe spaces" (or equivalent terms such as "free spaces," "protected spaces," "havens," or "free social spaces") to refer to "small-scale settings within a community or movement that are removed from the direct control of dominant groups, are voluntarily participated in, and generate the cultural challenge that precedes or accompanies political mobilization" (Polletta 1999, 1). Dozens of sociological studies of mobilization and activism have argued that these safe spaces produce counterhegemonic ideas and identities, thus building the resources that movements can mobilize for collective action.

Various scholars have claimed that safe spaces were crucial to developing strategies for the U.S. civil rights movement (Morris 1984) at the same time that these spaces allowed women in that movement to develop radical feminist identities and ideologies (Evans 1979; Robnett 1997). "Havens," as Hirsch (1993:160) called them, allowed German workers in Chicago to build a radical labor movement, and Fantasia and Hirsch (1995) claim that these spaces led Algerian revolutionaries to reimagine the veil. In the U.S. women's movement, safe spaces are said to have birthed the movement (Mueller 1994) and radicalized identities (Whittier 1995). The most stalwart supporters of safe spaces argue that they are necessary to democratic social movement activity, even though they often operate on the margins of those movements (Evans and Boyte 1986).

In Polletta's (1999) scheme, gay-straight alliances occupy a prefigurative safe space characterized by symmetrical associational ties. Such a space, according to this model, is external to the movement itself but has the capacity to develop new identities and claims, as it tries to live out its ideologies of equality and justice in the real world. These safe spaces accomplish these goals by providing some shelter from dominant ideologies, by creating physical (or virtual) spaces for like-minded people to meet and engage in dialogue, and by building skills for leadership or other activist roles. We build on Polletta's insights by identifying three important dimensions within this prefigurative category along which the characteristics of safe spaces can vary: contexts, membership, and activities.

The first of our questions, *safe from what?*, examines the contexts in which safe spaces are created. Stengel and Weems (2010, 507) claim that safe spaces are "deeply connected to affective states." They argue that when we consider safe spaces, we must also consider the role of fear. This echoes early studies of safe spaces, which tend to focus on settings ripe with potential violence, such as some towns in the U.S. South during the civil rights movement (Morris 1984). The dimension of *context* questions how levels of violence, harassment, discomfort, and social exclusion are a central component of theorizing safe space.

The second of our questions, *safe for whom?*, inquires about membership inclusivity or exclusivity. Polletta and Jasper (2001) consider the role of free space vis-à-vis boundary maintenance and collective identity development. Groch (2001) claims that oppositional identities require safe spaces, claiming directly that

members-only retreats from hegemonic views are a necessary feature of safe spaces. Hackford-Peer (2010) examines fear, exclusivity, and gay-straight alliances, claiming that students of color do not feel safe in these groups. The dimension of *membership* focuses on how our participants enacted boundary maintenance through inclusion and exclusion of members.

The third of our questions, *safe to do what?*, considers the relationship between safe spaces and the actions that emerge from them. This question interrogates the social movements literature's assumption that safe spaces are the incubators of collective action. This body of work makes a strong case that safe spaces are not only important sites to protect marginalized groups, but also to foster activism. It connects safe spaces with many of the social processes considered essential for mobilization. In this regard, Polletta (1999) considers the link between free spaces and collective identity building. Morris (1984) emphasizes their institutional and cultural supports for activism. The dimension of *activities* requires our participants to reflect on the kinds of actions that emerge from these spaces. Whether or not the safe spaces of gay-straight alliances will produce activism is an empirical question that we address directly in this study.

Methods

Between 2005 and 2008, we conducted 57 online interviews with young adults, ages 18 to 25, who had participated in gay-straight alliances or similar LGBTQ groups in high school. Of the 57 respondents, 38 were involved in gay-straight alliances in their high schools, while the other 19 were involved in similar school-based LGBTQ activism. Interviews were semi-structured, with consistent interview questions across participants as well as open-ended questions and invitations for participants to add other information. Recruitment involved multiple snowball samples born from a variety of social networks of LGBTQ youth and adults across the United States and Canada. Of the 57 participants, 26 went to high school in the United States and 31 in Canada.

Table 1 lists the identifiers that participants provided; participants were allowed to use their own language to describe their gender and sexuality.

Participants were interviewed online via instant messaging software, such as iChat and MSN Messenger. To be sure that our sample included those who had

Table 1 Breakdown of Participants.

Gender	Sexual Identity	Race and/or Ethnicity	Nation	Involvement
29 female	18 gay	35 White	31 Canada	38 gay-straight alliance recognized by school
23 male	7 lesbian	1 Black	26 United States	19 informal or external LGBTQ group
2 transgender	4 homosexual	3 Asian		
1 all genders	10 bisexual	1 Hispanic		
1 gender variant	5 straight	2 Jewish		
1 no response	5 queer	1 Armenian		
	3 pansexual	8 mixed background		
	2 asexual	4 no response		
	2 heterosexual			

closeted sexual identities during high school, we interviewed young adults (18–25 years of age) and asked them to reflect back on their experiences in high school. We chose instant messaging to broaden the geographic reach of our sample, which includes participants throughout Canada and the United States (for a discussion of qualitative interviews using instant messaging technology, see Kazmer and Xie 2008). Pseudonyms were assigned to all participants and others they referred to during the interviews. Identifying details were eliminated or slightly changed. Excerpted quotes were edited only for brevity; they are presented verbatim, including grammar and spelling errors.

Findings

We asked participants to comment on three elements of their experiences in gay-straight alliances. First, we asked about the hostile climate toward gay, lesbian, and gender variant students in school, as well as within families of origin and the larger community that created the social context that defined the need for safe spaces. Second, we asked about issues of membership in gay-straight alliances and the subculture that these organizations fostered. And third, we asked participants to comment on the ways that gay-straight alliances allowed students to engage in educational activities and activism on behalf of LGBTQ students. In the following subsections, we present the responses of our participants, as they speak to these three dimensions of safe spaces: *safe from what? safe for whom?* and *safe for what activities?*

Safe from What? Contexts for Safe Spaces

The first dimension of safe space is the level of hostility and even danger in the social context where this space is situated. Both the literature on safe spaces and the responses from our participants indicate that the perceived level of hostility or insecurity of the environment is a key factor in participants' need for safe spaces. Barriers to the formation of gay-straight alliances came from contexts both internal and external to the schools. Some school boards, parents, administrators, and fellow students opposed the formation of gay-straight alliances. This is not surprising, given that there has been a tendency for the education system to problematize and exclude homosexuality from its domain (MacDougall 2000, 100). The marginalization of homosexuality within the school system is evident in both the Canadian and American contexts.

In our study, subjects pointed out that the efforts of opponents kept some gay-straight alliances from being officially recognized. Some students formed groups informally or outside school. In other cases, students succeeded in forming gay-straight alliances and equity and/or diversity groups despite this opposition.

> [The biggest accomplishment] was being able to finally do things within the school . . . before that we couldn't even advertise . . . we couldn't do this when administration kept us underground. (Jamie, bisexual, transgender)

The struggles of this student proved worthwhile when a new administration came into the school and allowed the gay-straight alliance to become an official school club. Other participants report similar struggles, with teachers or members of the administration actively involved in either stopping the creation of the gay-straight alliance or trying to shut it down after it had started:

> well actually it had a huge impact on people at first, be-cause the administration didn't want a GSA there, and then we had to get student support together and peti-tion but then the administration gave up and our school newspaper wrote about the struggle we had / it was a big deal at the time even though we didn't think it was. (Morgan, pansexual, no gender identity)

The climate at some schools was such that student organizations in support of LGBTQ issues were not al-lowed to call themselves gay-straight alliances and in-stead had to use generic names that made invisible their connection to lesbian and gay students. There were at least five Canadian LGBTQ groups in our sample that were unable to call themselves gay-straight alliances and were forced to broadly identify as "equity and di-versity" groups.

Once a group was formed, many alliance members faced limits on their ability to promote events, finding that their posters were subject to vandalism:

> when we were advertising . . . we had to put up our post-ers again each day because they were being torn down. We got our own board now, but it had to be in a place where there was a camera because our stuff was still be vandalized and torn down. (Catherine, pansexual, female)

This incident was echoed by a student at another school, who states, "When the posters for the GSA first went up, they were torn down and spit upon" (Patrick, male, straight). Some students found that their participation in gay-straight alliances provoked a backlash, making visible some of the hostility to LGBTQ people that had previously been hidden. For example,

> the day after [an event sponsored by the gay-straight al-liance,] their was tagging on the front of the school and the sidewalk between buildings/antigay comments/many people were accused of being gay who partici-pated too. . . . (Jaime, bisexual, transgender)

The safe space of a gay-straight alliance student club is bounded by the structure of school regulations,

the policy decisions of school authorities, and the cul-tural climates that vary greatly in their acceptance of LGBTQ students. In addition to these administrative challenges in the formation of gay-straight alliances, students also experienced verbal harassment and physi-cal abuse from their peers, teachers, administration, and parents. Antigay graffiti appears to be a common struggle that many LGBTQ youth in our study dealt with at school. The following participant states, ". . . I generally kept to the theatre room . . . there did seem to be a lot of homophobic graffiti around whenever I ven-tured into the rest of the school" (Becky, queer, female). In some cases, peers created an antigay culture through verbal harassment and physical abuse. For example, one participant recalls:

> Also, a majority of people in my school are very into the whole "that's so gay" thing. And the whole calling people "faggots" and "queers." They say they don't mean it in a negative way towards gay people. . . . But if you think about it, that's exactly what they're saying. (Melissa, pansexual, female)

Coupled with these day-to-day instances of verbal abuse were instances of physical harassment by peers, including rape:

> well [friend X] had some verbal harassment . . . actually a lot of it from what i remember, both inside and out-side of school. at one point, he was raped. (Michelle, lesbian, female)

> I remember one meeting . . . one of the new mem-bers asked if he could speak, and divulged that he had been raped by another student at the school and was trying to decide whether or not to tell the police. I mean, you can't have that kind of experience and not be significantly changed for life. (Ryan, gay, male)

Instead of addressing issues of harassment, teachers were often the source of antigay harassment. In some cases, this took the form of ongoing harassment, such as running jokes at the expense of LGBTQ students:

> that class had a running gag about lindsey lohan, so they had a calendar of her up in the classroom / there was one [picture] where she was not conservatively clad, and the teacher took it and went up to him (while he was sitting) and he was like "this doesn't do *any-thing* for you???" . . . then there were jokes from class-mates and that sort of thing. (Jason, queer, male)

At other times, harassment from teachers involved physically separating students they believed to be dating or intimately involved.

The hostile climate found in many schools also extended beyond the confines of high school, into the families and communities of many respondents. Not only did participants encounter difficulties with their parents accepting their sexuality, but some were also discouraged from hanging out with LGBTQ friends.

> Interviewer (I): Did anyone ever give you a hard time for hanging out with any of your gay/queer/bi/lesbian friends?

> Respondent (R): well . . . my mom does . . . its gotten bad lately and i'm moving out from it . . . she's having issues with my hanging out with gay friends all the time. (Jaime, bisexual, transgender)

The larger community also posed problems for the following participant, who lived in a city in the United States that he described as "ultra-conservative":

> My high school . . . had invited the founder of the city's PFLAG [Parents, Families, & Friends of Lesbians and Gays] organization to speak to students. Well, some alumni . . . held a protest vigil across the street from the school because of their "concern" that the school was promoting "homosexuality" through the religion curriculum. (Quinn, queer, gender variant)

The participant adds, "[t]he anti-gay vigil organizers also brought in at least two anti-gay national personalities and ex-gay types who spoke on some conservative (but popular) talk radio programs in [large city]." The vigil did spark conversation among students who felt a need for a supportive network or club where they could connect. This participant and some fellow students formed an underground "dance club," basically, their version of a gay-straight alliance. However, their club was later investigated for "promoting homosexuality."

Participants connected their experiences with antigay comments both within school and in the larger community with a need for safe spaces, and just about everyone we interviewed indicated that gay-straight alliances did provide the kind of safe spaces they needed to withdraw from this hostile climate. For example, one participant suggests,

> We all need a sanctuary. I'm extremely grateful I was involved since it [the gay-straight alliance] helped me come to terms with being different. (Amanda, asexual, female)

Given the verbal and physical forms of harassment that students encountered from fellow students, teachers, and administrators, and the pressures from family and friends, gay-straight alliances and other LGBTQ organizations did indeed provide a safe space from internal and external threats to their safety. In addition, we found evidence of a connection between the amount of hostility in the school—from administrators, teachers, or fellow students—and both the type of safe space and the meaning of that space to group members. For example, extremely hostile contexts, in which there was a strong consensus in antigay opinions, such as in private religious schools or conservative towns, contained groups that were underground rather than official, in which members were closeted. In these cases, our participants reported deeply felt ties to fellow group members and to the group itself.

Safe for Whom? Membership in Safe Spaces

The second dimension of safe spaces is membership—who is welcome and who is left out. As collective identity formation is a key cultural process associated with safe spaces in the scholarly literature (e.g., Polletta and Jasper 2001; Robnett 1997; Whittier 1995), membership in gay-straight alliances is an important site of boundary maintenance. In our interviews, we asked participants to speak directly to the issue of membership in gay-straight alliances. Previous research on gay-straight alliances and safety have clearly illustrated how gay-straight alliances and other LGBTQ organizations may be safe for some students while unsafe for others (Griffin et al. 2004; McCready 2001). For example, one student notes that not all identities were acknowledged in the gay-straight alliance she helped form:

> we didn't really acknowledge the T in LGBTQ. . . . it was [a] GSA and that had no room for people with different gender identities . . . not that we hated trans people, but that we felt there was no one on campus that could possibly fit that letter and so didn't acknowledge that we might be wrong, that there could have been someone out there with gender identity issues. (Morgan, pansexual, no gender identity)

Furthermore, many students in gay-straight alliances were unwilling to disclose their sexual identities during meetings. They feared repercussions from fellow students:

> actually, really hilariously, no one really identified themselves because if we did, it would go around the school and someone might be harassed by other students. (Morgan, pansexual, no gender identity)

One of our more surprising findings was the large extent to which participants hailed the sexual diversity of the group as a positive aspect of the safe space that the group created. In particular, the role of straight students, which might be expected to undermine the sense of community and solidarity among LGBTQ students, was for the most part lauded as a particularly useful, helpful, or encouraging aspect of the gay-straight alliance. For example, one queer man says:

> I don't know what the straight/nonstraight breakdown of that group was, but I was happy that a straight guy was willing to be out front in support of queer issues. (Mark, queer, male)

For others, the inclusion of straights was seen as a way to make connections and educate the larger heterosexual community:

> umm to go back to the straight people being involved in a GSA, I also think that they need to be there because the gay community needs a sort of bridge if you will between them and the heterosexual community, and these straight members act as that bridge. (Jen, bisexual, female)

The inclusion of straight allies in the club provided cover for students who were not ready to disclose their sexual identity, or who were questioning their sexual identity. Straight allies were crucial to creating a space in which closeted kids could participate. As one respondent notes:

> I think that in larger schools . . . the closet became less of an issue because the group was large enough that it made sense that some extremely confident straight kids might be involved—so they could still be involved and even lead without that label being implicit. . . . So just having out kids may have made it easier for closeted kids to be involved. (Logan, gay, male)

Another important aspect to note is that all of the LGBTQ participants in our study were pleased by the support and involvement of straight allies. This participant sums up the common sentiment:

> Because any queer will stand up for their own rights. But when you can get a straight person to fight and be vocal for a right that doesn't affect them and that sometimes, they don't even really understand? well / it kind of made the "ally" part of the GSA really. (Lisa, lesbian, female)

Our respondents make clear that, while they felt that gay-straight alliances were safe spaces for themselves, there was not necessarily a full range of students participating in these groups. In particular, students of color were not present in great numbers, and racism was raised as a discussion topic more often among those student groups that were designated as diversity or anti-oppression groups rather than as gay-straight alliances. While this was disappointing to some of our respondents who felt that their LGBTQ identities were being made invisible, it also seemed to bring greater attention to racism. In terms of membership, students of color and transgender students were most likely to be marginalized in these groups, while straight students were welcomed.

Safe to Do What? Activities Emerging from Safe Spaces

Our third question considers the kind and quality of activities that gay-straight alliance produces. This is especially salient to the social movement literature, which is concerned less with the quality of the space than with its potential to mobilize participants. Our respondents describe how gay-straight alliances opened the door for a number of activities aimed at raising awareness of LGBTQ people and educating others about difference but did not create much policy change in their schools and communities.

In spite of the previously noted pressures from principals, the administration, parents' associations, and other students, there were many gay-straight alliances in schools that were able to promote a wide range of activities. For example, the "day of silence" and "pride prom" were events held by gay-straight alliances at some high schools in order to raise awareness of LGBTQ issues. During the "day of silence," participants refuse to speak for the day to draw attention to the

cultural silence around LGBTQ issues. As this participant explains:

> It [the day of silence] has brought gay rights to the fore-
> front of our minds, and has opened people's eyes about
> GLBT people. We have become a more tolerant, open
> school, partially as a result of this. (Katie, bisexual,
> female)

Other activities included students making pro-gay
buttons, which students at one U.S. high school created
in addition to participating in the day of silence, as this
student discusses:

> but I think recognizing the day of silence and wearing
> pro-gay rights buttons that we made ourselves to show
> our support in getting rid of the antigay marriage
> amendment was what hit our school the hardest as far
> as proud impact on young minds. (Morgan, pansexual,
> no gender identity)

For this student, the issue of gays being able to
marry was about freedom of choice, as well as the possibility of marrying and having children someday,
which this participant equates with the ability to lead "a
normal, young life." This demonstrates students' persistence and their effectiveness at drawing attention to
larger issues within their school community. The distribution of "slurring tickets" was another creative idea, as
this student describes:

> we collaborated and made these explanations of why its
> offensive to use terms like "gay" to refer to anything that's
> "bad.". . . we all give them out to make our point but to
> avoid being put on the spot. (Megan, bisexual, female)

Efforts of other students extended beyond their
immediate high school to reach students from other
high schools. In one Canadian city, students threw a
"pride prom," which LGBTQ students from various
high schools could attend. As many schools forbid students from bringing same-sex dates to the prom, the
students involved felt this was a much-needed act of
inclusion:

> the fact that we threw the first EVER Rainbow Prom :)
> [was especially important] because a lot of my friends
> couldn't bring who they wanted to their proms. ours was
> not only veryyy affordable for kids who no longer live at
> home for whatever reason, but you could obviously
> bring any date you wanted :). (Ashley, bisexual, female)

Other gay-straight alliance members participated
in activities that benefited the larger community. This
included raising supplies for a local women's shelter,
starting an AIDS fundraising campaign, participating
in and raising money through AIDS walks, assisting in
the development of education packages for a local
school board, and publishing an article regarding
LGBTQ issues in a local newspaper. Perhaps one of the
most ambitious activities was carried out by students at
one U.S. high school who were able to organize a statewide gay-straight alliance conference:

> The biggest single-event thing was holding a GSA con-
> ference for any schools in the state. . . . We brought in
> presenters from all kinds of different organizations in
> the city, had keynote speakers, all kinds of things. It
> was absolutely amazing. (Ryan, gay, male)

Students involved in gay-straight alliances were instrumental in planning and carrying out a variety of
activities, many of which brought a profound sense of
accomplishment to those involved. Through the support
of other students, teachers, and administrators, these
students felt empowered to engage in education and activism, in addition to social activities. This does not discount the fact that for many students who were involved
in gay-straight alliances, the social support garnered
through their involvement was satisfying on its own.
For many, the sheer existence of the group and access to
a comfortable social space was what made high school a
bearable experience. As this account demonstrates:

> We accomplished permanent and dedicated members.
> What I was proud of was the dedication of those mem-
> bers who came every week and brought their friends
> along with a smile and were always ready to do what-
> ever activity was planned. (Mike, gay, male)

The safe spaces of gay-straight alliances, however,
failed to achieve many of the goals that participants had
for their groups. When asked what kind of impact the
gay-straight alliance had on the school, one student who
had founded a gay-straight alliance in his school replied, "to tell the truth not much" (Jack, gay, male).
When asked why, this participant spoke of the newness
of this gay-straight alliance and the students' self-
professed lack of organization in planning events. So,
while many students wanted their alliance to create an
LGBTQ-friendly school, to reverse some heterosexist

policies like restricting prom dates by gender, or to launch some activism in their larger communities, this was seldom possible among our respondents. Overall, gay-straight alliances provided opportunities for limited activism, social exchange, and dialogue, though the kind and quality of activities produced in these spaces greatly varied depending on external factors (such as pressures from parents' groups) and internal factors (such as pressures from administrators, principals, and students), in addition to the unique demands and concerns of the gay-straight alliance members.

Discussion

The three dimensions we put forth are: context (safe from what?), membership (safe for whom?), and activity (safe to do what?). Safe spaces can vary along each of these dimensions to produce a wide variety of social settings, all of which feel like safe spaces to our participants. In addition, we suggest that these dimensions interact with each other to shape safe spaces. More hostile contexts, for example, are likely to restrict membership practices and the activities in which students participate. Further research should be conducted on how the dimension of context, membership, and activity may contribute to a better understating of safe spaces in and around other social movement organizations, such as antipoverty groups, social justice groups, feminist groups, LGBTQ groups, and antiracism groups, among others. These three dimensions will add much-needed specificity to the concept while remaining flexible enough to apply to a wide variety of spaces.

We also consider the extent to which the safe spaces produced by gay-straight alliances mobilize students and encourage activism, as the social movement literature would claim. We find that activism is not the inevitable outcome of gay-straight alliances. High schools' concerns with discipline and order, and especially their restrictive policies on student behavior, limited the activities that were feasible or even imaginable among our participants.

Our study also deepens our knowledge of gay-straight alliances in high schools across Canada and the United States. This growing body of work on gay-straight alliances considers the extent to which these groups reduce stress on LGBTQ students, eliminate bullying, improve LGBTQ dropout rates, or prevent LGBTQ teen suicides. Our study demonstrates that gay-straight alliances are not all the same. The wide variety of experiences reported by our participants serves as a useful reminder that consideration must be given not only to whether high schools have gay-straight alliances, but also to the variation in the qualities of these groups and the safe spaces they create for LGBTQ students and their straight allies.

References

Birkett, Michelle, Dorothy L. Espelage, and Brian Koenig. 2009. "LGB and Questioning Students in Schools: The Moderating Effects of Homophobic Bullying and School Climate on Negative Outcomes." *Journal of Youth and Adolescence* 38:989–1000.

Carragher, Daniel J. and Ian Rivers. 2002. "Trying to Hide: A Cross-National Study of Growing up for Non-Identified Gay and Bisexual Male Youth." *Clinical Child Psychology and Psychiatry* 7(3): 457–474.

Cortese, Daniel K. 2006. *Are We Thinking Straight? The Politics of Straightness in a Lesbian and Gay Social Movement Organization.* New York: Routledge.

Cruz, Cindy. 2008. "Notes on Immigration, Youth, and Ethnographic Silence." *Theory into Practice* 47:67–73.

Diaz, Elizabeth M. and Joseph G. Kosciw. 2009. *Shared Differences: The Experiences of Lesbian, Gay, Bisexual, and Transgender Students of Color in Our Nation's Schools.* New York: GLSEN.

Espelage, Dorothy L., Steven R. Aragon, Michelle Birkett, and Brian W. Koenig. 2008. "Homophobic Teasing, Psychological Outcomes, and Sexual Orientation among High School Students: What Influence Do Parents and Schools Have?" *School Psychology Review* 37:202–216.

Evans, Sara M. 1979. *Personal Politics: The Roots of Women's Liberation in the Civil Rights Movement and the New Left.* New York: Vintage Books

Evans, Sara M. and Harry C. Boyte. 1986. *Free Spaces: The Sources of Democratic Change in America.* New York: Harper and Row.

Fantasia, Rrick and Eric L. Hirsch. 1995. "Culture in Rebellion: The Appropriation and Transformation of the Veil in the Algerian Revolution." In *Social Movements and Culture* (ed. H. Johnston and B. Klandermans), 144–162. Minneapolis: University of Minnesota Press.

Fetner, Tina and Kristin Kush. 2008. "Lesbian and Gay Activism in High Schools: The Emergence of Gay-Straight Alliances." *Youth and Society* 40:114–140.

Griffin, Pat, Camille Lee, Jeffrey Waugh, and Chad Beyer. 2004. "Describing Roles that Gay-Straight Alliances

Play in Schools: From Individual Support to School Change." *Journal of Gay and Lesbian Issues in Education* 1:7–22.

Groch, Sharon. 2001. "Free Spaces: Creating Oppositional Consciousness in the Disability Rights Movement." In *Oppositional Consciousness: The Subjective Roots of Social Protest* (ed. Jane J. Mansbridge and Aldon Morris), 65–98. Chicago, IL: University of Chicago Press.

Hackford-Peer, Kim. 2010. "In the Name of Safety: Discursive Positionings of Queer Youth." *Studies in Philosophy and Education* 29:541–556.

Hatzenbuehler, Mark L. 2011. "The Social Environment and Suicide Attempts in Lesbian, Gay, and Bisexual Youth." *Pediatrics* 127:896–903.

Hirsch, Eric L. 1993. "Protest Movements and Urban Theory." *Research in Urban Sociology* 3:159–180.

Kazmer, Michelle M. and Bo Xie. 2008. "Qualitative Interviewing in Internet Studies: Playing with the Media, Playing with the Method." *Information, Communication and Society* 11(2): 257–278.

Kosciw, Joseph G., Emily A. Greytak, Elizabeth M. Diaz, and Mark J. Bartkiewicz. 2010. *The 2009 National School Climate Survey: The Experiences of Lesbian, Gay, Bisexual and Transgender Youth in our Nation's Schools.* New York: Gay, Lesbian and Straight Education Network (GLSEN).

Lee, Camille. 2002. "The Impact of Belonging to a High School Gay/Straight Alliance." *The High School Journal* 85:13–26.

MacDougall, Bruce. 2000. *Queer Judgments: Homosexuality, Expression and the Courts in Canada.* Toronto, ON: University of Toronto Press.

McCready, Lance T. 2001. "When Fitting In Isn't an Option, or Why Black Queer Males at a California High School Stay Away from Project 10." In *Troubling Intersections of Race and Sexuality* (ed. Kevin Kushamiro), 37–54. Lanham, MD: Rowman and Littlefield.

Miceli, Melinda. 2005. *Standing Out, Standing Together: The Social and Political Impact of Gay-Straight Alliances.* New York: Routledge.

Morris, Aldon. 1984. *The Origins of the Civil Rights Movement: Black Communities Organizing for Change.* New York: Free Press.

Mueller, Carol. 1994. "Conflict Networks and the Origins of Women's Liberation." In *New Social Movements: From Ideology to Identity* (ed. Enrique Larana, Hank Johnston, and Joseph R. Gusfield), 234–263. Philadelphia, PA: Temple University Press.

Polletta, Francesca. 1999. "'Free Spaces' in Collective Action." *Theory and Society* 28:1–38.

Polletta, Francesca and James Jasper. 2001. "Collective Identity and Social Movements." *Annual Review of Sociology* 27: 283–305.

Robnett, Belinda. 1997. *How Long? How Long? African-American Women in the Struggle for Civil Rights.* Oxford, UK: Oxford University Press.

Rotheram-Borus, Mary J., Joyce Hunter, and Margaret Rosario. 1994. "Suicidal Behavior and Gay-Related Stress among Gay and Bisexual Male Adolescents." *Journal of Adolescent Research* 9:498–508.

Russell, Stephen T. 2003. "Sexual Minority Youth and Suicide Risk." *American Behavioral Scientist* 46(9): 1241–1257.

Saewyc, Elizabeth M., C. L. Skay, Sandra L. Pettingell, Elizabeth A. Reis, Linda Bearinger, Michael Resnick, Aileen Murphy, and Leigh Combs. 2006. "Hazards of Stigma: The Sexual and Physical Abuse of Gay, Lesbian, and Bisexual Adolescents in the United States and Canada." *Child Welfare* 85:195–213.

Stengel, Barbara S. and Lisa Weems 2010. "Questioning Safe Space: An Introduction." *Studies in Philosophy of Education* 29:505–507.

Szalacha, Laura. 2003. "Safer Sexual Diversity Climates: Lessons Learned from an Evaluation of Massachusetts Safe Schools Program for Gay and Lesbian Students." *American Journal of Education* 110:58–88.

Taylor, Catherine, Tracey Peter, Kevin Schachter, Sarah Paquin, Stacey Beldom, Zoe Gross, and T. L. McMinn. 2008. *Youth Speak Up about Homophobia and Transphobia: The First National Climate Survey on Homophobia in Canadian Schools. Phase One Report.* Toronto, ON: Egale Canada Human Rights Trust.

Walls, N. Eugene., Sarah B. Kane, and Hope Wisneski. 2010. "Gay-Straight Alliances and School Experiences of Sexual Minority Youth." *Youth and Society* 41: 307–332.

Wells, Kristopher. 2006. *Gay-Straight Alliance Handbook: A Comprehensive Resource for Canadian K-12 Teachers, Administrators and School Counsellors.* Ottawa, ON: Canadian Teachers' Federation.

Whittier, Nancy. 1995. *Feminist Generations: The Persistence of the Radical Women's Movement.* Philadelphia, PA: Temple University Press.

Williams, Trish, Jennifer Connolly, Debra Pepler, and Wendy Craig. 2005. "Peer Victimization, Social Support, and Psychosocial Adjustment of Sexual Minority Adolescents." *Journal of Youth and Adolescence* 34: 471–482.

Questions

1. Why have researchers and advocates argued that "safe spaces" are important for certain groups of people? What do people get from being in safe spaces? What makes a space "safe"?

2. Why, specifically, are "safe spaces" important for LGBTQ youth? What statistics and information do the authors offer as evidence of this need?

3. The authors put forth three dimensions and questions to consider about safe spaces. What are these dimensions and corresponding questions? Why are these important to ask and answer?

4. What answers do the authors find? What are the implications for social change and the reproduction of inequality? In what ways do safe spaces in this study challenge and contest inequality? What are the ways in which these organizations and safe spaces could do a better job at challenging inequality?

5. Superordinate group members often criticize subordinate group members for "self-segregating" and creating spaces just for their group. Provide some examples. What narratives do people use to press their point? Do they have a point? Why or why not? Why do people from subordinated groups insist on having safe spaces in the face of these criticisms?

6. Where and for whom are safe spaces in your community? How are safe spaces maintained and by whom? What role do people from dominant groups play? How is information about a safe space spread to others? What happens if the safeness of the space is challenged? How can this study help bolster safe spaces in your community?

7. How have social media shaped the need for and nature of safe spaces? What platforms have been used most effectively and how? How else might people use social media to create safe spaces?

I. Data Analysis Exercise: What Causes the Wage Gap?

In Chapter 26, Crowley showed how women and men work in different jobs where employers exert different strategies to control workers. Gender segregation in the workplace is just one social process that contributes to unequal wages. Social scientists have also shown that women are denied promotions or tracked into jobs with little chance for promotion by employers because of their real or perceived positions as mothers. Women also hit a glass ceiling that blocks them from access to the top jobs. In this data analysis exercise, you will analyze historical trends in the gender wage gap and the ten most common occupations for women. The tables and charts presented here provide information on full-time workers only. That is, they exclude stay-at-home moms and part-time workers from the analysis.

Part I.

Questions:

1. How has the gender wage gap in median weekly earnings changed across time? During what times were there the greatest shifts in the wage gap? How has the wage gap changed across the last 10 years?

2. If the wage gap continues to change at the same rate as it has for the last 10 years, when would you estimate that the wage gap would completely disappear? How old would you be?

3. What policies or programs could be implemented to increase the speed at which the wage gap closes?

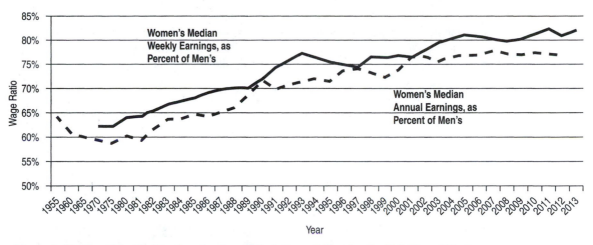

Figure I Median Weekly Earnings by Race/Ethnicity and Gender for Full-Time Workers.
Source: Hegewisch, Ariane, and Heidi Hartmann. 2013. *The Gender Wage Gap: 2013 Differences by Race and Ethnicity*. Washington D.C.: Institute for Women's Policy Research. http://www.iwpr.org/publications/pubs/the-gender-wage-gap-2013 (accessed January 3, 2015).

Part 2.

In the next part of this data analysis exercise, you will examine the gender wage gap among the most common occupations held by women in 2013. Use Table 1 to answer the questions that follow.

Questions:

1. Of the top ten occupations, which one has the smallest wage gap? Which occupation has the largest?

2. Of these occupations, in which one do women have the highest median weekly earnings? What is the wage gap for that occupation? In which occupation do women have the lowest median weekly earnings? What is the wage gap for that occupation? Calculate how much more—in real dollars—men earn per week for the occupation with the largest gap and the smallest gap. How many more dollars do they earn in a year? About how much more would men earn across a 35-year career if those earnings gaps held steady?

Table I The Wage Gap for the Top Ten Most Common Occupations for Women 2013.

	Women's Median Weekly Earnings	Women's Earnings as a Percent of Men's
Elementary and Middle School Teachers	$937	91.4%
Secretaries and Administrative Assistants	$677	87.7%
Registered Nurses	$1,086	87.9%
Nursing, Psychiatric, and Home Health Aides	$450	90.2%
Customer Service Representatives	$616	96.4%
First-Line Supervisors of Retail Sales Workers	$612	78.7%
Accountants and Auditors	$1,029	81.2%
Cashiers	$379	89.0%
Managers, All Other	$1,105	79.0%
First-Line Supervisors of Office & Administrative Support Workers	$748	88.4%

Source: Hegewisch, Ariane, and Maxwell Matite. 2013. *The Gender Wage Gap by Occupation*. Washington D.C.: Institute for Women's Policy Research, Retrieved (http://www.iwpr.org/publications/pubs/the-gender-wage-gap-by-occupation-2). (accessed January 3, 2015).

3. Before doing this exercise, would you have expected the gender wage gap to be the size it is for women's most common occupations? Why or why not? What accounts for these gaps?

Part 3.

In the last part of this data analysis exercise, you will examine the gender wage gap among different race/ethnic groups in the United States in 2013. Before looking at the following table, what race/gender categories do you think have the lowest median wages? Which do you think will have the highest?

Questions:

1. Calculate the average wage gap in real dollars and fill in this table:

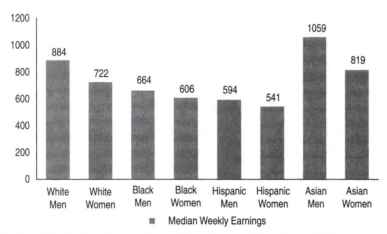

Figure 2 Median Weekly Earnings by Race/Ethnicity and Gender in 2013.
Source: Bureau of Labor Statistics, *Usual Weekly Earnings of Wage and Salary Workers. Third Quarter 2014.* Washington D.C.: United States Department of Labor. http://www.bls.gov/news.release/wkyeng.toc.htm (accessed January 3, 2015).

How much more do white men earn on average than . . .?

White women:	Black women:	Hispanic women:	Asian women:	Black men:	Hispanic men:	Asian men:

How much more do men earn on average than women of their same race?

Whites? Blacks? Hispanics? Asians?

2. Whose wage gap is biggest? Smallest? Why? How much of an earnings boost do white men get over others across a year? Across a lifetime?
3. How does this chart illustrate the importance of taking an intersectionality approach to understanding inequality? When answering this question be sure to discuss how women's earnings compare to those of men in their own race/ethnicity and men across other race/ethnicities.
4. Why is it important to use full-time workers in the analysis? Who is excluded from the analysis? What inequality-infused processes influence who can and does work full-time and year-round?

References:

Bureau of Labor Statistics. 2014. *Usual Weekly Earnings of Wage and Salary Workers. Third Quarter 2014.* Washington, DC: United States Department of Labor. http://www.bls.gov/news.release/wkyeng.toc.htm (accessed January 3, 2015).

Hegewisch, Ariane, and Heidi Hartmann. 2013. *The Gender Wage Gap: 2013 Differences by Race and Ethnicity.* Washington, DC: Institute for Women's Policy Research. http://www.iwpr.org/publications/pubs/the-gender-wage-gap-2013 (accessed January 3, 2015).

Hegewisch, Ariane, and Maxwell Matite. 2013. *The Gender Wage Gap by Occupation.* Washington, DC: Institute for Women's Policy Research.http://www.iwpr.org/publications/pubs/the-gender-wage-gap-by-occupation-2 (accessed January 3, 2015).

J. Data Analysis Exercise: Living Together or Living Apart?

In the reading by Roscigno, Karafin, and Tester in Part III, you read about discrimination that contributes to continued racial segregation. The reading focused on Ohio, but what does racial segregation look like in different cities across the country? In this data analysis exercise you will first view maps of the top ten most segregated cities in the country. You will then examine racial segregation in metropolitan areas near where you attend school. Remember that the index of dissimilarity measures racial segregation, where low scores indicate low segregation and high scores indicate high segregation. Scores can range from 0 to 100, where a score of 100 would indicate that 100 percent of the people living in the area would need to move to create a racially integrated neighborhood.

Part 1.

Go to the article "The 10 Most Segregated Urban Areas in America" (Denvir 2011) on Salon's website (http://www.salon.com/2011/03/29/most_segregated_cities/slide_show/10). Then use the maps to answer the following questions.

Questions:

1. What is the most segregated city in the United States? What is the index of dissimilarity for this city? Explain what the index of dissimilarity score means.
2. Looking at the different urban spaces, are there any that surprise you? Why or why not?
3. Taking the top 10 most segregated urban spaces as a whole, are certain geographic regions of the country over- or underrepresented in the list? Be sure to support your answer with evidence.
4. What pattern can you observe in the location of where different race/ethnic groups live in the different segregated cities?

Part 2.

Next you will use census data to examine metropolitan areas in the state where you attend school. Please note that in any area with less than 1,000 people of a given race/ethnic group the results will not be reliable. Be sure that you only discuss cities that have enough people in the race/ethnic group to accurately discuss their segregation.

Step 1: Begin by going to the Census Scope's segregation website (http://www.censusscope.org/segregation.html).

Step 2: Under the tab "rankings and comparisons" on the left side of the page make the following selections:
   - Pick "White – Black" in the dropdown menu under dissimilarity index.
   - Pick "Cities" under "geographic units," and then use the drop-down menu to select your state.

Questions:

1. What city in the state where you attend school has the highest dissimilarity score? Which city has the lowest dissimilarity score? What is the dissimilarity score for the city in which you attend school? Do these results surprise you? Why or why not?
2. Now examine the dissimilarity score for other race/ethnic groups. How does the level of segregation differ between these groups and whites in comparison to the white/Black dissimilarity index scores? Are the same cities the most segregated across the different race groups? Make sure you use evidence to support your answer.
3. What consequences do you believe the continued racial segregation has for the reproduction of inequality? Why?

Reference:

Denvir, Daniel. 2011. "The 10 Most Segregated Urban Areas in America." *Salon.* http://www.salon.com/2011/03/29/most_segregated_cities/slide_show/10 (accessed January 3, 2015).

K. Data Analysis Exercise: Are Student Loans the Great Equalizer?

In Part IV, you read about how U.S. and British business schools cultivate international social networks to enhance their students' social capital. In this sense, going to college is a way to build human capital (skills and job training), social capital (networking), and cultural capital (knowledge of group norms). However, every year since 2002, both public and private colleges and universities across the United States have raised tuition, making it difficult for lower class students to pay for their educations. For many students, the price of tuition is too high for them or their family members to afford on their own, leading them to borrow money. In this data analysis exercise, you will examine how student loan debt has shifted across three time periods: 1992–1993, 1990–2000, and 2007–2008. The data were published in a report by the U.S. Department of Education (Woo 2013) and uses data from the Baccalaureate and Beyond Longitudinal Studies. Use the information provided in the figures to help answer the following questions.

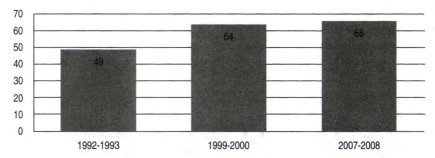

Figure 1 Percentage of Students Who Borrowed for Their Undergraduate Education.
Source: Woo, Jennie H. 2013. "Degrees of Debt." Washington, DC: U.S. Department of Education. http://nces.ed.gov/pubs2014/2014011.pdf (accessed January 3, 2015).

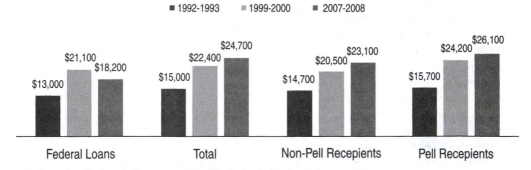

Figure 2 Average Amount Borrowed for Bachelor's Degree Across Time.
Source: Woo, Jennie H. 2013. "Degrees of Debt." Washington, DC: U.S. Department of Education. http://nces.ed.gov/pubs2014/2014011.pdf (accessed January 3, 2015).

Questions:

1. What were the reasons that you decided to go to college? What types of skills and resources do you hope to gain? Are the skills and resources you describe social, cultural, or human capital?

2. Drawing from Figures 1 and 2, how has the percentage of people with loans and the amount that they borrow changed across the three time periods?

3. Figure 2 separates the average amount borrowed by students who obtained their bachelor's degree by

students who did and did not receive Pell Grants. A Pell Grant is only given to students with lower household incomes who qualify for government aid. Thus, from this figure, we can get an idea of how much students in different financial situations borrowed. How does the student loan debt differ between students who received Pell Grants and those who did not?

4. Students who take on massive amounts of student debt face other challenges that students without debt do not. Like what? How might debt affect people's abilities to finish school, find work, begin families, or purchase homes?

5. Student loan debt is a crisis for this generation in a way not experienced by previous generations. Why is that? What is different about this time period? What broader economic and political changes have occurred to increase the cost of and shift the burden for paying for college? What long-term consequences might there be for this indebted generation? What are the consequences for the reproduction of inequality?

Reference:

Woo, Jennie H. 2013. "Degrees of Debt." Washington, DC: U.S. Department of Education. http://nces.ed.gov/pubs2014/2014011.pdf (accessed January 3, 2015).

Projects and Resources to Make a Difference

In Part III, we learned about women's and non-traditionally gendered men's experiences of sexual and sex-based harassment at work. Further, in Part IV, we learned about how dominant groups control space and how social policy can affect inequality. What can we do about it?

Workplaces are not the only place harassment based on gender and sexuality occurs. There is increasing attention to experiences of street harassment and numerous cases of sexual assault and rape in high schools and on college campuses. These forms of harassment do not go unchallenged. Many groups have emerged to document and combat street harassment (e.g., Stop Street Harassment, http://www.stopstreetharassment.org/; and Hollaback!, http://www.ihollaback.org/).

While Title IX of the Education Amendments was enacted in 1972 (http://nces.ed.gov/fastfacts/display.asp?id=93), schools still fail to offer women equal opportunities in education because they fail to protect women from assault and harassment. Students on campuses across the United States have demanded that their universities adopt programs that promote healthy learning environments and healthy, consensual relationships in efforts to hopefully lessen

instances of sexual assault. The American Association of University Women even provides an "Ending Campus Sexual Assault" toolkit (http://www.aauw.org/resource/campus-sexual-assault-tool-kit/).

One group, Girls for Gender Equity (GGE; http://www.ggenyc.org/), a non-profit organization in New York City, challenges harassment on the streets and in schools. Student leaders in the group train other student leaders to challenge sexism and harassment in secondary schools. Members of the group even worked together to write the book *Hey, Shorty!* (Smith, Van Deven, and Huppuch 2011), which documents their struggles and their successes.

There are so many ways you can get involved and make a difference. Here are just a few:

1. All of these organizations provide tips or toolkits for creating change. Read up, learn more, and educate others. Post links to social media you participate in to help educate others.

2. Oftentimes when we read about harassment or sexual assault, we learn about all the ways women should change their behavior. In what ways can we encourage *men* to change their behavior? Investigate options and promote these strategies

when you hear suggestions for how women should change their behavior.

3. Check out the options for change from these organizations or the many others and implement small things into your daily life. One potentially easy step is to NOT be a bystander, meaning do not go along with the group or a peer, but instead speak out when you see sexism or gendered harassment occurring. To learn more about bystanding, check out the following: http://www.eyesonbullying.org/bystander.html

4. If you have the time and motivation to take on more, find out what programs, if any, are available in your area. The groups listed here provide many models for effective ways to engage in social change. What would work in your area: for groups on your campus or in your town?

5. Other ideas:
   a. Ask your professor if your semester paper can be a social change project.
   b. Get involved with campus organizations that are already challenging harassment and assault.

Reference:

Smith, Joanne N., Mandy Van Deven, and Meghan Huppuch of Girls for Gender Equity (GGE). 2011. *Hey, Shorty! A Guide to Combating Sexual Harassment and Violence in Schools and on the Streets.* New York: Feminist Press at the City University of New York.

PART

V

Why Do People Go Along with Inequalities?

In Part V, the readings examine why people become invested in identities despite the fact that the behavior associated with these identities reproduce inequality. We have talked about how the reproduction of inequality is socially constructed and intersectional, and discussed how it often seems invisible or natural. Thus, it is not surprising that people would not critically evaluate something that they perceive to be natural—their selves. People do, however, put a lot of effort into successfully accomplishing their identities, since some identities carry privileges while others do not. Further, other people have the option of accepting our identities, helping us accomplish them, or challenging them.

The way that we talk and the way we feel are other things we take for granted. However, while they may seem natural, they are also important sites for the reproduction of inequality. Cohn (1987) argues that our language shapes what we are capable to think and feel. In her article of defense intellectuals, she shows how terms such as "collateral damage" conjure up completely different images than "burned bodies." The readings in this section examine not only what is said but also the ways in which it is said. Additionally, they will examine the way that inequality influences the types of emotions that people feel, and also the amount of effort they need to invest in how they present their emotions and manage other people's emotions. Language and emotions are social constructions and they are, of course, important to understand if we wish to learn about how people create shared meanings and ways to organize the world. Language and emotions are also experienced intersectionally, as we learn language and emotions become powerful tools in the reproduction of inequality.

Specifically, in Part V we will learn that:

- *People do identity work to gain privileges and avoid marginalization.* Previously you have learned about "othering." This section expands on this concept and illustrates a specific type, "defensive othering" (Schwalbe et al. 2000). Defensive othering refers to when people in marginalized groups do identity work where they attempt to establish themselves as better and more deserving of resources than other marginalized people. However, in doing so, the readings show that their strategies reproduce ideologies that lead to their own disadvantage.

- *Everyday discourse can be used to reproduce or challenge inequality.* Blatantly racist or sexist statements are often easy to identify. However, people also use language that reproduces inequality in ways that may not always be as apparent. In this section, you will be introduced to the concept of colorblind racism. Colorblind (Bonilla-Silva, 2006; Carr, 1997) racism refers to an ideology where racism is viewed as morally wrong but where people simultaneously deny the existence of racism. People discount structural factors that reinforce persistent racial inequality and instead blame racial disparities on the shortcomings of marginalized individuals. This way of thinking is expressed and reinforced through specific discursive strategies. For example, one way that individuals neutralize racist beliefs is by providing disclaimers. Bonilla-Silva (2002) found that white college students prefaced racist statements with phrases such as, "I'm not racist, but" and "some of my best friends aren't white."

- *Power elites have more power to control public discourse.* In addition to how ideology is reproduced through language, this section also shows that some people have a greater power in controlling debates regarding key issues than others.

- *Inequality influences the ways in which we manage our own and other peoples' emotions.* Although we think about our emotions as being "natural," they are also learned. Similar to other norms, we learn "feeling rules" or the correct way to feel in different situations (Hochschild 1979). For instance, we learn that we should show sympathy to people who have lost a loved one. Also, the emotions we want to express may not always be the emotions that we feel. This causes people to engage in what Hochschild (1979) calls "emotion work." In this section, readings show us how marginalization leads different people to engage in different types of emotion work. In order to avoid negative reactions in others, marginalized individuals must manage their own emotions. In some instances, doing this emotion work fails to challenge inequality more broadly.

Finally, Part V ends with readings that explore how people in marginalized groups attempt to challenge the marginalization associated with their identities.

References

Bonilla-Silva, Eduardo. 2002. "The Linguistics of Color-Blind Racism: How to Talk Nasty about Blacks without Sounding 'Racist.'" *Critical Sociology* 28(1–2): 41–64.

Bonilla-Silva, Eduardo. 2006. *Racism without Racists: Color-Blind Racism and the Persistence of Racial Inequality in the United States Second Edition.* New York: Rowman & Littlefield.

Carr, Leslie G. 1997. *"Color-Blind" Racism.* Thousand Oaks, CA: Sage Publications.

Cohn, Carol. 1987. "Sex and Death in the Rational World of Defense Intellectuals." *Signs* 12(4): 687–718.

Hochschild, Arlie. 1979. "Emotion Work, Feeling Rules, and Social Structure." *American Journal of Sociology* 85:551–575.

Schwalbe, Michael, Sandra Godwin, Daphne Holden, Douglas Schrock, Shealy Thompson, and Michele Wolkomir. 2000. "Generic Processes in Reproduction of Inequality: An Interactionist Analysis." *Social Forces* 79(2): 419–452.

34

Cultural and Cosmopolitan: Idealized Femininity and Embodied Nationalism in Nigerian Beauty Pageants

OLUWAKEMI BALOGUN

On September 15, 2013, Nina Davuluri became the first Indian American woman to be crowned Miss America. While she was born in Syracuse, New York, and would later receive her bachelor's degree from the University of Michigan, some people took to social media to protest Davuluri winning the title. For example, Tweets collected by Buzzfeed said, "I swear I'm not racist but this is America," "9/11 was 4 days ago and she gets miss America?" and "Miss America? You mean Miss 7–11." If Miss America represents U.S. idealized beauty, the people tweeting did not approve of a woman of Indian American descent representing the nation. If that is the case, what does the idealized woman look like? How do different beliefs about race and ethnic groups continue to shape beauty norms in the United States?

In her ethnographic study presented here, Oluwakemi Balogun examines the idealized beauty reinforced by the organizers of two different Nigerian beauty pageants. In the first pageant, "Queen Nigeria," contestants compete within Nigeria by demonstrating their Nigerian cultural competence. In "The Most Beautiful Girl in Nigeria" contest, contestants rely on consultants from the United States and South Africa—and go on to represent Nigeria in international contests. Idealized womanhood in this pageant is cosmopolitan. The two pageants demonstrate how nation, ethnicity, class, and gender come together to shape two different ideals regarding what it means to be a Nigerian woman within a globalized context.

This chapter examines gendered nationalism through the lens of two national beauty pageants in contemporary Nigeria that [. . .] engage in different projects of idealized femininity bolstered by separate nationalist claims. Beauty pageants, particularly national ones, provide a unique case for studying how gendered ideals play a role in nation-building discourses since they are tangible sites in the production of gendered national identity (Banet-Weiser 1999). Based on ethnographic research of two Nigerian national pageants, this chapter asks: How and why are gendered nationalist messages framed differently? This study suggests that beauty pageants perform an important dual role in emerging nations like Nigeria by creating both a unifying vision of Nigerian femininity within Nigeria and a more cosmopolitan vision of femininity that places Nigeria squarely in the international arena.

The gender and nation literature, through a focus on the relationship between gendered ideologies and the reproduction of the cultural and political boundaries of nations, examines how masculinity and femininity are differentially positioned to represent nations (Alarcon, Kaplan, and Moallem 1999; Enloe 1990; Kondo 1990; McClintock 1995; Nagel 1998; Sinha 1995). Transnational feminist scholars have theorized this mutual constitution of gender and nation by arguing that women in particular serve as both cultural bearers of tradition and symbols of progress and modernity (Yuval-Davis 1997). Tradition has

Excerpted from Balogun, Oluwakemi. 2012. "Cultural and Cosmopolitan: Idealized Femininity and Embodied Nationalism in Nigerian Beauty Pageants." *Gender & Society* 26(3): 357–381. © 2012, © SAGE Publications.

often been framed as a means of ensuring protection from or struggle against foreign influences (Chatterjee 1990; Kandiyoti 1996; Moallem 2005). Modernity, on the other hand, is primarily understood as a sign of the failure or success of nation building in the global arena (Gal and Kligman 2000). This literature, however, has also problematized this binary between tradition and modernity, focusing on how these categories are produced in tension with each other to construct distinctions between nations, ethnic difference within nations, and boundaries of "the West" in opposition to the "Third World" (Alarcon et al. 1999; Choo 2006; Grewal 1996; Grewal and Kaplan 1994; Moallem 2005; Mohanty 2003; Radhakrishnan 2005).

Nigeria: Geopolitical Context of an "Emerging Nation"

While all nations must contend with the task of appealing to domestic and international agendas, this process becomes especially heightened in emerging nations who run the risk of pulling the nation apart if they fail to manage these competing interests. By using the term *emerging nation*, I am not referring to newly formed states (i.e., political units) but rather to newly developing nations (i.e., a shared sense of cultural affiliation) which are vying to become major players in the international arena. Nigeria is a useful place to study gendered nationalism because of the profound economic, political, and cultural changes that the country has witnessed since attaining independence in 1960. As the seventh most populous country and one of the largest oil suppliers in the world, Nigeria's vast human and natural resources highlight Nigeria's potential as a major global player (Apter 2005; Rotberg 2004). Despite its resources, well-known images of corruption, poverty, and communal conflict in Nigeria mar its international reputation and appear to be major roadblocks to nation-building and unity (Obadare 2004; Ukiwo 2003; Watts 1997). These shifts provide a broader context for understanding how Nigeria negotiates the dilemma of staking a claim in the global political economy while remaining attuned to its internal sensibilities.

The Two Pageants
Queen Nigeria

Queen Nigeria evolved from a popular game-show that incorporated mini beauty contests to a national pageant first held in 2008. It is a joint venture between Silverstone Communications, a privately run events management firm, and TV Enterprises, the commercial arm of the government-owned Nigerian Television Authority responsible for organizing public lectures and live cultural events and initiating business ventures. The Nigerian Television Authority is the largest broadcast television network in sub-Saharan Africa, with about 100 stations covering all states in the nation, and includes international transmissions to North America and Europe, which target the Nigerian diaspora. Contestants must first enter and win a state-level competition. Winners from the various states then go on to compete at the national finale. All contestants must have a cultural tie to the state they represent either through ethnic heritage (i.e., as an indigene), birth, or residence. In addition to the judges, a group of invited elders and dignitaries are asked to certify the final results at both the state and national contests.

The Most Beautiful Girl in Nigeria

The Silverbird Group, a Nigerian-based media conglomerate with branches in Ghana and Kenya, has coordinated the Most Beautiful Girl in Nigeria (MBGN) since 1986 and sends delegates to the top international beauty contests such as Miss World and Miss Universe. Silverbird's operations include cinemas, shopping malls, television and radio stations, and live shows and events, including beauty pageants. While its organizers are primarily Nigerian-based, MBGN relies on grooming and production experts from outside of Nigeria, most notably from South Africa and the United States. Judges and special guests are drawn from celebrities in the Nigerian entertainment business (modeling, acting, music, and performing arts worlds), business leaders (oftentimes expatriates), and members of the political elite.

Contestants are chosen at various urban cities throughout Nigeria, primarily in the southern part of the country (Benin in the South-South, Lagos in the South-West, Port Harcourt in the South-South, and Abuja, the capital in 2010). Semifinalists selected from these screening venues then compete in Lagos, where 30 finalists are chosen to compete in the final show. Since contestants are screened and chosen without regard to where they are from, contestants do not necessarily represent the states they are actually from. The finale and a reality show series are broadcast on Silverbird Television.

Contesting Representations: Tests and Models of Idealized Femininity

This chapter considers the formation of gendered national representations primarily through the perspective of Nigerian beauty pageant organizers who, as cultural producers, employ a *relational* discourse of idealized femininity (e.g., "true Nigerian womanhood") to bolster their broader nationalist claims. That is, organizers push forward a gendered nationalist vision in direct competition with the rival national pageant. I use the term "idealized femininity" to highlight the public cultural construction of femininity in these beauty pageants, which emphasizes distinct sets of skills, divergent ways of managing appearance and dress, and varied classed strategies. By looking at how organizers mold competing visions of their contestants, through either a *cultural-nationalist* ideal focused on valuing Nigerian customs and unifying Nigeria's diverse population or a *cosmopolitan-nationalist* paradigm oriented toward highlighting Nigeria's compatibility with a global community, I argue that gendered national identities are produced for specific audiences and constrained by the systems within which they are created.

While contestants were aware on some level of the symbolic differences between the two pageants, and readily adapted to the demands and expectations of each contest, it was organizers (who are mostly male) who were the most invested in framing contestants' femininity and their embodied representations of the nation in divergent ways. Contestants approached both pageants from a much more flexible standpoint, stressing a "beauty diplomacy" narrative, which values charity, development, and goodwill in order to connect to everyday Nigerians and promote their own voices and that of the general public in the national arena.

Serving Up a "Touch" of Africa

A key component integrated into the Queen Nigeria pageant, to show its commitment to producing a "true" Nigerian queen, is a cooking competition. Each contestant is allotted a N1000 ($7) budget to spend on ingredients for a regional dish that represents her state. The judging criteria included speed, cleanliness, taste, and service (e.g., presentation of the dish and interaction with the judges). On the day of the cooking contest, the contestants, the organizers, and I gathered outside of the hotel, preparing to head over to the market to buy the necessary ingredients for the upcoming cooking contest to be held later that afternoon. As one of the organizers, Mr. Richard, handed a N1000 note to each contestant, he launched into a lecture. "We are going to be watching you closely," he began. "We are going to be paying attention to how you interact with the sellers. How you bargain. How you choose your ingredients. And, when you're cooking, we will be looking at how clean you keep your station. These are things you all should know. I shouldn't even be telling you this." Mr. Richard's insistence that he should not openly inform the contestants about the judges' expectations signaled that they should already be aware that their assessment extended beyond the flavor and presentation of their meals.

Queen Nigeria's focus on a culinary test as a symbol of "authentic" Nigerian femininity taps into a widely held idea outside of the beauty pageant world that conventional markers of domesticity such as cooking Nigerian meals, childrearing, or housekeeping are standard elements of femininity. As such, the cooking competition connected contestants to a recognizable domesticated element of femininity that would resonate with a broad Nigerian audience. Organizers labeled those who could not cook "spoiled" or "out of touch." As Lovett lamented, "It would amaze you that some are 20, 18, and they have never cooked. [The cooking test] is telling them you don't have to depend on mummy and daddy for everything or a fast food joint." Although multinational fast-food franchises like KFC have only recently begun to enter Nigeria, more established homegrown and South African imported fast-food corporations are often viewed as a sign of Westernization and middle-class convenience. By showing off their cooking skills with regard to specific local cuisines and demonstrating their ability to navigate one of the many open-air markets typical of the area, contestants highlighted their cultural competency with Nigerian traditions and also warded off the threat of being seen as spoiled by their parents or overly dependent on Western-derived influences like fast-food joints. As such, Queen Nigeria contestants are presented as the national custodians of Nigerian cultural identity, hedging against foreign influences.

Modeling the Self-Confident Nation

Queen Nigeria's cooking test assumes a preexisting knowledge of traditional African dishes, which highlights access to an intrinsic cultural skill and emphasizes differences from Western culture. In contrast, MBGN's organizers and groomers worked on carefully cultivating skills needed for the modeling segment of their competition, in part through the prism of internationalism. During the show, one contestant would be crowned the "Face of Select Pro," serving as an endorsement ambassador for one of the sponsors of the event, Select Pro Cosmetics, a makeup and styling line. Gina, the African-American producer flown in each year to drill the contestants on poise, etiquette, cat-walking, and posture, spent most of rehearsal periods teaching the choreography needed for the modeling sequence as a Lady Gaga track pulsed in the background. During an interview, she emphasized that international pageants were becoming increasingly focused on modeling and as a result she had to train contestants not only in the mechanics of walking, posing, and grooming but also in gaining self-confidence and professionalism, qualities needed to be successful in the field. When I asked her to describe her ideal candidate, Gina responded forcefully, "Someone really competitive. It's a game they play, and it's about learning to play that game and playing it well."

Learning to "play the game" of self-confidence was woven into the 10-day preshow training and rehearsal period (referred to as "camp"). On the night of the first day of camp, the panel of organizers and groomers sat in a row of chairs facing the 30 contestants. After all the organizers and key members of the production crew were introduced and the national director made his opening remarks, Gina stood up and stated, "I only have one question, which one of you is my queen?" About five hands shot up immediately and a couple more were tentatively half-way up in the air. "I only saw a couple of you raise your hands," Gina continued,

> A lot of you seem unsure. We have to work on that. Part of this process is about having confidence. You have to be sure that all of you can say you can be a queen. I'm going to work on instilling that confidence. If you don't want to win, you might as well go home now. I want you all reaching for that crown!

She ended her pep talk with, "Again I want to ask, Who's my queen?" This time all hands shot up. Through such tactics, Gina continually instructed contestants on the rules of the game. The skills contestants were supposed to acquire—especially those promoting self-confidence, professionalism, and competitiveness—were meant to be translated off the stage. One lunchtime discussion revolved around how African contestants are perceived to be at a disadvantage at contests like Miss World or Miss Universe because they lack self-confidence. Eliza, a South African production specialist, pointed out, "African girls are so soft. They are trained to be quiet and obedient. They have to be trained to be firm. They

can be a lady on the catwalk, but firm off of it." While "African" women are conventionally imagined as soft, weak, and dutiful, this clashes with constructions of "modern" women as strong, assertive, and confident. Eliza insists, however, that contestants still can be *trained* to be firm, a process that MBGN directly engages by "grooming" contestants through "international experts" who are thought to provide a competitive edge at subsequent phases of the competition. As agents of internationalism, MBGN contestants were supposed to embody firmness and self-confidence, traits that are expected to signal a cosmopolitan nation.

The Politics Of Embodiment

Bodily practices and markers of appearance such as dress, makeup use, accent, and grooming are vehicles of collective identity, and women's bodies are often the terrain where national identities are produced, maintained, and resisted (Banet-Weiser 1999; Choo 2006; Gal and Kligman 2000; Huisman and Hondagneu-Sotelo 2005). By looking at specific bodily practices and ideologies such as debates about beauty, bodily display, and embodied class trajectories, I argue that specific framings of the body shape how the nation is managed and configured. While Queen Nigeria seeks to accommodate national differences, MBGN remains oriented toward securing an internationally competitive edge.

Challenging and Strategizing against "International" Beauty Standards

For both competitions, organizers and judges evaluate contestants' bodies based on similar factors such as height, body size, hair style, skin color and texture, and teeth and smile. While Queen Nigeria and MBGN had a fairly similar range of contestants in terms of skin color and negligible differences in body size, they framed their beauty ideals in different ways.

While "international standards" matter to Queen Nigeria organizers, they are critical of Western preferences, insisting that the "international" should be expanded to include more than Western criteria. When I asked one organizer of Queen Nigeria about what specific beauty traits they looked for, he responded: "In Igboland it is someone who is large that is considered beautiful, because it shows she is well taken-care of. But here it doesn't play a role. We are not looking for 'Miss Big and Bold.'" He insisted that international standards of tall and thin beauty queens mattered because organizers had to "move with the trend" within the beauty pageant industry. At the same time, he noted that while MBGN is bound to follow international rules and regulations, if Queen Nigeria were to host an international pageant of their own, other nations would have to abide by Nigerian-derived guidelines, which would directly challenge Western dominance.

In contrast, MBGN does not openly question these international standards. Gina explained that her involvement in the pageant, which resulted in MBGN (as "Miss Nigeria") winning the Miss World title in 2001, had successfully pushed their standards toward thinner and taller contestants, in line with international criteria. A couple of days before we headed for the auditions, one of the organizers warned, "We don't want any big leg girls. If you have any of those local guys pick the contestants, they will just be looking for girlfriends. We don't want that, so watch out for that." By cautioning screeners to be weary of "big leg girls," his comments suggest a distinction between local-based desirability and the quest for a candidate that would fit internationally defined notions of attractiveness.

MBGN plays within "international standards," strategizing and picking delegates who tapped into two different kinds of beauty, appealing to niches within international pageantry. MBGN chooses five winners who go on to represent Nigeria at different beauty, modeling, and promotional contests within the country and around the world. The winner and first runner-up continue on to Miss World and Miss Universe, respectively. Organizers revealed that for Miss World, a British pageant organized and privately owned by the Morley Family, they chose "a girl next door type" and were a little more flexible with height and body shape. The winner tends to be lighter-skinned. They explained that, since Miss World is focused primarily on raising money for charity events through its "beauty with a purpose" tagline, they pick a fresh-faced, innocent-looking candidate with mass appeal.

Debating Bodily Display: Banning Bikinis versus Bikini Barbie-Turns

Organizers for Queen Nigeria spent time policing the amount of skin contestants showed in public. Their costumes and attire were inspected prior to the final show to make sure they were not too revealing, and during excursions to visit public officials and sponsors, contestants were instructed to either wear "native" attire

(a colloquial term that refers to African-styled clothing) or to cover up with a shawl if they were wearing tight-fitting or skimpy "English dress." Queen Nigeria is specifically branded as a no-bikini show. Wearing a bikini, or nothing more than "bra and pants" as it is often referred to, was frequently brought up as un-African and representative of a major roadblock in pageants' gaining greater acceptance throughout the country.

By barring bikinis from the show, organizers believed they could attract girls who normally would not enter a beauty competition and assuage some of the sensitivities some felt about bodily display in pageantry. Raul, an organizer of a state-level pageant, explained why Queen Nigeria did not want to include bikinis:

> Especially in Africa, we believe that nudity is wrong, women should not be exposing their body; they [Queen Nigeria] didn't want to celebrate nudity and especially as a national brand. It's family TV, where the young, the old, and children would be able to watch. . . . We want to celebrate our culture, without celebrating bikini.

By banning bikinis and remaining attuned to regional, religious, and cultural concerns over bodily display, Queen Nigeria sought to present itself as a legitimate arbiter of Nigerian culture through an inclusive stance that recognized local-based differences, unified the country, and helped establish an African-centered national brand.

Whereas Queen Nigeria drew a firm line against including bikinis in their show and policed bodily display, MBGN included a bikini segment and contestants often wore short, tight cocktail dresses throughout camp. During the initial screening process, one of the first things those who auditioned are instructed to do is to change into their bikinis and five-inch high heels. Contestants are asked to come up one by one and introduce themselves while in their bikinis and then stand in a lineup and turn around in a "Barbie turn" (a slow, 360-degree spin) so that screeners can inspect their bodies. Bikinis were used to "weed out" contestants according to body type (e.g., uneven skin texture, disproportionate bodies, cellulite, and stretch marks) and the presence of scars. Scars from accidents (e.g., exhaust pipe burns from motorbikes were commonly referenced), protruding belly buttons, and "tribal markings" were pointed out, scrutinized, and debated over the course of the screening process. Markings on the body, either in the form of "tribal markings" or scars, served to indicate specific ethnic traits or membership in lower status communities (Ford 2008; Rogers 1998) and were thus seen as inconsistent with a cosmopolitan femininity.

Discussions over whether scars could be simply hidden also highlighted that readily visible scars would somehow betray Nigeria's lack of access to good surgery or resources to travel abroad, thus relegating Nigerian beauty contestants to an unmodern status internationally.

The organizers recognized that including bikinis in the program made some Nigerians apprehensive about the pageant, but they insisted that it was necessary in order to be in line with international standards both in terms of format and body ideals. Organizers dismissed concerns by asking, "What is a beauty pageant without a swimsuit section?" or "When you go to the beach what do you wear? A bathing suit." Through such matter-of fact statements, organizers sought to normalize the inclusion of bikinis in a context where seeing women in bathing suits, even at public beaches, is rare (Nigerian women often wear jeans, shorts, T shirts, and tank tops at the beach). By doing so, MBGN closes itself off from internal hesitations over bodily display and instead emphasizes how bikinis visually show off which bodies are more in line with "international" standards based on body type and lack of scarring, and thus ripe for inclusion in international contests.

Classed Trajectories: Cultured Beauties and Jet-Setters

Nationalist projects are always class-specific. Both contests mold a particular class version of their participants that is shaped by their target audience. Queen Nigeria makes class distinctions based on local references, which promote a cultured middle-class Nigerian woman. In contrast, MBGN focuses on the speedy upward trajectory of their contestants who through winning or even just participating in the pageant gain entrance into an otherwise impossible-to-penetrate jet-setter echelon of Nigerian society who are aligned with transnational capital and culture. These classed paths of nationhood manifest in shifts and varied emphases in the body.

Queen Nigeria organizers specifically targeted college students as ideal candidates and as an unwritten prerequisite for entry, in part to highlight their educated, middle-class trajectories. They also invoked specific tropes of "market women" to create an implicit class distinction between the contestants and other women that they should actively distance themselves from. Late one evening during dance rehearsals, Will, the

choreographer, asked the contestants to walk one by one to form two lines for the opening sequence of the dance number. As one contestant walked by he bellowed, pointing at her, "You! Why are you walking like that? You look like a woman carrying firewood on her head. Start over!" Throughout the rehearsal he scolded, "You are all dancing like market women!" Will's repeated statements invoking images of "women carrying firewood on her head" or "market women" were meant to serve as a reference point for women living in rural villages or women working in poor, urban environments. Market women have a long history of trading in urban Nigeria and other areas of West Africa (Byfield 2002; Clark 1994) and as such serve as a recognizable symbolic figure. In the context of beauty pageants, market women are imagined as rough and brash—characteristics that a beauty queen should not exhibit. Instead, contestants were expected to maintain a refined beauty queen stance, maintaining excellent posture in high-heeled stilettos, even while dancing. Women were expected to have skills traditionally associated with Nigerian women that gestured toward an "authentic" African context by showing competency, at traditional cooking for example, but not be *wholly of that* context, allowing Queen Nigeria to construct a class-specific cultural ideal. Jane Collier's (1997) work deals with how an ambivalent stance toward "tradition" features in modernity, in which embracing "traditions" serve as a means of symbolizing region and identity, but the actual way of life is rejected. In this case, rejecting "market women's" embodiment and emphasizing the educated middle-class lifestyles of contestants presents a hierarchy of who can serve as a cultural icon for the nation, elevating the social standing of contestants.

MGBN focuses on signaling the rapid upward mobility of their contestants. The process of "grooming" during camp was noted as having a profound impact on the contestants. "Grooming" contestants focused on changes in both demeanor and physical embodiment, which was directly linked to the class mobility of contestants. People would constantly comment that contestants would change over the course of the 10-day camping (training) period that led up to the finale. I was chatting with one of the chaperones, Ada, as the contestants were having their photographs taken for the brochure. She motioned toward the group of contestants gathered outside the pool of the five-star hotel which served as host for camp, "They will all change. You'll see them next year and you won't even recognize them." With access to hairstylists and makeup artists provided by MBGN and the opportunity to interact with some of the top Nigerian fashion designers, contestants' physical embodiments were expected to change over the course of the contest and beyond.

During the audition process, a couple of the chaperones pointed out a woman who had auditioned for the past two cycles of MBGN. While she had made the cut in the past, she did not go on to win the crown. "Each year she comes back cleaner and cleaner." When I asked her what she meant by this statement, she responded that each time she returns to audition her skin looks fairer. This observation was just one of many which pointed to how contestants' bodies physically shifted as a result of participating in the pageant, which in this case was linked to access to exclusive skin and makeup treatments that seemingly made their skin "cleaner." This finding is similar to other scholars' work that shows how lighter skin not only serves as a means of promoting dominant beauty ideals but also secures and verifies upward mobility (Hunter 1998; Pierre 2008; Rahier 1999). Contestants were also expected to eschew secondhand and counterfeit clothing and accessories that flood the Nigerian market and instead wear Nigerian couture and shop at malls with brand-new American or European merchandise.

What others pinpointed as the core change the contestants undergo is the cultivation of a new polished image that directly translates into increased social status and a newly acquired jet-set lifestyle. The day before the finale, during the dress rehearsals while all the contestants practiced onstage, Mr. Oke, a staff member at Silverbird, commented, "I'm always scared of these girls. They are powerful. That's why I'm always nice to them. They're all going to dump their boyfriends after this is over. You'd be surprised, one of them might be the future wife to a minister [head of national ministries]; they might just be the one to make that phone call to make or destroy a deal." Newly formed relationships with business leaders, celebrities, and politicians were touted as signs of emergence into new elite circles centered on transnational culture and capital to which most contestants would otherwise not have access. Mr. Oke's reference to contestants was meant to signal their acquired access to the political elite who are well connected to the international business world. Since oil is nationalized and the federal government controls nearly 90 percent of oil revenues that it distributes to federal, state, and local governments, aligning with politics is the fastest means of gaining access to capital. Organizers stressed how contestants moved into new

accommodations (usually on the Island), gained access to chauffeurs, and consumed the trendiest luxury brands. Through shifts in embodiment and lifestyle, contestants, and especially winners, were said to embrace a newfound status that indicates the nation's compatibility with an international political economy.

Conclusion

This chapter has focused on sets of practices that construct two representations of femininity and, by extension, two visions of national identity. By focusing on differing sets of skills, debates over appearance and dress, and diverging modes of economic mobility, I argue that the two national pageants I studied construct distinct versions of gendered nationhood. Queen Nigeria constructs a *cultural-nationalist* model of femininity that emphasizes *testing* cultural competency, primarily through a cooking contest. This cultural competency test serves as a means of connecting contestants to a broad Nigerian community and showing appreciation for Nigerian culture, with the ultimate aim of unifying the nation. In contrast, by focusing on a modeling competition that emphasizes *cultivating* skills viewed as integral to success at the international phases of the pageant, such as self-confidence, MBGN's *cosmopolitan-nationalist* model stresses Nigeria's compatibility with an international community in order to globalize the nation. I argue that through the cultural production of idealized femininities, contours of the nation—as inclusive of cultural and ethnic diversity for a local audience *and* part of global community for a transnational audience—are consolidated in tandem through the multilayered process of nationalism.

References

Alarcon, Norma, Caren Kaplan, and Minoo Moallem. 1999. "Introduction: Between Woman and Nation." In *Between Woman and Nation: Nationalisms, Transnational Feminisms, and the State* (ed. Caren Kaplan, Norma Alarcón, and Minoo Moallem), 1–16. Durham, NC: Duke University Press.

Apter, Andrew H. 2005. *The Pan-African Nation: Oil and the Spectacle of Culture in Nigeria.* Chicago: University of Chicago Press.

Banet-Weiser, Sarah. 1999. *The Most Beautiful Girl in the World: Beauty Pageants and National Identity.* Berkeley: University of California Press.

Byfield, Judith. 2002. *A Social and Economic History of Women Dyers in Abeokuta (Nigeria), 1890–1940.* Portsmouth, NH: Heinemann.

Casanova, Erynn Masi De. 2004. "'No Ugly Women': Concepts of Race and Beauty among Adolescent Women in Ecuador." *Gender and Society* 18(3): 287–308.

Chatterjee, Partha. 1990. "The Nationalist Resolution of the Women's Question." In *Recasting Women: Essays in Indian Colonial History* (ed. Kumkum Sangari and Sangari Vaid) 33–53. New Brunswick, NJ: Rutgers University Press.

Choo, Hae Yeon. 2006. "Gendered Modernity and Ethnicized Citizenship: North Korean Settlers in Contemporary Korea." *Gender and Society* 20(5): 576–604.

Clark, Gracia. 1994. *Onions Are My Husband: Survival and Accumulation by West African Market Women*. Chicago: University of Chicago Press.

Collier, Jane Fishburne. 1997. *From Duty to Desire: Remaking Families in a Spanish Village*. Princeton, NJ: Princeton University Press.

Enloe, Cynthia H. 1990. *Bananas, Beaches and Bases: Making Feminist Sense of International Politics*. Berkeley: University of California Press.

Ford, Kristie A. 2008. "Gazing into a Distorted Looking Glass: Masculinity, Femininity, Appearance Ideals, and the Black Body." *Sociology Compass* 2(3): 1096–1114.

Gal, Susan, and Gail Kligman. 2000. *The Politics of Gender after Socialism: A Comparative-Historical Essay*. Princeton, NJ: Princeton University Press.

Grewal, Inderpal. 1996. *Home and Harem: Nation, Gender, Empire, and the Cultures of Travel*. Durham, NC: Duke University Press.

Grewal, Inderpal, and Caren Kaplan. 1994. "Transnational Feminist Practices and Questions of Postmodernity." In *Scattered Hegemonies: Postmodernity and Transnational Feminist Practices* (ed. Inderpal Grewal and Caren Kaplan), 1–36. Minneapolis: University of Minnesota Press.

Huisman, Kimberly, and Pierrette Hondagneu-Sotelo. 2005. "Dress Matters: Change and Continuity in the Dress Practices of Bosnian Muslim Refugee Women." *Gender and Society* 19(1): 44–65.

Hunter, Margaret L. 1998. "Colorstruck: Skin Color Stratification in the Lives of African American Women." *Sociological Inquiry* 68(4): 517–535.

Kandiyoti, Deniz. 1996. "Identity and Its Discontents: Women and the Nation." In *Colonial Discourse and Post-Colonial Theory* (ed. Patrick Williams and Laura Chrisman), 376–391. London: Harvester Wheatsheaf.

Kondo, Dorinne K. 1990. *Crafting Selves: Power, Gender, and Discourses of Identity in a Japanese Workplace*. Chicago: University of Chicago Press.

McClintock, Anne. 1995. *Imperial Leather: Race, Gender, and Sexuality in the Colonial Contest*. New York: Routledge.

Moallem, Minoo. 2005. *Between Warrior Brother and Veiled Sister: Islamic Fundamentalism and the Politics of Patriarchy in Iran*. Berkeley: University of California Press.

Mohanty, Chandra Talpade. 2003. *Feminism without Borders: Decolonizing Theory, Practicing Solidarity*. Durham, NC: Duke University Press.

Nagel, Joanne. 1998. "Masculinity and Nationalism: Gender and Sexuality in the Making of Nations." *Ethnic and Racial Studies* 21(2): 242–269.

Obadare, Ebenezer. 2004. "In Search of a Public Sphere: The Fundamentalist Challenge to Civil Society in Nigeria." *Patterns of Prejudice* 38(2): 177–198.

Pierre, Jemima. 2008. "'I Like Your Colour!' Skin Bleaching and Geographies of Race in Urban Ghana." *Feminist Review* 90(1): 9–29.

Radhakrishnan, Smitha. 2005. "'Time to Show Our True Colors': The Gendered Politics of 'Indianness' in Post-Apartheid South Africa." *Gender and Society* 19(2): 262–81.

Rahier, Jean Muteba. 1999. "Body Politics in Black and White: Señoras, Mujeres, Blanqueamiento and Miss Esmeraldas 1997–1998, Ecuador." *Women and Performance: A Journal of Feminist Theory* 11(1): 103–120.

Rogers, Mark. 1998. "Spectacular Bodies: Folklorization and the Politics of Identity in Ecuadorian Beauty Pageants." *Journal of Latin American Anthropology* 3(2): 54–85.

Rotberg, Robert I. 2004. *Crafting the New Nigeria: Confronting the Challenges*. Boulder, CO: Lynne Rienner.

Sinha, Mrinalini. 1995. *Colonial Masculinity: The "Manly Englishman" and the "Effeminate Bengali" in the Late Nineteenth Century*. Manchester: Manchester University Press.

Ukiwo, Ukoha. 2003. "Politics, Ethno-Religious Conflicts and Democratic Consolidation in Nigeria." *Journal of Modern African Studies* 41(1): 115–138.

Watts, Michael. 1997. "Black Gold, White Heat: State Violence, Local Resistance, and the National Question in Nigeria." In *Geographies of Resistance* (ed. Steve Pile and Michael Keith), 33–67. London: Routledge.

Yuval-Davis, Nira. 1997. *Gender and Nation*. London: Sage.

Questions

1. How did the two beauty pageants differ?
2. Why does Balogun argue that scars are not acceptable at the MBGN pageant? What role does this have in the reproduction of inequality?

3. Balogun refers to Nigeria as an "emerging" nation. What does she mean by this? How does this influence the pageants?

4. How do race and class influence perceptions of beauty in the United States?

35

"Barbie Dolls" on the Pitch: Identity Work, Defensive Othering, and Inequality in Women's Rugby

MATTHEW EZZELL

In 2013 Brittney Griner, an award winning basketball player at Baylor University who went on to play in the Women's National Basketball Association (WNBA), mentioned in an interview that she was a lesbian. The media attention regarding Griner's sexuality was underwhelming. For example, an article by Sam Borden (2013) in the *New York Times* was titled, "Female Star Comes Out as Gay, and Sports World Shrugs." In contrast, when Michael Sam, a defensive end who played football for the University of Missouri, stated in a press conference that he was gay just before the start of the 2014 draft, the announcement gained notable media attention, with all the major networks covering the story. The South Eastern Conference defensive player of the Year and All-American was drafted into the NFL with the 249th pick by the St. Louis Rams—and the coverage continued with reporters questioning whether he would have been picked higher if he wasn't openly gay. Why would Brittney Griner's sexuality gain so little attention while Michael Sam's continues to make headlines?

Part of the answer to this question rests on traditional gender and sexuality expectations. Women in sports traditionally viewed as masculine challenge expectations that women are weak. Since women who are not traditionally feminine are associated with same-sex behavior, Griner's sexuality is perhaps less unexpected than Sam's, whose performance in a highly masculine sport is consistent with gender norms. The example of Griner and Sam illustrates the ways in which gender and sexuality are conflated in our culture. When someone violates a gender norm, people often assume that the individual is not heterosexual.

In the following piece, Matthew Ezzell examines how women on a college rugby team manage their involvement in a masculine sport while attempting to avoid a lesbian stigma. Ezzell argues that while the women challenge traditional gender norms by their engagement in a sport considered masculine, they also behave in ways that reinforce traditional femininity and heterosexuality in order to

Excerpted from Ezzell, Matthew B. 2009. "'Barbie Dolls' on the Pitch: Identity Work, Defensive Othering, and Inequality in Women's Rugby." *Social Problems* 56:111–131. Copyright © 2009, Oxford University Press.

maintain their relationships with and appeal to men. That is, the college rugby players were invested in the privilege associated with successfully accomplishing gender and heterosexuality in socially valued ways. Ezzell's study demonstrates how people in marginalized groups draw on and reinforce status structures, even when they themselves are subordinated by them. Please note that in order to protect the privacy of the people discussed in the chapter, Ezzell uses pseudonyms when referring to athletes and "Comp U" is a fictitious University name.

Reference

Boden, Sam. 2013 "Female Star Comes Out as Gay, and Sports World Shrugs." *New York Times,* April 19.

Identities are the "meanings one attributes to oneself as an object" (Burke and Tully 1977, 883). Michael L. Schwalbe and Douglas Mason-Schrock (1996) expound on this understanding by focusing on identity claims as "indexes of the self" (p. 115). By this they mean that identities are not meanings in and of themselves, but signs that individuals and groups use to *evoke* meanings in the form of responses from others. Identities, then, are signifiers of the self. They are not fixed, as if they were personality traits, but mutable consequences of reflection and interaction (Blumer 1969; McCall and Simmons 1978; Strauss 1959). Accordingly, individuals and groups can *work on* their identities. Identity work is "anything people do, individually or collectively, to give meaning to themselves or others" (Schwalbe and Mason Schrock 1996, 115).

Race, class, and gender, as Candace West and Don H. Zimmerman (1987) and West and Sarah Fenstermaker (1995) have argued, are interlocking systems of oppression; moreover, they are the social arrangements from which we derive our core identities. This view implies that identity creation and affirmation are parts of the process whereby inequality is reproduced. The study of identity work, thus, has the potential to yield insight into the processes that uphold large-scale inequalities.

What happens when, as part of their identity work, members of subordinated groups act in ways that challenge dominants' expectations for their groups, yet seek approval from dominants? How do they manage this potential dilemma? I examine these questions through an ethnographic analysis of collegiate female athletes, addressing how they resist and reproduce inequality through interaction. Specifically, I analyze how a group of female rugby players, responding to subordinated status and the stigma that arose from their transgression of conventional gendered norms, managed their identities as women, as athletes, and, for most of them, as heterosexuals. Some of their strategies fall into the category of "defensive othering." This occurs when subordinates

"[accept] the legitimacy of a devalued identity imposed by the dominant group, but then [say], in effect, 'There are indeed Others to whom this applies, but it does not apply to me'" (Schwalbe et al. 2000, 425). Michael Schwalbe and associates include defensive othering as one of the generic processes in the reproduction of inequality. I expand on the work of Schwalbe and associates by adding two subcategories of defensive othering, offering insights into how inequality is reproduced through face-to-face interaction. In particular, I analyze how the players (a) *identified with dominants* (identifying with the values associated with dominant group members) and (b) engaged in what I call *normative identification* (identifying with the normative values prescribed by dominants for subordinated group members). Also, I discuss how the players deflected stigma through a boundary maintenance process I call *propping up dominants* (reinforcing the idea that dominant group members are, and should be, dominant).

Setting and Method

From September 2002 to October 2003, I studied a women's rugby team at Competitive University (Comp U), a large, public university in the southeastern United States. The Comp U Women's Rugby Football Club was nonvarsity, yet it was nationally ranked (in the top 15 of 300 teams). Over the course of the research, it was made up of 33 to 50 female players and two male coaches. During my research, the team was 90 percent white (45 players), 6 percent Black (3 players), and 4 percent nonwhite Hispanic (2 players). The players were from predominantly middle- and upper middle-class backgrounds.

I spent 13 months working with the team as a participant observer. This included attending and helping out at weekly practices, weekend games, three team social events, and two fundraisers (for the men's team and the women's team). I was on the team's listserv, which had 1,085 postings during my membership. In addition to numerous informal interviews (Lofland et al. 2006) with players and other participants over the course of the study, I conducted 13 in-depth, semistructured interviews with players, both coaches, and a former player.

Identifying with Dominants

Given the historical association between (white, middle-class) women and physical weakness and passivity, many women have interpreted their sport practice as an act of resistance (see, e.g., Heywood and Dworkin 2003). The female ruggers at Comp U, however, did not do this. Even as their success on the pitch (the rugby playing field) shattered the belief that all women are passive, the players used their athleticism to suggest that only *they*, and not women *as a class*, were tough and aggressive. Further, they used their status as ruggers to position themselves above women in general, whom they dismissed as weak. In doing so the players identified with dominants, claiming a heightened status relative to other members of their subordinated group (women) through closer identification with the behavior and traits associated with members of the dominant class (men).

To contest the image of themselves, as women, as being weak, the female ruggers distinguished themselves from women in (white) sororities. Frequently, the Comp U players referred to these women as "sorostitutes." This term—combining "sorority" and "prostitute"—implied promiscuity on the part of sorority women. Yet, the Comp U players commonly engaged in bantering, joking, and bragging about drunken sexual escapades. They did not believe, moreover, that the women in sororities literally sold sex acts. In fact, it was the ruggers themselves who held an eroticized mud wrestling fundraiser annually, selling access to the sexual display of their bodies as the most lucrative fundraiser of the year. Why, then, did the Comp U ruggers sexually libel women in sororities?

The players' reasons for setting up "sorostitutes" as a foil became clearer when they created a t-shirt listing the "Top Ten Reasons to Play on the Comp U Women's Rugby Football Club." One reason was: "You just laugh when people ask what sorority you're in." I asked Frankie, a vet player, what this meant and she explained that (white) "sorority girls in general are stereotyped to be, you know, like, pansy girly-girls, makeup all the time, and that kind of stuff." Yet most, if not all, of the Comp U players wore makeup (for some, even during games) and were invested in the same conventionally feminine appearance that sorority women projected.

Moreover, women on the rugby team spoke glowingly about how rugby offered the same benefits for which sororities are often celebrated (see Robbins 2004): a sense of community and belonging, social outlets in the forms of parties and dances, and social networks that could offer payoffs in the future. Also, both groups were predominantly white and middle to upper middle class. These similarities with nonathletic ("girly-girl") sorority women potentially threatened the Comp U players' identities as tough and aggressive. In response, they asserted that despite similarities in their gender presentation, they were different from—and superior to—women in sororities because they were not "pansies" (weak). The Comp U players, then, claimed a closer association to the dominant (masculine) persona.

Toughness, for the players, was not just something that they *did*; it was part of who they *were*. The game of rugby supported this claim and enabled them to strategically use other athletic women, in addition to nonathletic women in sororities, in their defensive othering. Specifically, female athletes who did not play rugby were set up as an inferior other.

The establishment of sex-specific rules within sport is one means of institutionalizing inequality (Messner 2002). Such distinctions between men's and women's rules do not exist within rugby. For many of the Comp U players, this was a source of pride. Jana, a vet player, said, "I think rugby is definitely unique in that sense because there is no separation [in terms of rules and equipment], and I love that." Tammie, another vet player and one of the team officers, agreed: "I just really appreciate that. People don't feel like they have to bend the rules just because of the change in sexes playing the game." The players used this uniqueness to position rugby, and female rugby players by extension, as superior to other sports and other athletes. When male athletes, and men's style of play, are the standard in those sports played by both men and women (Messner 2002), good play and good athletes are defined by the men's games. Thus, playing by the same rules as the male rugby players enabled the women at Comp U to claim more respect as athletes.

The players put forward the identity of "rugger," and its attendant toughness, as an expression of their true athletic self. They did this by creating a life narrative in which their previous sport participation, though extensive and positive, was lacking. As they spoke, the players cast themselves as too competitive for the less (physically) demanding sports they had played in high school. Many noted that they were "always angry" as children, were "too aggressive" for other sports, or "always wanted to hit people." Finding rugby, they claimed, was finding the home they never knew they could have.

When I asked in interviews about what made a good rugby player, the women responded: "an aggressive personality," "an anger management problem to work out," "someone really intense," "a competitive personality," "it's just in their genes," or someone "with that little bit of craziness in 'em." The players thus justified their claim to the rugger identity by naturalizing aggression and competition: This is who I am. Female rugby players, in this account, are not just different from other female athletes; they are *better*. Carter, one of the coaches, echoed these sentiments in an interview: "You get girls who play soccer and play basketball and you get them to come out here and stand on the sidelines and watch this and you tell me how many of them will raise their hands and say they want to try it: Not very many."

Were the players tough? They valorized hard tackles and played through pain and injury, sometimes incurring permanent damage to their bodies. They policed dirty play by opponents with targeted hits and other forms of retribution that sometimes left opposing players unconscious or sent them to the hospital. And, they taunted their defeated opponents. Tammie, who refused treatment for torn shoulder ligaments for over a year in order to continue playing, famously tackled a player who had been "talking trash" during the game, then stood over her and yelled, "Get up, bitch; I'm not done with you yet!" Words like "bitch" are used in traditionally male sports to denigrate boys and men who show a lack of aggression or masculinity (Messner 2002).

By using this word to subordinate her opponent, however, Tammie adopted and reinforced this sexist theme of the larger institution of sport and positioned the Comp U team, and Comp U players, as masculine (tough) in relation to their feminine (weak) opponents. The female ruggers at Comp U positioned themselves as "tougher" than women generally and nonrugger female athletes specifically. They also adopted the style of play and aggression, along with the denigration through feminization of opponents ("Get up, bitch!"), associated with men's rugby. In doing so, they identified with dominants, reinforcing stereotypes of passive femininity for others and positioning themselves as stronger in contrast.

Normative Identification

Marilyn Frye (1983) notes that the socially constructed lines dividing dominant and subordinated groups are vigilantly policed, often by members of both groups. When members of subordinated groups cross these lines, they may experience backlash and social sanction. She notes that homophobia is used as a policing resource to maintain sex inequality. Faced with such threats, women (or members of other subordinated groups) may engage in *normative identification*, aligning themselves with the norms and values prescribed by dominants for a subordinated group.

To the extent that the Comp U players made successful claims to an essential toughness in comparison to women in general as well as other female athletes, they created a dilemma for themselves. Historically, athletic women have been stereotyped as masculine lesbians (Blinde and Taub 1992; Griffin 1992). The very things that made rugby attractive as a resource for the players' identity work—its pervasive physicality and its similarity to the men's game—made the Comp U players vulnerable to such labeling. The players were keenly aware of this. When I asked them about the dominant view of female ruggers, they said, in matter-of-fact or angry tones: "scary, butch lesbians," "she-males," "he-shes," "lesbian man-beasts," and "butch, big—definitely gay." Many players reported experiencing intense resistance from their parents. One player told me that when she told her mother she was playing rugby her mother responded, "Isn't that a dyke sport?" They also ran into social sanction from friends. Peg, a fourth-year player known on the team for her aggressive play, told me that when one of her male friends heard her talking about playing rugby he said, "Peg, if you turn out to be a lesbian, I'll kill you." He was "joking," but Peg received the message of his sanction loud and clear. Comp U players did not say that these stereotypes were false or try to strip them of their stigmatizing power. They asserted only that the stereotypes did not apply to them.

Comp U players positioned themselves as the exception to the rule by emphasizing their conformity to traditional notions of white, middle class, heterosexual femininity—what Griffin (1992) calls "promoting a heterosexy image (p. 252)"—in their style of dress and appearance on and off the pitch. They thus engaged in normative identification. The players essentialized their femininity and heterosexuality, claiming them as natural expressions of their selves. Additionally, they privileged their smaller physical size—in comparison to female rugby players on other teams—as a mark of their hard work and dedication to the sport, treating their bodies as social projects—objects that are shaped, scrutinized, and negotiated (see Bourdieu 1984; Brumberg 1997; Foucault 1977). They saw themselves as both *essentially* different (heterosexual and feminine) from other female ruggers, as well as relationally superior athletes as a result of their *accomplished* fitness.

Essential Femininity and Heterosexuality

Conventional femininity carries with it compulsory heterosexuality (Frye 1983; Griffin 1992; Rich 1994). One way for women to engage in normative identification as an attempt to please the dominant group (or at least not alienate them) while breaking other gendered norms is to make an appeal to their own "natural" femininity and heterosexuality. More than simply "apologizing" for the transgression by emphasizing other conventional gendered norms, this strategy involves claiming those norms as an essential aspect of the self. The women on the Comp U rugby team, coming up against expressed and internalized sanctions for their tough and aggressive (unfeminine) rugby play, did exactly this.

During interactions at practices and games, the players negotiated and policed acceptable gender and sexual performances for each other and for the team as a whole. For example, at a game early in the season, Doris, a newbie, saw an opposing player whose biological sex she could not clearly identify. She asked Carter, one of the coaches, if there were any coed teams: He answered,

"No, there are no coed teams. In women's rugby, you'll see a lot of *interesting* looking women, but they *are* always women." Maeve, a vet player, said, "They're all *technically* women." Doris laughed.

At a practice a few weeks before the team left for nationals, the competition for the best team in the United States, a group of veteran players asked me if I would be able to travel with them. I told them that I could not, but said jokingly that I was sure there would be "lots of data" to collect:

Sandy said, "Great data, and a chance to compare us to the other 'women's' teams. And by 'women,' I mean 'she-males.'" [When she said "women," she used her fingers to make quotation marks in the air.] Opal, Kent, and Mo laughed. Kent said, "Huge, scary women with goatees!"

Mo said, "Bigger than my dad!" Then, turning to me, she said, "Don't expect to get checked out [looked at sexually] at all, because *we're* the ones getting checked out!"

Maeve's qualification that women who were masculine in appearance were only "technically" women, Sandy's use of quotation marks around the word "women," and Mo's comments about getting "checked out" suggest that *real* women (should) look feminine and date men. Such comments positioned the Comp U team as the exception and, as the comments came from veteran players, modeled acceptable gender performances for the newbies. A few of the Comp U players self-identified as lesbian or bisexual, and two of the players were openly dating one another, but the team, as a collectivity, presented itself as heterosexual. Susie commented on this:

We have, um, obviously there's a larger number of lesbians in this sport than a lot of other sports. They're very attracted to this sport. But, um, I don't know if that's because they're just more aggressive people by nature. I have no idea. I haven't really studied any of that. But, um, they, we just don't have that on our team, at all. I mean, we do, but not in the same numbers as most other teams. And, just, we tend to be effeminate people. I have no idea why. Susie says that lesbians may just be "more aggressive by nature."

Yet, as noted earlier, naturalized aggression was the most common account I heard from players when I asked how they came to play rugby. This account worked to validate the athletes' claim to the identity of tough rugby player; but, it also came close to outsiders' beliefs that all lesbians are aggressive, hence all female rugby players are lesbians. Susie dealt with this problem by essentializing the feminine gender performance of *this* team: "we just tend to be effeminate people."

Comp U players often claimed that they were special because, in addition to being tough, they were also heterosexual *and* feminine—closer to normative expectations of (white, middle-class) women than other female ruggers. Importantly, the overwhelmingly white status of the team enabled their use of this strategy. Black women are typically stereotyped as more "masculine" than white women (Collins 2004; Kaplan 1987), and may not have been able to draw on this strategy in the same ways. Thus, the players used their racial identities, here and elsewhere, as a buffer in their identity work.

Time and again, in practices and in interviews, players touted the "diversity" on the team and noted how welcoming the club was to anyone who was serious about the sport. Seeing the team as "open" may have been important for the players because it suggested that they were good people. Despite their claims of inclusivity, though, the players were disproportionately "feminine" in appearance, white, and heterosexual. This had not always been the case.

The third- and fourth-year players remembered a time when the team was less heterosexual and feminine identified and fractured along lines of sexuality (the racial makeup of the team, though, had consistently been white dominated). According to Susie: "There was a big division on the team between the straight girls and the lesbians on the team. . . . I mean, they wouldn't stay in the same rooms in the hotels and stuff. It was a big issue." Donna, a former player, lesbian identified, who left the team prior to my research because of injuries and a growing "feminist consciousness," spoke to me in an interview about the climate on the team while she played:

> There was definite internalized homophobia and sexism and, like, people didn't want to look certain ways, they didn't think that certain ways of expression in your, in your, I don't know, in your body image were okay—even if you were a lesbian. . . . [L]ike, body hair—that was not okay. That was *not* okay. I mean, they would be like, "I don't care how much of a lesbian you are, you should shave your legs."

Individual players, Donna learned, should support the collective image of the team and shield the group from stigma.

Sherry, who also played during this time, discussed tensions among the players surrounding issues of sexuality. It came up when I asked about the relationship between Comp U's men's and women's teams. Sherry answered:

> That changes year to year, and it changes based on how "hot" [conventionally attractive] the team is, the girls' team is, which is very noticeable. . . . My sophomore year when all of the drama was going on and most of the team was lesbian it wasn't necessarily that they weren't hot, it was that they were all lesbian and very anti-man. There was a huge—the teams did not get along. . . . When [the straight players] felt like the lesbian girls were ruining [our relationship with the men's team] it got, you know, it was like a big point of contention. It was like: They're our guys and you're pissing them off.

Sherry's comments suggest that, for at least some of the players at Comp U, there was a conscious decision to move away from a lesbian, or lesbian-*perceived*, collective identity (and lesbian-identified players) in order to attract and please rugby men. Vet players socialized the newbies to adopt this account. When I asked Tina, a newbie, what she had heard about the previous tension, she said, "Somebody told me one time the whole reason was because the team used to be composed of all angst-ridden, butch, man-hating lesbians."

Two players, both respected and valued athletes on the team who fit the privileged heterosexy-fit presentation of self, began openly dating during my research. Importantly, they did not self-identify as lesbians. Hannah, one of the women, explained to me, "I'm *not* a lesbian, but I'm dating Wendy. . . . That's our major thing. We're like, why do you need the label?" Still, after they went public with their relationship, Frankie, who was Christian identified, told them they were "going to hell." Her intervention was not well-received by the team. Joanne, a respected fourth-year player, said, "That was tough for a while. People were really angry with Frankie because of that. We don't want that."

How can the lack of support for Frankie's denunciation of Hannah and Wendy, given the history of the team, be explained? In one sense, Frankie's public disapproval challenged the team's image of itself as "open." Framed through religion, it may also have clashed with aspects of the team's social activities (parties, drinking, etc.). Yet her words were in keeping with the actions of vet players in the past who had also policed the sexual performances of the players. What shifted was the sexual balance of the team; two dating players were not enough of a threat to the *collective* heterosexual identity of the team to warrant the negative reactions of previous years. Everyone but Frankie, at least openly, positioned these two women as an exception. Had a larger number of players been dating one another, the tensions of the past may well have resurfaced.

The Comp U female ruggers were invested in a collective heterosexual identity. They were not, however, intolerant homophobes allergic to any sign of lesbianism. The problem was the homophobic context that compelled them to publicly distance themselves from the stigma and stereotypes attached to their sport. Indeed, Tina's and Sherry's comments reveal that the specific reaction of Comp U's *men's* team to the lesbian-identified players in the past was the proximate cause of the women's negative reactions.

Why would the heterosexual-identified players give so much weight to the male players' response? Female athletes—and female rugby players in particular—are stereotyped as butch lesbians, so the heterosexual-identified players said they feared that most men would not be attracted to them. Male rugby players, in this context, became even more important as potential dating partners. Frankie put it simply: "I think that a girl rugby player is intimidating for a lot of guys, *except* for the guy rugby players." The women, then, tried to recruit players who would be deemed attractive to heterosexual men. Eden, a second-year player, said, "It's just like, we've kind of, over the years, weeded them [physically larger, lesbian-identified players] out and kind of replaced them with girls that are more like us and athletic and everything." This highlights the importance of recruitment as a resource for the team's collective identity.

The players' belief in an already reduced dating pool was compounded by the fact that female students were the majority at Comp U. The players reported that "the ratio" created fierce competition for men as dating partners. Mo, a second-year player, told me that a popular men's magazine had described the women at Comp U as "goddesses." Given the players' ages and the undergraduate culture of romance (see Holland and Eisenhart 1990), it makes sense that dating was important to them. Because outsiders stereotype female rugby players as masculine lesbians, and "goddesses" were their competition for dates, it is not surprising that they emphasized feminine and heterosexual signifiers on and off the pitch. Surprising or not, their use of defensive othering relied on and reinforced heteronormative ideals of body presentation and performance.

Accomplishing Fitness

In another example of defensive othering through normative identification, the players positioned themselves as better than other female ruggers because of their smaller physical size and greater commitment to fitness, qualities closer to normative understandings of "femininity." The players granted toughness, seemingly by default, to all female ruggers through their assertions of a naturalized aggression as the foundation of rugby play. But being "fit"—a body presentation that often necessitates the middle-class privileges of gym memberships,

flexible schedules, and access to sports teams and equipment—was an accomplishment reached through hard work. The players' idea of fitness (strong, yet smaller and thin) located them closer to conventional understandings of white, middle class femininity (and, thus, heterosexuality) and reaffirmed their claims of difference from nonathletic (unfit) women in general.

In an interview, Sherry noted how important being fit was to Comp U players, repeatedly using the word "big" to describe the players on other teams. I asked what she meant:

> "Big," I mean, like, a lot of them are fat, or—it's not a sport for them, it's a lifestyle. You know, they don't work out the way we work out. They don't—like, we're fit. Not every single girl on our team is, you know, a size-two. There are girls that aren't, but they're fit. They're in good shape and they're not big girls, you know. . . . If you're playing a sport you'd think that people wouldn't be fat, but then you have these big, fat girls [on other teams].

Being "fit" and not "fat" was something for which this team was known. In fact, as many players and both coaches told me with pride, Comp U players were called "The Barbie Dolls" within the national rugby community. Male players from opposing teams applauded the Comp U women during warm-ups before games, calling out: "Let's hear it for the hottest rugby team in the South!"

Players reinforced team norms for body size through their informal interactions. In the middle of the fall semester of 2002, the vet players on the Comp U team held an initiation for the newbies, attended by both the men's and the women's teams. As part of the evening's events, the vets required the newbies to dress up as characters and perform skits. At practice a few weeks later, Tracy, Jenny, and Flash, all newbies, had the following conversation:

> "Did you see me at Susie's house on Halloween in those sweatpants?" asked Flash. "They came all the way up to my shoulders!" Tracy responded, "So did your thong at initiation." Flash answered, "Well, it was a size-thirteen thong! It was a size thirteen thong on a size-zero body. That's what happens." Tracy asked, with a tone of disgust, "Who wears a size-thirteen here?" Jenny explained, "The vets went out and bought it at Wal-Mart." Tracy said, "Oh," sounding relieved. She continued, "Isn't that kind of gross, a fat woman in a thong? And someone's supposed to think that's sexy?" They all laughed.

Not being "fit"—being larger than the "size-zero bod[ies]" on the Comp U team—was regarded with derision and contempt.

In these ways the players used a rhetoric of accomplishment, in addition to their appeals to an essential toughness and heterosexuality, to position themselves as superior to other female ruggers, other female athletes, and nonathletic women—an updated version of emphasized femininity I call heterosexy-fit. The apparent contradictions of the identity, and its use to distance the players from imposed stigma, are visible in the following excerpt from my interview with Hannah:

> Like, if you look at other teams you can see the stereotype. But, if you look at our team you don't get that typical butch-rugger, like, lesbian-type deal, you know?
>
> [Interviewer: What do you think accounts for that?]
>
> Comp U has a lot of pretty girls and that's just how it is. And, we just got lucky with some that really want to hit other girls [laughs]. I don't know. I'm not really sure. I think it's weird, but it's kind of neat that we're unique, you know, because we have a reputation for kicking ass *and* looking good. So, that's kind of fun. It's like: "I'm a sexy bitch and I will kick your ass," basically [laughs].

This heterosexy-fit identity emerged out of the contradictions between "tough" and "feminine," the seemingly incompatible identities to which the players made simultaneous claim. It was enabled by the team's whiteness and middle-class privileges, and it was a rewarding identity in a variety of ways. Constructing it relied, however, on the devaluation of other female athletes and women in general. The defensive othering of the women ruggers thus helped to maintain women's status as others within the dominant gender order.

Propping Up Dominants

In addition to defensive othering, maintaining boundaries between dominant and subordinate groups is an essential component of the reproduction of inequality (Schwalbe et al. 2000). Boundary maintenance allows members of dominant groups to hoard resources, and is thus not usually in the interest of subordinates. But, because the Comp U players saw the rugby men as comprising a small and threatened dating pool, they had an investment in protecting their access to these men. Their identity work as tough athletes challenged the conventional equation of women with physical weakness and

passivity, thus pushing them closer to the status of men. This could have been interpreted as unattractive by rugby men, and the Comp U female ruggers worried that it did. To position themselves above other women by virtue of their toughness, but still below men, the players maintained the boundary between men and women by propping up dominants—(re)asserting the superiority of dominant group members. The female players, in short, put men forward as essentially superior athletes.

As mentioned earlier, the female ruggers at Comp U were proud of the fact that they played by the same rules as the men. However, they did not want to play *against* or *with* the men. Tammie said:

> I'm not this kind of person that thinks, "Oh, girls should be able to play with the boys if they want to." No. Like, I would never step on that field and play full-contact rugby with the boys. They're so much stronger than me I would get killed, you know? . . . 'Cause I mean, yeah, there is that level of difference there and nobody can do anything about it. . . . I'm just happy I can play exactly what they play, just on my level.

To the women, the men were the more valued rugby players, and the women sought higher status by approaching, but not surpassing, the men's style of play as the standard. The men's valued status was evident when I asked Tammie why she liked playing by the same rules as the men: "I think it's a big deal because I think men's rugby teams really respect you for it." Joanne said, "Men's games are a lot more fast-paced. I mean, obviously, we're not ever gonna be able to sprint quite as fast." She, like Tammie, reinforced the idea of men's natural athletic prowess. Not wanting to be tackled by an opponent who is physically larger and stronger is understandable. And male athletes, on average, may be faster than female athletes. But reinforcing the men's superiority in these ways worked as a form of boundary maintenance that lessened the potential threat the women posed to the men, thus increasing the female players' desirability. Yes, the women were tough athletes on the pitch, but they were tough *with other women*, not with men. In addition to maintaining the boundary between women and men, this strategy reasserted the women's specialness by distancing them from other female athletes who believe that women can do anything that men do. Jana derisively described such players as "super unathletic" (unfit) and "definite feminists," in contrast to the "fit" and apolitical ruggers on the Comp U team. She continued:

> I've never consciously thought, "Okay, I'm gonna do this [play rugby] to prove that I'm equal to men." [Interviewer: There's no political motivation?] Oh, not at all. Not at all. . . . I never did it because I wanted to prove something. . . . I think most of the women on our team are that way.

The coaches also reinforced the superiority of male athletes. Carter put it simply: "There's a big gap between [men's and women's] playing ability." Jim, the other coach, said:

> [O]ne thing I'm going to do this year is just spend more time putting them in front of a television and making them watch the men's game. . . . Just watch great rugby. Yes, the men's game is played at a faster pace and, yes, it's not as technically proficient [focused on technical rugby skills like passing, kicking, etc.]; it's still very useful just to watch the very best players in the world play their game. . . . It's played at such a different pace.

I asked both coaches what accounted for the differences they had noted between the men's and women's games and styles of play. They highlighted a mix of nature and nurture. They said there were inherent differences between men's and women's physical abilities and "drives," but they acknowledged that social conditioning also played a role. Their message to the players, however, was clear: Real ruggers are men and the women's game is derivative and, thus, second class. Jim's comments, noted previously, clearly reinscribe the boundary between men and women. They also raise an interesting question: If the men are not as "technically proficient" as the women, why are the men considered the "very best players in the world"? Such comments expose the values of the institution of sport. Men's and women's bodies fall along a continuum of human differences; however, there are average differences between them. The most valued sports, in terms of media coverage and funding, are typically organized through rules, strategies, and norms that privilege men's bodies (Messner 2002). This does not mean that men are inherently better athletes. It only means that what is valued in sport reflects the premium put on size, strength, and masculine behavior. By propping up dominants, Comp U's female players (with help from their coaches)

strengthened their claim to a heterosexy-fit identity that did not threaten men or male dominance. They positioned themselves and their sport as exceptional in that they (and it) were tough and aggressive, while they were also feminine, heterosexual, and sexy. They "knew their place" (below men), and thus could be desirable to men.

Conclusion

The female rugby players at Comp U were successful athletes in high school but found themselves unable to compete in their chosen sports at the varsity level at Comp U. So they turned to rugby, an intensely physical yet nonvarsity sport, as an alternative. They stepped onto the pitch and met with success, only to find themselves stigmatized by outsiders as "butch lesbians." Instead of resisting and rejecting the power of such stigma, as others have found female rugby players to do, the Comp U players turned to defensive othering, casting themselves as the exception to the stereotype, and thereby unintentionally reinforcing the dominant heterosexist ideology. In doing so, they created a unique identity as heterosexy-fit—simultaneously tough, heterosexual, and conventionally attractive. The women's presentation of the heterosexy-fit identity helped them respond to sexist and homophobic stigma and backlash to women's participation in sport. They wanted to be seen as tough and serious athletes without sacrificing their sexual appeal to men. To some extent they succeeded. For example, the heterosexy-fit identity insulated them from outsiders' negative beliefs; granted them higher status relative to other women, other athletic women generally, and other female ruggers in particular; and promoted an individual and collective presentation of self they personally valued and saw as desirable to rugby men. The women did not create the conditions of inequality under which they acted, nor did they create the devalued identities imposed on them. Understandably, they managed their identities in ways that promoted a sense of self-worth and affirmation. However, their solution to the identity dilemmas they faced reinforced the stigmatizing power of the devalued identities they sought to deflect.

Members of subordinated groups seeking access to dominant institutions, however, may choose alternative paths. They may seek *access* to these institutions without seeking *approval* from dominants. For example, they may seek access in an attempt to change the institutions, to challenge institutional norms that privilege dominants, and/or to seek redress for structural or institutional discrimination. This may be most likely to occur when subordinates have achieved a sense of group consciousness around subordinated identity(ies), and solidarity among members. If a group identifies its struggles with those of the wider social category (e.g., women, people of color, the queer community), members have less incentive to become an "exception."

How else might athletes approach identity work? Similar to the work of scholars in higher education who seek to change institutional norms and values, Theberge (1997, 85) calls for sporting practice among male *and* female athletes that "rejects violence and the normalization of injury in favor of an ethic of care." And, Michael Messner (2002) describes a "social justice model" of empowerment in sport available to all athletes: "leveling the playing field and simultaneously *changing the rules of the game* to make the world more just, equitable, and healthy for all" (p. 166; emphasis added). This involves moving beyond a focus on individual empowerment and addressing institutional inequality and harm within sport. What this social justice model of empowerment could mean in men's and women's rugby, or any other sport, is for teams to challenge institutional values that privilege violent masculinity and men's bodies. Male and female athletes could challenge sex segregation in their sports or seek segregated play that was not organized around violent masculinity and the "survival of the fittest." If and when female athletes were targeted with homophobic backlash, they could not be so quick to "correct" those who label them by (re)asserting their heterosexuality. Male and female athletes might take the risk of confronting those who perpetuated these stereotypes, challenging issues of heterosexism in sports. And, they could refrain from using homophobic or misogynistic slurs themselves. Further, those interested in issues of inequality and justice could turn a critical eye toward the institution of sport itself, making the links between inequality in sport and broader questions of structural inequality (see, e.g., Birrell and MacDonald 2000; Eitzen 2006; Frey and Eitzen 1991; and Theberge 1981). How might sport reflect and reinforce other social problems? Structural racism and sexism within the larger culture, for example, are evident within sex and race disparities in coaching and sports administrative

positions (Messner 2002). The hypersexualization of female athletes, as evidenced in *Playboy*'s 2004 "Women of the Olympics" pictorial, reflects and reinforces the sexual objectification of women in other spheres (Jhally 2002). Further, sport as socialization into the use of the body as a weapon and indoctrination into violent masculinity can be seen as an enabling condition of militarism and violence in other arenas (Schwalbe 2004). Sport, in short, is more than entertainment. It is a core social institution built around competition, hegemonic masculinity, and the suppression of empathy. What happens on the field has consequences for life off of it.

References

Birrell, Susan, and Mary G. McDonald, eds. 2000. *Reading Sport: Critical Essays on Power and Representation.* Boston: Northeastern University Press.

Blinde, Elaine M., and Diane E. Taub. 1992. "Women Athletes as Falsely Accused Deviants: Managing the Lesbian Stigma." *Sociological Quarterly* 33:521–533.

Blumer, Herbert. 1969. *Symbolic Interactionism: Perspective and Method.* Berkeley: University of California Press.

Bourdieu, Pierre. 1984. *Distinction: A Social Critique of the Judgment of Taste.* London: Routledge.

Brumberg, Joan Jacobs. 1997. *The Body Project: An Intimate History of American Girls.* New York: Vintage Books.

Burke, Peter J., and Judy C. Tully. 1977. "The Measurement of Role Identity." *Social Forces* 55:881–897.

Collins, Patricia Hill. 2004. *Black Sexual Politics: African Americans, Gender, and the New Racism.* New York: Routledge.

Eitzen, D. Stanley. 2006. *Fair and Foul: Beyond the Myths and Paradoxes of Sport,* 3rd ed. New York: Rowan and Littlefield Publishers.

Foucault, Michel. 1977. *Discipline and Punish.* London: Allen Lane.

Frey, James H., and D. Stanley Eitzen. 1991. "Sport and Society." *Annual Review of Sociology* 17:503–522.

Frye, Marilyn. 1983. *The Politics of Reality: Essays in Feminist Theory.* New York: The Crossing Press.

Griffin, Pat. 1992. "Changing the Game: Homophobia, Sexism, and Lesbians in Sport." *Quest* 44: 251–265.

Heywood, Leslie, and Shari L. Dworkin. 2003. *Built to Win: The Female Athlete as Cultural Icon.* Minneapolis: University of Minnesota Press.

Holland, Dorothy C., and Margaret A. Eisenhart. 1990. *Educated in Romance: Women, Achievement, and College Culture.* Chicago: University of Chicago Press.

Jhally, Sut. 2002. "Playing Unfair: The Media Image of the Female Athlete." Northampton, MA: Media Education Foundation (MEF). http://www.mediaed.org/assets/products/208/transcript_208.pdf (accessed September 18, 2015).

Kaplan, Elaine Bell. 1987. "'I Don't Do No Windows': Competition between the Domestic Worker and the Housewife." In *Competition: A Feminist Taboo?* (ed. V. Miner and H. E. Longino), 92–105. New York: The Feminist Press.

Lofland, John, David Snow, Leon Anderson, and Lyn H. Lofland. 2006. *Analyzing Social Settings: A Guide to Qualitative Observation and Analysis.* Belmont, CA: Wadsworth/Thompson Learning.

McCall, George and J. L. Simmons. 1978. *Identities and Interaction.* 2d ed. New York: Free Press.

Messner, Michael A. 2002. *Taking the Field: Women, Men, and Sports.* Minneapolis: University of Minnesota Press.

Rich, Adrienne. 1994. *Blood, Bread, and Poetry: Selected Prose (1979–1985)*, Reissued ed. New York: W. W. Norton & Company, Inc.

Robbins, Alexandra. 2004. *Pledged: The Secret Life of Sororities.* New York: Hyperion.

Schwalbe, Michael. 2004. "The Sport of Empire." *Commondreams.org*, January 6. http://www.commondreams.org/views/2004/01/06/sport-empire (accessed September 18, 2015).

Schwalbe, Michael, and Douglas Mason-Schrock. 1996. "Identity Work as Group Process." In *Advances in Group Processes*, Vol. 13 (ed. B. Markovsky, M. Lovaglia, and R. Simon), 115–149. Greenwich, CT: JAI Press.

Schwalbe, Michael, Sandra Godwin, Daphne Holden, Douglas Schrock, Shealy Thompson, and Michele Wolkomir. 2000. "Generic Processes in the Reproduction of Inequality: An Interactionist Analysis." *Social Forces* 79:419–452.

Strauss, Anselm L. 1959. *Mirrors and Masks: The Search for Identity.* Glencoe, IL: Free Press.

Theberge, Nancy. 1981. "A Critique of Critiques: Radical and Feminist Writings on Sport." *Social Forces* 60:341–353.

———. 1997. "'It's Part of the Game': Physicality and the Production of Gender in Women's Hockey." *Gender and Society* 11:69–87.

West, Candace, and Sarah Fenstermaker. 1995. "Doing Difference." *Gender and Society* 9:8–37.

West, Candace, and Don H. Zimmerman. 1987. "Doing Gender." *Gender and Society* 1:125–151.

Questions

1. What does Ezzel mean by a heterosexy-fit presentation of self? When the rugby players reinforce a heterosexy-fit presentation of self as ideal, how do they challenge or reinforce inequality? What are the ways that the ruggers adapt to their subordinate position? Explain identifying with dominants, normative identification, and propping up dominants. How are they related to gender inequality more broadly?

2. What reasons does Ezzel give for why the women reinforce the superiority of male rugby players? How does this reinforce gender norms that support inequity between men and women?

3. What is Ezzell's argument about how marginalized people respond to being in subordinate positions? What other groups do you see engaging in identifying with dominants, normative identification, and propping up dominants? Give a specific example of each. What do people have at stake that draws them into reproducing inequality? What are the unintended consequences of engaging in these behaviors? Are there alternative ways to respond to one's own subordination that do not reinforce hierarchy?

4. Do sports, such as football, boxing, hockey, and mixed martial arts, encourage a larger culture that supports violent masculinity? Why or why not? What implication does your answer have for how sports are valued in our culture? What other social institutions sponsor violent masculinity? How is violent masculinity inflected by social class?

36

"Anyone Can Be an Illegal": Color-Blind Ideology and Maintaining Latino/Citizen Borders

KATRINA BLOCH

While we often hear the United States referred to as a nation of immigrants, the history and politics surrounding citizenship and migration are complex. Today immigration reform provokes heated debate among politicians and within the media. Interest groups have formed on different sides of the debates, arguing for the humane treatment of migrants and clear paths to citizenship or stricter policies and enforcement of laws that restrict migration into the country. Recent events catapulted immigration into the mainstream media, especially protests of buses carrying unaccompanied migrant children from Central American countries. Hundreds of protestors in California successfully blocked three busses, while chanting and holding signs stating that migrant children pose health risks, are invaders, and do not deserve tax dollars. Meanwhile, opponents argue that the children should be granted asylum, because they are refugees attempting to escape severe poverty, violence, and death. They stress that parents have sent the children because they fear for their lives. These events call into question what belief systems people use when making claims regarding access to the United States and the rights attached to citizenship.

The next reading focuses on a group that advocates for stricter immigration policies. Previously in Part V, you read about how people reinforce hegemonic idealized images. The readings examined why and how different beauty norms, sexualities, and class groups are either relegated to a stigmatized status or hailed as the morally correct identities. This next reading continues this discussion with a focus on how these distinctions are made through how people talk. In it, Katrina Bloch examines the discourse used in an anti-immigrant online discussion forum to examine how members use color-blind racist techniques to argue for the restriction of immigration into the United States. Bloch argues that the immigrant restrictionists engage in boundary work that racializes Latinos and makes "Hispanic" incompatible with "citizen." Thus, the groups reinforce a white hegemonic idealized citizen.

Construction of a National Identity as White and the Nonwhite Immigrant

The ability to be considered a citizen in the United States, and receive full citizen privileges, has been limited throughout history to characteristics including place of birth, race, gender, and class (Cacho 2000).

As Haney Lopez (2006) shows, the separation of "white" from "nonwhite" played an integral role in birthright and naturalization laws. In the 1790s Congress limited naturalization to only "whites" and subsequent laws continued to use race as a deciding factor in immigration law. In 1882 Congress passed the Chinese Exclusion

Excerpted from Bloch, Katrina. 2014. "'Anyone Can Be an Illegal:' Color-blind Ideology and Maintaining Latino/Citizen Borders." *Critical Sociology* 40 (1): 47–65.

Act. This act barred immigration of Chinese laborers, which was later expanded in 1917 to include all persons from Asia. In the 1920s and 1950s we saw the law focus on Mexican immigrants, with mass deportations that included large numbers of U.S. citizens. Further, even birthright citizenship was limited to "whites" up until the 1940s (Haney Lopez 2006).

Naturalization cases during this time forced courts to rule on what constituted "white" and hence who qualified for the privilege of citizenship. The courts used either anthropological classification systems or relied on the "common knowledge" of race to make decisions on whether or not immigrants qualified as "white." For example, in the early 1920s the district court ruled to grant Thind, an immigrant from India, naturalization based on previous court cases that followed the anthropological classification that Indians are Caucasian and therefore "white." However, the federal government appealed this decision and the case went before the Supreme Court, which ruled with "common knowledge" that Indians are not "white." This resulted in Thind's naturalization being denied and other immigrants from India having their naturalization stripped (Haney Lopez 2006). It wasn't until 1965 that Congress passed the Immigration Act of 1965, which eliminated quota laws that privileged immigrants from Europe. The focus shifted to family reunification, including the spouses, children, and siblings of current immigrants, with only 20 percent of visas set aside for work-related migration (Hing 2006). However, since previous quotas led to a higher percentage of white immigrants, the 1965 law was intended to attract more relatives of white than nonwhite immigrants and, thus, lead to the same proportion of white and nonwhite migration as had existed under previous law (Reimers 1985). Instead, Asian and Latino migrants to the United States disproportionately took advantage of the family reunification policy, and by the 1990s they became the largest immigrant groups (Hing 2006). Recent changes in immigration policy have become increasingly punitive in nature and continue to be influenced by racial prejudice. The public sentiment largely associates immigrants with Mexicans (Hing 2010), and media and political debates are coded with racial messages (Cacho 2000).

In 1994, President Clinton launched the program "Operation Gatekeeper" and began construction of a 14-mile wall between California and Mexico intended to curb illegal immigrants crossing the United States border (Walker 2007). This was shortly followed by the 1996 Antiterrorism and Effective Death Penalty Act (AEDPA) and the Illegal Immigration Reform and Immigrant Responsibility Act (IIRIRA) passed by the House of Representatives. These laws increased deportable offenses and expenditures on border control (Walker 2007). While these immigration laws were constructed without the stated intention of differentiating between racial and ethnic groups, the increasing criminalization and militarization of immigrants calls attention to the southern border, thus constructing Mexico as dangerous. The construction of Mexico as dangerous, and Mexican immigrants as threatening, was further heightened by the government's response to 9/11 which linked terrorism and immigration. The "War on Terror" led to the criminalization of being undocumented when Immigration and Customs Enforcement (ICE) and the Customs and Border Protection came under the supervision of Homeland Security. This shift led to an increase in deportations, especially for undocumented immigrants with minor infractions (Akers Chacon and Davis 2006). The policy also increased border patrol and enforcement along the Mexican border, which did not reduce migration but did lead to huge increases in the number of migrants who died in the desert (Hing 2006).

Since 9/11 there has also been an increase in nativist groups (Buchanan and Holthouse 2007), vigilante border groups in particular (Walker 2007), and nativist websites (Sohoni 2006). Groups such as the Anti-Defamation League (2007) and the Southern Poverty Law Center (Beirich 2008) have noted that nativists have increasingly become mainstream with organizations such as the Federation for American Immigration Reform, founded by well-known nativist John Tanton, building ties with politicians and testifying in Congress. However, the ideology purported by these organizations and adopted in the mass media racializes Latinos (Chavez 2008; Johnson 1998; Romero 2008). For example, Romero (2008) argues, in her study of Mothers Against Illegal Aliens (MAIA) and its leader Michelle Dallacroce, that the symbolism of mothers is used to hide the racist messages of the organization. MAIA and Dallacroce stereotype Latino immigrants as less than human. Specifically, Latino women are portrayed as selfish and criminal breeders, while white mothers are constructed as idealized Madonnas (Romero 2008). Further, Chavez (2008) finds that racial threat is played out on magazine covers, such as a 1990 *Time* magazine titled "America's Changing Colors," whereby whites are warned of their imminent descent into minority status.

The racialization of nonwhite noncitizens has important consequences for domestic citizens. As Johnson (1998, 1154) notes, "The punishment of noncitizens of color suggests just how society might zealously attack domestic minorities of color absent legal protections" and provides the Japanese internment camps for Japanese American citizens during World War II as a clear example. The negative attributes of a nonwhite immigrant other are generalized to the larger nonwhite other, including nonwhite citizens (Johnson 1998).

Color-Blind Racism

While whiteness brings privileges, blatant verbal support of inequality *because of* race is discouraged. Scholars have suggested that the post–civil rights era is marked by color-blind (Bonilla-Silva 2001; Carr 1997) or "laissez-faire" (Bobo and Smith 1998) racism, whereby whites verbally denounce racism and simultaneously deny the existence of continued racial discrimination. Racist ideas are covered and neutralized to appear less malignant (Feagin 2000). For instance, interview studies with whites find that participants argue that they are opposed to racial inequality, yet they also oppose social policies and programs that would reduce racial inequality (Feagin and O'Brien 2003; Wellman 1977). In the new racism, racial disparity is attributed to individual failures and cultural shortcomings, as opposed to problems with the ideology of meritocracy (Bobo and Smith 1998). Whites diminish the importance of race in explanations for disparities in the distribution of wealth across racial groups and the continued economic marginalization of nonwhites (Bonilla-Silva 2002). Color-blind ideology isn't just a way of thinking; it is also a way of speaking (Bonilla-Silva 2001, 2002; Bonilla-Silva and Forman 2000; Bonilla-Silva, Lewis, and Embrick 2004). On one hand people proclaim that they are not racist, while simultaneously freeing themselves to say racist things (Bonilla-Silva 2001; Bonilla-Silva and Forman 2000; Bonilla-Silva et al. 2004; Van Dijk 1992, 1993). Color-blind racist discourse includes phrases such as "I'm not racist, but. . ." and "Some of my best

friends aren't white" (Bonilla-Silva 2002; Bonilla-Silva and Forman 2000). This general climate of color-blind racism is evident in debates regarding immigration.

Mass media is an important site for the reproduction of color-blind ideology (Collins 2006). Coutin and Chock (1997) illustrate how journalists used racial and ethnic stereotypes to separate illegal immigrants into the undeserving illegal and those deserving amnesty in the media accounts of the U.S. Immigration Reform Control Act of 1986. When journalists gave accounts of immigrants placed into the "good" category, they stressed their likeness to citizens and diminished the immigrants' racial or ethnic difference. They were constructed in opposition to "other" criminal and threatening immigrants, thus reinforcing whiteness as normative. Similarly, Ono and Sloop (2002) find that the media makes distinctions between good and bad immigration by relying on the concept of legality. Immigrants of today are juxtaposed with historical waves of legal immigrants. Immigrants now are portrayed as overwhelmingly illegal, and immigrants being referred to as "good" by the legal distinction are European. Hence a dichotomy between good and bad separates European and white immigrants as "good" and today's nonwhite immigrants as bad (Ono and Sloop 2002).

However, the reliance on "legality" is a color-blind tactic that only appears race neutral. Calavita (1998) argues that "legality" is itself created by people and, thus, is informed by ideology regarding who is and who is not welcome into the nation. Laws can be used to reproduce a racist structure (Feagin 2000); hence, relying on legality does not preclude one from espousing racist ideology. Further, Akers Chacon and Davis (2006) argue that the term "illegal" has become a pejorative term associated with Mexicans that reproduces negative stereotypes while appearing non-racist.

Methods

In this study I focus on the website and the online general discussion forum of the group Americans for Legal Immigration Political Action Committee (ALIPAC). ALIPAC is one of the organizations identified by the Southern Poverty Law Center (SPLC) as "nativist extremist." However, the group self-identifies as pro–legal immigration, with a focus on creating social change through legislation. The organization's website lists a four-point platform: "1. Secure our borders; 2. Crack down on employers that intentionally hire illegals; 3. Remove incentives and rewards to illegals such as licenses, welfare, and other taxpayer benefits; 4. Enforce our existing laws and deport illegal aliens when convicted of crimes or detected during routine law enforcement activities." The headquarters of ALIPAC are in Raleigh, North Carolina; however, the group considers itself to be a national organization. The organization was founded in 2004 by its current leader and spokesperson, William Gheen. The Southern Poverty Law Center's 2008 Intelligence Report lists William Gheen as one of 20 most influential nativists in the United States.

Data Collection and Analysis

The data for this chapter come from the main website for ALIPAC (http://www.alipac.us/) and a sample of threads from the group's online general discussion forum. Threads are online conversations about one topic within a discussion forum that can be traced to an original post. I obtained a sample of 200 threads by sampling every fifth thread. All but three (98.5%) of the threads in the sample were first started in November or December of 2007. The oldest thread began on 14 June 2006. On the website, threads are arranged by most recent post date, not starting date. Hence, the three threads with older start dates were threads that had been started earlier but recently posted to. My sample of threads includes a total of 2,168 posts, with a median post of six per thread. The length of the threads ranged greatly, from only the one original post to as high as 191 posts per thread. Of the 274 unique aliases, 150 (55%) of the sample listed their "location" in their user information. Among those who did provide this information, 32 different states plus "Mexifornia" ($N = 4$) were listed. The states with the highest frequencies were California ($N = 34$), Texas ($N = 19$), and North Carolina ($N = 14$).

I approached the data inductively, without a set coding schema. I began with open coding, where I assigned a code to each line of data (Charmaz 2006; Lofland and Lofland 1995). After 30 threads, I began to develop a more focused coding schema based on themes that emerged from the open coding (Charmaz 2006).

Language of Legality as a Race Diminutive

Consistent with the dominant color-blind ideology, being racist threatens the legitimacy of both the group and individuals. This is a problematic identity dilemma

since group members reinforce racist ideology, some more explicitly than others. For example, in one instance, a forum participant posted discussions from a perceived pro-immigrant organization. The members referred to this as a Chicano forum. This post prompted an example of a more explicitly racist statement. EX_OC writes, "They resort to that because (a) their level of sanity is limited and (b) the macho rapist/tough guy image makes up for their pigmy stature and mental midget failure of Mexico to achieve what America has." In this statement, EX_OC is connecting the physical makeup of Chicanos (pigmy stature) with mental abilities, "mental midget failure." In response, No2illegals posts, "Wow . . . I couldn't have said it any better. . . . Awesome!" and wilro writes, "It's amazing how childish the chicken forum—ooops, I mean chicano forum is. Only small minds like theirs can produce something so moronic." The preceding quotes attach negative attributes with genetic characteristics and liken Mexicans to animals. However, comments that are so blatantly racist, referring to physical features, are rare. They are also inconsistent with today's color-blind ideology. Less explicit statements that reinforce racist ideology are much more common.

Consistent with today's color-blind ideology, group members maintain that they are not racially motivated. There were 67 posts across 25 threads where forum participants explicitly state that they, or nativists in general, are not racist. Diminishing the importance of race as an explanation for inequality is one form of color-blind racist discourse (Bonilla-Silva 2002). Bonilla-Silva (2002, 62) notes that white students interject "anything but race" phrases into their stories to stress that their color-blind story is truly devoid of racial explanations. This is a central tactic used by the ALIPAC forum members to attempt to neutralize any part of their explanations regarding immigration that have racial messages in them. For members of ALIPAC the specific "anything but race" strategy is to rely on rhetoric of legality. When nativists rely on "the law" as the moral measuring stick, the discourse suggests some level of rational decision making because it relies on seemingly immutable laws. This is despite the fact that laws themselves are socially constructed, and in such a way that has historically excluded nonwhites from full citizenship (Calavita 1998) and reinforced white as the conceptualization of a "national" community (Collins 2006). While racial groups are socially constructed

(Omi and Winant 1987), people are classified into racial groups based on physical features present at birth and outside the control of the individual. However, legal citizenship status is seen as an achieved status, an identity that someone can acquire through social action. In this sense, if the law is unquestionably rational and rule breakers are morally inferior, illegal immigrants can be deemed morally inferior others who should be blocked from crossing "the border."

Both the main website and the forum members make claims that they are not racists because they welcome *legal* immigrants and people of all races and ethnicities. For example, the platform provided on the main website of ALIPAC illustrates the emphasis placed on legal status. It states, "ALIPAC supports those that legally immigrate, but we DO NOT support any amnesty, visa expansion, or 'Guest Worker' program designed to reward illegal aliens or legalize their presence in the US." The platform stresses that legal immigrants are welcome, but that the organization opposes intervention by the government in an already existing process that would change the law in such a way that would make some current illegal immigrants legal. These changes to the law are perceived as rewarding those who break the law. While the statement on one hand recognizes the mutable nature of law, the forum participants treat the legal status of immigrants as fixed.

In the forum, stressing legality becomes immediately linked with accounts that neutralize racist labels. For example, in a thread titled "Is Illegal Immigration about Racism," Joazinha writes, "Jim Gilchrist, founder of the Minutemen Project, told me that illegal immigration is a LEGAL, NOT a RACIAL/ETHNIC issue because ANYONE can be an illegal!" This statement is exemplary of how forum members use legal status as a measure of morality, while denying that certain racial or ethnic groups could be disproportionately affected by the law. It portrays illegal immigrants as choosing to break the law, while ignoring the structural constraints that limit what choices different types of people have. The stress placed on "legal" immigrants is a deliberate move by ALIPAC to racial rearticulation whereby they draw from ideas in the broader culture to apply and construct racial meanings (Omi and Winant 1987). Here, the ALIPAC forum members draw from a color-blind frame of "anything but race" to ensure that the word "legal" cannot be deemed openly racially motivated, despite the

fact that the converse "illegal" becomes associated with "criminal" and "Latino" (Johnson 1998), consequentially racializing all Latinos.

While the focus on border protection provides legitimation for a conceptualization of illegal (De Genova 2002), it becomes an even more powerful discursive tool of boundary maintenance when criminality is stressed. The connotation and meaning behind "illegal" is very different from "undocumented." "Illegal" stresses criminality, while "undocumented" suggests lack of paperwork. The term "illegal" is used expressly for the imagery that it evokes. The ALIPAC members are cognizant of this. For instance, one forum participant posted, "Calling an illegal alien an undocumented worker is like calling a robber an unwanted houseguest." The poster stresses the belief that immigrants who are in the country illegally are not just breaking the law, but they are causing harm to citizens. This statement associates immigration with people who violate homes and steal from the owners.

Seventy-three of the 200 threads contained references to immigrants engaging in criminal activity beyond documentation status, including murder, rape, and drunk driving. The overall consequence of the ideology is the construction of a dangerous and criminal immigrant "other." Since 9/11 and the association of immigration with terrorism, national discourse and more punitive laws have set a framework for interpreting undocumented workers as criminal and threatening just by their presence. Further, instead of the focus being on an action, this new framework suggests that the very identity of the person is criminal (Akers Chacon and Davis 2006). Drawing on criminality is coded with both class and racial messages. Crime is associated in the United States with poor black men, and policies and policing have focused on the crimes of the poor as opposed to white-collar crimes committed by the upper class (Cacho 2000). Cacho (2000) further argues that claims of immigrant criminality attempt to reverse the historical relationship where whites have hoarded resources and persecuted nonwhites. Here, forum participants are constructing a threatening nonwhite perpetrator in relationship to a white citizen victim.

Welcoming Legal Immigrants

Another way that the color-blind rhetorical strategy of legality manifests in conversations is through stressing that legal immigrants are not just welcome but supported by other members.

Similar to the findings of Coutin and Chock (1997) that the media separates "good" and "bad" immigrants, the construction of good and bad immigrant categories is also played out in the conversations on the ALIPAC forum. However, when ALIPAC forum participants accept immigrants in the forum, their difference from "other" immigrants is stressed. There were two individuals who started conversations in the forum by announcing their status as legal immigrants. Following is an exchange between forum participants on the ALIPAC website and one of the two posters.

> **sbi** – Do I have a place here? Been here **legally** for over 11 years, started green card process 6 years ago, **never** overstayed my visa. My name check (part of the green card process) is pending with the FBI for 5 - yes, five - years. I wish Washington (AKA McCain and Kennedy) would devote time to deal with this nonsense as much as they do to help those crimeallians.
>
> **PinestrawGuys** – You most certainly DO, sbi, and WELCOME TO ALIPAC!!!! Jump right in and give 'em hell, you're the kind of immigrant we're fighting for.
>
> **Cliffdid** – Welcome sbi. People like you are one of the reasons I become so infuriated with people who break our laws and sneak in. I commend you for doing things the legal way. For any trolls reading this who have cut in line . . . I hope your ashamed of yourselves!

On the surface, by welcoming a legal immigrant, the forum members reinforce the message from the title of their organization Americans for *Legal* Immigration. Welcoming legal immigrants underscores ALIPAC's claim that they oppose only illegal immigrants. In the quote, sbi notes the long, hard process of getting legal status. He or she states a six-year visa process and five-year waiting period for the government to verify his or her name. Further, sbi uses the language of ALIPAC when labeling undocumented immigrants, calling them crimeallians. PinestrawGuys responds that sbi is "the kind of immigrant that we're fighting for." This reinforces the difference between immigrants who go through legal channels and those who do not, and it reinforces the connection between undocumented

immigrants and criminality. It also describes ALIPAC members as moral champions of legal immigrants. In addition, Cliffdid suggests that illegal immigrants have "cut in line" and are not only illegal but contributing to a much harder and longer process for immigrants who attempt to gain citizenship status through acceptable legal channels. Illegal immigrants are portrayed as rule-breakers who are merely unwilling to seek citizenship through legal channels, which downplays the different levels of hardship and opportunity that individual undocumented immigrants face. It simplifies "good" and "bad" in order to easily place people into simplified categories and ignore complex questions regarding the creation and enactment of the law itself (Coutin and Chock 1997). As Johnson (2009) argues, current immigration law currently disadvantages poor, and thus nonwhite, immigrants by requiring potential immigrants to prove that they have the education and employment to ensure that they will never need public assistance. Employers who sponsor immigrants must likewise agree to pay for the public assistance should the immigrant need it. This blocks immigrants who lack education and the opportunity to get a well-paying job; these are more likely to be from poorer countries such as Mexico. Meanwhile, immigrants who are more likely to meet these requirements are more likely to come from wealthier, predominantly white countries such as Great Britain. Further, current yearly caps on the number of immigrants who can come from one country lead to long lines that can last 20 years from countries with high demand, while there are short or no waits for immigrants coming from wealthy countries that do not have high levels of out-migration (Johnson 2009).

The exchange between the participants just presented also illustrates claims of likeness and group membership. For instance, Cliffdid refers to "our laws" which suggests a group membership and conversely a group boundary. Cliffdid constructs the in-group as law-abiding citizens and calls attention to a border by referring to those who "sneak in." With the advent of Homeland Security and the connection between immigration and terrorism, this draws attention to the Mexican/United States border. Further, as noted previously, the reference to "crimealliens" by sbi draws on culturally coded images of poor people of color. Since U.S. laws promote white privilege and reinforce a white national identity, this highlights a white normative in-group in relation to immigrant others regardless of the actual race of sbi (Collins 2006).

Additionally, welcoming legal immigrants also does not mean that they are given full inclusion into the nation. Collins (2006) argues that whites tolerate historically oppressed racial/ethnic groups as long as they do not challenge white privilege. Similar to the media analyses of Chavez (2008) and Ono and Sloop (2002), the reliance on legality reinforces the creation of a racialized immigrant other, because ALIPAC forum members conflate illegal immigrant and Hispanic. This becomes even more evident when the cultural threat of immigrants is linked with illegality.

Culture and the Case of Puerto Rico

Another color-blind racist frame is to rely on cultural explanations for differences between racial and ethnic groups (Bonilla-Silva 2006). In this frame, people identify perceived negative traits of racial and ethnic minorities. This tactic was also used by members of the online forum. In particular, the forum members do focus on the cultural inferiority, especially perceptions of an immoral Hispanic or Latin o/a and, in some instances, "Mexican" specifically. For example, one ALIPAC forum participant posted a message arguing that Mexicans are cruel toward horses. In response to the posting, members discussed the overall moral shortcomings of Mexicans and/or "Hispanics." Specifically, one forum member wrote:

> Culture or not, its against the law, since it is cruelty to animals. That they believe it is ok because of their culture, doesn't speak well for their culture. Culture is also used as the high number of hispanics that drink while driving, or drink underage. Neither of those are made "ok" just by some idea of culture either.

In the preceding statement, the conceptualization of illegal and criminality is not completely ignored. However, the "legal" status of the individual as an immigrant is no longer the underlying premise. This argument is no longer necessary, because the link between illegal immigrant and Mexican is strong enough to free individuals to merely associate Mexican with criminal. The expectation that immigrants should assimilate and fear that new waves of immigrants are incapable of assimilating is historically a core component of nationalism in the United States (Feagin 1997). Chavez (2008) argues

that the cultural stigmatization of Latinos is one component of the racialization of Latino in nativist discourse. Latinos or Hispanics are seen as naturally different by virtue of "their culture," incapable of assimilating, and thus threatening to and incompatible with the white in-group. This is consistent with Bonilla-Silva's (2006) finding that cultural racism is a central tenet of today's color-blind ideology. While explanations for racial inequality diminish the importance of discrimination, people instead focus on perceived flaws in the culture of racial and ethnic minorities. These perceived cultural flaws explain their marginalized status and place blame on racial minorities, thereby relieving whites of responsibility.

Another example of the cultural racism theme is illustrated in a thread where members discuss Puerto Rico. The thread was longer than the 10-post average for this forum, with 19 posts by 13 members. It started with one forum member, AmericanPatriot23, asking, "Why Cant English Be Made the 'Official Language' of the USA? I hear one of the obstacles is Puerto Rico since their 'main' language is Spanish, rather than English. What do you guys think?" To this question, Jimpasz responds,

> Puerto Rico teaches English in all public schools and has done so for 40+ years. Puerto Ricans are U.S. Citizens if they choose to speak Spanish that is their right. Puerto Ricans are not immigrants or illegal immigrants, no visa or passport is needed for U.S. Citizens (including Puerto Rican born) folks who travel between the mainland U.S. and the U.S. possession of P.R. The U.S. Military is proud to have thousands of men and women from the enchanted Isle.

In this quote, we see Jimpasz relying on the definition of legal vs. illegal immigration as the standard for who to include as a citizen and who not to include. This fits with the arguments forum members and websites give supporting their claims to being race/ethnicity neutral. However, all but one of the other forum members in this thread argue that Puerto Ricans are different from other citizens. AmericanPatriot23 responded, rebutting Jimpasz's argument with the following:

> . . . but recently Puerto Rican organizations have protested against making English our official language. If you do some search you will see that has been one of the obstacles. Also, les not forget that some Puerto Rican organizations are "branches" with the racist "National

Council of La Raza." I don't know if you know this but in the town of Hazletown Pennsylvania the 2 main organizations suing not to crack down on illegal immigration and to not make English the official language of Hazletown were the ACLU and a Puerto Rican organization since the small Puerto Rican population said it would make them feel uncomfortable having English as the official language of Hazletown.

AmericanPatriot23 ignores Jimpasz's argument that Puerto Ricans can speak Spanish if they desire, because they are citizens. He criticizes Puerto Ricans for opposing English as the official language of the United States. Santa Ana's (2002, 235) analysis of immigration metaphors in mainstream media shows that people perceive the English language to be "an emblem of being 'truly American'" and that speaking any other language is "unpatriotic and un-American." In this sense, adopting the English language is perceived as key to full assimilation into the culture of the United States. Thus, it is not surprising that language was one of the cultural aspects that ALIPAC forum members focused on when drawing from the cultural inferiority color-blind racist frame.

The cultural racism theme is perhaps exemplified by statements that create an explicit boundary between Latino and U.S. citizens. For instance, Joanzina replied to the thread regarding Puerto Ricans and English-only policies with the following statement: "I believe we should just DITCH Puerto Rico! Then on their own, they can be Latino ALL they WANT to!" Similarly, in a different thread, Rockfish writes about an Illinois politician who was born on the mainland but has Puerto Rican heritage. Rockfish posts, "He is latin before he is American." In both Joanzina's and Rockfish's comments, Latino and "American" appear incompatible. Further, we see ethnicity, "Latino," being used as a proxy for nationality and "American" as the proxy for white.

Reverse Racism

The final color-blind racist rhetorical strategy that emerged from the data was making claims of reverse racism (Bonilla-Silva 2006). This tactic neutralizes claims that whites are racist by projecting the claim of racism to nonwhites. In this instance, the National Council of La Raza (NCLR), a civil rights organization for Latinos in the United States, and the ACLU are implicated as racist. In addition, the Mexican American Legal Defense and Education Fund (MALDEF) and the

League of United Latin American Citizens (LULAC) are also charged by forum members with being racist. For example, Jamesw62 responds to comments made by Janet Murgula, President and CEO of NCLR:

> **Jamesw62** – here is my post on the commentary by the LaRaza hate bating racist woman a Raza meaning "the race" or "the people" along with LULAC and MALDEF think that anyone who wants the borders secured is racist. . . . I did not know that being illegal means your a race of people. Especially when one considers the Border Patrol report that came out a few months ago where they reported that citizens of 140 different countries were arrested crossing illegally into the US from Mexico. So the Minuteman Civil Defense Corps is a vigilante group? i find this to be the best joke I have heard today. Does Ms. Murguia know that the true racist and vigilante group is hers?

In this example of reverse racism, Jamesw62 denies accusations that immigrant restrictionists are racist and then returns the racist label to La Raza. In addition, Jamesw62 cites the English translation of La Raza, the race, as evidence that the group is racist.

While forum participants use this color-blind racist tactic to justify opposing immigration, it is part of a larger frame for interpreting race relations in the United States. Similar to the criminalization frame, reverse racism similarly inverts what Cacho (2000) describes as the perpetrator/victim binary. Despite evidence that immigration policing targets and harasses people who "look" Mexican, regardless of citizens status (Hing 2006; Romero 2011b), these statements not only deny white racism but reverse the relationship so that whites are victims. Through what Bonilla-Silva refers to as abstract liberalism, white people use rhetoric of equality to suggest that any laws or policies meant to reduce racial inequality are not color-blind and are therefore racist. For example, 1_paint writes, "Members of white racist groups are prosecuted and removed from positions of power in both the political and private sector. Why are the 'brown' racists groups treated any differently." Similarly, in response to a story about a boy who called a classmate "brown" being suspended from school for a "hate crime," NOamNasty writes, "Ths bill was to protect the real haters. Haters of good morals and values. We already have hate crimes aaginst racist, bigots, it's called civil law !" In these statements, the belief that nonwhites in the United States are given special treat-ment, while whites are disadvantaged, is extended to in-clude all "brown" people. In this sense, we see again the abandonment of rhetoric on legality and citizenship status, and see that white becomes an in-group symbol-izing the right to privileges such as jobs and political power through a perceived superiority in morals in com-parison to nonwhites, the general out-group.

Discussion

The online forum is an important place where individu-als can reinforce color-blind ideology through using colorblind terms in interactions and finding others who confirm those beliefs. The main color-blind frames used by the forum members were: diminishing the impor-tance of race through rhetoric of legality, cultural racism through the stigmatization of Latino, abstract liberalism, and the use of reverse racism. Throughout these frames, the forum members drew from coded messages that reference racial stereotypes such as crim-inality and the "welfare queen."

In a post–civil rights era, a color-blind ideology frames white people's interpretations and understand-ings of race. While white people denounce racism as morally wrong, they simultaneously do not support policies that would reduce racial inequality. Addition-ally, while they use discursive tactics to stress how race is not part of their reasoning for opinions, they then go on to say very racist things (Bonilla-Silva 2001, 2006; Bonilla-Silva and Forman 2000; Bonilla-Silva et al. 2004; Van Dijk 1992, 1993). Bonilla Silva (2006) cleverly refers to this as "racism without racists." While color-blind racism has been shown to legitimate continued racial inequality among citizens by race, it is also clear that color-blind ideology also shapes how people view immigrants, especially nonwhite immigrants.

These rhetorical devices are particularly important, because there are clear contradictions within and across the frames. For instance, one of the major color-blind frames argues that forum participants distinguish be-tween citizens and immigrants solely on the basis of le-gality. This frame ignores the social construction of the law itself and how immigrants have become increasingly criminalized under the law. There are also contradic-tions between this frame and the second frame where forum members draw from cultural racism. While

forum participants may argue in one thread that "anyone can be illegal," forum participants in other threads sug-gest that one cannot be Latino and "American" at the same time. This is especially highlighted by some forum members who argue that Puerto Ricans should not be citizens, because they are Latino. Here, Latino trumps legality as the marker of who can be American. However, it appears that the other color-blind tactics free these members to also make distinctions based on ethnicity without threatening their identity as non-racist.

Whites have traditionally used cultural racism as a way to explain why Blacks have not succeeded and to jus-tify opposition to programs that would reduce and elim-inate racial inequality. Whites have argued that racial disparities in economic outcomes are the results of Blacks' poor family values, failure to stress education, laziness, and a culture of poverty instead of a racist social structure (Bonilla-Silva 2006). For the forum members, the perceived negative cultural traits of Latinos are used to justify laws that disadvantage Latino immigrants and keep them from gaining citizenship. However, this also operates to stigmatize all Latinos regardless of citizen status, illustrating that while some Latinos may be able to reach honorary white status, they are not granted full citizen status. Further, racialized Latinos face racial pro-filing and discrimination in their daily lives (Romero, 2011b). Similar to Coutin and Chock's (1997) findings that journalists use assimilation to separate "good" and "bad" immigrants, some forum participants stress the assimilation of legal immigrants and Puerto Ricans to argue their inclusion. However, honorary status can be revoked, and the national ideal citizen remains white Anglo (Collins, 2006).

Another way that whites have used color-blind racism to explain racial disparities, especially in the criminal justice system in the United States, is to stereo-type Blacks as dangerous and criminal (Anderson1990). The rhetoric of legality allows forum participants to extend this stereotype to Latino immigrants as well. Not only do ALIPAC forum participants stress that being undocumented makes an immigrant's main identity an "illegal," this illegality is associated with a host of other crimes ranging from drunk driving to murder and rape. This association of immigrants with crime is made de-spite the fact that research finds no association between immigrant population and crime rates (Reid et al. 2005) and in some instances, even an inverse relationship (Graif and Sampson 2009). It neatly categorizes immigrants into a stereotypical bad other and undermines efforts of immigrant rights groups who attempt to gain resources and improve their treatment (Honig 2001).

The final frame of reverse racism neutralizes nonwhite immigrants' and citizen's claims of discrimination by painting whites as the true victims. However, this reversal of the victim/perpetrator relationship (Cacho 2000) ignores how previous immigration law specifically excluded "nonwhites" from the ability to become naturalized citizens (Haney Lopez 2006) and current trade agreements that draw resources from Mexico to the United States. Specifically, as Hing (2010) argues, while the policies of the Mexican government have certainly had a role in the poverty faced by Mexican workers, the NAFTA trade agreement led to major job losses as Mexican farmers could not compete with the price of government-subsidized corn from the United States.

My research finds the same nativist tactics as found by Feagin (1997), whereby forum members stress racial and ethnic inferiority and present immigrants as non-assimilative. These nativist tactics are also used by the mainstream media toward "other" immigrants and create a boundary between citizen and Latino (Chavez 2001, 2008; Ono and Sloop 2002). However, the nature of my data—discussion posts—illustrates the importance of the color-blind rhetoric. While one might expect that group members would not feel it necessary to give disclaimers that they are not racist, this is not the case. Even in discussions with other forum participants, posters specifically state that they, the group, and nativists in general are not racist.

References

Akers Chacon, J., and Davis, M. 2006. *No One Is Illegal: Fighting Racism and State Violence on the U.S.–Mexican Border*. Chicago, IL: Haymarket.

Anderson, Elijah. 1990. *Streetwise Race: Class and Change in an Urban Community*. Chicago, IL: University of Chicago Press.

Anti-Defamation League. 2007. "Immigrants Targeted: Extremist Rhetoric Moves into the Mainstream." http://www.adl.org/civil_rights/anti_immigrant/ (accessed March 15, 2012).

Beirich, Heidi. 2008. "John Tanton's Private Papers Expose More Than 20 Years of Hate." *Intelligence Report* November. https://www.splcenter.org/fighting-hate/intelligence-report/2008/john-tanton%E2%80%99s-private-papers-expose-more-20-years-hate (accessed September 21, 2015).

Bobo, Lawrence D., and Ryan A. Smith. 1998. "From Jim Crow Racism to Laissez-Faire Racism: The Transformation of Racial Attitudes." In *Beyond Pluralism: The Conception of Groups and Group Identities in America* (ed. W. F. Katkin, N. Landsman, and A. Tyree), 182–220. Urbana: University of Illinois Press.

Bonilla-Silva, Eduardo. 2001. *White Supremacy and Racism in the Post-Civil Rights Era*. Boulder, CO: Lynne Rienner.

Bonilla-Silva, Eduardo. 2002. "The Linguistics of Color-Blind Racism: How to Talk Nasty about Blacks without Sounding 'Racist.'" *Critical Sociology* 28(1–2): 41–64.

Bonilla-Silva, Eduardo. 2006. *Racism without Racists: Color-Blind Racism and the Persistence of Racial Inequality in the United States*, 2nd ed. New York: Rowman & Littlefield.

Bonilla-Silva, Eduardo., and Tyrone A. Forman. 2000. "'I Am Not a Racist but. . .': Mapping White College Students' Racial Ideology in the USA." *Discourse and Society* 11(1): 50–85.

Bonilla-Silva E., Amanda Lewis, and David G. Embrick. 2004. "'I Did Not Get That Job Because of a Black Man. . .: The Story Lines and Testimonies of Color-Blind Racism. *Sociological Forum* 29(4): 555–581.

Buchanan, Susy, and David Holthouse. 2007. "'Shoot, Shovel, Shut Up': 144 'Nativist Extremist' Groups Identified." *Intelligence Report* 44–47.

Cacho, Lisa M. 2000. "'The People of California Are Suffering': The Ideology of White Injury in Discourses of Immigration." *Cultural Values* 4(4): 389–418.

Calavita, Kitty. 1998. "Immigration, Law, and Marginalization in a Global Economy: Notes from Spain." *Law & Society Review* 32(3): 529–566.

Carr, Leslie G. 1997. *"Color-Blind" Racism*. Thousand Oaks, CA: Sage.

Charmaz, Kathy. 2006. *Constructing Grounded Theory: A Practical Guide through Qualitative Analysis*. Thousand Oaks, CA: Sage.

Chavez, Leo R. 2001. *Covering Immigration: Popular Images and the Politics of the Nation*. Berkeley, CA: University of California Press.

Chavez, Leo R. 2008. *The Latino Threat: Constructing Immigrants, Citizens, and the Nation*. Stanford, CA: Stanford University Press.

Collins, Patricia Hill. 2006. *From Black Power to Hip Hop: Essays on Racism, Nationalism, and Feminism*. Philadelphia, PA: Temple University Press.

Coutin, Susin. B., and Phyllis P. Chock. 1997. "'Your Friend, the Illegal': Definition and Paradox in Newspaper Accounts of U.S. Immigration Reform." *Identities* 2:123–148.

De Genova, Nicholas. 2002. "Migrant 'Illegality' and Deportability in Everyday Life." *Annual Review of Anthropology* 31:419–447.

Feagin, Joe R. 1997. "Old Poison in New Bottles: The Deep Roots of Modern Nativism." In *ImmigrantsOut! The New Nativism and the Anti-Immigrant Impulse in the United States* (ed. J. F. Perea), 13–43. New York: New York University Press.

Feagin, Joe R. 2000. *Racist America: Roots, Current Realities, and Future Reparations*. New York: Routledge.

Feagin, Joe R., and E. O'Brien. 2003. *White Men on Race: Power, Privilege, and the Shaping of Cultural Consciousness*. Boston, MA: Beacon.

Graif, Corina, and Robert J. Sampson. 2009. "Spatial Heterogeneity in the Effects of Immigration and Diversity on Neighborhood Homicide Rates." *Homicide Studies* 13(3): 242–260.

Haney Lopez, I. 2006. *White by Law: The Legal Construction of Race*. New York: New York University Press.

Hing, Bill. 2006. *Deporting Our Souls: Values, Morality, and Immigration Policy*. New York: Cambridge University Press.

Hing, Bill. 2010. *Ethical Borders: NAFTA, Globalization, and Mexican Migration*. Philadelphia, PA: Temple University Press.

Honig, Bonnie. 2001. *Democracy and the Foreigner*. Princeton, NJ: Princeton University Press.

Johnson, Kevin R. 1998. "Race, the Immigration Laws, and Domestic Race Relations: A 'Magic Mirror' into the Heart of Darkness." *Indiana Law Journal* 73(4): 1111–1159.

Johnson, Kevin R. 2009. "The Intersection of Race and Class in Understanding Immigration Law and Enforcement." *Law and Contemporary Problems* 72(1): 1–35.

Lofland, John, and Lyn Lofland. 1995. *Analyzing Social Settings: A Guide to Qualitative Observation and Analysis*. Belmont, CA: Wadsworth.

Omi, Michael, and Howard Winant. 1987. *Racial Formation in the United States: From the 1960s to the 1980s*. New York: Routledge & Kegan Paul.

Ono, Kent A., and J. M. Sloop. 2002. *Shifting Borders: Rhetoric, Immigration, and California's Proposition 187*. Philadelphia, PA: Temple University Press.

Reid Lesley Williams, Harald E. Weiss, Robert M. Adelman, and Charles Jaret. 2005. Immigration–Crime Relationship: Evidence across US Metropolitan Areas. *Social Science Research* 34:757–780.

Reimers, David M. 1985. *Still the Golden Door: The Third World Comes to America*. New York: Routledge.

Romero, Mary. 2008. "'Go After the Women': Mothers Against Illegal Aliens' Campaign against Mexican Immigrant Women and Their Children." *Indiana Law Journal* 83(4): 1356–1389.

Romero, Mary. 2011b. Not a Citizen, Only a Suspect: Racialized Immigration Law Enforcement Practices. In *State of White Supremacy: Racism, Governance, and the United States* (ed. M. Jung, J. H. Costa Vargas, and E. Bonilla-Silva), 189–210. Stanford, CA: Stanford University Press.

Santa Ana, O. 2002. *Brown Tide Rising: Metaphors of Latinos in Contemporary American Public Discourse*. Austin: University of Texas Press.

Sohoni, Deenesh. 2006. "The 'Immigrant Problem': Modern-Day Nativism on the Web." *Current Sociology* 54(6): 827–850.

Southern Poverty Law Center. 2008. "The Nativists: Profiles of 20 Anti-Immigrant Leaders." *Intelligence Report* 129.http://www.splcenter.org/get-informed/intelligence-report/browse-all-issues/2008/spring/the-nativists?page=0,8 (accessed March 15, 2012).

Van Dijk, Teun A. 1992. "Discourse and the Denial of Racism." *Discourse and Society* 3(1): 87–118.

Van Dijk, Teun. A. 1993. "Stories and Racism." In *Narrative and Social Control* (ed. D. Mumby), 121–142. Newbury Park, CA: Sage.

Walker, Christopher J. 2007. "Border Vigilantism and Comprehensive Immigration Reform." *Harvard Latino Law Review* 10:135–174.

Wellman, David T. 1977. *Portraits of White Racism*. New York: Cambridge University Press.

Questions

1. In Ezzel's chapter on women rugby players, he argues that the women engage in three types of defensive othering which reproduce inequality. Do the ALIPAC forum members in this reading also engage in defensive othering? Why or why not? In what ways could the concept be applied, and what consequence does it have for inequality more broadly?

2. Why do the forum members argue that their motivation for supporting restricting immigration is solely based in a value for the law? How does this argument reinforce the idea that inequality is natural and unchangeable?

3. In the chapter by Balogun regarding Nigerian beauty pageants, you read about how class, race, and cultural norms interact to construct two different ideals of womanhood. Do the members of ALIPAC similarly use class, race, and cultural norms to construct an idealized citizen? How so, or how not?

4. Research news articles that cover the protests of the buses carrying unaccompanied children into California and Arizona. What are the specific signs and chants that protestors present? What narratives and ideologies do they draw on and advance? Which do they argue against? What can we learn about how narratives about inequality get constructed and advanced? What counter-narratives are most successful?

37

The Knowledge-Shaping Process: Elite Mobilization and Environmental Policy

ERIC BONDS

When constructing what is right or wrong, people engage in what Howard Becker (1963) refers to as the moral enterprise. According to Becker (1963) this is the process where moral entrepreneurs attempt to bring awareness to and create legislation regarding social issues. Power influences how successful moral entrepreneurs are in attempting to gain the support of important political and media allies. Some people will have more power to have their social issues presented in the way they desire. In Chapter 37, you learned about the importance of discourse for the reproduction of racist ideology. This chapter expands our understanding of the importance of controlling discourse for the reproduction of inequality. In particular, it focuses on the power of elites with strong social networks to engage in a successful moral enterprise.

Earlier you read about C. Wright Mills (1956) and the power elite. In the Hall chapter, you read about how U.S. and British business schools form elite networks. In this chapter, we return to the concept of the power elite and the importance of social capital. Eric Bonds pulls from William Domhoff's theory on power networks and their influence on state policy-making. Domhoff is a scholar who has done significant research documenting the resources and interlocking web of the power elite. On his website, http://www2.ucsc.edu/whorulesamerica/power_elite/interlocks_and_interactions.html, Domhoff, along with Clifford Staples and Adam Schneider, provides a comprehensive analysis of elite business members, their links to multiple company boards of directors, and government committees.

Bonds focuses on the case study of the political debates surrounding ammonium perchlorate, a contaminant found in rocket fuel. Bonds shows how government officials and industry leaders controlled the debate about what level of ammonium perchlorate in the environment represents a health hazard. He argues that power elites were successful in lessoning the level of regulation by limiting the amount of information available and influencing the scientific dialogue. Thus, a few powerful people were able to influence what amount of a harmful contaminant is considered safe, while experts and the general public had little knowledge or say in the outcome.

References

Becker, Howard. 1963. *Outsiders: Studies in the Sociology of Deviance.* New York: Free Press.

Domhoff, William, Clifford Staples, and Adam Schneider. 2013. "Interlocks and Interactions among the Power Elite: The Corporate Community, Think Tanks, Policy-Discussion Groups, and Government." *Who Rules America?* University of California at Santa Cruz. http://www2.ucsc.edu/whorulesamerica/power_elite/interlocks_and_interactions.html (accessed January 1, 2015).

Mills, C. Wright. 1956. *The Power Elite.* New York: Oxford University Press.

Elite Political Mobilization and Environmental Policy

Power structure research is a sociological perspective holding that the corporate wealthy exercise a disproportionate influence in public policy-making; in other words, they constitute a power elite (Domhoff 2006; Dye 2001; Useem 1984). Elite dominance, however, does not come automatically; it is not simply "built in" to the state. Rather, elites must continuously mobilize in order to exercise the power needed to enact the policies that best suit their interests (Domhoff 1990).

Domhoff (2006) argues that elites organize four different power networks in order to influence state policy-making:

1. *The special-interest process,* in which specific corporations and specific business sectors formulate policy proposals and attempt to implement them by lobbying legislative assemblies and by colluding with executive agencies.

2. *The policy-planning process,* in which the general interests of the corporate community are formulated in think tanks. Policy proposals, once formulated, are brought to the attention of the White House and high-ranking congressional committees. They are also broadly disseminated through high-status newspapers and magazines.

3. *The candidate-selection process,* in which the corporate community influences the selection of political candidates most sympathetic to its needs and wants.

4. *The opinion-shaping process,* in which corporations utilize public relations techniques to influence public opinion in ways that promote corporate interests.

By organizing and channeling resources through these networks, elites influence environmental policy. But Domhoff's typology of power networks is not comprehensive. Environmental policy is also likely influenced by a fifth process proposed in this chapter, *the knowledge-shaping process,* which is similar to and closely interrelated with the power networks identified by Domhoff. In the knowledge-shaping process, elites actively work to influence what is known about a particular subject in an effort to achieve their policy goals. Environmental science, from this perspective, is not a pure reflection of a biophysical world that is separate and distinct from environmental politics. Rather, environmental science and environmental politics are co-produced (Forsyth 2003). For this reason, environmental knowledge is often a political contest, one into which elites may allocate substantial resources and often prevail.

The knowledge-shaping process involves four distinct exercises of power:

1. *Information suppression*, in which elites purposively act to suppress knowledge damaging to their interests.

2. *Contesting knowledge*, in which elites fund experts to attack and disqualify knowledge that poses a threat to their power base. Elites may also fund diversionary efforts attacking those who have produced or who uphold potentially "damaging" knowledge (Freudenburg 2005a; Freudenburg and Alario 2007).

3. *Knowledge production*, in which elites fund or otherwise promote the production of particular knowledges, either through peer-reviewed scientific research or governmentally administered tests and analyses.

4. *Knowledge administration*, in which elites influence the selection of what information counts as knowledge and what information does not count.

In this chapter I present evidence of an elite knowledge-shaping process in a case study regarding the policy debate over rocket fuel contamination.

An Introduction to the Case and Its Analysis

The U.S. military and the corporations that manufacture its weapons and provide military services are connected through self-reinforcing relationships of mutual dependence, creating a network of organizations called the military-industrial complex. This network of organizations is capable of exerting major influence on U.S. policy-making.

The following case constructed around the policy debate over rocket fuel contamination indicates as much: Elites can mobilize substantial resources to determine U.S. environmental policy. The chemical of concern is ammonium perchlorate, both a natural and a manufactured chemical that is the primary constituent of solid rocket fuel. According to the U.S. Environmental Protection Agency (EPA), "wastes from the manufacture and improper disposal of perchlorate-containing chemicals are increasingly being discovered in soil and water" (U.S. EPA 2007, 1). There have been, according to the U.S. EPA (2007), at least 25 confirmed releases of the chemical in the United States into ground and surface waters. But the total amount of perchlorate released is likely much more because, according to the U.S. EPA (2002b, 37), perchlorate has a "shelf life" as a rocket fuel, and so "must be washed out of the USA's missile and rocket inventory to be replaced with a fresh supply. Thus, large volumes have been disposed of in various states since the 1950s."

Perchlorate is a common contaminant throughout the United States. According to a report by the National Research Council of the National Academies' Committee to Assess the Health Implications of Perchlorate Ingestion, perchlorate exists in the drinking water of at least 11 million people (National Research Council 2005). Further, perchlorate has been measured in Lake Mead and the Colorado River system, water from which is drawn a portion to irrigate much of America's supply of winter lettuce (Sharp and Lunder 2003); this is of potential concern because lettuce concentrates perchlorate taken from irrigation water. A U.S. Food and Drug Administration (FDA) survey found perchlorate in 123 of 137 samples of lettuce taken from different locations in the Southwest (U.S. FDA 2007a). The FDA, however, assures the public that the amount of perchlorate in winter lettuce is, as a whole, below limits established to protect human health (U.S. FDA 2007b). But just how much perchlorate, or rocket fuel, can a person ingest without harm? This question has been a matter of intense scientific and political debate in the past decade.

This much is agreed upon: In the human body, perchlorate, in sufficient levels, disrupts the intake of iodine by the thyroid gland and influences the production of thyroid hormones (U.S. FDA 2007a). How much perchlorate is needed to produce this effect within different bodies (for instance in a healthy male compared to a newborn, a pregnant woman, or a person with a thyroid abnormality or iodine deficiency) has been a matter of intense dispute. The U.S. Department of Defense (DoD) and various corporate manufacturers and users of perchlorate have been particularly important players in this conflict.

In order to chart the ways these players exercised power to influence the outcome of the policy debate over perchlorate contamination, I constructed a case study using archival data (including websites, official documents, and news stories), which is a method often employed by power structure researchers (see, for instance, Domhoff 1990, 1996; Gendron and Domhoff 2008).

During the course of this chapter, I report a number of "reference doses" for perchlorate, or amounts of perchlorate the EPA has determined are safe for daily ingestion. These reference doses change over time, some being much higher than others. Each reference dose is, in effect, a truth claim: a claim that such and such amount of perchlorate, ingested daily, does not pose a significant risk to the well-being of Americans. As a social scientist I cannot speak to which of these claims is the closest approximation of reality, and for this reason I make no attempt to do so. My goal is less ambitious: I attempt to demonstrate that elites associated with the military-industrial complex organized a network and mobilized resources that influenced the course of the EPA's policy-making, or, in other words, influenced the final reference dose the EPA settled on.

Secrecy as a Dimension of Power

This case best begins in the 1950s, when the U.S. military began using tremendous amounts of perchlorate in explosives and as a major constituent of solid rocket fuel. For several decades, waste perchlorate was disposed of when it was dissolved in water and then poured out onto the ground or into waterways. At the time, military officials did not believe that, when ingested in small amounts, it posed a public health risk (Lee 2004). The American public, given the chance, might have believed differently. While the environmental consciousness of Americans was very different during the 1950s, 1960s, and even 1970s than it is today, some amount of awareness did exist that human-manufactured chemicals may pose health risks and so cannot be released untreated into the nation's ground and surface waters without environmental consequences (Carson [1962] 2002; Gottlieb 2005). The military, however, did not allow the American public to exercise its developing environmental consciousness in relation to perchlorate. It instead exercised secrecy and kept the public ignorant of its rocket fuel disposal practices. In this way, we can see that ignorance about threats to the biophysical world is not something that just happens to organizations or

publics in modern industrial societies. It is an achievement and a direct outcome of existing social relations (Bonds 2007; Flyvbjerg 1999).

Secrecy, as here practiced by the military, is an important way elites exercise agenda power to keep knowledge that challenges elite interests out of the public sphere and to avoid the social construction of environmental problems that may pose challenges to the status quo. This is, according to Freudenburg and Alario (2007, 146), part of "the dark side of legitimation, which depends heavily on evading attention." Importantly, elite power, exercised here through secrecy, prevented any attempts to rectify past mishandling of perchlorate from emerging for several decades.

The Department of Defense has not abandoned secrecy as an exercise of power since the era of perchlorate dumping. In 2000, the EPA asked the DoD to test all groundwater beneath its bases for perchlorate. In 2002, the DoD prepared standards for testing. In 2003, upon direction from the White House, the Department then made a determination to forgo such tests, claiming that they would be unnecessary and too costly (Waldman 2003a). When releasing the new policy, the Undersecretary of Defense for the Environment told reporters "testing is something we should do, and probably will do eventually, but it's a question of priorities" (quoted in Waldman, 2003a). To this day, the Department of Defense has practiced secrecy regarding the extent of perchlorate contamination of groundwater at bases by refusing to conduct a comprehensive survey. The DoD has very simply, and actively, chosen not to know and chosen to keep such knowledge out of the hands of others. But secrecy, as an exercise of power, is not a foolproof plan for elites working to secure their interests and maintain the status quo.

Constructing the Problem of Rocket Fuel Contamination

Despite the Department of Defense's secrecy, the issue of perchlorate was eventually brought to the public's attention and carried into public policy debates by the EPA and civil society groups. In the early 1980s, the Agency identified perchlorate in municipal drinking water sources and classified it as a potential contaminant. In 1992, the EPA declared it a probable danger to human health and set a provisional "safe dose" at 3.5 parts per billion (Madsen and Jahagirdar 2006). Native American tribes utilizing Colorado River water to irrigate lettuce fields were among the first civil society groups to express concern, calling on the EPA to study the potential health effects of perchlorate on food crops (Sharp and Lunder 2003). At an "eco-summit" organized by the EPA in 1999 in response to Native American concerns—which was attended by five tribes, several major manufacturers and corporate users of perchlorate, and the Air Force—representatives of the DoD pledged $650,000 to evaluate environmental risks posed by the use of perchlorate-contaminated irrigation water (Sharp and Lunder 2003).

Though the Department of Defense never carried out this research, in this sense again actively choosing not to know potentially damaging information, the EPA continued to pursue the issue. In 1999 the Agency made a decision to list perchlorate under its Unregulated Contaminants Monitoring Rule to gather evidence about the effects of exposure, to gather evidence about the extent to which perchlorate is present in public drinking water systems, and to begin a formal process determining whether or not the contaminant should be regulated (U.S. EPA 2007).

Environmental groups also played a role in the EPA's policy-making process, demonstrating that environmental science and decision-making is a contested arena in which competing actors work to influence what is known about particular topics and what such knowledges should mean. These organizations educated the public about perchlorate contamination and worked to pressure the EPA to impose strict regulations. The Environmental Working Group, an independent non-profit organization, played an especially important role when it paid University of Texas researchers to sample lettuce and spinach from grocery store shelves; the researchers did indeed find perchlorate in 18 percent of the food they tested (Sharp and Lunder 2003). The study made headlines around the country and put further pressure on the EPA and the Food and Drug Administration to protect public health from the contaminant. Meanwhile, weapons-making corporations and the Department of Defense were organizing on this issue to make the task of regulating perchlorate more difficult, if not politically impossible for the time being.

The Beginnings of a Knowledge-Shaping Network

Soon after the EPA took notice of perchlorate contamination, the Department of Defense, weapons-makers

using perchlorate, and perchlorate manufacturers established the Perchlorate Study Group (Madsen and Jahagirdar 2006). The Perchlorate Study Group is, in its own words, "a coalition of aerospace, defense, chemical, and allied industries," which includes Lockheed Martin, Aerojet, and the chemical manufacturer Kerr-McGee. The Perchlorate Study Group was not incorporated as an official non-profit organization, but rather, records indicate, more of an informal way to funnel resources toward scientific research, public relations, and policy influence (Madsen and Jahagirdar 2006).

In the words of its founders, the Perchlorate Study Group was created to work "cooperatively with the US Environmental Protection Agency to increase scientific and medical understanding of perchlorate's risk to human health" (Council on Water Quality, 2008). The evidence stands, however, to the contrary; all evidence points to a very hostile relationship between the Perchlorate Study Group and the EPA.

What, exactly, these goals are becomes readily apparent by considering the Perchlorate Study Group's earliest efforts. In 1995, the Perchlorate Study Group advocated a "safe level" of perchlorate at 42,000 parts per billion (Beeman and Danelski, 2004). This proposed level was astronomically higher than the EPA's proposed level of less than 4 parts per billion. The Perchlorate Study Group, along with scientists and officials at the DoD, later came to advocate a "safe dose" of perchlorate at 200 parts per billion. Both recommendations would exempt the Department of Defense and perchlorate manufacturers and users from a great deal of liability regarding clean-up, as most perchlorate levels that exist in drinking water sources are between the levels of 4 and 100 parts per billion (Lee 2004).

Both the Department of Defense and the corporations that use perchlorate or manufacture (or have manufactured) it have interests in avoiding regulation and liability. The DoD has long sought to avoid public interference or oversight of its operations, including on issues relating to the environment (Durant 2007). And corporations dealing with perchlorate have a structured interest in avoiding liability to maximize, or to at least ensure, their own profitability.

In an attempt to avoid the environmental regulation of perchlorate, elites associated with the military-industrial complex created the Perchlorate Study Group as something similar to a think tank in the policy-planning process. Sociologists have produced a good deal of work examining the power of think tanks in public policy formation (Altheide and Grimes 2005; Domhoff 2006; McCright and Dunlap 2003). The largest, most well-known think tanks are funded by the corporate community to generate policy proposals for consideration by executive branches and legislative committees. They are also funded to attack and discredit policy proposals or existing governmental programs that do not serve the interests of the corporate community (Domhoff 2006). Think tanks have in the past mobilized the resources of the corporate wealthy in order to achieve particular environmental policy outcomes; McCright and Dunlap (2003), for instance, found that think tanks played an integral role in the defeat of the Kyoto Protocol in the United States. The Perchlorate Study Group is something similar to a think tank, but not quite the same. In the knowledge-shaping process such an organization is perhaps best called a "science tank," in which I intend the militarized sense of the word; that is, a science tank is a vehicle that is built to attack and defend. Unlike think tanks, science tanks do not necessarily work publicly, but channel money surreptitiously behind the scenes. And unlike a think tank, its purpose is not so much to generate policy proposals but to generate scientific research and fund experts, who attempt to appear unaffiliated, to produce particular knowledges and to contest competing claims. The Perchlorate Study Group is one such organization that fulfilled both roles.

Producing and Contesting Knowledge

Some organizations have a much greater ability to produce knowledge, compared to others, because they are replete with resources and/or legitimacy. The Perchlorate Study Group was well-funded but short on legitimacy. In U.S. society, however, legitimacy is something that can often be bought and sold. Between 1996 and 2005, the Perchlorate Study Group or its individual member companies funded at least 16 studies to assess the human health implications of perchlorate exposure, which were all peer-reviewed and published in scientific journals (Madsen and Jahagirdar, 2006). By 2005, these studies accounted for more than half of all published works on the health impacts of perchlorate. While the Perchlorate Study Group states that it funded these studies to "help" the EPA understand what the health impacts from perchlorate might be, such statements are misleading, or, at best, incomplete.

Corporations do not exist to help. Their purpose, as defined by their charters and necessitated by the social organization of capitalism, is to maximize profit for shareholders. The Perchlorate Study Group did not fund scientific research to "help" the EPA, but—for better or worse, depending on one's perspective—to help its member corporations avoid regulation and liability. And the organization's studies were helpful. The Perchlorate Study Group continuously cites these studies in its advocacy against regulation, while ignoring or contesting other studies that present findings that suggest perchlorate may be a public health risk. For instance, numerous industry-affiliated experts and scientists presented or reviewed an impressive array of industry-funded research at the EPA's 2002 Peer Review Workshop on perchlorate contamination (U.S. EPA 2002a). The CEO of American Pacific Corporation might have well summarized the industry-affiliated presenters when he told the EPA,

> Since 1997, our company alone has spent over three million dollars in funding human health studies and in characterization work [regarding perchlorate] . . . The data and conclusions of these human health studies support our belief that the [EPA proposed] reference dose could be safely set at a higher level than indicated in the subject review and risk characterization. (U.S. EPA 2002a)

More generally, the companies that manufacture and use perchlorate employ the research they have funded to make such public statements as: "Data from human studies shows that low levels of perchlorate being detected in some drinking water supplies have no adverse health effects on adults, children and newborns" (Perchlorate Information Bureau 2009a). Similarly companies use this research when making other public statements such as: "There is no evidence that minute levels of perchlorate pose any health risk to anyone. Credible, peer-reviewed science consistently shows no adverse health effects from perchlorate, which has actually been used as a medicine for more than 50 years" (Perchlorate Information Bureau 2009b).

Corporations seek out opportunities to fund helpful research that is publishable in peer-reviewed journals, for instance research that may assist corporations in efforts to avoid regulation or limit liability. When corporations do so, they almost always respect the professionalism of scientists; rarely would we expect them to urge researchers to falsify evidence or make unsupported claims. But this does not mean corporate funding does not produce biases within bodies of scientific knowledge. On the contrary, according to Freudenburg (2005b, 3), "the corporation's most effective techniques of influence may have been provided not by overt pressure, but by encouraging scientists to continue thinking of themselves as independent and impartial." Freudenburg (2005b) calls this "seeding science" and "courting conclusions." Corporations seed science by providing incentives for researchers to study some particular phenomena out of the infinite milieu of possible research topics, which of course have particular relevance for the corporations involved. And corporations are, of course, not interested in giving this seed money to just any researcher, but to those whom they believe will study the particular topic from a perspective that is useful. Furthermore, to Freudenburg (2005b), corporations court conclusions when they express a willingness to continue funding research as long as the results are helpful. Conclusions are further courted when corporate funders and researchers form professional and congenial relationships with one another, such that researchers may unintentionally anticipate the needs of corporate funders and so feel uncomfortable when results are produced that let friends and colleagues down (Freudenburg, 2005b).

Industry funding of perchlorate research introduced such biases into the body of knowledge regarding the potential human health risks of the contaminant. According to two environmental advocates, the studies funded by the Perchlorate Study Group had designs ill-suited for determining whether or not perchlorate posed a health risk to the American public (Madsen and Jahagirdar 2006). These advocates note, for example, that some of the studies used very small sample sizes, which makes establishing statistically significant differences more difficult. Officials at the Environmental Protection Agency found industry research lacking for different reasons. In the Agency's 2002 Draft Risk Assessment, its authors stated that no research had been done regarding perchlorate's potential effect on the neurological development of fetuses, infants, or effects on persons with thyroid deficiencies, which are all groups considered more vulnerable to perchlorate contamination (U.S. EPA, 2002b). It is for this reason, the Agency stated, that

it was proposing a more stringent recommendation based on its review of available scientific information. In its draft review, the Agency proposed a "reference dose," or a safe daily allowance, of 1 part per billion (U.S. EPA, 2002b), a standard lower than its earlier proposal of 3.5 parts per billion.

The experts at the Department of Defense and experts funded by the Perchlorate Study Group, while working simultaneously to produce "helpful" scientific research, also began work to contest and discredit the EPA's Draft Risk Assessment. Freudenburg, Gramling, and Davidson (2008) report a long history of corporate efforts to cast doubt upon scientific knowledge in order to reduce liability and/or thwart increased governmental regulation. Corporations often utilize a technique these authors call SCAMS—or scientific certainty argumentation methods—to exploit the uncertainty necessarily part of the scientific method (Freudenburg et al. 2008). The Perchlorate Study Group also used this tactic. It hired the public relations firm APCO Worldwide, which formerly had managed the Philip Morris campaign to avoid health-related tobacco liability, and formed the Council on Water Quality to publicly downplay potential risks associated with perchlorate (Madsen and Jahagirdar 2006). Other governmental organizations took a more direct approach in efforts to discredit the EPA's work (Waldman 2003b). For instance, a U.S. Air Force colonel told the press, "We have reviewed the EPA risk assessment, and we think the document is biased, unrealistic and scientifically imbalanced," while a NASA official, also a major user of perchlorate, told the press, "We do not believe the EPA has used good science" (Reported in Lee 2004).

But the DoD and the Perchlorate Study Group went beyond working to downplay potential risks and to discredit the EPA's assessment; they also began working to pressure the White House to intervene and take the decision of a final reference dose away from the EPA. In 2003, the Perchlorate Study Group paid lobbyists to advocate that the White House create a committee from the National Academy of Sciences to conduct a review of the literature and to propose a reference dose—as opposed to letting the EPA continue its own work toward these ends (Beeman and Danelski 2004). Documents submitted in a response to a Freedom of Information Act request from the Natural Resources Defense Council (NRDC) reveal that representatives from Lockheed

Martin and the Department of Defense met with White House officials during this time to discuss perchlorate, though the White House refused to disclose the actual content of the discussions (NRDC 2005). It seems the weapons manufacturers and the Department of Defense got what they wanted. In 2003 the George W. Bush administration intervened in the EPA's decision-making process and asked the National Academy of Sciences to instead conduct a review of the potential toxicity of perchlorate and to propose a reference dose (Beeman and Danelski 2004).

This point brings the case to the fourth important dimension of power in the knowledge-shaping process, the administration of knowledge. Elites do not only organize networks and devote resources to fund "helpful" research and to attack "damaging" research, they also work to influence the selection of what counts as knowledge and what does not (Flyvbjerg 1999). Scientific information and environmental data do not, after all, have a pure meaning. Its meaning, like the meaning of all objects in the human universe, is subject to a process of interpretation (Freudenburg and Gramling 1994). Interpretation is often influenced by position within social structures, which means that *who* gets to interpret what counts and what does not count as scientific knowledge is a political battle fought between individuals and organizations of differing structural locations (Bonds 2007). Elites organize to win the battle of science administration through lobbying efforts and funding decisions, and via personal and business relationships. The Perchlorate Study Group won this particular battle by convincing the White House to intercede and take decision-making powers away from officials at the EPA. Agency officials had not administered knowledge in ways deemed suitable to the military-industrial complex because they had discounted research funded by industry and relied instead on research that made threatening claims to the military and weapon industry's interests.

Beyond taking decision-making authority away from the EPA, the Bush administration White House took further steps to ensure that the science surrounding perchlorate would be administered in ways amenable to the military-industrial complex. Public documents requested under the Freedom of Information Act by the Natural Resources Defense Council indicate that the White House acted to influence the National Academy of Sciences' review. For instance, the documents indicate that officials from the White House, including the Director and other high-ranking officials from the Office of Management and Budget, were involved in writing and editing the "charge" for the Academy's review, which is a document that frames the issues to be addressed by the Academy's committee (NRDC 2005). The extent to which the White House was involved in developing and editing the "charge" cannot be determined because it refused to disclose such information to the public (NRDC 2005). The public documents released also indicate that the White House influenced or at least sought to influence the selection of the Academy's committee members. The documents indicate that the White House held discussions to develop lists of potential candidates and to discuss "selection dynamics" (NRDC 2005). But here again, the extent to which the White House was involved in selecting the review committee's members cannot be clearly determined because the White House withheld this information from the public. However, it may not be coincidence that two individuals appointed to the Committee, including its director, formerly worked as paid consultants to Lockheed Martin, a major perchlorate user and member of the Perchlorate Study Group (NRDC 2005).

Elite Knowledge-Shaping

The EPA became fairly silent in the public policy debate surrounding perchlorate after the National Academy of Sciences took up its review. The Bush Administration had, in fact, imposed a gag rule prohibiting Agency officials from talking to reporters about perchlorate (Waldman 2003c). The Perchlorate Study Group, however, was far from silent. Quite the contrary: The Study Group sought to influence the National Academy of Science's review process. The best example is a conference, entitled Perchlorate State-of-the-Science Symposium, held at the University of Nebraska's Medical Center. Though the University's involvement gave the symposium an air of authority and neutrality, it was largely paid for and organized by the Perchlorate Study Group. The Group paid the University $75,000 for its involvement (Waldman 2005). It also paid the private consulting firm Intertox $128,000 to plan the conference and use the Symposium's outcome for advocacy purposes (Madsen and Jahagirdar, 2006).

The Symposium's planning committee later wrote to the National Academy of Sciences review committee on perchlorate and stated that:

> The Perchlorate State-of-the-Science Symposium was designed to be an *independent and impartial* review of four fundamental science issues related to the potential risk from low-level exposure to perchlorate. Researchers who performed the most important recent studies published since 1999 were asked to present their work. (Report of the Planning Committee 2003, emphasis added)

There is good reason to doubt these claims of independence and impartiality. The framework of the symposium was arranged by the owner and director of Intertox, who billed the Perchlorate Study Group for his work. The owner and director of Intertox was also involved in selecting the presenting scientists, many of whose work was funded by the Perchlorate Study Group or its individual member corporations. The planning committee, however, never disclosed this information to the National Academy's review committee (Waldman 2005).

The Symposium held two sessions of note. In one session the presenters promoted the value of research conducted on healthy adult subjects that found perchlorate posed little health risk in small amounts. In another session, presenters, including one paid industry consultant, worked to discredit the research used by the EPA when it conducted its 2002 draft review (Waldman 2005). The organizers of the conference then worked to communicate these proceedings, sending six Symposium participants to share their conclusions with the National Academy's committee, while also sending transcripts and a written report (Waldman 2005).

It may well be that the National Academy's committee was listening. It gave industry, as well as the Department of Defense, much of what it wanted. In its review, the committee chose to give little weight to the studies utilized by the EPA when it proposed its more stringent 1 part per billion reference dose of perchlorate. It also chose to rely heavily on a study promoted at the industry symposium (Greer et al. 2002) and perhaps not incidentally funded in part by the Perchlorate Study Group (Madsen and Jahagirdar 2006). In its report, the Committee proposed a reference dose of 24.5 parts per billion, more than 20 times higher than the "safe" dose

proposed by the EPA in 2002. In 2005, the EPA adopted the National Academy's proposal and designated a reference dose of perchlorate at 24.5 parts per billion.

Power Structure Research, Environmental Sociology, and the Knowledge-Shaping Process

In the aftermath of this policy debate, there is much evidence to indicate that military and corporate elites were able to achieve their interests. But their success was not unconditional. For instance, the EPA did end up adopting a reference dose for perchlorate much smaller than the 200 parts per billion standard advocated by industry and the military. And the states of California and Massachusetts have since designated their own standards, both well below that of the EPA's 2005 rule: Massachusetts set a standard at 2 parts per billion, while California implemented a standard at 6 parts per billion.

All the same, weapons manufacturing companies and the DoD did gain much in the sense that state standards often pose less of an imposition than federal standards, and the federal standard is much higher than it would have been without military and corporate involvement. Furthermore, the EPA has since ruled against regulating perchlorate, opting instead to keep it on its list of "unregulated contaminants" indefinitely (Environmental Working Group 2008), something surely in the interests of perchlorate-using corporations concerned about profitability, and also something in the interests of a military establishment that has a history of working to avoid regulation and citizen oversight. The military and industry were able to achieve these "successes," I have argued, through organization and the allocation of resources.

This case illustrates how power structure research can inform and benefit environmental sociology. Power structure research can contribute to the treadmill of production model, which strongly emphasizes the expansionary logic of capitalism to explain contemporary environmental degradation (Gould, Pellow, and Schnaiberg 2008; Schnaiberg 1980). Freudenburg (2005a, 89) critiques the model by arguing that "contrary to common assumptions, much environmental damage is not economically 'necessary'"—necessary, that is, for the continued functioning of a capitalist economic system. Quite the opposite, Freudenburg's (2005a) analyses show that the biggest polluters in the United States release a highly disproportionate amount of pollution compared to their contribution to the gross domestic product or national employment. Moreover, he found, these major polluters are not producing "critical materials" for the U.S. economy that might make such tremendous amounts of pollution unavoidable (Freudenburg 2005a).

The widespread contamination of perchlorate is a complementary example of pollution that cannot be considered economically necessary. The case study of the policy debate over perchlorate then informs environmental sociology by cautioning theorists against explaining all varieties and rates of environmental degradation as being economically necessary for the continued functioning of capitalism. While treadmill of production and Marxist theorists have convincingly argued that the social organization of capitalism necessarily degrades the environment (Foster 2002; Gould et al. 2008; Schnaiberg 1980), the rates of resource use and pollution can vary dramatically between different capitalist economies (Freudenburg 2005a). This case suggests that elite mobilization is an important variable determining environmental policy and, consequently, amounts of pollution and resource use. While treadmill of production theorists are attentive to the environmental consequences of inequality, more attention to elite political mobilization is warranted because the capacity of elites to organize and exercise power to protect their disproportionate access to the environment means that environmental degradation can occur at far greater rates than that which is necessitated for the reproduction of capitalism.

Power structure research can also inform ecological modernization theory, which was developed to explain the ways societies are responding to contemporary environmental degradation and argues, in opposition to the treadmill of production model, that capitalism is not inherently environmentally destructive (Mol 1996; Mol and Spaargaren 2002). The potential contribution can be made most clear by again building from Freudenburg's work, in which he argues that:

> Contrary to the widespread assumption that environmental improvement could only be achieved at significant cost to jobs and the economy, significant improvements could be made if a small fraction of all economic actors were to reduce their emissions-per-job ratios simply to the average for the economy as a whole. (Freudenburg 2005a, 91)

Freudenburg (2005a) bolsters his claim by citing the example of one of the biggest polluting companies in the United States, which significantly reduced its toxic releases by simply putting dirt and planting grass on its waste piles. Perchlorate contamination is another case in point: Its cleanup is technically achievable and, while it might be expensive to the weapons-manufacturing companies responsible for some of its release, could be achieved with relatively little cost to the U.S. economy as a whole.

The Knowledge-Shaping Process as a Power Network

Evidence in the case of the perchlorate policy debate supports the contention that elites can achieve major influence in state policies by creating and utilizing what I have termed knowledge-shaping processes. Elites first influence policy through secrecy by suppressing the production of knowledge that may disrupt profitable, even if environmentally harmful, behaviors. Weapons manufacturers and the Department of Defense suppressed information for decades about the widespread perchlorate contamination in America's water systems. Information suppression, however, is never a fail-safe plan to avoid liability or prevent increased regulation in complex industrial societies.

For this reason, elites organize themselves in networks (connecting mutually aligned corporations together along with scientific consulting firms, public relations firms, university researchers, and government decision-makers) to mobilize resources in order to shape what is known about a subject of concern. Elites begin to do so by forming and funding "science tanks," or private affiliations that channel money to researchers who produce knowledge useful to elites. Elite-funded science tanks also channel money to experts who discredit or raise doubts about "damaging" scientific research. This was the work of the Perchlorate Study Group.

Finally, elites work to influence policy outcomes through knowledge administration, or by influencing the selection of what counts as knowledge and what does not. This may be accomplished through lobbyists or through the personal and business relationships of elites themselves. It may be that such efforts are further augmented through past or promised campaign contributions or educational endowments. Perchlorate users and manufacturers were able to influence knowledge administration regarding the contaminant by convincing the Bush Administration to take decision-making authority away from the EPA and granting it instead to a National Academy of Sciences committee, the charge for which it sought to influence and the members of which it likely helped select.

References

Altheide, David L., and Jennifer N. Grimes. 2005. "War Programming: The Propaganda Project and the Iraq War." *The Sociological Quarterly* 46(4): 617–643.

Beeman, Douglas A., and David Danelski. 2004. "Perchlorate: Cost, Risks Fuel Debate over Safety; Impact on Health Weighed against Billions for Clean Up." *The Press-Enterprise*, December 19.

Bonds, Eric 2007. "Environmental Review as Battleground: Corporate Power, Government Collusion, and Citizen Opposition to a Tire-Burning Power Plant in Rural Minnesota, U.S.A." *Organization and Environment* 20(2): 157–176.

Carson, Rachel. [1962] 2002. *Silent Spring*. New York: Houghton Mifflin.

Council on Water Quality. 2008. *The History of Perchlorate: Evolving Science, Technologies and Regulations*. http://www.councilonwaterquality.org/science/history.html (accessed January 9, 2008).

Domhoff, G. William. 1990. *The Power Elite and the State: How Policy Is Made in America*. New York: Aldine de Gruyter.

Domhoff, G. William. 1996. *State Autonomy of Class Dominance?* New York: Aldine de Gruyter.

Domhoff, G. William. 2006. *Who Rules America? Power and Politics, and Social Change*. Boston, MA: McGraw-Hill.

Durant, Robert F. 2007. *The Greening of the U.S. Military: Environmental Policy, National Security, and Organizational Change*. Washington, DC: Georgetown University Press.

Dye, Thomas R. 2001. *Top Down Policymaking*. New York: Chatham House Publishers.

Environmental Working Group. 2008. *Last Minute Mischief: EPA Employed Suspect Chemical Industry Lab to Declare Perchlorate Safe*. http://cpeo.org/lists/military/2008/msg00697.html / (accessed September 20, 2015).

Flyvbjerg, Bent. 1999. *Rationality and Power: Democracy in Practice*. Chicago, IL: University of Chicago Press.

Forsyth, Tim. 2003. *Critical Political Ecology: The Politics of Environmental Science*. London: Routledge.

Foster, J. Bellamy. 2002. *Ecology against Capitalism*. New York: Monthly Review Press.

Freudenburg, William R. 2005a. "Privileged Access, Privileged Accounts: Toward a Socially Structured Theory of Resources and Discourses." *Social Forces* 84(1): 89–114.

Freudenburg, William R. 2005b. "Seeding Science, Courting Conclusions: Reexamining the Intersection of Science, Corporate Cash, and the Law." *Sociological Forum* 20(1): 3–33.

Freudenburg, William R., and Margarita Alario. 2007. "Weapons of Mass Distraction: Magicianship, Misdirection, and the Dark Side of Legitimation." *Sociological Forum* 22(2): 146–173.

Freudenburg, William R, and Robert Gramling. 1994. "Bureaucratic Slippage and Failures of Agency Vigilance: The Case of the Environmental Studies Program." *Social Problems* 41(2): 214–237.

Freudenburg, William R., Robert Gramling, and Debra J. Davidson. 2008. "Scientific Certainty Argumentation Methods (SCAMs): Science and the Politics of Doubt." *Sociological Inquiry* 78(1): 2–38.

Gendron, Robert, and G. William Domhoff. 2008. *The Leftmost City: Power and Progressive Politics in Santa Cruz*. Boulder, CO: Westview Press.

Gottlieb, Robert. 2005. *Forcing the Spring: The Transformation of the American Environmental Movement*. Washington, DC: Island Press.

Gould, Kenneth., David Pellow, and Allan Schnaiberg. 2008. *The Treadmill of Production: Injustice and Unsustainability in the Global Economy*. Boulder, CO: Paradigm.

Greer, Monte A., Gay Goodman, Richard C. Pleus, and Susan E. Greer. 2002. "Health Effects Assessment for Environmental Perchlorate Contamination: The Dose Response for Inhibition of Thyroidal Radioiodine Uptake in Humans." *Environmental Health Perspectives* 110(9): 927–937.

Lee, Jennifer (2004) "Second Thoughts on a Chemical: in Water, How Much is Too Much?" *New York Times*. 2 March, p. F1.

McCright, Aaron M., and Riley E. Dunlap. 2003. "Defeating Kyoto: The Conservative Movement's Impact on US Climate-Change Policy." *Social Problems* 50(3): 348–373.

Madsen, Travis, and Sujatha Jahagirdar. 2006. *The Politics of Rocket Fuel Pollution: The Perchlorate Study Group and Its Industry Backers*. Los Angeles: Environment California Research and Policy Center. http://www.

environmentcalifornia.org/reports/clean-water/clean-water-program-reports/the-politics-of-rocket-fuel-pollution (accessed January 9, 2008).

Mol, Arthur P.J. 1996. "Ecological Modernization and Institutional Reflexivity: Environmental Reform in the Late Modern Age." *Environmental Politics* 5(2): 302–323.

Mol, Arthur P.J., and Gert Spaargaren. 2002. "Ecological Modernization and the Environmental State." In *The Environmental State under Pressure* (ed. A. Mol and F. Buttel), 33–55. Oxford: Elsevier Science.

National Research Council. 2005. *Health Implications of Perchlorate Ingestion*. Committee to Assess the Health Implications of Perchlorate Ingestion, National Research Council of the National Academies. Washington, DC: The National Academies Press.

National Resources Defense Council. 2005. *White House and Pentagon Bias National Academy Perchlorate Report. National Resources Defense Council Press Backgrounder.* http://www.nrdc.org/media/pressreleases/050110.asp (accessed January 10, 2008).

Perchlorate Information Bureau. 2009a. *Summary of Scientific Studies*. Perchlorate Information Bureau. http://www.perchlorateinformationbureau.org/science/studies.html (accessed July 7, 2009).

Perchlorate Information Bureau. 2009b. *The Facts about Perchlorate and Milk*. Perchlorate Information Bureau. http://www.perchlorateinformationbureau.org/facts/milk.html (accessed July 7, 2009).

Report of the Planning Committee. 2003. *Perchlorate State of the Science Symposium 2003: Report of the Planning Committee and Reports of the Expert Review Panels.* Provided by the National Resources Defense Council. https://www.nrdc.org/media/docs/050110UNReview.pdf (accessed September 20, 2015).

Schnaiberg, Allen. 1980. *The Environment: From Surplus to Scarcity*. New York: Oxford University Press.

Sharp, Renee, and Sonya Lunder. 2003. *Suspect Salads: Toxic Rocket Fuel Found in Samples of Winter Lettuce.* Oakland: Environmental Working Group. http://www.ewg.org/reports/suspectsalads/ (accessed January 9, 2009).

U.S. Environmental Protection Agency. 2002a. *Peer Review Workshop on EPA's Draft External Review Document "Perchlorate Environmental Contamination: Toxicological Review and Risk Characterization."* http://cfpub.epa.gov/si/si_public_record_report.cfm?dirEntryId=51762 (accessed July 7, 2009).

U.S. Environmental Protection Agency. 2002b. *Perchlorate Environmental Contamination: Toxicological Review and Risk Characterization*. Washington, DC: U.S. Environmental Protection Agency.

U.S. Environmental Protection Agency. 2007. *What is Perchlorate*. Washington, DC: U.S. Environmental Protection Agency. http://safewater.supportportal.com/link/portal/23002/23015/Article/22493/What-is-perchlorate (accessed September 20, 2008).

U.S. Food and Drug Administration. 2007a. *2004–2005 Exploratory Survey Data on Perchlorate in Food*. U.S. Food and Drug Administration. http://www.fda.gov/Food/FoodborneIllnessContaminants/Chemical-Contaminants/ucm077685.htm (accessed September 20, 2015).

U.S. Food and Drug Administration. 2007b. *Perchlorate Questions and Answers*. Washington, DC: U.S. Food and Drug Administration. http://www.fda.gov/Food/FoodborneIllnessContaminants/Chemical-Contaminants/ucm077572.htm (accessed September 20, 2015).

Useem, Michael. 1984. *The Inner Circle: Large Corporations and the Rise of Business Political Activity in the U.S. and U.K.* New York: Oxford University Press.

Waldman, Peter. 2003a. "Pentagon Backs Off Water-Test Plan: Fuel-Ingredient Perchlorate Is Center of Fight with EPA on Evaluations Near Bases." *Wall Street Journal*, June 20.

Waldman, Peter. 2003b. "Bush Seeks Liability Shield on Water Pollutant." *Wall Street Journal*, March 14.

Waldman, Peter. 2003c. "EPA Bans Staff from Discussing Issue of Perchlorate Pollution." *Wall Street Journal*, April 28.

Waldman, Peter. 2005. "On Campus, Industry Set up a Perchlorate Confab." *Wall Street Journal,* December 29.

Questions

1. Bonds argues that the power elite engage in a knowledge-shaping process when influencing environmental policy. What are the different ways in which elites shape environmental knowledge?

2. Why does Bond argue that even peer-reviewed articles may be skewed by researchers accepting money from elite interest groups, even if there is no explicit pressure to produce specific types of

results? What evidence does Bond provide to support his claim that this occurred in the case of perchlorate?

3. In what way did President Bush influence which side of the perchlorate debate could be heard? What interest did the government have in the final regulatory outcome?

4. Bonds provides Freudenburg's argument that the scale of current environmental degradations is neither natural nor a required outcome for modern capitalism. What evidence does the author provide to support Freudenburg's argument? Do you agree with this conclusion? Why or why not?

5. Watch the film *Toxic Sludge Is Good for You: The Public Relations Industry Unspun*. What are some of the similar processes used by the elite to control information shown in the documentary that Bonds found in his research on perchlorate? What additional tactics did you learn about in the film? What local examples can you find of the power elite controlling speech and knowledge production?

38

"For the Betterment of Kids Who Look Like Me": Professional Emotional Labor as a Racial Project

CARISSA FROYUM

Just as inequality may seem natural, we also tend to view our emotions as things that we just naturally feel. However, throughout our lives we learn what Hochschild (1979) refers to as "feeling rules." Feeling rules are the norms for what to feel and express in different situations. For example, feeling rules dictate that we feel sadness and nostalgia at funerals, and that we express those sentiments through crying and storytelling. Feeling happy and relieved, however, is inappropriate. So is laughing hysterically. What's more, our emotions do not always match what we are supposed to feel, and we may find ourselves trying to stir up particular feelings in ourselves or others, what Hochschild called "emotion management." For instance, my very large and sensitive dog once accidently knocked her tail into my soup, overturning it onto my computer keyboard. While I felt angry, I knew that she had not purposely done this or even understood what had happened. Because of this, I attempted to manage my emotions to mask my anger. I tried to change my emotional state from anger to acceptance. Over the course of each day, we may attempt to repress or change how we and others feel many times. This can be as

Excerpted from Froyum, Carissa. 2012. "'For the Betterment of Kids Who Look Like Me': Professional Emotional Labour as a Racial Project." *Ethnic and Racial Studies* 36 (6): 1070–1089 (2013).

simple as smiling and saying we are "good" to a passing acquaintance, even though our computer was just ruined, we got a parking ticket, and we are running late to class. We may also work in a job that requires that we manage our emotions. Customer service jobs, for example, come with the expectation that we present ourselves as happy to help and the customer is always right, when in reality we want to tell rude people to take their business elsewhere. We hide our feelings to keep our jobs and our paychecks.

This reading examines the role that emotions play in the reproduction of inequality. Do marginalized people have to control their emotions more or differently than people in power? Can this lead to the justification and reproduction of inequality? What role do those in power have in this, and do those in marginalized statuses reproduce their own inequality by following prescribed feeling rules? To get at these answers, Carissa Froyum examines the way that workers at an after-school program reinforce different types of feeling rules. Her results illustrate the ways in which feeling rules around professionality can contribute to the reproduction of racial inequality. As you have learned previously, the reproduction of racial inequality does not require malicious intent. Froyum provides an instance where whites who mean well and have devoted their time to a good cause unintentionally reinforce hierarchy.

Reference

Hochschild, Arlie. 1979. "Emotion Work, Feeling Rules, and Social Structure." *American Journal of Sociology* 85:551–575.

For the Betterment of Kids Who Look Like Me

Work often includes emotional labor, or conjuring emotional states in others and managing one's own emotions for pay (Hochschild 1983, 7). Research has demonstrated how stratification systems shape emotional labor and criticized the consequences for workers. Workers with high status enjoy a range of emotional expressions and control "feeling rules," the scripts to evoke particular emotional states (Hochschild 1983; Pierce 1995; Sloan 2004). They more often expect emotional deference than give it, producing positive emotional experiences. Organizations prescribe deferential feeling rules for lower-status workers, alternatively, creating negative or conflicted emotions (Hochschild 1983; Leidner 1999). Managers suppress criticism of inequality by conditioning workers' emotional subjectivities (Kunda and Van Maanen 1999; Schwalbe et al. 2000; Jocoy 2003). Despite their connecting emotions to inequalities, studies have rarely examined emotional labor processes in relation to race, leaving a misimpression of race neutrality or inconsequentiality.

This study examines an emotion-based racial project in a workplace where whites prescribed deferential emotional labor but Black youth workers internalized it. It uses Schwalbe et al.'s (2000) concept of regulating discourse to analyze how administrators used professionalism to define and police deferential emotion work in ways that reinforced racial structuring. It asks: Why did Black workers engage in deferential emotional work? How did workers resolve conflicts stemming from racializing feeling rules? How did emotional labor stabilize racial organizing? In answering these questions, this study illustrates how emotional labor elicited the participation of Black workers in their own racial subordination.

Kidworks

Kidworks (KW) was a non-profit youth agency with a mission of cultural change: to help disadvantaged children become productive adults. It provided life-skills and recreational programs at six locations in a mid-sized U.S. city with moderate levels of racial residential segregation. My analysis focuses on two sites in a neighborhood disproportionately Black and poor. . . . These sites served mostly low- and middle-income Black girls and boys, ages 6 to 12, in gender-segregated facilities I call Girlworks and Boyworks.

KW's workplace was racially stratified. The direct-care workers who carried out the mission of the organization primarily identified as Black. Between both sites, the direct-care workforce consisted of a couple dozen Black workers. Two or three usually Black full-time salaried "professionals," most with college degrees, worked at each site at any time. They earned between $28,500 and $47,000 yearly and had little chance for promotion. Boyworks employed men and women, while Girlworks employed only women. A dozen part-time college students worked both sites; Black and some white women worked with girls, while women and men worked with boys. Most made about seven dollars an hour. A young Black woman was the volunteer coordinator. She also handled "accountability" to benefactors and hosted fundraisers; she earned $32,000 yearly.

Yet, those with high status and policy-making authority were nearly universally upper-middle-class and upper-class whites. The director, a well-connected white man, earned $103,000. The assistant director, a white man, earned $75,000. White women served as resource developer, government relations officer, and personal assistant. Thirty-four whites (26 of them men) and 1 Black man constituted the board of directors. Its members were established white businessmen with social networks in real estate, finance, and banking. The board made policy, networked, and fundraised to secure KW's $4.5 million annual revenues. In 2006, the top board fundraiser solicited over $33,000. Younger white lawyers and financial officers created another group that planned and hosted fundraisers. At KW, then, whites nearly exclusively dictated policy and standards of behavior for Black workers who carried out KW's mission.

Data

I volunteered and conducted participant observation at KW between October 2004 and June 2006. Around 300 hours at life-skills groups, art classes, volunteer events, fundraising events, and interviews produced 2,000 pages of field notes and transcripts.

I also conducted semi-structured in-depth interviews with 40 workers, administrators, volunteers, fundraisers, board members, and kids. The relevant interviewees included 10 self-identified white volunteers and administrators, 15 self-identified Black workers or volunteers, and 1 self-identified Latino worker. Interviews focused on work and volunteer experiences, relationships between kids and adults, and actors' interpretations.

Findings

Emotional Experiences to Overcome Cultural Dysfunction

Kidworks created an informal code of conduct around professionalism. Professionalism attests to workers' skill and expertise (Harris 2002), and workers feel compelled to act professionally in order to demonstrate competence (Erickson 2004; Lewis 2005). At KW, administrators appropriated professionalism as a regulating discourse (Schwalbe et al. 2000) that promoted deferential forms of emotional labor which conjured feelings of "belonging" among children, emotional release among white volunteers, and devotion among Black workers. KW administrators, board members, and official documents labeled full-time workers "trained, professional staff." The label was so ubiquitous and valued that professionalism standards applied to both full-time and part-time direct-care workers, who routinely called themselves "professionals," even though their positions did not rise to professional status. Workers learned professionalism at regional and local trainings and through interactions with administrators.

Professionalism prescribed emotional labor among Black workers in order to overcome what whites perceived as poor Black kids' social disadvantage. White administrators and volunteers at Kidworks drew on long-standing racist stereotypes about Black cultural dysfunction (Collins 2004) when describing the challenges that KW children faced. A primary problem, from their perspective, was neighborhood and home instability: environments marred by drugs, violence, parental instability, and neglect. Wanda, a white fundraiser, characterized KW kids' backgrounds as "socially weaker" and "economically weaker." She explained further: ". . . there's shootings, the police cars . . . even those things that those kids have to go through whether it's verbal abuse, maybe other kinds of changes, being in foster homes or God knows what." Whites believed these circumstances undercut kids' life chances by divesting them from achieving. Kidworks' challenge, in turn, was to help children overcome the cultural dysfunction around them. A white board member explained: She wanted kids to "know that the world is larger than what they experience every day, and they don't have to let their family circumstances hold them back."

Creating an Emotional Refuge

Whites thought kids needed to connect with adults in order to motivate them to change their lives. KW materials explained that the agency provided "a safe place to learn and grow," "ongoing relationships with caring, adult professionals," and "life-enhancing programs and character development experiences." Administrators tasked direct-care workers, largely Black, with creating an emotional refuge through professionalism. Wanda espoused this perspective when she juxtaposed the security that KW "professionals" created to the "majority" of homes of the children, which "probably don't have that:" KW provided "a safe place," where children "get a relationship with a KW professional [knowing] that when they go there [to Kidworks], [they're] being heard, they have a sense of belonging. . . ." According to KW discourse, feelings of comfort and connectedness made personal development possible by fostering emotional stakes among children. Then kids felt obligated to act as the adults, who presumably had their best interests at heart, directed. Belonging also offered a sense of purpose and meaning. Edward, a white administrator, described emotional connection as an agent of change:

> Nowadays to get [kids] to respond to you, they have to have . . . that connection with you individually . . . so that they don't want to disappoint you. . . . [Otherwise] they don't have a stake in Kidworks. . . . And so you try to build that feeling of "I'm part of something."

Administrators similarly touted emotional connection between children and workers as the foundation for long-term influence: "When kids come back years later, they always tell us that they forget the programming, but they remember the people" (Richard, white administrator, during a presentation to white donors).

Professionalism generally allows workers emotional autonomy and control over their feeling scripts, but at KW professionalism dictated deferential emotional labor that set the "right" priorities—the kids and KW's brand, as a place of change, over self. Tasha, a Black worker, explained that KW's code of conduct was "about protecting the brand, protecting kids, and protecting yourself. So kids come first, brand comes second, you come last." The code established connecting emotionally with children as a primary requirement of direct-care work, one that further involved employees devoting themselves to their jobs and integrating their personal identities with their worker role. Relating this way involved transforming KW into a home-like atmosphere filled with familiarity, comfort, and emotional availability. In a report's description of KW's "highest priority," a board member explained: "We believe that Kidworks provides a 'home away from home' for many children, where young people receive the guidance and support to overcome the most daunting obstacles, and where children learn to live honorably." Workers created a "home" or "family" at work by integrating children into their emotional lives and making themselves readily available. Libby, a Black worker, stated:

> [Kids] can call me anytime they need to talk . . . they're not always able to talk to their parents about everything. "So you can call me if need be. Or give me your number and I'll call you.". . . sometimes on the weekend, I'll just go get [two specific girls] and they stay at my house all day and Miss Casey [another worker] comes over . . . we'll just sit there, laugh and talk. . . . I try to get them as much as I can, so they feel some type of love and some type of support in things they do because they don't get the attention they need at home.

By giving out their cell numbers and bringing girls home with them, Libby and Casey extended themselves emotionally so that girls' problems became their own. They positioned themselves as the girls' confidants, and they tried to fill their emotional needs by making them feel loved. Other workers acted like family by meeting with kids' teachers and intervening when their relationships or lives took a wrong turn. Ben, a Black employee, "kept tabs" on Eric, whose mother was seriously ill. Ben worried that Eric "wouldn't know what to do" if his mother died because "nobody from his family would take [him and his brother] in. . . . Pretty much Eric is taking care of himself." Ben fretted about "his sad situation." Because Eric's family did not help him, Ben made a point to: "I will do anything for the guy, like I donate clothes and shoes to him. . . . I do things so they can stay positive so they won't have to go out here and do the wrong thing." Consistent with KW's dictate of professionalism, Ben took his work home with him.

Professionalism also encouraged workers to find fulfillment through emotionally investing in children. A mailing described KW professionals as "men and women who use their education, training and energies to help young people. They enjoy being with kids, they understand them and get satisfaction from seeing them become responsible citizens and leaders." Employees internalized this call; they routinely described loving the children. Libby, for instance, described the rewards of her job as worth the frustration she felt with some of the girls: "I get joy just being around them every day. . . . I love them all like if they were mine. I really do. It's a few bad ones that get on my nerves. But you know what? I love them all." According to professionalism, love and making a difference were their own rewards.

But integrating work and family was one-sided: While professionalism prescribed emotional labor that integrated children into workers' lives, it proscribed letting employees' emotional lives intrude on their jobs. This was part of what Tasha meant by putting the needs of kids first. Here, professionalism discourse treated the workers' personal lives as potential pollutants to be contained and controlled. To prevent workers' own emotions from becoming overbearing or their own needs from interfering, workers were to separate the personal from the professional: "If you're having a bad day at home, you gotta leave that outside that door," Ben learned from his training. "Because once you come in here, you gotta go to work. . . . You gotta come in with a positive attitude." Maintaining a "positive attitude" entailed compartmentalizing in order to prioritize the children. Ben explained: "Working here at Kidworks and [having a] family, you have to keep those separated because here you have to have your full attention on the kids in this building." For Sharice, a Black worker, professionalism encouraged workers to give kids their due attention rather than "bad attitude":

> You can't come into Kidworks with your head held down acting like you know the weight of the world is on your shoulders. Like I tell [workers] every day, "We all go through personal stuff, but [kids] have not done anything to us. So when you come through those doors, whatever problems you have brought with you to work, you need to leave them beside those doors."

Not taking one's personal frustration out on the kids, furthermore, entailed suppressing negative emotions. Edward, a white administrator, looked to employees to temper these emotions, demonstrating what he called "temperament" and "aptitude," especially during "mad moments" when kids acted out or staff became frustrated. After Warner, a Black worker, lost his temper during a confrontation with a kid, a white administrator challenged him to control himself: "Warner, you just, you've got to learn to humble yourself. And when you learn to do that, [kids] will do the same thing."

Fostering Whites' Investment

Additionally, prioritizing the kids and brand meant fostering whites' commitment to KW through emotional labor. The professional code of conduct existed in part to maintain a funding stream to KW, which primarily depended on individuals, corporations, and foundations. This is what Tasha termed prioritizing KW's brand, as a nonprofit that truly influenced lives. Changes in resource allocation have led nonprofits to adopt capitalist business models where donors are clients and fundraisers are marketers (Dees and Battle Anderson 2003). Because of their dependence upon public patronage, nonprofits cultivate emotional experiences that invest donors in organizations. The most effective strategies (Merchant, Ford, and Sargeant 2009) situate donating as a release from negative emotions and source of positive ones. KW fit these patterns. Fundraising and volunteer recruitment were major enterprises at KW, which tapped into elite white real estate and finance networks to garner personal and financial support. Nearly all Kidworks' donors and the vast majority of volunteers, especially those who fundraised, were middle-class to upper-class whites. Emotional experiences made Kidworks their "charity of choice" (June, a white volunteer fundraiser, who worked in sales and marketing). Whites became attached to KW when they felt a "warm glow" (Andreoni 1990) by altering the life course of children—when they felt generous, important, and socially conscious.

In experiencing these emotions, however, whites othered the kids as needy, in turn framing themselves as redemptive. Like administrators, white donors and volunteers attributed poor and Black kids' vulnerability to culturally dysfunctional backgrounds. Miranda, a white volunteer fundraiser who worked in finance, stated: "I can't imagine what it's like for kids who not only don't have someone pushing them to achieve in life but . . . they don't even have the basics to learn how to be a good person." In contrast to Black workers below, white donors and volunteers distinguished their "lucky," "privileged" childhoods full of love, encouragement, and opportunity from what they understood as the deprivation experienced by "underprivileged" kids. June juxtaposed her experiences to the kids' using a framework of cultural function versus dysfunction: ". . . I had such a happy family life. I can't understand how people grow up without a happy family life. . . . KW sorta piles all types of people from all types of different, challenging backgrounds into one pot." After I asked her what made her volunteer work meaningful, she stated:

> The kids, the "thank-you's," the hugs, the "I love you," how much they need attention, how it tugs on your heart strings that they might not get the attention at home and how much Kidworks is a source for them to get the attention and the guidance and the affirmation, to me is tops. . . . it does your heart good and breaks your heart a little bit to be there at the same time.

For whites who "can't imagine" or "understand" what they perceived as neglectful backgrounds, KW elicited pity through othering, and giving made them feel important and influential.

Essential to these emotions was observing results personally but without losing control over the emotional experience. KW did not expect or require volunteers or donors to expose themselves emotionally by creating a home, becoming like family, or overlooking their own emotional needs. Rather, it employed its direct-care staff to create an emotional experience that cultivated emotional release for whites by facilitating seeing kids change, interacting with grateful children, and viewing programs and facilities in use and well cared for. These results made giving time and money feel worthwhile. As Miranda put it: "It really brings it home if I can feel what I'm working for." Professionalism at KW, thus, also tasked creating an emotional experience for potential volunteers and funders so they could feel what they were working for.

One strategy was to charge professional employees with preparing triumphant stories (Merchant et al. 2009) for public consumption at fundraising events and scholarship contests. These stories gave whites a feel of their influence by eliciting pity about kids' backgrounds and attesting to the potential for change with their resources. They followed this narrative: Marlesa came from a broken background that led her down the wrong path, KW gave her the support she needed, now she is headed the right way, you can help girls like her. Administrators invited workers to share their own stories, and they assigned them with finding and telling kids' stories.

An annual report featuring Jeremiah, a Black boy around ten, modeled for Black workers how to, in the terms of a white fundraiser, "tell a success story" and personalize. The report described him as struggling in school and delinquent. Staff, it read, worked until closing for a year until Mark improved academically and behaviorally. "Proof again," it concluded, "that KW changes, enhances—even saves—the lives of young people." Employees became skilled in describing the work of KW as saving so that potential donors *felt* influential without actually knowing the kids. Ben grew up in the neighborhood and attended KW. Of his close friends, a handful graduated from high school:

> Everybody else was just caught up in the streets. . . . I believe that Kidworks was a good, positive way for me to learn the right things and . . . to teach you how to be a responsible young man. Kidworks was really influential in my life.

More impressive, however, were children testifying themselves. Workers recruited kids to testify and coached them how under the rubric of practicing public speaking or getting recognition or scholarship money. Samuel, a white volunteer fundraiser, learned the story of Marcesha at a KW event. He juxtaposed her success to the troubles of her brother due to her involvement in KW: "He really wasn't as active as she was and didn't really participate in everything like she did. And she felt like if it wasn't for KW, she'd be down that same road." For a scholarship contest, employees nominated kids and helped them prepare extensive applications which testified about their background, KW involvement, and influence of KW. They coached kids how to dress and present themselves, and they drove kids to the contest where a group of 26 mostly upper-middle-class whites acted as judges who questioned the kids about their deservedness through several rounds of interviews. Among the criteria KW supplied to judges were "obstacles overcome," which elicited the triumphant storylines that contestants then relayed at fundraising events. June, who served as a judge, described learning about a boy whose

> mom was single, pregnant, been through four husbands. . . . Certainly there was nobody waiting for him at home. But if he didn't have anywhere else to go, then he probably would have ended up a little bit misguided. And he'll probably look back one day and know how much Kidworks has done for him.

One scholarship winner, Carl, a teenage Black boy, especially made lasting impressions on white volunteers. He told the judges: "When I was seven, I was adopted. I think my biggest obstacle in life was trying to put my past behind me. I witnessed a lot of alcohol and drugs, physical abuse. And I feel like I never want to be that way." Miranda was so moved by this testimonial that she recalled it a year later: "I think he has every opportunity to come from that unhealthy lower-class-struggling-to-get-by-type-of-existence into the American dream." Carl's story was known throughout the organization because, as Warner, a Black employee, explained, workers enlisted him "to speak at just about every big event we have." Staffers had invested considerable resources into his success by securing tutors, jobs, and scholarships for college. As Warner stated: "We're really working on him and putting a lot of time in him."

Darin invited another "respectful" boy, Martin, with "positive attitude" to represent KW "every time we have a speaking engagement." One event was a major fundraiser featuring a jewelry auction at an upscale department store. Workers prepared several kids by renting tuxedoes and coaching them to greet whites by opening the door, hanging their jackets, and ushering them onto a red carpet. While other kids represented KW's importance in speeches, Martin, dressed in his tuxedo, mingled with white donors who gathered around him, saying: "You're so handsome! Look at you. What a cutie!" For much of the night, he danced for his admirers, evoking Jim Crow era caricatures of Blacks as entertaining exotic others. These strategies had their desired emotional effect, as Miranda shows:

> To see the kids and know these are some of the kids that we are helping by being here and having a good time, bidding up the auction to support, I think it makes a big impact.... I see the kids at the door and I hear the little boy talk about what Kidworks means to him and all of a sudden I'm thinking I need to buy more.

Finally, administrators charged Black workers with creating a personal experience for whites who came to visit or volunteer. Administrators instructed them to use the term "we" rather than "I" whenever discussing KW so that they felt vital to KW's functioning. A white administrator mentored a Black worker to make volunteers feel special by learning their names and showering praise and thanks at elaborate "volunteer celebrations."

She routinely sent cards with personalized messages. When potential donors entered the buildings, administrators had workers immediately accommodate them: greet them with a smile, invite them in, provide tours, and describe the programs that made KW successful.

In sum, professionalism at KW prescribed deferential emotional labor for Blacks working directly with kids and white donors and volunteers. Based on the racist assumptions that Black kids were culturally dysfunctional, white administrators employed a professionalism discourse that framed workers as family members who loved the children and devoted themselves to them. Not letting their personal lives impede on the work added additional layers of deferential emotion work. Administrators, furthermore, required Black workers to facilitate cross-race interactions, which left whites feeling a warm glow. These personalization strategies were unidirectional and unreciprocated (Lewis 2005) across race lines. They reinforced stereotypes of Blacks as exotic others.

Effects of Professionalism on Workers

Black workers often internalized KW's standards of professionalism. Workers adopted the discourses administrators professed in public, routinely word-for-word, as Darin did. He adopted the "remember the people" language mentioned previously: "That's where the impact comes in. That's what we hope when the kids leave here," he explained. "They won't remember every tournament they were in, but they will remember Ben or Warner . . . and the positive impact they had on their lives." Professional emotional labor made the work feel important.

Loving the children and creating a home, then, were no longer what administrators wanted from workers; they were what workers wanted for themselves. Workers' devotion to children aligned their interests with the organizations. Through professional emotional labor, workers identified closely with children. Compare the workers' descriptions of "giving back" to the othering accounts of white volunteers discussed earlier. Workers wanted children to experience the same benefits they experienced at KW. Darin stated:

> I grew up here in southwest Sherburne where the kids are served. So the same streets and community and houses that they live in, I lived in. . . . [Working here] was an opportunity to give back to kids like I was given back to.

Others wanted to make life easier than they had it. Yolanda, a Black volunteer, struggled after her mother died: "I try to help children to get what I didn't get." No whites related to kids this way.

But loving the kids facilitated overlooking racial meanings and the degrading emotion work employees performed. They understood humbling themselves to be part of the job and necessary, and they were willing to sacrifice to help children they related to so closely. Two examples illustrate the processes.

Even though each KW facility had custodians, administrators ordered direct-care workers to clean floors and take garbage around the outside of the building rather than through the administration area. Workers and kids picked up garbage in the ditches along KW's property, a task I found dangerous. These beautification strategies were part of KW's efforts to make volunteers feel comfortable and their resources well invested. When Casey, a Black worker, did not maintain the gym to white administrator Richard's satisfaction, he sent her an email holding her accountable, using professionalism:

> Casie [sic], I walked in the gym this morning in preparation for a site visit with a new Board Member and was appalled by its condition. . . . it still looks like a trash dump. . . . There are many people who have given of their resources to ensure that these children have a facility in which they can take pride. . . . As a Kidworks professional you have the responsibility to ensure the safety and cleanliness of your program areas. You have until I come to work at 7:30 AM Friday morning to make the gym the cleanest, most orderly, and safest facility in Sherburne.

Casey was "really offended" and confused. Had she really done something wrong? Was she not a professional? Casey tried to meet with Richard to seek some clarity, but he did "not have time." She crafted an email that expressed concern over "a lack of communication between employees and the administration" and requested he address future concerns in person. But Casey's superiors policed her into interpreting the situation less critically. Her Black supervisor told her: "You have to take stuff with a grain of salt. You have to let it roll off. You've got to not show your emotions on your face and that type of stuff." A white administrator instructed her to not take it personally because being rebuked happens to everyone. He explained the reprimand would have been worse in

person. While she did not regret sending the email, these conversations led Casey to conclude: "I need to work on being submissive. I do." The next day, Richard reinforced Casey's new interpretation after a brief meeting: "He said I'm doing a good job. The gym looks good now. The request to meet with him in person was a part-time person's complaint. . . . I can see his point."

This exchange taught Casey the importance of deferential emotional labor as part of her job. When she challenged administrators' interpretation of her work and their methods for conveying criticism, supervisors quickly reinforced that others' emotional experiences mattered more than hers. They framed her reaction as overreacting and insisted that being a professional required emotional restraint and muted criticism of superiors. Professionalism regulated Casey into reinforcing a racist structure she wanted to challenge by fostering self-doubt and challenging her interpretation of mistreatment. Richard did the same with Warner, as discussed previously, when he told him to "humble" himself. In practice, then, professionalism policed workers into *wanting* to submit to white authority.

Tamera's experiences with a white volunteer who claimed racial discrimination illustrate a second process. In a form of symbolic boundary maintenance (Schwalbe et al. 2000), Black workers contrasted their commitment to kids to "wrong priorities": self-interestedness and self-promotion. Warner criticized: "There are people who come here for pay checks. . . . They're here just to get that check and go home. They're not here for the kids." To "come for a pay check" was to be "fake." Personal gain did not matter, conversely, to "genuine" people "with a heart" who were "here for the kids." Staff, in turn, measured their own importance as workers through their self-sacrifice and child-centeredness. This practice led to color-blindness and muted criticism, particularly during conflicts. Tamera relayed:

> [White volunteers] felt like they were being picked on because they were the minority in the group now. . . . Lisa was white and she felt like she didn't get any respect from the Black staff. Or no one tried to really help her.

According to Tamera's account, volunteer Lisa was "really, really concerned with the kids, and they weren't accepting her." She wanted the staff to help her connect better with them, but when they did not, she charged racism. Tamera tried to broker a meeting with the relevant workers because "we don't want people unhappy." But Lisa refused and instead emailed administrators, saying, "she would never step foot back in KW again and that she would continue to support the organization but that we should look at how we treat minority [white] people."

Professionalism guided Tamera's response to this and other problematic whites. Lisa provoked frustration, skepticism, and an interpretation of racism. Tamera stated: "I really doubted that that was the situation [Lisa was mistreated as a white] because we have great employees and that doesn't really make a lot of sense." Instead, she thought Lisa had unrealistic expectations that disrespected the staff: "She wanted to be patted on the back *constantly*" and "You can't come in here and expect that someone's going to baby you." She thought Lisa was like other volunteers, whose expectations were racially offensive—"I think they want to feel like I saved this poor little Black kid"—and who espoused stereotypes that Black kids "be like needy, can't function, semi-brain-dead, [disheartened] kids that they can hold and rock and tell them that everything is going to be okay." Other workers shared her frustration: "[An administrator] wants us to raise all this money. That's *their* job. . . . Don't ask me to go to these events. Don't make me parade kids around for all these rich people. I don't want to do it" (Darin). Tamera wanted to challenge Lisa directly. But despite her claims that "volunteers are not VIPs" and workers "don't want to" or "have time to kiss their butts," she did not. She instead fostered Lisa's commitment so that Lisa worked events where "she can be thoroughly recognized" and "around other white people."

In this example, what Tamera wanted to do, based on her feelings of frustration due to her interpretation of racism, conflicted with what she was supposed to as a professional employee. Tamera transformed her negative feelings into positive ones based in self-sacrifice:

> I deal with a lot of non-minorities [whites] on a daily basis that I wouldn't ever deal with in my regular life. But it's for the betterment of kids who look like me. . . . If I have to smile in somebody's face that I know may not really like me and would never hang in the same circles as I or speak to me in the street . . . I'm going to smile 'cause . . . it's about creating opportunities for these kids.

When Sharice hit her breaking point, she similarly stated, "I'll go on record: the only reason that I'm still here is for my girls." After discussing Lisa's situation with

her bosses, Tamera altogether abandoned the racism interpretation of the volunteer deemed "really important to the organization" in favor of a new, color-blind interpretation. She attributed Lisa's complaints to a personality flaw: "We understood that it's important to maintain that relationship with her but we knew some people are just happy to be unhappy." Professionalism, thus, conditioned workers to self-regulate and overlook race.

Discussion and Conclusion

Previous research too often treats emotional labor as racially neutral, neglecting its racial foundations and implications. This study demonstrates how emotional labor functioned as a racial project that contributed to racial hegemony through its appropriation of professionalism. I identify three social processes that fostered the consent of racial subordinates to degrading racial meanings and structuring.

First, appropriated professionalism aligned Black workers' interests with white administrators' goals. Like many others, Kidworks' organizational hierarchy itself was racialized: white administrators dictated feeling rules for Black, direct-care workers, even though administrators considered employees professionals. Accordingly, workers signified their competence by fulfilling the emotional labor prescribed to them rather than through freedom of expression. Opposite its "professional" designation, this emotion work was deferential in nature. Creating a refuge for kids and fostering whites' emotional investment required prioritizing others' needs, even when it created conflict. Thus, although professionalism generally provides emotional freedom, it had the opposite effect here: It legitimized the subordination of Black employees by framing their emotional deference as necessary to the work. Staff who invested themselves in their work, thusly, believed in the importance of acting deferentially—for the children's sake. They *wanted* to be devoted and loyal to KW because self-sacrifice signified their worth as workers. Emotional labor reinforced racial subordination by investing Black workers in submitting to whites.

Second, professionalism diffused negative emotions, which cultivate discontent with racial structuring. Emotional labor itself drew on long-standing racist stereotypes about Black cultural dysfunction and white superiority and paternalism, creating resentment and frustration among Black workers. These emotions fuel disruptions to stratification systems, while satisfaction, complacency, and resignation stabilize them (Jocoy 2003). But feeling scripts often deny Blacks the expression of "negative" emotions (Wingfield 2010). At KW, workers learned to consider them contagions. When negative emotions did surface, supervisors used professionalism to police them. Employees repressed them, emphasizing the children's needs instead. Even though emotionally relating is often unevaluated and uncompensated, devotion made the work *feel* meaningful and important. Black employees, moreover, felt morally superior when they juxtaposed their self-sacrifice to the superficial priorities of whites, even though emotional labor subordinated them structurally. Professionalism, consequently, mediated workers' negative emotions, thereby stabilizing the racial structure.

Third, professionalism muted racial critiques and fostered color-blindness. Under the guise of acting professionally, workers transformed their racially laden interpretations into racially neutral ones while repressing frustration. Testimonials were no longer stereotypical but an opportunity for kids to speak publicly. Accommodating whites was not racially insulting but a fundraising necessity. Even racial interpretations of whites' belittling actions were labeled overreactions.

Thus, professionalism served as a racial project that not only drew on and reinforced racist meanings but also conditioned the emotional subjectivities of Black workers so that they consented to race-based organizing. This finding has implications beyond KW to other workplaces that are racially stratified or have racialized emotional content. In the globalized capitalist economy, workplace stratification often coincides with race, and workers of color, especially women, routinely perform devalued carework.... Under these circumstances, emotional labor can have insidious racial consequences.

References

Andreoni, James. 1990. "Impure Altruism and Donations to Public Goods: A Theory of Warm-Glow Giving." *The Economic Journal* 100:464–477.

Collins, Patricia Hill. 2004. *Black Sexual Politics: African Americans, Gender, and the New Racism.* New York: Routledge.

Dees, J. Gregory, and Beth Battle Anderson. 2003. "Sector-Bending: Blurring Lines between Nonprofit and For-Profit." *Society* 40(4): 16–27.

Erickson, Karla. 2004. "To Invest or Detach? Coping Strategies and Workplace Culture in Service Work." *Symbolic Interaction* 27(4): 549–572.

Harris, Lloyd C. 2002. "The Emotional Labour of Barristers: An Exploration of Emotional Labour by Status Professionals." *Journal of Management Studies* 39(4): 553–584.

Hochschild, Arlie Russell. 1983. *The Managed Heart: Commercialization of Human Feeling.* Berkeley: University of California Press.

Jocoy, Christine L. 2003. "Vying for Hearts and Minds: Emotional Labour as Management Control." *Labor and Industry* 13(3): 51–72.

Kunda, Gideon, & John van Maanen. 1999. "Changing Scripts at Work: Managers and Professionals." *The Annals of the American Academy of Political and Social Science* 561:64–80.

Leidner, Robin. 1999. "Emotional Labor in Service Work." *The Annals of the American Academy of Political and Social Science* 561:81–95.

Lewis, Patricia. 2005. "Suppression or Expression: An Exploration of Emotion Management in a Special Care Baby Unit." *Work, Employment and Society* 19(3): 565–581.

Merchant, Altaf, John B. Ford, and Adrian Sargeant. 2009. "Charitable Organizations' Storytelling Influence on Donors' Emotions and Intentions." *Journal of Business Research* 62(7): 754–762.

Pierce, Jennifer L. 1995. *Gender Trials: Emotional Lives in Contemporary Law Firms.* Berkeley: University of California Press.

Schwalbe, Michael, Sandra Godwin, Daphne Holden, Douglas Schrock, Shealy Thompson, and Michele Wolkomir. 2000. "Generic Processes in the Reproduction of Inequality: An Interactionist Analysis." *Social Forces* 79(2): 419–452.

Sloan, Melissa M. 2004. "The Effects of Occupational Characteristics on the Experience and Expression of Anger in the Workplace." *Work and Occupations* 31(1): 38–72.

Wingfield, Adia Harvey. 2010 "Are Some Emotions Marked 'Whites Only'? Racialized Feeling Rules in Professional Workplaces." *Social Problems* 57(2): 251–268.

Questions

1. What is meant by "emotional labor"? How is emotional labor different from unpaid forms of emotion work? How do employers exploit emotions for profit?

2. What was Kidworks? What did the organization look like, and why is that important? What feeling rules accompany the expectation to be "professional"? In what ways was professionalism racialized?

3. How did workers deal with the expectation that they act professionally? Why was it hard? How did emotion work contribute to racial and class hierarchy at Kidworks?

4. Why did workers engage in emotional labor, even though they felt exploited? What would happen if workers refused to manage emotions in the ways expected of them? Could they resist doing it without losing their jobs? How so?

5. In what ways do stratification systems produce unique requirements for managing emotions? What costs accompany those requirements?

6. What is the most emotionally challenging job you or someone close to you has held? What was so difficult about it? How did you cope? What was the most emotionally rewarding work? What made it so great? How did you express yourself? Now compare the circumstances of the worst and best. What social circumstances produce rewarding emotion work versus exploitive emotion work? How can we take those lessons into the organizations we work and volunteer with?

39

Gender Labor: Transmen, Femmes, and Collective Work of Transgression

JANE WARD

In Chapter 12 by David Grazian, you learned about the concept of "doing gender." People give performances using clothing, hairstyles, and body language to accomplish masculinity or femininity. For the men in Chapter 12, this meant engaging in a "girl hunt." In this chapter, we revisit the idea of doing gender. However, the author, Jane Ward, also suggests that we give performances that help others accomplish their gender performance. She introduces the concept "gender labor." Gender labor refers

---

to the emotion work and gender performances that people do in order to help others accomplish their gender. How do you help others accomplish their gender performance? For example, when one of the editors was in college, she had a friend inform her that she may have been having a hard time finding "a man" because she had a habit of opening car doors for men and not allowing them to open doors for her. In this statement, her friend wasn't just pointing out that she was doing gender incorrectly—but that she interfered with men properly doing masculinity, too. In this instance, performing femininity was necessary for men to correctly perform masculinity.

Ward examines the way that people help others do gender through an examination of transgender men and their women partners. For the transmen in Ward's study, accomplishing a masculine presentation of self is especially important because their status as "men" is tenuous. In a culture where people stress a binary sex and gender system, people who play with gender can face harsh discrimination and violence. As of October 2014, only 18 states and Washington, D.C., had laws that make employment discrimination based on gender identity illegal. This means that in 32 states, people who are transgender or gender queer can be fired purely because of how they choose to perform gender regardless of how good they are at their jobs. However, even something as simple as using a public restroom can become a hostile experience for transpeople. These are concerns that people who are cisgender (people whose gender presentation matches their sex) do not have to think about. In the Ward reading, pay attention to the types of gender labor that are accomplished. In what ways does this labor challenge some forms of inequality, and in what ways does it reproduce other inequality? Why is this so important for the men in the reading?

This project takes femme/FTM sexual relationships as a point of departure to consider gender itself as a form of labor, or to illustrate how gender subjectivities are constituted by various labors required of, and provided by, intimate others. My analysis focuses on examples of work that women do in relationships with transgendered men, specifically the work that they do to validate and celebrate their partners' masculinity and to suppress the complexity of their own gender and sexual subjectivity in the service of this goal. Though numerous theorists have accounted for the ways in which gender is constructed, performed, and disciplined, such approaches have yet to theorize fully the relational and feminized labors that reproduce gender and nurture new genders (or new gender formations) into public and private being. These collective labors are distinct from the repetitive and involuntary acts that constitute the subject, or that take form as unwilled labors of the *self* (Butler 1990, 1997). In contrast, I use the term "gender labor" to describe the affective and bodily efforts invested in *giving gender* to others, or actively suspending self-focus in the service of helping others achieve the varied forms of gender recognition they long for. Gender labor is the work of bolstering someone's gender authenticity, but it is also the work of

co-producing someone's gender irony, transgression, or exceptionality.

Gender as Labor

My first aim here is to consider the relational, intimate, and sexual labor that has produced transgender subjectivity and to show how this labor is undertaken by people who fall both within and outside of the boundaries of transgenderism.

My second aim is to reveal the applications of linking gender and labor not only for queer analyses but also for understanding the collective work that produces masculinities and femininities in all of their various iterations. Indeed, examples of gender labor abound. Women friends, across the lines of race and class, rehearse for one another the self-effacing scripts associated with female validation ("I wish I had your body," or "No, you don't look fat, but I do"). Women of color come home from work and care for men of color, helping to ease their partners' presumably greater racial burden. Femme dykes labor to treat butches and FTMs like men; and butches and FTMs labor to treat femmes (and sometimes all women) like queens. That these efforts are often "labors of love" enacted for and by people who are denied gender validation within mainstream culture (women, men of color, queers) must not elide the ways in which gender is reproduced through routinized forms of carework. As I will show, these routine efforts—akin to the emotional labor enacted by service workers and described by Arlie Hochschild ([1983] 2003)—often result in the recurring misrecognition or diminishment of the laborer. As I will demonstrate, all genders demand work, and therefore all people both give and require gender labor. However, some genders, principally those that are masculine and especially those that intersect with other forms of power (such as wealth and whiteness), make their demands less visible and more legitimate, or deliver them with more coercive force. Gender labor, like other forms of caring, weighs down most heavily on feminine subjects, the people for whom labors of love are naturalized, expected, or forced (Nakano Glenn 2004).

Giving Gender

As Viviana Zelizer has explained, intimate labor frequently involves the work of providing support in the face of denials of dignity or compensating for someone's shortcomings—shortcomings that may be emotional, interpersonal, physiological, or otherwise material in nature. Intimate labor, most commonly done by women, also includes offering temporary connection and authenticity (Bernstein 2007), which can involve "faking" or giving someone what they want, even when the lack of "realness" is implicitly recognized by both participants (Augustin 2007). Though these feminized labors are integral components of social life and subject to increasing demand, they are also regularly denied the status of work due to "social expectations about what women should undertake out of love, kinship, or obligation" (Boris and Parreñas 2007).

To the extent that gender is always a shortcoming or never-achieved ideal, I want to suggest that gender is always already bound up with the search for people and things that will offer relief, compensate for failure, enhance dignity, and create moments of realness. In this sense, gender labor is the act of giving gender to others in an attempt to fulfill these needs. Though these acts of giving, like carework in general, are performed by people across the spectrum of feminine and masculine genders, feminine subjects (straight women, femme lesbians, transwomen, feminine gay men, faggy boys/bois, and so on) are held particularly responsible for the work

of gendering. This is because the duties that comprise gender labor—witnessing, nurturing, validating, fulfilling, authenticating, special knowing, and secret-keeping—have long been relegated to the sphere of female work (Hochschild [1983] 2003).

That both normative and transgressive genders are made possible by feminized labor has important implications for queer theory, in particular, which has often aligned the feminine with the non-queer, or the homonormative. Queer studies has embraced those utopic ways of life made most possible or necessary for masculine subjects—mobility, independence, extended identification with youth culture, grungy/ alternative modes of consumption, risk-taking—and disavowed those ways of life made most possible or necessary for feminine subjects—reproductivity, caretaking, shopping, homemaking, and safety-making (see Halberstam 2005, 1–2). In contrast, to investigate gender labor is to reconnect these two seemingly distinct cultural and productive spheres; it is to see the ways that the construction of the former (the queer) has depended upon the latter (the feminine)—even, and especially, for assistance in enhancing its capacity to reject the feminine upon which it depends.

Introducing the Study

This project began in 2004 as an interview-based study of FTMs' relationships with queer women, primarily women who identify as femme. In the course of these interviews, several FTMs spoke about having a hope or expectation that their partners would have sex, speak, dress, and think about gender and gender politics in ways that would bolster their masculinity. Conversely, femme interview participants described their relationships with FTMs as sites of frequent confusion, resentment, and hard work. It was during these interviews that I first began to think about gender labor, but I was dissatisfied with interviews as my only source for understanding these dynamics and I expanded the project to include related forms of cultural production. Consequently, the current project is based on transdisciplinary analysis of three sources: (1) a set of interviews I conducted in 2004 with 13 FTMs and eight femmes living in Los Angeles, San Francisco, Seattle, or New York; (2) four documentaries addressing FTM or genderqueer identities, spanning the years 1994 to 2005 (*Shinjuku Boys*; *Mind If I Call You Sir?*; *Boy I Am*; *The Aggressives*;

see Filmography at the end of the References); and (3) two websites in which participants discuss FTM-related articles from two lesbian magazines (*On Our Backs* and *Curve*). All interview participants for this research have been given pseudonyms and each signed a consent form agreeing to the recording, transcription, and publication of their interviews. Comments taken from public websites are cited by website only and without names or other identifying information, whereas subjects in nationally distributed documentaries have been identified by the names they use in the films.

My analysis focuses on three forms of gender labor that femme partners do to co-produce trans masculinity: the labor of being "the girl," the labor of forgetting, and the labor of alliance. These labors are in many ways particular to the temporal, regional, and subcultural context of trans/queer relationships in major cities of the United States in the mid-2000s; however, as I will illustrate, each also serves as an example of general mechanisms used to produce gender coherence for others.

The Labor of Being "The Girl"

In FTM identity narratives, trans masculinity has frequently been described as the experience of not being, or not wanting to be, a girl. As has been explored in other research on FTMs (Devor 1997; Dozier 2005), "not wanting to be a girl" speaks to an awareness, often beginning in childhood, of a gendered self and body that does not fit social, cultural, and familial expectations associated with girlhood: "I didn't want to wear dresses," "I always felt more like a boy," "I hated my breasts," and so on. Yet beyond not wanting to be *a* girl, many FTM (and butch) identity narratives also describe the experience of not wanting to be *the* girl in a particular relational context, often during sex. In Dozier's (2005, 312) study, for example, "Dick," a white FTM, explains why his transition led to a new sexual interest in men by stating, "what I figured out a lot later was that it wasn't about not wanting to be with a guy; it was about not wanting to be the girl."

Similarly, avoidance of being the girl—and reference to women who, in contrast, embrace being the girl—is a recurring theme in the 2004 documentary *Mind If I Call You Sir?: A Video Documentary on Latina Butches and Latino FTMs*. The film centers on butches and FTMs from the San Francisco area who are filmed discussing the contours of their masculinity while sitting around a table in an office-like setting. Scenes from

this discussion are interspersed with more in-depth footage of individuals recounting stories of gender dysphoria, outsiderness, and/or transition, and, in one case, an interview with a femme who is filmed preparing food in a kitchen while speaking about her partner's transition. During the discussion between butches and FTMs, Yosenio, a Latino FTM, tells the group that he is hesitant to "bottom" to his sexual partner because, as he states, "then I'll be a girl." Such narratives, which link "bottoming" with femininity, define girlhood, in part, by a comfort with sexual submission and lack of sexual control. Other scenes from the film illustrate that being a/the girl refers to more than sexual receptivity or submission. In one scene, Diane, a Latina butch, describes her early awareness of her masculinity by telling the story of her difference from other Chicana political activists with whom she had worked. These women, Diane implies, were satisfied with their ancillary role in the Chicano movement:

> In my soul, I knew I was different. I wasn't like the rest of the Chicanas in the movement. . . . I was more man. I wanted to hang out with the men. I wanted to talk politics with the men. I didn't want to be in the kitchen. I didn't want to be stuffing envelopes. . . . So I was different.

Similarly, Yosenio, an FTM, explains his difference from women:

> I was always taught, women are less than. You don't want to be a woman. . . . the poor lot in life of women. They struggle, and they struggle, and they struggle. . . . And it's like, I don't want to be like that. But all the people that I gravitated to were women, all the people that I felt the closest to were women, and all the people that I always wanted to be around were women. And all the people who ultimately gave me the love to survive all the crap I went through as a child were women. And so it was a push me, pull you thing. I always want to be around you, but I don't ever want to be like you.

Although butches and FTMs are often theorized as stand-alone figures who are not reliant upon femmes (or the feminine other) for public recognition, such accounts construct trans and butch masculinity by citing the existence of a satisfied feminine other, or a female subject who may be queer, but is different from butches and FTMs in that she is happy to occupy the role of the girl. Diane describes her butch masculinity through an account of her disidentification not only with the costume of femininity, but with the women she presumes were happy in the kitchen, happy stuffing envelopes, happy being barred from political talk. Yosenio describes dis-identification not only with femininity but also with women's "struggle" and with being "less than." He says, in a kind of address to the women who nurtured his own escape from girlhood: "I always want to be around you, but I don't ever want to be like you." In Diane's and Yosenio's narratives, butch and FTM subjectivities are not only those that reject feminine appearances or embodiment; they are also those that cannot tolerate sexism.

The film highlights the ways in which the coherence of butch and FTM identity narratives depends upon the existence of a feminine subject who experiences female embodiment, sexual submission, and sexism as more natural or trouble-free than the butch/trans subject. My interest here is the way this reliance on the satisfied feminine other—whether as an abstraction ("somewhere out there, other women like being girls") or specified within a relationship ("my girlfriend loves being a girl")—has produced a demand for the labor of becoming this satisfied girl. Needless to say, many butches and FTMs do not have relationships with femmes (or feminine people, for that matter); however, the figure of the girl nonetheless remains an important element of the narrative of trans and butch difference. In cases in which FTMs do have femme partners, the interviews I conducted suggest that the latter are often compelled to embody this girl subjectivity, or to work to enhance their own femininity and its apparent seamlessness in order to reinforce the masculinity of their partners. Keaton, a 32-year-old white FTM, told me:

> [I think some transguys] want their girlfriend or their partner, if they're dating a woman, to re-emphasize their masculinity. These two FTMs [I know] who are both dating women . . . apparently had both asked their girlfriends to grow their hair out long since their transitions. . . . And [my girlfriend] has long hair, so they asked her if I did the same thing, and she's like, "No, and if he did, I'd cut it all off."

Jimmy, a 40-year-old Asian American FTM, told me about a conflict that he and his femme-identified partner had with one of their FTM friends. He said:

> We had a friend who was . . . very warm and loving and wonderful in a lot of ways, but has this very clear sense of what he feels he needs to be as a man, as an FTM

person, and has really imposed his sense of the world on us as a couple. . . . And I think he saw my wife as, "OK, you're the female, you need to be the one who's doing clearly feminine tasks in support of your man." . . . He really wanted to disregard her and put her in her place, and like snap at her or whatever, and disrespect her.

Femmes also told similar stories about being compelled to occupy the position of the girl so as to bolster trans masculinity. For example, Melinda, a 37-year-old white femme, talked about her experience meeting transmen online (through dating websites). She said:

> I heard from three transguys in a row who all made comments about liking my photographs, and specifically aspects of my appearance that were super feminine. And they all said, "I want to learn more about you" and followed up . . . with some variation of "Tell me why trans-people do it for you" and in one case "Tell me why trans-people are better for you, hotter for you than anybody else on the planet." That was a very explicit solicitation for my femininity to prop up their masculinity or validate it in some way, and it was really revolting and at that point I decided, "no trans-people, no trans-men."

Similarly, another femme named Jennifer told me:

> In my relationships with people who are trans-identified, there's been less room for the politics around *my* gender. . . . They really wanted my identity to be femme, and they really wanted the person they were with to help bolster their own gender.

In femme–FTM relationships, being the girl produces scenes and intimate spaces in which FTMs become more clearly, or more easefully, the boy or the man. In the documentaries *Mind If I Call You Sir* and *Boy I Am*, femmes are shown engaged in very material forms of carework, such as binding their partners' chests and cooking in the kitchen. In *Shinjuku Boys* and *The Aggressives*, femmes are shown in constant pursuit of intimacy—calling, clinging, asking questions, hoping for more—while butches and FTMs appear to forge their most intimate or long-term relationships with one another. In other cases, femmes work to facilitate their partners' ability to experience a lost boyhood or male adolescence, often through a synthesis of sexual exploration and maternal nurturing. A femme writing on a website called transensualfemme.com explains the femme/FTM "dynamic" by invoking the image of an erotic mommy figure who gently guides a young boy through his first sexual experiences:

> We are the pioneers. We are discovering what a femme trans-guy dynamic means. Thus far, for me it has mostly felt like a mothering role. In many ways, I'm acknowledging, encouraging, fulfilling and validating my partner's adolescent urges. I'm nurturing his maleness. I'm sexually initiating him, if you will.

Curve magazine has described transensualfemme.com as a website for "partners of people in transition—particularly femme-identified lesbians—[who] often get left in the dust when it comes to dealing with their own gender and sense of self" (Szymanski 2003, 14). Yet most comments on transensualfemme.com suggest that the site provides an online community designed precisely for femmes to trade information about caring for FTM partners sexually, physically, and emotionally, and to redefine themselves in relation to this work. Much akin to the 1970s spate of self-help books designed to teach straight women how to probe the male psyche—how to catch him, understand him, care for him, and keep him—femmes avoid being left in the dust by becoming the "pioneers" of masculine territories.

Undoubtedly there are cases in which being the girl is a reflection of femmes' own sense of comfortable alignment with the conventions of femininity (with being in the kitchen, having long hair, and so on). Yet the foregoing narratives also indicate that being the girl is a form of intimate labor that is undertaken to produce the masculinity of the other and to keep the social, emotional, and erotic structure of femme/FTM relationships intact. Femme labor not only involves embodying feminine contrast (if I'm the girl, then you are the boy), but also discovering, acknowledging, encouraging, fulfilling, validating, nurturing, and initiating masculine complexity. Like other forms of intimate and sexualized labor, femmes *give gender* to FTMs through efforts that augment masculine authenticity, offer moments of realness, and compensate for gendered shortcomings.

The Labor of Forgetting

Several of the FTMs interviewed for this project explained that new sexual relationships with femmes go through a kind of testing phase in which FTMs assess whether or not they can trust their new partner to interact with them, and their bodies, as male. In some cases, this involves developing trust that the femme partner has forgotten, or does not see, signs of femaleness. Travis, a 27-year-old white FTM, described how he prefers women partners to relate to his childhood as a girl:

> *Travis:* Most of the time, I think I want them to know, but not know. Like they know and they get it, but they don't talk about it. I'm allowed to talk about it, but it doesn't mean anything when I do talk about it. I know it's incredibly complicated and a lot to ask of a person. Like if I slip and say, "when I was a little girl" you have to be able to hear that without even batting an eye, but understand what that means to me, and how that might get me to where I'm at now. Like I said, I know I'm asking a lot. I'm asking for the person I'm dating to be able to do a lot of work without me.
> *Author:* Are you comfortable if the person you're dating wants to be in a partners' support group?
> *Travis:* I feel like on one level she would need that, and I would want her to have that outlet. But like, I want her to know, but not know. So I don't know how I would deal with that if she wanted to go to SOFFA meetings [meetings for "significant others, friends, family, and allies"] once a week. You know, I think that on that one day a week I would be freaked out all day. It would mean it was on her mind.

Like Travis, several participants explained that they are most comfortable in relationships with women who can demonstrate that they have forgotten their partners' past femaleness and are not preoccupied with being in a "transgender relationship," even though their relationships require particular kinds of work and expectations related to trans identity. Some participants explained that they teach femme partners to learn a new trans vocabulary of the body, including ways of talking about sex, talking about the past, gender code-switching when FTMs are not out to family or co-workers, and a new gendered division of labor (such as asking femmes to always buy the tampons, place them in the bathroom, but never speak about them). Forgetting, in this case, is not the opposite of having knowledge but is a new kind of gendered knowing that includes a new vocabulary and a new set of gendered practices (Halberstam 2006). These relations of forgetting and knowing are marked by many of the elements Zelizer (2007) attributes to intimate labor: trust, privacy, secret knowledge, and special access. For some FTMs, straight women and "high femmes" play a central role in erasing femininity and offering masculine realness, primarily through their participation in heteronormative sex.

The corollary of the labor of forgetting femaleness is the labor of establishing trust that femmes see, know, and understand trans masculinity and can deploy and communicate this understanding through particular sex acts. Countless sex columns in queer magazines and websites now instruct readers on how to have sex with the trans or genderqueer body ("how to fuck a boi," "how to suck cock," "mommy/boy role-play," and so on). These advice columns often stress the importance of relating to trans masculinity as authentic, as well as the importance of ensuring that one's sex cannot be mistaken for lesbian feminist sex (circa 1970), which is typically represented as boring, unsexy, power-neutral, or passé. For example, the magazine *On Our Backs: The Best of Lesbian Sex* instructs readers about "how to suck cock" by stating: "Get Real: treat the dildo like a real penis—focus on the things that feel good to bio men; stroke the vein along the bottom, tongue the slit, gently tickle the balls" (Venning 2002). Femmes can learn how to affirm the gender identity of FTM partners not simply by forgetting or de-emphasizing their partners' past femaleness, but also by demonstrating knowledge of male physiology and desire. In some cases, interview participants shared stories of successful male recognition, such as R. J., a 42-year-old African American FTM:

> My girlfriend tells me, "You're not a lesbian. . . . When I talk to you there's no woman there. . . . You're just male, you know. I don't relate to you like I've related to butch lesbians." She says, "I don't relate to you the same way. Nothing's the same." So I feel very lucky in that sense.

Yet, in other cases, femmes described the trans/femme erotic script as a site of negotiation, confusion, and hard work, one that is subject to an unspoken and often changing set of rules, particularly with respect to sex. Bridgette, one 26-year-old white femme dating an FTM in Los Angeles told me:

> The question of breasts and what I'm allowed to do to them has always felt very confusing to me. . . . I can remember moments where every so often [one of my partners] would sort of be like, "Hey, I have boobs too,"

and I would be like "Oh, right, right, right," but I think there was this way that I had been given other messages. . . .

My review of femme websites indicated that femmes are keenly aware that not seeing femaleness and understanding maleness are central aspects of their role in the trans/femme erotic script. Among the women who post on *transensualfemme.com* and *femme.com*, successful femininity is often linked to a seemingly effortless or natural ability to see only her partner's maleness. As one woman states on *femme.com*:

> No one ever "trained" me on how to understand their maleness. I just knew. I relate to my butch's female body as if it is male. In fact, thinking of or relating to a TG [transgender] butch as if he were female would be utterly confusing to me. I absolutely see TG butches as guys. It is difficult to express, yet it is extremely profound to me . . . very deep . . . deeper than words.

Many transensual femmes express their innate desire for trans masculinity in somewhat mystical terms that position this expression of desire outside of its social and political context. Such accounts obscure the ways in which trans-sensual femininity, like other forms of gender labor, is scripted, routinized, and hierarchical (and learned through advice columns, SOFFA groups, and other authoritative sources); the more you can "automatically" see maleness and forget femaleness, often the more desirable and valuable you are as a transensual femme.

The Labor of Alliance

One of the effects of the aforementioned labors is that they solidify a trans-gender/fixed-gender binary in which femmes are firmly located outside of a gender dysphoric experience, and often outside the realm of the queer or transgressive. Femme activists in the United States, such as Amber Hollibaugh (1997), have asserted femme as a form of transgenderism that is marked by a constructed and ironic engagement with femininity, and femme scholars have suggested that femme subjectivity is defined by its own form of gender dysphoria and unintelligibility (Walker 2001). However, within trans subculture, femmes have been positioned in the outsider categories of "ally" or "SOFFA." In order to be understood as legitimate stakeholders in trans politics, some accounts suggest that femmes are compelled to participate as "gender supporters," quietly celebrating female masculinity while remaining silent as femininity is de-queered or pathologized. A zine written by Rocko Bulldagger about misogyny in trans communities in New York discusses this dynamic:

> When I first heard about *Venus Boyz*, a documentary about drag kings and trannies, I was so excited to see some queerly gendered people on screen. . . . When the movie got started. . . . [we heard] so much contempt for femininity from the mouths of the very same people we consider our community. . . . The final straw (for the girls I was with) was when one supposedly liberated genderqueer declared righteously that not everyone can be blonde haired and ditzy. The laughter of this huge auditorium packed with queers, so delighted in their shared disdain for femininity, was just painful. . . . It's brave for femmes to persist in their support for butches and trannies who could comfortably sit down and name a thousand different genderqueer, masculine sub-identities but would experience serious discomfort at the thought of sitting down and having a long conversation about the meanings and complexities of femininity.

In emphasizing the work of alliance, my aim is to show the ways in which femmes labor at being gender supporters not only within intimate, sexual relations, but also within the more collective realm of FTM political and cultural public space. The laborious quality of alliance stems primarily from the silences and misrecognitions that femmes manage in order to help preserve the momentum of FTM exceptionalism. The femme-as-ally or SOFFA construction typically erases feminine forms of gender fluidity or dysphoria, an erasure that causes many femmes to assert and reassert their experiential alignment with trans narratives. For instance, Jennifer, a femme in Los Angeles who also identifies as a "tough broad" told me that being an ally does not capture her own identification with the trans experience. She said:

> When I was partnered with folks who were FTM identified, sometimes it was complicated for me to understand "Ok, what is this ally thing?" . . . Because [in the trans community,] I found for the first time a real comfort in my own queerness. I had similar feelings [as trans folks] about walking into dyke space and [being] both an insider and an outsider. I came into the trans community not as a partner to anybody, but as an

individual. But it felt like I was being pigeonholed as, "Well, the only way a bio female can be in this community then is as an ally or as a SOFFA." But my only place wasn't as an ally, because the trans relationship to gender and sexuality and queerness was really familiar to me . . . Just because it's femininity and not masculinity, I [still] had similar things going on.

As Jennifer points out, feminine forms of gender trouble pose a challenge to the very construction of FTM community by drawing attention to the permeability of trans identification. Given the fixity of trans boundaries, femmes' efforts to locate themselves within trans politics frequently involves adopting, and adapting to, the ill-fitting role of gender supporter. Like other forms of affective labor, performing the role of SOFFA not only entails elements of scripted "faking," it also requires suspending truer accounts of oneself in the service of the other.

Femmes who are critical of being assigned the position of gender supporter have drawn heavily upon feminist frameworks to intervene in the sexism they experience in their relationships with transmen or within trans political spaces. In contrast, many FTM discourses place the FTM subject outside or beyond feminist analysis, emphasizing instead the ways in which FTMs' refusals of femininity and/or the forces of sexism stem from a natural calling to masculine gender rebellion. The resultant polarization of feminist and trans frameworks has dissonant effects within femme/FTM relationships, particularly given the ways in which FTMs' disidentificatory narratives about female embodiment and objectification often ring true for femmes (and for women in general). Though it has become something of a taboo to draw comparisons between the gender dysphoric feelings of FTMs (i.e., I hated my female body and the sexism it elicited) and those of non-trans women (i.e., I hate my female body and the sexism it elicits), both femmes and FTMs reported in interviews that such comparisons nonetheless emerge, especially when two female-coded bodies share intimate sexual space. For instance, R.J., an African American FTM, explained:

> [My girlfriend] says, "You make [being female] sound so disgusting. I hope you don't think that of me." And I was like, no . . . it's not that I think that about you. It's just that, you know, I love these things about you, but I

don't want them on me. Like my chest, I call them cow sacks, you know. Something like that. I use those kind of really negative terms.

In *Mind If I Call You Sir*, Prado's comments about his breasts raise similar questions about the extent to which FTMs' experiences of femaleness differ from those of many women. Prado accounts for his decision to transition by explaining his rejection of the societal dictate that breasts are "who he was":

> My breasts were . . . like a constant presence that felt like all attention, all eyes, all focus, and everything about who I was, that's what it was about. And that was always at the forefront of people's minds . . . it just became this psychological burden of womanhood that just wasn't true for me.

Referring back to the figure of the satisfied girl, such accounts gesture toward the female subject for whom the burden of womanhood must, at some level, be "true." In many cases, these origin stories ("I knew I was trans because the burden of womanhood wasn't true for me.") produce conflict and alienation between FTMs and femme partners, especially when femmes foreground the ways in which they are implicated in FTM narratives (e.g., "I hope you don't think that of me. . . ."). As in most forms of service work, the story about the needs of the recipient also tells a story about the satisfied laborer. The laborer not only fulfills others' needs, but also arrives on the scene satisfied and ready to work, presumably without possessing similar needs of her own. As Hochschild explains ([1983] 2003), this is the justifying logic that naturalizes the "second shift": women manage their own emotional needs throughout the course of a day's work, and arrive home from paid labor ready to provide intimate care for others. Similarly, the SOFFA construction implies a resolved and natural gender, one that arrives on the scene ready to nurture masculinity into being.

Discussion

Focusing on gender labor draws attention to the collective work that produces and sustains gender. Though we already know that genders exist inside an interdependent gender system, little attention has been given to the laborious quality of reproducing other people's genders in daily life, and we remain without a clear mapping of the training, skills, duties, and specific efforts that various genders require. Here I have shown that in many cases, FTM identities remain reliant upon the labors of femininity that nurture and witness them, both within and outside of intimate sexual relations. It is not simply that femmes provide support to transmen (and butches); they also reproduce a trans/not-trans binary by training to be the girl in new and particular ways, many of which they are compelled to experience as easy and natural. In some cases, femmes learn to actively forget their partner's differently gendered past, to study up on male desire and male physiology, and to master a new set of sexual practices and erotic scripts. Transsupportive and feminist-identified femmes also learn how to occupy the role of ally or SOFFA, often through silence regarding their own gender dysphoria. In sum, femme labor describes not only the emotional, physical, and sexual work of reproducing FTM subjectivity; it also refers to the work of adjusting one's own gendered self in relation to this process—such as the work of transitioning from femme to transsensual femme.

While this chapter has focused on the gender labors femmes do to produce trans masculinity, a similar chapter could have explored the opposite relationship, as femininity requires very particular labors of masculinity to sustain it. However, I have attempted to show the ways in which many elements of gender labor—offering sexual validation, co-constructing realness, forgetting other possibilities, maternal nurturing, keeping one's complex personhood to oneself—mirror the practices of intimate labor generally assigned to women. This confluence reveals the ways in which gender itself takes form through feminized acts of service done for others, often at the expense of the laborer's own recognition, dignity, or assistance with gendered shortcomings. To the extent that these labors are performed within intimate spheres and through gestures of bodily, emotional, and sexual care, they are embedded in the historical and political-economic structures of women's work. Women do a disproportionate amount of the commercial care and sex work in the United States, but they are also held responsible—sometimes through legal and other structural channels—for relationship-based forms of caring (Nakano Glenn 2004) and relationship-based sex work (Cacchioni 2007). Though I have not undertaken a comparative study that could demonstrate the ways in which gender labor weighs down most heavily on feminine subjects, I have attempted to underscore the ways in which all genders may be bound up in intimate dependencies and feminized relations of nurture, giving, and collectivity.

References

Augustin, Laura Maria. 2007. "A Multiplicity of Acts, Acting and Caring: The International Sex Industry." Paper presented at *Intimate Labors: An Interdisciplinary Conference on Domestic, Care, and Sex Work*. University of California, Santa Barbara, October 4–6.

Bernstein, Elizabeth. 2007. *Temporarily Yours: Intimacy, Authenticity, and the Commerce of Sex*. Chicago, IL: University of Chicago Press.

Boris, Eileen, and Parreñas, Rhacel. (2007) "Conference Program." *Intimate Labors: An Interdisciplinary Conference on Domestic, Care, and Sex Work*. University of California, Santa Barbara, October 4–6. http://www.ihc.ucsb.edu/intimatelabors/ (accessed December 20, 2009).

Butler, Judith. 1990. *Gender Trouble: Feminism and the Subversion of Identity*. New York: Routledge.

Butler, Judith. 1997. *The Psychic Life of Power: Theories in Subjection*. Stanford, CA: Stanford University Press.

Cacchioni, Thea. 2007. "Heterosexuality and 'the Labour of Love': A Contribution to Recent Debates on Female Sexual Dysfunction." *Sexualities* 10(3): 299–320.

Devor, Holly [Aaron]. 1997. *FTM: Female-to-Male Transsexuals in Society*. Bloomington: Indiana University Press.

Dozier, Raine. 2005. "Beards, Breasts, and Bodies: Doing Sex in a Gendered World." *Gender and Society* 19(3): 297–316.

Halberstam, Judith. 2005. *In a Queer Time and Place: Transgender Bodies Subcultural Lives*. New York: New York University Press.

Halberstam, Judith. 2006. "Notes of Failure." Keynote address at the *Failure: Ethics and Aesthetics Conference*, University of California, Irvine, March 3.

Hochschild, Arlie Russell. ([1983] 2003). *The Managed Heart: Commercialization of Human Feeling*. Berkeley: University of California Press.

Hollibaugh, Amber. 1997. "Gender Warriors: An Interview with Amber Hollibaugh (interviewed by Leah Lilith Albrecht-Samarasihna)." In *Femme: Feminists, Lesbians, Bad Girls* (ed. Laura Harris and Elizabeth Crocker), 210–222. New York: Routledge.

Killmermann, Sam. "30+ Examples of Cisgender Privilege." *It's Pronounced Metrosexual*. http://itspronouncedmetrosexual.com/2011/11/list-of-cisgender-privileges/ (accessed January 1, 2015).

Nakano Glen, Evelyn. 2004. *Unequal Freedom: How Race and Gender Shaped American Citizenship and Labor*. Cambridge, MA: Harvard University Press.

Szymanski, Zak. 2003. "Out on the Web: Affirm Your Identity." *Curve Magazine*, February 14.

Venning, Rachel. 2002. "How to Suck Dyke Cock." *On Our Backs* December/January:11

Walker, Lisa. 2001. *Looking Like What You Are: Sexual Style, Race, and Lesbian Identity*. New York: New York University Press.

Zelizer, Viviana. 2007. "Caring Everywhere" Keynote address presented at *Intimate Labors: An Interdisciplinary Conference on Domestic, Care, and Sex Work*. University of California, Santa Barbara, October 4–6.

Filmography

Aggressives, The. 2005. Directed by Daniel Peddle.

Boy I Am. 2005. Directed by Sam Feder and Julie Hollar.

Mind If I Call You Sir?: A Video Documentary on Latina Butches and Latino FTMs. 2004. Produced by Karla Rosales, StickyGirl Productions.

Shinjuku Boys. 1994. Directed by Kim Longinotto and Jano Williams.

Questions

1. What does Ward mean by "gender labor"? When have you done gender labor? Be specific. Why?
2. What types of gender labor did femmes do for their partners?
3. How can the gender labor that some of the women do be seen as both challenging inequality but also reproducing other forms of inequality?
4. Do you think that the rugby players in Ezzel are doing gender labor? Why or why not? How does this concept change our understanding of gender?
5. On Sam Killermann's website, he discusses cisgender privilege. (Go to his website at http://itspronouncedmetrosexual.com/2011/11/list-of-cisgender-privileges/.)
6. What are some examples of cisgender privilege? How are these privileges similar to or different from white privilege? Able-bodied privilege? What does the concept of cisgender add to our understanding of inequalities? How is cisgender privilege enshrined in law and practices?

40

Fitting In and Fighting Back: Stigma Management Strategies among Homeless Kids

ANNE R. ROSCHELLE AND PETER KAUFMAN

It is difficult to estimate the number of homeless in the United States. Homelessness can be temporary. Additionally, not all homeless people seek shelter assistance, and it is nearly impossible to accurately count the street homeless. According to the National Coalition for the Homeless, national estimates of homelessness range from 1.6 million to 3.5 million people, with up to a third of that population being children. In this chapter, Anne Roschelle and Peter Kaufman share the experiences of homeless kids in San Francisco who participate in programs run by an organization called A Home Away From Homelessness. The chapter shows how the kids cope with the stigma associated with being homeless.

The chapter draws from Goffman's (1963) work on stigma management techniques and shows how the youth attempt to "pass as normal" and manage a deviant identity. People are stigmatized when others view them as different from "normal" and negative. This leads to what Goffman refers to as a "spoiled identity." The kids in Roschelle and Kaufman's study are cognizant of the fact that outsiders view people who are homeless as having a host of character flaws, and they develop strategies to deal with the negative emotions that result from their stigmatization. While some of the stigma management techniques work to foster healthy relationships, other strategies are exclusionary. Similar to the rugby players discussed in Chapter 35, these kids engage in defensive othering techniques. The authors demonstrate how the location of these kids in the social structure influences their behavior. They have limited resources to challenge the stigma they face in everyday situations. What do you think the consequences of their behavior will be for these youth?

Reference

Goffman, Erving. 1963. *Stigma: Notes on the Management of Spoiled Identity.* New York: Simon and Schuster.

Our work is an ethnographic account of kids who are or have been homeless in a variety of settings. We use a broader definition of homelessness than just living on the streets or in a shelter, because families, unlike childless adults, are more likely to receive services that provide housing (even if it is substandard). We look specifically at the stigma management strategies homeless kids use and consider how these strategies are both informed by and interpreted through their devalued social structural location. Like all social actors, kids who are homeless construct and manage their behavior on the basis of the meanings they have assigned through

Excerpted from Roschelle, Anne R., and Peter Kaufman. "Fitting in and Fighting Back: Stigma Management Strategies among Homeless Kids." *Symbolic Interaction* 27.1 (2004): 23–46. ©2004 Society for the Study of Symbolic Interaction.

social interaction (Blumer 1986). Because their homelessness is a "pivotal category" and is therefore a defining aspect of their identity (Lofland 1969), their social interactions are largely mediated through the lens of homelessness. This effect of homelessness is not surprising in light of sociologists' general agreement that "individuals' locations in the social hierarchy have a major influence on their life experiences, personal development, and behavior" (Kerckhoff 1995, 476).

Research Site

The research site is an organization in San Francisco called A Home Away From Homelessness. Home Away serves homeless families living in shelters, residential motels, foster homes, halfway houses, transitional housing facilities, and low-income housing. The program operates a house in Marin County (called the Beach House), provides shelter support services, a crisis hotline, a family drop-in center (the Club House), a mentorship program, and, in conjunction with the San Francisco Unified School District, an afterschool educational program (the School House). Home Away is neither a typical homeless service agency nor a shelter. Home Away serves a population of approximately one hundred 5- to 18- year-old children annually. Fifty percent of the participants are boys and 50 percent are girls. The racial-ethnic breakdown of homeless families participating in Home Away programs is 40 percent African American, 30 percent white, 20 percent Latino, and 10 percent multiracial. All the kids participating in Home Away programs lived with at least one parent (none are runaways or homeless youth living independently), although some were essentially on their own as a result of parental neglect.

Methods and Data

The ethnographic component of our research included participant observation at the Beach House, the School House, and the Club House where Anne Roschelle collected the data and did volunteer work for four years (1995–1999). During this time, she also attended meetings of relevant social service agencies at which she took copious notes and conducted observational research at residential motels, transitional housing facilities, and homeless shelters throughout the San Francisco Bay area. In addition, she conducted thousands of hours of informal interviews, sometimes

asking leading questions (Gubrium and Holstein 1997) and sometimes just listening. Many of the informal interviews were taped and transcribed. In addition, she conducted and transcribed verbatim formal taped interviews with 97 kids and parents who were currently or previously homeless.

Stigma Management Strategies

Goffman (1963, 3) suggests that stigma should be understood as "a language of relationships" as opposed to the attributes a person possesses. Moreover, he notes that "the stigmatized are not persons but rather perspectives" (138). These ideas are particularly relevant for understanding the stigmatization of kids who are homeless. While these kids do not necessarily exhibit physical manifestations of their stigma, they are stigmatized because of their marginalized status in society. The discourse surrounding poverty and homelessness has a long history of blaming individuals for their predicament. Kids who may have been defined in the past as deserving of societal sympathy have more recently been recast as part of the legions of the undeserving poor (Gans 1995; Katz 1989). Home Away kids were aware of their relationship to normative society and understood that others generally saw them as undesirable. Because of the large numbers of homeless in San Francisco and the visibility of the street homeless, there were numerous negative public discussions about the issue. The local newspapers constantly featured articles that were contemptuous of the homeless, and mayoral races often focused on ridding the city of its unsightly homeless population. The kids in the sample were attuned to the negative discourse surrounding homelessness and often expressed their anxiety about being demonized by the public. In fact, the kids spent many hours sitting in front of the fireplace discussing how hard it was for them to be routinely disparaged. As Dominic, an articulate 16-year-old, said, "Everyone hates the homeless because we represent what sucks in society. If this country was really so great there wouldn't be kids like us." A more developed expression of this political awareness is evident in the following conversation:

> MARTA: Man, I'm so sick of the nasty shit people say about the homeless.
>
> JORGE: Yeah, me too. They talk about us like we were garbage.

WANDA: I know and it ain't our fault we poor.

MARTA: Yeah, my dad lost his job cuz he got hurt and then we got kicked out of our apartment cuz he couldn't pay the rent. It's not like he's some lazy crack head.

JORGE: My mom works two jobs and we still can't afford an apartment.

MARTA: Yeah, but that don't matter. Willie Brown and them other politicians—they just keep saying how lazy homeless people are and that we are all drug addicts and criminals. It ain't right and you know it ain't true.

WANDA: Damn straight.

Kids who are homeless manage their stigma in a variety of ways. We observed that the kids displayed two sets of strategies. The first set conformed to societal norms of appropriate behavior and aimed at creating a harmonious environment with both peers and strangers. In other words, these strategies represented attempts at establishing self-legitimation in both hostile and supportive environments. We refer to these as *strategies of inclusion* because they reflected the kids' desire to eradicate the boundary between a homeless and a nonhomeless identity. Through these inclusive strategies, Home Away kids hoped to be recognized simply as kids—without the stigmatizing label and discredited status of being homeless. The most common strategies of inclusion among Home Away kids were forging friendships, passing, and covering. The second set of strategies were also attempts at gaining social acceptance but were not necessarily aimed at creating a harmonious atmosphere. We refer to these as *strategies of exclusion* because Home Away kids use them to distinguish themselves from both peers and strangers. With these strategies, kids who are homeless attempted to redress their spoiled identity by declaring themselves tougher, more mature, and better than others. These exclusive stigma management strategies included verbal denigration and physical and sexual posturing. Unlike strategies of inclusion in which kids used conciliatory tactics to be accepted, strategies of exclusion were aggressive and forceful attempts by the kids to blend in. These strategies largely reflected the kids' interpretations of socially acceptable behavior. However, given their disenfranchised social position, these behaviors were often perceived as maladaptive and threatening. As a result,

when kids engaged in strategies of exclusion, they provided members of the dominant culture with a seemingly legitimate justification to further disqualify and disparage them.

Strategies of Inclusion

Forging Friendships

At the Beach House, the kids attempted to construct a positive identity. Children were treated with dignity and respect by volunteers and were included in important decision-making processes. The services provided by Home Away gave kids an opportunity to experience childhood in a way most individuals take for granted. In addition to providing a break from the difficulties of living in shelters, transitional housing, residential motels, and so on, Home Away gave the kids a place to forge friendships with caring adults. Many of these relationships offered the only opportunity for homeless kids to obtain positive self-appraisals from nondisenfranchised adults. This supportive environment allowed for greater self-legitimation, gave the kids a respite from their stigmatization, and provided them with a sense of belonging (Brooks 1994). As a result of this inclusive strategy, many of the kids developed more favorable self-images. Silvia's discussion of her friendship with Tami, a volunteer, illustrates the importance of forging friendships as a way to manage stigma.

SILVIA: I call her whenever I feel really bad. She is so nice. She makes me feel better when I'm depressed and she never makes me feel like a freak because I'm homeless.

ANNE: Is that important to you?

SILVIA: Yeah. Most of the time I feel pretty bad about my life. I mean my mom has a new boyfriend every few weeks, we live in this nasty ass hotel, and I feel like everyone knows I'm a loser. Tami is always trying to make me feel better about my life. She tells me how smart and pretty I am and that I should feel good about being such a great older sister. Tami really cares about me and makes me feel better about myself. I don't know what I'd do without her.

Home Away also provided these kids with the opportunity to befriend other impoverished youths. By embracing other disenfranchised children, Home Away kids created a safe space where they could construct a positive identity and manage their stigmatized status. For example, when new kids were incorporated into Beach House activities, instead of rejecting them, the "old-timers" served as mentors and attempted to create a harmonious climate. Old-timers initiated the new kids into the program by teaching them the rules, showing them around, and introducing them to secret hiding places. Much like the traditional African American role of "old heads" and "other mothers" documented, respectively, by Anderson (1990) and Collins (1991), this mentor relationship allowed the old-timers to gain self-esteem. By initiating newcomers, they became experts at something and shared their wisdom with other impoverished kids. In addition, as the following conversation suggests, old-timers took great pride in their knowledge of the surrounding environment:

> CARLOS: Hey, Hernán, don't go in the water without your life jacket.
> HERNÁN: *No hay problema*—I'm a great swimmer.
> CARLOS: It doesn't matter, man, the undertow is really strong and you can get swept under really easily.
> HERNÁN: Don't be such a pussy.
> CARLOS: Seriously man, people drown here all the time. Last week some kid almost died.
> HERNÁN: Really?
> CARLOS: Yeah, man. Listen I been coming here for two years and I've seen a lot of shit—you gotta believe me.
> HERNÁN: *Gracias*, Carlos—thanks for watching my back. You really are a cool dude. I guess I better to stick close to you so I don't get into any trouble.
> CARLOS: Hey, after we finish swimming Marcus and I can show you the secret hiding place.
> HERNÁN: Cool.

Forging friendships with newcomers is an important stigma management strategy because it enables kids who are homeless an opportunity to transcend their discredited status and assume a role invested with interactional legitimacy. Through forging friendships, Carlos is able to negate feelings of worthlessness bestowed on him by society and feel like a valuable member of the kids' community. Similarly, Hernán's stigma is mitigated because he now feels like a legitimate member of Home Away.

Passing

Goffman (1963) suggests that visibility is a crucial factor in attempts at passing. To pass successfully, an individual must make his or her stigma invisible so that it is known only to himself or herself and to other similarly situated individuals. Unlike their nonhomeless peers who have legitimate access to the public domain, kids who are homeless must often pass as nonhomeless as a means of appropriating heretofore unavailable and legitimate public space. One "passing" strategy kids in our study used entailed adopting the dress and demeanor of nonhomeless kids. Whenever clothing was donated to Home Away, the kids selected outfits based on style rather than function. It was extremely important that clothing and shoes looked new and were "hip." On numerous occasions, kids refused to take donated coats during the winter because they were ugly and out of style. The importance of fitting in is evidenced by the following conversation between Anne, Jamie, and Cynthia (Jamie's mom) while they were hanging out at Stonestown Mall:

> JAMIE: Hey, do you think these people can tell we are homeless?
> ANNE: No, how could they possibly know?
> JAMIE: I don't know. I always feel like people are looking at me because they know I am poor and they think I am a loser.
> CYNTHIA: I feel like that a lot too—it makes me feel so bad—like I'm a bad mother and somehow being homeless is my fault. I feel so ashamed.
> JAMIE: Me too.
> ANNE: Jamie, what are some of the ways you keep people from knowing you are homeless?
> JAMIE: I try and dress like the other kids in my school. When we get clothes from Home Away, I always pick stuff that is stylin' and keep it clean so kids won't know I'm poor. Sometimes it's hard though because all the kids try and get the cool stuff and there isn't always enough for everyone. I really like it when we get donations from people who shop at the Gap and Old Navy. I got one of those cool vests and it made me feel really great.
> ANNE: Is it important for you to keep your homelessness a secret?
> JAMIE: Yeah, I would die if the kids at school knew.

Implicitly, homeless kids know that their appearance situates them within or outside group boundaries (Hunt and Miller 1997; Stone 1970). In this sense, passing is a strategy of inclusion that allows them to fit in and be accepted by mainstream society. By dressing in a style that conforms to adolescent norms, Home Away kids hide their stigmatized status, avoid social ostracism, and experience a momentary affinity with the non-homeless world. Home Away kids also attempt to pass by using code words:

ROSINA: I hate that kid Jamal that lives with us in Hamilton [Family Shelter], you know his cot is three over from mine.

SHELLEY: Sssh, be quiet, someone will hear you and then people will know we are homeless.

ROSINA: I don't care.

SHELLEY: I do.

LINDA: So do I. You should say that you don't like Jamal who lives three houses down—that way people will think you are talking about a kid in your neighborhood.

ANNE: Is that how you guys talk in school?

SHELLEY: Yeah, we say things like that and we make up other stuff so people don't know we live in the shelter.

LINDA: Or in the motels.

SHELLEY: When we talk about our caseworkers we say our aunts and when we talk about shelter staff we call them our friends.

ANNE: That is a really clever way of keeping people from knowing you're homeless.

ROSINA: It totally is, but then you can't invite friends over after school because they think you live in a house.

LINDA: We can't hang out with kids who are not poor. There is no way I would invite a kid from school over to my room in that skanky motel we live in, I'd be so embarrassed.

SHELLEY: Yeah, we can't make friends with a lot of kids because how can we bring them to the shelter after school?

This example illustrates how homeless kids use words to construct a positive identity, protect their sense of self, and feel integrated with the larger society. Moreover, it shows that language reflects and reproduces power relations in society. Interestingly, although these kids use code words to mask their stigmatized status and construct a positive identity, their language choices disqualify them from participating in normative social interactions. These verbal gestures reflect the extent to which homeless kids are in danger of having their homelessness revealed. When they do not use code words, their stigmatized identity will be evident, and they will be unlikely to befriend middle-class children. Alternatively, when they do use code words, they reduce their chances of befriending nonhomeless kids because they risk exposing their stigma. In managing stigma through passing, the threat of discovery is ever present.

Covering

Individuals engage in covering when they attempt to minimize the prominence of their spoiled identity. Covering allows individuals to participate in more normative social interactions by reducing the effects their stigma elicits (Goffman 1963). Unlike passing, the point of covering is not to deny one's stigma but rather to make it less obtrusive and thereby reduce social tension (Anderson, Snow, and Cress 1994). Home Away kids often engaged in this stigma management strategy when they became friends with nonhomeless kids who knew about their predicament. Home Away kids would especially use this strategy around the parents of their nonhomeless friends, and they would often ask the staff to advise them on appropriate dress or behavior when they were going out with nonhomeless kids and their families. One Home Away kid, Ellie, became a close friend of an affluent schoolmate, Carol, who lived in the Marina district of San Francisco. Ellie was honest with Carol and her family about where she lived. Still, when Ellie went to Carol's house for dinner, she wore the least tattered, cleanest clothes she owned and would eliminate her ghetto swagger and jargon. As she said to Anne, "They know I'm homeless and all, but I don't want to act like I'm homeless. I don't want to embarrass them. You know my clothes aren't that fancy and I'm used to eating at the shelter where everyone is talking really loud and eating with their hands and being kinda sloppy." To fit in and be "normal," Ellie decided to minimize the obvious manifestations of her homelessness. These efforts subsequently enabled her to manage her stigma, maintain her friendship with Carol, and feel included in her friend's "normal" family structure.

Strategies of Exclusion

Verbal Denigration

When individuals face a social world that labels them deviant, they are likely to fight back by maligning others as a way to augment their self-esteem. Termed "defensive othering" by Schwalbe et al. (2000), this type of stigma management strategy was common among Home Away kids. Many kids in the sample protected their sense of self by verbally denigrating other stigmatized groups such as homosexuals and homeless street people. This was a form of identity work that allowed homeless kids to distance themselves from the stigmatized "other" (Snow and Anderson 1987) and proclaim their superiority over these similarly disparaged groups. Because homeless kids recognize that they are problematic in the eyes of society, their denigration of other stigmatized groups is a "largely verbal effor[t] to restore or assure meaningful interaction" and align themselves with the dominant culture (Stokes and Hewitt 1976, 838). Along these lines, many of the kids were homophobic and freely expressed their disgust for homosexuality. This attitude can be attributed to the kids' (arguably accurate) interpretation of societal norms and values with regard to homosexuality. By portraying gays and lesbians as "freakin' faggots" and "child molesters," the kids were placing others lower than themselves in the social hierarchy. The kids' stigmatized status was deflected onto others, thereby bolstering their own sense of self. This exclusionary strategy was especially interesting in the context of San Francisco—a city in which there is a large population of gay and lesbian activists and citizens, many of whom have achieved positions of power and prestige and who themselves often denigrate the homeless. The following conversation illustrates the pejorative discourse Home Away kids often used when talking about gays and lesbians:

ANTOINE: Look at those homos, they make me sick.
FRED: Yeah, they be all trying to grab your ass when you walk by.
ANTOINE: I know man, they'd love a piece of us but I'd make 'em suck on a bullet before I'd let 'em suck on my thang.
FRED: People think we are nasty because we live at the Franciscan, but at least we don't do little boys. I mean those guys are freaks.

Homeless kids also spoke disparagingly about homeless street people. Homeless kids in our sample lived in shelters, residential motels, transitional housing, foster homes, and other institutional settings. Though many of them have spent a night or two sleeping in parked cars, in a park, or on the street with their parents, their homeless experience has taken place primarily in some type of sheltered environment. The main reason they have not spent the majority of their lives on the streets is because there are many more programs for homeless families in San Francisco than there are for childless homeless adults. Essentially, the only factor preventing their parents from becoming part of the homeless street population is them. Despite this, Home Away kids often made fun of homeless street people.

ROSITA: Man look at those smelly street people, they are so disgusting, why don't they take a shower.
JALESA: Yeah, I'm glad they don't let them into Hamilton with us.
ROSITA: Really, they would steal our stuff and stink up the place! [Laughter]
JALESA: Probably be drunk all the time too.
ROSITA: Yeah, and smokin' crack all night long!

Ironically, the mothers of both these girls have struggled with drug and alcohol addiction and have had several episodes of homelessness. By distancing themselves from the "true" social pariahs of San Francisco, Jalesa and Rosita mitigate their own stigmatized status and maintain some semblance of a positive self. Further, identifying a group as more discredited than themselves allows the girls to feel superior to "those losers on the street."

Physical Posturing

Physical posturing is another form of identity work that grants homeless and non-homeless kids a momentary degree of empowerment. Kids who are homeless use physical posturing to feel powerful in their interactions with nondisenfranchised kids, a feeling that is rarely available to them. It has long been recognized that many adolescents are filled with insecurity as they attempt to establish their identities (Erikson 1968). However, middle- and upper-class kids have more socially acceptable means than low-income ones to demonstrate to others (and to themselves) that they are important. As Anderson (1999, 68) notes, privileged kids "tend to be more verbal in a way unlike those of more limited resources. In poor inner-city neighborhoods verbal prowess is important for establishing identity, but physicality is a fairly common way of asserting oneself. Physical assertiveness is also unambiguous." In this sense, Home Away kids' use of physical demeanor is a stigma management technique that emerges from their social structural location and protects them from a hostile world.

One common manifestation of this physical posturing was the use of body language. When encountering nonhomeless children, kids in our study often adopted threatening postures by altering their walk, speech, and clothing to mimic "gangsta" bravado. In short, these kids adopted what Majors (1986) refers to as the "cool pose." For example, to get from the parking lot to the beach, we had to walk over a very small, narrow wooden bridge. As we crossed the bridge, we often passed kids coming from the opposite direction. As soon as the Beach House kids spotted other kids coming toward them, they would immediately change their demeanor. They metamorphosed from sweet cuddly kids to ghetto gangstas. The kids grabbed their pants and pulled them down several inches to mimic the large baggy low-riding pants of the gangbanger. They turned their baseball caps around so that the brim was in the back and swaggered in exaggerated ways. Their speech became filled with ghetto jargon, and they spoke louder than usual. When encountering other kids, the topic of conversation on the bridge would also suddenly shift from how much fun we just had to the fate of a gang member they knew who had just been arrested. These self-presentations mirror what Anderson (1990, 175) calls "going for bad." Anderson argues that this intimidation tactic is clearly intended to "keep other youths at bay" and allow disempowered kids to feel tougher, stronger, and superior. Like verbal denigration, this strategy of exclusion also helped Home Away kids to lessen their stigma. Interestingly, these behaviors clearly imitate images of adolescence that pervade popular culture. In music videos, movies, television shows, video games, and so on, images of baggy pants, baseball caps, and swaggering walks abound. Although this strategy had the intended effect of empowering Home Away kids by intimidating their nonhomeless peers, it also reinforced their stigmatization. As Nonn (1998, 322) notes, "While the coping mechanism of cool pose weakens the stigma of failure, it undermines identity . . .

and contribute[s] to their own alienation from other groups in society." Though some kids recognized that their behavior may stigmatize them further, they still engaged in such posturing because it was one of the few areas in their lives over which they had some control.

Sexual Posturing

Some Home Away kids used sexuality to validate themselves. Although nonhomeless youth also engage in sexual posturing to establish a sense of self in their social groups, Home Away kids engage in it more explicitly and overtly than their nonhomeless peers. For Home Away kids, sexual posturing and promiscuity articulate the sexual exploitation and violence they experienced both within and outside the family. As researchers have documented, victims of child sexual abuse often resort to promiscuity in adolescence and adulthood (Beitchman, Zucker, and Hood 1991; Rotheram-Borus and Mahler 1996). Molestation by older men was not uncommon, and many of these kids learned at an early age to use their sexuality to gain status among their peers. For example, several young women in the sample dressed and behaved in overtly sexualized ways that surpassed what we expect from the budding sexuality of "normal" adolescents. In one poignant incident, a 14- year-old girl was teaching a younger girl how to perform oral sex on an 11-year-old boy. By bragging to his friends about his newfound sexual prowess and achieving prominence among his peers, this boy exhibited an exaggerated masculine alternative commonly found among lower-income racial-ethnic males (Oliver 1984). The girls involved increased their status by demonstrating a level of sexual maturity that is typically associated with older women. In another example, Patti, a 13-year-old, discussed the self-esteem she gained through her sexual posturing:

> I mean not everyone is pretty enough to get a man to pay for a room for the night. At least I know that I can get anything I need from a man because I am totally hot. I get lots of attention and some of my friends are jealous of me because they know I got it going on.

As these examples illustrate, sexual posturing is an exclusionary tactic kids use to distinguish themselves from their peers and to lessen their stigmatization. Research has shown that some poor racial-ethnic girls invoke a discourse of sexuality in order to negotiate and construct a more empowering identity (Emihovich 1998), and others may attempt to achieve similar results through motherhood (Luker 1996). In a society bombarded with images of hypersexuality, it is not surprising that Home Away kids imitate these sexual scripts in an attempt to strengthen their social standing. Although middle-class youth also use these strategies, the consequences are not as profound for them. Unlike middle-class kids, Home Away kids occupy a stigmatized position in the social structure that severely limits their life opportunities (Anderson 1990; Kaplan 1997). As Anderson (1990, 135) poignantly notes, "the economic noose restricting ghetto life encourages both men and women to try to extract maximum personal benefit from sexual relationships." In short, Home Away kids engage in physical and sexual posturing to affirm their social existence in a society that often denies them opportunities for self-legitimation.

Conclusion

In this chapter, we examined the stigma management strategies of kids who are homeless. Although researchers of stigma management have studied a variety of populations, our work contributes to existing knowledge by including this previously neglected group. By examining the stigma management strategies homeless kids use, we address a number of gaps in the literature. First, our work emphasizes the need to acknowledge stigma and homelessness as structural locations. Much like homelessness, we must posit stigma not as an individual attribute but as a relationship to the social structure (Goffman 1963; Link and Phelan 2001). This perspective is noteworthy because it attends to how individuals' behaviors are both informed by and interpreted through their social structural location. This insight is particularly true of homeless kids who are oppressed socially because of their age, race, ethnicity, and social class. Kids who are homeless encounter and interpret a world that is characterized by hunger, uncertainty, chaos, pain, drug abuse, violence, sexual abuse, degradation, and social rejection, among other things. This social reality epitomizes the violence of poverty and ultimately results in a lack of consistency, stability, and safety in their lives. Furthermore, these kids exist in a constrained public domain and are forced to carve out their own space in a limited urban environment that is generally hostile to them. It is in this environment that kids who are homeless engage in social interactions that

aim to construct positive identities and overcome their discredited status.

References

Anderson, Elijah. 1990. *Streetwise: Race, Class, and Change in an Urban Community.* Chicago: Chicago University Press.

Anderson, Elijah. 1999. *Code of the Street: Decency, Violence, and the Moral Life of the Inner City.* New York: Norton.

Anderson, Leon, David A. Snow, and Daniel Cress. 1994. "Negotiating the Public Realm: Stigma Management and Collective Action among the Homeless." *Research in Community Sociology* (Supplement 1):121–143.

Beitchman, Joseph, Kenneth Zucker, and Jane Hood. 1991. "A Review of the Short-Term Effects of Child Sexual Abuse." *Child Abuse and Neglect* 15(4): 537–556.

Blumer, Herbert. 1986. *Symbolic Interactionism: Perspective and Method.* Berkeley: University of California Press.

Brooks, Robert B. 1994. "Children at Risk: Fostering Resilience and Hope." *American Journal of Orthopsychiatry* 64(4): 545–553.

Collins, Patricia Hill. 1991. *Black Feminist Thought: Knowledge, Consciousness, and the Politics of Empowerment.* New York: Routledge.

Emihovich, Catherine. 1998. "Body Talk: Discourses of Sexuality among Adolescent African American Girls." In *Kids Talk: Strategic Language Use in Later Childhood* (ed. S. M. Hoyle and C. Temple Adger), 113–133. Oxford: Oxford University Press.

Erikson, Erik H. 1968. *Identity: Youth and Crisis.* New York: Norton.

Gans, Herbert J. 1995. *The War against the Poor: The Underclass and Antipoverty Policy.* New York: Basic Books.

Goffman, Erving. 1963. *Stigma: Notes on the Management of Spoiled Identity.* New York: Simon and Schuster.

Gubrium, Jaber F., and James A. Holstein. 1997. *The New Language of Qualitative Method.* New York: Oxford University Press.

Hunt, Scott A., and Kimberly A. Miller. 1997. "The Discourse of Dress and Appearance: Identity Talk and a Rhetoric of Review." *Symbolic Interaction* 20(1): 69–82.

Kaplan, Elaine Bell. 1997. *Not Our Kind of Girl: Unraveling the Myths of Black Teenage Motherhood.* Berkeley: University of California Press.

Katz, Michael B. 1989. *The Undeserving Poor: From the War on Poverty to the War on Welfare.* New York: Pantheon Books.

Kerckhoff, Alan C. 1995. "Social Stratification and Mobility Processes." In *Sociological Perspectives on Social*

Psychology (ed. K. S. Cook, G. A. Fine, and J. S. House), 476–496. Boston: Allyn and Bacon.

Link, Bruce G., and Jo C. Phelan. 2001. "Conceptualizing Stigma." *Annual Review of Sociology* 27:363–385.

Lofland, John. 1969. *Deviance and Identity.* Englewood Cliffs, NJ: Prentice-Hall.

Luker, Kristine. 1996. *Dubious Conceptions: The Politics of Teenage Pregnancy.* Cambridge, MA: Harvard University Press.

Majors, Richard. 1986. "Cool Pose: The Proud Signature of Black Survival." *Changing Men: Issues in Gender, Sex and Politics* 17:5–6.

Nonn, Timothy. 1998. "Hitting Bottom: Homelessness, Poverty, and Masculinity." In *Men's Lives* (ed. M. S. Kimmel and M. S. Messner), 318–327. Boston: Allyn and Bacon.

Oliver, W. 1984. "Black Males and the Tough Guy Image: A Dysfunctional Compensatory Adaptation." *Western Journal of Black Studies* 8:201–202.

Rotheram-Borus, Mary Jane and Karen A. Mahler. 1996. "Sexual Abuse History and Associated Multiple Risk Behavior in Adolescent Runaways." *Journal of Orthopsychiatry* 66(3): 390–401.

Schwalbe, Michael, Sandra Godwin, Daphne Holden, Douglas Schrock, Shealy Thompson, and Michele Wolkomir. 2000. "Generic Processes in the Reproduction of Inequality: An Interactionist Analysis." *Social Forces* 79(2): 419–452.

Snow, David A., and Leon Anderson. 1987. "Identity Work among the Homeless: The Verbal Construction and Avowal of Personal Identities." *American Journal of Sociology* 92:1336–1371.

Stokes, Randall, and John R. Hewitt. 1976. "Aligning Actions." *American Sociological Review* 41:838–849.

Stone, Gregory P. 1970. "Appearance and the Self." In *Social Psychology through Symbolic Interaction* (ed. G. P. Stone and H. A. Faberman), 394–414. Waltham, MA: Ginn-Blaisdell.

Questions

1. What were the strategies of inclusion and exclusion used by the homeless youth in this study?

2. Often times we discuss social class as static categories that people simply fit in such as: lower, middle and upper. How does Roschelle and Kaufman's analysis of the homeless youth illustrate that class is also a performance? What about the fluidity of class?

3. How do gender norms influence how the homeless boys and girls behave?

4. How is the defensive othering done by the homeless youth similar or different from the othering done by the rugby players in the chapter written by Ezzell?

5. Ami Stearns wrote a blog for www.sociologyinfocus.com titled, "Hot Pants in the Frozen Aisle: Shaming and Norming the POWM." She argues that the popular "People of Walmart" website, which makes fun of the way people dress while shopping at Walmart, ultimately reflects and reinforces the stigmatization of poor people. How are derogatory comments regarding the clothing worn by people who shop at Walmart is rooted in and reinforces class inequality? What role does the Internet play in stigmatizing subordinated groups?

41

Toward an Affirmation Model of Disability

JOHN SWAIN AND SALLY FRENCH

One goal of social movement activism of marginalized groups has been to be able to define one's own identity. What does it mean to be Black, pan, gay, trans, fat, etc. in a culture where people in the dominant group devalue these identities? The common assumption of people without disabilities is that having particular physical or mental needs is something negative and pitiable rather than something different or valuable. As alluded to in previous chapters, language reflects and shapes the construction of disability. For instance, people may say that someone is "confined to a wheelchair," instead of that someone "uses" a wheelchair or moves around using one of many different forms of transport. The word "confined" suggests some level of restriction or imprisonment, where "uses" redefines the wheelchair into a tool. "Confined" also calls attention to limitations associated with an individual, which renders the ways in which the social structure creates unnecessary obstacles for people with disabilities invisible. For instance, by focusing on the individual person's capacities, the human-made components of disability, such as building stairs instead of ramps, fades into the background.

The ideology that supports the notion that having a disability is something tragic limits the representativeness of people with disability in the broader culture. For instance, people with disabilities are rarely presented positively in the media. How often do stores display mannequins with walking aids? How often is deaf culture presented on its own and as valuable? People with disabilities have formed movements to challenge these belief systems and redefine their identities as positive. In this chapter, John Swain and Sally French argue for an affirmative model of disability. This model challenges the association of disability with tragedy. The disability movement seeks to redefine a positive collective identity from the experiences and voices of people with disabilities. In addition, the authors suggest that education and structural change is necessary to create equality. The authors state that the Disability Arts Movement is one place where this work could be accomplished.

Across the Divide: Existing Models

The divide we are discussing here is not in the categorization of people as disabled and non-disabled. Despite the evident personal, social, and political reality of this conception of a divide, we believe it is problematic in a number of ways, two of which are particularly pertinent to this chapter. Firstly, a division cannot be made on the grounds of impairment. The divide between disabled and non-disabled people is not that one group has impairments while the other does not. Indeed, many non-disabled people have impairments, such as short and long sight, and impairment cannot be equated with disability. Secondly, the divide between two groups cannot be sustained on the basis that one is oppressed while the other is not. Non-disabled people can be oppressed through poverty, racism, sexism, and sexual preference, as indeed are many disabled people. Furthermore, oppressed people can also be oppressors. Disabled people, for instance, can be racist. Whatever definition of oppression is taken, it will apply to some non-disabled, as well as disabled people.

The divide we are addressing is in perceptions of disability, in terms of the meaning it has in people's lives and social identities. Perceptions and the experiences on which they are founded vary considerably, not least as many people become disabled in later life having constructed understandings and lifestyles as non-disabled people. Nevertheless, there is a divide in perceptions which is most clearly related to a divide in experiences, being disabled or non-disabled.

The first question, then, is one of conceiving this divide in different models of disability. The opposition of the social model to an individual, particularly medical, model of disability is well established (Oliver 1996; Priestley 1999) and is clearly crucial to understanding the disability divide. The social model was borne out of the experiences of disabled people, challenging the dominant individual models espoused by non-disabled people (French and Swain 1997). Nevertheless, it is our experience that many non-disabled people readily accept the social model, albeit superficially and at a basic conceptual level. Non-disabled people can generally accept that a wheelchair user cannot enter a building because of steps (i.e., the person is disabled by barriers in an environment built for non-disabled people). Non-disabled people are much more threatened and challenged by the notion that a wheelchair user could be pleased and proud to be the person he or she is.

Better Dead than Disabled?

The tragedy model is so dominant, so prevalent, and so infused throughout media representations, language, cultural beliefs, research, policy, and professional practice that we can only hope to cover a few illustrative examples. In terms of media representations, disabled characters (played by non-disabled actors) were featured in two major family films televised during the 1998 Christmas period when we were planning this chapter.

The first was *A Christmas Carol* which included two disabled characters. The best known is, of course, the pitiable and pathetic Tiny Tim whose tragedy of using a crutch is miraculously overcome at the end of the picture when he runs to meet the enlightened Scrooge. The other is a blind man, with both a dog and a white stick, who appears as a beggar. In the final scene, the humanized Scrooge can donate money in the proffered hat, for which the tragic figure of the cap-in-hand (handicapped) blind man is clearly grateful. The other film, again widely celebrated for the general sentiments it portrays, was *It's a Wonderful Life*. This features just one disabled character, Mr. Potter, who is rich, evil, twisted, frustrated, and in a wheelchair. No other explanation for his inhumanity, which includes theft, is offered other than his response to a life as a wheelchair user (despite the fact that he is the richest man in the town). It is the tragedy that has twisted him. The only other evil character, a minor character, in the film is the man who pushes the wheelchair. The tragedy, it seems, begets evil even by association.

Perhaps the most intrusive, violating, and invalidating experiences for disabled people emanate from the policies, practices, and intervention, which are justified and rationalized by the personal tragedy view of disability and impairment. The tragedy is to be avoided, eradicated, or non-disabled (normalized) by all possible means. Such are the negative presumptions held about impairment and disability, that the abortion of impaired fetuses is barely challenged. As Disability Awareness in Action (1997) states, there is considerable and growing pressure on mothers to undergo prenatal screening and to terminate pregnancies in which an impairment has been detected. The use of genetic technology in its different forms in so-called "preventative" measures is, for many disabled people, an expression of the essence of the personal tragedy model, better dead than disabled. The erroneous idea that disabled people cannot be happy, or enjoy an adequate quality of life, lies at the heart of this response. The disabled person's problems are perceived to result from impairment, rather than the failure of society to meet that person's needs in terms of appropriate human help and accessibility. There is an assumption that disabled people want to be "normal," although this is rarely voiced by disabled people themselves who know that disability is a major part of their identity. Disabled people are subjected to many disabling expectations, for example to be "independent," "normal," to "adjust" and "accept" their situation. It is these expectations that can cause unhappiness, rather than the impairment itself.

Indeed, within the disabling context we have outlined here, the expression of an affirmative model by disabled people flies in the face of dominant values and ideologies. It is likely to be denied as unrealistic or a lack of "acceptance," distorted as an expression of bravery or compensation, or simply ignored. The tragedy model is in itself disabling. It denies disabled people's experiences of a disabling society, their enjoyment of life, and their identity and self-awareness as disabled people.

Towards a Positive Individual Identity

An affirmative model is developing in direct opposition to the personal tragedy view of disability and impairment. The writings and experiences of disabled people demonstrate that, far from being tragic, being impaired and disabled can have benefits. If, for example, a person has sufficient resources, the ability to give up paid employment, and pursue personal interests and hobbies, following an accident, may enhance that person's life. Similarly, disabled people sometimes find that they can escape class oppression, abuse, or neglect by virtue of being disabled. We interviewed Martha, a Malaysian woman with a visual impairment. She was separated from a poor and neglectful family and sent to a special school at the age of five. She states:

> I got a better education than any of them (brothers and sisters) and much better health care too. We had regular inoculations and regular medical and dental checks.

She subsequently went to university and qualified as a teacher. Similarly, many visually disabled people became physiotherapists, by virtue of having their own "special" college, at a time when their working-class origins would have prevented them entering other physiotherapy colleges. None of this is to deny, of course, that many disabled people who are educated in "special" institutions receive an inferior education and may, in addition, be neglected and abused (Corker 1996).

A further way in which disability and impairment may be perceived as beneficial to some disabled people is that society's expectations and requirements are more difficult to satisfy and may, therefore, be avoided. A disabled man quoted by Shakespeare, Gillespie-Sells, and Davies said, "I am never going to conform to society's requirements and I am thrilled because I am blissfully released from all that crap. That's the liberation of disfigurement" (1996, 81).

Young people (especially women) are frequently under pressure to form heterosexual relationships, to marry, and have children (Bartlett 1994). These expectations are not applied so readily to disabled people who may, indeed, be viewed as asexual. Although this has the potential to cause a great deal of anxiety and pain, some disabled people can see its advantages. Vasey states:

> We are not usually snapped up in the flower of youth for our domestic and child rearing skills, or for our decorative value, so we do not have to spend years disentangling ourselves from wearisome relationships as is the case with many non-disabled women. (1992, 74)

Though it is more difficult for disabled people to form sexual relationships, because of disabling barriers, when they do any limitations imposed by impairment may paradoxically lead to advantages. Shakespeare et al., who interviewed disabled people about their sexuality and sexual relationships, states:

> Because disabled people were not able to make love in a straightforward manner, or in a conventional position, they were impelled to experiment and enjoyed a more interesting sexual life as a result. (1996, 106)

For some people who become disabled their lives change completely though not necessarily for the worse. A woman quoted by Morris states:

> As a result of becoming paralysed life has changed completely. Before my accident it seemed as if I was set to spend the rest of my life as a religious sister, but I was not solemnly professed so was not accepted back into the order. Instead I am now very happily married with a home of my own. (1989, 120)

The experience of being impaired may also give disabled people a heightened understanding of the oppressions other people endure. French found that most of the 45 visually disabled physiotherapists she interviewed could find advantages to being visually impaired in their work. An important advantage was their perceived ability to understand and empathize with their patients and clients. One person said:

> The frustrations of disability are much the same inasmuch as it is a physical limitation on your life and you think, "If only." . . . Having to put up with that for so long, I know ever so well what patients mean when they mention those kinds of difficulties. (French 1991, 1)

Others believed that their visual disability gave rise to a more balanced and equal relationship with their patients, that patients were less embarrassed (e.g., about undressing) and that they enjoyed the extra physical contact the visually disabled physiotherapist was obliged to make. One person said:

> Even as students when we had the Colles fracture class all round in a circle, they used to love us treating them because we had to go round and touch them. They preferred us to the sighted physios. I'm convinced that a lot of people think we are better. (French 1991, 4)

As for non-disabled people, the quality of life of disabled people depends on whether they can achieve a lifestyle of their choice. This, in turn, depends on their personal resources, the resources within society, and their own unique situation. The central assumption of the tragedy model is that disabled people want to be other than as they are, even though this would mean a rejection of identity and self. Nevertheless, the writings of disabled people demonstrate that being born with an impairment or becoming disabled in later life can give a perspective on life which is both interesting and affirmative and can be used positively. Essentially, impairment, which is social death and invalidates disabled people in a non-disabled society, provides a social context for disabled people to transcend the constraints of non-disabled norms, roles, and identity and affirm their experiences, values, and identity. Phillipe explains:

> I just can't imagine becoming hearing, I'd need a psychiatrist, I'd need a speech therapist, I'd need some new friends, I'd lose all my old friends, I'd lose my job. I wouldn't be here lecturing. It really hits hearing people that a deaf person doesn't want to become hearing. I am what I am! (Shakespeare et al. , 184)

Watson writes of Phil, a disabled participant in research he is conducting:

> Phil sees his acceptance of his impairment as central to his sense of self and well-being. . . . (1998, 156)

Toward a Positive Collective Identity

As a member of a poetry group of young disabled people, Georgina Sinclair wrote the following poem:

Coming Out
And with the passing of time
you realise you need to find

people with whom you can share.
There's no need to despair.
Your life can be your own
and there's no reason to condone
what passes for their care.
So, I'm coming out.
I've had enough
of passing and playing their game.
I'll hold my head up high.
I'm done with sighs
and shame.

(Tyneside Disability Arts 1999, 35)

In his introduction to the anthology of poetry in which this poem is published, Colin Cameron writes:

> We are who we are as people with impairments, and might actually feel comfortable with our lives if it wasn't for all those interfering busybodies who feel that it is their responsibility to feel sorry for us, or to find cures for us, or to manage our lives for us, or to harry us in order to make us something we are not, i.e. "normal." (Tyneside Disability Arts 1999, 35)

The affirmation of positive identity is necessarily collective as well as individual. The growth of organizations of disabled people has been an expression not only of the strength of united struggle against oppression and discrimination, but also of group identity. Disabled identity, as non-disabled identity, has meaning in relation to and constructs the identity of others. To be disabled is to be "not one of those."

Group identity, through the development of the Disabled People's Movement, has underpinned the development of an affirmative model in a number of ways:

1. The development of a social model of disability has re-defined "disability" in terms of the barriers constructed in a disabling society rather than as a personal tragedy. Through group identity the discourse has shifted to the shared experience and understanding of barriers. "Personal tragedy" has been reconceptualized as frustration and anger in the face of marginalization and institutionalized discrimination.

2. Simply being a member of a campaigning group developing a collective identity is, for some disabled people, a benefit of being disabled in its own right. It can feel exciting being part of a social movement which is bringing about tangible change.

3. Frustration and anger are being collectively expressed. They are expressed through Disability Arts and campaigns of the Disabled People's Movement, rather than being seen as personal problems to be resolved, say, through counseling. The roots of Disability Arts lie in the politicizing of disability issues. As Shakespeare et al. state:

> Drama, cabaret, writing and visual arts have been harnessed to challenge negative images, and build a sense of unity. (1996, 186)

The activities are so diverse it is difficult to talk in general terms. However, Vic Finkelstein, who was one of the founders of the London Disability Arts Forum (LDAF) in 1987, stated in his presentation at the launch that his hopes for the future were "disabled people presenting a clear and unashamed self-identity." He went on to say that it was "essential for us to create our own public image, based upon free acceptance of our distinctive group identity" (Campbell and Oliver 1996). This development of identity has indeed been central to Disability Arts, challenging the values that underlie institutional discrimination. Through song lyrics, poetry, writing, drama, and so on, disabled people have celebrated difference and rejected the ideology of normality in which disabled people are devalued as "abnormal." They are creating images of strength and pride, the antithesis of dependency and helplessness.

4. Through group identity it is recognized that just because there are benefits from being excluded from non-disabled society (which is capitalist, paternalistic, and alienating) does not mean that disabled people should be excluded. From this way of thinking, disabled people enjoy the benefits of being "outsiders" but should not be pushed out; that is, they should have the right to be "insiders" if they so wish.

5. Finally, group identity has been, for some, a vehicle for revolutionary rather than revisionist visions of change, often under the flags of "civil rights" and "equal opportunities" (Shakespeare 1996). The inclusion of disabled people into the mainstream of society would involve the construction of a better society, with better workplaces, better physical environments, and better values including the celebration of differences. As Campbell and Oliver conclude in their history of the Disabled People's Movement:

> In building our own unique movement, we may be not only making our own history but also making a contribution to the history of humankind. (1996, 180)

Disabled people, encouraged by the Disabled People's Movement, including the Disability Arts Movement, are creating positive images of themselves and are demanding the right to be the way they are—to be equal but different.

Toward an Affirmative Model of Disability

In this concluding section, we first summarize the basic elements of an affirmative model of disability, particularly in relation to the tragedy model and the social model. An affirmative model is being generated by disabled people through a rejection of the tragedy model, within which their experiences are denied, distorted, or re-interpreted, and through building on the social model, within which disability has been redefined. The affirmative model directly challenges presumptions of personal tragedy and the determination of identity through the value-laden presumptions of non-disabled people. It signifies the rejection of presumptions of tragedy, alongside rejections of presumptions of dependency and abnormality. Whereas the social model is generated by disabled people's experiences within a disabling society, the affirmative model is borne of disabled people's experiences as valid individuals, as determining their own lifestyles, culture, and identity. The social model sites "the problem" within society. The affirmative model directly challenges the notion that "the problem" lies within the individual or impairment.

Embracing an affirmative model, disabled individuals assert a positive identity, not only in being disabled, but also being impaired. In affirming a positive identity of being impaired, disabled people are actively repudiating the dominant value of normality. The changes for individuals are not just a transforming of consciousness as to the meaning of "disability," but an assertion of the value and validity of life as a person with an impairment.

The social model has empowered disabled people in taking control of support and services, the establishment of Centres for Integrated Living and the struggle for direct payment being clear expressions of this empowerment. The development of an affirmative model takes his fight squarely into the arena of medical intervention. Some impairments, such as diabetes, epilepsy, and those involving pain, can respond to intervention. Just as the social model signified, for disabled people, ownership of the meaning of disability, so the affirmative model signifies ownership of impairment or, more broadly, the body. The control of intervention is paramount. This is an affirmation by disabled people of the right to control what is done to their bodies. It includes the right to know the basis on which decisions of medical intervention are made, the consequences of taking drugs (including side effects), the consequences of not taking drugs, and the alternatives. Disability Action North East states:

> Our movement should campaign for effective healthcare treatments that are under our control, treatments that are Holistic and see our differences not as Geneticists do (as "defective traits") but as a *positive* sign of our human diversity. (1998, 3)

It has been argued, as mentioned in the first section of this chapter, that the greatest danger for disabled people in addressing impairment is political, with the possibility that impairment is seen to be "the problem," as in the tragedy model. The danger is clearly apparent in the following quotation from a book entitled *An Introduction to Disability Studies*. Writing about the social model, Johnstone states:

> As an explanation it must somehow begin to incorporate, rather than stand in opposition to the medical/deficit model of disablement. (1998, 20)

Yet on the previous page he also recognizes that:

> The medical model encourages the simplistic view that disability is a personal tragedy for the individual concerned. (Johnstone 1998, 19)

Indeed, it is for this reason that the social model cannot "incorporate" the medical model and for this reason, too, that the affirmative model is emerging to strengthen the opposition of the social model to the personal tragedy model.

Oliver states:

> This denial of the pain of impairment has not, in reality, been a denial at all. Rather it has been a pragmatic attempt to identify and address issues that can be changed through collective action rather than medical or other professional treatment. (1996, 38)

The affirmative model, however, is not about the "pain of impairment," but on the contrary the positive experiences and identity of disabled people from being impaired and disabled. The social model is collectively expressed, most obviously, through direct action and campaigns in the struggle of the powerless for power. The affirmative model again builds on this particularly through the development of the Disability Arts Movement within which disabled people collectively affirm their positive identity through visual arts, cabaret, song, and, as in the following extract by Colin Cameron, poetry:

Sub Rosa
Fighting to establish self-respect . . .
Not the same, but different . . .
Not normal, but disabled . . .
Who wants to be normal anyway?
Not ashamed, with heads hanging,
Avoiding the constant gaze of those who assume
that sameness is something to be desired . . .
Nor victims
of other people's lack of imagination . . .
But proud and privileged to be who we are . . .
Exactly as we are.

(Tyneside Disability Arts, 1998.)

Rather than being politically threatening to disabled people, the affirmative model builds on and strengthens the Disabled People's Movement, not least by bringing disabled people, who would not otherwise engage in political action, into the Disability Arts Movement.

Finally, in terms of visions of the future, the affirmative model is building on the social model, through which disabled people envisage full participative citizenship and equal rights. Disabled people not only look toward a society without structural, environmental, or attitudinal barriers, but also a society which celebrates difference and values people irrespective of race, sexual preference, gender, age, or impairment.

In this chapter, we have summarized an affirmative model and the social and historical context in which it is emerging. The broader significance of this view of disability and impairment has yet to be fully realized. We conclude by suggesting two directions for development. First, it is central to the concept of "inclusion." Policies, provision, and practice, whether in community living or education, can only be inclusive through full recognition of disability culture and the affirmative model generated from the experiences of disabled people (Oliver and Barnes 1998). Secondly, an affirmative model also has a role to play in the development of a theory of disability. In his book *Social Identity*, Jenkins (1996) writes of resistance as potent affirmation of group identity:

> Struggles for a different allocation of resources and resistance to categorization are one and the same thing. . . . Whether or not there is an explicit call to arms in these terms, something that can be called self-assertion—or "human spirit" is at the core of resistance to domination. . . . It is as intrinsic, and as necessary, to that social life as the socialising tyranny of categorisation. (1996, 175)

As is so often the case, however, in relation to sociology generally and feminist theory, for instance, existing theory and concepts are rarely explicit in the validation of the experiences of disabled people and are often explicit in invalidation. Jenkins rarely mentions disability, and when he does the same old questions arise:

> Perhaps the most pertinent questions arise out of perceived, typically bodily, impairments: is the neonate to be acknowledged as acceptably human? (1996, 55)

Better dead than disabled? Quintessentially, the affirmative model is held by disabled people about disabled people. Its theoretical significance can also only be developed by disabled people who are "proud, angry, and strong" in resisting the tyranny of the personal tragedy model of disability and impairment.

References

Bartlett, Jane. 1994. *Will You Be Mother? Women Who Choose to Say No*. London: Virago Press.

Campbell, Jane and Mike Oliver. 1996. *Disabling Politics: Understanding Our Past, Changing Our Future*. London: Routledge.

Corker, Mairian. 1996. *Deaf Transitions: Images and Origins of Deaf Families, Deaf Communities and Deaf Identities*. London: Jessica Kingsley.

Disability Action North East. 1998. *Fighting Back Against Eugenics and the New Oppressors*. Newcastle-upon-Tyne: Disability Action North East.

Disability Awareness in Action. 1997. *Life, Death and Rights: Bioethics and Disabled People*. Special Supplement. London: Disability Awareness in Action.

French, Sally. 1991. The Advantages of Visual Impairment: Some Physiotherapists' Views. *New Beacon* 75(872): 1–6.

French, Sally and John Swain. 1997. It's Time to Take Up the Offensive. *Therapy Weekly* 23(34): 7.

Jenkins, Richard. 1996. *Social Identity*. London: Routledge.

Johnstone, David. 1998. *An Introduction to Disability Studies*. London: David Fulton.

Morris, Jenny. ed. 1989. *Able Lives: Women's Experience of Paralysis*. London: Women's Press.

Oliver, Michael. 1996. *Understanding Disability: From Theory to Practice*. Basingstoke: Macmillan.

Oliver, Michael and Colin Barnes. 1998. *Disabled People and Social Policy: From Exclusion to Inclusion*. Harlow: Longman.

Priestley, Mark. 1999. *Disability Politics and Community Care*. London: Jessica Kingsley.

Shakespeare, Tom. 1996. Disability, Identity, Difference. In *Exploring the Divide: Illness and Disability* (ed. C. Barnes and G. Mercer) 94–114. Leeds: Disability Press.

Shakespeare, Tom, Kath Gillespie-Sells, and Dominic Davies. 1996. *The Sexual Politics of Disability*. London: Cassell.

Tyneside Disability Arts. 1998. *Sub Rosa: Clandestine Voices*. Wallsend: Tyneside Disability Arts.

Tyneside Disability Arts. 1999. *Transgressions*. Wallsend: Tyneside Disability Arts.

Vasey, Sian. 1992. Disability Culture: It's a Way of Life. In *Disability Equality in the Classroom: A Human Rights Issue* (ed. R. Rieser and M. Mason) 74. London: Disability Equality in Education.

Watson, Nicholas. 1998. Enabling Identity: Disability, Self and Citizenship. In *The Disability Reader: Social Science Perspectives* (ed. T. Shakespeare) 147–162. London: Cassell.

Questions

1. Describe the tragedy model of disability. Why do the authors critique this approach? What do the authors mean when they state that within the tragedy model is an ideology of "better dead than disabled"? What examples do they give to back up this claim? What role does essentialism play in this conceptualization of disability? Do other forms of inequality fit a tragedy model, or is it unique to disabilities?

2. What is an affirmative model of disability? Why is it so important? In what ways did people in the reading claim that their disability was an advantage? How does it challenge dominant discourses and images regarding disability?

3. How are the tragedy model and affirmative model embedded in social policy or normative practices of schools, workplaces, and other institutions? What role can the Disability Arts movement have in the development and success of an affirmative model of disability? How can social policy build on an affirmative model of disability? Be specific.

4. Sometimes, disabilities do arise from traumatic events: car accidents, genetic mutations, war, acts of violence. How does the tragedy model influence people's responses to disabling events? How might other conceptualizations better prepare people to be resilient in the face of difficulty?

5. List as many TV or movie characters with disabilities as you can. What disabilities were represented? How? Did the characters reproduce or challenge the tragedy model of disability? Why?

L. Data Analysis Exercise: Does Money Make Us Happy?

People often think that having more money will make them happier. Do you think that there is a relationship between money and happiness? Why? How much money do you think people need to be happy? In this data analysis exercise, you will use data from the General Social Survey (GSS) 2010 (Smith et al. 2011) to examine how people responded to a question on general happiness.

In 2010, GSS respondents were asked, "Would you say that you are not too *happy,* pretty *happy* or very *happy*"? Here, you will analyze how people with different family incomes, genders, and education answered this question.

Part 1. Income and Happiness

The first table examines how people reported their level of happiness and total family income. Use Table 1 to answer the following questions.

Questions:

1. A Pearson's Chi Square shows that there is a statistically significant association between income and the level of reported happiness. However, the Chi Square does not automatically tell us the direction of the relationship. Are people with higher incomes reporting that they are happier than those with lower

Table 1 Crosstab for the Level of Happiness by Total Family Income*.

	0–$19,999	$20,000–39,999	$40,000–59,999	$60,000–74,999	≥$75000
Very Happy	102 (23.6%)	66 (20.9%)	53 (27.9%)	33 (33.7%)	108 (33.6%)
Pretty Happy	255 (58.9%)	201 (63.6 %)	117 (61.6%)	54 (55.2%)	181 (56.4%)
Not Too Happy	76 (17.6%)	49 (15.5%)	20 (10.5%)	11 (11.2%)	32 (10.0%)
Total	433 (100%)	316 (100%)	190 (100%)	98 (100%)	321 (100%)

*Pearson Chi Square = 25.621, p = .001. A Pearson's Chi Square suggests that this relationship is statistically significant.

incomes? Use the percentages to support your answer. What income group reports the highest level of happiness? What income group reports the lowest level of happiness?

2. Is your answer to question 1 what you expected before analyzing the data? Why or why not?

Table 2 Crosstab for the Level of Happiness by Gender*.

	Men	Women
Very Happy	223 (25.1%)	315 (27.4%)
Pretty Happy	516 (58%)	668 (58.1%)
Not Too Happy	151 (17%)	166 (14.4%)
Total	890 (100%)	1,149 (100%)

*Pearson Chi Square = 3.11, p = .212 The Pearson's Chi Square is not statistically significant. This suggests that there is not a meaningful relationship between perceptions of happiness and the respondent's gender.

Part II. Gender and Happiness

Table 2 shows how men and women answered the same question about their levels of happiness. Before analyzing the data, do you think there will be a relationship between gender and happiness? Why or why not?

Questions:

1. Is there a relationship between gender and level of reported happiness? Use the percentages in the table to support your answer.
2. Is the relationship between gender and reported happiness what you predicted? Why or why not?

Part III. Education and Happiness

The final table shows the relationship between the highest degree held by respondents and their reported happiness. Do you expect there to be a relationship between education and happiness? Why or why not? Use Table 3 to answer the following questions.

Table 3 Crosstab for the Level of Happiness by Respondent's Highest Degree*.

	Less than High School	High School	Junior College	Bachelors	Graduate Degree
Very Happy	69 (22.8%)	245 (24.5%)	35 (24.1%)	116 (31.0%)	73 (33.5%)
Pretty Happy	156 (51.7%)	589 (58.9.6 %)	88 (60.7%)	228 (61.0%)	123 (56.4%)
Not Too Happy	77 (25.5%)	166 (16.6%)	22 (15.2%)	30 (8.0%)	22 (10.1%)
Total	302 (100%)	1,000 (100%)	145 (100%)	374 (100%)	218 (100%)

*Pearson Chi Square = 51.087, $p < .001$. A Pearson's Chi Square suggests that this relationship is statistically significant.

Questions:

1. What group of people had the highest percentage who reported being "not too happy"? What is the percentage?
2. What group of people had the highest percentage who reported being "very happy"? What is that percentage?
3. Using percentages from the table, would you argue that there is a relationship between education and reported happiness? What type of relationship? Why do you think that this relationship exists?
4. Do you believe happiness is a right or a privilege? Taking all of the information from Tables 1, 2 and 3,

would you conclude that inequality influences happiness? Why or why not?

Reference:

Smith, Tom W., Peter V. Marsden, and Michael Hout. *General Social Survey, 1972–2010* [Cumulative File]. ICPSR31521-v1. Storrs, CT: Roper Center for Public Opinion Research, University of Connecticut/Ann Arbor, MI: Inter-university Consortium for Political and Social Research [distributors], 2011-08-05. http://doi.org/10.3886/ICPSR31521.v1

Projects and Resources to Make a Difference

In this section, some of the chapters discussed ways that people speak that reproduce inequality. Specifically, you read about color-blind racism, a way that people say racist things while appearing race neutral. In addition, you read about how power elites control what is said and what is known about environmental hazards. Thus, if what we say can reproduce inequality, we can also use language to dismantle inequality. The first step is to become knowledgeable about the way sexist, ableist, and racist ideology is reinforced through discourse. Next, you can adapt your own language to challenge the reproduction of inequality. Finally, you can educate others about the importance of language. Here are some places to get started:

1. Read Sherryl Kleinman's article, "Why Sexist Language Matters." It was originally published in a newsletter of the Orange County [North Carolina] Rape Crisis Center, but has since been reproduced in multiple places across the Internet. In this article Kleinman argues that male-generics reinforce an ideology that makes women invisible and denigrates them to second-class citizens. She argues that sexist language ultimately supports the reproduction of gender inequality and domestic violence. You can find a copy of the article at the following link: http://

www.alternet.org/story/48856/why_sexist_language_matters.

2. Learn about the movement to end the use of the term "retarded" as a slur. While many people use the term without intention to hurt people with physical or learning disabilities, using the term as a synonym for "stupid" or "dumb" reproduces an ideology that marginalizes individuals with disabilities. Read more about this at the website "R-Word: Spread the Word to End the Word" and watch the public service announcement with Lauren Potter and Jane Lynch from *Glee*.
http://www.r-word.org/Default.aspx
http://www.r-word.org/Not-Acceptable-R-word-PSA.aspx

3. Similarly to the campaign to end the use of the word "retarded" as a slur, there has been a movement to end the use of gay slurs. The Gay, Lesbian and Straight Education Network (GLSEN) has created a website, "Think Before you Speak." You can learn more at the campaign's website and then watch Wanda Sykes's public service announcement.
http://www.glsen.org/participate/programs/thinkb4yourspeak
https://www.youtube.com/watch?v=sWSoGVOQPso